THE STATISTICAL ACCOUNT OF SCOTLAND

General Editors: Donald J. Withrington and Ian R. Grant

VOLUME X

FIFE

THE
STATISTICAL ACCOUNT OF SCOTLAND

GENERAL EDITORS' INTRODUCTION

The *Statistical Account of Scotland* has been used by generation after generation of social historians enquiring into the local or national affairs of Scotland in the later 18th century. It is an unrivalled source, and historians of other countries, as well as their sociologists, geographers and natural scientists, have long regretted having no similar body of evidence available to them. Sir John Sinclair, determinedly cajoling the parish ministers of the Established Church to respond to his long list of over 160 queries, intended his statistical enquiry to enable the country, and its government, not only to assess its current state but to prepare better for a better future— "ascertaining the quantum of happiness enjoyed by its inhabitants and the means of its future improvement", moral as well as economic or political. The quality of the returns he received was generally good and was often excellent, and the parochial reports provided the Scots of the 1790s with a uniquely valuable analysis of their own times: the same reports provide us today with an incomparable view of Scotland two centuries ago, through the sharp eyes and the often sharp words of men who knew their localities very well indeed.

However, the original *Account*, printed in twenty-one volumes in the course of the 1790s, is difficult and often exasperating to use. Sinclair published the parish returns just as they came in to him; therefore the reports for one county or for part of one county may be scattered throughout a dozen volumes or more. Readers of the original printing must have the index in volume xx in order to search out easily the particular returns they want, and even then they may overlook the supplementary replies eventually published in volume xxi. Furthermore, Sinclair's indexes of subjects and persons in volume xxi are woefully inadequate.

In this new edition we have brought together the parish returns in groupings by county and have printed them in alphabetical order, thus avoiding a major difficulty in using the earlier compilation. This new arrangement will not only assist those who wish to use the *Account* as a whole, it will also be especially useful to local historians and to others engaged in local or regional researches with an historical basis: and the new format makes much easier a direct comparison of the Sinclair *Account* with the *New Statistical Account*, published by counties in 1845. So large is the volume of material for Aberdeenshire and Perthshire, however, that these counties have required two volumes each in this reissue. And we have decided to gather together in one volume all the returns from western island parishes, in the Inner and Outer Hebrides and in Bute, rather than leave them scattered among the returns from mainland Ross-shire, Inverness-shire and Argyll: these have a coherence in themselves which would be lost if placed with their respective counties.

Each of the twenty volumes in this reissue is being edited by a scholar who contributes an introduction showing the significance of the *Statistical Account* reports for the region and assessing their importance for modern historical and other social studies. Each volume will also contain an index (of the more important topics discussed in the returns, but not of persons or places) which will make the *Account* more accessible to and more immediately useful to all students, not least to pupils in schools where Scottish local studies are being introduced or extended. We are grateful to James Hamilton for his help in preparing the indexes.

We believe that the significantly improved format of this reissue will make more widely useful, and more widely used, an already acknowledged vital work of standard reference.

Ian R. Grant   Donald J. Withrington

THE

STATISTICAL ACCOUNT

OF

SCOTLAND
1791–1799

EDITED BY SIR JOHN SINCLAIR

VOLUME X

FIFE

With a new introduction by
R. G. CANT

EP Publishing Limited
1978

This is volume X of a reissue in twenty volumes of *The Statistical Account of Scotland*, originally published between 1791 and 1799. In this reissue all the parish accounts for individual counties are printed together for the first time, with a new introduction and index in each volume.

Volume I of this reissue carries a general introduction by Donald J. Withrington.

ISBN 0 7158 1000 6 (set)
      0 7158 1010 3 (vol. X)

British Library Cataloguing in Publication Data
The statistical account of Scotland, 1791–1799.
   Vol. 10: Fife. – [New ed.]
   1. Scotland – History – 18th century
   I. Sinclair, *Sir* John, *bart*, b. 1754
   941.107′3   DA809
   ISBN 0-7158-1010-3

Printed in Great Britain by
The Scolar Press Limited, Ilkley, Yorkshire

CONTENTS

vii

Contents

(map a last page of with (Appendix))

viii

INTRODUCTION

WITHIN Scotland Fife holds a unique position in physical and political geography alike. Occupying a sizeable peninsula between the Firth of Tay on the north and the Firth of Forth on the south, it is also separated from its neighbours on the west by an area of mountainous country. At first glance, then, it conveys an impression of compact isolation. Yet the Firth of Forth has never formed a serious barrier between Fife and Lothian and both the earlier and later history of Scotland shows how relatively easy it was for political and cultural influences to pass from one side of the estuary to the other. On the north, admittedly, the situation was rather different. Filled with treacherous shoals and lacking the multiplicity of safe harbours that line both shores of the Forth, the Firth of Tay has, until its comparatively recent bridging, proved a formidable obstacle to communication across its waters[1].

When the Kingdom of Scotland assumed recognisable form in the eleventh and twelfth centuries the most influential centres of its political life came to be in Fife and Lothian, at Dunfermline and Edinburgh respectively, and if Edinburgh subsequently grew to a position of unique dominance the Scottish kings maintained their interest in Fife which still held, in St Andrew's, the chief religious centre of the country. Hence, far from being isolated from the mainstream of

---

1. The point must not, of course, be pressed too far. In the process of 'agricultural improvement', for example, the minister of Kennoway (426) reported that Small's improved plough "was lately introduced from the coast of Angus into the north side of Fife and has become pretty general over the county".

Scottish life, Fife was deeply involved in its activities. And the growth of a multiplicity of thriving townships along its southern shores – more numerous than those in Lothian and backed by comparable agricultural and mineral resources – meant that it also held a key position in the economy.

Although so influential in the life of Scotland Fife has tended to lack effective unity within itself. Its people have certainly had a strong sense of identity, but the geological structure of their homeland has divided it into several distinct areas, none powerful or central enough to dominate the others. In comformity with that of the whole of central Scotland this structure is aligned from north-east to south-west and the two great estuaries that give Fife its characteristic outline are part of the same pattern. In the north, extending some five miles inland from the Firth of Tay, is a great mass of andesite, igneous rock of the Old Red Sandstone period that forms the eastmost section of the Ochil Hills. Although their highest summit, Norman's Law, rises to no more than 935 feet, these hills ascend steeply from the firth and form a quite serious barrier. Indeed, the only significant ports here are Newburgh opposite the 'Lindores gap' in the west and Ferryport-on-Craig or Tayport in the east where the alluvial plain of the Motray Water and the sand-dunes of Tents Muir provide a more level hinterland.

To the south of the Ochils the softer sedimentary rocks of the upper Old Red Sandstone provide a basis for the fertile valley of the River Eden, some twenty-five miles in length and between two and six miles in breadth. This is by far the most extensive stretch of continuous lowland in Fife and although it lies appreciably to the north of its geometrical centre it is easy to understand how Cupar, with the religious focus of St Andrews nine miles to the east and the royal palace of Falkland ten miles to the south-west, should for long have held the position of county town.

Southwards of the Eden valley almost the whole of the remainder of Fife consists of varieties of carboniferous rock. Although this is comparatively soft, its more northerly section, between Loch Leven and Fife Ness, is overlaid by harder dolerite sills or penetrated by volcanic intrusions which form a series of sizeable hills descending in altitude from the West and East Lomonds (1,713 and 1,394 feet) to Largo Law and Kellie Law (952 and 597 feet). In the surrounding uplands fertility is limited, communications difficult, and population sparse, but the coastal area of the 'East Neuk', below the last two hills, has a strip of good farmland twelve miles long and three miles wide, with a group of small harbours well-placed for fishing and for trade across the North Sea.

In the south-west of Fife another series of dolerite sills and volcanic intrusions has produced such hills as Benarty (1,167), Saline (1,178), and the Binn of Burntisland (632 feet). In the centre of this area (some 18 by 10 miles in extent) lies the old royal capital of Dunfermline, strategically set at the intersection of the route northwards from the Queen's Ferry across the Forth narrows with others running to the east and west. Eastwards of this area is what comes as near as any part of Fife to constituting its geographical 'heartland'. This is the wide triangular plain, some ten miles in extent along each of its faces, that embraces the valleys of the Leven and the Ore with a southern extension towards the Tiel. Combining great fertility with great mineral wealth, it has several good ports and in Kirkcaldy what has come to be the largest town in Fife.

In effect, then, the social and economic life of Fife has always had a marked local emphasis. And it may have been partly because of this that the upland area of Kinross, separated from Perthshire by the Ochils and having stronger geographical and historical links with Fife, should have developed a separate political identity. In early times it seems to have been associated with west Fife as the district of *Fothreve* or *Fothric*. This, in turn, with east Fife, formed part of the regional kingdom of *Fib*, one of the major constituents of the 'Pictish confederation' which preceded the medieval Scottish kingdom. Within this kingdom the original Sheriffdom of Fife was of similar extent and the old 'shire' of Kinross seems to have had little more significance than other comparable units in Fife. In 1685, however, it was considerably enlarged and although still generally associated with Fife for ecclesiastical and legal organisation[1] must for the next two and a half centuries be regarded as a distinct entity. The modern association of Kinross with Perth dates only from 1918. As partial compensation, in 1891 the parishes of Culross and Tulliallan, previously in Perthshire, were transferred to Fife, but for this new edition of *The Statistical Account* they have been left as they were at the time of its compilation, as have the smaller areas affected by later boundary changes. In this form Fife had an area of 328,427 acres or 513 square miles, with an estimated population of 87,250 for the sixty parishes comprised within it.

The survey of the county provided by the sixty-one parochial returns to Sir John Sinclair's "statistical inquiries" was not the first of its kind. In 1710 Sir Robert Sibbald, himself a member of a landowning family in Fife, had published a *History of the Sheriffdoms of Fife and Kinross*, its descriptive sections constituting approximately half of the completed work[2]. In 1755 all the Fife parishes had featured in Dr Alexander Webster's plan to compile the first systematic census of population for the whole of Scotland[3]. But there had been nothing to compare with the wealth of information assembled in the 1790's for *The Statistical Account*. Like Webster Sinclair addressed his "inquiries" to the parish ministers of the Established Church and in Fife all but four of the accounts were supplied by the current incumbents. Of the remainder one was provided by a neighbouring minister, one by the parochial schoolmaster, and two by "a friend to statistical inquiries"[4]. As might be expected, the accounts

1. Fife and Kinross formed a single sheriffdom from 1748 to 1807 and again from 1870 to 1975. The Synod of Fife included Kinross continuously until 1975, from 1856 to 1929 as a distinct presbytery, at other times as part of the Presbyteries of Dunfermline and Kirkcaldy.
2. Sir Robert Sibbald, *The history, ancient and modern, of the Sheriffdoms of Fife and Kinross, with the description of both, and of the Firths of Forth and Tay* (Edinburgh, 1710).
3. J. G. Kyd (ed.), *Scottish Population Statistics, including Webster's Analysis of Population* 1755 (Edinburgh: Scottish History Society, 1952).
4. While it is sometimes possible to penetrate this anonymity, all that can be said here is that the account of Abdie, with its sharp criticism of its non-resident proprietors (11), must have been written by someone extremely well-informed on local conditions.

vary considerably in length and quality, but the material assembled is impressive in its coverage and the comments, however cautious and conventional in some respects, are quite often remarkably observant.

The ministers owed their appointment to patrons, to whom this right had been restored in 1712[1]. At an earlier stage there had been a close association between the landed aristocracy and the ministry, but among Sir John Sinclair's correspondents in Fife whose parentage can be identified only two were the sons of lairds[2]. Of the remainder by far the largest group consisted of ministers' sons and since they, and a good many others, quite often married ministers' daughters, the profession tended to become something of a hereditary caste. The other main sources of recruitment were sons of tenant farmers and of schoolmasters, the latter being not infrequently disappointed candidates for the ministry.

If the ministers thus no longer belonged to the same social group as the landowners, and were sometimes in conflict with them over their stipends and the provision of church, manse, and glebe, all the responsibility of the latter as *heritors*[3], they nevertheless regarded themselves as part of the same general 'establishment' dedicated to the maintenance of the existing political and ecclesiastical order. This was particularly the view of the 'moderate' party in the church to which the great majority of the ministers belonged. Thus the tone of their observations was apt to be strongly conservative. At the same time they had a genuine concern for the wellbeing of their parishioners and could on occasion be quite sharply critical of landlords and other vested interests. Furthermore, since most were content to remain in the same parish throughout their entire ministry they could write with great knowledge and also a certain independence. Admittedly, when

1. It should be emphasised that by far the largest patron was the Crown, which controlled 21 parishes in Fife, including all those of major importance.
2. These and other particulars relating to ministers are derived mainly from the entries in Hew Scott, *Fasti Ecclesiae Scoticanae*, vol.v (Edinburgh, 1925).
3. Leslie (582n–5n) has a lengthy disquisition by the minister on the general inadequacy of stipends.

Introduction

The Statistical Account was being compiled, several of these prolonged ministries were only in their early stages, but a significant proportion of the parochial reports were by incumbents whose memories extended over many years.

As one of the strongest aspirations of the reformed church in Scotland was to have 'an educated ministry', all these men had attended a full course in arts and theolgy at one of the Scottish universities. Fife had, of course, a university of its own at St Andrews, but the strong division in local organisation that have been mentioned meant that its effective 'province' extended only to the northern and eastern parts of the county, that is to the presbyteries of Cupar and St Andrews[1]. In the presbyteries of Dunfermline and Kirkcaldy there were certainly ministers with a St Andrews connection, but most had been educated at Edinburgh and maintained close links with its professional and commercial families, from which indeed many of the lairds in this part of Fife were drawn.

An aspect of the parochial organisation of Fife deserving of comment is the fact that, although by the late eighteenth century the presbyteries of Dunfermline and Kirkcaldy contained approximately half the population of the county, the number of parishes here was no more than twenty-two compared with thirty-nine in Cupar and St Andrews. This was because their parishes originated in the Middle Ages and were based more on political influence than actual population. Between 1600 and 1650 efforts were made to ameliorate the situation by the division of large parishes and the amalgamation of smaller ones[2], but very little had been done in the eighteenth century when the distribution of population

1. See R. N. Smart, "Some observations on the provinces of the Scottish Universities 1560–1850" in G. W. S. Barrow (ed.), *The Scottish Tradition* (Edinburgh, 1974), 91–106.
2. In this period, new parishes of Abbotshall, Anstruther Easter, Cameron, Elie, Ferryport-on-Craig, Kingsbarns, and Pittenweem were formed, the parish of Abercrombie was enlarged to include St Monans, and Tarvit was incorporated in Cupar, but as this involved a net increase of five parishes in the east and only one in the west the effect was to accentuate still further the disparity between the two halves of Fife.

had begun to alter quite drastically and economic changes created problems which the old parochial system was ill-adapted to meet. Of all this there is surprisingly little in *The Statistical Account* and even the two overworked ministers of Dunfermline, serving a widespread population of close on 10,000, made no firm proposal for an addition to their number although this had been considered as far back as 1713[1].

While it is possible to make a broad distinction in the parochial accounts between 'urban' and 'rural' conditions, the only completely urban parish in Fife was the minute one of Anstruther Easter carved out of Kilrenny in 1641[2]. Parishes such as Dunfermline and St Andrews, containing important urban centres, also had quite extensive 'landward' areas. But beyond this there was a considerable overlap in the eighteenth century and even later between what might be regarded as 'agricultural' and 'industrial' pursuits. Most burghs embraced farming activities of some kind[3], while the traditional craft of handloom weaving was generally conducted in villages[4]. Coal-mining took place wherever the most accessible deposits were to be found and collier-villages, however inadequate in other respects, might exist in a largely unspoiled countryside. The same was true of early iron-works, although the group of forty-three smiths manufacturing six million nails a year at Pathhead near Dysart obtained their raw material in the form of scrap-iron imported from Holland[5]. On a smaller scale, every country community had a wide range of artisans and craftsmen, not only masons, joiners, and

1. Dunfermline, 278. There was at least a second place of worship (additional to the Abbey Kirk) in a chapel of ease authorised in 1779 (ibid 285). The charge here, as at Cupar, Dysart, and St Andrew's, was 'collegiate' with two ministers sharing parochial responsibilities. In Wemyss (800) the minister had the assistance of a "catechist" with special responsibilities for "the coaliers and salters".
2. This is the correct date (*otr* Anstruther Easter, 27). With a land area of no more than 5½ acres this was by far the smallest parish in Scotland.
3. Kirkaldy, 515, 517.
4. Even when, in the next period, large mills were introduced, with machines operated by water or steam power, they might have the same location (as at Freuchie and Kingskettle) or (as at Dura Den in Kemback parish) one predominantly rural in character.
5. Dysart, 355.

smiths of all kinds, but millers, coopers, shoemakers, tailors, and many more beside[1].

It may seem surprising that in what is often regarded as a relatively advanced phase of the industrial revolution the change that interested the ministers of Fife most was the process of 'agricultural improvement'. It was, of course, a matter with which the originator of *The Statistical Account*, 'Agricultural Sir John', was particularly concerned. Moreover, quite a few of the contributors were themselves 'improvers' of their glebe-lands[2]. But beyond such considerations it is evident that the ministers in general tended to regard a society based on the land as the most 'natural' and beneficial for mankind, that they feared the social consequences of industrialisation, and hoped that a more enlightened use of material resources might make it possible to maintain a growing population in something like its traditional form[3].

Already, however, it was apparent that 'improvement' might involve wholesale dispossession of tenants and an actual reduction of population. An extreme case was that of the parishes of Ballingry and Beath in the hill country of west Fife where it was reckoned that the population was less than half what it had been in 1755 through the conversion of marginal agricultural land into grazing[4]. But even where land remained under tillage the way in which it was cultivated was completely transformed.[5] In place of the untidy 'run-rig' of 'infield' and 'outfield' were trim fields of moderate size enclosed by hedges or stone dykes and grouped in farms generally of between 50 and 300 acres. The heavy wooden ploughs dragged by teams of six oxen[6] were

1. Kilconquhar (449) had the remarkable number of 46 shoemakers.
2. Auchtermuchty, 58–9; Beath, 87.
3. See, e.g. Kilmany, 471.
4. Ballingry, 75; Beath, 88. In the former case, however, it was conceded that the soil was "better calculated for grass".
5. There are good descriptions of "improvements in husbandry" in Denino, 251–7; Dunfermline, 303–5; Kemback, 411–5; Kilconquhar, 446–8; Kirkaldy, 514–6; Largo, 567–9; Markinch, 625–8; St Monance, 734–5; See also the interesting reference in Inverkeithing, 396–7 to a "Farmer Club . . . to consider and improve the different modes of agriculture".
6. The oxen were sometimes replaced by black cattle (Auchterderran, 42).

replaced by light iron ploughs drawn by two horses directed by one man. For the rough alternations of cropping prescribed by custom there was introduced a balanced rotation supplemented by a scientific manuring of different types of soil for different crops.[1] Among the latter oats and barley remained by far the largest, with peas and beans as the main 'green' variant, but wheat was becoming more common, together with potatoes and turnips.[2] Among stock black cattle generally retained their popularity but sheep were on the decline.[3]

If the methods adopted to 'improve' the form of agriculture were roughly similar, the speed with which they were introduced might vary considerably. In certain parts of Lowland Scotland including Fife, the process was already under way quite early in the eighteenth century.[4] Yet almost all the parochial reports indicate that the main development had only come in the preceding thirty years (since about 1760) and in certain areas at least had made but limited progress. In Crail, for example, "a great proportion of the parish" was still un-enclosed, while in Auchterderran, despite almost complete enclosure, only one-third of the ploughs were of modern design.[5]

Clearly the process of change depended not only on the physical character of each locality but on its tenurial organisation and social structure and it might well proceed by

1. "The ground is well dunged for the turnips and well limed for the wheat" (Torryburn, 779). There was also some use of seaweed for this as well as for industrial purposes (see Anstruther Wester, 30-1).
2. In Leuchars (596) it was feared that "the sowing of wheat may be carried too far". In Kilconquhar (446-7) the 5th Earl of Balcarres was credited with the introduction "about 40 years ago" of the field turnip, an example "little followed . . . till within these 25 years".
3. Most parishes reported an increase in cattle; where they did not it was usually because of their disuse for ploughing. In many places there were no sheep whatsoever (see Leuchars, 605-6).
4. This was certainly true of the estates of Carslogie, Rankeillor and Rossie to the west of Cupar, and in case of the last the draining of its loch, said to have been completed in 1741 (Collessie, 153), had been envisaged and may have been begun as early as 1653 (Rossie Papers, MS, St Andrew's University Library).
5. Crail, 169; Auchterderran, 42.

stages extending over a prolonged period. While Fife contained estates pertaining to great nobles like the Earls of Balcarres, Elgin, Kellie, Leven, Moray, and Rothes, none was of a size approaching the holdings of magnates of this rank elsewhere in Scotland. In popular reckoning and in actual fact Fife was a land of small lairds, some of ancient lineage, others 'incomers' from the professional and mercantile classes of adjoining towns. On such estates, where the laird or his factor lived on terms of some intimacy with the agricultural tenants, there might be a desire to avoid undue social dislocation in the process of improvement. Hence, initially, a landlord might accept new tenant-farms of relatively small scale. But when the leases fell in he would then amalgamate these in larger units and at a rent that the old tenant could ill afford. Many of the ministers were bluntly critical of this practice as well as of the short leases and inadequate farm buildings on certain estates and of the perpetuation of such antique survivals as the 'thirlage' of tenants to the lairds' mills.[1]

The agricultural revolution might thus be more complex and slow-moving than the conventional description of the process suggests, and in Fife at least it would be some time before agricultural society assumed the pattern familiar to the nineteenth and early twentieth centuries of landlord, tenant-farmer, and farm-servant. What is at least clear is that the 'husbandmen' who stood immediately below the laird were becoming fewer in number and more substantial in status as the size of holdings increased while the 'cottars' and 'pendiclers', who commonly held their small plots in terms of labour services, were tending to disappear. The parochial accounts contain references to the "suppression of cot-houses"[2] and the new "cottagers", living in groups on the farms, seem to have been what would later be termed "farm-servants".[3] To a great extent, however, work on farms was

1. See, e.g., Aberdour, 25–6; Crail, 159; Dysart, 330.
2. See, e.g., Crail, 159.
3. This was clearly the case in Ceres (141), but the situation is confused by the application of the terms "cottar" and "cottager" to both the old "pendiclers" and the new "farm-servants".

performed by "day-labourers" finding their own accommodation and often eking out a living in other ways.

While the ministers approved the notion that a better use should be made of the land, and the disappearance of the "cottaries" seem to have occasioned no particular regret, the reduction of opportunities for agricultural employment was viewed with a good deal of misgiving. In the parish of Ferryport-on-Craig where the minister, Robert Dalgleish, was also the sole proprietor and superior of a growing township, it was possible to make the transition without undue social or economic distress.[1] Elsewhere, however, the redistribution of population had no such systematic basis and was liable to create serious problems in town and country alike. In the completely rural parish of Creich in north Fife the "disappearance" of a cottar village and the union of farms meant that "many of our young people leave us to go to the neighbouring towns of Dundee and Perth to learn handicraft trades".[2] If a sense of regret is no more than implied here, in the case of Auchtertool the minister was eloquently outspoken in his condemnation of a like development there:

"This taste for enlarging and uniting farms . . . forces the people from the active healthy employments of a country life to take refuge in manufacturing towns and populous cities which may literally be said to be the graves of the human species."[3]

In certain localities the estates of the major proprietors were interspersed with independent small-holdings in the form of *feus*. Many of these had originated on old monastic lands; others might be held from a nearby burgh or even from the Crown. In Ceres, where the minister had to report the departure of many young men to service in the army or navy or to "other pursuits", he found satisfaction in "the great number of freeholdings" which enabled the parish to maintain a "general populousness" it might not otherwise have had.[4] In Falkland, on the other hand, the existence of

1. Ferryport-on-Craig, 372, 376.
2. Criech, 185.
3. Auchtertoul, 66–7.
4. Ceres, 150.

numerous small proprietors engaged in some craft or similar occupation was regarded as a serious obstacle to agricultural improvement.[1] In Newburgh this problem was resolved by the buying up of similar small feus by an adjoining proprietor who then absorbed them in the improved farms of his estate.[2]

The situation in Falkland and Newburgh illustrates a point already mentioned, namely, that agriculture was by no means the only occupation in the eighteenth century countryside of Fife. Even at the time of the compilation of *The Statistical Account* the linen industry was still predominantly "domestic" in character, both spinning and weaving being conducted within or alongside the dwellings of the workers.[3] Out of a total population of 2,198 the parish of Falkland had 231 weavers, Balmerino had 50 in its 162 houses, and in Kennoway "every person almost that is not engaged in the labours of the field is employed at the loom".[4] With an industry so rooted in the countryside it is surprising that a greater proportion of its raw material, flax, was not produced in the locality. In Kettle, admittedly, three-quarters of what was used was raised in the parish, the remainder being "$\frac{1}{8}$ Dutch and $\frac{1}{8}$ Riga".[5] But this was exceptional, and the case of Dysart supplies a partial explanation. Here "more flax was formerly cultivated, but in the late leases the farmers have been restricted in this article, from a mistaken notion of its being too scourging". Hence "not above a fourth of the yarn used in the parish is spun in it".[6]

Without getting involved in the technicalities of a highly complex industrial process, it may be said that its object was to turn the flax or "lint" into yarn by a sequence in which spinning formed the final element. Thereafter the yarn was woven into a variety of fabrics ranging from the fine "da-

1. Falkland, 359; also Kirkcaldy, 513.
2. Newburgh, 673.
3. See D. I. A. Steel, "The Linen Industry in Fife in the later 18th and 19th century" (St Andrew's University Ph.D. thesis, 1975).
4. Falkland, 358; Balmerino, 81; Kennoway, 427.
5. Kettle, 439.
6. Dysart, 330, 332.

masks" and diapers" for which Dunfermline had a well-established reputation[1] to the more general run of coarse or "brown" linens, "tickings", and "osnaburgs". The spinners – almost uniformly women – worked for the weavers.[2] The weavers, by tradition, worked for themselves and marketed their product in the nearby towns, often at the periodic traditional 'fairs'.[3]

By the time of The Statistical Account, however, there was already a trend towards closer organisation. In Kettle, for example, there were 170 looms superintended by about 60 master-weavers with the product being sold "as it comes out of the loom" (unbleached, that is) in Cupar or Auchtermuchty.[4] At Newburgh, among a strongly independent community, there were now "workshops" housing a dozen looms under a "master".[5] In Largo some of the weavers "of less stock" were employed by manufacturers in neighbouring towns who supplied them with their raw materials and marketed the complete article.[6] Changes in organisation were accompanied by changes in production,[7] one being the development of lint-mills for the preparation of the flax. There was also a greater use of fulling and dyeing to perfect the manufacturing process before marketing, while bleach-fields were now employed to a far greater extent, not only in the preparation of yarn but even in the completion of the coarser fabrics. Within a few years the introduction of power-looms would mark the beginning of the end of the traditional form of the industry, but for the moment it remained broadly intact.[8]

Although the handloom weavers formed part of the social structure of the communities in which they worked they had

1. Dunfermline, 273–4.
2. But in Crail (172) yarn was spun "for the manufacturers in other places".
3. Kingsbarns, 501; Leslie, 581.
4. Kettle, 439.
5. Newburgh, 673–4.
6. Largo, 569. In Kirkcaldy the "manufactures" were said to employ about 810 looms, only 250 of these being in the parish itself (Kirkcaldy, 533–4).
7. For details see Steel, *op.cit.*
8. The first power-loom in Fife to have been brought into actual production appears to have been at Kirkcaldy in 1821 (Steel, *op.cit.*).

at the same time a very distinctive identity of their own. Engaged as they were in a sedentary occupation, laborious but to a great extent repetitive and automatic, and commonly conducted in adjoining dwellings, they had more contact with their fellows than most workers of the time and developed a formidable capacity for religious and political discussion, generally of a strongly anti-authoritarian character.[1] At the time of *The Statistical Account* their political radicalism was no more than incipient but their passion for religious controversy had contributed powerfully to the secessions from the Established Church of the preceding period and to the growth of what the parish ministers termed "a spirit of schism".[2]

An industry in which the workers were to develop an even more powerful and persistent radicalism was that of coal-mining but at this period they played little part in the life of their localities. The reason for this was the servitude which had applied to both colliers and "salters" as late as 1775. And even the Emancipating Act of that year did no more than provide a procedure for liberation which advanced somewhat slowly and unevenly until the more revolutionary act of 1799. How far emancipation had proceeded in Fife is hard to determine through an almost studied disinclination of the ministers to discuss the matter but the impression is that it was far advanced if not complete.[3] Even so, the colliers and their families remained a race apart, in their separate settlements adjacent to the mines in which they worked. Their houses seem often to have been of the most elementary construction, some of them mere huts intended to provide the minimum of shelter during the expected period of extraction.[4]

1. The same was generally true of shoemakers, quite a few of whom, like certain weavers, had entered on the occupation through some physical deformity.
2. Largo, 573.
3. In Pittenweem the colliers were certainly "all free" and "engaged by the year" (Pittenweem, 695). In Wemyss the minister reported the remarkable degree of support among the inhabitants (mainly colliers, salters, weavers, fishermen, and farm-workers) for a negro servant, baptised in the parish church in 1769, who raised an action in the Court of Session to prevent his master returning him to slavery in the West Indies (Wemyss, 806n).
4. Carnock, 131.

Since, under the feudal system, all minerals pertained to the land in which they were located, the organisation of coal-mining was primarily a matter for the proprietors. Hence, as with agricultural improvement, its development depended on their individual enterprise but also on the accessibility of deposits and the degree of technical assistance available. Where seams were near the surface they could be worked 'open-cast' or by a simple 'adit' or incline, but deeper levels involved the sinking of a vertical 'pit' with attendant problems of access and egress for the workers and the extraction of the coal. There were also increased hazards of flooding, inadequate ventilation, and explosions. Beyond such difficulties of production were others of distribution. With inland communications as poor as they were generally reckoned, the output of collieries at any distance from the coast was usually for local consumption.[1] Near the sea, however, as many of them were, prospects of export were good and in some cases special "waggon-ways" were run from a mine to a port to assist this.[2] The most telling evidence of the importance of this trade is the fact that of ships leaving Kirkcaldy between 1743 and 1792 "92% showed coal as part of the cargo and in the vast majority coal was the sole item exported".[3]

Once again space does not allow of any detailed discussion of the technicalities of the industry at this stage of its development but the proprietors and lessees of mines in Fife seem to have shown a reasonable enterprise even if there might be occasional suspension of production while new methods were being devised. In Scoonie parish, for example, the excellent Durie seam was exhausted "so far as it could be drained by the

1. Markinch, 633–45. There were fears here that reserves might be exhausted.
2. One waggon-way ran from Halbeath colliery to Inverkeithing (399), another from Fordell to St David's (Dalgety, 246), and another from Kirkland to Methil (Wemyss, 792). With remarkable prescience the minister of Wemyss thought "it would not be at all surprising to see, in a few years, Methil rank among the first coal-ports in Scotland". There was also a waggon-way from workings west of Dunfermline to Lord Elgin's new lime-works near Charlestown (Dunfermline, 312n).
3. R. Douglas, "Coal-mining in Fife in the second half of the eighteenth century" in G. W. S. Barrow (ed.), *The Scottish Tradition* (Edinburgh, 1974), 211. There were also considerable exports of coal from Dysart (337–8).

present water engine" and inferior seams were being worked
local consumption, but an additional engine was envisaged
which would tap "a large field of the principal or better
seam" and secure the resumption of its export from Leven to
Holland.[1] Along the coast, in an old working between
Pittenweem and St Monans, "Sir John Anstruther, about 20
years ago, erected a fire engine, and has since that period put
out an immense quantity of coal".[2] But at Torryburn in
west Fife, where there were "great seams" of "the best
quality", extraction was in suspense since they were "all
under level" and "cannot be wrought but with the assistance
of a powerful engine".[3] In consequence, "numbers of the
workmen went to collieries in the neighbourhood, and at
present very few families of them remain in the parish".[4]

With such uncertainties added to the arduous labour of an
occupation in which the colliers' wives and children might
also be involved, the mining communities of Fife lived on the
outermost edge of society and sometimes, it would almost
seem, beyond it altogether. Yet in some places at least conditions were more tolerable, and in Dalgety the parish
minister was prepared to give credit, with obvious sincerity
however stilted the language, to the way in which the mining
community of Fordell had raised itself by its own efforts.

"It is pleasing to observe that the colliers, who compose a
considerable part of the population of the parish, and who
in former times were less enlightened and civilised, have
for a long while been making progress in religious knowledge and moral improvement; and so anxious are they to
give education to their children that for many years they
have maintained a teacher by subscription, as they are a
great distance from the parochial school".[5]

Closely associated with the colliers, yet inherently different
from one another, were the salters and the quarrymen. In
Fife a large part of the coal produced was used to work the

1. Scoonie, 767-8.
2. Pittenweem, 695.
3. Torryburn, 780.
4. *Ibid.*, 781.
5. Dalgety, 242.

salt-pans that lined the shores of the Forth in close proximity to many of the mines. Wemyss parish had no less than sixteen separate salt-pans while the small parish of Pittenweem had nine and nearby St Monans "one of the neatest and best contrived salt-works on the coast" of which vestiges may still be seen.[1] In these works similar conditions of servitude to the colliers had prevailed until 1775 but in the period since then a like emancipation seems to have taken place. By contrast the quarrymen, whose most valuable product was the fine sandstone to be found in the carboniferous deposits, enjoyed formal freedom, although the villages in which they lived often had something of the isolated and ingrown character of their colliery counterparts. The same was true of the lime-workers whose product played an important part in agriculture, alike in its older and "improved" form, as well as in building and the manufacture of iron.[2]

Another occupation tending to create self-contained communities was that of fishing.[3] Leaving on one side the special case of the salmon-fisheries in the Tay and other estuaries[4] and the incidental 'catches' in inland waters, the fishing industry of Fife was concentrated in the Firth of Forth with haddock and the less predictable herring as its most important constituents. Unfortunately, as almost all the accounts emphasise, it had recently suffered a catastrophic decline. The minister of Kilrenny, which included the important fishing centre of Cellardyke, could recall the "vast quantities of fish" formerly caught there which had involved no fewer than fifty boats, each with a crew of six.[5] But here, as at St Andrews, Crail, Anstruther, and St Monans, "the fish have in a manner quite deserted these places".[6] At Dalgety, however, it was thought that more might have been made of the opportunities that still existed,[7] an argument

1. Wemyss, 793; Pittenweem, 695; St Monance, 739.
2. Burntisland, 99; Dunfermline, 308–10.
3. Wemyss, 791.
4. See especially Ferryport-on-Craig, 369–70; Newburgh, 665–6, where the fishing was already being operated by "a company at Perth".
5. Kilrenney, 476.
6. St Monance, 739.
7. Dalgety, 239.

supported by the example of Buckhaven where, despite a general decline in resources, the local fishermen found a good market for their catches in Edinburgh.[1] In Crail, again, considerable quantities of lobster were supplied to London.[2] And in Kingsbarns, which shared in the same trade, older men could revert to their other occupation of weaving while young men found employment in the Greenland whaling based on Dundee.[3]

If a precise distinction between urban and rural is hard to sustain in Fife, even at the close of the eighteenth century, the county did contain no less than seventeen communities which claimed the status of royal burghs, among them four which formed focal points of the surrounding districts. These were Dunfermline, with a reputed population of 5,192, Kirkcaldy with 2,607 (or perhaps 3,500 if its associated villages are included), Cupar with 3,135, and St Andrews with 2,754.[4] Even by the standards of the period these were not large figures, so that it is easy to understand the attraction of centres like Edinburgh, with over 80,000, Dundee with some 23,000, and Perth with 16,000, for the adjacent areas of Fife. Even so, its four principal towns were, within their limits, well-equipped to provide marketing facilities, technical services, and a wide variety of professional expertise for their neighbourhoods. The same was true of lesser burghs such as Inverkeithing and Burntisland, Auchtermuchty and Newburgh, Crail and the Anstruthers.[5]

Although these were very ancient communities, with a corporate life extending back over many centuries,[6] they were beginning to assume a more 'modern' character. It would, of course, be some time before this process made any great impact on the character of municipal government, the town councils being almost without exception 'self-perpetuating oligarchies' of the burgh merchants and crafts-

1. Wemyss, 790.
2. Crail, 162.
3. Kingsbarns, 502.
4. Dunfermline, 278; Kirkaldy, 511; Cupar of Fife, 199; St Andrew's, 718.
5. See, e.g., Newburgh, 674–6.
6. The account of Kirkaldy (519–29) includes a quite lengthy "History of the Burgh".

men and themselves controlling the election of members of
parliament for the 'districts of burghs'.[1] Despite this,
elections were occasions of public excitement severely criti-
cised by the ministers of Cupar, Inverkeithing, and Kinghorn,
while in Scoonie it was thought "no small advantage . . . to
the town of Leven that they have no connection with corporation or borough politics which, for the most part, are
attended with such bad effects upon the industry and morals
of the people".[2] A particular obstacle to industrial development was the right claimed by the crafts – despite an act of
1751 – to control "manufactories" within the burghs and in
Kirkcaldy, to avoid it, some of the earlier works were
deliberately sited in suburban villages beyond the burgh
'royalty'.[3]

Despite difficulties of this kind, by the 1790's quite a few
industries were operating within the Fife burghs in something
like a 'modern' manner. Kinghorn had shown particular
initiative in using the water-power of a stream passing through
its bounds to establish four mills for spinning flax and cotton
"by means of the Arkwright and Darlington machinery".[4]
In the part of Kirkcaldy within Abbotshall parish there were
"five cotton manufacturers of the name of the Spinning
Jeanies, the heavy parts of which are driven by a horse
engine",[5] and at St Andrews in 1792 "Messrs Robertson of
Glasgow established a factory for sewing and tambouring
muslin".[6] At Inverkeithing "an iron foundry was lately set
up . . . They make beautiful chimney grates, waggon wheels,
and all kinds of cast iron work for machinery and house
utensils".[7] Burntisland had "a sugar house" belonging to a
Glasgow company and a vitriol work about to be extended.[8]
Cupar had two tanneries supplying saddlery in increasing

1. The precise constitution depended on the *sett* of each burgh. At Kirkcaldy (544) the council consisted of "10 mariners, 8 merchants, and
   3 craftsmen".
2. Cupar of Fife, 205; Inverkeithing, 404; Kinghorn, 495; Scoonie, 770.
3. Steel, *op.cit.*
4. Kinghorn, 790.
5. Abbotshall, 5.
6. St Andrew's, 707.
7. Inverkeithing, 399.
8. Burntisland, 92.

quantity to the surrounding country and a brick-works "not yet able to answer the great demand for tiles".[1]

These examples suggest that if the industrial revolution had appeared in the burghs of Fife it was still in its early stages. Another revolution, likewise at an early stage, was that of public sanitation, but in Dunfermline at least a beginning had been made with the appointment of an officer to superintend the cleaning of the streets, now better paved and lit, and other similar matters.[2] Here, as at Cupar, Newburgh, and St Andrews, there was considerable re-building, and in Dunfermline "several streets" of new houses,[3] but it would be some time before the burghs acquired the handsome "public edifices" which were to make this whole period one of the most distinguished in Scottish urban architecture. Even at this stage, however, they comprised an educated society of some size and accomplishment, this in turn sustained by "grammar" and "english" schools providing advanced instruction in both an academic and more practical form.[4] And at St Andrews it was recognised that "the chief support of this city is the University and the conflux of strangers who here find excellent teachers in all different branches".[5]

These towns, forming as they did the principal centres of population in the county, were the obvious focal points of its system of communications. And as all the accounts emphasised the difficulties of travel and transport by land the fact that most of them were seaports increased their significance in this respect. Even inland centres like Dunfermline and Cupar had notions of obtaining access to the sea by means of canals.[6] Among the seaports Kirkcaldy was by far the most important, exporting coal and textiles and importing raw materials for building and industry.[7] But other lesser ports might carry a considerable trade through a preference for using the harbour

1. Cupar of Fife, 205.
2. Dunfermline, 275–6.
3. Ibid., 275; Cupar of Fife, 199–200; St Andrew's, 710; also Newburgh, 672.
4. See, e.g., Cupar of Fife, 212–3.
5. St Andrew's, 707.
6. Dunfermline, 277; Cupar of Fife, 206–7.
7. Kirkaldy, 529–30.

or landing-place nearest to hand with ships of relatively small burden. Largo, for example, exported farm produce to Leith and the West Country together with salt to Dundee and Perth and imported timber and iron direct from Norway.[1] On the east coast the somewhat decayed harbour of St Andrews had recently revived for "from this port chiefly is the eastern part of Fife, for 9 or 10 miles, supplied with wood and iron, which formerly were purchased at Dundee or Ely".[2] In the north of Fife the chief port was Newburgh which had a thriving export of wheat and barley from its fertile hinterland in the Howe of Fife "chiefly for the Edinburgh and Glasgow markets".[3] At most ports there were yards for the building and repair of vessels, also such auxiliary facilities as roperies and sail-making works.[4]

Where the shores of the two great estuaries came closest to one another there were ports which had a special function as ferry terminals – Woodhaven, Newport, and Ferryport-on-Craig on the Tay, Pettycur (Kinghon) and North Queensferry on the Forth. The ferry-boats were sailing vessels, none of any great size, and were used according to conditions of wind and tide and the type of cargo to be carried.[5] At the terminals, and in nearby towns, horses and post-chaises could be hired, the great days of the public mail coach being yet to come. Despite the almost universal criticism of the roads under the statute-labour system,[6] and the hopes entertained of the new turnpikes,[7] it is noteworthy that Samuel Johnson, not much given to praise of things Scottish, had a different impression when he passed through Fife just twenty years before: "The roads are neither rough nor dirty; and it affords a southern

1. Largo, 570–1. By contrast the much better harbours of Burntisland (93–4) and Elie (349) were under-used.
2. St Andrew's, 706–7.
3. Newburgh, 675–6.
4. Anstruther Easter, 28; Dysart, 334–5; Kirkaldy, 540; Scoonie, 768; St Andrew's, 707; Wemyss, 791.
5. Ferryport-on-Craig, 366–7; Forgan, 382–3; Inverkeithing, 397–8; Kinghorn, 494.
6. The 'statute labour' was regulated by the Justices of the Peace for the county but it might be commuted for a money payment.
7. Turnpikes were established in terms of a *Report of the Committee appointed by the . . . Heritors of the County of Fife* (n.p., 1788).

stranger a new kind of pleasure to travel so commodiously
without interruption of toll-gates".[1] If there were no
public passenger vehicles there were at least public carriers
who conveyed goods at regular intervals, generally twice a
week between the major towns, once a fortnight between
other places.[2] There were also official "post-boys" (pro-
ceeding on foot as much as on horse) who carried mail
between the government post-offices.[3]

Of all the questions addressed to Sir John Sinclair's correspondents the ones that affected them most directly related
to the "ecclesiastical state" of their parishes. These involved a
discussion not only of the provision made – in church, manse,
glebe, and stipend – for the official establishment but the
extent to which it could count on the active support of the
local community.

Like much else in this period the fabrics of Scottish parish
churches were in a state of transition well exemplified in Fife.
What may seem surprising is that in half the parishes of
medieval origin (all but seven of the total) the pre-reformation
building was still in use, a state of affairs by no means to the
taste of all the ministers. At Leuchars, admittedly, the fine
romanesque structure was described as "an ancient lofty
building . . . more than sufficient to hold the parishioners".[4]
But at Dalgety the church was "an old building very much
out of repair and not well adapted in construction or situation
as a place of worship for the parish".[5] At a grander level, the
arcaded design of St Serf's, Dysart was regarded as an obstacle
to preaching and as it accommodated "not above half of the
congregation" parishioners drifted away, "some to the
sectaries", others "taking advantage of this circumstance to
forsake public worship altogether".[6] At Cupar, however, a

1. S. Johnson, *A Journey to the Western Islands of Scotland*, ed. R.W . Chapman
    (London, 1924).
2. See, e.g., Leuchars, 613.
3. See, e.g., Wemyss, 805.
4. Leuchars, 607.
5. Dalgety, 242.
6. Dysart, 340. On non-attendance at public worship see also the obser-
    vations in Newburgh, 680–1.

rather similar building had been replaced in 1785 by a new church, hailed as "the most elegant structure of its kind in the county",[1] and within a few years all but a handful of parishes had been similarly equipped. There was also an even more comprehensive replacement of manses in the elegant classical manner which only a few, like that of Wemyss (1791), had achieved in the preceding period.[2]

While the Presbyterian Establishment commanded the support of the great majority of the population of Fife, and its historical rival, 'the episcopal interest', could now muster no more than three places of worship,[3] a serious problem was posed by secessions from within its own ranks. Of such there were two of more than passing significance. The first was the 'Original Secession' of 1733 which produced an 'Associate Presbytery'[4] and then a Synod which divided in 1747, over the question of the burgess oath, into 'Burghers' and 'Anti-Burghers'. The second major secession arose from the deposition in 1752 of the saintly Thomas Gillespie, minister of Carnock, who nine years later at Colinsburgh formed the 'Presbytery of Relief' or 'Relief Church'. All these bodies were well represented in Fife, the total of 36 congregations comprising 18 Burgher, 9 Anti-Burgher, and 9 Relief.[5]

The distribution of these "sectaries" was distinctly uneven. In places as different in character and location as Abdie, Balmerino, Ferryport, Markinch, Saline, Scoonie, and Wemyss they were said to amount to no more than a minute fraction of the parishioners. In Scoonie, for example, with a very varied population of 1,675, "there are not above 150 seperatists from the established church", and in Markinch the

---

1. Cupar of Fife, 200-1.
2. Wemyss, 799.
3. At St Andrew's, Cupar, and Pittenweem.
4. This presbytery, formed at Gairney Bridge in Kinross-shire, attracted the support of three Fife ministers, including the influential Ralph Erskine of Dunfermline, brother of Ebenezer, leader of the movement.
5. R. Small, *History of the congregations of the United Presbyterian Church from 1733 to 1900* (Edinburgh, 1904). Occasional congregations of Cameronians, Independents, and Baptists are also mentioned.

proportion was put at "about one 16th part only".[1] But in Auchtermuchty, Ceres, Dunfermline, Inverkeithing, Kennoway, Kilconquhar, Largo, Leslie, Newburgh, Newburn, and Strathmiglo between a quarter and a half of the population had left the establishment. In Auchtermuchty, where the parish church had to compete with three "sectarist" meeting-houses, the references to the latter are particularly bitter.[2] In Inverkeithing, on the other hand, where the minister put the proportion of adherents of the establishment at not much more than "the half of the inhabitants", he was able to speak with tart urbanity of the "spirit and zeal" with which the sects retained their followers.[3] But beyond the element of ecclesiastical competition some parish ministers resented the way in which the secessionist bodies drew off "the ignorant and unwary" from their care to "make up a salary" for their own ministers and their practice of sending back members "in need of charity" to the parish session for relief.[4] And when the French Revolution entered on its more radical phase they were further accused of "forming societies, which consisted if not wholly yet mostly of persons of these sects, for circulating seditious pamphlets and disseminating disaffection to King and Government".[5]

Despite these tensions, most ministers of the Established Church were able to speak of their ecclesiastical opponents with a fair measure of charity. Even in Newburn, "for many years past . . . a nursery of seceders", the minister observed that "diversity of religious sentiment does not preclude social intercourse and mutual good offices". But beyond this he was assured that "rational religion seems to be gaining ground".[6] Such a belief in the reconciliation of religion and reason was a basic element in 'moderate' thought and it explains, in part at least, the importance which its adherents attached to an effective system of education at the parochial

1. Scoonie, 763; Markinch, 630.
2. Auchtermuchty, 56–8.
3. Inverkeithing, 402.
4. St Monance, 749. At Dunfermline (280) "the poor belonging to the sectaries are not admitted to the parish funds".
5. St Monance, 750n.
6. Newburn, 688.

level. As the minister of Auchtermuchty put it with characteristic asperity: "The youth in this place have been, and now
are, ruined by bad schoolmasters; and to this may be attributed
the narrow and uncharitable dispositions of the inhabitants".[1] His ideal clearly was what was said to have
been achieved in Saline where the views of the parishioners
were reported to be "tolerably sound and rational".[2] But
more impressive than such special pleading was the exposition
by the minister of Falkland of the traditional Scottish view
of the advantages of general education:

"The lowest classes of the people were taught to read the
scriptures, instructed in the first principles of religion and
morality, and thus prepared in schools for being further
enlightened and improved by the theological and moral
lectures of the churches. Hence the distinguished superiority
of the common people of Scotland in knowledge and
sobriety. Parish schools have hitherto been the great
nurseries of the church and other learned professions."[3]

The organisation of parochial schools was regulated by the
well-known act of 1696 which bound the heritors to provide
a schoolhouse together with a salary for the schoolmaster.[4]
As has been noted, in parishes containing a royal burgh there
was usually a grammar school maintained by the town
council.[5] The accounts confirm that this arrangement was
generally in force, though in many cases a single school was quite
inadequate, particularly if the parish was of any size and there
had been a significant growth or redistribution of population.
But beyond such problems – which were alleviated in some
parishes by the existence of privately sponsored "subscription"
or "venture" schools[6] – there was recurring criticism, in

1. Auchtermuchty, 62.
2. Saline, 758.
3. Falkland, 362.
4. The interest of the church was recognised in the right of the local
   presbytery to insist on the provision of a school and to approve the
   appointment of schoolmasters who functioned to a great extent under
   the supervision of the parish ministers and kirk sessions.
5. There was also the special case of the country parish of Newburn which
   had a grammar school of "considerable repute" deriving from a bene-
   faction by John Wood of Orkie in 1660 (Newburn, 688–9).
6. These were most numerous in the towns and, by most accounts, varied
   very considerably in quality.

account after account, of the inadequacy of the salary provided for the parochial schoolmaster.[1] Although nearly a century had elapsed since the act of 1696, in the majority of parishes this salary stood at the minimum then prescribed of 100 merks Scots, or, as the minister of Dalgety put it, "somewhat below £7".[2] In most cases, admittedly, the schoolmaster had additional emoluments as session clerk, and in a few instances there were special mortifications which might raise the total salary to around £20.[3] But there was general agreement that, even so, schoolmasters were grossly underpaid. The point was well expressed by the minister of Kinghorn:

"We cannot help observing with regret that a body of men so highly useful to the community as country school-masters . . . should be in general so poorly provided for by the country".[4]

Most of the schoolmasters had in fact received a university education and not a few were men of outstanding scholarship, like Robert Duncan of Inverkeithing who had translated Boethius into English and was said to teach "besides the common branches of education, the languages, navigation, and the other parts of mathematics."[5] At Anstruther Wester the schoolmaster was esteemed "the best teacher of navigation on the coast" but otherwise seems to have confined his instruction to "English and the principles of the Christian religion".[6] At Kilconquhar, out of a total enrolment of between 30 and 40 "four are at present learning Latin".[7] Thus the varying needs of the pupils were met with reasonable efficiency. And at Newburgh, which had two schools, one officially provided, the other "taught by a Seceder", it was

1. See especially Auchtertoul, 72; Cameron, 104; Carnock, 126; Dalgety, 243–4; Denino, 258–9; Dunbog, 268.
2. Dalgety, 243.
3. Ceres, 145–6; Largo, 573; Leuchars, 608; St Andrew's (Boarhills), 728; Saline, 756–7.
4. Kinghorn, 493.
5. Inverkeithing, 401 and n.
6. Anstruther Wester, 33. While religious instruction was accepted as an inherent function of the parochial school, some parishes had special "Sunday schools" primarily (though not exclusively) for this purpose. (Dysart, 340–1; Kingsbarns, 503; Torryburn, 783).
7. Kilconquhar, 450.

reported that "during the winter months both are resorted to, after ordinary hours of labour, by a considerable number of grown up persons, for the purpose of learning English, writing, arithmetic, book-keeping, and navigation".[1] But despite all this the minister of Auchterderran considered that "the parochial schools are by no means supplied with such enlightened teachers as formerly".[2] The statistics of attendance further confirm that many children were untouched by the educational system, but as schooling was neither compulsory nor free it might be counted something of an achievement that it embraced as high a proportion of the population as it actually did.

There was one other area in which the parish ministers held a special responsibility, that of "poor relief". Like education this was supposed to be regulated by statute, especially two acts of 1579 and 1597, which provided for the assessment of the 'indwellers' of each parish to maintain its own poor and placed the supervision of the system under the kirk session. There were also arrangements for the suppression of "sturdy beggars" and vagrancy. The reports of the Fife minister confirm that here as elsewhere in Scotland this system was largely inoperative. Responsibility for poor relief undoubtedly rested with the sessions but instead of being financed by a "poor rate" they depended primarily on the voluntary contributions of church attenders. To these there might be added such items as "mortcloth dues" and the income from special mortifications,[3] but the total amount available was almost always less than was requisite, even under normal conditions.[4] In a crisis like that occasioned by the harvest failure of 1782 special measures had to be taken, and in some places at least parochial assessments were made.[5]

1. Newburgh, 681.
2. Auchterderran, 49.
3. These were particularly numerous in Dunfermline (282n–284n). There were also special "charitable societies", like those organised for the sailors, trades, and colliers of Pittenweem (698).
4. See especially Kinghorn, 487–8.
5. Carnock, 127–8.

Introduction

While there was broad agreement among the ministers that the funds for sustaining the "deserving poor" were generally inadequate, they were not in favour of an undue increase, and there was certainly no thought that any encouragement should be given to "vagrant beggars" who seem to have been a particular problem in Cupar and areas adjoining the ferry terminals.[1] Believing as they did in individual self-reliance, and having a semi-biblical notion that justification for relief should arise from some manifest misfortune, the authorities wished to keep assistance to the absolute minimum, defined by the minister of Leslie in the bleak statement that since 1759 (the year of his own settlement) "no person in this parish hath perished from hunger, nakedness, or want of lodging; nor have any taken to begging".[2]

On the question of how these minimal funds were best raised and administered there was some divergence of opinion. Most felt that it was unjust that the greater part of the burden should fall on the charitable benevolence of worshippers at the parish church, with dissenters and heritors as such being excused. The ministers of Burntisland and Largo were particularly forceful in arguing for "a general assessment".[3] On the other hand Dr George Campbell of Cupar thought that this system – in effect that which operated in England – was "attended with such pernicious effects" that the best solution was for landholders to make appropriately generous donations to the sessions of "those parishes where their property lies" and leave the administration of relief in their hands.[4]

If the ministers appear here and elsewhere in a somewhat unsympathetic light, there is ample evidence in the accounts of a concern for the quality of life of their parishioners as a whole. A problem on which Sir John Sinclair was particularly anxious to obtain precise information was that of

1. Cupar of Fife, 210; Forgan, 391; Kinghorn, 494. In Cupar they may well have been displaced agricultural workers.
2. Leslie, 586.
3. Burntisland, 98–9; Largo, 573.
4. Cupar of Fife, 210–12; also Kirkaldy, 554.

wages and prices and his correspondents did their best by supplying him with meticulous particulars, often with comparative figures for preceding periods.[1] That the price of most "necessaries of life" had increased sharply in recent years was undeniable,[2] but despite this, in Dr Campbell's view "the labourer at present is better lodged, better fed and clothed, and can give a more decent education to his children than his father", the chief reason being because "the proportion of the price of his own labour . . . is more in his favour than at any preceding period". He also had the advantage of more continuous employment and, in the potato, access to "a vast additional supply of food".[3] At Anstruther Wester it was also thought that labourers "when they are frugal and industrious . . . live very comfortably. Thrice the quantity of butcher meat and wheat bread are used now than were twenty years ago in this parish".[4] Elsewhere, however, it would seem that meat was a rarity,[5] the chief foods consumed being "meal, potatoes, milk, and small beer, with kail".[6] But the old Scots ale – of which ministers in general had a good opinion – was being steadily adulterated under the pressure of the Malt Tax and replaced by whisky, regarded as "pernicious both to health and morals".[7]

The most moving presentation of this sombre view of the condition of "the day labourer and his family" was by the minister of Auchterderran: "The greatest evils of their situation arise from the lowness of their diet and the wretchedness of their lodging . . . exposing them to a numerous class of diseases incident to such a condition".[8] And beyond these, and maladies peculiar to particular localities and occupations,[9] there were periodic visitations by epidemics,

1.   See, e.g., Monimail, 656.
2.   A notable exception to this trend, in some places at least, was oatmeal, "the principal food of the common people" (Beath, 87).
3.   Cupar of Fife, 229.
4.   Anstruther Wester, 32.
5.   Largo, 574.
6.   Kinglassie, 499.
7.   Saline, 758; also Dunfermline, 472.
8.   Auchterderran, 47.
9.   See, e.g., Aberdour, 25; Leuchars, 594-5.

especially small-pox. The last was now mercifully reduced by the use of inoculation,[1] but it was thought that "the indiscriminate practice of visiting the sick" was responsible for a needless spreading of infection.[2] Despite such hazards, which severely curtailed the normal expectation of life, almost every parish could produce examples of individual longevity.[3]

Over and above this wealth of "statistical particulars" relating to the condition of their parishioners, the ministers were encouraged to make such "miscellaneous observations" concerning their "manner of life" as seemed appropriate.[4] They were also asked to supply details of natural phenomena, history, and antiquities, which produced a miscellany of highly variable quality. In this by far the most reliable as well as the most attractive element is to be found in the descriptions of landscape, like the charming account of "the prospect from Kellie Law" by the minister of Carnbee, who, with several others, also supplied valuable information on migratory birds.[5] But it was with the quality of human life that both Sir John Sinclair and his correspondents were primarily concerned, and it is on this theme that this introduction should most appropriately end.

What struck the more observant ministers was the desire and the capacity of quite ordinary people to seek out information and to reach their own conclusions on a variety of problems. As was noted in Auchterderran, "they endeavour to form opinions, by reading as well as by frequent conversation, on some very metaphysical points connected with religion. They likewise read, occasionally, a variety of other books".[6] There was, of course, no great wish that this independence of thought should express itself in religious or

1. See, e.g., St Monance, 738.
2. Newburn, 686.
3. The extreme case would seem to be that reported in Collessie, 153–4. On "expectation of life" see the elaborate calculations for Kettle (435–8) by David Wilkie, minister of the adjoining parish of Cults (193–4).
4. As an example of this, in Auchterderran (50) the minister regretted that "the people have scarcely any sports after they are grown up".
5. Carnbee, 110–1; also Kilconquhar, 453n.
6. Auchterderran, 48–9.

political dissent, and most ministers were obviously happiest when they could report, as at Strathmiglo, that "the people . . . are in general disposed to industry and economy; they enjoy the comforts and advantages of society and seem contented".[1] Again, although there was frequent emphasis on what were thought to be distinctive Scottish virtues, in a society still overwhelmingly indigenous in composition,[2] and an occasional note of regret at the passing of traditional usages, it was the almost universal opinion that the latter, including the replacement of spoken Scots by English,[3] was the necessary price to be paid for "that civilisation which has recently produced so great a change on the manners of the nation at large".[4]

R. G. CANT
Centre for Advanced Historical Studies
University of St Andrews

1. Strathmiglo, 776–7.
2. See, e.g., Anstruther Wester, 35.
3. See, e.g., Denino, 265.
4. Newburgh, 682.

APPENDIX

1791	Monimail	884	1101	1066	+25	+21
1793	Moonzie	249	171	201	−31	−19
1792–3	Newburgh	1347	1664	1936	+24	+44
1794	Newburn	438	456	412	+4	−6
1790–1	Pittenweem	939	1157	1072	+23	+14
1793	St Andrews and St Leonard's	4913	4335[11]	4203	−12	−14
1790	St Monance	780	832	852	+7	+9
1793	Saline	1285	950	945	−26	−26
1791	Scoonie	1528	1675	1681	+10	+10
1790	Strathmiglo	1095[12]	980	1629	−11	+49
1791	Torryburn	1635	1600	1403	−2	−14
1791	Wemyss	3041	3025	3264	−1	+7
		80970	87224	93071	+8	+15

† The dates given in this first column indicate, as nearly as possible, the actual year in which the count of population was made. The parish account itself often gives this information: failing that, the date is either that indicated by Sinclair at the start of each volume of the published *Account* or is the date of publication of the appropriate volume in the 1970s.

1. The minister gives a population of 494 "on the roll, of all ages", i.e. those expected to be able to read, learn and be examined on the catechism: the non-examinable children usually numbered about one-fifth of the population – hence the estimate of 600, although it still seems too low.
2. The population in 1764 is reported to have been 900.
3. The population is given as between 400 and 500.
4. An estimate of 1100 is refined in a second submission to 1210.
5. A figure of 1151 in 1780 is also recorded.
6. A figure of 910 in 1781 is recorded.
7. The later account reports a population of 1624 in 1797–8.
8. Population "from the age of going to school" said to have been 1200 in 1785, and by and large unchanged since.
9. 1643 in 1778.
10. Population reported as 1096 in 1756, 1165 in 1769, 1189 in 1775, 1211 in 1781 and 1212 in 1785 since which date it "has not materially altered".
11. In 1755 and 1793 these parishes were reported separately – in 1755, there were 4590 in St Andrew's and 323 in St Leonard's; in 1793 the figures were respectively 3950 and 385.
12. The figure given by Webster in 1755 is 1695: the minister is adamant that this was "probably a slip of the pen for 1095", which seems a much more likely estimate of the population.

FIFE

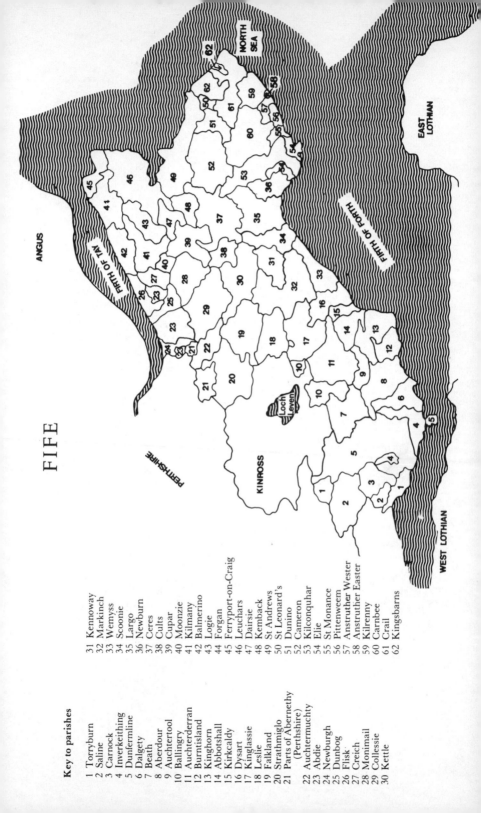

Key to parishes

1 Torryburn
2 Saline
3 Carnock
4 Inverkeithing
5 Dunfermline
6 Dalgety
7 Beath
8 Aberdour
9 Auchtertool
10 Ballingry
11 Auchterderran
12 Burntisland
13 Kinghorn
14 Abbotshall
15 Kirkcaldy
16 Dysart
17 Kinglassie
18 Leslie
19 Falkland
20 Strathmiglo
21 Parts of Abernethy (Perthshire)
22 Auchtermuchty
23 Abdie
24 Newburgh
25 Dunbog
26 Flisk
27 Creich
28 Monimail
29 Collessie
30 Kettle
31 Kennoway
32 Markinch
33 Wemyss
34 Scoonie
35 Largo
36 Newburn
37 Ceres
38 Cults
39 Cupar
40 Moonzie
41 Kilmany
42 Balmerino
43 Logie
44 Forgan
45 Ferryport-on-Craig
46 Leuchars
47 Dairsie
48 Kemback
49 St Andrews
50 St Leonard's
51 Dunino
52 Cameron
53 Kilconquhar
54 Elie
55 St Monance
56 Pittenweem
57 Anstruther Wester
58 Anstruther Easter
59 Kilrenny
60 Carnbee
61 Crail
62 Kingsbarns

PARISH of ABBOT's HALL,

(COUNTY OF FIFE.)

By the Rev. Mr GEORGE SHAW.

Name, Situation, Soil, &c.

IT is faid that an Abbot of Dunfermline built a fummer-houfe near the place where the church of Abbot's Hall now ftands, and called it the Hall of the Abbot. Abbot's Hall is in the county and Synod of Fife, and prefbytery of Kirkaldy. Its form is very irregular, being interfected in feveral places by the neighbouring parifhes. In the broadeft and longeft corners it may be about 2 miles each way. It is bounded by Kirkaldy on the E. Kinghorn and Auchtertool on the W. Auchterderran on the N. and the frith of Forth on the S. The general appearance of the country is very pleafant; it is flat for about near half a mile north of the coaft; from thence rifes into pretty high grounds, or beautiful banks, floping gently. The air is dry and healthy. The foil, immediately by the town, is light and fandy, but very fertile, efpecially in fhowery fummers. It can fcarcely be hurt by rain, but eafily by drought. As it rifes northwards, it is deeper and ftronger,

but

but thin and cold on the north fkirts. The extent of fea-
coaft is about half a mile, lying along the weft fide of the
Bay of Kirkaldy. It is very flat and fandy, but exceedingly pleafant; moft of the towns and villages on the coaft
are pleafantly fituated.—The lands of Abbot's Hall, which
belong to Mr Fergufon of Raith, abound in coal of different feams, it is faid, fome 3, 5, and even 14 feet. Part
of the crop-coal only was wrought about 40 years ago.

Population.—The ancient extent of the population is not
eafily traced, but was much lefs than at prefent. The return to Dr Webfter, about 40 years ago, was only 1348
fouls. In 1791, the total population is 2136; males 1061,
females 1075. The number of inhabitants in the town is
1660, in the country 476. The annual average of births
is 50, of deaths 44, of marriages 22. Under 10 years of
age there are 249 males, 239 females; only a few perfons
are between 80 and 90. There are 6 heritors, 2 of whom
refide. Farmers 25, their families about 200; 8 principal
manufacturers, befides a few fmaller ones; apprentices 50;
feamen about 10 or 12; male houfehold-fervants 63; female 60; merchants 12. The great bulk of the inhabitants
are tradefmen, being wholly employed in manufactures.
Families of gentry 3; 1 in the town and 2 in the country.
One minifter of the Eftablifhed Church, and a perfon who
preaches to a fmall Cameronian meeting. The number of
the Eftablifhed Church 1338, of Seceders 798. Within
thefe 20 years, the population of the town is increafed between 300 and 400; but the country part of the parifh is
decreafed above 100. The increafe of the former is owing
to the manufactures, and the decreafe of the latter to a
coal-work being entirely given up, and 7 or 8 farms being
taken into one. Batchelors 27, married men 187, widowers

·ers 20, widows 87. At an average, each marriage produces 3 children.

Agriculture, &c.—Extenſive plantations have been for
ſeveral years, and are ſtill carrying on by Mr Ferguſon of
Raith. There being in this pariſh about 143 acres occupied by plantations, little or none of theſe grounds are a-
rable, and are ſo ſteep that they are fit for nothing elſe.
The number of horſes, cows, cattle and young beaſts may
be about 1250. The acres in the pariſh are about 3165.
In corn 530, in turnip and cabbage 85, in potatoes 84, in
wheat 85, in barley 250, in peaſe 176, in ſown graſs 164,
in common paſturage 1278, for feeding cattle 300, in ſummer fallow 70. Oats and peaſe are ſown from the beginning of March to the middle of April; barley from the
beginning of May to near the end of it; wheat in September and October, and turnip from the middle of July,
&c. They reap ſometimes in the end of Auguſt, and the
beginning of September. The pariſh imports articles of
proviſion. The valued rent of this pariſh is L. 798 : 9 : 9.
The real rent may be about L. 3165. The arable land
near the town is about L. 3, 10 s. the acre. Beſt paſture
upwards of L. 2, 10 s. On the north ſkirts of the pariſh,
ſome as low as 5 s. the acre. In general, the ſize of farms
is from 200 to near 300 acres. The rent about L. 200.
There may be a few ſmaller. The number of farms is
decreaſing conſiderably, owing to their being larger. Except the land immediately by the town, the pariſh is wholly incloſed, and the farmers are ſo much convinced of the
advantage thereof, that they do not think they would be
able to pay their advanced rents, if it were not ſo. There
are 50 ploughs, of which the one half is the old Scotch
plough, improved by being made lighter, and the other
half the Engliſh plough made by Small, or after his conſtruction,

ftruction. There are alfo 50 carts in the country part of the parifh, and 20 more in the town; 3 carriages, 1 of which is a coach, and the others 2 four-wheeled chaifes.

Stipend, School, Poor, &c.—The ftipend, except 100 merks in money, being paid in victual, varies with the prices. It is 46 bolls of barley, 34 of meal, and 36 of oats; but taken at the lateft valuation, of L. 100 Scots the chalder, including the manfe and glebe, which is $6\frac{1}{2}$ acres, may be about L. 80. Mr Fergufon of Raith is patron. A new, larger, and more elegant church was built 4 years ago, in the fame place where the old ftood. The firft manfe in this parifh was built in the 1772, the minifter having till then only an allowance of L. 5 for a houfe.—The falary of the parochial fchool is about L. 7; perquifites a-rifing from baptifms and proclamations about L. 5; from the feffion and at the communion L 2; L. 5 for teaching poor fcholars, being the intereft of L. 100, mortified about 30 years ago, by a Mr Dundas, who lived at Raith. The number of fcholars at an average is about 60. There may be 2 or 3 fmall private fchools in the town.—There are 6 poor on the roll, and feveral others are fupplied according as their need requires. The annual amount of the contributions for their relief, arifing from the collections at the church, the intereft of money, &c. is about L. 50; and the parifh is well able to fupply its own poor, were they not oppreffed with vagrants from almoft every quarter, efpecially from the North, going to and from the Infirmary at Edinburgh.

Prices, Wages, &c.—The prices of provifions are near double what they were 30 and 40 years ago. Beef, mutton, veal, lamb, and pork, &c. are $4\frac{1}{2}$ d. and 5 d. the pound, according to the different feafons, all Troy or heavy weight.

Pigs

Pigs 4 s. geefe 2 s. 6 d. ducks 8 d. each, chickens 6 d. and
8 d. the pair, butter 9 d. cheefe, fuch as is commonly fold,
3 d. the pound, all heavy weight; wheat and barley at 4 s.
Sterling below the Mid-Lothian fiars, &c. Day-labourers
get 1 s. carpenters, mafons, &c. get 1 s. 6 d. tailors, when
they work out, 6 d. and their meat; but they moftly work
in their own houfes, at fo much the piece. The only fuel
is coal, price paid on the fpot, 6 d. the load, weighing 22
ftone. On different coal-hills the weight is different, and
fo are the prices. Some within half a mile, 2 and 3 miles,
&c. Such as are frugal and attentive, feem to live comfortably in their fituation, and bring up large families in general. Their children coft them little, and as foon as
they can do any thing, are employed in manufactures;
their wages are exceeding good, and double of what
they were formerly. The wages of male-fervants are L. 6
and L. 7, of female L 2, 10 s. and L. 3 a-year. There are
but about 8 livery-fervants, and their wages vary from
L. 10 to L. 20, L. 30, &c. according to their ftations, &c.

Mifcellaneous Obfervations.—In general, the people are of
the middle fize. The greateft height which any have attained, is about 6 feet 2 inches. They are very much difpofed to induftry.—In the town are 3 principal manufactures, under the name of Checks and Bed-tikes. Thefe
employ between 200 and 300 looms in the parifh, and a
great number in the parifhes around. Two of thefe have
each an extenfive bleachfield near by, where they whiten
their own yarn. Befides thefe, are a few who do a little
in the fame branches. There are befides 5 cotton manufactures of the name of the Spinning Jeanies, the heavy
parts of which are driven by a horfe-engine. Thefe employ neat 200 hands, feveral of whom are children, &c.
Other buildings are prefently erecting for the fame, &c.—
The

The roads are tolerably good. There are only 2 ſmall
bridges, which ſeparate the pariſh from the neighbouring one on the weſt, both in good caſe, and lately
repaired, made and kept by the county. The ſtatute-
labour is exacted partly in kind and partly in money.—
Though the harveſt was late in 1782, and the weather very
unfavourable, ſo that the prices roſe much above what they
uſed to be, yet it was not ſo ſeverely felt in this part of
the country as in ſome others, owing partly to the dryneſs
of the ſituation, and to a conſiderable quantity of corn being
imported ſtraight from the Baltic into the harbour of Kirkcaldy, &c. The poor had very liberal ſupplies. Mr
Ferguſon gave L. 50 to be diſtributed among them, and
the ſeſſion, at the deſire of the heritors, lifted L. 40, and
diſpoſed of it to the ſame purpoſe, over and above their ordinary diſtribution.—There are 4 brewers in the town.
Theſe keep decent houſes, and good company. But there
are ſeveral that are commonly called Tapſters, becauſe they
ſell ale to theſe brewers, that are nuiſances to ſociety.—
Within theſe 20 years, above 100 new houſes have been
built in the town. About the one half of theſe are on new
foundations, and the other on old ones, made much larger
and better; and in the country part of the pariſh are upwards of 20. Some ſtill employ cottagers, and others do
not, preferring hired ſervants to them, and conſequently
differ in their ſentiments concerning the effects.

PARISH of ABDIE.

(County and Synod of Fife, Presbytery of Cupar.)

By a Friend to Statistical Inquiries.

Name, Surface, Climate, &c.

NO fatisfactory account can be obtained of the name of this parifh. It is probable, however, that it is of Celtic origin. The extent of this parifh is confiderable; but, from the circumftance of its being feparated by the intervention of other parifhes, into 3 parts, it is not eafy to afcertain its precife length and breadth. It is fituated between Abernethy and Monimail on the S. of the river Tay, in the heart of the range of high lands, which, to weftward, is known by the name of Ochil Hills. The middle part, where the church and manfe are placed, is larger than either of the other two parts, and is bounded on the W. and S. W. by Newburgh; on the

the N. by the Tay ; on the N. E. and E. by Dunbog and
Fliſk ; on the S. E. by Monimail ; on the S. W. by Colleſſie. The E. part of the pariſh is bounded on the W.
N. W and N. by the Fliſk ; on the N E., E. and S. E.
by Criech ; and on the S. and S. W. by Dunbog. The
W. part is bounded on the E. by Newburgh ; on the N.
by Newburgh and Abernethy ; on the W. and S. by A-
bernethy. Dunbog on the E. and Newburgh on the W.
lying thus in the boſom of Abdie, favour the tradition of
their forming, at ſome diſtant period, parts of that pariſh. No traces, however, of the diſjunction of Dunbog
can now be diſcovered ; but the curious article, at the
bottom of the page, confirms the tradition reſpecting
Newburgh *.

The

* Apud Holyroodhouſe, 3tio. die menſis Februarii 1632 years. Anent
the ſupplication preſented to the commiſſioners for the ſurrender of teinds,
for Mr. David Orme, miniſter a Newburgh, making mention, that where
the kirks of Ebdie and Newburgh have been ſeparat theſe manie years by-
paſt, by act of ſynodal aſſemblie, ſpecial conſent of the patron, gentlemen
of the parochin, and all others parties having interes for the time, for manie grave and weighty reaſons contained in the foreſaid act, and likewiſe,
ſeeing his majeſtie has preſented the ſupplicant to the kirk of Newburgh,
where he preſently ſerves the cure, by virtue of his Heines's preſentation
and the Biſhop of St. Androis admiſſion, and collation thereupon ; and
ſeeing the ſaid commiſſion are now ſettling an maintenance and proviſion
for the kirk of Ebdie ; humbly defiring therefor the ſaids commiſſioners
to ratify the ſaid ſeparation, like as at mair length is conteined in the
ſupplication : quhilk being read, heard and confidered by the commiſſioners ; and they having likewiſe h ard Mr. Andrew Murray miniſter at Ebdie,
and the ſaid ſuppliant, who were perſonally preſent ; hereupon, and being
well advyfit, with all that was propoſed and allegit by them heiranent,
the Lords, and others of the commiſſion, for the ſurrender and teinds, with
conſent of the ſaids twa miniſters, and heritors preſent, has ratified, and
be the tenor heirof, ratifies the act above written ; whereby the ſaid kirk of
Newburgh is ſeparat from the kirk of Ebdie ; and declares the ſame to be
an ſeparat kirk be itſelf in all time coming ; without prejudice always to
the ſaid Mr. Andrew Murray of his right of patronage of the ſaid kirk, as
accords of law

The face of the country, in all parts of the parifh, par-ticularly towards the E. and W. extremities, is remark-ably uneven. The quantity of arable land, however, is probably not lefs than in any equal extent of furface throughout the whole length of the Ochil Hills. From the free circulation of air among thefe hills, and the pre-vailing drynefs of the foil below, the climate, in moft parts of the parifh, proves very falubrious. The fituation of the minifter's manfe is, perhaps, as unfavourable to health, as any other houfe in the parifh ; for it ftands clofe by a lake of confiderable extent in low and wet ground.

Hills, Woods, Rivers, Lakes, &c.—Of the many hills in the parifh, 2, Clatchart-Crag and Norman's Law, are remarkable ; the one for its abrupt precipitous front, the other for its height. Abdie is bare of wood, there being only one confiderable fpot in the whole extent of the parifh planted with trees. It is to be hoped, how-ever, that the proprietors will be induced to convert the inarable fummits of fome of the hills to ufe and beauty, by covering them with wood. The grounds, in many places, require fhelter ; and there is good reafon to be-lieve, that the feveral fpecies of fir planted in the neigh-bourhood with fuccefs, will thrive in the high lands of Abdie. No river runs through this parifh : It is, not-withftanding, well watered. It contains feveral lakes or lochs, the principal of which, in point of largenefs and beauty, is the loch of Lindores : this is a fine fheet of water in the middle divifion of the parifh, of nearly a mile in length, and of unequal breadth : It belongs to Mr. Simfon of Brunton. Its perch and pike, its ducks

and

and other water fowls, contribute to the amusement of the gentlemen in the neighbourhood, whom the proprietor politely admits to the privilege of fishing and fowling. Were the rising grounds, with which this lake is surrounded on all sides, covered with plantations, disposed in a proper manner, a prospect, it is believed, would be furnished not inferior, in point of beauty, to those presented by lakes, which have attracted much notice, and acquired celebrity. Ill supplied, as the country at present is, with wood, no traveller, in passing along the road which leads from Cupar to Perth, can survey the loch of Lindores, when it opens at once on his view, without being both surprised and pleased. The small wood of Wood-Mill, just showing its northern extremity on the S. W., the manse, church, and church-yard, standing solitary on the W., and the old mansion-house of Old Lindores, with the trees that surround it on the N., have a very fine effect. Taken altogether, they justify the following lines occasioned by the death of the late minister, Mr. Millar *.

" 'Tis not the site that fixes my regard,
　Nor lake, nor grove, nor hills, inspire the bard:
　　　　　　　　　　　　　　　　Though

* Short biographical sketches, it is believed, are not foreign from the design of this work. Respect for the young man, whose death the epistle laments, prompts his friend and neighbour, to preserve his memory in this more lasting and public manner, and to say, Mr. Millar was, from early life, distinguished for sedateness, application and engaging manners: he officiated as assistant preacher at Perth with much approbation : he was received with cordiality as minister of Abdie: he performed his duty among his people with diligence and credit. But, so it pleased God, he died in the beginning of the 5th year of his ministry, in the 28th year of his age. A monument is erected over his grave, with proper inscriptions by his father, Mr. Millar, minister of Inchture.

Though nature here might warm a Thomſon's lay,
Or a Salvator Roſa's powers diſplay;
And richly grants, as genius may chooſe,
Helvetian manners, and Helvetian views;
Another hour may note the varying face
Of vale and mountain, and their beauties trace;
Our morning walks renew and frequent ſtand,
To mark that Abdie is a Switzerland."

Antiquities.—If gentlemens ſeats uninhabited, negleᢗed, or in ruins, may be included under this article, the pariſh of Abdie has many antiquities, there being 8 manſion-houſes in it, Den Mill, Den Muir, Kinnaird, Ayton, Lindores, Wood Mill, Berry Hole, Ormiſton, either to-tally deſerted, or inhabited by tenants. The manſion-houſe of Kinnaird, mentioned by Sibbald as a large new houſe, is now in ruins. The manſion-houſe of Den Mill, built 1679, is in the ſame ſtate, and ſhows the havock of time, and the more waſteful and deplorable ſteps of ad-verſity, ſupineneſs and negleᢗ. Indeed, while one looks around him in the pariſh of Abdie, and marks the many halls now ſilent, which, in a former century, were the ſeats of hoſpitable feſtivity and joy, he finds ſome diffi-culty in admitting, that Scotland is, at preſent, in a ſtate of higher improvement than it had attained in any for-mer period. The antiquities of Abdie extend beyond the æra of the ſeats now mentioned. On the ſummit of Clatchart Crag, are the evident veſtiges of a fortifica-tion, or place of ſtrength. Sibbald ſays it had been a ſtrong caſtle. Traces of fortifications on a larger ſcale, are more viſible on the top of Norman's Law, which, from the ſituation, and height, and name, one is led to con-ſider as either the work of ſome of the northern invaders,

or

or as a place of strength and observation, occasioned by their hostile visits *.

Population.—According to Dr. Webster's report, the number of souls in 1755, was 822. Since 1789, no exact account of the parish has been taken. The minister's roll of that year contains 494 of all ages. The decrease of population must be accounted for, from the enlargement of farms, from diminishing the cottagers, from the non-residence of the principal heritors.

Agriculture.—The farmers of this parish practise the same modes of labouring the fields, and cultivate the same kinds of crops, which have been repeatedly described in the

---

* Near the village at Lindores, are pointed out the supposed remains of a castle, said to have belonged to the celebrated M'Duff, Thane of Fife. Tradition adds, that in the view of its being demolished, much of the plate and wealth of it were cast into an adjoining lake, still known by the name of the Sillar Lake. Attempts have been made to connect these traditions with scenes immortalized by Shakespeare, in his tragedy of Macbeth. But M'Duff, like Wallace, and other favourite characters, has had too many places of residence assigned him by the fond admiration of his countrymen. At no great distance from the church, and on the way to it from the Abbey of Lindores, there are a few stones called the Licker-Stones: Antiquaries have conjectured licker to be a corruption and contraction of lecturer, and with much show of probability have observed, that formerly, when Bibles were scarce, and the capacity of reading them was confined to a few, the people might assemble at such stones to hear the scriptures read to them. Not many yards N. W. of the Licker Stones, and nearer to the abbey, is a rising ground called the Teind Know ; at which, tradition represents the ecclesiasticks belonging to the abbey, collecting the teinds, or tithes. A little farther N. on the grounds of Den Mill, and in full view of the mansion house, appears the Witch Tree, a large spreading plane, of more than one century, which, had it fallen under the observation of a late traveller, might have saved the county of Fife from one of his hasty misrepresentations.

the ſtatiſtical accounts of neighbouring pariſhes: like their neighbours they have meliorated the ſoil by their improvements, and much increaſed the annual returns of grain. On one farm containing a conſiderable quantity of low ground, adjoining to the Tay, and ſubjected formerly to the tides, the tenant, a young man of laudable enterpriſe, and perſevering induſtry, has, in a great meaſure, excluded the tides, by running a bank of earth along the whole length of his fields parallel to the river ; his returns are nearly double. There are examples of ſimilar exertions and improvements in the neighbourhood ; and one cannot help ſaying, Are not ſuch men entitled to attention, at the expiration of their preſent leaſes ? The ſubject of embanking, to which this Article has led, is a very ſerious and important one on the ſides of the Tay. The current of the river, alas ! gradually wears away many acres of the fineſt ſoil in this part of the country. Within the memory of ſome perſons living, whole fields have been waſhed away, and theſe depredations have much increaſed ſince the running out of ſtone heads on the oppoſite ſide, for the purpoſe of protecting the lands belonging to the eſtate of Errol. The farms are 28 ; 6 conſiderably larger ; 22 of different extent and value, wrought by about 60 ploughs : two horſe-ploughs are moſt in uſe. Some farmers uſe oxen in the plough : Moſt of them rear occaſionally black cattle, and draught horſes for ſale.

There are no ſheep-farms, properly ſo called, within the pariſh, though ſeveral of the farmers keep ſmall flocks of ſheep, as in the contiguous pariſhes, for paſturing their high grounds, amounting, in whole, to about 60 ſcores. Formerly, the number of ſheep was much greater, and the management of them more carefully

ſtudied

ſtudied. Were the grounds ſubjected to agriculture, properly encloſed, the farmers might return to the practice of keeping greater flocks, as many parts of the pariſh ſeem well adapted for ſheep-fields. What ſpecies ſucceeds beſt, cannot be certainly affirmed, as no proper experiments have hitherto been made. Notwithſtanding the evident and acknowledged improvements and melioration of the ſoil, ſtrangers coming from the valley in which Cupar ſtands on the E., or from Strathearn from the W., muſt conſider Abdie as in a ſtate of inferior cultivation. Allowance, however, ought to be made for the untowardneſs of a hilly country ; and they are here informed, that the farmers have little acceſs to the quickening example and animating influence of proprietors. Of 10, the number of heritors, only 1 reſides on his grounds, whoſe fields have of late become highly improved.

Trade in Stones.—Since the year 1788, 3 quarries have been opened on the riſing ground immediately S. of the town of Newburgh, at which the rock is cut into pavement for the ſtreets of London. From 30 to 50 quarriers and cutters are employed in this work : as the demand for the ſtones increaſes, there is reaſon to conclude, that the number of hands will be augmented. The ſtones are ſhipped at the ſhore of Newburgh, and carried to London chiefly by the veſſels employed in the ſalmon trade. Already the returns amount to between 500l. and 600l. Sterling.

Eccleſiaſtical State, School, Poor, &c.—The pariſh is at preſent vacant. Earl Mansfield is patron. The church is an old narrow building, low in the walls, and poorly lighted. The manſe is lately repaired, and tolerably commodious.

commodious. The ſtipend conſiſts of 55¼ bolls bear ;
62¾ oats ; 20¾ oat meal, and 10l. 5s. Notwithſtanding its near neighbourhood to Auchtermuchty and Newburgh (ſee Statiſtical Accounts of theſe pariſhes), there
are few ſeparatiſts from the church of Scotland in Abdie.
Perhaps obſervation of the ill conſequences ariſing from
the levity, inconſiſtency and folly of too many in theſe
pariſhes, has contributed to confirm the bulk of the
people in their adherence to the Eſtabliſhed Church, and
reſpect for its miniſters.—The ſchoolmaſter's ſalary is
4l. 10d., 2 bolls bear, 2 bolls oats, a houſe and ſmall garden. In ſummer, the number of ſcholars is about 30 ;
in winter 40. They are taught reading, writing, arithmetic and Latin.—The ſtock for the poor is about 600l.
Sterling ; the reſult of legacies, collections at the church
doors and other caſualties. The neceſſitous are few, and
ſufficiently cared for and aſſiſted.

Character.—Peaceableneſs of diſpoſition, and ſimplicity
of manners, have long been regarded as diſtinguiſhing
features in the character of the inhabitants. They who
know them ſpeak warmly of their kindneſs and civilities,
and praiſe their perſevering induſtry. More detached than
other pariſhes, in which there are large villages, or towns,
from intercourſe with ſtrangers, they retain the modes of
thinking and acting of their fathers : If, therefore, they
have not the vivacity, neither exhibit they the artful-
neſs of the preſent times.

Advantages and Diſadvantages.—The proximity of the
port of Newburgh is favourable for the exportation, or
ready ſale of the grain. Cupar, Auchtermuchty, and
Newburgh, are markets at hand for their cattle and
ſheep.

ſheep. Its various lakes, and the ſtreams iſſuing from them, render Abdie an eligible ſituation for maltſters, manufacturers, bleachers. That it is well adapted for that kind of machinery that is moved by water, appears by the mills at preſent working in the pariſh : they are meal mills 5 ; fulling mills 2 ; lint mills 2. On conſidering theſe circumſtances, and the vicinity of the populous towns named above, one may well be ſurpriſed that no manufacturing work of any extent has yet been eſtabliſhed in Abdie. The ſituation and command of water is inviting, materials are at hand, and labourers would not be wanting.—Good is balanced here with ſome evil. From the unevenneſs of the grounds, many places are difficult of acceſs; the roads are in bad repair ; ſome of the marſhes cannot be eaſily drained ; the harveſt on the high grounds is often late. By the induſtry of the inhabitants, the examples and improvements of the age, and the police of the country, many of the diſadvantages that now preſs upon our obſervation, may be removed at ſome future period; but the hills, and coldneſs, and difficulty of acceſs to many places, muſt remain. And from the preſent ſtate of property, there is little reaſon to expect, that the gentlemen, in whoſe hands it is placed, will ſoon reſtore, and return to the ſeats of their predeceſſors, to ſpread a portion of their wealth over the barrenneſs of the mountains, and to gladden the vallies with their preſence.

PARISH of ABERDOUR,

(COUNTY OF FIFE.)

By the Rev. Mr ROBERT LISTON.

Name, Situation, Extent, Soil, &c.

ABERDOUR, in Gaelic, fignifies ' the mouth of the water.' The name is taken from a rivulet, which empties itfelf into the Forth, a little below the village. The
parifh lies in the Synod of Fife, and prefbytery of Dunfermline. It is bounded by the parifh of Dalgety, on the
W.; by thofe of Beath and Auchtertoul, on the N.; by
Kinghorn and Burntifland, on the E.; and by the Forth,
on the S.; being, at an average, about 3 miles from E. to
W. and as much from N. to S. A fmall part of the parifh is detached from the reft, by the intervening parifhes
of Burntifland and Kinghorn, and lies at the diftance of 4
or 5 miles. The number of acres may be about 5000. The
parifh is divided by a ridge of hills, running nearly from
E. to W. The north part is a cold and bleak track, being
confiderably above the level of the fea, and excepting
what has been done by one of the heritors on the N. W.
corner of the parifh, altogether unfheltered, either by
hedges or plantations. The foil is cold and four. On the
south

ſouth of this ridge, both the ſoil and the climate are much
more kindly. The cold winds in Fifeſhire blow from the
N. and the E. The Collello Hills, which form the above
mentioned ridge, afford ſhelter on the N.; the Gorry Hills,
and a track of high ground, on the E. Theſe fall gradually
towards the W. running out into different branches, with
little ſtraths between them. The ſoil here is generally a
black loam, more or leſs mixed with ſand. The air is
dry and healthy.

Agriculture and Rent.—The north part of the pariſh is
but poorly cultivated. Little has been done in the way of
draining or incloſing the fields. Where farms are ſmall and
leaſes ſhort, little improvement can be expected upon poor
lands. The ſouth part is well cultivated, and generally incloſed. The real rent of the pariſh may be above L. 2600
Sterling. The valued rent is L. 7015, 10 s. Scots. The
beſt arable grounds are worth 40 s. the acre. Some of the
lands about the village have been recently let at 50 s. and
L. 3, 5 s. The farmers are 23 in number. They ſow their
wheat in the months of Auguſt, September and October;
beans and oats in March; barley in the end of April and
beginning of May. Harveſt begins about the end of
Auguſt, though it is not general till about the middle of
September, and the crop is commonly got in by the end of
October. The north part of the pariſh is conſiderably
later. The old Scots plough continues to be uſed. *Small's*
plough has been lately introduced. There are about 58
ploughs in the pariſh; 18 of which are upon the village
acres. There may be as many carts as ploughs, and perhaps 160 horſes, and about 130 milk-cows. The rotation
of crops obſerved by the farmers is various. Some ſow
wheat, beans, barley and oats in ſucceſſion, after ſummer-
fallow; others leaving out the oats, ſow graſs-ſeeds with
the

the barley; fome take wheat after drilled beans or potatoes, and then barley and oats; after turnips they fow
barley, and then oats with grafs-feeds. The parifh in general exports wheat and barley, and imports oats and meal.
The prices are much the fame as in Mid Lothian, or fomething lower. Farms are from 50 to 150 acres. There
are about 200 acres planted in the parifh. The trees
thrive well, and much more may be done this way. The
rugged fpots, which are frequent, and generally covered
with furze, if they were planted, would beautify the face
of the country which they now deform.

Roads and Minerals.—The roads in this parifh are generally bad, as in other parts of Fife. The gentlemen of
the county are now paying attention to the direction and
the formation of the roads. Toll-bars are erecting, and a
great change for the better muft foon take place. The
village of Aberdour, like many others, has fuffered by its
caufeway being changed into a common road. Such a
road in a narrow village continues long moift, and is hurtful to the health of the inhabitants. They fuffer great inconveniencies too, in winter, from the depth of the road,
and in fummer, from the duft. Neither does a common
road laft in a village, being exhaufted by the attempts which
are made to keep it clean. A paved caufeway endures,
and no inconvenience which the travellers can find from
it, can balance the daily inconveniencies to which the refidenters are fubjected by the other. The parifh abounds with
coal, lime and free ftone, and fome iron ftone. The coal
is not wrought at prefent. The inhabitants are fupplied
with this neceffary article from collieries in the neighbouring parifhes. The price paid on the hills is 6 d. the load,
of 18 ftone, of chews or fmall coal; the great coal is refer-
ved at prefent for the fea-fale. The limeftone on the coaft
is

is fhipped at a commodious harbour, which the Earl of Morton has lately built for the purpofe. It is a ftone of a ftrong and fuperior quality. It is ufed at Carron for fmelting. It is alfo difpofed of in fhells, or flacked. The fhells are put on board at 1 s. o$\frac{1}{4}$ d. the boll, and the ftones at 2 s. 8 d. the ton.

Coaft.—The parifh ftretches along the fhore above two miles. From the eaft boundary the coaft is rugged and fteep, and generally covered with wood to the water's edge. The trees have been planted with a proper regard to the variety of fhade, and the jutting rocks which appear in different places, render the whole extremely picturefque and beautiful. This wood is interfected with walks cut out on the face of the hill, from which the profpects are rich and varied. On the weft, there is a beautiful white fandy bay, furrounded with trees. Here the grounds rife gently to the weft, bordered by thriving plantations; and ftretching fouthward, they terminate in a perpendicular rock wafhed by the fea.—By this rock on the E. and by headlands on the S. W. the fmall harbour of Aberdour is well fhelter-ed from all winds. The fhipping at prefent confifts of a few fmall veffels. There is one ferry-boat to Leith, which is principally employed in carrying grain. The fhipping here, as in moft towns on the coaft of Fife, was formerly much more confiderable than at prefent. To the N. W. of this harbour, the ground again rifes into a little hill, co-vered with trees, above whofe tops an obelifk yet appears; beyond this, fome corn-fields ftretch to the weftern boun-dary of the parifh on the coaft. The profpects to the fouth are beautiful. On the right hand lies the ifland of Inch-colm, with the ruins of its monaftery. On the left ap-pears the town of Burntifland, which here feems to be feated on the fea. The iflands of Inchkeith, Cramond,
Mickry

Mickry and Carcary, vary the appearance of the frith. The coaft of Lothian is juft diftant enough to be feen with advantage. The city of Edinburgh and its environs rife in view, and the diftant Pentland Hills terminate the profpect.

Village and Manufactures.—The village of Aberdour lies about a quarter of a mile from the fea. It is quite furrounded by rifing grounds, except towards the fouth. Between the village and the fea are rich corn-fields, and the fharpnefs of the fea-air is kept off by a great number of fine old fpreading trees. The venerable old caftle of Aberdour, rifing amidft trees, ftands on the eaftern bank of the rivulet, which, taking a winding courfe below it, falls into the frith in front. The fituation is beautiful, and the profpects from it magnificent. To the north of this ruin ftands the houfe of Hillfide, commanding different views of the Forth, and exhibiting the richeft and moft diverfified fcenes. Between this and the village, the rivulet runs in the bottom of a little rich ftrath, and its borders in fummer are covered with cloth and yarn, which gives a pleafing idea of the induftry of the people. There are 36 weavers in the village, who are employed principally in making coarfe cloths and tickings. The only manufacture for export is the coarfe tickings, of which there are made about 520 webs annually, of 70 or 80 yards each. There is a fmall manufacture of fpades, fhovels, &c. lately erected in the parifh. The great hammer is driven by water. There are about 15 tons of kelp made annually upon the coaft and the ifland of Inchcolm.

Population.

Population.—According to Dr Webſter, the population
was   -   -   -   -   1198
In the end of the year 1790,   -   -   1280
Males in the village,   -   -   368
In the country part,   -   -   -   221
Females in the village,   -   -   472
In the country part,   -   -   -   219
Total males,   -   -   -   589
Total females,   -   -   -   691
Aged under 10,   -   -   -   320
between 10 and 20,   -   -   240
between 20 and 50,   -   -   482
between 50 and 70,   -   -   191
between 70 and 100,   -   -   47

They are all of the Eſtabliſhed Church, except 263 Seceders. The average of baptiſms is 32 ; of marriages 9 ; of
deaths 23.

Inchcolm.—The pariſh of Aberdour belonged to the monaſtery of Inchcolm. This monaſtery was founded about
the beginning of the 12th century, by Alexander I. in
conſequence of a vow. · Sibbald ſays, that the weſter part
of Aberdour was given by one of the Mortimers to this
monaſtery, for the privilege of burying in the church.
There is a tradition, that the corpſe of one of the family
was thrown overboard in a ſtorm, which gives name of
Mortimer's Deep to the channel between the iſland and the
ſhore, according to the account which I have from a gentleman connected with this pariſh. This weſter part of Aberdour, together with the lands and barony of Beath, are ſaid
to have been acquired from an Abbot of Inchcolm, by
James, afterwards Sir James Stuart, ſecond ſon of Andrew
Lord Evandale, grandfather by his daughter to the admirable
Crichton, and by his ſecond ſon, Lord Doune, to Sir James
                                                    Stuart,

Stuart, who married the daughter of the Regent Murray. Lord Doune was Commendator of the monaitery of Inchcolm at the Reformation. The whole of the above mentioned property, together with the ifland itfelf, is ftill in the family of Moray, with the title of St Colme. The prefent Earl of Moray attempted to cover the ifland with trees, which would have increafed its picturefque appearance, but the attempt did not fucceed.

Stipend, School, Poor, &c.—The Earl of Morton is patron of the parifh. The prefent Earl is a grandion of James Earl of Morton, who was Prefident of the Royal Society. He was a Nobleman of diftinguifhed literature and abilities.—The ftipend confifts of 63 bolls 3 firlots of meal, 50 bolls 1 firlot of barley, 15 bolls of oats, L. 200 Scots of money, and L. 5 for elements, with manfe and glebe.— The fchoolmafter's falary is L. 100 Scots. The fchool-fees are from 1 s. 3 d. to 2 s. 6 d. for Englifh, writing, arithmetic and Latin. The ordinary number of fcholars is from 60 to 90, or upwards. As feffion-clerk, he has the perquifites of 2 s. 6 d. for proclamation and regiftration of marriages, and 10 d. for regiftration of baptifms.—The funds for the poor are from L. 25 to L. 27 a-year. During the general fcarcity in the years 1782, 1783, the people were enabled to live by the generofity of the heritors, who brought meal into the parifh, and fold it confiderably lower than the market-price. To the poor it was diftributed *gratis.*—There is an hofpital in the village for 4 widows. It was founded by Anne Countefs of Moray. The Earl of Moray and the Clerks to the Signet prefent the widows. The Earl of Moray prefents 3 of them, and the Clerks to the Signet the 4th.

Antiquities.

Antiquities.—Not far from the village of Aberdour, on a flat on the top of a hill, there is one of thoſe cairns or tumuli ſo frequently met with in Scotland. The farmer on whoſe farm it is ſituated, when carrying away the ſtones ſome years ago, diſcovered a ſtone coffin, in which were found the ſkeleton of a man, the head of a ſpear made of copper, with the copper nails by which it had been fixed to the ſhaft, and a piece of clear ſubſtance, like amber, ſuppoſed to have been an amulet. The coffin, with a great part of the cairn ſtill remain. The tumulus has been conical, the coffin being exactly in the centre of the baſe, from which, to the circumference, it meaſures 20 paces. The height cannot now be aſcertained. There have been found in the ſame cairn ſeveral earthen veſſels, containing human bones. The veſſels were flat, narrower at the bottom than top, and without any covering. The farmer digging in the ſame field, in another place, found ſuch a quantity of human bones, that he was obliged to deſiſt.

Miſcellaneous Obſervations.—It is ſaid that there were only three parſonages in Fife, Aberdour, Dyſart, and Balingry; and that there were only two nunneries in Scotland of the order of St Francis, the one at Dundee, the other at Aberdour; the field contiguous to the miniſter's garden bears the name of the Siſterlands to this day.—The people of Aberdour are ſober and induſtrious, are contented with their ſituation, enjoy in a conſiderable degree the advantages of ſociety, and while in health, they are able to maintain their families. In ſickneſs and in old age, many need relief.—Labourers receive from 8 d. to 1 s. 2 d. according to their ability; carpenters and maſons, 1 s. 6 d. tailors, 6 d. and their victuals; the wages of men ſervants employed in huſbandry, are from L. 5 to L. 8 a-year, with victuals, of women ſervants from L. 2 to L. 3, with victuals.

tuals. A good fpinner on the two-handed wheel, may earn from 6 d. to 8 d. the day.—The food of the common people confifts principally of oat-meal, potatoes, garden-roots, and a little butcher meat. There are 5 alehoufes in the village. The people are fond of a feafaring life, and enter willingly into the navy. There are about 60 failors in the village. The common people here, and generally through Fife, are not fond of the army.—The village is in general healthy. A very epidemical fever appeared here June 1790, and continued till January 1791. It was not materially different from the fevers that are common in this country, except in the prevalency of it. It was more general than in any former period in the memory of man. Nearly a fourth part of the parifh was infeeted during thefe 7 months. The frequency of this fever was fuppofed to proceed from two circumftances, very favourable to contagion : Its commencing in the hotteft feafon of the year, and among the children at fchool, who were crowded in a low damp room.—The croup fometimes appears among the children, as it generally does in places near the fea. It often proves fatal, unlefs affiftance is immediately pro-cured.—Inoculation is frequent, and fuccefsful among the better fort of people ; yet the common people are ftill a-verfe to it. This is not fo much owing to their prejudices, as to their poverty. A workman, with a fmall family, hath very little to fpare to the furgeon.—It is afked, what can be done to improve the condition of the people? One anfwer to this may apply to a great part of Scotland. There is no doubt but it would much improve the ftate, both of the people and of the country, if the proprietors of land, where they have it in their power, were to give long and encouraging leafes to their tenants. This ufeful body of men, who, by toil and expence, improve the fields, fhould be enabled to live comfortably, and, by the induftry of

their

their youth, to lay up a proviſion for the ſeaſon of old age. To improve the condition of the people, care ſhould be taken to improve their morals; and particularly to eſtabliſh their virtue upon religion, the only ſtable foundation of good morals. The higher ranks of life might do much good in this reſpect. They who, by their practice, weaken the influence of religion among the people, do much hurt in ſociety; but they who give their countenance to religion, are public bleſſings, and do honour, both to the ſoundneſs of their own heads, and the goodneſs of their own hearts.

PARISH OF ANSTRUTHER EASTER,

(COUNTY AND SYNOD OF FIFE, PRESBYTERY OF ST ANDREW'S).

By a Friend to Statiſtical Inquiries.

Situation, &c.

THIS pariſh is ſituated on the ſea-coaſt, between Kilrennie and Anſtruther Weſter, (from which it is divided by a ſmall river), in the Preſbytery of St Andrew's.
The obſervations that occur in the Statiſtical Account
of theſe two pariſhes, as to the ſoil, climate, fiſhing, price
of proviſions, equally apply to Anſtruther Eaſter, and need
not be repeated here.

Church, Stipend, &c.—Till the year 1636, the town of
Anſtruther, and the barony, was in the pariſh of Kilrennie ;
but though the church was at Kilrennie, the miniſter reſided at Anſtruther, and was ſtyled the miniſter of that
town.   In the above mentioned year, the town of Eaſter
                                                    Anſtruther

Anſtruther was erected into a ſeparate charge, and a church
built. The ſtipend ariſes from the tithes of the fiſh, a grant
from his Majeſty of part of the biſhops rents, and ſome
money mortified for that purpoſe, and may be reckoned
between L. 70 and L. 80. Sir John Anſtruther is the
patron.

Population.—In 1744, the number was 1000; in 1764,
it was 900; at preſent, it is ſuppoſed rather above 1000.
The average of births 36 ; deaths 24.

Port, Shipping, &c.—In 1710, Anſtruther, which formerly was a creek of the cuſtomhouſe of Kirkcaldy, was
made a port, and a cuſtomhouſe eſtabliſhed.

In 1753, a new key was built; and to defray the expence an act of Parliament was procured, laying a tax of
two pennies Scots upon every pint of ale brewed or ſold in
the burgh. For ſome years of late the produce has not
been more than a third of what it was at the beginning.

In 1768, the tonnage belonging to Anſtruther Eaſter was
80 ton ; it is now 1400.

Ship-building has been carried on for ſome years to a
conſiderable extent.—There is a thread-manufacture.

Poor.—The poor are ſupported by the weekly collections; beſides which the ſhipmaſters have a large fund, from
which they are able to make a decent proviſion for the
widows and orphans of their Society. The trades have a
fund for their poor.

Longevity.—In 1761, Robert Arnot, blackſmith, died,
aged 99 years and ſome months ; Mr James Nairne, late
miniſter, 92 ; his ſon, the preſent incumbent, is 84.

PARISH OF ANSTRUTHER-WESTER.

(*County of Fife.*)

By the Rev. Mr JAMES FORRESTER.

Name, &c.

ANSTRUTHER-WESTER is situated on the sea-coast, in the east part of the county and synod of Fife, and presbytery of St Andrews. The name is derived from its situation, *Struther* being a Celtic word which signifies a place lying in a valley, as Anstruther does.

Anstruther-Wester became a borough of barony in 1554, and a royal borough in 1583. The magistrates are three bailies, a treasurer, and any number of counsellors, from six to eleven.

Extent, Boundary, Soil, &c.—The parish is of a very irregular form. There is no map of it; but, from the best information, it contains about 540 acres of arable land, and about seven or eight acres of common, on which the burgesses have the privileges of pasturage and of casting turf. It is bounded on the south by the sea, for about half a mile; on the east by Easter-Anstruther; on the north by Carnbie and Kilrennie; and on the west by Pittenweem. Near the sea, the soil is either a black loam, or a light sand mixed with shells,

ſhells, both of which, though ſhallow, are very fertile. In the higher grounds there is ſome light ſoil, but the greateſt part of it is a deep ſtubborn clay, that neither agrees with a wet nor a dry ſeaſon, but yields conſiderable crops in favourable weather. About the town the ground is flat, but it riſes gently from the coaſt. From the vicinity of the ſea, and from the eaſterly fogs, which come from the German ocean, the air is moiſt ; yet the pariſh cannot be ſaid to be unhealthy. Agues, which from the above mentioned circumſtances might be ſuppoſed to be prevalent, are totally unknown ; and no epidemical diſeaſes, except the ſmall-pox, have appeared within theſe laſt twenty years. The practice of inoculation is increaſing, and has been attended with ſuccefs.

Rivers, Fiſheries, and Produce of the Coaſt, &c.—A ſmall river divides the two Anſtruthers, in which, it is ſaid, there was once a conſiderable ſalmon fiſhery, whence the arms of the town, bearing three ſalmon. is ſaid to be derived. Cod, ling, turbot, hollybut, ſkate, haddocks, herrings, flounders, and lobſters, are caught here and ſent to Cupar, Edinburgh, Stirling, and Glaſgow. Lobſters are the only fiſh ſent to London, for which, it is ſuppoſed, that above L. 1000 is annually brought into this and the neighbouring towns. Great quantities of ſea weeds are thrown on ſhore after ſtorms, and are uſed as manure. Once in two years, the ſea weeds, growing on the rocks, are cut and burnt into kelp ; ten ton of which is thought a good produce for the two years. The firſt mention of kelp in the records is in the year 1694, when an Engliſhman offered the town-council L. 4 for the privilege of cutting and burning it for one year, which one of the bailies proteſted againſt, as being prejudicial to the health of the inhabitants, and his own family ; but at length they

they accepted the offer, on condition that the kelp should be burnt at the west end of the town, and only when the wind blew from the east.

The harbour does not admit ships of burden; but a little to the westward is a creek, called Westhaven, which, at no great expence, might be made an excellent harbour. Nature seems to have fitted it for that purpose, as boats can come into it almost at low water. It is singularly useful in the fishing season.

Migratory Birds, &c.—The woodcock, fieldfare, and curliew, visit the coast regularly in the winter, and the Bohemian jay is sometimes seen in the neighbourhood; as are also wild geese, when the higher grounds are covered with snow. The swallow, cuckoo, water-wagtail, and plover, make their appearance in summer. The early arrival of the woodcock and Bohemian jay, indicates the severity of the winter on the continent, while the cuckoo's early visit is a sure mark that fine weather may be soon expected.

Agriculture.—The rotation most approved by the best farmers on the strong clay soil of the parish, is, 1st fallow, 2d wheat, 3d beans, 4th barley, 5th oats, with grass, 6th hay; on the light soil, 1st turnips, potatoes, or flax, 2d wheat or barley, 3d oats or drilled-beans, 4th barley with clover, 5th hay; part of the outfield is pasture for the young cattle. This plan is pursued with advantage, on a farm of 148 acres, of which about 50 are outfield. The largest farm in the parish is 148 acres, the smallest 70. Formerly every farmer in the parish had cottagers besides his hired servants, and the present farmers have not more servants than their predecessors; hence the cottagers were supernumeraries. The parish,

riſh, beſides ſupporting itſelf, exports a conſiderable quantity of wheat, barley, and beans; but the light and ſoft grounds being unfavourable for oats, a quantity of oatmeal is annually imported. Peaſe and beans are ſown in February; oats in March; barley in May, and wheat in October. The earlieſt harveſt begins in the firſt week of Auguſt, and the lateſt in September.

Cattle.—The breed of cattle has, of late, been much improved, by croſſing with the Lancaſhire, Holderneſs, and Dutch kinds; by houſing them in winter, and by feeding them on turnip. The farmers find, by experience, that there is not a more profitable application of turnips, than giving them liberally to young cattle; and the fame which the Fife breed of cattle has acquired, is probably owing to this method of rearing them. A young ox of 20 months old, ſold lately for 7 guineas. It was much ſtouter, and fitter for work, than a three year old one fed in the common way, with ſtraw in the winter.

Price of Labour and Proviſions.—In 1764, the wages of a day-labourer were 6 d. in winter, and 7 d. in ſummer. They are now 10 d. in winter, and 1 s. in ſummer. Men in harveſt, 9 d. *per* day, and their victuals, women 7 d. They are now more conſtantly employed than at the former period. When they are frugal and induſtrious, they live very comfortably, and their children are well fed and educated. Thrice the quantity of butcher meat and wheat bread are uſed now, that were 20 years ago in this pariſh. In 1695, the wages of a man ſervant was L. 20 Scots; a maid ſervant, from L. 5 to L. 8 Scots, for the year. In the year 1768, the wages of a man were from L. 4 to L. 5 Sterling *per annum*; of a woman, from 32 s. to 40 s. *per annum*. The pre-

ſent

fent wages of men are from L. 6 to L. 7 Sterling *per annum*;
and of women, from L. 2 to L. 3 Sterling.

Prices of Proviſions.—Proviſions have riſen one third in the
courſe of 20 years. Mutton, lamb, veal, and beef, are from
3 d. to 4 d *per* pound; a hen, 1 s.; ducks, 8 d.; geeſe, 3 s.;
eggs, 3 d. a dozen. The only kind of proviſions that have
not riſen are pork, which is 4 d. *per* pound, and rabbits 6 d.
a-piece, owing to the common people having an averſion to
pork and rabbits.

Church.—The pariſh church appears to be a very antient
building, from the remains of a large choir, and the gothic
ſtructure of the ſteeple. It was new-roofed in the year 1761.
The manſe was built in 1703, and repaired in 1761. Sir
John Anſtruther of Anſtruther, Bart. is patron of the pariſh.
The preſent incumbent was ordained in 1768, is married, and
has a ſon and two daughters. The ſtipend, valuing the victual at 12 s. *per* boll, is about L. 90 *per annum*, excluſive of
the manſe and glebe.

School.—The ſchoolmaſter has a ſalary of L. 8 : 6 : 8 *per
annum*. The heritors pay the rent of his dwelling houſe and
ſchool, and the ſeſſion pays him 10 merks a year for teaching poor children. The dues are, for reading Engliſh, 14 d.
a quarter; writing, 1 s. 6 d.; Latin, 2 s. 6 d; and navigation, L. 1 : 1 : 0. As the ſchoolmaſter is eſteemed the beſt
teacher of navigation on the coaſt, his chief attention is directed to that branch. All the young people in the pariſh,
without a ſingle exception, are taught to read Engliſh, and the
principles of the Chriſtian religion.

Rent.

Rent.—The valued rent of the parish is L. 1185 Scots. The rent of land has risen greatly within these 20 years, viz. from 7 s. and 10 s. *per* acre, to 21 s. and 30 s.

Poor.—The collections at the church, the interest of the poor's funds, and the savings in years of plenty, make an annual income of L. 25 or L. 30, which is sufficient for the maintenance of the poor, of which there are at present five on the list. Besides the maintenance of these, occasional supplies of money are given to widows, orphans, or persons who, from sickness or accident, are unable to support themselves.

Population.—Total inhabitants,	370
Males,	200
Females,	170
Inhabitants in the burgh,	324
—— —— in the country,	46
Families in the burgh,	80
—— in the country,	6
Average of births in the parish,	12½
—— deaths,	8
Mariners,	36
Carpenters and wrights,	9
Weavers, with journeymen and apprentices,	15
Shoemakers,	4
Taylors,	3
Baker,	1
Brewers,	2
Dyer,	1
Miller,	1
Smith,	1
Officers of the customs,	2
—— of the excise,	1

Farmers,

Farmers,	-	-	-	-	4
Mason,	-	-	-	-	1
Day-labourers,	-	-	-	4
Land-labourers,	-	-	-	5
Gardener,	-	-	-	1
Milliner,	-	-	-	-	1
Mantuamakers,	-	-	-	-	2
Shopkeepers,	-	-	-	-	7
Ale-fellers, the brewers included,	-	-	3
Widowers and widows,	-	-	-	20

All the inhabitants are of the Established Church, except one man and his wife, who attend the Relief Congregation at Pittenweem ; and they are all natives of Scotland, except one English woman.

The population is rather increasing at present, owing to the revival of the coal and salt works at Pittenweem, and the consequent increase of shipping.

Four new houses have been built within these last 20 years. One of them is uninhabited, owing to the high rent of L. 10 which is demanded for it.

Sir John Anstruther is proprietor of a third part of the parish ; Sir Robert Anstruther has one farm, and the remaining part is divided among 15 small proprietors.

Antiquities.—At the west end of the town, there is a large mound, called the *Chesterhill,* in the middle of which is a fine well. Two or three years ago, in digging, on the side of this mound, a foundation for a house, two skeletons were found in the most perfect preservation, at a small distance
from

from each other. They were incloſed in a kind of coffin, conſiſting of a large ſtone at each end and ſide.

Iſle of May.—South-eaſt from Anſtruther-Weſter, and ſix miles diſtant from it, in the mouth of the Frith of Forth, ſtands the Iſland of May; which, after the deſolation of the Abbacy of Pittenweem, was ſuppoſed to belong to the pariſh of Anſtruther-Weſter, the mother church, and in this light it was annually viſited by the miniſter of Anſtruther-Weſter, while it was inhabited by 14 or 15 families.

It is computed to be one mile long, and three quarters of a mile broad ; it has a well of fine water, and a ſmall lake, and affords excellent paſture for ſheep. It is frequented by a great variety of ſea fowl, ſuch as kittiewakes, ſcarts, dunters, gulls, ſea-pyets, marrots, &c.

On the iſland is a light-houſe, erected upon a tower 45 feet high ; it was built in the reign of King Charles I. and a duty is exacted, of 2 d. *per* ton, upon all ſhips which paſs the iſland. The architect, who planned and built the tower, periſhed in his return to his houſe, in a ſtorm, which ſome old women, then ſuppoſed to be witches, were burnt for raiſing. There was a priory on this iſland, for ſome monks of the order of St Auguſtine ; it belonged firſt to the abbacy of St Andrews, and afterwards to Pittenweem. There was a chapel dedicated to St Adrian, who was murdered by the Danes, in one of their incurſions, and buried here in the 870. There is a ſtone coffin which has ſtood expoſed to the injuries of the weather, time immemorial, in the church-yard. Tradition ſays that it once contained the reliques of St Adrian.

A very intelligent farmer, who has dealt in ſheep above
thirty

thirty years, and has had them from all the different corners of Scotland, ſays, that he knows no place ſo well adapted for meliorating wool, as the Iſland of May; he adds, that the fleeces of the coarſeſt woolled ſheep, that ever came from the worſt paſture in Scotland, when put on the Iſland of May, in the courſe of one ſeaſon, become as fine as ſattin; their fleſh alſo has a ſuperior flavour; and that rabbits bred on this iſland have a finer fur than thoſe which are reared on the main-land.

While employed in drawing up this account, a very melancholy accident happened, which ought to be recorded, as a warning to future times. The keeper of the light-houſe, his wife, and five children, were ſuffocated. One child, an infant, is ſtill alive, who was found ſucking at the breaſt of its dead mother. Two men, who were aſſiſtants to the keeper, were ſenſeleſs, but got out alive. This truly mournful event was owing to the cinders having been allowed to accumulate, for more than ten years. The cinders reached up to the window of the apartment where theſe unfortunate people ſlept. They were ſet on fire by live coals falling from the light-houſe, and the wind blowing the ſmoke into the windows, and the door below being ſhut, the conſequences were inevitable. Theſe perſons were the only inhabitants, and all of them lodged in the light-houſe. The families, who formerly reſided there, lodged in houſes detached from it. The old plan is to be again adopted; and houſes are preparing for lodging the keeper, and a boat's crew, which will be of advantage to all the coaſt, as they will be ready to give intelligence when the herrings come into the Frith. The revenue ariſing from the light-houſe, was formerly let at L. 360 *per annum;* it was let laſt year at L. 970.

Miſcellaneous

Miscellaneous Observations.—What the state of the fisheries once was, and how much they have declined, will appear from the following facts, which are either taken from the records, or related on undoubted authority. The minister drew the teinds (i. e. tythes) of fish, as part of his stipend; the town generally farmed them at the rate of ten, twelve, or sometimes fifteen pounds a year. For these last twenty years they have never let for more than 13 s., and have been sometimes so low as 5 s. The late Mr Nairne, minister of Anstruther-Easter, drew L. 55 *per annum* for the teinds of the herring fishery alone; but his son the present minister let them to the town for L. 22 : 4 : 5 Sterling.

The town of Anstruther, and many others on this coast, suffered much in the civil wars, in the reign of Charles I. both by sea and land. They were zealous covenanters, and there are few old inhabitants of the parish, who do not talk of some relations, that went to the battle of Kilsyth, in the year 1645, and who were never afterwards heard of. In this disaster, and in temporary failures of their fishing, Anstruther shared the fate of its neighbours, about the year 1670, by an inundation of the sea, which destroyed or chocked up the harbour, washed away the bulwarks, and rendered many of the houses unsafe to dwell in. An inundation of a similar kind happened about the end of last century; when about a third of the town seems to have been destroyed. A long street, called the fore street, was totally destroyed; scarce a vestige of it now remains. The rock on which the town house once stood, is covered by the sea every spring tide, and every tide the sea washes the street, where the principal houses of the borough were situated.

The old people date the decay of the towns on this coast

to

to the Union with England. It is evident, that that event did undoubtedly give a great ſhock to the trade of theſe towns. Their ſtaple commodities were malt, herrings, and cod. Before the Union, there were 24 ſhips belonging to Eaſter and Weſter Anſtruther, and 30 boats employed in the fiſhery. In 1764, there were only two ſhips, each 40 tons burden, and three fiſhing boats belonging to Anſtruther-Eaſter, and one of 20 tons, and two fiſhing boats to Anſtruther-Weſter. At preſent the number of ſhips belonging to Eaſter and Weſter Anſtruther, is 20, their tonnage 1172, men employed 94, of which ſix in the foreign, 13 in the coaſting, and one in the fiſhery trade; eight of theſe belong to Anſtruther-Weſter, whoſe tonnage is 532, and they employ 36 men. At preſent there is not a ſingle perſon in the pariſh, who can properly come under the denomination of a fiſherman; yet in the herring ſeaſon there are four boats, which are manned by the tradeſmen of the place, and ſome mariners, and fitted out for fiſhing. Ever ſince the battle of Kilſyth, the people here have a ſtrong averſion to a military life; in the courſe of twenty-one years, there is only a ſingle inſtance of a perſon inliſting, and it was into the train of artillery. There has not been a ſuſpicion of murder for theſe 50 years. A ſingle inſtance of ſuicide is remembered about the 1744. No perſon has been tried before a criminal court ſince the 1732, and he petitioned for baniſhment. This is the only inſtance even of baniſhment.

Agriculture is much improved; the cattle employed are of a better breed, and in finer order, and the tenants enjoy more of the comforts of ſociety, and are in a more affluent ſtate than their predeceſſors. This change is probably owing to the following cauſes: Formerly the rent was all paid in victual, which the tenants were obliged to drive ſix Scots

miles,

miles, at any time between Chriſtmas and Candlemas; they
were obliged to lead the proprietors coals during the ſummer; beſides a ſtated number of other carriages, ſuch as
ſtone, lime, and timber; if required, they paid a certain
number of hens and chickens, and they were allowed to
ſubſet or let off part of their farms to inferior tenants. In
many places the proprietor drew the teind on the field. No
tenant, however favoured, was allowed to lead any part of his
corn, till the whole was ready; and in ſome places they
were obliged to make the barley into malt, and to pay their
rent in the grain thus manufactured. The great prices of
cattle and grain, and the market of Glaſgow, of late opened
to this county, by the canal, which takes off vaſt quantities
of wheat, barley, and beans, have given a ſpur to induſtry,
which, joined to the improved mode of culture, have meliorated the face of the country, and added to the wealth of the
farmers. It is well known, that this country was viſited with
a great famine in the year 1699. It had been preceded by
ſome years of late and rather ſcanty crops, and it was attended with a great mortality. From an account publiſhed
in the beginning of this century, and from tradition, it is
probable, that in ſome pariſhes nearly one third of the inhabitants died. The only manufactures exported, are Oſna-
burgs and green linen. There are three ale-houſes in the
pariſh, which do not ſeem to have any bad effect on the
morals of the people. The peculiar diſadvantages of the pariſh are, the encroachments of the ſea, and the harbour not
admitting ſhips of burden. The people in general are ſober
and induſtrious. They enjoy in a reaſonable degree the
comforts and advantages of ſociety, and are contented with
their ſituation.

PARISH OF AUCHTERDERRAN.

By the Rev. Mr ANDREW MURRAY.

Name, Situation, Extent, Soil, and Surface.

THE name of the parish, as well as many places in it, is said to be derived from the Gaelic. This parish is situated in the county of Fife, presbytery of Kirkcaldy, and synod of Fife. It is of an irregular form, about 4 miles long, and 3 broad. It is bounded by Auchtertool on the south, Abotshal on the south-east, Dysart on the east and north, Kinglaffie and Portmeak on the north, and Ballingry on the west. A great part, if not the whole, of the fields are upon coal. Where the stratum connected with the coal comes near the surface, the ground is barren ; and, even where this is not the case, it is not remarkably fertile. It is moist throughout. Part of the soil is clay, and part black earth. The valley in which this parish lies is bounded on the south and east by a ridge of ground, and on the west by a similar ridge. Though the height of the ground excludes the view of the Firth of Forth, yet the highest part of it, which can scarcely be called a hill, is under tillage. There are many little inequalities in the fields, so that they appear rather broken and disjointed. The same is the case with a great part of Fife. There are some rocks of a singular appearance. What strikes the eye most

moſt is a number of detached pillars ſtanding perpendicularly on the baſe of the rock, and ſeparated both at the ſides
and behind from the general maſs. They are of a regular
fiɡure, reſembling the trunk of a large tree. The riſing
grounds are all green, but rather of a duſky tinge, as if
the plant did not delight in its ſituation.

Agriculture, &c.—About a fifth of the ground in the pariſh is
employed in raiſing corn, roots, &c. There is very little wheat.
Oats, barley, and peaſe, are the common grains. Green crops
of pɔtatoes, turnips, and cabbages, are introduced ; but, except potatoes, they are not in any great quantity The ſowing
of oats is begun about the 1ſt of March, and finiſhed about
the 2cth of April. The ſowing of barley is begun about the
20th of April, and finiſhed about the 20th of May. The
harveſt, in a good ſeaſon, begins about the 1ſt of September,
and ends about the middle of October. In a bad ſeaſon, it
continues till the beginning of November. The paſture, including ſown graſs, comprehends 4-fifths of the pariſh.
There are 51 ploughs, 17 of which are drawn by horſes
only ; and black cattle are uſed in the reſt. Small's new
plough is introduced here. There is generally a cart to every plough, and about 18 more employed in leading coal, &c.
They are all two-horſe carts. The beſt arable ground taken
through a whole farm does not exceed 20 s. an acre when
incloſed ; and the ſame farm will let for as much on the ſame
leaſe when in graſs and paſture. The poorer farms are let at 8
or 10 s an acre when incloſed. The rent of one-half of the
farms is from L. 10 to L. 20. There are ſix whoſe rent at preſent is about L. 30 each, which, at the expiration of the old
leaſe, will let at L. 100. Only five are let at L. 100 at preſent.
The land-rent of the pariſh is about L. 2000 Sterling *per annum.* The number of farms rather diminiſhes, which is
partly

partly owing to life-rents and feus. They are, in general, inclofed ; and the ground is fo much more fuited to grafs than
corn, that the moft of the remainder of the arable land will
be foon converted into grafs. The people and proprietors
are fufficiently convinced of the benefits of inclofing. Inclofing has banifhed fheep from the neighbourhood ; for fheep
cannot be confined within the fame inclofures as black cattle.
On one large farm there are rows of hedges and ftrips of planting throughout, which is a complete fence ; and this mode of
inclofing adds to the beauty of the country ; and the plantations
thrive. But the cheapeft, the moft valuable, the moft fpeedily raifed, the moft lafting, and moft general fence, is the
Galloway dike. The ftones are either found on the furface,
or got from quarries in the neighbourhood. A field of 10
acres may be inclofed for L. 20 ; and the money is generally
repaid in additional rent in 4 years. Fallow is not fo general as in a more advanced ftate of hufbandry. Of late, the
arable lands are fcarcely ever left in grafs without fowing artificial graffes in them. The farmers pay their rents chiefly
by raifing and feeding a great number of black cattle, by
which the circumjacent markets of Dunfermline, Kinghorn,
Dyfart, &c. are fupplied. Agriculture has advanced greatly
within thefe few years ; and the face of the country begins
to change rapidly. The rife of rents has contributed to the
progrefs of agriculture, by promoting additional induftry, and
calling forth exertion. The rents are all paid in money, except a few poultry to the proprietors, and 50 bolls of grain
to the minifter. Winter provender is fcarce and dear, owing
to the number of cattle ; but the farmers are beginning to
provide ftacks of hay from their fown fields, which will prove
the beft remedy for the evil. Good hay, at an average, fells
from 3½ d. to 4 d. a ftone. The parifh does more than fupply itfelf with provifions. It exports particularly live-cattle,
butter,

butter, cheeſe, and poultry. It imports rather more wheat bread than could be made of the wheat that grows in it. It raiſes oats nearly equal to the conſumption of oat-meal. No remarkable hardſhip was ſuffered here from the ſeaſon of 1782, although the harveſt did not yield above 4 months proviſions. The late Baron Stewart Moncrieff remitted rents to his tenants. The patron of the pariſh, with a well timed benevolence, directed the grain of the vacant ſtipend to be ſold at a cheap rate among the poor. The corn is ground by water-mills ; but the rude cuſtom of thirlage ſtill remains on ſome eſtates. Landed property in Fife changes more than in any other county in North Britain ; and the land ſold of late in this neighbourhood has generally been about 35 years purchaſe. Leaſes of farms are in general for 19 years.

Roads.—The roads hitherto made were done by ſtatute-labour, but are very indifferent. The ſtatute-labour is of late partly commuted ; and turnpike roads are making. One of them is to paſs through this pariſh, leaving the great road between Kirkcaldy and Cupar of Fife at the inn called the *Plaiſterers.* It takes a weſtern direction, through the pariſhes of Leſlie, Kinglaſſie, and Auchterderran, and lands the paſſengers on the Queensferry road at the kirk of Beathe. This line of road is already in uſe in the ſummer months ; but a free communication through this inland diſtrict would be highly advantageous. The general opinion of the common people is not againſt turnpikes. This pariſh has hitherto been diſtinguiſhed for bad roads, and is inacceſſible on the north for 6 months in the year. Hence the farmers on the oppoſite ſide muſt ſell their commodities at an under rate, being ſhut out from the coaſt towns.

Population.—The number of inhabitants, according to Dr Webſter's ſtate, is 1194 ; at preſent they are 1200.

Inhabited

Inhabited houfes	293
Eftablifhed minifter	1
Burgher ditto	1
In 1783 the families of the eftablifhed church .	105
—— Individuals belonging to it . .	430
—— Families of feceders, and other fectaries .	188
—— Individuals belonging to them . .	770
Heritors, befides feuers, (only one refides in the parifh)	12
People in their families, including themfelves .	322
Farmers	47
Families of colliers nearly . . .	31
Cottagers houfes built within thefe 10 years .	17
Houfes become uninhabitable . . .	7

There is 1 village called Lochgellie, containing 342 people.

Poor.—There are no poor belonging to this parifh that are vagrant. The poor are fupplied in their ufual refidences. Pride prevents our poor common people from making themfelves burdenfome to the public, which in general they never do but from neceffity. The number of poor in the monthly lift at prefent is 22. There are about L. 600 left in legacies, &c. in the management of the feffion ; the intereft of which, with the collections, is applied to the fupport of the poor. Their fituation is much better than that of the poor in many of the neighbouring parifhes. The kirkfeffion give their fervices *gratis*, (as every where in Scotland), and are from their fituation well qualified for pointing out the proper objects of charity. The weekly contributions for the poor does not exceed 2 s.

Provifions and Labour —There is no weekly market in the parifh. Kirkcaldy is the chief market. Beef, the long
weight,

weight, at an average, is 4½ d. a pound ; a hen 1 s. ; a dozen eggs 4 d. A day-labourer not retained gets 1 s. a day. When promiſed work from one perſon, at one place, throughout the year, he gets 11 d. ; but this is not general, and is thought the better bargain for the labourer. The average prices of artificers work differs according to their trade ; ſome get 1 s. 3 d.; ſome 1 s. 6 d. ſome 1 s. 8 d. a day.

Annual earnings of a day-labourer, his wife, and three children ; deducting four weeks earnings of the man on account of holidays, bad health, attendance on funerals, &c. and exceſſive bad weather ; and four weeks earnings of the woman, on account of holidays, bad health, and lying-in.

To 48 weeks labour of a man at 1 s. a day   L. 14 8 0
To 48 weeks labour of a woman, in ſpinning,
    beſides taking care of her houſe and chil-
    dren 3 12 0
To the earnings of 3 children at the age of ſix,
    ſeven, and eight years, nothing.

                          L. 18 0 0

Annual expence of a day-labourer, his wife, and three children.

By 2 pecks oat-meal a week, at 11½ d. per peck L. 4 19 8
By 2 pecks barley or peaſe-meal a week, at
    7½ d. a peck   .   .   .   3 5 0
By 6 bolls potatoes, at 5 s. a boll   .   .   1 10 0
By barley for kail, at 3 lb. a week   .   0 16 3
By a kail-yard, and a wretched houſe   .   0 13 0
                                          By

By milk, at 4 d. a week . .	L.	0 17	4
By falt, cheefe, and butter		0 12	6
By foap for wafhing clothes . .		0 2	6
By coals in a year, with carriage . . .		1 0	0
By fhoes to the whole family . . .		1 0	0
By body-clothes to the man . . .		1 10	0
By ditto to the woman and children . .		1 5	0
By worfted thread for mendings . . .		0 7	0

L. 17 18 3

The preceding ftatement is favourable for earnings, from the number of children, which is rather fmall ; and particularly on account of the ages of the children, as at that period of their lives it is fuppofed in the calculation that the woman has it in her power to work half work at fpinning, and yet take care of her houfe and children. The day labourer of this diftrict, and his family, are more decently clothed than a family of the fame defcription in England, and therefore it is fomewhat more particularly ftated than in the Printed Extract accompanying the Queries. The fuel is alfo higher charged. They are obliged to ufe coals, a much finer fuel than that mentioned in the Extract, and, at the loweft, it amounts to the expence above mentioned; but it ferves them for light, as well as heat, in the winter feafon. The greateft evils of their fituation arife from the lownefs of their diet, and the wretchednefs of their lodging, which is cold, dark, and dirty ; expofing them to a numerous clafs of dufafes incident to fuch a condition. The meagre food of the labouring man, too, is unequal to oppofe the effects of inceffant hard labour upon his conftitution, and, by this means, his frame is often worn down before the time of Nature's appointment.

That

That people continue to enter voluntarily upon ſuch a hard ſituation, ſhows how far the union of the ſexes, and the love of independence, are principles of human nature ; and, from ſuch cauſes, this ſituation is not thought, by the people themſelves, to be wretched, nor without ſome ſhare of comfort. Within theſe laſt twelve years, the wages of a man have riſen from 8 d. to 1 s. without a proportional riſe upon his expence. When this claſs of people have got ſuch additional wages as will enable them to have better lodging, and to have that quantity of animal and other foods, which their labour and the climate require, they will then have nearly their ſhare of human enjoyment. About the year 1755, the yearly wage of a domeſtic man-ſervant was L. 28 Scots, of a woman ſervant L. 16 Scots. The wages of ſervants, when maintained by the employer, in different branches of huſbandry, is now L. 3 Sterling a year for a woman, and L. 6 a year for a man The wages of domeſtic ſervants is the ſame. Work people are rather ſcarce, owing to the drain of wars, and the increaſing induſtry of the country.

General Character of the People.—The inhabitants are very regular in their attendance on public worſhip Formerly they were fond of long church ſervices, and conſidered it as a point of duty to continue long in religious exerciſes. Perhaps the ſervices, though ſhorter than before, are ſtill too long for anſwering the ends of devotion and ſpiritual edification. The people are not illiterate. In common with the reſt of Scotland, the vulgar are, for their ſtation, literate, perhaps, beyond all other nations. Puritanic and abſtruſe divinity come in for a ſufficient ſhare in their little ſtock of books ; and it is perhaps peculiar to them, as a people, that they endeavour to form opinions, by reading, as well as by frequent converſation, on ſome very metaphyſical points connected with religion,

gion, and on the deeper doctrines of Chriftianity. They likewife read, occafionally, a variety of other books unconnected with fuch fubjects. The parochial fchools are by no means fupplied with fuch enlightened teachers as thofe that were formerly inftrumental in diffufing this knowledge. No one of good education and ability now accepts of this reduced pittance, where the fituation is not favourable for procuring lucrative fcholars: And the village teacher, brought in by the fubfcription of needy people, is a ftill more unqualified perfon. In fuch cafes, the people do not propofe feeking out the beft, but the cheapeft. The confequence will be, that the poorer diftricts of the country, and the poor claffes of the people, muft become more ignorant. Although the parifh confifts wholly of the poorer ranks of fociety, newfpapers are very generally read and attended to: The defire for them increafes; and the reading of them feems to be attended with advantage. With regard to the intellectual character of the people : They are deficient in imagination, vivacity, humour, &c. ; their apprehenfion and judgment are very good, and they make a decent figure in the common profeffions of life. With refpect to their moral and religious character, they have all a profeffion of religion; but, in the points where their fituation more immediately leads to temptation, they too frequently and even habitually contradict their profeffion. Their civil character is excellent: They feem in fome degree capable of reflecting on the advantages of government; and they obey it peaceably, and on principle. They could, however, be eafily ftirred up to fedition in matters of religion. There is one Burgher meeting in this parifh. The religious toleration granted feems to anfwer, in this diftrict, the full ends of good government and public utility : It could hardly ftand on a better footing. Seceffion now begins to diminifh; and the

bitternefs

bitternefs of contending fects is greatly fubfiding : This partly proceeds from the novelty being over; partly from the great variety of fects which have taken place; and partly, it is hoped, from more enlightened views of true religion. As to holidays for recreation or merry-making, the people have only one in the year, called Handfel-Monday ; and even the manner in which this is employed fhews the fober mindednefs of the people. Inftead of meeting in large affemblies for diverfions, each family collects its own kindred from the different parts of the diftrict, provides a feaft, and fpends the time in eating, drinking, and converfation. The holidays, befides Sabbaths, for religious fervices, in the Eftablifhment, are three days in the year; among the Seceders fix. The people have fcarcely any fports after they are grown up. Among the infinite advantages of the Reformation, this feems to have been one difadvantage attending it, that, owing to the gloomy rigour of fome of the leading actors, mirth, fport, and chearfulnefs, were decried among a people already by nature rather phlegmatic. Since that, mirth and vice have, in their apprehenfion, been confounded together. Some of the fectaries punifh attendance on penny weddings, and public dancing, with a reproof from the pulpit, in the prefence of the congregation : So that the people muft either dance by themfelves, or let it alone. This cenfure, in feveral congregations, is falling into difufe. There are a few perfons, called *tinkers* and *horners*, half-refident, and half-itinerant, who are feared and fufpected by the community. Two of them were banifhed within thefe fix years. Strangers complain of the pronunciation in this diftrict being drawling, and that it impreffes them with a belief that the perfon fpeaking is four and ill tempered. The inhabitants are improving in their mode of living and drefs. Intemperance from fpiritous liquors is by no means frequent among them; but, unluckily,

luckily, the ufe of whifky is increafing, and that of beer diminifhing. The blue bonnet, a national badge, is difappear-
ing rapidly. The prevalent colour of the mens drefs is blue.

Church, School, &c.—For feven years paft the ftipend
has, at an average, been L. 100, including the glebe, which
is large, befide the houfe and garden. Claud Bofwell, Efq;
of Balmuto, is patron. A new manfe was built in 1784,
and a new church in 1789. The income of the fchoolmafter
may be about L. 10, independent of the fcholars fees, which
are from 1 s. 3 d. to 2 s. a quarter; the number of fcholars
from 50 to 60. There are, befides, two private fchools: The
fcholars at both, taken together, may amount to 80.

Mifcellaneous Obfervations.—The air is moift, but not unhealthy: Fogs are not frequent, nor of nearly fo long continuance as in the fouthern parts of the ifland. There is a mineral well at the bottom of the rocks formerly mentioned,
recorded in Camden's Britannia, and Gordon's Itinerarium,
for its medicinal qualities; but it has not been reforted to for
fome time paft. The lake called Lochgellie is 3 miles in circumference; that called Camilla about 2 miles. There is a common free-ftone quarry for houfe-building, &c. There is peat
in the parifh, but it is little ufed for fuel. Coal is to be dug
in every corner of the parifh, and fcarcely exceeds a farthing a
ftone at the pit mouth. There is likewife great abundance of
lime-ftone, which, when burnt and flaked, fells at 7d. a boll.
The ufe of it in agriculture is increafing; but not fo much here
as in other places where the price is perhaps double or triple.
Induftry is increafing; and there are very convenient fituations
on which manufactures might be eftablifhed. Several weavers living at Lochgellie, and neighbourhood, connect themfelves with the manufactures of Kirkcaldy. There is a thriving

ving bleachfield here.   The inhabitants have no predilection
either for the army or the navy; but more of them go to the
latter.   They enjoy, in a tolerable degree, the comforts and
advantages of ſociety.   The muſic here is between the quick
ſprightly muſic of the north, and the ſlow plaintive muſic of
the ſouth.   A peculiar ſourneſs of aſpect is obſerved in the
people here, and a ſeeming unwillingneſs to converſe with, or
ſhew expreſſions of good will to ſtrangers.

There are 6 alehouſes, or inns, chiefly ſupported by the
tryſtes at Lochgellie, i. e. fairs or markets where no cuſtoms
are exacted on the commodities ſold; the chief of which is
black cattle.   The number of Lochgellie tryſtes is 5 in the
year.

A collier earns, or can earn, about 10 s. a week.   The coal-
works juſt now working in this pariſh draw for coals L. 1700
a year; L. 500 of which is for coal exported, the reſt for the
conſumption of the neighbourhood.   Private families here
never brew their own beer ; but private baking is ſtill in uſe.
There are but 2 public bake-houſes in the pariſh.

The advantages and diſadvantages of employing unmarried
hired ſervants, or married cottagers, are, to the immediate
employers, pretty nearly balanced : A mixture of each, where
the farm is large, is moſt convenient.   The preference beginning to be ſhewn for married cottagers is far more beneficial in its conſequences.   The beſt ſervants for huſbandry
are raiſed from theſe cottagers families ; otherwiſe they become ſcarce, dear, and unſkilful.

This neighbourhood and county were long diſtinguiſhed
for excellent pigeons and well ſtocked pigeon-houſes, but
                                                      which,

which, of late, have been falling off. It has been doubted whether our law authorising pigeon-houses is not, in some degree, contrary to natural equity; as it does not seem reasonable that any one should keep a house furnished with a multitude of animals, over which he has no government, and which prey on his neighbour's corn as freely as on his own, while he alone has the profit. It has also been doubted, whether, on the whole, pigeons are not detrimental to the public, by devouring more corn than the profit of them is worth; it having been stated as a fact, that a pigeon house of an ordinary size, moderately stocked, will consume 200 quarters of seed in a year.

As an instance of remarkable industry, it may be mentioned, that a young man of this parish went into the north of England as a labourer, and laid by, out of his earnings, in the course of somewhat more than 20 years, L. 400 Sterling. He then returned to his native parish, purchased and furnished a pretty extensive feu, upon which he has lived with his family 28 years.

PARISH OF AUCHTERMUCHTY.

(PRESBYTERY OF CUPAR, SYNOD AND COUNTY OF FIFE.)

By the Rev. JAMES LISTER, A. M.

Name, Extent, and Surface.

THE town, from which the parish takes its name, is called Auchtermuchty; which, as those who are acquainted with the Gaelic language say, signifies, ' the cottage of ' the king.'—If so, it is more than probable, that this town had been originally intended for the accommodation of the king's servants, during his residence at Falkland. The parish is 2 miles in length, and 1½ mile in breadth.

The general appearance of the country in this parish is extremely various. Towards the S. the ground is so low and flat that were it not for drains, a great part would be covered with water after heavy rains.—Towards the N. and N. W. the country assumes a hilly appearance. There nature is seen in its wildest forms, and those fond of romantic scenes are much gratified by contemplating " the goodly prospect of hills and " dales that spread around." But though mountainous, and covered with heath in general, it is not altogether barren or
useless.

ufelefs. Some fpots have been cultivated within thefe few years; and there is a large plantation of firs, interfperfed with fome larix, in a very flourifhing ftate, the property of Mr Gourlay of Kilmarron, a gentlemen well known in this country, not only for his enterprifing fpirit, but alfo for his judicious and extenfive improvements.

Soil, Climate, &c.—Around the town the ground is rather light, loofe, and black, fomewhat gravelly and ftony. Towards the S. and S. E. there is a mixture of black clay, loam and mellow earth, fo exceedingly fertile, that there is perhaps not a richer fpot in Scotland. Some inclofures lying towards the N. W. of the parifh have been particularly remarked for the production of excellent pafture, fingularly calculated for feeding cattle, and confequently have rented very high to graziers for fome years paft *.

There is plenty of free ftones and other forts commonly ufed in building.—There are four remarkable echoes in the parifh †.

Cattle.

---

* The air is good and healthy. Confumptions are the moft prevalent diftemper, particularly among young women, which perhaps may be attributed to their ftaying at home, fpinning at two-handed wheels, and not enjoying that comfortable diet, and moderate exercife, the refult of being in fervice.

† The migratory birds are the wild goofe, the lap-wing and the fieldfare.— The wild geefe make their appearance about the firft of November, and leave this place about the firft of April. The lap-wing is as it were the harbinger of fpring.—When that is early, they appear in February, but if the weather is fevere, they come not till March; they go for England or Ireland about the end of September. They are much diminifhed in numbers within thefe few years, becaufe the gentlemen in this neighbourhood are now draining their moffes and cultivating their muir grounds, the ufual haunts of this beautiful though gloomy bird. The fieldfare comes from the northern countries in the month of December; but when the winter is mild it makes a very fhort ftay.

Cattle.—Much attention is paid to the breed of cattle; a great many are reared of good ſize and great value. Of late the cattle dealers from England have been in the habit of purchaſing them privately, which has injured the markets confiderably. They give from L. 6 to L. 12. before they are fattened ; and calves new dropt, which could have been purchaſed a few years ago at 4s. to 5s. laſt ſeaſon gave from 10s. to 12s. It is ſo far well for the country, that there is ſuch a demand ; for, confidering the advanced price of labour, and the high rents given for land, if either the cattle or grain were to diminiſh much in value, none of thoſe tenants who have got new tacks could poſſibly pay their rents ; a circumſtance to which gentlemen of landed property would do well to attend, if they regard their own intereſt, and the comfort of ſuch a reſpectable and uſeful body of men.

Population.—On account of the different ſectariſts in this pariſh, which will be afterwards more particularly taken notice of, it is difficult to aſcertain with precifion the increaſe of population ; as theſe ſectariſts ſeldom regiſter the births of their children in the books appropriated for that purpoſe ; but it is the opinion of ſome aged inhabitants, whoſe veracity may be depended upon, that the number of the inhabitants and houſes within the town, has encreaſed at leaſt one half within theſe 60 years.

Number of ſouls in 1755		halt	-	-	147
- - -	1308	Males	-	-	61
——— in 1792 -	1439	Females	-	-	86
In the town - -	1134	In the country	-	158
Males - -	527	Males	-	-	75
Females - -	607	Females	•	-	83
In the village of Danes-		Total males	-	- 663
				Total

Total Females	-	776	Butchers - -	4
Annual average of births,			Hairdreffer (who acts oc-	
for 10 years preceding			cafionally as a player)	1
1792, as nearly as can			Barbers - -	2
be computed	-	35¼	Surgeons - -	2
——— of marriages*		18	Their apprentices -	4
——— of deaths	-	21	Writer - - -	1
Age of the oldeft man		92	Merchants - -	6
Confiderable farmers		12	Shopkeepers - -	10
Linen manufacturers		205	Eftablifhed clergyman	1
Taylors	-	20	Relief feceding do. -	1
Blackfmiths	-	7	Burgher do do. -	1
Wrights	-	15	Antiburgher do. do. -	1
Saddler	-	1	Eftablifhed church, not	
Shoemakers	-	18	including children	620
Wheelwrights	-	3	Relief church, do†.	284
Coopers	-	3	Burghers, do. - -	189
Heel-makers	-	2	Antiburghers, do. -	93
Dyers	-	2	Batchelors above 25 years	
Bakers	-	6	of age - - -	16
				Inftead

* It is to be regretted that little attention is paid to the regiftration of marriages and deaths, as this neglect not only injures the feffion clerks, but the revenue itfelf. The tax indeed is very unpopular; and the act of Parliament which impofes it ought either immediately to be enforced or repealed.

† The divifions in this parifh commenced foon after the depofition of Mr Gillefpie. Thefe furely are among the greateft judgements which can befal any place. They are a judgement temporally, as they take away the fubftance of families to fupport minifters, and thus often prevent the juft claims of others being paid. They are a judgement fpiritually, as they extinguifh that fpirit of love and charity, the diftinguifhing characteriftics of our holy religion. At the fame time, the parifh minifter lives on very good terms with their clergy, who feem to be well difpofed men, and he defires to love all who are lov-

Inftead of any leaving the parifh for want of employment, or there being any uninhabited houfes, a demand for both daily encreafes, although upwards of 40 new houfes have been built within thefe few years.

Natural Productions.—Comparing the fertility of the land in this parifh to what it was in former times, a very remarkable difference will be found ; there is no reafon to doubt but that one fifth more of provifion is annually produced, than what was raifed in the fame time, on the memory of many yet alive. To account for this, recourfe muft be had to the hiftory of fociety in its progrefs from a rude to a civilized ftate. It is acknowledged by all, that when mankind were in an uncultivated ftate, every individual provided for himfelf all the neceffaries of life ; but as the manners of the human fpecies improved, the arts were divided among different hands, and individuals, with the fruit of their refpective employments, purchafed from the manufacturers of other commodities whatever they ftood in need of. Thus every thing was not only procured at a much eafier rate, but finifhed in much greater perfection. It was but lately that Scotland, efpecially this part, and places adjoining to populous towns and villages, arrived at a proper knowledge of agriculture. The learned Dr. Anderfon's treatife, and others on this fubject, begin now to be read with advantage by farmers ; and confequently the modern fyftem of hufbandry is generally adopted. The minifter too, who farms about twenty acres, flatters himfelf that he has been of fome
ufe

ers of the truth, though they may differ in leffer matters. It is well for the minifters of the eftablifhed church, that their fubfiftence does not depend on the caprice of the people, as the relievers here lately turned off an inoffenfive old man who had preached to them upwards of twenty years ; and who muft have fuffered in the evening of life, had not their injuftice been compenfated by the benevolence of a fon.

ufe to his parifh in this refpect; as within thefe three years
he has raifed turnips, potatoes, wheat, and barley on a fpot
where they were never before feen in the memory of man.
The crop on that ground this feafon is furpaffed by none in
the country. There are in the parifh only one fmall flock of
fheep, about 160 horfes, and 230 cows, in general of a good
breed. The parifh contains upwards of 3000 acres, 90 of which
are generally appropriated to the raifing of flax. Although
the crop this feafon promifes well, yet for thefe fome years paft
it has been very indifferent, which makes it the more to be regretted that the Honourable Board of Truftees fhould have
curtailed the bounty on that article. There are about 70 acres
in turnips and cabbage, 150 in wheat, 200 in-fown grafs, and
160 in pafture; the remainder is occupied in raifing oats,
barley and potatoes. All the wafte grounds, to the extent of
between 6 or 700 acres, are planted with fir. In general
beans and peafe are fown in the end of March, oats in April
and barley in the beginning of May. Confidering the backwardnefs of the feafons of late, fowing ought to commence
more early; yet fome of the old farmers ftill delay it, alledg-
ing, that they did not begin laft year till fuch a week, or fuch
a day; as if providence always limited the feafon to a week or
a day. The wheat which is fown in the months of September
and October, is generally cut down along with the barley in
the months of Auguft and September following.

There is marle, but no other kinds of minerals have yet been
difcovered. The gardens produce every neceffary vegetable and
root, together with all kinds of common fruits. A fmall rivulet flows directly through the town and falls into the river
Eden, a little below the village of Danefhalt, which terminates
the fouthern part of the parifh.

Manufactures.—Auchtermuchty is well calculated for
manufactories,

manufactories, being ſituated in a healthy fertile country.—A gentleman from Glaſgow propoſes to eſtabliſh a tambour branch immediately, which muſt contribute to the proſperity of the town, as thereby a number of children, who at preſent can be of no ſervice either to themſelves or their parents, will find employment. It muſt alſo be an eligible ſituation for an woolen branch, conſidering its vicinity to the Lomond hills, and the frequent opportunities of conveying wool from the Ochils. Such is the ſpirit of induſtry and enterprize, which now actuates the inhabitants, that a manufactory of that ſort could not fail to ſucceed. From the books of the ſtamp-maſter of Auchtermuchty, it appears that, from 1ſt November 1790 to 1ſt November 1791, he ſtamped

239,244¼ yards of 35 inch wide brown linen, valued at 9¼d. per yard   L. 9470   1   8⅓
260,093 yards of 30 and 27 inch wide brown
  Sileſia linen, valued at 8d. per yard   8669 15 10
2,212¾ yards of white linen, at 8d.   73 15   2
                                 ——————————

               Total L. 18,213 12   8⅓

Great part of the above muſt be manufactured in the town, and the immediate neighbourhood, as there are ſtamp offices in Falkland and Newburgh, which are within two and three miles of Auchtermuchty. An ordinary journeyman weaver will work 9 ſpindles in a week, at 1s. per ſpindle, but others who are more expert at their buſineſs, will weave 17 ſpindles at the ſame rate. L. 50,000 ſterling is annually expended by green linen merchants in this town for that article *.

                                  Eccleſiaſtical

* Wages within theſe 20 years are more than double, at that period 5d. halfpenny per ſpindle, was the ordinary price. Labourers now receive 1s. per day, wrights 1s. 2d. maſons 18d. taylors who work out of their houſes
                                         8d.

Ecclefiaftical State, Town, &c. Auchtermuchty was conftituted a royal burgh by James the IV. which charter was renewed by James the VI. It enjoys all the privileges of a royal burgh, but that of fending a reprefentative to parliament.
It has 3 bailies chofen annually at Michaelmafs, 15 councillors,
(one of them treafurer) and a clerk. The annual income of
the town's property is L. 106 : 14 : 6, which arifes from the
cuftom of fairs, rent of the mills, &c. How that money is difpofed of is beft known to thofe to whom the management of
it is intrufted. By the charter there was a market appointed
to be held every Tuefday, which it is to be regretted is now
done away. There are four confiderable fairs in the year, the
one held on the 13th of July, by the fame charter, was to
continue 8 days. It is now one of the moft confiderable in
Fife, for the fale of black cattle, horfes, fheep, wool, &c.

The church was built in 1780. The patronage belongs to
Moncrieff of Reedy, an antient and refpectable family, who
received fome fignal tokens of favour from one of the Scottifh
kings, when refiding at Falkland. The ftipend is 3 chalders
of barley, 3 chalders of oats, and L. 36 : 13 : 4. fterling. The
glebe is now let at L. 19. Sterling.—There are 65 heritors, of
whom 57 refide in the parifh. A new manfe is juft now finifhed, and much to the honour of the heritors is inferior to
none in the country; the church too is well finifhed, and fuperior to the generality in the neighbourhood. There is a
flour mill, a corn mill, and 2 lint mills. Within thefe few
years there was a cotton work; but one of the partners dying
before it had well commenced, it is converted into a mill for
dreffing

8d. and their victuals. When a common labourer is frugal and well married,
he can do more than fupport himfelf and family. The ufual wages of male
fervants in hufbandry are from L. 6 : to L. 7. *per annum.* A female fervant
L. 2 : 10s. befides as much ground as will fow 2 lippies of flax feed.

dreſſing flax. The price of beef and mutton is generally
about 4d. and 4½d per lib.

Miſcellaneous Obſervations.—The chief diſadvantages conſiſt
in being at a diſtance from coal, there being none nearer than
Balbirnie and Balgony, 6 miles off ; but were the proprietors
of theſe mines to erect a coal yard here, they would find their
account in ſo doing. · Another is, the want of a proper ſchoolmaſter and ſchool-houſe ; and without an augmentation of ſalary, which at preſent is only L. 5 : 11 s. it can never be expected that a man of merit will devote his time and talents for
ſuch a trifle. It is worthy of remark that the youth in this
place have been, and now are, ruined with bad ſchoolmaſters ;
and to this may be attributed in a great degree the narrow and
uncharitable diſpoſitions of the inhabitants, and that bigotry
and party ſpirit which manifeſts itſelf in all the actions of
thoſe who are given to diviſive courſes.—The rent of tradeſmen's houſes is, from 20s. to 50s. The valued rent of the pariſh is L. 5782 Scots, and the land-rent of L. 4000 ſterling.
The lands immediately around the town let from L. 2 : to
L. 3 : 10s. per acre, though it muſt be acknowledged that thoſe
who pay ſuch rents have other means of ſubſiſting themſelves
and families than from the produce *.

The

* Several places take their names from ſome remarkable circumſtances,
which had happened at or near them. Daneſhalt is ſuppoſed to ſignify the
ſhelter of the Danes, as it is ſaid that formerly the Danes having made an invaſion into the country, were repulſed in Falkland muir, fled, and concealed
themſelves in the lower part of the pariſh of Auchtermuchty. Daneſhalt is
half a mile diſtant from Auchtermuchty ; and the road to Falkland, Kirkaldy,
and Kinghorn lies directly through this village, which is the property of E-
benezer Marſhall, Eſq. of Hill Cairny, who is doing every thing to encreaſe
the number of its inhabitants, by feuing out ground for building, &c. The
great M'Duff is ſuppoſed to have lived once in Auchtermuchty, in a houſe

now

The roads and bridges are getting into high repair; and the advantage of the turnpikes which are now eftablifhed in this county, will foon be felt by all ranks, though at prefent, the common people do not relifh them, as they deem the ftatute-labour a great hardfhip. It is in contemplation to repair the road from Perth to Kinghorn, through Auchtermuchty-hill, which will add to the profperity of the town; for travellers will naturally come this way, inftead of going by the Ferry, as it will fave them twenty miles journeying. The poft ought alfo to come this way, and the poft-office for this diftrict to be eftablifhed here, rather than at Falkland; as this is not only a more centrical place, and more bufinefs carried on, but it is alfo in a direct line from Kinrofs to Cupar, and St. Andrews.

The inhabitants of this parifh, with a few exceptions, are very induftrious, and rather economical than otherwife; in fo much that there are only 6 on the poor's lift. There is here a fociety diftinguifhed by their focial habits, their hofpitality, and their benevolence to the poor. Upon the whole, if Sir John Sinclair wifhes that his *patriotic exertions* fhould be effectually crowned with fuccefs, and the condition of the country meliorated, he muft devife fome means of increafing the falaries of country fchoolmafters; fo that men of merit may be induced to take upon them that important charge, the education of youth; for as the poet fays.

" 'Tis education forms the human mind.

" Juft as the twig is bent, the tree's inclin'd."

now the property of William Marfhall, Efq.—In the South Eaft end of the parifh, there are the remains of a road: it commences at the eaft end of Rofie-brae, and runs in a direct line to Falkland. In ploughing the lands where it lies, the plough is frequently obftructed by large ftones; and what makes it more remarkable is, that thefe lands about 50 years ago were over-flown with water.

PARISH OF AUCHTERTOUL.

(County and Synod of Fife—Preſbytery of Kirkcaldy.)

By the Rev. Mr. JOHN SCOTT.

―――――――

Name, Extent and Proſpeɛt.

*A*UCHTER is ſaid to be an Erſe word, ſignifying a height; and *toul*, or *tool*, ſeems to be a corruption of *Teel*, the name by which a ſmall ſtream of water, that riſes in the pariſh, and runs into the ſea toward the eaſt, is diſtinguiſhed. Thus Auchtertoul ſeems to ſignify the heights, or higher grounds upon the Teel. The pariſh is about 2 miles in length, and 1 mile in breadth. There is a ſmall village in the pariſh, and the church is ſituated about half an Engliſh mile to the weſt of it. The ground about the church and manſe is elevated and commanding, and takes in a fine view of the ſea to the eaſt, as far as the eye can reach, comprehending in it, the Iſle of May, the Baſs, North-Berwick Law, and a point of the Lothian coaſt, which ſtretches a conſiderable way into the ſea.

Surface and Soil.—The ſurface of the ground is very un-equal, and varied with eminences and little hills, which cauſes a conſiderable difference in the nature and quality of the ſoil; the land being light and thin towards the tops of the riſing

grounds,

grounds, and richer and deeper as you defcend. The foil is light, free and open; and fuch parts of it, as have a warm fouthern expofure, are of a good quality: But the ground toward the N. W. end of the parifh, is of a worfe nature, being a four, wet, clayey foil, and better fitted for pafture than for cultivation. A few acres, in the neighbourhood, are covered with heath, and a few are foft and marfhy. Thefe laft have occafionally been burnt, and for 2 or 3 years afterwards produced good crops; but they are not of fuch a quality as to render them fit for the purpofes of general cultivation, or productive for any length of time. Several of the faces and tops of the hills and rifing grounds, are interfperfed and covered with whins, which render them not only unfit for cultivation, but of a trifling value even for pafture. If thefe were inclofed and planted, they would both ferve to give a warmth and fhelter to the neighbouring ground (things very much wanted in this climate), and tend greatly to improve and beautify the face of the country, by giving it a more romantic and picturefque appearance. Some gentlemen, in the neighbourhood, are beginning to plant a little on their eftates. The plan, however, is making but a flow progrefs.

Minerals.—There are both free-ftone and lime-ftone in the parifh; but none of them are wrought. The tenants, however, have liberty from the Earl of Moray, the proprietor, to ufe as much of the lime-ftone as they pleafe, for manure to their lands; a circumftance which is of material advantage to them. The ground is moftly inclofed, partly with ftone dikes, and partly with hedges.

Climate and Lake.—The parifh of Auchtertoul, is about 5 miles diftant from the fhore to the eaft, and 4 to the fouth. In confequence of this fituation, the air is reckoned good and healthy;

healthy ; being neither fo near the fea, as to render it too
thin and penetrating, nor at fo great a diftance from it, as to
render it thick and unwholefome. There is only one fmall
lake in the parifh *(Camilla Loch)*, in which there are fome
perch. The lake takes its name from the old houfe of Camilla *, adjacent to it ; which was fo called after one of the
Counteffes of Moray, whofe name was Campbell.

Population.—With refpect to the ancient ftate of the population, it cannot be exactly afcertained. But from the regifter
of marriages and baptifms, which extends as far back as the
year 1675, compared with the regifters that are kept at prefent, it appears to have been formerly confiderably more populous than it is now. This feems owing to the practice of
uniting farms, which has taken place here, as well as in many
other parts of the country. What ufed formerly to be 2 or 3
farms, is now thrown into 1, and rented by the fame tenant ;
fo that the number of families in the parifh, is thereby decreafed ; and as there is no trade or manufactures carried on
in the village, to draw the people in from the country, the
population is confiderably diminifhed. Since 1755, that diminution has amounted to 55, the population, at prefent, being
334, and according to Dr. Webfter's return, having been 389
fouls. This tafte for enlarging aad uniting farms, which
feems

---

* Its ancient name was *Hallyards,* when it belonged to the family of the
Skenes. It is faid to have been the rendezvous of the Fife lairds at the rebellion
in the year 1715. When James Vth of Scotland was on his road to the
palace of Falkland, after the defeat of his army on the Englifh border, under
the command of Oliver Sinclair, his favourite, he lodged all night in the houfe
of Hallyards, as he paffed, where he was courteoufly received by the Lady of
Grange, " *ane ancient and godlie matrone,*" as Knox calls her. It feems then to
have belonged to the Kirkcaldies of Grange, a family of confiderable note in the
hiftory of Scotland. It is now a ruin.

feems to be on the increafe throughout Scotland, will perhaps, eventually, be unfavourable to the population of the country, and moft undoubtedly to the perfonal character and morals of its inhabitants. It forces the people from the active, healthy employments of a country life, to take refuge in manufacturing towns and populous cities, which may literally be faid to be the graves of the human fpecies. It is accordingly obferved, of towns in general, and of large manufacturing towns in particular, that the inhabitants are of a more fickly and delicate appearance, than their neighbours in the country. This may arife from the operation of various caufes. From the fedentary life, to which they are accuftomed, which enervates and enfeebles the conftitution ; from the impure and unwholefome air, which they are conftantly breathing; and above all, from the habits of diffipation and profligacy, which are always too certainly contracted, in any great concourfe of people. And, as it is from towns like thefe, that our armies and navies are moftly fupplied with recruits, it is eafy to fee, how ill fitted, men, of fuch a defcription and mode of life, will, in time, become for defending the liberties and deareft rights of their fellow citizens, and enduring the watchings, the dangers and the toils, which are incident to the profeffions of the foldier and the failor. It was the fame body of men, that, on the banks of the *Thrafymenus*, and the *Aufidus*, humbled the pride of the Roman eagle, and empurpled the field with patrician blood, who were afterwards routed on the plains of *Zama*, though ftill fighting under a leader the foremoft in the world, whofe very name was almoft fufficient to fecure him of victory. But the luxuries of *Saguntum*, according to the Roman hiftorian*, had enervated and enfeebled the victorious Carthaginians, and rendered them an unequal match for the hardy Romans, over whom they had fo often triumphed.

Evils

* Livy.

Evils like thefe, may not indeed be very fenfibly perceived or felt, for a confiderable time : But, though their operation may be flow, yet it will not, on that account, be the lefs certain; nor the lefs to be dreaded in its tendency and confequences, as an accelerator of national weaknefs and decline. But in our ardour to extend our manufactures and our commerce, and thereby to multiply the delicacies and luxuries of life, as well as to increafe our tafte and defire for the ufe of them, we perhaps but too readily forget, that human nature is but too liable to temptation and corruption, and that infirmity of body, and depravity of mind, are, fooner or later, the almoft certain confequences of every great affemblage of our fpecies. We perhaps but too readily forget, that the profperity, the ftability, and the glory of nations, do not confift fo much in the *wealth*,—no, nor even in the *numbers*, of their inhabitants—as in their political, their military, and their perfonal character and virtues ;—as in the penetration and the depth of mind, which they are able to difplay, in difcovering where their true interefts lie ; in the promptitude and the ardour, with which they are, at all times, prepared to guard and to defend their rights ; and in the practice of thofe private and public virtues, which are alike conducive to the welfare and ftability of kingdoms, and the perfection and aggrandifement of the fpecies.

The prefent ftate of the population, and the divifion of the inhabitants, in this diftrict, is pretty nearly as follows :

Number of fouls,	- -	334	Number from 20 to 50,	-	140
———— of males,	- -	148	———— —— 50 to 70,	-	43
———— of females,	-	186	———— —— 70 to 100,	-	10
———— in the village,	-	231	———— of farmers,	-	9
———— in the country,	-	103	Average number of their families,		9
———— under 10 years of age,	89		Number of male fervants, includ-		
———— from 10 to 20,	-	52	ing cotters,	-	31

Number of female ditto, - 14

——— of day labourers, - 8

———- of wrights, - 2

——— of fmiths, - 1

———- of fhocmakers, - 1

◄——— of tailors; - 2

——— of millers, - 1

———- of brewers, ⁓ 1

——— of innkeepers, - 2

———- of bakers, - 1

——— of weavers*, - 17

Number of examinable perfons of

the Eftablifhed Church, 105

——·— of Seceders, - 20

The proportion between

bachelors and

married men, is

as - - 36 to 48

The proportion between the annual births and the population, is, as - 10 to 334

——— between the annual marriages and the po- lation, as - - - 3 to 334

Each marriage, at an average, produces children, - 5

Annual average of births, 10

——— of marriages, - 3

——— of deaths, as nearly as can be colleded, - 4

Number of inhabited houfes in the parifh, - - 80

Average number of perfons in each houfe, - - - 4

The population, in 1755, was 389

Decreafe, - - - 55

Produdions, Agriculture, &c.—There is no map of the parifh; but, in as far as can be afcertained, there are in it from 1700 to 1800 acres; which are laid out nearly as follows:

In pafture, - 1135

— fown grafs, - 110

— oats, - - 293

— barley, · - 81

— wheat, - - 33

In turnips and cabbage, 56

— peafe, - - 14

— flax, - - 15

— meadow, - - 45

There

* The reafon, wny there is fo much greater proportion of weavers in the parifh, than of any other trade, is, the weaving manufadures, which are carried on, in the neighbouring towns of Kirkcaldy and Link-town of Abbotfhall. It is from thefe, that the greateft part of our weavers receive their employment; and it is this, which draws in fo many of them to fettle in the village. A great part of the women too, who refide in the village, are employed in fpinning lint to the fame manufaduries. They fpin on the two-handed wheel, and are able to earn from 6 d. to 8 d. per day, according to their particular alertnefs and dexterity.

There are paftured in the parifh,

Sheep,   -   -   106   Cattle,   -   -   338

There are ufed in agriculture,

Carts,   -   -   24   Ploughs,   -   -   20

There is one threfhing machine lately erected.—The ftile of farming is, in general, carried on after the new plan of hufbandry, and is much improved of late years. This feems chiefly owing to the introduction of fown grafs, cabbage and turnips. The former ferves to give reft and folidity to the foil, and prepares it for the production of future crops ; the latter cleanfes and pulverifes it, and opens it to receive the influences of the fun and air, the great quickeners and fofterers of vegetation. The hay, thus raifed, is fold, at an average, about 4 d. per ftone, and brings a good profit to the farmer. Cattle are brought into the houfe, fome time between Michaelmas and Martinmas, and fed on turnips for feveral months, when they are fold to the butcher, about the end of winter, or beginning of fpring. This practice, independent of the advantage, which the ground receives, by preparing it for the turnips and cabbage, together with the weeding and hoeing which are afterwards given it, and independent of what profit is to be made of the cattle, which are fometimes bought cheap, and fold dear, gives, moreover, a great command of dung to enrich the reft of the land ; a circumftance of capital importance to the country farmer, who cannot find manure to buy ; and which is, of itfelf, perhaps, fufficient to recommend the feeding of cattle, although few other advantages attended it.

The land is generally plowed with 2 horfes ; except where it is wet or fteep, when 3 are ufed. But there is a divifion of opinion as to the ufe of the new and the old plough ; fome

preferring

preferring the one, and fome the other. It is however likely, that the new will foon become the moſt prevalent.—The pa-riſh does more than ſupply itſelf with proviſions.

Church, &c.—The Earl of Moray is patron ; and to that noble lord the whole pariſh belongs, excepting 1 farm, which is the property of William Wemyſs, Eſq. of Wemyſs. Nei-ther of the heritors reſide in the pariſh. The ſtipend is, 53 bolls 3 firlots of meal; 26 bolls 3 firlots 1 peck 2¼ lippies of bear ; and 150 merks in money. The manſe has been lately repaired. The church is old ; but it cannot be aſcertained when it was built. The glebe is ſmall.

Schools.—The ſchoolmaſter's ſalary is 100 merks. The annual average number of ſcholars is about 25. The ſchool wages are 1 s. *per* quarter for reading, and 1 s. 6 d. for writ-ing and arithmetic. The ſchoolmaſter is alſo ſeſſion-clerk. The appointments for this are 13s. 6d. Sterling of ſalary; with the perquiſites on marriages, viz. 5 s. for feuers and tenants ; and 3 s. 6 d. for ſervants and houſeholders. The records of the ſeſſion extend as far back as the year 1670.

It is truly amazing, that ſo uſeful and laborious a body of men, as the ſchoolmaſters of Scotland, ſhould, in general, be not only ſo poorly appointed in ſalaries, but oppoſed ſo keen-ly by the gentlemen of landed property, in their attempts to better their ſituation. If it be chiefly owing to education, that man is rendered ſuperior to the animals around him, and one man to another ; if it be a principal mean of advancing his happineſs and beſt intereſts, both in this world, and that which is to come ; if, moreover, in a political view, it opens the mind to a ſenſe of the advantages and bleſſings, which men derive from order and good government, in oppoſition to anarchy and confuſion, and renders a nation leſs apt to be

miſled

misled or convulsed, by designing and seditious men; if the rise and the fall of kingdoms, have, in all ages, been chiefly produced by moral causes ; and if the morals, the opinions, and the behaviour of men, be intimately connected with the instructions they receive, and the principles they imbibe, during their early years ;—if these things be so, the instruction and education of youth ought certainly to be reckoned a matter of primary concern, in every well regulated state ; more especially by those, who sit at the helm of government, and are entrusted with the management of public affairs. But how is it possible, that the purposes of public instruction should be properly attained, in the present situation of many of our schoolmasters, with respect to salaries and appointments ? Is it in truth to be expected, that any person, who has been at the expence of an education, sufficient to qualify him for being a teacher and instructor of youth, should betake himself to that irksome and laborious profession, when the emoluments are so poor, (in country parishes especially, where the school wages are small, and there is no opportunity of raising a large school), as to be inferior to the wages of a day labourer, or a common servant ? The time will certainly come, when the eyes of the nation will be opened to their own best interests, as well as to those of their fellow creatures; and this useful body of men will be placed in circumstances, more likely to ensure the great ends of education, and public instruction, both to individuals, and the community.

Poor.—The number of persons receiving charity, at present, is 6; and they are supplied by the session, as their situation and necessities seem to require. The annual average amount of contributions at the church door, is 4 l.; the money received for the use of the mort-cloth, and fines for irregular marriages, 3 l. ; and there is a fund of about 80 l. lent out at interest.

Miscel

Miscellaneous Observations.—The parish is supplied with coals from the neighbouring parish of Auchterderran : The distance may be from 2 to 3 miles. The price is 18 d. for as many as 2 horses can easily draw on a cart ; and the same sum for driving them home.—There is 1 public road goes through the parish from E. to W. It is kept in repair by the statute labour. Each plough of land pays to it annually 10s. Sterling ; half a plough pays 5 s., and downward in the same proportion. Each householder, not on the poor's roll, pays 18 d. annually.—Both men and women servants wages have risen greatly of late. Men servants used to get 6 l. Sterling for the year ; and women, 2 l. 10 s. : But a man servant, now, receives 8 l. ; and a woman 3 l., for the year. The cause of this sudden rise in the wages, is the manufactures, which are carrying on in the sea coast towns, together with the repairing and making the roads through the country, which employ a great number of hands, and render servants scarce as well as dear. A day labourer's wages are 14 d. or 15 d. *per* day.

PARISH OF BALLINGRY.

(County of Fife.—Presbytery of Kirkaldy.—Synod of Fife.)

By the Reverend Mr THOMAS SCOTT.

Origin of the Name.

BALLINGRY fignifies the Village of the Crofs. It is a compound of the Gaelic word *Bal*, which is a village, and *inri*, being the initials found on thofe croffes erected often in the fields, in honour of Chriftianity, on which were infcribed J. N. R. J. *Jefus Nazarenus Rex Judicorum*, Jefus of Nazareth King of the Jews.

Appearance and Soil.—The figure of this parifh is irregular, its utmoft length being 3 miles, its utmoft breadth not above one. The foil, in this parifh, is in general reckoned good, though not ftrong ; there is not more than a fourth of it in tillage, the reft is employed in pafturage. In general, this part of the country is very imperfectly improved, and extremely naked of planting, excepting the eftates of Lochore, Ballingry, and Navity, which have attained a confiderable degree, both of cultivation and of beauty.

Crops generally raifed, and Times of fowing.—Oats is the grain moft generally fown here, and it is efteemed the moft

advan-

advantageous crop ; they fow alfo a mixture of rough bear
and barley, peafe and beans and fome wheat ; but of this laft,
very little. The time of fowing oats is towards the end of
March, or the beginning of April ; they fow their bear from
the beginning to about the middle of May. The rotation
of crops here in general is, after breaking up ground, to
take two crops of oats, and one of bear ; with this laft crop
they fow grafs feeds, and the ground then commonly remains
in grafs 3 or 4 years before it is again broke up. There is,
in this parifh, one mill, that of Inchgaw, to which the different eftates are bound *thirle*, that is, muft have ground at
that particular mill what quantity of victual is confumed by
the families living on the eftate.

Population.—In 1755, the numbers were rated at   464

At prefent, the number of fouls in this parifh, is   220

Families, - - - - -   55

Being, to a family, - - - -   4

Of the above there are, males, - -   94

Females, - - - - -   126

Of the above there are 80 Seceders. About 30 years ago, it
appears this parifh contained above double the number of inhabitants, which it does at prefent. The obvious caufe of
this decreafe of population, has been the throwing the principal eftates into grafs farms, which are now in the hands of
a few confiderable dealers in cattle.

Productions.—Although there is a confiderable quantity of
grain raifed in this parifh, yet the foil being better calculated
for grafs, the rearing of cattle forms the moft confiderable
employment of the tenants, and is one of the principal productions of the parifh. There are alfo in this parifh both
coal and lime ; the laft hath only been wrought fince Captain
Park

Park purchaſed Lochore, upon which eſtate they both lie. They are of an excellent quality; and will be of conſiderable benefit to this part of the country, as affording the means of improvement at a convenient diſtance, and at a moderate price.

Church and Poor.—The living conſiſts of 48 bolls of victual, one third being bear, and two thirds meal, and 48 l. in money. The manſe and offices are in very good repair.—In ſo ſmall a pariſh, the number of poor cannot be conſiderable; at preſent there are 7 upon the poor's liſt. The funds for their maintenance are extremely good. The collections at the church door may amount to 5 l. *per annum;* but there is an income beſides the collections, of about 30 l. Sterling annually, ariſing partly from money, and partly from land, the property of the poor. The poor receive according to their neceſſities, from 6 d. to 2 s. *per* week.

Waters.—There are no rivers of any conſequence in this pariſh. There is one ſmall rivulet named *Orr,* which iſſues from a conſiderable lake, called *Lochore,* from which the eſtate takes its name. The preſent proprietor hath formed a plan for draining this lake, which is already far advanced, the ſucceſs of which will gain about 150 acres of excellent land, beſides draining the ſurrounding grounds, which at preſent are annually overflowed. Towards the eaſtern extremity of the lake, there is a ſmall iſland, upon which is ſituated an old caſtle, ſurrounded by a high wall. The building conſiſts of an old tower, and ſeveral lower houſes. It was built by Duncan de Lochore, former proprietor of the eſtate, in the reign of Malcolm III.; but the eſtate paſſing into the hands of the Wardlaws of Torry, it from them received conſiderable repairs; and the name of *Robertus Wardlaw,* is
upon

upon the chief entry to the tower. At prefent it is ruinous, but forms a very beautiful object in the lake.

In this parifh there is a Roman camp, a little to the weft-ward of the houfe of Lochore, which is ftill remarkably en-tire, although, in fome places, it is levelled and defaced. Its form is nearly fquare. There appear, on the north and weft fides, three rows of ditches, and as many ramparts of earth and ftone. There is a round turret on that fide which is next the loch, the total circumference meafuring about 2020 feet.

It has been conjectured, with much probability, that this was the fpot where the ninth legion was attacked, and nearly cut off, by the Caledonians, as we have it narrated by Taci-tus, in his life of Agricola. The prefent proprietor of Loch-ore, in profecuting the plan mentioned above, for draining the lake, having occafion to cut fome ditches immediately under the camp, the workmen have dug up feveral antiqui-ties, which are evidently Roman, particularly the head of a Roman fpear. Juft by the camp is a village called *Blair*, which, in the original, is faid to fignify *locus pugnae*, or a place where a battle has been fought.

PARISH of BALMERINO,

(County and Synod of Fife, Presbytery of Cupar.)

By the Rev. Mr Andrew Thomson.

Name, Extent, Climate, &c.

THIS pariſh takes its name from a ſmall village upon the banks of the river Tay, anciently ſpelt *Balmure-nach,* ſignifying, as would appear from the Gaelic, " Sailors " Town ;" and the old abbey of that name is called by Leſlie *Balmuræum,* and by Fordun, *Habitaculum ad Mare.* This pariſh ſtretches along the banks of the Tay in 2 ranges of hills. The medium length from E. to W. by a pretty exact meaſurement, about 3½ miles, and its breadth from N. to S. nearly 2¼ miles. It is almoſt a ſemicircle, with the church in the centre, and the northern half of the circle cut off by the Tay. From the above meaſurement, it muſt exceed 3000 Scots acres; about 2-3ds of it is arable, and ſupports more than 700 people old and young. There are no diſeaſes peculiar to the pariſh; on the contrary,

trary, the people may be faid to be healthy. There were
4 perfons who died within thefe 10 years upwar.. of 90;
and there are feveral now alive above 80 years of age.
The wholefomenefs of the climate appears alfo from the
fruitfulnefs of the females. The prefent incumbent has
often, in the courfe of 10 years, had an opportunity of
baptizing twins; and there are 2 families in it at prefent,
1 of whom has had thrice twins, and the other has five
fons, now alive, at 2 births : The twins are youngeft, and
were baptized in the 1789.

Soil and Culture.—As the lands lie on rifing banks, they
are for the moft part dry. The foil in general is thin and
fharp, but very productive, lies on a gravel, or what is
called here a rachelly bottom, except in fome places where
it is tilly, or upon rock, and confequently wettifh; and
even this is much improved by draining, (which is now
begun to be better underftood), though indeed it is to
be wifhed that the Highland, or fome other fociety, would
pay attention to that great improvement in agriculture, by
offering a premium for the beft effay on the moft effectual
mode of draining lands. The method of culture and cropping varies even in this fmall parifh. The ploughing is
now generally carried on by two horfes, managed by one
fervant with a pair of long reins, and oxen are feldom
yoked; yet fome keep and work them both in the plough,
by themfelves, and in carriages. In cropping, fome adopt
the following rotation : Four years in grafs, kept the 2
firft years for hay, and the 2 laft laid out into pafture, oats,
barley, green crop, or fummer fallow, with a top dreffing
of lime, wheat, barley, and grafs-feeds, and fo on, having
always 5-9ths in green crop and fummer fallow, 4-9ths
in white crop, and never more than 2 white crops in fucceffion. Others, with what they call infield land, take 2
years

years grafs, 1 year in hay, and the other in pafture, oats, barley, oats, green crop, or fummer fallow, wheat, and barley, with grafs-feeds; outfield, 2 years grafs paftured, oats, barley, oats and grafs-feeds. Thofe that adopt this mode of hufbandry, generally lime on the grafs from 30 to 40 bolls of fhells an acre, and which, they think, will not admit of more lime for 20 or 30 years afterward. At the fame time, it muft be obferved, that moft of the outfield is now coming to be infield, from the fuperior mode of management adopted by the farmers. Some pre-pare with green crop, fuch as turnips, potatoes, or peafe for barley, with grafs-feeds, 3 years grafs cut for hay 2 years, and pafture the 3d; oats, barley, green crop, and fo on in rotation; and fome grafs and oats alternately.

Produce.—The foil here is remarkably fitted for barley, and frequently produces large returns from the acre. The wheat, though of a good quality, feldom produces fo much. The oats are good, and have often been known to give 8 ftone of meal the boll, Linlithgow meafure. The turnips feldom fail to produce a heavy crop. Peafe and beans are precarious, and cultivated chiefly with a view of preparing the foil for the after crop. Potatoes are good in quality, and often give large returns from the acre. Flax, efpecial-ly in new-drained lands, a weighty crop. The lands pro-duce more of every fort of grain than is fufficient for the inhabitants. Moft of the wheat and barley is fent by the Tay to the Forth and Canal, and the oats are fold in the neighbourhood. This parifh, till within thefe 30 years, did not produce fo much grafs as to afford pafture for the cattle neceffary for labouring the foil. At that time the farmers were forced to graze out a part, and depended chiefly upon their marfhy grounds for the fubfiftence of the remainder through the fummer. Now the bogs are

almoft

almoſt all drained, and by the means of artificial graſſes, the farmers are become remarkable for their fine breed of cattle, which are generally ſold off at high prices, from 3 to 4 years old; and what are kept till they are full growth, are not to be excelled by any of the Fife breed. One farmer ſold his 3 year old black cattle laſt ſummer, for fattening, at L. 9, 12s. and the ſtock on hand this year is eſteemed to be much ſtronger and more valuable. There is a gentleman who reſides in the pariſh, who ſold laſt ſeaſon in Cupar fair, the 2 beſt oxen, both for weight and beauty, that were in it.

It is impoſſible to ſay what are the real rents of the pariſh, as they are paid part in victual, part in money; and hence riſe and fall with the price of grain. Beſides there are ſome 100 acres occupied by ſeveral of the proprietors themſelves, the rents of which cannot be aſcertained. The valued rent is L. 3944 : 9 : 2 Scots; and the lands let as high as any in the neighbourhood.

Population.—According to the return made to Dr Webſter, the population was then 565. The number of ſouls, when taken laſt ſummer, was, males 334; females 369; in all 703. The pariſh contains 162 houſes, 28 of which are occupied by widows and unmarried women. There are 12 heritors, 3 great ones, and 9 poſſeſſed of ſmall property. Two of the principal heritors have their conſtant reſidence in it, and likewiſe 3 of the leſſer ones. There are 50 weavers, 4 wrights, 2 blackſmiths, 2 maſons, 7 tailors, 9 ſhoemakers, 1 miller, and 2 boatmen; about 20 Seceders; the remainder are farmers and labourers. There has been no regular regiſter of burials for a great number of years. The regiſter of baptiſms and marriages for the 10 years preceding 1782, is as follows :

Baptiſms.

	Baptiſms.		Marriages.
	Males.	Females.	
1772,	9	1	1
1773,	4	4	7
1774,	11	6	6
1775,	11	6	2
1776,	7	7	3
1777,	7	7	7
1778,	7	4	5
1779,	14	6	7
1780,	8	9	5
1781,	10	10	5
	88	60	

Total Baptiſms, - 148   Ditto Marriages, - 44

Stipend, School, Poor, &c.—The ſtipend is 8 chalders of victual, and 200 merks Scots, (out of which the miniſter has to furniſh the communion-elements) ; a glebe of about 9 acres, with a manſe, garden, and office-houſes.—Schoolmaſter's ſalary is 100 merks Scots; and the pariſh-dues, which may amount to L. 3 Sterling, with a houſe and garden.— There are no beggars ; ſuch as are infirm by diſtreſs or old age, and unable to procure a maintenance, either by help of their friends, or by their own hands, are provided for out of a ſmall fund, from former ſavings, from the weekly collections, and from private beneficence*.

Advantages.—Theſe are, 1ſt, Its being ſituated on the banks of the Tay, where there is a ferry boat which paſſes twice

---

* Servants wages are from L. 6 to L. 8 Sterling. Day-labourers earn from 1 s. to 1 s. 3 d. ; maſons and wrights have generally through the county, the ſame wages. Butcher meat and poultry, the ſame as the Dundee prices.

twice a-week to Dundee, and it is within two miles of Woodhaven, a public ferry, where boats conftantly ply; thus cheefe, butter, poultry, eggs, &c. are eafily conveyed to a good market. By means of the Tay likewife, coal and lime are brought to Balmerino in fuch quantities, as to ferve all the purpofes of fuel and agriculture. And what is of the greateft importance, the harbour of Balmerino, a creek belonging to the cuftom-houfe of Dundee, is the chief place on the fouth fide of the Tay for fhipping wheat and barley for the Forth and Canal. The quay was at firft defigned for fhipping lime from the Fife hills to Dundee; now there is not a boll that comes from thence, but, on the contrary, fome thoufands from Charleftown on the Forth, and from South Sunderland, are delivered annually to the parifh and neighbourhood. This trade has been much on the increafe of late. The trade of fhipping wheat and bar-ley at this port began about 30 years ago; at firft, only fome farm-bolls were fhipped, and afterward the mer-chants began to buy from the farmers at the weekly mar-ket in Cupar, and received their grain at Balmerino. Be-fore that period, the farmers carried their victual either to Dundee, where the merchants fhipped the furplus, or tranfported it upon horfeback to the fouth coaft. The number of bolls fhipped here laft year muft, from the near-eft calculation, have exceeded 7000. The harbour is but trifling, and may, no doubt, be improved; but, as the bot-tom is good, fhips lie to and take in and deliver with eafe. 2d, This being in the neighbourhood of Dundee, a great manufacturing town, the weavers find plenty of work, and the factory-work finds conftant employment for all the women, who generally fpin with both hands, and are at prefent receiving at the rate of 17 d. the fpindle. 3d, There are eight falmon-fifhings in the parifh, upon the banks of the Tay. Thefe fifhings are carried on by means

of

of yairs or ſcaffolds with poke-nets, and in ſummer with
ſweep and toot nets. The firſt are hauled when the fiſh
ſtrike the nets in their way up with the flowing tide. The
ſecond are payed off and drawn in at a certain time of the
tide, without knowing whether there are ſalmon or not;
and the laſt are ſet in the water, and never drawn till the
watchman, or *tootſman*, as he is called here, obſerves the
fiſh to have got within the net. Theſe fiſhings are become
very valuable of late, and bring in money to the country
from our neighbours in England. There is likewiſe a ſpir-
ling fiſhing carried on here through the winter, and as
they catch great numbers of ſpirlings, garvies, herrings,
flounders, &c. they are ſold at low prices, and are eaſily
come at by the pooreſt in the pariſh. The ſpirlings are
taken with poke-nets tied between two poles, and anchored at the back end. The ebbing tide forces the fiſh into
them, and they are ſhaken out at low water *. The fiſhers, who are extremely induſtrious, likewiſe catch ſeals, in
the ſummer months, with long nets, for which, beſides the
value of the oil and ſkins, they draw a ſmall premium
from the ſalmon-dealers in Perth.

Antiquities.—The firſt thing that deſerves our notice
here, is the ruins of the Abbey of Balmerino. Some pillars of excellent workmanſhip, and moſt durable ſtone, e-
very one ornamented in a different manner, and covered
in by a beautiful arch, are ſtill to be ſeen. There are alſo
ſome ſemicircular vaults, one of which ſeems to have been
a place of worſhip, as there is a row of ſtone-benches all
round it, and nigh the entrance two baſons cut out in the
ſtone, probably for holding holy water, as the buſt of the
Virgin,

---

* The reaſon why I do not mention the fiſhers in my deſcription of the
people is, that they are all either tradeſmen or labourers, and follow their
occupation when the fiſhing is over.

Virgin, with the Holy Child in her arms, ftood in a niche above them. This buft was dug out of the ruins fome years ago, and given to Mr David Martin, painter and antiquarian. There are alfo the ruins of the church, and what appears to have been a fmall chapel upon the end of a houfe, within the precincts of the Abbey, where Lord Balmerino fometimes refided. This Abbey was begun by Alexander II. and his mother Emergarda, daughter to the Earl of Baumont, and widow of William, firnamed the Lion, in the year 1229. This lady in the year 1215, purchafed the lands of Balmurenach, Cultrach, and Balindean, from Richard de Rule, for 1000 merks Sterling, upon which ground they founded the monaftry near the fhore, about 8 Englifh miles above where the Tay empties itfelf into the bay of St Andrew's. It is pleafantly fituated upon the banks of the Tay, noted for their romantic fhelving and perpetual verdure, and commands a beautiful view of the river, with Dundee, and the rich vale of the Carfe of Gowry on the oppofite fhore. It has a fmall running water to the eaft of it, which turns a mill, and runs through a den or glen, well ftocked with venerable trees, confifting of afh, beech, elm, &c. In the old garden there is a chefnut-tree, the bole of which meafures 15 feet in the girth, and not above 5 feet to the fetting out of the branches, two of which run horizontally the whole length of the chapel, formerly mentioned, ftanding at the end of the houfe. A beech-tree was meafured to 12 feet 7 inches in the girth ; and an elm to 7 feet 9 inches, their height from 30 to 40 feet. It is well fheltered from the northeaft wind by the Scurr hill, which rifes to a great height above the river, has Naughton on the eaft, and Birkhill on the weft, both of them modern houfes, with rifing pleafure grounds of confiderable extent. At this laft place there is, befides fome extenfive plantations lately made, a confiderable

able coppice wood, extending above a mile along the banks of the Tay, confisting moftly of oak, and in which there are feveral groves of beech and oak, which may now be reckoned tolerable timber *.

* The abbey-church, wherein Queen Emergarda is faid to be buried, *ante magnum altere,* ferved as the parifh-church till the year 1595 when it was removed to the eaft fide of the Den; it ftands upon a little eminence. The manfe was likewife in or near the abbey, till fome time after the year 1618, when a houfe, built of that date by T. and J. Chrichton, whofe names and arms are ftill to be feen on ftones that ftood on the ftorm-windows, was given in lieu of it. This abbey belonged to the Ciftertian or Bernardine Monks, was dedicated to St Edward, and, as all the other houfes of this order were, to the Virgin Mary alfo. It feems to have been well endowed. David de Lindfay gave to it an annuity out of his mill in Kirkbuet, in the year 1233; Simon de Kinnear gave to it Little or Wefter Kinnear, in the 22d year of Alexander's reign; and Corbeck, fignifying a den with birks, or Birk-hill, as it is now called, was given to it by Laurentius de Abernethy. The preceptory of Gadvan, in the parifh of Dunbog, alfo belonged to it.—After the Reformation, King James VI. erected Balmerino into a temporal lord'*ip, in favour of Sir James Elphinfton of Barnton, then Principal Secretary of State, on the 20th of April 1604.—There are alfo two places in the parifh, one of them called the Battle-law to this day, where the Scots are fuppofed to have given battle to the Danes, after their retreat from Luncarty, where they again defeated, and forced them to fly with precipitation on board their fhips, then lying in the mouth of the Tay. One of the places was dug up a few years ago, at the defire of two gentlemen, where they found fome ftone coffins and arms, or pieces of broken fwords; but no further difcoveries have fince been made.—The dates of the abbey. and the gifts made to it, are taken from Sibbald's Hiftory of Fife, and Hope's Minor Practics.

PARISH OF BEATH.

(*County of Fife.*)

By the Rev. Mr JAMES REID.

Extent, &c.

BEATH is a fmall inland parifh, about four Englifh miles
long, and three broad, fituated on the weft end of the
county and fynod of Fife, and prefbytery of Dunfermline.
The Earl of Moray is patron. The value of the living is
about L. 80 Sterling, including the glebe.

Productions.—The only crops it produces are oats, barley,
peafe, beans, potatoes, and turnips; but no wheat, except what
the minifter fows in his glebe. It is believed, however, that
a great deal of wheat might be raifed, were the ground properly prepared; but the farmers feem to have a prejudice
againft it. A great proportion of the land is in grafs, and
produces excellent hay and pafture. The largeft of the cattle bring about L. 10 or L. 12 a head. Provifions of all kinds
have rifen nearly one half within thefe 20 years, except oat
meal, which is the principal food of the common people.
There is only one coalliery in the parifh at prefent, belonging to John Symes, Efq; of Cartmore; feveral other feams
of coal have been wrought formerly, and may ftill be wrought,
as moft of the ground feems to contain that mineral.

Heritors.

Heritors, &c.—There are 15 heritors in the parish, four of whom are non-resident. Many of them farm their own lands, so that the real rent of the parish cannot be easily ascertained; but there are about 30 farms in the parish, great and small, which, taken at L. 50 each, at a medium, would make the whole rent L. 1500. About two thirds of the ground are inclosed, partly with stone dykes, and partly with hedges and ditches.

There is no lime here, but plenty of stone for building. The whole of the surface is rugged and uneven, consisting of a great variety of little hills, or rising grounds, but nothing that can be called a mountain.

Population.—The parish contains about 100 families, which, allowing somewhat more than four to a family, may amount in all to from 400 to 500 souls. In Dr Webster's report, the number is 1099. The population has decreased considerably within these 20 years; owing, not to any epidemical distemper, for the people are very healthy, but principally to the practice of laying so much ground into grass, by which means the farmers carry on their labour with fewer hands than formerly.

Poor.—There are no begging poor here, and only a few pensioners, generally from 10 to 12. These are supplied either quarterly, or occasionally, as they need. The funds are the ordinary collections, dues upon marriages, and burials, and the interest of L. 100 due by bond to the session.

Rivers, &c.—There are only two small rivers in the parish, one of which rises out of Loch Tilly, and drives two corn mills, the only two in the parish; there is also a lint mill,

mill, lately erected on a new conſtruction, which is drawn
by a ſingle horſe without water, and ſerves for a barley mill
at the ſame time : this is conſidered as a great improvement
in this part of the country. Loch Tilly is a ſmall lake, or
piece of water, which ſeparates Beath from Dunfermline, and
abounds with pikes and perches.

Curioſities.—The greateſt curioſity in the pariſh is the hill
of Beath, the ſouth weſt part of which which affords a moſt
delightful and extenſive proſpect of the Frith of Forth,
the three Lothians, and many of the neighbouring counties ;
it is covered with a beautiful green ſward, and affords excellent ſheep paſture. From the top, there is certainly one of
the fineſt landſcapes in Scotland. This hill is frequently
viſited by ſtrangers, for the ſake of the extent and beauty of
the proſpect.

School.—The parochial ſchool is the only one in the pariſh:
the ſalary is 100 merks Scots. The number of ſcholars is
about 30; the living altogether does not exceed L. 15 or
L. 16 a year.

PARISH OF BURNTISLAND.

(COUNTY OF FIFE.)

By the Rev. MR. JAMES WEMYSS.

Name, Situation, &c.

IT is difficult to ascertain the origin of the name. The traditional story is, that it arose from the burning of a few
fishermen's huts, upon a small island on the west side of the
harbour, which induced them to take up their residence, where
the town now stands. Originally, however, the parish was
designed Kinghorn-wester. It is situated in the county of
Fife, on the firth of Forth, north and by west, from Leith, a-
bout 6 miles It is in the presbytery of Kirkaldy, the synod and
county of Fife. From east to west it may extend about 3 miles,
and nearly as far from south to north.

Town and Climate.—The town of Burntisland is pleasantly
situated, upon a peninsula, surrounded by hills to the north,
in the form of an amphitheatre. They lie at the distance of a-
bout half a mile, and happily occasion much warmth and shelter. The climate is very healthful. The air, dry and clear,
rather sharp. Many of the inhabitants live to a good old age.
They enjoy the benefit of fine dry walks of great extent, and

can

can go abroad at all seasons, when it is fair. To those who are fond of the healthful and manly diversion of the golf, there is adjoining, one of the finest pieces of links, of its size, in Scotland. A great part of it is like velvet, with all the variety of hazards, necessary to employ the different clubs, used by the nicest players. A golfing club was instituted lately, by the gentlemen of the town and neighbourhood.

Bruntisland was constituted a royal burgh, by King James VI. The government of it it vested in 21 persons, of whom 14 are termed Guild-counsellors, consisting of merchants tradesmen, skippers, seamen, and land labourers; of whom 3 are chosen yearly at Michaelmas, by the old and new council, to be bailies; the other 7 are trades-counsellors, being one of each trade. There is also a provost chosen yearly at Michaelmas. If he is a nobleman, he is a supernumerary; but if a burgher, he is included in the above number.

It appears, at some former period to have been fortified. On the south-east side of the harbour, part of the walls of a fort is still standing entire. And on the top of a small hill, immediately to the north of the town, there are to be seen, the remains of a trench. It is also said, that when Cromwell had an army in this country, it held out against him, till he he was obliged to enter into a compromise, with the inhabitants, on certain conditions: part of which were, that he should repair the streets and the harbour. In consequence of this, the quays, as they presently stand, were built by him, and the streets have never been mended since, which their present state too clearly proves. There is, however, every reason to hope, that they will soon be put into better condition, as the gentlemen of the county have lately proposed, to make the public ferry from Burntisland to Leith, or rather to Newhaven, where it is intended, to build a pier, in order to secure a passage for travellers, at any time of tide.

Trade

Trade.—Before the union, the trade of this place ſeems to have been very conſiderable. A number of ſhips belonged to it. Large quantities of malt were made, and exported to England, and the north, which yielded great profits. Many of the ſhipmaſters, and inhabitants appear to have been wealthy. But ſince that period, little buſineſs of any kind has been done, till within theſe few years, when trade has again begun to revive a little. Some branches of manufactures have been eſtabliſhed. There is, at preſent, a ſugar houſe, belonging to a Glaſgow company, in a very thriving condition; and a vitriol work, upon a ſmall ſcale, but, having lately become the property of ſome gentlemen of much induſtry and ſpirit, it is to be extended, and will moſt likely do well.——An attempt was alſo recently made, to eſtabliſh a ſilk manufactory. This, however, did not anſwer the wiſhes of the projectors; which, perhaps, was more owing to the want of capital, and ſome other cauſes, than to the badneſs of the trade, or any thing unfavourable in the ſituation of the place. Ship-building is carried on by a few hands, and might be increaſed to any extent.—— It is much to be regretted, that manufactures are not eſtabliſhed here. Indeed, it is rather ſurpriſing they have not, as the town is doubtleſs equally, if not more, favourable, for theſe, than many others on the coaſt of Fife, where they are carried on to a great extent. No place can be better ſituated for export and import; houſes are low rented; fuel is reaſonable; coals may be had both by ſea and land; 18 ſtone, heavy weight, from 1s. to 1s 3d. Many hands could eaſily be had, from among the young and the poor, particularly for the cotton branch, who are, in a great meaſure, loſt, for want of employment.— And though the water in the town is moſtly hard, yet there are ſome wells of it ſoft; and, in the neighbourhood, there is a conſiderable run of ſoft water, with many copious ſprings, along the foot of the hills, by which bleaching might be carri-

ed

ed on. Beſides, the manufacturers will now have the benefit
of good roads, and carriers to all parts of the country.

The Harbour.—What next merits particular notice, in this
place, is, the harbour, which certainly is one of the beſt in
Scotland. By way of excellence it is called, in ſome of the
town's charters, *Portus Gratiæ* and *Portus Salutis.* It is here,
that ſhips generally take ſhelter, when driven up by ſtorms,
and hard gales of eaſterly wind. It is eaſily entered, and affords the greateſt ſafety, let the wind blow from any quarter.
It is very capacious, and of great depth of water. The Cham-
pion frigate came lately in, with all her ſtores, and got as conveniently cleaned, as in a dock. Much improvement might
ſtill be made upon it. Were the quays extended, (which could
eaſily be done at no great expence) ſmall ſhips could come
in, and go out, at any time of tide. In the opinion of profeſ-
ſional men, docks ought to be eſtabliſhed here, capable of receiving the largeſt ſhips of war. This is ſurely an object, well
deſerving the attention of government. It might be done at a
ſmall expence. And, in the event of our ever being at war,
with our northern neighbours, would be a vaſt ſaving and conveniency; as the ſhips that happened to want cleaning and repair, would not need to return to England for that purpoſe;
which they muſt always do at preſent. Even for the ſhips that
are ſtationed in this Firth, and ſuch as may occaſionally come
into it, an eſtabliſhment of this kind would be a great ſaving
of time and money. Here too, houſes and yards for the
King's ſtores might be had, much more conveniently, and at
far leſs expence, than at Leith. They could be had at the very entrance of the harbour, or along the quays. And as the
houſes would be cheap, and the acceſs eaſy, an annual ſaving
of ſome hundreds of pounds might reaſonably be expected.
There is another thing, reſpecting this harbour, which deſerves

to be pointed out to Government, and may at leaſt merit their conſideration. It is this ; that it might be made one of the ſafeſt and moſt convenient *watering-places* poſſible, for his Majeſty's ſhips in this Firth. At no great expence, a run of the fineſt water might be introduced, by a pipe, and carried to any of the quays, thought moſt proper, where the king's boats might receive it, without the leaſt trouble or danger. This may be thought the more worthy of notice, as, it is well known, that the preſent mode of watering the King's ſhips, either by going to Leith, or Harly burn, a place on the north ſhore, about a mile to the weſtward of Burntiſland, is often attended with danger, and ſometimes with loſs. And, it is to be hoped, it would be no ſmall inducement to adopt this plan, were it to be properly ſtated to Government, that the ſame pipe, that ſupplied his Majeſty's ſhips, could eaſily furniſh the town of Burntiſland, with ſoft water, of which it ſtands much in need. It would be juſt, or at leaſt, it would be generous, to accommodate a place, at preſent unable to help itſelf ; a place, eſpecially, that, upon every occaſion, has furniſhed a very large proportion of brave men, for the navy ; and, where many of the lame, and the wounded, and many of the widows and the fatherleſs, of thoſe who have ſuffered in the ſervice of their country, now reſide.

It is ſurpriſing, that the advantages of this harbour, ſhould have ſo long been overlooked by the public ; and no leſs ſo, that, in the preſent enterpriſing mercantile age, they have not been laid hold of, and improven. It is doubtleſs equal, if not preferable to any in Scotland, for dry docks. Its vicinity to Edinburgh, the capital of the kingdom, and its ready acceſs, by ſea, to every quarter of the globe, certainly renders it eligible for every ſort of mercantile purſuit.

Shores.—To the weſtward of the town, towards Aberdour,
the

the fhore is all rocky; and, from a quarter of a mile eaftward, it is all fandy, till it joins the Pettycur harbour, near King-horn. Oppofite this fandy beach, the fea has made great in-croachments, within thefe hundred years, and ftill continues to gain ground. Near the town, however, the rocks are a perfeſt defence. From thefe rocks, there is as much fea weed cut, every two years, as produces about 12 or 15 ton of kelp. After gales of eafterly and foutherly winds, there fre-quently come on fhore, large quantities of tangles and fea weeds, which are ufed as manure, and anfwer well for a feafon.

It might be mentioned here, how beneficial the rocks and fhores are to the inhabitants of this place, particularly the poor, from the large quantities of fhell-fifh, that may be ga-thered, of one kind or another, at all feafons; efpecially cockles, which abound in the extenfive fands between Burntifland and Kinghorn. A boy or girl may gather to the value, perhaps, of 3d. or 4d. in a few hours. Excellent oyfters are alfo to be had near the town. The bed belongs partly to the borough, and partly to the Earl of Morton.

Hills.—The moft remarkable hill, is that which lies about half a mile north of the town. It is very fteep, and elevated between 500 and 600 feet above the level of the fea. It yields moft excellent pafture in any feafon; is well watered and fhel-tered, and withal, very extenfive. It would make one of the fineft inclofures in Scotland, particularly for fheep. From its appearance, one would almoft be induced to believe, it had undergone fome violent commotion, and that the rocks on each end were incrufted with fome thing like volcanic mat-ter.

In the fame line, to the eaftward, there is another very high hill, called Dunearn, remarkable for having a fmall loch, or

lake,

lake, upon its top, which never dries in any feafon. On the north fide it is very fteep and rugged ;—the appearance frightful, from the projection of the ftones, and the immenfe number that have tumbled down. The ftones, of which this hill is compofed, feem to be of the Bafaltic kind. They are moftly of a regular figure, ftand upon end, and are generally from 2 to 4 feet long: All this makes it probable, that it has once been the feat of a volcano, and the loch might be the crater.————There is alfo, on the very fummit of this hill, a flat piece of ground, furrounded with an immenfe number of loofe ftones, called Agricola's camp, or garrifon. The ftones appear once to have been built, but not with mortar, or cement of any kind. It is highly probable this tradition is true: —If we may believe Tacitus, it is certain, that the Romans explored the north coaft of the Forth with their fhips. It is no lefs fo, that fome of the legions were garrifoned during the winter, near the coaft. Dunearn hill, from its fituation, would moft naturally invite them, to take up their refidence on it. Befides, the country from this, all the way to Benartiehill, near the Lommonds, exactly anfwers the defcription which that hiftorian gives of it, in his account of the Roman expedition on the north of Bodotria, i. e. Forth. It was full, he fays, of hills, rocks, marfhes, woods, and lakes. ————A little way to the north-eaft, is the hill of Orrock, of confiderable extent, but not fo fteep as the two former. It affords alfo excellent pafture. It is faid diamonds have been found on it, and that it produces capillary herbs. There is alfo a vitriolic fpring upon it.———Next to Orrock is the farm of Babie ; moft of which is hilly and high ground, but yields good crops, both of corn and grafs. On thefe hills of Orrock and Babie, feveral barrows or tumuli are to be feen, but too large to be eafily removed. Some of them have, however,

been

been dug up, and diſcovered the bones of thoſe antient warriors over whom, they had been raiſed.

With reſpect to the hills above mentioned, it may be obſerved, that they are peculiarly adapted for ſheep; being verdant the greateſt part of the year. The proprietors turn them to good account, by the rearing and feeding of black cattle; but doubtleſs, turning them into ſheep walks, would render them ſtill more beneficial to themſelves, and uſeful to the country. The Bin moſtly belongs to Roger Ayton, Eſq. of Inch-dairny; Dunearn to Dr Charles Stuart of Edinburgh; Orrock to the Earl of Morton; and Babie to William Ferguſon, Eſq, of Raith.

Soil.——Between the hills and the ſea, the ſoil is moſtly very rich, and when properly cultivated, produces excellent crops. The rent is generally from 4 to 4¼ bolls of barley, or from L. 3 to L. 3 : 3 an acre. Wheat, barley, and beans, are moſt cultivated. The grain is of the beſt quality, from the warmneſs of the climate, owing to the ſurrounding hills. The grounds, in the higher part of the pariſh, are of a much inferior value, as may be ſuppoſed, from the lightneſs of the ſoil, and their more elevated ſituation: Notwithſtanding which, they bring a good rent to the proprietor. Few of the tenants have regular tacks, and extenſive farms.——They, in general, follow the new mode of farming.—The burdenſome and injurious effects, of the feudal, ſyſtem are totally aboliſhed among them.

Ecclefiaſtical State of the Pariſh.——The place of worſhip for the pariſh, was formerly, about half a mile north of the town. The remains of it are ſtill to be ſeen, with the old manſe, and burial yard. It evidently appears to have been originally a Popiſh chapel, but when built, is not known.

In

In 1592, the parifh growing more numerous, and, it may be fuppofed, the inhabitants of the town, more wealthy, they built a new church within the borough, afking nothing from the heritors but their confent. And, at the fame time, as an inducement, granted them proper feats, with certain privileges, taking the whole burden of building and repairing upon themfelves. It is a ftately fquare ftructure, with a pavilion roof; and, with a little more finifhing, would be a moft handfome place of worfhip. That it is capacious, will appear from a fact well known in this place, that it once held within its walls, between 3000 and 4000 Heffians, that were lying encamped near the town, in the year 1746.——There is alfo a meeting-houfe for the Antiburgher Seceders.

The king is patron.——The ftipend confifts of 2 chalders of barley, 2 of oats; L. 60 in money, with a manfe and glebe; and L. 5 for communion elements. An augmentation was obtained within thefe 20 years. The free teind is ftill very confiderable.

Population.——The number of fouls, in the parifh, may be about 1100. In the report made to Dr Webfter, An. 1755, they are called 1390. The inhabitants of the borough are often fhifting. No regifter of burials has ever been kept.

State of the Poor.——The poor, within the borough, are rather numerous. None of them, however, beg. There being no funds, they are fupplied by weekly, and extraordinary collections at the church-doors. Such of them, as have their names put on, what is called, the poors roll, get from 6d. to 1s a week. Their fupport muft be fmall, confidering from whence it arifes. Moft of the heritors are non-refidenters, which makes the burden fall heavy upon fuch as are any way able, or rather well difpofed, to relieve the neceffities of the poor. Such a
general

general aſſeſſment ſhould certainly take place in this, and in e-
very other pariſh, as would affect the landlord and his tenant, in
ſome juſt proportion, according to their ability, whether inclined to be charitable or not, and whether of the eſtabliſhed
church or diſſenters : and, till this takes place, there is little
doubt, but that both the uncharitable and the Seceder, will
take but ſmall ſhare in the ſupport of the poor.

Quarries.—There is a very fine quarry of free ſtone, a ſmall
diſtance north from the town, on the Grange eſtate. Moſt of
the new buildings along the coaſt, to a conſiderable diſtance,
are furniſhed with hewn work from that quarry. About a mile
to the eaſtward, and alſo to the weſtward, there are inexhauſtible quarries of lime ſtone, which is ſent off in great quantities to the works at Carron, and other places. There is alſo
upon the ſhore, near the town, excellent quarries of hard
ſtone, which is uſed for oven ſoles, and chimney grates ; as
they endure the greateſt heat, and will laſt for many years.—
There is alſo, on the eſtate of Grange, a ſort of marble, which
has been wrought, and takes a very fine poliſh.

Coal.——At one period, it is certain, coal has been wrought
in this pariſh ; but how, or on what account it was given up,
is not now known. Of late, ſome attempts have been made, by
Mr Wemyſs of Cuttlehill and others, to find coal ; but theſe
have been ſo feeble, as by no means to be reckoned a ſufficient
trial. But it is to be hoped, the proprietors will be induced to
renew their attempts, with more ſpirit, and ſucceſs.

Miſcellaneous Obſervations.——There are 2 mills cloſe to the
town, employed in making flour, meal, and barley. One of
them is erected *upon the ſea*, which comes into a bay, on the
north ſide of the eſtate of Roſſend. At an average it works the

year

year round, about 14 hours each day. On the same water, other profitable works might be erected.——There is also a distillery in the neighbourhood of the town, in high repute for making good whisky. But however profitable this, and other works of the same kind, may be, to the manufacturer, the landlord, and the farmer, there can be little doubt of their being most pernicious to the health, the morals, and the industry of the people at large.——There are at present 3 large stout boats, with a small one, that goes at half tide. They cross every day, when passengers cast up. And when once the quays are extended, as now resolved on, there will be passage at all times, wind and weather serving.——It is also proper to mention, that about 5 years ago, an ingenious foreign gentleman, in his researches about this country, discovered in this parish, a sort of mould, (which appears to be rocks reduced by time to earth) ; of which he afterwards sent to France two ship loads. He was very tenacious of making any discoveries respecting its quality.—It is now known, however, that the court of France prohibited the importation of it. It is thought this stuff was used either in the porcelain manufactory, or for making crucibles. The ships were loaded from the earth on the top of a small hill, immediately to the north of the town.

Parish of Burntisland.

Additional Communications from the Rev. James Wemyss.

I had the honour to receive yours some weeks ago, and since that time have made out an exact numeration of the parish, and find the whole to be 1210. Still, however, there is a deficiency of the number made in the return to Dr. Webster. This, I apprehend, may be accounted for from the decrease in shipping since that period, and also from the tenants and proprietors having fewer cottars upon their grounds than formerly—this I think a bad plan, and an evil attending large farms.

PARISH OF CAMERON.

(Preſbytery of St. Andrews—Synod and County of Fife.)

By the Rev. Mr. JOHN MAIR, *Miniſter.*

Erection, Situation, and Extent.

THIS pariſh was disjoined from St. Andrews about 160
years ago. The church and manſe lie almoſt in the centre,
about 3 computed miles S. W. from the city of St. Andrews.
Its extent, from N. to S., is 3 computed miles ; and 4 from
E. to W.; but, from N. E. to S. W., and from N. W. to
S. E., 4 computed miles each way.

Cultivation, Minerals, Soil, &c.—About 30 years before
the disjunction, there was plenty of game ; and long after that
period, even no farther back than 60 years ago, almoſt all eaſtward from the church, there was one continued tract of heath ;
but at preſent nothing of that kind is to be ſeen, excepting upon
the lands of Lathocker, belonging to Miſs SCOTT, who, it is
to be hoped, when ſhe arrives at majority, will give proper
encouragement to cultivate that barren ſpot. What has been
of

of fingular fervice in making fuch an alteration is the lime-ftone and coal, with which this parifh abounds. The foil differs very much through the whole parifh ; and though fome very good grain is produced, (efpecially on the farms to the north-ward of the church), yet, in general, it is better adapted for pafturage. The proprietors are fo fenfible of this, that more than one half of the parifh, which was all open fields 30 years ago, is now inclofed ; and fimilar improvements are daily making upon the reft of it.

Farm Rents, Prices of Labour, &c.—Rents are confiderably raifed within thefe 30 years. All the farms, of which leafes have been lately granted, produce to the proprietor double, and fome of them triple, of what they did formerly. The price of labour, in fome meafure, keeps pace with the rents. Tailors, whofe wages were no more than 4d. per day, demand 10d. ; mafons, who ufed to work for a merk, (13s. 4d. Scotch), look for 1s. 8d. Ster.; day labourers cannot be got under 1s. ; common ploughmen have raifed their wages, from 40s. and a pair of fhoes, to 5l. Sterling; and they who fow and *bigg*, expect 7 guineas. Women fervants, who ufed to be fatisfied with 20s. in the year, will not now engage under 2l. 10s. at the loweft, and few can be got under 3l. The article of coals is very much advanced in price within thefe 40 years : A cart load at the hill coft only 1s. 4d. ; but now, for the fame quantity, 3s., and fometimes 3s. 6d. is paid. Indeed, it muft be owned, that the expence of working coal is greatly increafed. Two fire engines are employed for that purpofe, in this parifh, by Mr. DURHAM of LARGO, and the coal-hewers receive more wages. Adjacent to one of thefe fire engines, he has lately erected a number of houfes to accommodate the workmen.

Population.

Population.—Though this be a new village, the number of inhabitants in the parifh has increafed very little within thefe 13 years, and has decreafed confiderably within thefe 40 years, as appears from the following

POPULATION TABLE of the Parifh of CAMERON.

Number of fouls in 1755,	1295	Number of weavers, -	20
Ditto in 1793, - -	1165	——— tailors, - -	4
——		——— wrights, - -	7
Decreafe in 38 years,	130	——— fhoemakers, -	2
══		——— millers, - -	2
Population in 1780, -	1151	——— mafons, - -	5
——		——— fmiths, - -	6
Increafe within the laft 13 years,	14	——— flax dreffers, -	1

The above decreafe is to be attributed to the many inclofures which have taken place, which naturally operate in diminifhing the neceffity of having a number of fervants.

Climate and Longevity.—There is no difeafe peculiar to this parifh ; and when any become epidemical in the neighbourhood, they feldom find their way fo high as to reach this, excepting the fmall-pox and the meafles, which the ftraggling poor fometimes introduce. The climate is remarkably healthy ; and as an evidence of this, fix perfons, within thefe 40 years, were all alive about the fame time, aged upwards of 90. At prefent, a few can reckon 80 years ; and the minifter himfelf (who writes this narrative) is 71 complete, and has been 41 years in the parifh, having been ordained in March 1752.

Church.—The ftipend is made up by 10 bolls and 3 firlots of bear ; 29 bolls, 2 firlots and 6 lippies of *fufficient* oats, (the exprefiion expreffion in the decreet of locality), and by 98 bolls 2 firlots of black oats, at half price, with 158l. 13s. 4d. Scotch, as the parfonage tithes, and the vicarage of St. Andrews and Cameron parifhes; the colle&ting of which is both expenfive and troublefome, being paid by 110 perfons, and fome of the articles not exceeding *one penny and three farthings;* a very trifling income! Indeed, under the denomination of communion elements, one particular farm is faddled with 12 bolls and 2 firlots of black oats, at half price; and there is a fufficiency of unexhaufted tithes to anfwer a tolerable augmentation, which will certainly be obtained, whenever an incumbent fhall purfue for it.

Rent, School, and Poor.—The valued rent is 5859l. 7s. 10d. Scotch, and yet affords no more than 100 merks of falary to the fchoolmafter.—The minifter and elders have hitherto maintained the poor by the weekly colle&tions in the church, and the emoluments arifing from the mort-cloth.

PARISH of CARNBEE,

(County and Synod of Fife, Presbytery of St
Andrew's.)

By the Rev. Mr Alexander Brodie.

Name, Extent, Surface, Soil, &c.

THEY who are judges of the Gaelic, fay, That Carnbee takes its name from two words, *carn* and *bee*, or
bray, which fignify, " Birch-hill." This derivation feems
the more probable, as there is immediately to the north
of the church, which ftands high, a pretty large inclofure,
which to this day goes by the name of the Birch-park,
though there is no one alive who remembers having feen a
fingle birch growing in it. This parifh is near 4 ftatute-
miles in length, and about the fame in breadth. From the
church, all the way to the weft end of the parifh, there is
a ridge of rifing ground, which ftretches in a pretty ftraight
line, nearly through the middle of the parifh. Upon this
rifing,

riſing ground, there are ſeveral little hills, of a conical
form, of which the moſt conſpicuous are, Carnbee-Law,
Kellie-Law, Gellandſhill, and Cunner-Law. Upon the
top of ſome of theſe, particularly Kellie-Law, is an im-
menſely large cairn of ſtones, of various kinds and ſizes,
which evidently appear to have been collected with much
labour, and thrown together, probably for the purpoſe of
perpetuating the remembrance of ſome great event, or
with a view to kindle a fire upon the top of the cairn, to
warn the country at a time of public danger. On the
ſouth ſide of theſe high grounds, all the way down towards
the coaſt, you have a great extent of fine rich fertile
ground, which commonly produces moſt luxuriant crops of
all kinds. The ſoil here, has, in general, a mixture of
clay in it; ſome of the fields are of a loamy nature; others
conſiſt of deep rich black earth; and almoſt all of them
have a gentle ſlope towards the ſouth and eaſt. That part
of the pariſh, which lies to the north of the riſing grounds
above mentioned, is much more adapted for paſture than
tillage, though there are ſome of the lands, (thoſe particularly at Caſſingray), where, in dry ſeaſons, they raiſe as
rich crops of bear and oats as in any part of the pariſh.

Agriculture, &c.—Two farmers, (out of 32), pay a-
bout L. 300 Sterling of yearly rent; the reſt from L. 30
to L. 120. On their farms, in whole, they employ about
248 work-horſes, many of them in value about L. 20. One
farmer lately refuſed 100 guineas for 4 of his beſt work-
horſes. Oxen are not much uſed here for the plough, though
the kinds they raiſe are large, and very fit for the purpoſe.
When ſold to the graziers at 4 year old, or ſo, they generally fetch from L. 8 to L. 12. After the month of March
comes in, the farmers here commonly carry on all their
                                                        labour

labour with horfes, and feldom above 2 to a plough. The old Scots plough is ftill ufed by fome, but in general thofe of a more modern conftruction are preferred. They have fown for fome time paft, at an average, about 350 bolls of wheat, 360 of barley, 300 of peafe and beans, and upwards of 900 of oats; very few tares, and no rye. Upon every farm, you fee a field of turnip, and even thofe, who do not in common ufe them for the purpofe of feeding for the butcher, find great advantage in giving a few of them every day during the winter and fpring to their young cattle, and milk cows. Every farmer fows a confiderable quantity of clover and rye-grafs; were it not for this and his turnip crop, it would be impoffible for him to keep his farm in good heart. There are no fheep bred in the parifh for the market; but in the beginning of this century, there were fome thoufands. The few fed in it at prefent, during the fpring, fummer, and harveft months, are all for the ufe of private families. There are nearly two thirds of the whole parifh inclofed and fubdivided; and thofe who let their parks from year to year to the graziers, generally draw from L. 1, 5 s. to L. 2, 5 s. the acre. Confiderable quantities of flax-feed are fown here, but it does not commonly yield a plentiful return, excepting in the north part of the parifh. Potatoes are raifed in great abundance upon every farm; they feldom export any; at an average, it is fuppofed every farmer raifes from 20 to 60 bolls of this moft ufeful root. Laft crop, however, owing to the wetnefs of the harveft, they had fcarce a third of their ufual increafe. When their horfes are not at hard work, they commonly give them one feed a-day of potatoes, which it is thought has a fine effect in keeping the belly open. They were wont to boil the potatoes, but now generally give them raw, and think they do fully as well in that ftate. Some

of

of the farmers, who have made the trial, find, that when given in fmall quantities to their young cattle, in February and March, they have a fine effect in fharpening their appetite for the dry ftraw, and preparing them for being put out to grafs in the fpring. The valued rent of the parifh is L. 10,202 Scots *.

Population, &c.—According to Dr Webfter's report, the population then was 1293. At prefent, the number of fouls is 1041.

Males,

* *Price of Labour* &c.—Men fervants hired for the purpofe of hufbandry, generally have from L. 5 to L. 8 of wages, and their victuals, befides what they call bounties, which commonly confift of as much ground as will fow two or three lippies of flax-feed, or as as many pecks of potatoes; articles thefe which ufually turn out greatly to their account; as after work hours, they are very induftrious in weeding and keeping the ground clean. The farmers are in ufe of paying to their women-fervants, hired by the year, only L. 2, 10 s. but with their perquifites, or bounties, they make about L. 3, which are the common wages given them in the families of gentlemen refiding in the parifh. The demand for yarn from Elie, Kirkcaldy, Dundee, and other manufacturing places, is fo great, that the women here who earn their bread by fpinning upon the two-handed wheel, can, it is faid, with great eafe, make from 5 d. to 7 d. a-day. The price of labour of all kinds is increafed about ⅓ within thefe few years. A fhilling is now the common wage of a day-labourer, during the fpring and fummer-months. In the time of harveft, they pay to the man-reaper the fame wages as above, and give him his victuals befides. A woman-reaper gets 9 d. or 10 d. and her victuals. A few years ago, Sir Robert Anftruther, who had a large farm in the parifh in his own poffeffion, cut down almoft all his oats and barley with the fcythe; but his example has not as yet been much followed by the farmers in general, though many of them employ the common fcythe with great fuccefs in cutting down thofe fields of barley or oats, which have been intentionally fown thin, to let the clover and rye-grafs come up thick.

Males,	- -	502	Widows *,	- -	43
Females,	- -	539	Bachelors, who have		
Of the above are mar-			houfes,	- -	18
ried,	- -	348	Wrights,	- -	5
Who have of fons,		217	Smiths,	- -	8
Daughters,	- -	272	Weavers,	- -	15
Men-fervants, hired by			Tailors,	- -	9
the year,	- -	82	Mafons,	- -	3
Women-fervants, do.		50	Farmers,	- -	32
Widowers,	- -	11			

There are 21 heritors. The only nobleman who has a landed intereft here, is the Earl of Kellie; a family, who, for near two centuries, have had their principal refidence in this parifh, and been univerfally efteemed and refpected by all ranks. The caftle of Kellie, where his Lordfhip refides, is a very large and ftrong building, with ftately apartments, which the prefent Earl has lately fitted up in a moft elegant manner, and laid out the pleafure-ground about the place with great tafte. This parifh, about 70 years ago, was much more populous than at prefent; as at an average of the births between the years 1713 and 1725, there appear from the records to have been yearly about 46 baptifms; and it is probable, there were a few more, as the parents then were not under fuch neceffity of having their children regiftered as they are now, in con-fequence of the act, laying a duty of 3 d. upon each mar-riage, baptifm, and burial, in every parifh, paupers ex-cepted.

* It may be worth remarking here as a pretty uncommon cafe, that there is at prefent refiding in the parifh, a widow woman, who in her married ftate, about 20 years ago, brought forth three children at a birth. All of whom are alive, and in good health.

cepted. But from the average of births, taken from the year 1781 to 1793, there have been only 27 births yearly. This decreaſe of population is evidently to be aſcribed to the two following cauſes. The firſt is, that at preſent, the whole lands in the pariſh, (excepting what ſome of the proprietors keep in their own hands), are let in tack to 32 farmers; whereas, in the beginning of this century, they were divided among at leaſt 5 times that number. The ſecond cauſe to be aſſigned, is, that ſome years ago, there were coals wrought to a pretty conſiderable extent, at Over-Carnbee, Balcormo, Caſſingray, and in ſome other lands in this pariſh, whereas now there is not any one coal-work going on within the bounds of the pariſh; the neceſſary conſequence of which has been, that a great many of thoſe colliers, and other work-people in that line, who were wont to find conſtant employment here, found themſelves under the neceſſity of going elſewhere for buſineſs, in the way to which they had been accuſtomed.

Proſpeƈt from Kellie-Law, &c.—The proſpeƈt from the church of Carnbee is uncommonly fine; it ſtands high, and is comfortably ſheltered from the north by a clump of fine old trees; but when, in clear weather, you go weſt, and aſcend to the top of Kellie Law, which is about 800 feet above the level of the ſea, and near three ſtatute-miles from the coaſt, you have then one of the moſt delightful views to be ſeen in almoſt any part of Scotland. Imme-diately below to the ſouth, the eye is delighted with the near view of a rich beautiful ſtretch of country, a great part of which is encloſed and ſubdivided, and in a high ſtate of cultivation. The ſmall towns and royal boroughs upon the coaſt, though far from being in ſo flouriſhing a ſtate as before the Union, add greatly to the beauty and richneſs of the proſpeƈt; ſo does the range of towns on the

oppoſite

oppofite coaft from Edinburgh, all the way eaft to St Abb's head, and the frith of Forth, with the fhipping conftantly going up or down, prefent a grand object always varying. It is remarkable in this hill, that the foil of it in general is equally good and deep with the moft fertile grounds below, and the afcent fo gradual from the weft, that carriages, with fafety, may go to the top of it.

Birds of Paffage, &c.—The birds of paffage here are dotterel, woodcock, fwallow, cuckoo, and lapwing. Of thefe laft, it is obferved, that they have of late returned much earlier in the feafon than they were wont to do, probably owing to the uncommonly open winters we have had for fome years paft. But all thefe birds of paffage, the gentlemen and farmers too would heartily welcome to a longer vifit among them, could they only get free of the crows, which are very deftructive in the fpring to the wheat, and every other kind of grain. At the fame time, the deftruction they do in this way, very probably is in a great meafure balanced by the very effectual affiftance they give in deftroying the cob-worm: Of this there was a fatisfying proof lately in this parifh. A fervant of the Earl of Kellie, who had juft finifhed the fowing a rich field with oats, was much vexed to fee it in a little covered all over with crows; in various ways did he endeavour to drive them off, but all in vain, till at laft he fhot fome of them, when, to his great aftonifhment, upon opening up their ftomachs, he found them quite full of cobworm, and not one grain of oats.

Church, Stipend, School, Poor, &c.—The church of Carnbee is a very old building of Gothic conftruction, with pillars, &c. It has undergone many expenfive repairs within thefe

thefe 40 years, and from the faulty ftate of fome parts of it, the heritors it is probable will find it more for their intereft to build a new one, than to keep in good repair the old fabric. The Earl of Kellie is patron. The manfe and office-houfes were built about 60 years ago. It is a commodious houfe, beautifully fituated, but will alfo foon need repair. The minifter's ftipend at prefent is, 5 bolls of wheat, 40 bolls 1 peck and 2 lippies of bear; 66 bolls 3 firlots 2 pecks and 2 lippies of meal; and L.243 : 16 : 10 Scots money, of which L. 60 Scots for communion-elements, with a glebe between 7 and 8 acres.—The parochial fchool-houfe was built about 50 years ago, and is in good repair. The mafter's falary is L. 6. He has befides L. 7, 10 s. yearly, being the rent of a few acres of land, mortified by a predeceffor of his for behoof of the fchoolmafter of Carnbee. His fchool fees are, 1 s. 6 d. for teaching Englifh, 2 s. for writing, and 2 s. 6d. for Latin or arithmetic, the quarter; his income may be about L. 40.—From the lift kept of the poor, it appears, at an average, there are 8 yearly upon the public funds of charity in the parifh. Some of thefe have allowed them 5 s. and others only 2 s. a-month. When induftrious houfeholders come to be in want, as foon as the feffion have proper information of the fame, they generally get conveyed to them what will buy a firlot or two of meal, a cart-load of coals, or help to pay the furgeons bill for medicines and attendance, when they have been long in bad health. Poor however as they are, they feem very averfe at firft to take any affiftance from the public funds, in fo much that inftances have occurred of their returning the money, though not many months after they found themfelves under the neceffity of applying for it. About 60 or 70 years ago, it was very common here for houfeholders in rather poor circumftances, to apply to the kirk-feffion for the loan of a fmall fum of money, for which they granted bill.

bill Frequently it happened, owing to a variety of different causes, that these bills turned out good for nothing. The kirk-session therefore, about 10 years ago, judged it expedient, that instead of lending out any small sums for the future to parishioners in the above predicament, that they would rather at once give them in charity, according as the funds would admit, a part or perhaps the whole of what they humbly proposed to borrow. This plan has had a very good effect, in so far as it has prevented some from borrowing of the kirk-session, what it is too probable they never would have been able to repay, and what was, perhaps, too great a sum to have been allowed them out of the funds upon the head of charity. Besides it has prevented the minister and elders, from being under the disagreeable necessity of prosecuting any of their fellow parishioners, for the recovery of small sums due the fund, at the same time that they know now, with more certainty, what annual-rents, &c. they have to deburse. At present, besides the Sunday collections, (which one day with another through the year amount to about 3 s.), they have L 255 of a capital at interest. It may in some respects be considered as a loss to the poor in the parish, that there are only two of the heritors who reside in it, the Earl of Kellie, and Sir Robert Anstruther of Balcaskie. The loss, however, is in a great measure made up by the charity of those respectable families, who at present occupy the houses of some of the non-residing heritors, and by the kind attention of some of the non-residing heritors themselves, who in years of scarcity have most seasonably contributed to their support.

Character of the Parishioners, &c.—They are in general a sober and industrious people, religiously disposed, and mind their own affairs. In the last age, when smuggling

was

was carried to a great length in this neighbourhood, many
of the farmers and others were, by various means, induced
to give affiftance to the fmugglers, in carrying away and
difpofing of vaft quantities of foreign fpirits, which had a
very bad effect upon their health and morals. Happily, however, that illicit trade is in a great meafure abandoned,
and the farmers, with their fervants, now employ themfelves
to much better purpofe in improving their lands.

Mifcellaneous Obfervations.—There are 4 refpectable families of the Epifcopal perfuafion ; alfo 6 families who attend an Antiburgher meeting, and about 50 more who join
themfelves to the Kirk of Relief ; but when they have no
fermon there, they commonly attend the Eftablifhed Church;
and it is but juft to remark here, what muft give pleafure
to any one poffeffed of the benevolent fpirit of Chriftianity,
that there is nothing of that blind furious zeal among the fectaries in this age which too often difgraced the former. The
fectaries and thofe who attend the Eftablifhed Church, live
together in Chriftian charity, and act very differently to
one another in fociety, from what the Jews of old did to
the Samaritans.—It would be much for the advantage of
the parifh in general, were more attention paid to the crofs
roads, and a greater proportion of the ftatute-work allowed for putting them in fome better repair. Were the proprietors, while enclofing and fubdividing their lands, to allot
more of their ground for planting, it would in a few years
be a confiderable advantage to themfelves and the public,
as there are large tracts of ground in many parts of the parifh which cannot be employed to better purpofe. Sir Robert Anftruther, and John Patullo Efq; commiffary of St
Andrew's, have of late fhown a very proper example in
this way, which it is to be hoped will foon be followed by
other

other proprietors. There are not many trees of great fize in the parifh, but near the caftle of Kellie are fome fine old ones, particularly a <u>beech</u>, which is 16 feet in circumference, and 30 feet high before it branches. There are fome excellent lime and free ftone quarries, and plenty of coal in different grounds in the parifh. There is one lint and three corn mills.

PARISH OF CARNOCK.

(County and Synod of Fife—Prefbytery of Dumfermline.)

By the Rev. Mr. ALEXANDER THOMSON.

———————————————

Origin of the Name.

IT is not known, when, either the parifh, or the village from which it is denominated, received the name of *Carnock.* But it is probable, that this happened at the time when the Gaelic was the prevailing language in the Lowlands of Scotland. In that language, the words *Cair,* or *Cairn,* and *Knock,* (of which *Carnock* is fuppofed to be a compound), fignify a *Village,* or *Collection of Houfes adjoining to a fmall hill,* which is very expreffive of its fituation. The adjoining eminence of, *Carneil Hill* feems to have been the fpot where a battle was once fought, probably during the time of the Danifh invafion, in 1039, or 1042 [*] ; and perhaps derived its name (Cairn-Neil) from one of the chieftains who fell on that occafion.

Situation,

[*] *Vide Buchanani Hift. Scot. lib.* VI.

Situation, Extent, Surface, and Hills.—This parish is situated in the western extremity of the county of Fife. Its form is nearly square, if we except an excrescence containing the barony of Pitdennies, which terminates in the village of *Cairney-hill,* and extends the whole breadth of the parish at its southern extremity. The length and breadth are about 3 English miles at a medium †. The ground is level towards the E., but has a gentle declivity towards the S., and is bounded on the N. and N. E. by some hills, which terminate in a precipice, called *Craig-Lufcar,* beyond the limits of the parish. Other hills, called *the Clums,* separate this parish from that of *Saline.* Most of the ground confifts of gentle declivities. The *Camp's Bank* on the S. and *Carneil Hills* on the W. are confiderable eminences, commanding extensive profpects of the Frith of Forth, and the country adjacent. The former has a fine expofure towards the S., confifting moftly of arable land greatly improved; the latter confifts of excellent pafture.

Soil, Produce, Woods, &c.—The foil is partly black earth, and partly clay or till. In feveral places there is a mixture of gravel near the furface; but the two firft fpecies of foil are moft prevalent, and the country is of confequence pretty fertile. The hills, except fuch as are in tillage, are in general covered with grafs; but the heath begins to appear upon the rifing grounds towards the N. The ground produces crops of oats, barley, peafe, wheat, turnips, and fown grafs, in confiderable quantities. There is alfo natural grafs, mixed with feveral herbs, and fit for pafture, on thofe grounds, which

either

† The precife number of acres is not afcertained, there being no map of the parifh, though it is pretty accurately delineated in STOBIE's map of Fifeshire, publifhed about the year 1779, or 1780.

either are not arable, or have not been tilled within the memory of man. There are pretty confiderable plantations of wood on the lands of Clune and Pitdennies, chiefly fir, with fome afh and larix trees intermixed. In *Lufcar Dean* (or *Den*) there are feveral pleafant walks among the trees, with very romantic fcenery ; and upon the banks of the rivulet, near the village of Carnock, there are fome trees which have ftood thefe 50 years, and afford a refrefhing fhade during the heat of fummer.

Climate and Difeafes.—The air is rather damp in winter and fpring, but in fummer it is abundantly falubrious. Epidemical diftempers are more rare in this, than in fome of the neighbouring parifhes. The moft common complaints are coughs and rheumatifms, which prevail moft in winter and fpring. Fevers and fluxes are rare. The fmall-pox generally vifits the parifh once in 3 or 4 years. The 4 laft returns were in 1780, 1783, 1787, and 1789. That of 1787 was by far the moft fevere, when 15 children out of 45 died of that diftemper ; and that of 1789, the moft favourable, when only three died out of 63; and, of thefe 3, one at leaft was in bad health before. In 1780 and 1783, the medium of deaths was from 4 to 6 each year, though a great many had that difeafe. Inoculation has as yet made but little progrefs, though the prejudices of the common people, againft that falutary practice, feem to be fubfiding.

Agriculture, Crops, Exports, &c.—The rotation of crops is much the fame here as in other parts of the country. After rye-grafs, oats, fometimes repeated, then peafe and beans, then turnips or potatoes, or fallow and lime, fucceeded by a crop of wheat. There feems to be a feventh part of the arable land in fallow and turnips, and about a feventh part under

fown

sown grafs. The ploughs employed by the farmers are the common Scotch plough and Small's plough. The latter was introduced here within thefe laft 10 years. When the ground is limed, 5 or 6 bolls of lime, mixed with dung or compoft, generally fuffices for an acre; but a much larger quantity is found neceffary on land taken in from moors. Upon part of the eftate of Clunè, about 50 bolls per acre were ufed, when it was firft improved. Inclofures have made great progrefs within the laft 30 years, above four 5ths of the arable land being already inclofed, and the remainder in the near profpeċt of being fo. The fences are partly ftone walls *teethed* with lime, partly ditches, with thorn hedges on the top, which thrive pretty well. The quantity of ground, laid out under the different crops, cannot be exaċtly afcertained, but the following is nearly the average of the arable land. Under clover and rye-grafs one 5th, wheat one 10th, barley one 5th, oats one 4th, peafe one 5th, turnips one 10th, potatoes one 8th, flax one 20th, and, in field cabbage, a few falls of ground *; befides about one 4th kept in pafture. There is no common, even the moor land being exaċtly divided among the different proprietors. Within thefe 2 years there has been more than ufual attention paid to the growth of flax, feveral acres being annually laid out in that way, by perfons who make it their bufinefs to attend to it during fummer. The produce, even when the crop is but indifferent, is fully adequate to the confumption of the inhabitants. When plentiful, it is exported in confiderable quantities. Barley is fent to Culrofs, Borrowftownnefs, Alloa, and Dunfermline, where it is manufaċtured into malt. Meal and potatoes are alfo fent to Dunfermline.

Minerals.——This parifh is plentifully fupplied with coals, there

---

* There is no rye fown in the parifh, nor any black oats; although confiderable quantities of the lalter were fown laft century in the N. E. part of the Parifh.

there being at leaſt 5 different coal mines in it, belonging to
as many different proprietors ; viz. Sir John Halket of Pitfirran—the Rev. Dr. John Erſkine of Carnock—Mr. Mill of
Blair—Mr. Mutter of Annfield—and Mr. Hogg of New Liſ-
ton. There is alſo ſome iron-ſtone on the eſtates of theſe
gentlemen. The produce of the mines is uncertain. Mr.
Mutter's coal lets at 100l. a-year, and Dr. Erſkine's at 40l. Mr.
Mill's, which is wrought for his own emolument, is ſuppoſed
to produce from 8ol. to 100l. per annum. The ſtone quarries on the N. part of Dr. Erſkine's eſtate are of great extent, and eaſily wrought without any *tirring*. They are ſituated within 3 miles of the port of Torry, and 5 of Limekilns, where they can be conveniently ſhipped for exportation. They conſiſt of 3 different kinds of ſtone, one of a
bluiſh black colour, with a fine *greek*, capable of receiving a
poliſh like marble. This ſtone will ſtand the fire, and the
longer it is expoſed, it becomes the more durable, and contracts the blacker hue. The ſecond is a white ſtone, of a fine
ſmall *greek*, ſoft when firſt raiſed from the quarry, but gradually hardening afterwards. Though, to appearance, not
very durable, it withſtands the ravages of rain and tempeſt.
Stones of both theſe ſpecies have been dug up, 24 feet long
and 5 or 6 broad ; and, it is not doubted, they might be raiſed of far greater dimenſions. The third is of a browniſh colour and a harder quality than the ſecond, well calculated for
building houſes, &c. Some of this kind have been raiſed 7
or 8 feet long. They take a fine poliſh. Double the quantity of ſtones can be quarried here, in the ſame ſpace of time,
that can be done in any of the other quarries in the country.

Springs and Rivulets.—There are a few mineral ſprings in
the pariſh, chiefly of the chalybeate kind, but they are little
attended

attended to. There are no lakes of any magnitude, but a few pools, called *dams*, such as, *Bonhead Dam*, *Carnock Dam*, *Carneil Dam*, &c. The first and last of these furnish the *leads* of the mill of Carnock. There are 3 rivulets, viz. the *Carnock Burn* or *Blair Burn*, the *Camps Burn*, and the *Burn of Pitdennies* or *Cairny-hill*. They all run from E. to W., and, after joining several other small streams, discharge themselves into the Frith of Forth beyond the bounds of the parish. There is a fourth on the northern boundary, which runs westward and afterwards to the S., where it obtains the name of *Henderson's Burn*, and at last joins that of *Carnock*, which produces a few trouts and eels.

Animals.—The quadrupeds are such as are common in the country. The horses and black cattle are of the middle size, and thrive in proportion to the richness of the pasture and goodness of the season. There are but few sheep, especially since sown grass became general in the parish. The birds, besides the common poultry and a few turkies, are magpies, sparrows, crows, and a few hawks, with swallows and cuckoos in their seasons.

Population.—With respect to the population of the parish in ancient times, we cannot now speak with precision, only it appears, that the southern part was much less populous formerly than it is at present. There are people yet alive, who remember only a few houses, (perhaps *two* or *three*) standing upon the ground which is now occupied by the populous village of Cairney-hill, where there are now more than 400 souls; and there are several adjoining farms on the property of Sir John Halkett in this parish, upon each of which there are families of children and servants probably as numerous

rous

rous as before the village exifted. In other parts of the parifh, the population is more fimila to what it was 30 or 40
years ago. The average of burials, from 1754 to 1761, is
about 11½, which, if multiplied by 36, gives 414 : perhaps
that regifter is not perfectly exact ; but if we fuppofe
that it is, and that the proportion of burials, to the number
of inhabitants, is the fame here as above, they were fcarce the
half of their prefent number. The population, at different
periods, and the proportion of marriages, births, and burials,
to the number of inhabitants in 1 81 and 1791, may be obferved by infpecting the following tables :

STATISTICAL TABLE OF THE PARISH OF CARNOCK.

Population in 1755,	- - -	583	*Increafe.*
————— in 1781*,	- -	912	
Increafe in 26 years,——		329	
Number of fouls in 1791*,	- -	970	
Increafe in 10 years,	-	58	
Total increafe in 37 years,		387	

Annual average of burials for 7 years, from 1754 to 1761, -	11½	Number of houfes, - -	260	
Ditto of births for the laft 10 years, nearly -	28	—————— ploughs†, -	36	
		—— —— carts, -	52	
		—————— horfes, - - -	140	
——— marriages, nearly -	8	—————— black cattle, -	620	
——— deaths, - -	19	—————— fheep, -	100	
Members of the Eftab. Church, including infants, - -	489	—————— farmers marrif,	22	
		—————— ditto unmarried, -	4	
Diffenters of various deno- minations, - -	481	—————— heritors refident,	5	
		—————— ditto non-refident,	4	
——970		—————— feuars in villages, -	80	
			Number	

* * Thefe furveys were made, and the lifts completed, the former in March
1781, and the latter in December 1791.

† Oxen are employed in about a third of thefe. The reft are entirely drawn
by horfes.   ‡ All of thefe have children.

Number of ditto in the country,	20	Number of miners, - -	6
———- weavers, maſters, -	35	———- colliers, about 35 or	40
——— ditto, journeymen and		———- miniſters, -	1
apprentices, -	35	——— antiburgher ditto.	1
———- ſmiths, -	5	——— ſtudents in divinity,	2
——— maſons, - -	4	———. poor on the rolls,	15
——— wrights, -	6	——— male ſervants, -	61
———- tailors, - -	5	——— female ditto, - - -	59
——— mariners, -	2	——— day-labourers, -	40

	MARRIAGES.	BAPTISMS.			DEATHS, OR BURIALS.		
	Couples.	Males.	Females.	Tot.	Males.	Females.	Tot.
1781, -	10	20	10	30	7	9	16
1782, - -	6	11	11	22	9	5	14
1783, -	7	13	11	24	12	13	25
1784, -	10	14	8	22	6	8	14
1785, -	17	16	15	31	4	9	13
1786, - -	8	20	16	36	6	4	10
1787, -	6	16	15	31	17	14	31
1788, -	10	17	12	29	7	8	15
1789, -	8	19	16	35	11	17	28
1790, - -	5	7	16	23	15	8	23
	87	153	130	283	94	95	189
Aver. for 10 years, }	$8\frac{7}{10}$	$15\frac{3}{10}$	13	$28\frac{3}{10}$	$9\frac{4}{10}$	$9\frac{5}{10}$	$18\frac{9}{12}$

Villages and Manufactures.—The two principal villages
are *Carnock* and *Cairney-hill*, both pleaſantly ſituated, the former upon a ſmall rivulet, the latter upon the great road leading from Dunfermline to Torryburn, Culroſs, Alloa, and
Stirling. The bridge, which joins the 2 diviſions of the village

lage of Carnock, bears date 1638. The village of Cairney-
hill forms part of the eſtate of Pitdennies, the property of
ิir John Halkett of Pitfirran, Baronet. The villages of
วowk-hall and *New Luſcar* are but ſmall, and moſt of the inhabitants live in hamlets of two, three, or perhaps ſix houſes
each. Our only manufacture is the weaving of cloth and
linens.

Eccleſiaſtical State *.—The church of Carnock appears, by
an inſcription ſtill legible upon it, to have been built in 1602,
by Sir GEORGE BRUCE of CARNOCK, who was one of the
Lords of Seſſion, and anceſtor of the preſent Earl of Elgin.

It

* It is remarkable, that 3 of the miniſters of Carnock were depoſed or ejected,
yet none of them for any alleged immorality; but all of them for what may be
charitably ſuppoſed to have been with them *matters of conſcience*. One was ejected by Archbiſhop Sharp in 1662, for refuſing to acknowledge the Epiſcopal form
of Church Government and Worſhip ;—another after the Revolution fell a mar-
tyr to Epiſcopacy, by ſuffering deprivation for not acknowledging King WILLIAM
and Queen MARY ;—and a third, in the preſent century, was ſolemnly depoſed
by the General Aſſembly of the Church of Scotland, for not bearing a part in
a violent ſettlement, to which he had been enjoined by the authority of that
Court. This was the famous THOMAS GILLESPIE, afterwards founder of the
PRESBYTERY of RELIEF, whoſe caſe has long been, and ſtill is reckoned by
ſome, a ſingular inſtance of *Preſbyterian perſecution.*——As the liſt of clergy
can be traced as far back as 1592, it may not be improper to ſubjoin the whole
ſeries.

		Years.
1. From 1592 to 1646, Mr. John Row,	- - - -	54
2. —— 1647 — 1663, Mr. George Belfrage,	- -	16
3. —— 1664 — 1679, Mr. L. Schaw,	- - -	15
4. —— 1679 — 1689, Mr. T. Marſhall,	- - -	11
5. —— 1693 — 1697, Mr. W. Innes,	- - -	4¾
6. —— 1699 — 1734, Mr. James Hogg,	- -	34¾

7. From

It was laſt repaired about the year 1772. The church bell bears date 1638, and the pulpit 1674, with this motto, *Sermonem vitæ præbentes;* PHILIPP. ii. 16. The manſe, and moſt of the offices, were built in 1742 ; and repaired, with ſome additions in 1781. The ſtipend, by a decreet of augmentation granted in 1792, conſiſts of 7¼ chalders of grain*, and 20l. 10s. 0¹⁄₁₂d. in money, (including communion elements). The glebe conſiſts of 9 acres, which are worth about 10l. a-year; and the manſe and offices, garden, and other privileges, may be worth about 12l. Sterling per annum. So that the whole may be eſtimated at an average of from 105l. to 107l. Sterling a-year ; but in the years 1782 and 1783, it was not worth above 103l. The augmentation in whole is about 24l. Sterling. The Reverend Dr. John Erſkine of Carnock is patron.

School.——The ſalary of the parochial ſchoolmaſter is 8l. 6s. 8d. Sterling, beſide a free houſe and yard. He alſo receives 20s. per annum as ſeſſion-clerk, with 12s. 6d. for his extraordinary trouble at the Sacrament. The ſchool fees are eſtimated

7. From 1734 to 1739, Mr. Daniel Hunter,	-	-	-	4½
8. —— 1741 — 1752, Mr. Thomas Gilleſpie,	-		-	10¾
9. —— 1753 — 1780, Mr. G. Adie,	-	-	-	25
10. —— 1780 — 1793, Mr. Alexander Thomſon,	-	-	-	13

Vacancies on different occaſions, - -

* Viz. 61 bolls, 1 firlot, 1 peck, 1 lippie and nine 5ths meal; 39 bolls, 3 firlots, 1 peck, 3 lippies and one 5th bear, and 19 bolls oats.

† The patronage was acquired, together with the eſtate, from the Earl of Kincardine, about the year 1697, by the late Colonel Erſkine, (who died in 1743), the grandfather of the Doctor.

eftimated at about 3l. a-year; and the perquifites paid for proclamations of marriages, and regiftration of baptifms, will amount to 2 guineas more; befides which, he receives a fmall annuity of 5 merks Scotch, (or 5s. $6\frac{8}{12}$d. Sterling), from a donation bequeathed to the kirk-feffion of Carnock, by the Reverend Principal Row, who, being a native of this parifh, left this as a fmall teftimony of his regard for the place of his birth. The fchoolmafter's whole income may be calculated to amount to 15l. 6s. 8d. Sterling; a fum by far too fmall, in the prefent expenfive age, to compenfate any man of letters and genius, for executing the laborious tafk of teaching youth.

Poor.---Though the number of poor upon our ordinary lift is at prefent only 15, yet, upon an average of 10 years, it appears to have been not lefs than 18 annually. To thefe there are 6 diftributions made in the year, befides occafional fupplies to others, whofe neceffities, occafioned by temporary indifpofition, or fudden calamities, require charitable aid. For thefe purpofes, there are 4 quarterly diftributions made, in February, May, Auguft, and November; befides 2 extraordinary meetings, viz. one about the beginning of the year, and another at one of the occafions of difpenfing the Lord's Supper, as that ordinance is celebrated twice a-year in this parifh. Sometimes, however, that coincides with one of our quarterly meetings, which is confidered by the kirk-feffion, and feveral of the *quotas* are increafed in proportion. The funds for the fupport of the poor are as follows:

Three

Three hundred pounds Sterling, lent out at 5
per cent., producing interest annually, a-
mounting to   -   -   -   L. 15   0   0
Weekly collections at church, rate per annum,
about   -   -   -   -   4   4   0
Average dues, paid for the use of the mort-
cloth,   -   -   -   1 10   0
Annual gratuity, from the principal heritor,   2   2   0
Collections at the two sacramental occasions,   6 18   5¼

In all,   -   L. 29 14   5¼

The total annual income of the poor's funds may, therefore, be stated at 30l., besides occasional donations: though,
indeed, we have had no legacies these many years. The annual average of disbursements to the poor, for these last 10
years, has been about 20l. Sterling *.

Heritors.

* The state of this parish, in 1782 and 1783, merits particular attention, as
extraordinary exertions were made on these occasions for the support of the
poor, who would otherwise have been in very deplorable circumstances. At the
desire of several of the proprietors, a meeting was called, on the 31st of December 1782, of the heritors and kirk-session conjunctly, when it was agreed,
that an assessment of the 10th part of the valued rent should be levied. This
was accordingly done, and 6l. being taken from the poor's funds, and several
private voluntary donations added to it, the sum of 30l. Sterling was raised,
with which meal was bought at the market price, and sold to the poor at the
reduced prices of 1s. per peck for the oat meal, and 8d. per peck for the bear
and pease meal. This sale continued for 8 months, from the 18th of January to
the 19th of September 1783, when the meal fell to the prices above-mentioned;
and, upon calculating the sum total of expenditure, it appeared that about 24l.
Sterling had been laid out for that benevolent purpose. On that occasion, too,
the

Heritors and Rents.—There are 7 great proprietors in this parifh, who pay ftipend and all public burdens ; befides one fmall feuer, who pays only a trifle of vicarage, one large feuer, who pays no ftipend, and a great number of others, who have no other property but their houfes, and a fmall fpot of ground (often lefs than an acre) adjoining to each. Their number is, therefore, uncertain and variable. The landed property (including that of the whole of thefe feuers) may be eftimated at about 110ol. per annum *. In this fum is included the rent of the feffion houfes on the feveral eftates ; and the rents of the gentlemens houfes, inhabited or habitable, within the parifh, may be computed at 5ol. more. ———The beft arable land lets at about 20s. per acre ; inferior grounds at 10s. 12s. and 15s. Pafture lands let at from 5s. to 7s. 6d. The average rent of farms is about 7ol. a-year, none of them being very large, few indeed exceeding 100 acres, and fome being much lefs. The fize of farms, however, and confequently the rents, are upon the increafe ; the greater part of the arable land being now enclofed, as both proprietors and tenants feem convinced of the advantage of enclofures.

Fuel.

the kirk-feffion were more liberal than ufual in their diftributions; and our patron and principal heritor evidenced his liberality by giving two Guineas to the poor in May 1782, and three more in December, befides his proportion of the affeffment, which amounted to upwards of feven Guineas. By thefe means, under the bleffing of God, the poor of this parifh were provided for, and not only prevented from rioting and *mobbing*, but pretty comfortably fupported, till the return of plenty fuperfeded any farther demands upon the generofity of the public.

* Landed property has not been very fluctuating in thi parifh, none having been difpofed of within thefe 20 years, except the eftates of *the Clune* and *th·Camps*; which, it is faid, were fold at about 30 years purchafe.

Fuel.—There is a ſmall quantity of moſs in the S. E. part of the pariſh, from which a few peats are dug, but theſe are ſolely appropriated to the kindling of fires, coals being the only fuel uſed in this diſtrict, as they abound both in this pariſh and in the neighbourhood. The average price of great coal is 2s. 6d. for 40 ſtones, and, for the ſame quantity of *chows*, or ſmall coal, is. 3d. The carriage paid for a ſingle horſe cart of coals is 4d. per mile. But here it will be proper to give a particular account of the coal mines on the different eſtates in this pariſh.

Blair Colliery.—There are two veins of coal, the one 4 and the other 7 feet thick ; both of which have been wrought ſome years, and are ſtill working. They are of a ſtoney quality, and emit a very confiderable heat when uſed as houſe fuel. They are ſold at 1s. 3d. per cart (of 40 ſtones weight), excluſive of carriage. The ſmall coal has been found to anſwer well for burning lime, and for ſalt-works. Under theſe two veins of coal there are other two ; the one 2 feet 10 inches, and the other 3 feet thick. The former is a *ſplint* coal, the latter a *ſmithy* coal of a good quality. Of theſe two veins only a ſmall part has yet been wrought, as they are under level. Preparations, however, are now making for working both *.

Merrylees Colliery.—This coal-work is the property of Mr. MUTTER of Annfield, and has been wrought to a confiderable extent for theſe 8 years paſt. The laſt leaſe taken of it was at the rent of 100l. Sterling, and a ſteam engine was erected
for

* On the Blair eſtate there is alſo iron ſtone, both of the *bed* and *ball* kind, but no proper trial has yet been made to aſcertain its quality.

for draining it. There are many veins of this coal, several feet thick, partly above level and partly below. It is principally ufed for drying corn and malt for the mills, for which it feems peculiarly well qualified, as the grain, dried by it, does not receive the fmalleft tinge, but is rather fairer after the operation than before it. But the moft valuable, as well as fingular property of this coal, is, that grain or malt dried by it, is proof againft the depredations of the weevil, and all other fmall vermin. And it is even faid to be afcertained, by repeated experiments, that if only a part of the grain be dried with this coal, and mixed with other grain, the vermin among the grain not dried with it will be deftroyed :—So powerful are its effects in deftroying thofe pernicious animals, without communicating any quality to the corn, in the fmalleft degree prejudicial to the health of man. On thefe accounts this coal is of confiderable ufe to maltfters and corndealers. When there is a great demand, it is fhipped at Torry pier, oppofite to Borrowftownnefs, where veffels are loaded with the greateft difpatch.

Whinny-hill Colliery.——This coal belongs to Sir John Halkett of Pitfirran, and has the fame qualities with that of Merrylees, as the two collieries are fituated very near each other, and are feparated only by a fmall rivulet, which forms the *march*, or boundary between the two eftates. This coal is at prefent (May 1791) wrought to a confiderable extent, and is delivered at Torry pier, and put on fhip-board, carriage free, at 30s. per chaldron. Notwithftanding the great abundance of coals, there are no coal waggons in the parifh.

Roads.—The fituation of this parifh is upon the whole advantageous ; but the inhabitants labour under one great inconvenience

convenience from the badneſs of the roads. In ſummer they are tolerable, but in winter, or during a long courſe of rainy weather, they are hardly paſſable, owing to the ſoftneſs of the ſoil, and the great number of heavy carriages. It is hoped, however, that this inconvenience will ſoon be remedied, by a proper application, or reaſonable commutation of the ſtatute labour, as well as by the erection of turnpike roads ; the advantages of which, being already felt in ſome of the neighbouring diſtricts, are now more generally acknowledged than formerly.

Inns and Ale-houſes.——There are about 10 ſmall inns and ale-houſes in the pariſh, viz. 4 in Carnock, 5 in Cairny-hill, and 1 in Blair. Although theſe, as well as moſt other accommodations, and enjoyments in life, are and may be abuſed to the purpoſes of intemperance, yet it muſt be admitted that ſeveral houſes of this kind are neceſſary in country pariſhes, for the convenience of travellers, and the accommodation of the people who come from a diſtance, to attend public worſhip on the Sabbath day. Perhaps, however, the number at preſent in this pariſh might be diminiſhed, without any great inconvenience, or rather, probably, with advantage to the inhabitants.

Houſes and Cottages, &c.——Within theſe 10 years, about 20 new houſes have been built in different parts of the pariſh. Scarce any have been pulled down, except ſome cottages belonging to the colliers, who frequently move from one colliery to another ; and the habitations being ſlight and ſuperficial ſoon go to ruin. Two or three huts, poſſeſſed by ſmall tenants, have alſo become ruinous, but the number of cottages erected within that period greatly counterbalances
them ;

them ; a very confiderable number of cottagers, being employed as day-labourers, from the villages of Carnock and Cairny-hill. The employing of cottagers has been found preferable to the hiring of fervants, being equally cheap and far lefs troublefome *. It is a fact, that improvements, profecuted in this manner, on feveral of the neighbouring eftates, have turned out to good account. And it may be added, that thofe gentlemen who thus employ the inferior ranks, do the moft effential fervice to their country, by not only beautifying and enriching the ground, but, at the fame time, giving encouragement to population and honeft induftry.

Improvements.—Within thefe laft 16 years there have been planted in the lands of Blair above 130,000 foreft trees, partly firs of different kinds, and partly hard wood. There are two parks on Carneil-Hill, in high cultivation, making about 100 acres between them. About five or fix bolls of lime (mixed with dung or compoft), are ufed for an acre. In the land of Clune, about 50 or 60 bolls of lime were ufed for an acre, when firft taken in from moor. Lime being plentiful,

---

* Day-labourers generally get 1s. per day in fummer and 10d. in winter, without maintenance. Men fervants receive from 6l. to 7l., and women from 2l. 10s. to 3l. Sterling, befides their board. The expence of a common labourer and his family may be eftimated at from 15l. to 18l. per annum, which is defrayed by the united induftry of the parents and their children, from the time they are able to do any thing. The wages of a day-labourer will be about 14l. Sterling a-year of clear gain, at an average. At hay-making the men get 10d. and the women 7d. Male reapers during harveft get 10d. per day, and females 7d., with their meat. Ditchers get 1s. per day without maintenance.——It may be added, that the wages of tradefmen are in proportion ; as houfe-carpenters get 1s. 2d. per day ; mafons 1s. 6d. for 9 months, and 1s. the other 3 ; flaters $\frac{1}{4}$. in fummer and 6d. in winter ; and tailors 5d. per day, befides maintenance.

plentiful, there is no demand for marl, though some of the latter has been dug from the moss in the S. E. part of the parish. The farm of Carneil was all enclosed since 1761, and likewise the Clune farm since 1757; the former being done by Mr. Colvill, the present farmer, and the latter by Mr. Chalmers, the late proprietor of these lands.

Language.—That the Gaelic or Erse was the ancient language of this part of the country, is evident from the names of most places in the parish; such as *Carnock, Luscar, Clune, Blair, Pitdenny, Carneil,* &c.; though others, indeed, of later date, are clearly of modern derivation; such as *Bonny-Town, Herd-Hill, Gowk-Hall, Wood-End,* &c. The language now generally spoken in this district, is the broad Scotch dialect, with the Fifeshire accent, which gives some words so peculiar a turn, as to render the speaker almost unintelligible to the natives of a different county.

Eminent Men.—Under this head, we can only enumerate as natives of this parish, or residents in it, the Rev. JOHN ROW, above mentioned, (whose father was minister of it in the beginning and middle of last century, and) who was promoted to be principal of King's College in Aberdeen; and the late Mr. JOHN ERSKINE of Carnock, professor of municipal law in the college of Edinburgh, and author of the larger and lesser *Institutes of the Law of Scotland.* Of Mr. Erskine's abilities we need say nothing. His eminence as a lawyer is universally known. He resided at his house of Newbigging, in this parish, during the summer season, for upwards of 30 years; but at last removed to Cardross, in Monteith, where he died in the year 1767, having, some years before that, purchased considerable property there,

there, which is now poſſeſſed by his ſecond ſon, JAMES
ERSKINE, Eſq. of Cardroſs.

Antiquities.—Of theſe we cannot boaſt that we have many.
There ſeems to have been *a camp* a little S. from the village
of Carnock, upon an eminence, which ſtill retains the name
of *Camps*; and probably another, in ſome remote period, upon *Carneil-hill.* Both ſeem well adapted for that purpoſe ;
the aſcent being ſteep and difficult upon two ſides at leaſt,
and the proſpect of the adjacent country noble and extenſive
from the ſummits. Upon opening a cairn upon Carneil-hill,
about 20 years ago, there was found *an urn* of earthen ware,
containing ſome ſmall copper coins, but they had no inſcription which could be read by thoſe into whoſe hands they
came. There are evidently the remains of *a camp* (probably
one of the Roman *Caſtra ſtativa*), upon *Craig-Luſcar Hill,* in
the pariſh of Dunfermline, adjoining to the N. E. boundary
of ours.—We have no *barrows* or *tumuli,* certainly known as
artificial. There are indeed ſome *Knows,* or *ſmall eminences,*
as *the Knows of Luſcar,* and the *Law Know* adjoining to Carnock. From the name of the laſt of theſe, we may be led to
believe, that it was a place for aſſembling the vaſſals and de-
pendants round their ſuperiors, in the days of the feudal ſyſtem, that differences might be decided and juſtice adminiſter-
ed. Several of the hamlets preſerve ſome traces of thoſe diſ-
tracted times in the names they bear, as they ſeem to indicate *war, confuſion,* and *noiſe.*——Among the antiquities of
Carnock may alſo be mentioned an *ancient croſs,* in the
middle of the northern diviſion of the village. This croſs is
of a circular form, containing ſix rounds of ſtone ſteps, riſing
one above another, and gradually diminiſhing in diameter as
they aſcend. In the middle grows a venerable *thorn tree,*
which

which was, even within thefe few years, covered with leaves
and bloffoms in fummer; but is now much decayed. It is
called *the Thorne* in our feffion records; about the middle of
the laft century; and is probably about 200 years old.

Ink Craig.—The *Ink Craig* of Carnock, adjoining to the
Dam Dike, deferves to be mentioned as a curiofity. It produces
a liquid, refembling ink, which drops almoft conftantly from
the rock. A chemical analyfis was made of this liquid, by
the ingenious Dr. Black, when it was found to contain a
mixture of coal, flinty earth, and clay.

Stature, Character, and Manner of Living.—The natives
of this parifh have nothing remarkable in their fize or ftrength:
neither are they difcriminated from their countrymen by any
peculiar qualities of the mind. Their fize is generally between 5 and 6 feet; and fcarce any one has been known to
exceed 6¼. A laudable fpirit of induftry prevails much
among the inferior claffes. The men are moftly occupied in
hufbandry, and the women in fpinning, fewing, knitting
ftockings, &c. There are very few who incline to go to fea,
though fome are engaged at the ports on the Frith. The natives are equally averfe to the land fervice; not above 9 or
10 having inlifted in the army thefe many years; and of
thefe, 2 or 3 only of late. In point of benevolence, it is
but juftice to fay, that the people of this parifh are at leaft
upon a par with their countrymen in the neighbouring diftricts; and in times of extraordinary fcarcity, exertions have
been made by many individuals in behalf of the diftreffed,
which did honour to their feelings. The common people
live

live rather too sparingly* ; although there is reason to believe, that, in this, as well as other respects, their manners, customs, dress, &c. have considerably altered within these 50, or even within these last 20 years ; and perhaps the extreme, into which some may now be in danger of running, is that of living rather beyond their income, the fatal consequences of which need not be prognosticated. As to crimes, no instance has occurred of any native of Carnock being subjected to a criminal process for these 10 years past. May the virtue, sobriety, industry, and regularity of the inhabitants continue and increase ! Amen !

* When they work hard, the country people should, in general, take more nourishing diet that at present, and malt liquors instead of spiritous ones.— The prices of provisions in our nearest market, are generally as follows:— beef, 4d. a pound ; veal and mutton ditto ; lamb, 4½d. ; pork, 4d.; (pigs and geese not sold) ; ducks, 1s. each ; chickens, 3½d. or 4d. ; (no rabbits) ; butter, 8d. and 9d. ; cheese, 3d. and 4d. Wheat, barley, and oats may be reckoned, at a medium, 1s. per boll under the Mid-Lothian high fiars.

☞ *The following list of inhabitants, taken in* 1781, *omitted in its proper place, may here be subjoined.*

Children under 6 years of age,	159	Antiburgher Seceders,	-	143
Males above that age,	385	Burgher ditto, - - -		103
Females, - - -	366	Members of the Church of Relief,		52
		Ditto of the Chapel of Ease, Dun-		
In all, - -	910	fermline, - - - -		31
Children of the Established		Cameronians, - - -		2
Church, - - -	106	Children of Dissenters,	-	53
Examinable persons of ditto,	420			
				384
In all, - - -	526			

PARISH OF CERES,

(COUNTY OF FIFE.)

By the Rev. ROBERT ARNOT, D. D.
Minister of that Parish.

Origin of the Name.

THE parish of Ceres is one of the districts, which constitute the presbytery of Cupar, within the bounds of the Synod and county of Fife. It takes its name from the village in which the church stands, situated 2 miles and a half S. E. of Cupar the county town, and presbytery seat. From records, and old papers, it appears, that the orthography of the name was very indetermined, previous to the present century. Sometimes it was written *Siras,* at other times *Sires, Cyres, Cyrus, Cires.*—It is now understood, that Ceres is the true orthography, and in this way the name is now almost always written. There is no reason for believing, that the name of the parish, although the same with that of the heathen goddess, believed to preside over corn, is derived from her. It is highly probable, that it

is,

is, like the names of moſt other places in this part of the iſland, of Gaelic original, bearing an alluſion to the ſituation of the village, or to ſome hiſtorical faƈt concerning it.

Extent, Soil, Minerals, &c.—The greateſt length of the pariſh, from Magaſk moor on the N. E. where it joins the pariſh of St Andrew's, to Clatto-den on the S. W. where it joins the pariſh of Kettle, is about 8 ſtatute miles. The breadth is various, from half a mile to 4 miles. The contents may be about 8000 acres. The ſoil, as may be expeƈted in ſo great an extent of ground, is of different qualities. Along the banks of the Eden, in the N. W. part of the pariſh, it is light, inclining to ſand, and lies upon freeſtone rock. The greater part of the pariſh, is a deep cold earth, lying upon whinſtone rock, limeſtone rock, or tilly clay. A ſmall extent, around the village, is a free earth lying upon gravel. There are two conſiderable moſſes, and ſeveral moors, ſome of greater, ſome of ſmaller extent. The pariſh, in general, is hilly; but none of the hills are of great height, or very ſteep : Almoſt all of them are cultivated to the ſummit. A beautiful little valley runs about a mile weſt, and about as far eaſt, from the village. Along the north ſide of the pariſh, there is plenty of freeſtone rock, not difficult to be wrought. The ſouth ſide abounds with whinſtone rock. On the farm of Newbigging of Craighall, there is a little hill called *Gather-cold-craig*, the weſt ſide of which conſiſts of a maſs of baſaltic pillars, of an hexagonal form, of various heights and diameters, and joined at irregular diſtances. There are 3 lime works, and 1 coal work in the pariſh, all wrought to a conſiderable extent. The value of the coal work is much diminiſhed by the expence of a ſteam engine, for drawing off the water. Two coal pits, wrought in the pariſh, about 10 years ago, are now given up.

Rivers,

Rivers, Fiſh, Climate, &c.—Eden, the principal river in the county of Fife, abounding with excellent trout, runs along the N. W. ſide of the pariſh about a mile and a half. Three burns or brooks, one from the eaſt, one from the ſouth, and one from the weſt, unite near the village of Ceres, and form what is called Ceres burn ; which, after running a mile and a half, in a N. E. direction, through this pariſh, turns north through the pariſh of Kemback, and falls into the Eden a little above Dairſie bridge. In Ceres burn there are a good many trouts, but the number is prevented from increaſing, by the ochre water from the coal mines, and by the great quantity of lint, ſteeped annually in the burn itſelf, or in the rivulets which fall into it. Every part of the pariſh, is well ſupplied, with ſprings or rivulets of excellent water ; and this advantage it derives from its hilly ſituation. On the banks of the Eden, and in the valley around the village of Ceres, the air is temperate and mild. Snow ſeldom lies long. Harveſt begins commonly about the 20th of Auguſt. But in the higher parts of the pariſh, the air is colder,—ſnow lies longer,— and harveſt does not begin till about the firſt week of September. The pariſh is healthy, and not diſtinguiſhed from the adjacent diſtricts by any particular diſeaſe. With regard to longevity, the inhabitants are on the ſame footing with thoſe in the neighbourhood.

Agriculture and Produce.—Within theſe laſt 30 years, much has been done in the way of incloſing ; in ſome places with ſtone dikes, in others with hedge and ditch. Within the ſame period, much has alſo been done in the way of planting : And this, together with incloſing, has added much both to the beauty and value of theſe eſtates, where they have taken place. Much, however, in both reſpects, yet remains to be done. The cultivation of
wheat

wheat, barley, oats, peafe and beans, flax, clover, rye-grafs, potatoes, and turnips, is general, according as the different foils are fuited to them, and in fuch rotations as experience has fhown to be moft profitable. Since the introduction of clover, the cultivation of peafe and beans, has been lefs attended to. The quantity of wheat, fown annually in the parifh, is ten times greater now, than it was 40 years ago ; and the confumption has increafed in equal proportion. The grofs produce of all kinds of grain in the parifh, may be about 12,000 bolls, which, after deducting the quantity neceflary for feed, will do a great deal more than fupply the inhabitants. Potatoes form a confiderable part of the food of the people, and are alfo ufed as food for horfes. The quantity raifed is about 2000 bolls yearly. The foil being excellently calculated for flax, a great deal is cultivated; the annual produce may be about 1500 ftone weight. It will not be wide of the truth to calculate, that three tenths of the ground in the parifh are yearly in tillage ; fix tenths in grafs for cutting, and for pafture ; and one tenth in mofs, moor, and planting. In ploughing, horfes are chiefly ufed ; where oxen are employed, 2, together with 2 horfes, are reckoned fufficient. Thirty or 40 years ago, 4 oxen and 2 horfes were employed in each plough ; 2 good horfes are now found fufficient ; and the fame man, that holds the plough, alfo drives it. Both the old Scotch plough, and the Englifh, with a curved mould-board, are ufed. The latter now, is the more frequent of the two.

The number of ploughs employed in the parifh, is about,   —   —   90

Number of horfes, employed in different kinds of work,   —   —   —   250

Number of young horfes not ready for work,   50
———— calves reared yearly,   —   250
———— oxen and cows,   —   1000
———— fheep *,   —   —   400

Farms, &c.—The farms in the parifh, are of various extents; from 20 to 400 acres, and the rents different, from 5 s. to L. 1, 10 s. the acre, according to the foil and fituation. A great many farms in the parifh, belonging to the eftate of Craighall, were feued about the beginning of the prefent century; thefe, owing to the rife of the value of land, and improvements in agriculture, although feued out at the full rent, are now become of greater value to the feuers than to the fuperior.—Upon the different farms, a cottager, or, as he is commonly called, a *cotter*, is kept for each plough employed on the farm. He is bound to ferve the farmer in all forts of neceffary labour, and is allowed, befides his houfe, a fmall yard for raifing kitchen ftuffs, ground for a certain quantity of flax and potatoes, has a cow kept for him throughout the year, and receives L. 4 or L. 5 in money. Experience has proved this plan to be advantageous both for mafters and fervants. Thefe cottagers are generally married, and have families, which afford a fupply of ufeful hands, both for agriculture and manufactures. The wages of a man fervant, not a cotter, are about L. 8 yearly; the wages of a maid fervant, L. 2, 10 s. or L. 3 a-year. Day labourers receive 1 s. a-day, in the time of harveft; and on preffing occafions, more is given.

Trade

* About 50 years ago, there were not fewer than 20 flocks of fheep kept in the parifh; which, allowing ten fcore to each flock, would make the whole number of fheep, 4000. The flocks are now reduced to two.

Trade and Manufactures.—The articles of trade in the parish are cattle, horses, corn, flax, linen, coal and lime. There are 138 looms employed in the manufacture of linen.

There are in the parish,

Flaxdressers,	- -	7	Tailors,	- -	8
Smiths,	- -	8	Brewers,* (who also keep inns,)		3
Wrights,	- -	11	Bakers,*	- - -	6
Wheel-wrights,	-	2	Grocers or Shopkeepers,	-	8
Mill-wright,	- -	1	Alehouses,	- -	6
Cooper,	- -	1	Corn Mills,	- -	6
Turner,	- -	1	Barley ditto,	- -	4
Masons,	- -	15	Lint ditto,	- -	5
Shoemakers,	- -	7			

There are two annual fairs held in the village; one on the 24th of June, which is reckoned one of the principal markets for cattle in the county; the other on the 20th day of October.

Population.—Within these 40 years, the population has, on the whole, decreased.

The return to Dr Webster in			Number of Males, -	1028
1755, was -	2540		—— Females, -	1292
The present number of souls			—— Persons residing in	
is - - -	2320		the village,	740
	——		—— Married persons,	744
Decrease, - -	220		—— Widowers, -	34
Number of families in the pa-	-		—— Widows, -	121
rish, -	589		—— Unmarried persons,	1421

Number

* * In the remembrance of many persons yet alive, there were 14 or 15 brewers in the parish, and only 2 bakers; the number of bakers is now double that of the brewers. There is no butcher in the parish, the inhabitants being supplied with butcher meat from Cupar, the county town. Several of the mechanics keep one, and some of them two apprentices or journeymen.

Number of Marriages in the course of 10 *years, from the* 31*st December* 1780, *to the* 31*st December* 1790.

Both parties refiding in the parifh, - - -	66
The man in the parifh, but not the woman, -	36
The woman in the parifh, but not the man, -	45 } 81

Total,   147

Number of Births, during the above 10 *years.*

Males, - - -	276
Females, - - -	254

Total,   530

Number of Burials within the same period.

Males, - - - 259	Perfons, who at their death refided in the parifh,	421
Females, - - 248	Perfons from other parifhes,	86
507		507

It is remarkable, that, in the courfe of 10 years, 86 perfons from different parifhes have been interred in the burial yard at Ceres, during which period, there have not been more than 4 or 5 perfons carried out of the parifh of Ceres, to be buried in other parifhes.

Yearly average of marriages, according to the whole number, - - - - 14.$\frac{7}{10}$

Yearly average, taking only one half of thefe marriages, in which there is but one of the parties in the parifh ; which appears to be the proper mode of computation, - - - 10.$\frac{65}{100}$

Yearly average of births, - - 53.

Yearly average of burials, according to the whole number, - - - - 50.$\frac{7}{10}$

Yearly

Yearly average, taking only the perfons refiding
in the parifh, and fuppofing 5 perfons carried out of
it in the courfe of 10 years,   - -   42.$\frac{6}{10}$

It would appear, that the population of the parifh had
increafed very faft towards the beginning of the prefent
century. But for a good many years paft, it feems to
have decreafed ; the return to Dr Webfter, in 1755, a-
mounting to 2540 fouls. The army, navy, and different purfuits in life, carry away many young men ; and
this, as it prevents the increafe of population, is likewife
the reafon, why the number of females is fo much greater
than that of the males, although the births of the latter exceed thofe of the former.

Ecclefiaftical State *.—The right of patronage, by a grant
from the Crown, is now vefted in the Earl of Craufurd, who
is

* Ceres parifh is a rectory, which, before the Reformation, belonged to
the provoftry of Kirkheugh, a religious houfe at St Andrew's, fome remains of which are ftill to be feen, immediately above the harbour, on the
weft, and feparated from the Abbay wall by a deep hollow way. A confiderable part of the eaft end of the parifh formerly belonged to the parifh
of St Andrew's, and about the year 1620, was annexed to the parifh of
Ceres, *quoad facra tantum*. The church is a very old fabric, to which
great additions have been made at different times. At fome remote period, an aile has been conjoined to it, on the eaft end, by the family of
Craufurd, and ftill continues to be their exclufive property. An aile has
alfo been conjoined on the fouth, which is the exclufive property of the
Hon. John Hope of Craighall. This, before the Reformation, was a chapel dedicated to St Ninian, and the fchoolmafter of Ceres, whofe place is
in the gift of Mr Hope, receives a prefentation to be chaplain of the chapel of St Ninian, founded within the church of Ceres, and to be reader
of that parifh. A fmall falary of L. 3 Scotch was payable in former times
to the chaplain, from certain houfes in Cupar, but thefe houfes cannot now
be difcovered, and the chaplainry has become a title without a benefice.
In the year 1722, on account of the increafed population of the parifh, a
large

is alfo titular of the teinds. The living, by a decreet of the court of teinds in 1786, was fixed at fix chalders victual, half meal, half bear, with L. 45 Sterling of money, and L. 5 for communion elements. The glebe confifts of 7 acres of very excellent ground. The inhabitants of the parifh are divided, with regard to religious opinions, as under :

Families who adhere to the Eftablifhed Church,	481
————— join the Affociate Congregation of Antiburgher Seceders,	80
————— the prefbytery of Relief,	25
————— the Burgher Seceders,	1
————— the Scotch Epifcopal Church,	1
————— the Anabaptifts,	1

The Affociate Antiburghers have a meeting-houfe in the village of Ceres, built in the year 1744 The congregation is made up of perfons of that perfuafion, in this and the neighbouring parifhes. Perfons of different opinions live peaceably and happily together, and the feuds and animofities, which formerly prevailed on that account, are now unknown.

School.—By a contract entered into *anno* 1631, between Sir Thomas Hope, advocate to King Charles I. on the one part, and Lord Lindfay patron of the parifh, the heritors thereof, the minifter and kirk-feffion, on the other part ; Sir Thomas Hope, in confequence of mortifying 100

merks

large aile was added by the heritors, on the north fide of the church. The whole will contain about 800 hearers, and is by far too fmall a place of public worfhip for the parifh. The manfe was rebuilt in the year 1788, the expence, exclufive of the materials of the old manfe, and the carriages, which were all furnifhed by the tenants of the parifh, amounted to L. 320 Sterling. In this fum what was laid out on the offices is not included.

merks Scotch yearly, for the benefit of the fchoolmafter, was to have the hereditary right of prefenting the fchoolmafter, but the right of trial and admiffion was to be vefted in the minifter and feffion. In this ftate the matter ftill continues. Befides the parifh fchool, there are feveral private fchools, one fupported by fubfcription, at which about 50 young perfons attend throughout the year; and 3 taught by women, at which there may be about 50 or 60 fcholars.

Poor.—The funds, for the fupport of the poor, arife from collections at the church-door; money for the mortcloths at burials; dues on marriages; the rent of 3 acres of land; the intereft of L. 80 Sterling lent out on bond, and the rents of fome feats in the church. The whole amounts to about L. 46 Sterling yearly. The number of poor, at an average, is about 20, who are relieved at their own houfes, as their fituations may require, according to the difcretion of the feffion. Occafional donations are made by fome of the heritors, of whom but few refide in the parifh. In the year 1782, the heritors affeffed themfelves in the fum of L. 25 Sterling; which, with the ordinary funds, proved fufficient for the relief of the poor, during the fcarcity occafioned by the failure of that crop.

Rent, &c.—The valued rent of the parifh is L. 8248, 1 s. 11 d. Scotch.—The teind, according to a valuation made in 1631, is fixed as follows : Wheat, 2 firlots, 1 peck, 2 lippies, two fifths of a lippie; bear, 32 bolls, 3 firlots, 2 pecks, 3 lippies, two thirds of a lippie; meal, 26 bolls, 1 firlot, 2 pecks, 3 lippies, two thirds of a lippie; oats 52 bolls, 2 pecks, one third of a lippie; money, L. 2046: 16: 2 Scotch; cheefe, 1 ftone and $\frac{4}{5}$ths; lambs, 2.

Remarkable

Remarkable Places.—STRUTHERS, or, as it is called in some old papers, *Auchter-uther-Struther*, formerly the feat of the Earls of Crawfurd, stands a mile and a half fouth weft from the village of Ceres. The houfe is old, with towers and battlements, which give it a venerable and a fort of warlike appearance.—In the defcription of Fife, in *Cambden's Britannia*, Struthers is faid to derive its name from the number of reeds growing around it. There is, indeed, a wet meadow to the fouth of the houfe, but no reeds are now to be feen. The park around the houfe, inclofed with a ftone wall, contains about 200 acres of ground; there are a good many trees in different places of the park, particularly fome venerable beeches of a very large fize.

Upon the eftate of Scot's-Tervit, or, as fome write it, *Scotftarvet*, (the property, from which Mifs Scott takes her title), there is a beautiful tower of free ftone, well hewn and nicely jointed. This tower is about 24 feet fquare, and about 50 or 60 feet high. It ftands upon an eminence, and is feen at a great diftance in different directions. It has evidently been intended for a place of ftrength; the walls are thick, and the few windows in it are very fmall. The tower is formed by one lofty vault, on the top of another; upon the top of the uppermoft, which is furrounded with a battlement, there is an apartment covered with flate. The tower ftands a mile and a half weft from the village of Ceres.

CRAIGHALL, now in ruins, formerly the feat of Sir Thomas Hope, already mentioned, (from whom the principal families in Scotland of the name of Hope are defcended,) continued to be the refidence of Sir Thomas's heirs, till the beginning of the prefent century; and it ftands half a mile S. E. of Ceres, upon the north bank of a beautiful den, planted with trees; and is fheltered on the north by a

little

little rocky hill, from which it takes its name. The fituation is beautifully romantic, and the extent of the ruins indicate its former magnificence.

MAGASK, or, as it is commonly called, *Magus moor*, famous for being the fcene of the death of Archbifhop Sharp,
who was killed on his way from Ceres to St Andrew's, in
the year 1679, lies in the north eaft of Ceres parifh.   In
the weftern extremity of St Andrew's parifh, near the
boundary of Ceres, ftand the tombftones of fome perfons,
who fuffered for the death of the Archbifhop. Being
regarded as fufferers in the caufe of religion, the ftones
erected over their graves, got the name, which they ftill retain, of the *Martyrs Stones*.

Eminent Perfons.—1. That branch of the noble family of
Lindfay, diftinguifhed by the title of *Byres*, which, after firft
attaining the title of Earl of Lindfay, acquired alfo that of
Crawfurd, had its chief refidence, for about two centuries
preceding 1774, at Struthers in the parifh of Ceres.   This
branch of the Lindfay family has produced many eminent
ftatefmen and foldiers, the account of whofe character and
tranfactions, may be found in the general hiftory of the country.
2. Lindfay of Pitfcottie, author of a very entertaining hiftory of Scotland, abounding with many curious anecdotes,
was a native of the parifh of Ceres, and proprietor of a
fmall eftate in it.   3. Thomas Buchanan, rector of Ceres
immediately after the Reformation, was a man of confiderable abilities, and of great influence in the church. Owing to
an emulation between him and Mr Andrew Melvill, Principal of the divinity college in St Andrew's, by which the
peace of the prefbytery of St Andrew's was deftroyed, it
was found neceffary to feparate from that prefbytery, a
good many parifhes formerly belonging to it, and, amongft
others, the parifh of Ceres ; which were erected into a new
                                                       prefbytery

prefbytery appointed to hold their meetings in Cupar, the
county town. By thefe means a diftinct field was afforded
to each of the rivals, in which he might difplay his abilities.
Spottifwood, in his hiftory of the Church of Scotland, mentions this, as having taken place in the year 1591. 4. Mr
Thomas Haliburton, minifter of Ceres, and afterwards Profeffor of divinity at St Andrew's, was efteemed both as a
divine and as a fcholar. Several treatifes, written by him,
give proof of his piety and learning.

Remarkable Occurrences.—On Wednefday the 5th day of
October 1785, Sig. *Vincentius Lunardi*, a Florentine, having afcended at Edinburgh, in an air balloon, at 3 o'clock
afternoon, defcended a mile to the eaftward of Ceres, at 20
minutes paft 4 P. M. This was the firft aërial voyage
made in Scotland, and the daring adventurer, in performing
it, paffed over about 20 miles of fea, and about 12 of land.

Advantages and Difadvantages.—The Excife laws, and
the execution of them, are fo heavy on brewers, that the
ale, called in Scotland twopenny, is fcarcely drinkable;
this has led to a hurtful ufe of fpirituous liquors. Were
the whole duty, at prefent laid on malt and ale, laid upon
malt only, this would leave the brewer at liberty to make
his ale as he pleafed; would fecure a good and wholefome
beverage to the country; would prevent the hurtful ufe of
fpirituous liquors; would fave the expence of one half of
the excife-officers at prefent employed; would increafe the
revenue, and be attended with no lofs, but that of a little
patronage to perfons in power.—The populoufnefs of the
parifh of Ceres, is owing to the lime and coal works, and
to the manufactures carried on in it, but, perhaps, more to
the great number of freeholdings in it, than to all the other
caufes. It may be confidered as an axiom in politics, that,

wherever

wherever men have safe and permanent habitations, with abundant supplies of the neceffaries and conveniencies of life, the population will increafe, in proportion as thefe advantages are enjoyed.——The highways in the parifh are in general very bad, owing to the depth and wetnefs of the foil through which they pafs. An act of Parliament has been lately obtained for making turnpike roads through the county of Fife, one of which is to pafs through the weft, and another through the eaft end of the parifh. Thefe, with the bridges to be built where neceffary, in the line of thefe roads, will be of great fervice to this neighbourhood *.

Miscellaneous Observations.——Within thefe 30 years, more than a half of the houfes in the country part of the parifh, have been rebuilt, and in the village a good many new ones erected ; all of them, in point of neatnefs and convenience of accommodation, far excelling the old ones. A great change has taken place in drefs, within the period above mentioned ; the plaid is now almoft wholly laid afide by the women, and the ufe of the cloak and bonnet has become general. Among the men, the Scotch bonnet has given place to the hat ; the fervant men are generally clothed with Englifh cloth, and many of them have watches in their pockets. The ufe of barley and peafe for making bread, is much on the decline ; and the ufe

* The parifh of Ceres cannot boaft of any remarkable antiquities. There are fome tumuli or hillocks in the parifh, in which, upon their being dug into, ftone coffins, compofed of thin broad ftones, fet on edge, for the fides and ends, and laid flat for the top and bottom, have been difcovered. The bones found in them were reduced to afhes. Some urns have alfo been dug up, in which the afhes of human bones were found. In an urn, dug up near the boundaries of the parifh of Ceres and Cults, a fmaller urn was found inclofed, and in it, befides fome afhes of bones, a fmall brafs inftrument like the iron of a fhoemaker's awl, and a fmall black bead cut in a diamond form, were found.

ufe of bread made from wheat is now very general. It may be fafely faid, that tea is ufed in three fourths of the families in the parifh. The quantity of butcher meat confumed, is at prefent double what it was 30 years ago *.

* In the year 1770, a young rook, commonly called a crow in Scotland, was taken out of a neft upon a tree at Struthers; the bird was perfectly white, without one black feather; the beak, legs and claws were alfo white; it was tamed, and lived about two years in Struthers houfe. In voice, manner of living, and feeding, it differed not from other birds of the fame fpecies.

In the year 1788, a white fwallow was feen by many perfons, at different times, through the whole of the fummer feafon, flying about the Tower of Scotftarvet in the weft end of the parifh. Both of the above particulars fell under the immediate obfervation of the compiler of this ftatiftical account.

PARISH OF COLLESSIE.

(COUNTY OF FIFE.)

By the Rev. MR. ANDREW WALKER.

Name, Situation, &c.

BOTH the antient, and the modern name of this parish, as far as it can now be ascertained, is Collessie, derived, it is supposed, from the Gaelic: in which language, *Col* is said to signify the *bottom*, and *leffie*, a *den*; and the village, indeed, is situated at the bottom of a den. ——It lies in the presbytery of Cupar, and in the synod and county of Fife. Its length is about 8 English miles, and its breadth about 5. —The south side of the parish is remarkably flat; and there is scarcely a stone, great or small, to be seen in it. The north-west side is somewhat hilly. The arable part is extremely fertile. The air is in general healthy. The most prevailing distemper, 50 or 60 years ago, was the ague. It now visits us but seldom, since the late improvements by draining, &c.

River, Loch, &c.—The Eden runs about 3, miles along the south side of the parish, from west to east. Thence it proceeds to Cupar, and empties itself into the German ocean,

near

near St Andrews. It abounds with fine trout. In feed-time
and harveſt, it uſed to overflow its banks, and to do conſiderable damage. But, about 5 years ago, its courſe was made
ſtraight; in conſequence of which, it flows without interruption, and the adjacent grounds have become quite ſecure. A
large loch, on the ſouth-weſt ſide of the pariſh was drained,
anno 1741. It contains upwards of 300 acres, which produces a conſiderable quantity of natural hay, and paſtures, during the ſummer ſeaſon, above 120 head of cattle. In winter,
however, it has ſtill the appearance of a loch, and is frequented by a great variety of wild fowl, ſwans, &c.

Population.—The number of ſouls, as reported to Dr Webſter, in 1755, was 989. After a very exact ſurvey this year,
(1791) they were found to amount to 949. The decreaſe is
owing to the junction of farms, and to the number of cot
houſes which have been ſuffered to fall into decay. In the
principal village, called Kinloch, there are 191 ſouls. For
theſe laſt ten years, ending 1790, the average of marriages is
6, of births, 17, and of burials, 11¼. The regiſter, however, is not perfectly exact; clandeſtine marriages often taking
place, and many of the Seceders give no information, to the
ſeſſion clerk, of the births of their children.

Longevity.—In the village of Colleſſie, there is a very old
man, (Thomas Garrick) who, from the beſt information that
can be got, is in the 108th year of his age. He has reſided
many years in this pariſh, but was born in Perth ſhire. He
was a ſoldier, in the Duke of Argyle's regiment, in the year
1715. For nearly 20 years paſt, he has never been known
confined to his bed by ſickneſs, for a ſingle day. He is of a
ſhort ſtature, thin make, wears his own hair, and has been
for ſome years paſt much afflicted with deafneſs. But, on the
whole,

whole, he is ftill very healthy, and, in a fummer day, will walk two miles from his own home, and back again. About 9 years ago he married his third wife, a woman of 45 ; but he ftill keeps the whole houfe under proper fubjection. He is principally fupported out of the public funds. Other inftances of longevity are not wanting in this diftrict. There are a few above 80, and 1 or 2 upwards of 90 years of age.

Ecclefiaftical State.—The living, when grain fells well, may be valued at L. 100 *per annum*, including the glebe. Mr Johnfton of Lathrifk is patron, and one of the principal heritors. There are many diffenters, of every denomination in the parifh ; but by far the greateft number adhere to the eftablifhed church.

Antiquities.—Not far from the village of Colleffie, to the weft, there are the remains of two caftles, or fortifications. The one is fituated in a wet, and marfhy fpot. Upon the weft fide of it, there is an earthen mound, of a circular form, about an Englifh mile in length, and about 30 feet high, above the level of the ground in the neighbourhood. Some fay, that it was a place of obfervation ; and there is indeed a very good view from it. Others imagine, that the mound was conftructed by an enemy for the purpofe of damming up the ftream that comes from Colleffie den, in order to force the caftle to furrender. This ftream runs, at prefent, through the middle of the mound, at a place called Gadding ; fo named, from the water burfting through it. About 8 years ago, an urn was found, near the mound, containing fome human bones, all of which feemed to have been burnt. —— The other fortification is called the *Maiden Caftle*. The tradition concerning it, is, that during the time of the fiege, the governor died, and his daughter, concealing his death, gave the neceffary or-

ders

ders in his name, and thus made the castle hold out, until the
enemy raised the siege.———In the middle of this ruin, there
are two stones fixed in the ground, (covering, it is supposed,
human bones,) but of no very remarkable size.

Miscellaneous Observations.—The number of the greater
heritors, is 12 ; of whom 6 reside in the parish.   There are
also a number of feuers, or small proprietors.———There are
no turnpikes ; but the roads and bridges, in general, are in good
repair.   The rent of the best arable land is, at an average, between 30 and 40s. the acre ; the next best about 20s.———The
number of ploughs may be about 60.———There are only 3
flocks of sheep, the largest of which belongs to Lord Leven.
————A considerable part of the parish is inclosed, and
inclosures are going forward.——The common fuel is coals,
brought about 6 miles from Balbirnie, or Balgonie.————
The schoolmaster's salary is about L. 8 Sterling, with a dwelling house, school house, and a small garden ; and the dues
paid him by his scholars, who, at an average, are about 40 in
number.   The poor who get supplies, either statedly or occasionally, are about 10.   The only funds for their relief, are,
the collections at the church doors, amounting, at an average,
to L. 11 or L. 12 yearly, and a mortification from the Rossie
family of a boll of meal *per annum.*———Upon the prospect
of a war, many of our young men have shewn themselves
ready to serve their country, both by sea and land.   None have
been under the necessity of emigrating from this parish, for
want of employment, and none have died of want.

PARISH OF CRAIL,

(COUNTY AND SYNOD OF FIFE, PRESBYTERY OF ST ANDREW'S.)

By the Rev. Mr ANDREW BELL.

Stiuation, Extent, Surface, Soil, &c.

THE parifh of Crail lies upon the eaft point of the county of Fife. It is bounded on the S. by the frith of
Forth, and on the E. by the German ocean; its form is
irregular, and breadth unequal; its greateft length from
Fife's Nefs to Kingfcavin Mill, is about 6 Englifh miles.
The number of acres cannot be exactly afcertained. The
valued rent is L. 13,682 : 13 : 4 Scots. As the valuation,
from the early cultivated ftate of this part of the country, is
in general high, it is probable that the real rent does not exceed it in fo great a proportion as in many other diftricts of
Scotland.—The general appearance of the country is flat and
naked. At a very little diftance from the high water mark,
the land rifes abruptly from 20 to 60 or 80 feet above the
level of the fea. From thence it fwells gently towards the
Weft,

Weſt, without forming any hill or remarkable acclivity. The few trees and hedges here are reared with difficulty, and have an unhealthy appearance. The ſtrong breezes from the ſea contribute much to retard their growth. They thrive beſt at Ardrie, which has encouraged the preſent proprietor to make ſeveral additional plantations. The ſoil is excedingly various. It is found of all kinds, from the richeſt deep black loam, and drieſt ſharp channel, to the pooreſt thin wet clay. The value is conſequently as various, from 3 s. or 4 s. to L. 1, L. 2, L. 3, L. 4, and in one inſtance to L. 5 an acre. The manures employed are lime, dung, and ſea-ware ; which laſt is caſt upon the ſhore in great quantities ; and upon many fields produces as good crops of barley, wheat, and turnips, as can be raiſed from dung.

Agriculture, &c.—In the mode of farming, there is nothing peculiar to this pariſh. The crops, and their rotation, are in general the ſame as along the reſt of the coaſt of Fife. The ploughs are of the new conſtruction, and univerſally drawn by two horſes. No threſhing mills are yet erected. Where the land is good, potatoes are generally planted as a preparation for wheat. An acre may produce from 40 to 60 bolls ; 1500 or 2000 bolls are annually exported to the foreign and Engliſh markets, from 4 s. to 6 s. the boll. The trades people frequently rent ſmall portions of land from the farmers, which they plant with this uſeful root. At their leiſure hours they hoe and dreſs their little lots, an exerciſe which contributes both to their intereſt and to their health. In this way, after ſupplying the family, a few bolls are frequently procured for ſale. The rent, when paid in money, may be at the rate of L. 3 or L. 4 an acre; but a more common way is for the tradeſmen to give the ſeed and labour, allowing the farmer half the produce. Drilled

beans

beans are raised in the neighbourhood of the town in great
quantities, and of an excellent quality. The crops of
wheat, oats, bear and barley, are plentiful. Partly perhaps
from prejudice, and partly from a wish to accommodate
their practice to the general nature of the soil, which is rather late, as lying upon a cold bottom, many of the farmers
in this and the neighbouring parishes, still prefer for seed a
mixture of bear or big and barley, in different proportions,
which they call Ramble. Though they admit, that when
equal quantities of these grains are mixed together, and
the produce repeatedly sown, the barley in a few years is
found generally to prevail; yet they are of opinion that
they can depend most upon this mongrel crop. They think
that the bear, as being the earlier and hardier plant, cherish-
es the tender barley, and pushes it forward in its various
stages; that from its superior strength of straw, it prevents
the barley from lodging so much as it is apt to do, when
sown unmixed, a circumstance peculiarly prejudicial upon
a damp soil, from the great quantity of undergrowth it is
disposed to send up; and that, from the same quality, it
assists much in winning and preserving the whole crop in
late and rainy seasons. Experience without doubt confirms
in some measure the truth of this train of reasoning; but
how far these advantages are counterbalanced by the infe-
riority of this mixed kind of grain to pure barley, yet remains to be ascertained. Great quantities of these grains,
with a full proportion of beans and wheat, are sent every
year to Glasgow, and its neighbourhood. The opening of the Canal between the Forth and the Clyde, has
been of immense advantage to the farmers and landholders
in this part of the country, who formerly could find no
good market for what corns they raised, beyond what was
required for home consumption. The principal farms, a-
bout 20 in number, are of a moderate size. Though several

ral fmall ones were united, when the laft leafes were granted, yet the population of the country has not been fo materially affected by this meafure as by the gradual fuppreffion of cot-houfes, and a reduction of the number of
hands employed in agriculture, by the changes which have
taken place in the mode of farming. A part of tw -
ftates is not under leafe, but let from year to year in pafture; and the principal heritors, with their families, are either gone from the parifh altogether, or at moft but occafional refidenters. A great proportion of the parifh ftill
continues uninclofed. Much has been done, but much ftill
remains in refpect of draining, which has always been
found a moft beneficial improvement. With a very few
exceptions, the farm-houfes and offices are bad; an evil
which, it is hoped, will be remedied when new leafes are
granted There is no doubt but in the end, the landholders
would find their advantage in this. The tenant, who, at the
rifk of a valuable ftock, is anfwerable for a rent of L. 100,
L. 200 or L. 300 a-year, is entitled to good accommodation.
In the prefent improved ftate of fociety, a man of fpirit or
property has no encouragement to engage with a farm,
where he and his family muft be obliged to live in a hovel,
deftitute of every convenience and comfort. About half
the valued rent of the parifh belongs to Mifs Scott of Scot-
ftarvit, a young Lady, whofe amiable difpofition affords the
faireft profpect, that her ample fortune will be directed in a
manner highly advantageous to the interefts of humanity in
general, and to the particular improvement of thofe parts
of the country, in which fhe has an immediate concern.
Befides the farmers refiding in the country, about 12 or 15
live in the town, who cultivate from 3 to 20 or 30 acres
each, partly rented, and partly their own property. Thefe
are an induftrious clafs of men, whofe numbers it is to be
wifhed may not be reduced. Several of them are in the

practice

practice of letting their carts and horfes for hire for various purpofes, particularly for bringing coals to the inhabitants either from the harbour or the neighbouring collieries.

Minerals.—In former times coal has been wrought both in the eaft and weft fields of Crail. Veftiges of the pits and mines are eafy to be traced. It is probable that no machinery was ufed, and that the crop-coal only, where it was level free, has been exhaufted. In times of fcarcity, the poor people have from time immemorial, been in the practice of digging the thin feams of coal among the rocks along the fea-fhore ; while they were thus employed a few weeks ago, within the high water mark, a gold coin of Queen Mary's was found, about 3 feet below the furface, under a ftratum of rock, from whence the coal had formerly been wrought. It is dated 1553, and is intrinfically worth 11 s. or 12 s. in the poffeffion of Captain Whyte of Dyfart. Limeftone is alfo found by the fea-fide in fmall quantities. There are feveral quarries of it in the interior part of the parifh, upon the town's moor, and the lands of Newhall, belonging to the Honourable Henry Erfkine. But though it is of a pretty good quality, yet, owing to its great depth, the working of thefe quarries has been productive of little profit to thofe who have opened them. There is plenty of freeftone ; but, in general, it is by no means remarkable for its goodnefs.

Borough of Crail.—Crail is a place of great antiquity. The name formerly written Carle, Caryle and Carraille, is fuppofed to fignify, in the Gaelic, its fituation upon a fmall winding or bending of the fhore. By fome of the old hiftorians, it is mentioned as a town of confiderable note, fo early as the middle of the 9th century. It confifts of two parallel ftreets, extending eaft and weft along the

fhore;

shore, which is here pretty steep and high. The one upon the N. is wide, tolerably well built, and paved. The
south or Nethergate is not paved; and though, in point of
situation, perhaps naturally pleasanter than the other, has
of late fallen greatly to decay. The whole town bears e-
vident marks of having seen better days. As almost every house has a yard or croft belonging to it, the town co-
vers a considerable space of ground. Owing to this circumstance, and to its high situation in the immediate vicinity of the sea, without trees or hills to afford occasional
shelter, it enjoys a pure, uniform temperature of air, highly favourable to the health of the inhabitants, without producing, however, any remarkable instances of longevity.
In the parish, there are several above 80, but none above
90 years of age. Crail is a royal borough, and sends a
member to Parliament, in conjunction with Kilrenny, the
two Anstruthers and Pittenweem. It received a charter
from Robert the Bruce, which was successively confirmed,
with several new grants, by Robert II. Queen Mary,
James VI. and Charles I. By these charters, its privileges extend from the middle of the water of Leven, to the
water of Puttekin, which falls into the sea at Pitmilly burn
mouth, with a right to the fishings, tolls, anchorage, &c.
in all the harbours and creeks within these bounds. Accordingly the customs are regularly collected between
Crail and Pitmilly. Pittenweem and Anstruther Easter
were burdened with an annualrent or reddendo, when they
were erected into royal burghs. The other places between
Crail and Leven do not appear ever to have been in use
of making any such payment for their anchorage and customs; but the question has never yet been decided, whether the Town of Crail has or has not lost these, with several other rights and privileges. About the beginning of
this century, Crail was the great rendezvous for the herring

ring fishery in the frith of Forth. Besides a great number of boats fitted out and manned by the fishermen and others belonging to the town, several hundreds assembled from different parts of the country, particularly from Angus, the Mearns and Aberdeenshire. These were supplied by the inhabitants with nets, for the use of which they received a certain proportion of what was caught. Immense quantities of herrings were cured for home consumption, and for exportation. The *Drave,* as it is here called, was seldom known to fail. The fisherman expected it as certainly as the farmer did his crop. Almost all the people in the place derived their support from it, the other fisheries, and the trade and manufactures which were immediately connected with them. A sad change has now taken place; and we listen as to a fairy tale, to the accounts given by old people of what they remember themselves, or have heard related by their fathers. For half a century, the fisheries here have been gradually declining. The herrings, for several years past, have neither visited the coast in any considerable quantity, nor remained long enough upon it to spawn as formerly. This is partly to be ascribed to unfavourable weather; partly to the shoals being broken by the buss fishing upon the N. E. coast of Scotland, which was not the case during the flourishing period of the fishery here; partly to the encroachments of our neighbours the Dutch, who occasionally sweep our coast with a *fleet* of nets, extending several miles in length, at no greater distance than 2 or 3 leagues from the shore; and partly perhaps to the industry of man, having thinned this species of fish. This conjecture is not so vague, as some at first sight may be apt to imagine. In addition to the havock made by the British and Dutch fishermen, immense quantities have of late years been killed upon the coasts of Sweden and Norway. The herrings, crowding

into

into the narrow bays and creeks, are there inclofed by nets, which are hauled upon the beach by the aid of cap-ftans, where after curing what may be required for the market, the reft *by millions*, are immediately boiled down into oil, in cauldrons erected for that purpofe on the fhore. To the circumftance, of the herrings not having fpawned for feveral years paft upon this part of the coaft, muft in a great meafure be afcribed the want of haddocks, which formerly ufed to be caught here in great quantities. About eight or ten years ago, the price was 2 s. 1 d. the long hun-dred, *i. e.* 132. At prefent, if one or two happen to be caught, they are greedily bought for 4 d. or 6 d. a-piece. The fisheries of great cod and skate are still good, but very precarious for open boats, as the beft fishing ground lies far off fhore. About 20 or 25 thoufand lobfters are fent e-very year to the London market. Ten years ago, there was double the number. The price is L. 12, 10 s. the thoufand.

Population.—By the return made to Dr Webfter, the po-pulation was 2173.

Table of births, marriages, and deaths, in the town and parish of Crail, from 1750 to 1756.

Years.	Births.	Marriages.	Deaths.
1750,	64	16	48
1751,	60	19	45
1752,	67	20	71
1753,	82	22	46
1754,	66	17	35
1755,	70	11	79
1756,	61	13	40
Total,	470*	118	364
Average,	67$\frac{1}{7}$	16$\frac{6}{7}$	52

The

* Of thefe 249 males, 221 females.

The excefs of males above females in this table is perhaps uncommon. There is every reafon to believe, that during the above period, the regifter was kept with great exactnefs.

Table of births, marriages, and deaths, in the town and parifh of Crail, from the year 1786 to 1792. The population in 1790-91 was 1710 fouls.

Years.	Births.	Marriages.	Deaths.
1786,	56	9	27
1787,	48	7	34
1788,	39	8	38
1789,	53	12	36
1790,	52	10	26
1791,	45	10	52
1792,	49	11	35
Total,	342	67	248
Average,	48$\frac{6}{7}$	9$\frac{4}{7}$	35$\frac{3}{8}$

As there were two long vacancies during the above period, this table is not perhaps very accurate.

Particular ftate of the Population of the Town and Parifh of Crail, as taken in 1790-91.

No. of fam. in the town 335, in the country 73, total 430.
No. of fouls in the town 1301, in the country 409, tot. 1710.
Of thefe 770 are houfeholders, 322 males, and 448 fem.
330 are child. under 8, 157 males, and 173 fem.
457 are child. above 8, 185 males, and 272 fem.
153 are houfe fer. &c. 74 males, and 79 fem.

Total males in the parifh, 728 } No. of females more than
Total females, 972 } males, 234.

Total population in 1790-91, 1710
Decreafe fince 1755, 463

All

All the inhabitants are of the Eftablifhed religion, except 8 Epifcopalians, 3 Burgher Seceders, and 3 Prefbytery of Relief.

The great excefs of the females above the males, in the article of children, above 8 years of age, is occafioned by the young men going to fea, &c. while a great proportion of the girls remain at home with their parents. In the town of Crail there are 7 incorporated trades. The number of freemen, journeymen and apprentices, as they ftood upon the roll in 1792, is as follows :

Smiths, 5 freemen, no journeymen nor apprentices.
Wrights, 8 freemen, 7 journeymen and apprentices.
Weavers, 35 freemen, 21 journeymen and apprentices.
Tailors, 12 freemen, 1 journeyman,
Shoemakers, 18 freemen, 11 journeymen and apprentices.
Coopers, 3 freemen, no journeymen nor apprentices.
Bakers, 7 freemen, 1 apprentice.

Several of thefe freemen are not engaged in their refpective trades. At prefent there is but 1 working cooper, though this trade was formerly very flourifhing. In the country there are 2 fmiths, 5 weavers, 1 fhoemaker, 1 mafon, and 1 miller. Befides thefe, there are in the town, 2 hairdreffers and barbers, 1 butcher, 11 mafons, 6 brewers, who alfo retail ale and Britifh fpirits, 1 vintner, and 3 others who retail ale, porter, and fpirits, 1 furgeon, 1 writer, 1 minifter, 1 fchoolmafter, 1 fuperannuated ufher, 6 retail fhopkeepers, and 1 miller.—Belonging to this port, there are 6 floops from 25 to 60 tons, 1 brig of 150 tons, and 1 floop upon the ftocks. Thefe veffels are navigated by 25 men. The number of failors belonging to the town, but failing from other ports, is very fluctuating. During the late French and American war, 72 men from the town and pa-

rifh

rifh of Crail, entered on board his Majefty's fleet; a fmall
proportion returned home. Six boats are employed in the
white or cod fifhing, and 6 fmaller ones in the lobfter fifhing. The number of men required to work them, is about
45 or 50. In 1791, 13 large boats were fitted out for the
herring fifhery, each carrying 7 men. Upon the ifland of
* May, which, *quoad facra*, has always been confidered fince
the Reformation as part of the parifh of Crail, there were
formerly 10 or 15 fifhermens families, with a proportionable number of boats. At prefent there are only 3 men
and 2 women upon it, for the purpofe of taking care of the
light. At Fife's Nefs there is only 1 boat, with 2 fifhermen. The little village which is fituated there, is not now
fo confiderable as it appears once to have been. In the prefent
generally decayed ftate of the fifheries along the eaft coaft
of Fife, the people employed about them deferve every
protection and encouragement from the country. Nothing
but the moft prefling neceffity fhould ever induce Government to make demands upon them for manning the Navy.
Upon the occafion of a late armament, one for every *five*
men was required by the regulating captain at Leith, before
                                                            he

* For an account of this ifland, fee the " Statiftical Account of Anftruther-Wefter." The melancholy accident there recorded, *viz.* the
fuffocation of George Anderfon, his wife and five children in the light-
houfe, between the night of the 23d and morning of the 26th of January 1791, is fuppofed to have been occafioned by a fermentation among
the immenfe heap of afhes, which for years had been accumulating round
the building, as the two men who were faved, declare that a fulphureous
fteam was obferved to iffue from it for feveral weeks before the fatal night
on which it burft out in flames. The infant that was taken from the
breaft of the dead mother, and the eldeft fon and daughter, who happened providentially not to be upon the ifland, are under the protection of
Mifs Scott, to whom the light-houfe belongs, and who doubtlefs will continue to patronife them, as they fhall be found deferving. For feveral
curious particulars concerning this, and the other iflands in the frith of
Forth, fee Sibbald's Hift. of Fife.

he would grant protections. The fiſhermen here furniſhed their quota at the expence of about *Eighty Pounds Sterling*, thereby incurring a debt which they have not yet been able to liquidate.

Ecclefiaſtical State, Stipend, School, Poor, &c.—It would appear that Crail was once the ſeat of a priory *. A ruin

evidently

* This priory is not to be found in the liſt of religious houſes in Scotland at the time of the Reformation. It was probably fuppreſſed long before that period. While this conjecture is ſtated with becoming diffidence, it is alfo proper to take notice of a tradition which ſome have heard, that the above mentioned ruin is the remains of a chapel dedicated to St Rufus. The kirk of Crail, with the teinds thereof, both parſonage and vicarage, anciently belonged to the priory of Haddington. In the year 1517, upon the petition and endowment of Sir William Myreton of Cambo, vicar of Lathriſk, Janet, Prioreſs of Haddington erected it into a collegiate church, with a provoſt, facriſt and ſeveral prebendaries. The provoſt had a right to the vicarage tithes, upon entertaining a vicar penſioner, for ſerving the cure of the pariſh within the ſaid collegiate church ; and ſix of the prebendaries had annuities, payable out of certain lands and tenements of houſes, lying in the town and neighbourhood, mortified for that purpofe by Sir William Myreton. The church, quire and veſtry, are ſtill ſtanding, and ufed as the place of public worſhip by the congregation. " An inventarie of the ornaments and of the fylver wark in the college-kyrk of Carraile." is in the poſſeſſion of the preſent miniſter. It ſeems to have been handfomely provided. Befides the high altar, there were eight others, dedicated to the Virgin, St Catharine, St Michael, St James, St John the Baptiſt, St Stephen, St John the Evangeliſt, and St Nicholas. It was in this church that the mob, inflamed by the preaching of the famous John Knox, began the work of aboliſhing the monuments of idolatry in Fife, as their brethren had done at Perth a few days before Having finiſhed their operations here, they followed their apoſtolical leader to St Andrew's, where they affiſted in leveling its beautiful and fuperb Cathedral to the ground. About the time of the Reformation, Lord Lindeſay ſeems to have obtained from the prioreſs and convent of Haddington, a *tack* of the tiends, both parfonage and vicarage, of the *parochi* a *pariſh kirk* of Crail, for the yearly rent of two hundred and fifty-five marks. By King James VI. the pariſh was disjoined from the priory, and erected into a ſeparate and independant rectory. The patronage was veſted in Sir William Murray of Belvaird, who preſented

Mr

evidently of great antiquity, the eaft gable of which is ftill ftanding, bears the name of the prior walls. A well in the neighbourhood is called the *briery*, without doubt a corruption of *priory well*; and a croft belonging to the burgh is defcribed in the valuation of the tiends 1630, as the *prior croft*. By the act of Parliament *, which disjoined the parifh of Crail from the priory of Haddington, a third part of the tiend-fheaves was affigned for fupport of ' the minifter ferving the cure. The parifh being found too extenfive it was judged expedient to divide it. Accordingly, in 1630, the lands of Kingfbarns and others were erected into a feparate parifh. A ftipend of 5 chalders of victual was affigned to the minifter, which was by the voluntary act

Mr William Murray to the benefice. He then refigned the patronage into the King's hands in favour of John Lord Lindefay, who in 1609 obtained from Mr Murray a confirmation of the former tack of the tiends, for three lives, and twice three nineteen years.

The town of Crail having by feveral charters obtained a grant of the *collegiate church* and its revenues, with the advocation, donation and right of patronage of its provoftry, *prebendure*, chaplainaries, and choriftry, difputes began to arife between them and Lord Lindefay concerning their refpective rights. To prevent law-fuits, a compromife was entered into in 1630. by which the town's right to the collegiate church, and the place called the college, with the right of patronage as above, was confirmed; but their claim to emolument was exprefsly reftricted to the tithe fifh, and the rents, fees and duties, which had been the efpecial property of the provoft and prebendaries. The parfonage and vicarage tithes excepting the tithe fifh, were declared to remain with his Lordfhip and his fuccefsors. In 1774-6, the queftion concerning the right of patronage to the *parifh church* was tried By an interlocutor of the Lord Ordinary it was given *againft the town*, and the Earl of Crawford, as fuccefsor to Lord Lindefay, is now confidered as undoubted patron.

* *Vide* Unprinted acts of King James VI. in the parliament houfe, Edinburgh. A more particular account of the collegiate church of Crail may be obtained by confulting its chartulary, which is depofited in the Advocates library, Edinburgh.

act of the heritors augmented to 8. The stipend of Crail was at the same time declared to be 10 chalders 2 firlots and 2 pecks of bear, which the minister accepted in full of all *tack-duties* formerly paid. No augmentation has hitherto been asked. In 1758 a decreet was obtained for L. 66, 18 s. 8 d. Scots of element-money.—The minister has a house, garden, and stable, with a glebe of 4¼ acres, which is let for 16 bolls of bear and L. 4 of money-rent.—The school of Crail has experienced a proportionable decay with the town. The number of scholars throughout the year is at a medium about 50. The fees are, for reading English 1 s. 6 d. reading and writing 2 s. writing and arithmetic 2 s. 6 d. Latin 3 s. Latin and arithmetic 5 s. the quarter. There are few Latin scholars, as the people in general are not able to afford their children a liberal education. There are several women who teach children to read. The late usher of the public school, who is superannuated upon his salary, has also a few scholars. There is properly no parochial schoolmaster. The Magistrates and Town-council are patrons, and the salary, which is L. 12 a-year, is paid from the *common good*. The income of the present incumbent, who is also precentor and session-clerk, may be about L. 40 a-year. There is no house, nor garden annexed to the appointment.—The number of begging poor is only 6 or 8; but there are upwards of 100 who receive stated or occasional charity. There are no poor rates: They are supplied from the following funds: 1*st*, The kirk-session funds, which arise from the rent of about 6 acres of land; the interest of L. 293 Scots; the rent of seats in the church; dues upon marriages when the bride is in the parish; the collections at the church-doors; some small feu-duties, and occasionally gifts from heritors and others. After paying necessary fees and expenses, these funds, upon an average of

the

the laſt 4 years, have afforded L. 30 a-year to 20 or 25 pen
ſioners at 6 d. each the week, and L. 33 more to theſe and
others in diſtreſſed circumſtances, in occaſional charities of
money, coals, clothes, &c. As benefactors to the poor, the
families of Scotſtarvit, Wormiſton, and Sauchop, are mentioned with peculiar pleaſure. It may be proper to notice
here, an excellent cuſtom which has been eſtabliſhed in the
pariſh for more than a century. An annual collection is
made at the church-door about Martinmas, for purchaſing
ſhoes and other articles of clothing for the poor. The ſum
collected varies according to circumſtances, from L. 3 to
L. 7. A few guineas are always added by the ſeſſion, ſo
that about L. 10 or L. 12 a-year are appropriated to this
uſeful charity. 2*d*, The fiſhing box. The funds of this
charity ariſe from a ſmall fee paid at entry into the ſociety,
the rent of ſome land, and a half tithe of fiſh granted by
the town. From theſe are paid about L. 30 a-year in
weekly penſions from 6 d. to 1 s. 6 d. and from L. 6 to
L. 10 in occaſional charities. 3*d*, The ſailors box. The
funds of this ſociety ariſe from the, rent of a few acres of
land, and the intereſt of a ſmall ſum of money. They
pay about L. 10 a-year in ſtated and occaſional charities.
4*th*, The intereſt of L. 500 in the 3 *per cent.* S. Sea annuities 1751, mortified by Robert Ramſay tailor in London
for behoof of the poor of the pariſh of Crail, under the
management of the miniſter and Town-council for the time
being. The intereſt of this ſum is divided yearly among
poor houſeholders. The whole funds for ſupporting the
numerous poor may be ſtated to be, one year with another,
L. 120 or L. 125 Sterling. It is to be wiſhed that all the
non-reſiding heritors would annually contribute their charitable mite, which in every point of view is a much better
plan than the legal eſtabliſhment of poor rates.

Seats,

Seats, Antiquities, &c.—The only gentlemens ſeats in the pariſh are Balcomie, Wormiſton and Ardrie; the houſes of Weſt-barns and Newhall have been demoliſhed. In the line of antiquities there is nothing very remarkable; the prior walls, which ſtand cloſe to the ſea below the eaſt end of the town, have been already mentioned. Upon the point of land, a little to the ſouth-weſt of the harbour, there are ſome traces of a building, which has given the name of *Caſtle Hyne* to a ſmall creek or inlet among the rocks. In the vicinity, ſome ſtone coffins have lately been found. The remains of an old caſtle overlook the harbour upon the eaſt. In it King David I. frequently reſided; hence Crail became a conſtabulary, extending weſtward to *Kincraig Nooke*. Sibbald, in his hiſtory of Fife, ſays, that this monarch died here; in general, he is ſuppoſed to have died at Carliſle in Cumberland. The ſimilarity of the names Carryle and Carliſle, has probably occaſioned the miſtake. Upon the ſite of this caſtle, a gentlemen has lately erected a neat ſummer-houſe, which commands a fine proſpect, and having a battery of ſmall cannon mounted upon its top, it makes an excellent appearance from the ſea *.

Manufactures,

* In the liſt of antiquities, *the Danes dike* muſt not be forgotten. It is the remains of a bulwark of *dry ſtones*, raiſed, it is ſaid, in one night by the Danes, who having been defeated by the Scots at the water of Leven in 874, retreated eaſtward till they came to the extreme point of Fife, which they fortified in this manner, to defend themſelves againſt the attacks of their victorious enemies, till they had an opportunity of embarking on board their ſhips, which were hovering in the mouth of the frith. The mound is quite overgrown with graſs, but it is diſtinctly to be traced for a conſiderable way acroſs the point. The large ſpace which it incloſes, with ſome other circumſtances which ſtrike an attentive obſerver upon the ground, might perhaps juſtify ſome degree of ſcepticiſm upon the ſubject. Near this dike is the ſmall cave in which the Danes put to death Conſtantine the Scottiſh King, whom they had taken priſoner in a ſkirmiſh as they retreated. The only other antiquity in the pariſh which
ſeem

Manufactures, &c.—The reader muſt not expect to hear of the flouriſhing ſtate of trade and manufactures in this pariſh. They are indeed in a very languiſhing ſituation. The natural migration of commerce from ſmall towns, where the ſtock of the trader is inconſiderable, and the demand for conſumption limited, to great towns, where the capitals of merchants are large, and the demands extenſive and conſtant, has deprived Crail of any little portion of foreign trade which it formerly enjoyed. The various mercantile articles which are required, are brought weekly by the carriers from Edinburgh or Dundee, and occaſionally from Leith by ſea. Properly ſpeaking, there is no manufacture eſtabliſhed here. The women, however, are generally employed in ſpinning lint-yarn for the manufacturers in other places, to the extent of many thouſand ſpindles every year. At preſent the price is from 1 s. 3 d. to 8 d. the ſpindle, according to the quality. A few ſhoes are made for the market; and nearly 40,000 yards of ſheetings, Oſnaburghs, coarſe brown linen, &c. are wrought by the weavers for ſale, over and above what is manufactured for private uſe. It is to be hoped, that by proper exertions, theſe, and other branches of buſineſs, will be gradually extended and improved.

Advantages and Diſadvantages.—The pariſh enjoys no peculiar advantages over thoſe in the neighbourhood along the coaſt of Fife. Its diſadvantages are, the want of ſhelter, which expoſes it to the blaſt from every quarter. Its angular ſituation, which circumſcribes its intercourſe to a ſmall diſtrict of country, and a ſcarcity of running water, which diſcourages the introduction of any manufacture which requires

ſeems deſerving of notice, is a ſtone which ſtands upon a ſmall tumulus between Crail and Sauchop. A croſs is rudely ſculptured upon it. Concerning the time or occaſion of its erection, there is no tradition.

quires the aid of powerful machinery. The greatest difadvantage of all is the badness of the present harbour,
which only admits small vessels, is dangerous to take in bad
weather, and in south easterly winds affords but indifferent
shelter. It has frequently proved fatal to the fishermen,
who often for many days together cannot go out or in with
safety, while boats from the harbours to the westward experience no inconveniency. A little to the east of the
town, there is a small bay or opening among the rocks,
called *Rome*, for what reason is not known, which at a moderate expense might be made an excellent harbour. It
would have a good depth of water, could be easily taken
in all weathers, would be advantageous for a more perfect
prosecution of the fishery, and of very considerable use to
the coasting vessels, when turning either up or down the
frith in blowing weather. This is probably the place called the *old harbour* in some of the charters belonging to
the town.

Character of the People.—Of the character of his people, a minister ought to speak with caution in a publication
of this kind. To record their vices would argue impru-
dence, as tending rather to irritate than to reform. To
trumpet forth their praise would savour of adulation. In no
material feature of their character do the people here differ from their neighbours. The credulity of former times
with respect to witches is almost extinguished, and the little
superstitious fancies, which so frequently prevail among the
commonalty, are gradually losing ground. The practice of
inoculating for the small-pox has been much retarded, partly by religious scruples, and partly by the expense of medical aid. To the cleanness and commodiousness of their
habitations, they are beginning to pay greater attention
than formerly. When dressed they are decently neat, rather

ther than fine. If they are not remarkable for fobriety
and induſtry, neither do they deferve to be ſtigmatized as
diſſipated and idle. Their ideas and fentiments are gradually acquiring a greater degree of liberality. The ordinances of religion are refpected, a tolerable decorum of
manners is obferved, though here there are exceptions as
well as in every numerous fociety ; as fubjects they are
peaceable and loyal, and by no means fond of " meddling
with thofe who are given to change."

Mifcellaneous Obfervations.—Formerly there were four
corn-mills in the parifh. At prefent there are only two ;
one of them is turned by falt water, admitted during flood-
tide into a refervoir, and difcharged upon the wheel after
the tide has ebbed. The parifh is rated at about 50 plough-
gates. For them the ſtatute-labour is generally paid in
kind. It is commuted to private houfeholders. The fum
may amount to L. 12 or L. 14 a-year. The road leading
from Anſtruther to St Andrew's, and paſſing through Crail,
is in tolerable repair. The ſtatute-labour is perfectly fufficient to uphold it ; and if applied with vigour, might annually do fomething to the other roads within the parifh.
If the middle road to St Andrew's were made, it would
tend greatly to the improvement of the interior part of the
country. The price of labour and provifions is nearly the
fame as in other parts of Fife. James Shairp was fettled
miniſter of Crail in 1648. He continued to hold the living
till he was confecrated archbifhop of St Andrew's, after
the Reftoration. From the feſſion records, it appears, he
was a ſtrict difciplinarian. The rigid prefbyterian parfon
differed in *circumſtances*, rather than in *character*, from the
rigorous metropolitan. Of the many refpectable gentlemen, who at different times received the rudiments of their
education at the fchool of Crail, Lord Dunfinnan, Sir
Charles

Charles Middleton, Sir William Erſkine, Colonel Mony-
penny and Colonel Moncrieff of the Engineers, have diſtinguiſhed themſelves in public life. This laſt gentleman
is a native of the pariſh. It would be difficult to ſtate with,
any degree of exactneſs, how many acres are under the
different kinds of crops, or what may be the produce.

NOTE.

Births, marriages and deaths of inhabitants in Crail, town and pariſh,
for the year 1792, ſtand as follows:

Births.	Marriages.	Deaths.
49	11	35
Males 23—Females 26.		Males 14—Females 21

Of thoſe who died, there were 8 under 20 years of age,

2 between	20 and 30,	7 between	60 and 70,
1 ——	30 ——40,	8 ——	70 —— 80,
2 ——	40 ——50,	3 ——	80 —— 90,
4 ——	50 ——60,		

Diſeaſes of which they died, claſſed according to the ideas of their friends:

I. Febrile Diſeaſes.		IV. Local Diſeaſes.	
Continued fever, -	3	Iliac paſſion, - -	1
Conſumption of the lungs,	3		
Nervous fever, -	1	V. Anomalous Diſeaſes.	
Putrid fever and ſore throats,	2	Diſeaſe unknown, -	1
Total, —		Caſualties, drowned, -	1
	9	Childbed, - -	1
II. Nervous Diſeaſes.		Hyſterical, - -	1
Apoplexy, - -	2	Decay of nature, or aged,	11
Palſy, - - -	2	Ulcer, - -	1
—		Sore face, -	1
Total,	4	Pain in the head, -	1
III. Cachectical Diſeaſes.			—
Dropſy of the belly, -	1	Total,	19
Jaundice, - -	1		
Total,	2		

Parijh of Crail.

Additional Anfwers and Corrections, by the Rev. Andrew Bell.

Prefent ftate of the population, according to an accolint taken in 1797-8 : viz.

In the town   -   -   1236
In the country   -   -   388

Total   1624

The real rent is fuppofed to be from 4000l. to 5000l. fterling per ann.

The ftipend was lately augmented 10 chald. 2 firl. 2 pecks, 1 lip. of bear ; 260l. Scots money, ftipend, and 100l. Scots for communion elements. The glebe confifts of 5 acres, with grafs for two cows and a horfe, defigned this year, after a procefs before the Court of Seffion : Glebe and foggage worth about 20l. per annum. At prefent the whole is let out ; the minifter having neither barn nor barn-yard to enable him to farm himfelf.

The poor's funds are pretty nearly the fame as in the former return ; only the feffion has at prefent no money at intereft ; having laid out what it had in erecting feats in the church, which are let out at from 6d. to 1s. per feat room. The collections at the kirk door amount to about 10s. per week. Including the collection at the facrament, and for cloathing the poor, the amount may be from 36l. to 40l. per annum.

For

For several years the fishery has been very bad, and the number of hands fewer than by the former return. The fishermen, during the summer, frequently take voyages to Greenland and the Baltic, in coasting vessels, &c. Tradesmen and day-labourers assist in manning the boats, when employed in the herring fishery; and a good many of our seamen, who are occasionally fishermen, are now in the navy.

Little kelp is made in the parish; the value not known; but the rent paid for liberty to make it is from 12l. to 20l. once in two or three years.

Two midwives; no surgeon. Little inoculation. In 1797, twenty children died in the natural small pox.

State of the Births and Marriages in the parish of Crail, for 1792, 3, 4, 5, 6, and 7.

Years.	Births.			Marriages.
	Males.	Females.	Total births.	
1792	24	24	48	11
1793	14	35	49	6
1794	23	27	50	7
1795	12	26	38	9
1796	24	23	47	11
1797	18	15	33	14
	115	150	265	58
Average .	19$\frac{1}{6}$	25	44$\frac{1}{6}$	9$\frac{4}{6}$

N. B. In general, there is a registration of marriages only when the bride is in the parish.

Burials.

Years.		Burials.
1794	-	41
1795	-	29
1796	-	33
1797	-	59 {—Of thefe, 20 children in the natural fmall pox.

In an old manufcript inventory among the Harleian MSS. in the Britifh Mufeum, there is mention made of the following charter, ' To the *prior* of Crail, of the fecond teinds of ' the lands between the waters of Neithe and Nith.' It is mentioned in the roll of charters of King David the Second. This information the minifter lately received from N. Hutton, Efq. who has been long employed in collecting materials concerning our old monafteries and religious foundations.

Corrections of the former report.

P. 156, l. 5. For ' Kingscavin mill,' read ' *Kingscairn* mill.'

P. 158. l. 16. The fentence fhould have been as follows : ' That it prevents the barley from lodging fo much as it is ' apt to do when fown unmixed ; a circumftance peculiarly ' prejudicial upon a damp foil, from the great quantity of ' undergrowth it is difpofed to draw up ; and that, from the ' *round* figure of the ear, and the drier quality of the ftraw, ' it affifts much in winning and preferving the whole crop ' in late and rainy feafons.'

P. 167, Note, l. 13. For ' fix,' read ' eight.'

Do. Do. l. 3d from the bottom. After ' 255 marks,' add, ' and eight chalders of victual'—A very material error.

P. 450—

P. 167—168.   The miniſter can now ſtate, that the ruin there mentioned, the *ſouth eaſt* gable of which is ſtill ſtanding, is *not* the ruin of the chapel of St. Ruff, or Rufus. That chapel appears to have been *infra caſtellum de Carrail,* or *in caſtello*; probably pretty near the place where Mr Coldſtream's ſummer houſe now ſtands.   Vide p. 171.

PARISH of CRIECH,

(COUNTY OF FIFE.)

By MICHAEL GREENLAW, *D. Ð.*

Name and Situation.

THE name is faid to exprefs fomething indelicate to be explained. The parifh lies in the prefbytery of Cupar, and Synod of Fife, about 6 miles weft of the eaft end of the Ochil Hills, which run from the mouth of the Tay weft, to within a mile of Stirling. It is from S. to N. about 3 miles, and from E. to W. about 2. It is bounded on the E. by Balmerino and Kilmeny, on the N. by Flifk, on the W. by Abdie and Dunbog, and on the S. by Monimail and Moonzie.

Agriculture, &c.—Farming in this parifh and neigh-bourhood is advancing faft in improvement, confidering our thin fharp foil. For many years paft, there was only rough bear, and no barley. But barley now is the ftaple grain. It is faid that Fife exports about 30,000 bolls of it yearly, befides what it confumes. And it is neceffary to import 6000 bolls of oats or meal a-year. The farmers find it more profitable to raife barley than oats. For 1 boll of
wheat

wheat ſown in this pariſh about 30, or even 20 years ago, there are, at a moderate computation, 10 ſown now. Formerly too, it was full of blacks, and needed to be waſhed before it was ſent to the mill ; now, by the attention paid to the ſeed, and the preparing of the ground, good wheat is produced from 8 to 12 bolls, after 1, without any blacks at all. The rents of many farms are doubled, and ſome tripled ; yet the tenants pay them, ride better horſes, wear finer clothes, and entertain their friends better than before. Several tenants in this pariſh are become proprietors, by mere ſucceſs in farming, and have far more general knowledge too than they had 30 or 20 years ago. There is 1 flock of ſheep, about 13 ſcore ; the wool ſells at between 16 s. and L. 1 the ſtone. The farmers have acceſs to lime, within 10 or 12 miles. The roads are good, and without turnpikes.

Population.—The population of this pariſh is diminiſhed one-fifth in the period of theſe 35 years paſt ; which is owing, probably, to 1 village being allowed to go to decay, the union of farms, and the uſe of two horſe ploughs.

Inhabitants, - - -	306	
Males, - - - -	134	
Females, - - -	172	
Males under 10 years of age, - -	33	
Females, - - -	41	74
Males between 10 and 20, - -	33	
Females, - - -	29	62
Males between 20 and 50, - -	46	
Females, - - -	81	127
Males between 50 and 70, - -	22	
Females, - - -	17	39
Males between 70 and 100, - -	0	
Females, - - -	4	4

The

The number of births, in proportion to the number of inhabitants, is increafed. From a comparifon of the number of births from 1726 to 1736, when the parifh was more populous, with that from 1776 to 1786, when it was lefs fo, the proportional increafe was found to be about one-tenth. The air is good, and the fituation dry ; the practice of inoculating children for the fmall-pox, is alfo favourable to population. The people are in more eafy circumftances, which encourages matrimony.

Stipend, &c.—The ftipend is between L. 80 and L. 90 Sterling, with 3½ acres of glebe, of a thin foil. Colonel Baillie is patron. There are 7 heritors, 5 of whom refide. —The weekly collections for the poor are very fmall; but the poor are few in number.—The fchoolmafter's falary is 80 merks, with the intereft of 2000 merks ; the perquifites are very trifling, and the number of fcholars fmall.

Antiquities.—There is a little hill near the church, with the veftiges of a Roman camp upon it. It has 2 lines of circumvallation; the one is much wider than the other, as an outwork, within a mile of the Tay. There is another of the fame kind, on a higher hill, weft of the former ; it is likewife within a mile of the Tay. This hill is feen from the north windows of the Old Town of Edinburgh. The lines about thefe camps are rough ftones. The higheft of thefe hills is called *Normans-Law*, or the Hill of Northern Men. The tradition concerning thefe camps is, that when the Normans invaded for plunder, and not for conqueft, they depofited their fpoils there, till they got intelligence of a force being raifed in the country, that was able to repel them; then they haftened to their boats in the Tay. Cardinal Beaton's caftle ftands by the church of Criech. The tradition is, that the Cardinal kept there a little country

try feraglio. It is defended on one fide, by a morafs ; and on the other fide, has had ftrong outworks. Being much defaced, and fome of the fineft ftones removed, no infcription can be found to mark its date. There were lately found, in a rifing fpot of ground near the manfe, 2 brown jars, with their bottoms upwards, and a broad ftone laid on each, containing human bones. The bones were much confumed, yet joints, &c. were difcernible. It muft have been long fince they were put there, as burning or in-urning the dead, is not a late practice in this country.

Thunder.—About 18 or 20 years ago, the lightning ftruck Pitcullo houfe, about 4 miles north of Cupar. It entered in 2 ftreams ; one came down the kitchen chimney, tore off the jack-cafe, and left 3 or 4 black fpots on the roof of the kitchen, at confiderable diftances from each other. A fervant fitting in a clofet off the kitchen, had a large hole burnt in the crown of her head-drefs. She was fome hours infenfible, but recovered. When the ftroke came, fhe thought that fhe was falling into a fwoon or faint. The other ftream entered by a fine fhell-clofet, ftripped a few fhells and fome frofting off, then went down the ftone-turnpike, and burft through the panneling of another room, where was a mahogany table. This table was picked, as if hit with very fmall fhot. Here its force was exhaufted.— Thunder broke within a mile of the manfe in fummer 1789, in a low-lying field of oats. It laid flat the corn for about 15 or 16 yards in length, and 7 or 8 in breadth. The ftraw that was before green, and full of fap, became yellow and withered. The earth on the fpot was ploughed up, though not deep. This field, though lying fo low, is near the Tay, and water is an attractor.—Four or 5 years ago, a tremendous flafh, accompanied with a dreadful peal of thunder, killed 2 tradefmen at Cupar. They were fitting

ting in one of the higheſt houſes there, and on the loft immediately above them were ſeveral pieces of old iron. The watch of one of them ſcarcely retained any of its former ſhape. It looked as if it had lain ſome time in a ſmith's furnace. The lightning ſeems to ſpread like ſmall ſhot when near ſpent. There is undoubtedly a ſtrong concuſſion of the air when it ſtrikes. In the room in Pitcullo houſe, the glaſs was all forced out of the windows, though the caſements were not marked. The houſe in Cupar, where the men were killed, had both ſide-walls a little ſplit, and burſt out from the flooring.

Hills.—The hills not only ſhelter, but by the rains waſhing them down in the courſe of ages, increaſe and meliorate the ſoil of the valleys. There is a narrow ſtrath, which runs through this pariſh, E. through Kilmeny, and W. through Dunbog and Abdie, the adjacent pariſhes, which is ſheltered by the Ochil Hills, and the dealers in barley prefer the grain to much that grows in other parts of Fife. The rich Carſe of Gowrie, oppoſite to this pariſh, is ſheltered in the ſame way. It, perhaps, deſerves notice, that the moſt remarkable ridges of hills in Scotland run E. and W. This holds with reſpect to the Grampian, as well as the Ochil Hills. It has been remarked, that the great ridges of mountains in England, extend generally E. and W. too. The ſame has been obſerved of the Alps, of Caucaſus, and Taurus, in Aſia ; and of Atlas, in Africa. Beſides affording ſhelter, they are ſaid to prevent the exhaled vapours from going too much N. or S. that there may be a ſufficiency of rain for the inland countries.

Miſcellaneous Obſervations.—There is one Seceder family here, and a few other individuals that are Seceders. It is ſuppoſed they are not increaſing along the banks of the
Tay

Tay and Forth, where they were at firſt moſt numerous. They, too, are leſs bigotted now, from the increaſe of knowledge.—Induſtry is inculcated both publicly and privately, as one of the cardinal virtues; and indeed it is more eaſy to perſuade to this, than to ſome other virtues, as the reward of it immediately follows.—Many of our young people leave us, to go to the neighbouring towns of Dundee and Perth, to learn handicraft trades.—There is only one ale-houſe.—It has been reported, that in a part of the pariſh of Leuchars, near this, there were a race of Daniſh ſhepherds, who kept their ſheep as well as themſelves in their original ſtate, and produced wool not inferior to that of Shetland; but I am informed, that the people do not keep themſelves ſeparate, but intermarry in the neighbourhood; and as to their wool, I do not hear that it is praiſed. Their ſheep are of a ſmall ſize, and feed on coarſe graſs or bent. When other ſheep fell at 14 s. or 16 s. theſe people are glad to get 6 s. or 7 s. for theirs.

Pariſh of Criech.

Additional Communications by the Rev. Michael Greenlaw, D. D.

| | Births. | | |
	Males.	Females.	Total.
From 1712 to 1721, both incluſive	66	71	137
From 1722 to 1731, both incluſive	64	59	123
From 1732 to 1741, both incluſive	40	57	97
From 1742 to 1751, both incluſive	51	36	87

From

	Births.		
	Males.	Females.	Total.
From 1752 to 1761, both inclusive	65	36	101
From 1762 to 1771, both inclusive	40	42	82
From 1772 to 1781, both inclusive	34	36	70
From 1782 to 1791, both inclusive	43	51	94

From 1783 to 1791, both inclusive, the number of marriages was 16, and of burials 38.

Above is a list of the births, distinguishing males and females in the parish of Criech from the year 1712; that is, as far back as our registers can be depended on. When I had the honour of writing to you formerly on this subject, the weakness of my eyes and the distress of our schoolmaster, disabled me from sending this part of the statistical account. This list shews this singular circumstance : that, though this parish is diminished about one fifth within these 40 years, through its vicinity to manufacturing towns and other causes I mentioned, yet the number of our births are by no means diminished in the same proportion. I ascribe this to the ease, affluence, and contentment, in which our people live under our present happy government. The flourishing of agriculture, trade, manufactures, always promotes matrimony and population.

I could wish to correct a small, but awkward, mistake, which the compiler or publisher had fallen into, in the printed account of this parish, concerning our Norman camps. In the printed account, they are called first Roman camps, and then they are immediately described as Norman ones. It might be a mere typographical mistake ; but it looks awkward. Norman camps they certainly were. One of the hills where they are is still called Normans' Law. Our vestiges of these camps are neither on the kind of ground the Ro-

mans

mans ufually chofe, nor of the fhape of Roman camps. The bold warriors of ancient Rome trufted more to their fword and their valour than to heights of difficult accefs. The Normans were mere plunderers; and chofe thefe heights to depofit their plunder, till they heard of a rifing in our country fufficient to beat them off, and then hurried down to their fhips in the Tay with what they had got. Befides, the Roman camps were fquares, or nearly fo; whereas our vestiges are all circles, which was the Norman form.

Our marriages and burials were not regiftered with any exactnefs till the tax commenced in 1782.

My parifh contribute for a complete copy of the Statiftical volumes. They embraced the propofal whenever I mentioned it, though we have only eight readers in this fmall parifh. I have endeavoured to perfuade my neighbours to adopt that fame plan, but they are flow.

In large parifhes where they would have many more readers, the expence would be a mere trifle. Itt were pity that every one were not active in fo ufeful and beneficent a plan, where you have fhown fuch difinterefted activity.

PARISH OF CULTS,

(COUNTY OF FIFE.)

By the Rev. MR. DAVID WILKIE.

Name, Situation, and Extent.

THE antient name of the parish was Qulkques or Quilkques ; which, in the Gaelic, fignifies, a " nook" or " corner."--it being disjoined from the large ftrath, which runs from E. to W. along the banks of the Eden. It is fituated in the prefbytery of Cupar, and in the fynod and county of Fife : being about $1\frac{1}{2}$ Englifh miles from E. to W. and about $2\frac{1}{4}$ from N. to S. it confequently contains about 3.5 fquare miles, and is nearly in the form of an oblong fquare. It lies in the very heart of Fife, and has eafy accefs to both the coafts of that county.

Surface, Soil, and Air.—The general appearance is, partly flat, declining to the north ; but partly mountainous towards the fouth. The parifh is remarkable, for a clear air and a light foil. The different kinds of foil are, gravel, a light black earth, and a ftrong clay ; with this particular circumftance, that, in the lower parts, along the Eden, it is gravel inclining to heath, and bent grafs ; from thence to the afcent of the hills, it is light earth, and upon their declivity, it is ftrong clay. Upon
the

the whole, the air is dry and healthy, except that the lower ground is ſubjeᴄᵗ to fogs. The moſt prevalent diſtempers, not to mention thoſe peculiar to children, are fevers and conſumptions; but this cannot be attributed to the local ſituation. The greateſt ſtorms of rain and ſnow are from the E. acroſs the German ocean ; the higheſt winds from the S. W.

River.——The Eden riſes about 8 miles to the W. and falls into the bay of St Andrews, about 7 miles to the E. Being fed by a number of rivulets, and having a pretty level courſe, it is never very low, even in the drieſt ſummer. It is not navigable at preſent, to any diſtance from its mouth, owing to the many mill-dykes, by which it is croſſed. Were it thought neceſſary, for promoting the commerce of the county, it might be made navigable, though at a conſiderable expence, for 12 or 14 miles; through which it has a fall probably of about 40 feet. Next to the want of commerce, to defray the expence, the greateſt diſadvantage would be, the danger of entering its mouth, on account of ſhoals and quickſands. Its banks being ſomewhat high on both ſides, in its courſe through this pariſh, there is little danger from land floods. The greateſt riſe of the river for theſe 50 years paſt, was in May 1782. From the exceſs of rain, our crops then failed ſo much, that had the culture of potatoes been unknown, and the importation of grain as little practiſed, as in the end of the laſt century, there would have been as great a famine, as in the former period. ——The Eden produces trout, pike, and a few ſalmon; which laſt are ſo much diminiſhed, by the number of ſeals, which frequent its mouth, that few are caught for ſale.

Hills.——On the ſouth-ſide of the pariſh, are the Walton and Pitleſſie hills ; not conſiderable for their height ; and connected with each other by riſing grounds. They are covered moſt-

ly

iy with grafs ; in part, with whins, and in part with heath.
The Walton hill has many *foſſæ* and ramparts cut along its fide,
which are fuppofed to be the remains of a Roman camp,
when Agricola invaded Scotland, and encamped one part of
his army here, and the other at Newtyle in Angus. Many urns
have been dug up, full of bones, on and near this hill.

Minerals.—There is abundance of free-ftone and lime-ftone
quarries ; both excellent; particularly the latter, for the lime
fhells of which, there is great demand, both in Fife and in
Angus. The ftrata are from 2 to 10 feet below the furface,
and are wrought, without having much recourfe to the affiftance of gun-powder. There were coal mines fometime ago
upon the eftate of Bonzion ; which were employed chiefly for burning lime. They might ftill be wrought to advantage.

Animals.—Horfes and black cattle have been much improved, in the courfe of thefe 20 or 30 years, owing to inclofing
ground, and fowing grafs-feeds. Horfes chiefly are employed, in agriculture, and fell from L. 12 to L 15 fterling. Oxen
fell from L. 7 to L. 12. The rearing of thefe, has diminifhed the breed of fheep fo much, that in place of 4 or 5 flocks,
there is now only one.

Population.—The number of the people has increafed
within thefe 40 years ; owing chiefly to the great number of
fmall feus, which have been granted during that period. If the
feffion record for baptifms may be depended on, the

Number of inhabitants, in 1751, was - 464
The return to Dr Webfter, in 1755, was - 449
Number of inhabitants at prefent (1791) is 534

Annual

Annual average of births, for 18 years paſt, is   17.6
     of deaths   10.
     of marriages - -   6.5
Proportion between annual births and the whole
     population,   -   -   as 1 to 30
           marriages -   as 1 to 81.7
           deaths -   as 1 to 53

Number of ſouls under 10 years of age -   110
     from 10 to 20 -   92
     from 20 to 30 - -   74
     from 30 to 40 - -   58
     from 40 to 50 -   59
     from 50 to 60 - -   58
     from 60 to 70 · -   57
     from 70 to 80 -   22
     from 80 to 90 - -   4
                            534

Acres, Culture, Rent, &c.——There are about 2100 Scots acres in the pariſh; of which there may be 720 employed in raiſing corn and roots; 20 in flax; 160 ſown with graſs ſeeds for hay or paſture; 800, including hill and muir, in paſture; and 400 in fir plantations. Rent per acre may be from 5s. to L. 2 ſterling. The rent of a farm of 200 acres, hill and dale, may be about L. 130. The ſize of farms in general, is 100, 200, or 300 acres. Their number has rather diminiſhed.—— There are a number of incloſures upon particular farms. In the pariſh are about 22 ploughs, moſtly two-horſe ploughs.— The real rent of the whole pariſh may be about L. 1060 ſter-ling; the valued rent is L. 2069 : 6 : 8 Scots.

Heritors, Stipend, School, Poor, &c.——There are 3 heritors, one

one of whom only refides.——The church and manfe are, at leaft 150 years old. The united college of St Andrews are patrons; and the living, including the glebe, may be worth a-bout L. 65 a year. The fchoolmafter's falary is 100 merks; the number of fcholars about 40 : the fee for teaching Englifh is 1s. per quarter, and other articles in proportion.——The number of poor is about 12; and the funds for their fupport, about L. 10 yearly.

Wages, Prices, &c—The wages of a day-labourer are 10d. befides which, he has little fpots of ground, for potatoes and for lint, by the manufacture of which his wife and daughters are ena-bled to contribute to the common fupport. As double-hecked fpinning-wheels are univerfally ufed, there is no county in Scotland perhaps, where fo much is made by fpinning as in Fife. The ufual wages of a male fervant, employed in huf-bandry are L. 5 or L. 6 yearly; of a female fervant, 20s or 25s. the half year. The common fuel is coal from Balbirnie, or Balgonie, which cofts at the hill 7d. per load, befides 2s 3d. per cart for carriage. Houfes for labourers let from 4s. to 20s. a year.

Mifcellaneous Obfervations—There are 3 corn-mills, 2 barley mills, 2 lint mills, 2 threfhing machines, and 1 malt mill driven by water. There is one ftone bridge acrofs the Eden. The public road from Kirkcaldy to Dundee has got feveral partial repairs, but is ftill nearly in a ftate of nature. The ftatute labour has been exacted moftly in kind; but there are now turnpikes whereby the roads may in time be improved. There is one inn, and four licenfed ale-houfes in the parifh.

Mr

Mr Wilkie (the writer of the preceding obſervations) is the perſon alluded to, in the Statiſtical Account of Scotland, vol. X (Pariſh of Kettle), page 437. In juſtice to whom, it is proper to mention, that there was a very material error of the preſs. Inſtead of " This table, upon trial, is found to anſwer better for Scotland than any yet publiſhed by Mr Wilkie," it ought to have been printed thus : " This table, upon trial, is found by Mr Wilkie, to anſwer better for Scotland, than any yet publiſhed." The fact is, Mr Wilkie himſelf conſtructed that very important table. ———It may be proper to add, that in a letter from Mr Wilkie on the ſubject of annuities, he communicates the following particulars, which ſeem to be highly worthy of being laid before the public. ——— " I have had an opportunity (ſays he) of forming a table of the probabilities of life, for the county of Fife, from the bills of mortality in the neighbouring pariſh of Kettle ; in which the ſeveral ages of the deceaſed, have been accurately recorded.— This table, I find, differs materially from all the Engliſh tables, upon the ſame ſubject. For example,

By my table	By Dr Halley's table.
$\frac{1}{30}$ of infants die the 1ſt year.	$\frac{1}{5}$ of infants die the 1ſt year.
$\frac{1}{13}$ die the 2d year.	$\frac{1}{7}$ die the ſecond year.
Expectation of an infant's life $=40.6$ years.	Expectation of an infant's life $=28$ years.
Greateſt value of a life at 4 per cent. correſponding to 5 years of age $=18.1$.	Greateſt value of a life at 4 per cent. correſponding to 10 years of age $=16.4$.

" My table not only agrees exactly with the preſent population of the pariſh of Kettle, but with the lives of miniſters and of their widows in Scotland at large : Suppoſing their mean age of ordination and of widowhood, to be reſpectively, 30

and

and 48 years. At 30 years of age, 32.27 years=a minifter's expectation of life. At 48 years of age, 19.44 years = widow's expectation of life; which laft, multiplied by 19.3, the number of widows left yearly, produces 375.2 = maximum of annuitants upon the widows fcheme."

" Farther, from 36 parifh accounts, publifhed in the firft volume of the Statiftical Account of Scotland, it appears, there are 46,625 fouls in thefe parifhes: the mean number of births and deaths is 1156. Hence $\frac{46625}{1156}$ =40.3, the expectation of an infant's life in thefe 36 parifhes; which agrees almoft exactly with the fame expectation by my table. Many of thefe parifhes are in different counties, and fituated widely remote from each other."

Mr Wilkie propofes foon to publifh a book " On the Theo-
" ory of Intereft fimple and compound, derived from firft
" principles, and applied to annuities: With an illuftration
" of the Widows Scheme in the Church of Scotland:"—A
work, which will probably throw much light upon thefe important fubjects of inquiry. In the mean while, the following table of the probabilities of life, derived from the bills of mortality, in the parifh of Torthorwald, County of Dumfries, for 27 years, ending anno 1790, publifhed in the appendix to this volume, is well entitled to be laid before the reader.

TABLE

TABLE of the Probabilities, of Life, &c.

Age.	Livg.	Dead	Age	Livg.	Dead	Age.	Livg.	Dead	Age	Livg.	Dead
0	280	32	24	204	1	48	169	2	72	88	6
1	248	10	25	203	1	49	167	2	73	82	7
2	238	2	26	202	1	50	165	2	74	75	7
3	236	2	27	201	1	51	163	2	75	68	7
4	234	2	28	200	1	52	161	2	76	61	7
5	232	2	29	199	1	53	159	2	77	54	6
6	230	2	30	198	1	54	157	2	78	48	6
7	228	2	31	197	1	55	155	2	79	42	5
8	226	1	32	196	1	56	153	2	80	37	4
9	225	1	33	195	1	57	151	3	81	33	3
10	224	1	34	194	1	58	148	3	82	30	3
11	223	1	35	193	1	59	145	3	83	27	3
12	222	1	36	192	1	60	142	4	84	24	3
13	221	1	37	191	2	61	138	4	85	21	3
14	220	2	38	189	2	62	134	4	86	18	3
15	218	2	39	187	2	63	130	4	87	15	3
16	216	2	40	185	2	64	126	4	88	12	3
17	214	2	41	183	2	65	122	4	89	9	2
18	212	2	42	181	2	66	118	4	90	7	2
19	210	2	43	179	2	67	114	4	91	5	1
20	208	1	44	177	2	68	110	5	92	4	1
21	207	1	45	175	2	69	105	5	93	3	1
22	206	1	46	173	2	70	100	6	94	2	1
23	205	1	47	171	2	71	94	6	95	1	1

By this Table, the number of inhabitants is to that of births or burials, as 14040—140 is to 280, that is as 49.64 is to 1. And the expectation of life, by the above Table, is as follows:

Age.	Expec.	Age.	Expec.	Age.	Expec.	Age.	Expec.
0	49.64	25	41.14	50	22.26	75	7.16
5	54.69	30	37.11	55	18.54	80	6.20
10	51.57	35	33.01	60	14.98	85	4.12
15	47.90	40	29.31	65	12.03	90	2.64
20	45.09	45	25.85	70	9.10	95	0.50

The

The most valuable age, by this table, is that of 2 years old, whose expectation of life is 56 years, which is exceedingly high, and can only be applied to a country district in Scotland.

The above table of probabilities of life is a striking evidence, that English or foreign tables of observation do not correspond with Scottish lives ;—seeing by these, the expectation of infancy does not exceed 25, or at most 28 years, whereas here, it wants but a trifle of 50. And if the value of life were computed by the above table, at a given rate of interest, the difference would also be considerable, which would still increase, did the practice of inoculation every where prevail. Hence, a table of equal decrements, constructed upon the supposition that 91 was the utmost extent of human life, would be better adapted to Scottish lives, than M. de Moivre's hypothesis, wherein that extent is fixed at 86 years.

It may be here observed, that if we had tables of observation, adapted to the several counties in Scotland, it would be easy to find the number of inhabitants, from the amount of births and burials. Thus, where they are equal, either of them multiplied by an infant's expectation, call it, for instance, 40, will produce the population. But where there is a difference, which is generally the case, the half of their sum, multiplied by an infant's expectation, adapted to the particular district, will give the number of the people. It would be very desirable, therefore, to have extracts from the registers of all the parishes in Scotland, where exact accounts are kept of the ages of the deceased, for the purpose of drawing up complete tables of the probabilities of lives, calculated for Scotland.

PARISH OF CUPAR OF FIFE.

(COUNTY AND SYNOD OF FIFE.—PRESBYTERY OF CUPAR).

By the Rev. GEORGE CAMPBELL, *D. D. Minifter.*

Situation, River, Extent, &c.

THE parifh of CUPAR is fituated in the middle of the peninfula of Fife. The river Eden divides it into two parts. It is of an irregular figure, meafuring from eaft to weft 5 miles, and nearly of an equal extent from north to fouth.

Etymologies.—The etymology of the name of the parifh is unknown. The names of different places in it are evidently of Gaelic original ; fuch as *Pittencrieff*, (Gaelic, *Pit-nan-craobh*), Englifh, the dale ; *Kingafk*, (Gaelic, *ceann-gaifk*), Englifh, the termination or ending of the lands of Gaifg or Gafk ; *Pitbladdo*, a hollow, named after fome perfon ; *Kilmaron*, (Gaelic, *Cill-Mha-Roin*), Englifh, the cell, or place of worfhip of St. Ron or St. Roan ; *Balafs, Balgarvie*, towns named after particular perfons.

Town of Cupar.—The burgh of Cupar, which is the county town, is beautifully fituated in the center of the parifh, on the northern bank of the Eden, in the fpot where it

forms

forms a junction with the water of St. Mary.—The town boasts of high antiquity. The Thanes of Fife, from the earliest times of which any account has been transmitted to us, held here their courts of justice *. It is at present governed by a provost, three bailies, a dean-of-guild, 13 guild counsellors, who choose one another, and 8 trades counsellors or deacons, elected by the 8 incorporations.—The town of Cupar is the most wealthy community in the county of Fife. Its annual revenue, at present, amounts to 430 l. Sterling. In conjunction with the towns of Perth, Dundee, St. Andrews, and Forfar, it sends a commissioner to Parliament. The revenue arising from the post-office, in 1763, was 20 l. per quarter; it now amounts to 90 l. Sterling per quarter.

Population.—The population, which was accurately ascertained in the month of June 1793, has increased greatly within these 40 years, as appears from the following table :

POPULA-

* In the chartulary belonging to the Benedictine Monks of Dunfermline, we find a precept by " *Willielmus, Comes de Rofs,* " *justitiarius ex parte boreali, maris Scoticani, conflitutus,*" directed, " *Davidi de Vemys, vice-comiti de Fyfe,*" warranting him to deliver, to the monastery of Dunfermline, the eighth part of the amercements of Fife, imposed in the courts held at Cupar, in the year 1239. In the rolls of the Parliament, assembled in the beginning of the reign of David II. may be seen the names of the Commissioners from the royal burgh of Cupar. The town, in antient times, depended on the Earls of Fife. The castle of Cupar was the chief residence of that powerful family for many ages. The town is in possession of several royal charters, conferring on them extensive property, and many valuable privileges.

POPULATION TABLE OF THE PARISH OF CUPAR OF FIFE.

	Males.	Females.	Total.
Inhabitants in the town	1464	1671	3135
———— in the country	255	312	567
Number of fouls in both	1719	1983	3702
Majority of females *	-	264	
The return to Dr Webfter, in 1755, was			2192
Increafe			1510

A more particular ftatement of the number of the inhabitants, ranked according to their different profeffions and
occupations, will be inferted, along with other articles, in
the STATISTICAL TABLE, at the conclufion of this account.

Buildings, &c.—Cupar, efpecially when approached by
the turnpike road from the eaft, has the appearance of a
neat, clean, well built, thriving town. The ftreets, within
the laft twelve months, have been all completely paved at the
expence of the corporation. There are no houfes in ruins,
and none untenanted. Upwards of a third part of the town
has been rebuilt, during the laft 25 years, in a neat and
handfome ftile. Confiderable additions have alfo been made.

No

* The number of females, fo much exceeding that of the
males, muft be accounted for chiefly from this circumftance,
that the youth of Cupar, at all times forward to engage in the
military life, are many of them, at prefent, abroad in the fervice of their country. The population has advanced rapidly
of late years, owing to the extenfion of the linen manufacture,
and to the increafed demand for hands employed in erecting
new buildings, and in carrying on important and extenfive im
provements in gardening and agriculture.

No leſs than 70 houſes, chiefly for manufacturers and labourers, have lately been built on *St Mary's Water*, or, as it is
called, *the Lady Burn*. A ſtreet, in a better ſtile, has begun
to be formed, on the road leading from the bridge on the
ſouth ſide of the town.

Church.—The parochial church of Cupar, in early times,
ſtood at a conſiderable diſtance from the town, towards the
north, on a riſing ground, now known by the name of *the
Old Kirk-yard*. The foundations of this ancient building
were removed by the preſent proprietor, in 1759; and many human bones, turned up in the adjoining field by the
plough, were collected and buried in the earth. In the year
1415, this ſtructure had become ruinous, or incapable of accommodating the numbers who reſorted to it. In the courſe
of that year, the prior of St. Andrews, (the head of all the
regular clergy in Scotland, and poſſeſſed of immenſe revenues), for the better accommodation of the inhabitants
of the town of Cupar, and that the rites of religion
might be celebrated with a pomp, gratifying to the taſte of
the age, erected, within the royalty, a ſpacious and magnificent church. The year in which this erection took place, is
aſcertained by the following extract from the Book of Paiſley:
—" *Sal: Hum.* 1415. *In Cupro de Fyfe fundata eſt nova*
" *parochialis eccleſia, quae prius diſtabat a Burgo ad plagam bo-*
" *realem.*" This church was built in the beſt ſtile of the
times, of poliſhed free ſtone, in length 133 feet, by 54 in
breadth. The roof was ſupported by two rows of arches,
extending the whole length of the church. The oak couples were of, a circular form, lined with wood, and painted
in the taſte of the times. In 1785, this extenſive building
was found to be in a ſtate of total decay. The heritors of
the pariſh reſolved to pull down the old fabric, and to erect,

on

on the fame fite, a church on a more convenient plan. This plan they have accordingly carried into execution, at a very confiderable expence ; and the new church of Cupar is by far the moft convenient and elegant ftructure of the kind, to be found at prefent in the county of Fife. It is to be regretted, however, that the new building was not joined to the fpire of the old church, which ftill ftands. The veftry, or feffion-houfe, by intervening between the church and fpire, gives a detached and aukward appearance to both. The fpire has always been confidered as a very handfome ftructure, and appears light and elegant when viewed from the eaft or weft. It was built by the Prior of St. Andrews, in 1415, only up to the battlement. All above that was added in the beginning of the laft century, by Mr William Scot *, who was for many years minifter of Cupar.

County Room.—During the period in which the church was erected, the gentlemen of the county, by fubfcription, and by an affeffment on their valued rents, built on a large fcale, and in the modern tafte, adjoining to the town-houfe, a room for their ufe at head courts, for their accommodation at balls, &c. A tea-room, and other apartments, have fince been added.

Prifons.—On the oppofite end of the town-houfe, and under the fame roof, there are apartments of a very different nature, not conftructed for the elegant accommodation of the rich and

---

* This gentleman was of the antient family of BALWEARIE, poffeffed of a confiderable eftate, and a great favourite with Archbifhop Spottifwood, with whom he paffed much of his time in the neighbouring delightful retreat of Dairfie. He died in 1642, in his 85th year, and his remains were interred in a handfome tomb, erected by his family, at the weft end of the church-yard.

and powerful, and to add to the ſplendour of their " gay-
" ſpent feſtive nights ;" but calculated for ſecuring and puniſhing thoſe, who, by their miſconduct or their crimes, have
ſubjected themſelves to the arm of the law, and which have
continued, in their preſent form, for ages paſt, the diſmal
receptacles of the accuſed, the profligate, and the guilty.
—The priſons of Scotland, (if with propriety we can give
that name to the dungeons in which, all over the kingdom, criminals are confined), accord but too well with the
barbariſm which marked and diſgraced that remote period, in which moſt of them were erected, and with that
ſavage and illiberal ſpirit, which ſeems to have dictated
no inconſiderable part of our criminal code. The priſon of Cupar, which is the public jail, for the very populous and wealthy county of Fife, yields perhaps to none, in
point of the meanneſs, the filth, and wretchedneſs of its accommodations. It is, in truth, a reproach to the town in
which it ſtands, a diſgrace to the county which employs it,
and a ſtain on that benevolent and compaſſionate ſpirit, which
diſtinguiſhes and dignifies this enlightened age, and which has
led it kindly to attend to " the ſorrowful ſighing of the pri-
" ſoner," to meliorate his ſituation, and ſoothe his woes.
How would the feelings of the benevolent Howard, who,
with unparallelled activity, and aſtoniſhing perſeverance, un-
ſhaken and unterrified, like a kind angel, went through every
land, demanding and obtaining comfort to the wretched, and
liberty to the captive !—How would his feelings have been
ſhocked, if, in his compaſſionate tour, he had turned aſide
into the peninſula of Fife, and viſited the cells of Cupar !

·The apartment deſtined for debtors is tolerably decent, and
well lighted. Very different is the ſtate of the priſon under
it, known by the name of " the Iron-houſe," in which perſons ſuſpected of theft, &c. are confined. This is a dark,
damp,

damp, vaulted dungeon, compofed entirely of ftone, without
a fire-place, or any the moft wretched accommodation. It
is impoffible, indeed, by language, to exaggerate the horrors
which here prefent themfelves. Into this difmal recefs, the
beams of the fun can with difficulty penetrate. Here " is
" no light, but rather darknefs vifible :" A few faint rays,
entering by an irregular aperture of about 9 inches fquare,
barely fuffice to difclofe the horrors of the place. An opening, or flit, on another fide of the dungeon, thirty inches in
length by two in breadth, but almoft filled by a large bar of
iron, ferves to admit as much frefh air as merely to prevent
fuffocation. As the affizes for the county are held at Perth
only in fpring and autumn, prifoners have frequently been
doomed to lie in this cold dungeon, during the rigour of the
fevereft winters.—The confequences may eafily be apprehended. It is to be hoped, however, that the period is now
happily arrived, when the landholders of Scotland, having
more humane fentiments and enlarged views, than thofe who
went before them, will attend to the wretched ftate of the
different county jails, and be difpofed to follow the example
of the neighbouring kingdom, in which, of late years, many
prifons, bridewells, &c. have been erected, on plans of the
moft extenfive benevolence, and of the foundeft and moft
enlightened policy. A fum of money, adequate to the expence of building a prifon on a modern improved plan ; a
penitentiary-houfe, with accommodations alfo for the deftitute fick, might, it is believed, without much difficulty, be
procured in the rich and extenfive county of Fife, were a few
men of rank and public fpirit to patronize and fupport the
benevolent attempt. Were the fum to be levied from the
three different orders of men, who are chiefly to be benefited by the new erection, namely landholders, manufacturers,
and farmers, the proportion neceffary to be advanced by individuals

dividuals would appear but ſmall, and the burden would ſcarcely be felt by the county. Perhaps they could adopt no plan which promiſes to be of ſo much public utility. A meaſure of this kind will appear every day of more preſſing neceſſity, when the Bridewell now building at Edinburgh ſhall be finiſhed. If Fife takes no ſtep to defend itſelf againſt the influx of pickpockets, ſwindlers, &c. which may natu‑ rally be expected, it will become the general receptacle of ſturdy beggars and vagrants; and the riſing induſtry of the county muſt be expoſed to the depredations of the deſperate and the profligate, from every quarter *.

Manufactures.—In Cupar, and the neighbouring country, a conſiderable manufacture of coarſe linens has been eſta‑ bliſhed. They conſiſt chiefly of *yard-wides*, as they are com‑ monly named, for buckram, glazed linens, &c. There alſo they manufacture Oſnaburghs, tow ſheetings, and Sileſias. About 500,000 yards are annually ſtamped in Cupar, which amount in value to about 20,000 l. Sterling. Cupar being the principal market in Fife for brown linens of the above deſcription, webs from the adjoining country, to the value of more than 20,000 l. come to be ſold there. All theſe are purchaſed with ready money, and ſent to London, Glaſgow, and other markets.—The linen merchants in Cupar pay an‑ nually

* Though, in deſcribing the priſons of Cupar, the writer may have been led to adopt terms ſeemingly harſh and ſevere, yet he means not to convey, in the moſt diſtant manner, reflections or cenſure on any body of men, or on any individual He has frequently had occaſion to praiſe the humanity of thoſe, to whoſe care priſoners at Cupar are committed, and to witneſs every kind attention paid to them, which the nature of the place in which they are confined would permit. He only wiſh‑ ed to embrace the opportunity, which the preſent publication affords, of turning the attention of the county, to objects which he deems extremely intereſting and important to ſociety.

nually to the manufacturers and weavers, betwixt 40,000 l.
and 50,000 l.—There are at present in the parish 223 looms,
employed chiefly in making linens of the description given
above.—There are two tan-works in Cupar, where confiderable quantities of leather are manufactured.—The demand
for faddlery from the furrounding country is increafed of late
years, in an extraordinary degree, and is fupplied from the
work-fhops at Cupar. The bleaching field on the Eden is
in good repute. The brick and tile work has long been profitable to the proprietors, and ftill continues to thrive, but is
not yet able to anfwer the great demand for tiles.

Obftacles to their fuccefs.—Cupar, though enjoying many
natural advantages; though fituated in the midft of a plentiful country; on a river that never ceafes, even in the fevereft drought, to flow in abundance; in the immediate vicinity of lime, free-ftone, and coal, yet poffeffes no confiderable manufacture, that of linen excepted.—This want of attention, induftry, and exertion in the inhabitants, in improving the happy fituation in which they are placed, may, in a
great meafure, be afcribed to the two following caufes. In
the firft place, *burgh politics* have ever operated here as a fatal
check to induftry. A fucceffion of contefted elections have
introduced, and, it is to be feared, confirmed, among the
members of the incorporations, habits of idlenefs, diffipation,
and vice. Mifled by that felf importance, which the long
expected return of the burgh canvafs beftows; feduced by
the flattering attentions and promifes of the great; accuftomed to the plenty and coviviality of the tavern, open to him
at all hours, the tradefman learns to defpife the moderate
profits arifing from the regular performance of his accuftomed toil: He quits the path which alone could have conducted him to peace, and comfort, and independence; he
feldom

feldom viſits his work-houſe or his ſhop, and when the election has at length taken place, and the ſcenes, which had ſo
much engroſſed and faſcinated him, have vaniſhed, he awakes
to ſolitude and want, and, with extreme difficulty, can prevail on himſelf again to enter on the rugged taſks of patient
induſtry.　But the ſucceſs of manufactures in Cupar has
hitherto been retarded by another cauſe, of a very different
nature, the great expence of land carriage.　St. Andrew's,
Leven, Newburgh, and Dundee, are the neareſt ſea-ports,
though all of them are diſtant 9 Engliſh miles.　Thus the
manufacturer muſt bring to Cupar the raw materials he uſes,
at a very heavy expence; and his different articles, when finiſhed, cannot be again conveyed to the ſea ſhore, but at an
additional charge.

Advantages to be derived from a Navigable Canal.—To enable the induſtry of the inhabitants to riſe ſuperior to this
natural diſadvantage, it has been ſuggeſted, that a navigable
canal might be formed, nearly in the courſe of the Eden, as
high as Cupar.　The river falls into the ſea about 9 miles
below the town.　The greater part of the channel is already
navigable.　The tide riſes as high as Lydox Mill, little more
than 3 Engliſh miles from Cupar.　The fall from the town
is very gradual, and to the place to which the tide riſes,
thought not to be more than 26 feet.　It is thus evident,
that a navigable canal might be formed, as far as Cupar, at
no very formidable expence.　The advantages to be derived
from this cut, to the inhabitants of the town and of the
neighbouring country, would be great indeed, and could not
be eaſily calculated.　Cupar is already the ſtore-houſe, to an
extenſive tract of country, for iron, tar, ropes, bricks, tiles,
wines, ſpirits, graſs ſeeds, ſoap, candles, tobacco, tea, ſugar,
fruits, and all kinds of groceries.　The ſaving in the carriage
of

of thefe articles, to thofe who deal in them, fuppofing the confumption to be no greater than it already is, would be immenfe. Vaft advantages would likewife be experienced by Cupar and its vicinity, in the eafier rate at which they would be fupplied with timber and flates for building, now brought, at a very great expence, from St. Andrew's, Dundee, &c.; by the farmers on both fides of the river, in the convenient fupply of lime and other manures; and by all ranks, in the reduction of the price of that expenfive, but neceffary article of daily confumption, coal.—Scotland has at laft opened her eyes, to the vaft advantages to be derived to her commerce and agriculture, from the eafe and fmall expence of water carriage. She now follows, with fpirit and fteadinefs, the bold and fuccefsful fteps of her fifter kingdom; and when thofe canals, on a grand fcale, which are now carrying on, fhall be finifhed, it is to be hoped, that this cut on the Eden, will be one of the firft, on a more humble plan, to be adopted and executed.

Ecclefiaftical State.—The diftrict of Cupar formed a parifh in early times, when the great parochial divifions of Crail, Kilrenny, Kilconquhar, St. Andrew's, Leuchars, and a few others, comprehended all the eaftern part of the county. The fmall parifh of St. Michael's, lying on the fouth of the Eden, was joined to that of Cupar in the beginning of the laft century. The church belonging to the parifh ftood on that beautiful fpot, now known by the name of *St. Michael's Hill.* Human bones are ftill occafionally difcovered in the field, when the operations of hufbandry are going forward. The ruins of a fmall chapel, fituated near the eaftern boundary of the lands of Kilmaron, were to be feen not many years ago.

The church of Cupar is collegiate. The King is patron

of

of both charges. The ſtipend, annexed to the firſt, conſiſts of 8¼ chalders of meal and grain, and about 25 l. in money, with a ſmall glebe. Of the grain and meal, there are only paid, within the pariſh of Cupar, 19 bolls. The ſtipend of the ſecond miniſter is about 1000 l. Scotch. There is no manſe belonging to either of the miniſters.

Religious Perſuaſions.—Till within theſe few months, there has always been an Epiſcopal meeting-houſe in Cupar, having a fixed paſtor reſiding in the town, or in the immediate vicinity. At preſent the people of that perſuaſion, who are now reduced to a very ſmall number, aſſemble for public worſhip only occaſionally, when the Epiſcopal miniſter from Pittenweem preſides. The ſect of Relief have a meeting-houſe in Cupar, built in 1769. The number of members in the pariſh, belonging to this congregation, cannot eaſily be aſcertained, as they are in a ſtate of conſtant fluctuation. There are alſo a few Burghers and Antiburghers, who belong to the congregations who meet at Ceres and Rathillet. About 7 or 8 perſons aſſemble on the Lord's Day, in a private houſe in town, for the purpoſes of devotion; but their principles and mode of worſhip are not known.—It is pleaſant to conclude this detail of the religious perſuaſions which prevail in this place, with remarking, that the ſectaries in Cupar live on good terms with their neighbours, the members of the Eſtabliſhed Church;—that their different opinions in religion ſeldom interrupt the ſocial intercourſe of life, or prevent them from doing kind offices to one another; —that a more liberal and benevolent ſpirit begins at laſt to prevail; and that, except among a few, that gloomineſs of aſpect, that bitterneſs of ſpirit, and that fierceneſs of zeal, which in former times marked and diſgraced the different ſects, are, at the preſent day, happily unknown.

Poor,

Poor.—Though the parish of Cupar is very populous, yet, during the last 20 years, there have never been, at any time, more than from 4 to 7 beggars belonging to it. The number of begging poor is at present 5. The number of poor house-holders, however, is very confiderable. Fifteen receive from the kirk-feffion a weekly allowance, proportioned to their various claims. A far greater number are fupplied occafionally. Parochial affeffments, for the maintainance of the poor, in this part of the kingdom, are yet unknown; yet a more decent and adequate provifion is made for the fupport of the indigent in Cupar, than in moft parithes, perhaps, where thefe obtain, and where the population is equally great. The poor receive annually, collected at the doors of the church, between 70 l. and 80 l.; and 16 l. as the intereft of a fund in money, which has long been their property.—In a building which ftands near to the church, known by the name of *the Alms-Houfes*, and under the management of the kirk-feffion, a few aged and infirm women are lodged, and, in part, fupported, out of the above fund.— But, befides the confiderable fupplies, which the poor thus receive from the ordinary parochial fund, they are indebted to the liberal fpirit of public bodies, and to the compaffion of individuals, for effential and feafonable fupport. The town of Cupar, greatly to their credit, give liberally out of the revenue of the burgh, to the indigent and diftreffed. The incorporations, too, as far as their fcanty funds will permit, contribute to the relief of their decayed members. A fociety has been formed, among tradefmen and mechanics, which has the happieft effects. By contributing, when in health, a very fmall fum weekly, they provide for their fupport in ficknefs and old age. The ladies of feveral of the principal heritors of the parifh, who conftantly refide in it, have each of them their lift of weekly penfioners,

fioners, to whofe wants they kindly and regularly attend; and
other individuals are not more diftinguifhed by their rank and
opulence, than by their extenfive charity, and exemplary benevolence *.—It may be faid with the ftricteft regard to truth,
(and to the honour of the humanity of the age, and of the
place, it ought indeed by no means to be concealed), that no
cafe of private diftrefs is made known, which does not here
meet with kind fympathy, and inftant relief; that no time
of general fcarcity occurs, which does not bear teftimony to
the virtue of individuals, and call forth the moft benevolent
exertions. Thefe acts of beneficence are by no means peculiar to thofe of high rank, and in affluent circumftances; inftances of compaffion to the afflicted, and of relief extended
to the indigent, frequently occur among thofe placed in the
humbler walks of life, which do honour to themfelves and
to humanity.

Vagrant Beggars.—Though the town of Cupar may be
                                                    faid

---

* In the year 1782, the price of meal rofe to an enormous
height. That the poor might be enabled to purchafe their ufual
fupply, the feffion added to their ordinary diftributions the fum
of 50 l. the favings of former years. They divided alfo to the
neceffitous 25 l. raifed for their ufe by the humane and benevolent, by the laudable and efficient fcheme of a *fubfcription ball*.
Owing to thefe and fome other donations of lefs confideration,
the poor in Cupar were happily preferved from the preffure of
want, during that year of general diftrefs.—In the courfe of the
laft wintner, (1793), coals, all over the kingdom, were extremely fcarce and high priced. That the poor might not fuffer
from the want of fuel, and that coals might be fold to them at
the ordinary rate, the town of Cupar generoufly gave 20 guineas, to affift in reducing the price of this neceffary article. A
nobleman, who probably would not wifh his name to be mentioned, fent to the town 15 guineas to purchafe coals for the
poor. The refiding heritors of the parifh alfo liberally contributed to the fame benevolent purpofe. One gentleman gave 5
guineas, another 3, &c.

said to have almoft no begging poor belonging to it, yet there is no town perhaps in Scotland, of the fame extent, where a greater number are daily feen infefting the ftreefs. Cupar being the principal thoroughfare, on the great turnpike road leading through the county of Fife, and no plan being fteadily followed, to prevent the numerous vagrants paffing from north to fouth, and from fouth to north, to beg the whole round of the town, the inhabitants are daily fubjected to their importunities and extortions. To the difgrace of the police alfo, feveral houfes are ftill to be found in Cupar, that harbour the idle and the profligate, from whatever quarter they come. In the day they prowl in the neighbouring country, giving out, that they are poor from the parifh of Cupar, and beg or plunder by turns, as opportunities offer. At night, they return to the infamous receptacles which they had left in the morning, difpofe there of their fpoils, and riot and caroufe, at the expence of the fimple, the fober, and the induftrious. In truth a fum of money could not be laid out by the community fo frugally, or fo much to the advantage of the town and of the neighbourhood, as in hiring a perfon, whofe fole bufinefs it fhould be to prevent foreign poor from begging in Cupar, and to apprehend all vagrant ftrangers, who cannot give a proper account of themfelves.

It is hoped, that it will not be deemed improper, or in any degree difrefpectful to the laws and conftitution of the country, to conclude this article with obferving, that the acts of the Parliament of Scotland, intended to operate for the regulation and maintenance of the poor, are many of them become of little ufe, and inapplicable to the prefent ftate of fociety. Whoever has lived in England; whoever has paid attention to the legal provifion made in that country, for the maintenance of the poor; whoever has witneffed the formidable amount to which the tax in fome diftricts rifes, how

fatally

fatally it ſometimes operates, as an encouragement to idleneſs, and check to induſtry ; whoever has paid attention to
theſe circumſtances, would never wiſh to ſee *poor's rates* eſtabliſhed in Scotland. Yet, every one who has been, during
any conſiderable length of time, concerned in the management of a pariſh fund in this country, muſt frequently, from
the imperfection and inconſiſtency of our acts of Parliament
relating to this buſineſs, have felt himſelf difficulted, and
muſt have wiſhed for a new law, containing proper regulations on this ſubject, ſo very important and intereſting to ſociety—particularly for a ſtatute, defining accurately theſe
two points :

1ſt, Who are the poor, or who are they who have a legal claim to maintenance in a pariſh ?

2dly, Who are the ſole and legal adminiſtrators of the
funds belonging to the poor * ?

Schools.—The ſchools of Cupar meet in a convenient and
                                                          hand-

* The arguments againſt the eſtabliſhment of poor's rates,
have often been ſtated to the public. It is unneceſſary here to
repeat them. From what has been repreſented, with reſpect to
the maintenance of the poor of Cupar, it is evident that a decent proviſion may be made for the indigent, without adopting
a practice, that has been attended with ſuch pernicious effects
wherever it has been eſtabliſhed. If the landholders of Scotland underſtand their own intereſt ; if they entertain a deep and
grateful ſenſe of the prudence, and purity, and diſintereſtedneſs
of miniſters and kirk-ſeſſions, in the management of the funds
belonging to the poor intruſted to their care ; if they are intereſted in the comfort of thoſe with whoſe welfare their own
proſperity is intimately connected—while they reprobate parochial aſſeſſments, and all their baleful conſequences to ſociety,
they will chearfully follow the only plan, which, in many pariſhes, can prevent their eſtabliſhment—they will regularly contribute, on the Lord's Day, to the relief of the poor in thoſe
pariſhes where their property lies, whether they reſide or not,
and whether or not they attend public worſhip.

handfome building, erected in the year 1727, by the Magiftrates and Council, who are patrons, in a very pleafant and airy fituation, on the Caftle-hill. The houfe is divided into two apartments, which have feparate entries, and which have no communication with each other. In the one are taught Latin, French, Geography, &c. ; in the other, Englifh, writing, arithmetic, book-keeping, menfuration, &c. The rector of the grammar fchool has a falary of 30 l.; the mafter of the Englifh fchool, a falary of 17 l. Both are paid by the town. The fees paid by the fcholars, as regulated by the Town Council, are 3 s. per quarter for Latin, 1 s. 6 d. for Englifh, 2 s. for writing and arithmetic, befides dues paid at the new year and Candlemas. The fchool of Cupar has, in different periods, been in high repute; and, from the attention, ardour, and abilities of the prefent teachers, bids fair to attain its antient celebrity.

Climate, Difeafes, &c.—The inhabitants of Cupar juftly boaft of the falubrity of the air in which they breathe. Situated in the dry bottom of a delightful vale, bleffed with many abundant fprings of the pureft water, wafhed by the river Eden on the fouth, and the ftream of St. Mary on the north, fenced from the violence of every tempeft, by the green and fertile hills which almoft encircle the town, and bound the plain of Eden, they often enjoy a happy exemption from thofe difeafes which lurk in marfhy diftricts, and which frequently vifit and afflict tracts of country, at no very confiderable diftance. The running waters, which never ceafe to fill the channels of the Eden, no doubt, in a particular manner, contribute to the health of the inhabitants, and to the beauty of the furrounding region. The placid ftream of the river, and the fcenery, which diverfifies

and

and adorns its banks, long ſince touched the imagination of
the Poet *, and found a place in his ſong.

" *Arva inter nemoriſque umbras, et paſcua laeta*
" *Lene fluens, vitreis, labitur* EDEN, *aquis.*"

The view from the Caſtle-hill, though it cannot boaſt of being extenſive, yet, in point of richneſs, beauty, and variety,
yields perhaps to few proſpects which are purely inland. On
all ſides, the chearful aſpect of a cultivated and thriving
country meets the eye. Numerous farm houſes ſtud and
enliven the ſurrounding gentle acclivities. At various diftances, buildings of a more magnificent form, elegant and
ſtately villas, tower on the riſing grounds †. It may with
truth be affirmed, that diſeaſes have ſeldom proved epidemic in Cupar. Few infants now die of the ſmall-pox, as inoculation, under the direction of excellent practitioners,
daily gains ground. Many of thoſe, who are cut off in the
early period of life, ſeem to fall victims to a cruel and fatal
diſeaſe, till of late but ſeldom noticed by phyſicians, the
croup, or inflammation of the wind-pipe. It belongs to
others to attempt to account for the frequency of this diftemper.—The vale in which Cupar is ſituated, though poſſeſſing many advantages, is ſometimes viſited by dreadful
thunder

* JOHNSTONE.

† Attracted by the pleaſant and healthful ſituation of the
vale in which the town ſtands, our kings, when they lived in the
neighbouring palace of Falkland, placed (ſays the current tradition) the family nurſery at Cupar; and the royal children
had apartments fitted up for them, in the religious houſe belonging to the Benedictines, adjoining to the caſtle, now the reſidence of the Hon. Lady Elizabeth Anſtruther.

thunder ſtorms. Fatal accidents from lightning have frequently been experienced *.

Longevity.—Many in the pariſh of Cupar have attained, if
not to the utmoſt period of human life, yet to a very great
longevity It is not to be doubted, that in every place, and
in every age, perſons have frequently reached a length of
days far beyond the period allotted to the ordinary race of
mortals. But we are diſpoſed to give too eaſy faith to the
many inſtances which are publiſhed to the world, from every
quarter, of perſons having attained to extreme old age, from
that love of the marvellous which is natural to man, and
from that fond deſire of protracting life to the utmoſt ſpan,
which, in defiance of the ſober dictates of reaſon, and the
frequent checks of experience, we fooliſhly and obſtinately
cheriſh. Whoever will take the trouble to inquire minute-
ly into the hiſtory of thoſe, within the circle of his own acquaintance, who have died in advanced age, and who have
been reported, in every publication of the day, to have
reached their hundredth, or hundred and tenth year, will
find, that in truth, in almoſt every inſtance, conſiderable de-
ductions muſt be made from the exaggerated account. Whoever attends to the numerous inſtances of longevity, collected by the late Dr Fothergill, muſt be ſenſible, that the evi-
dences

---

* On the 30th of April 1735, a black-ſmith, while employed
in ſhoeing a horſe before the door of his work ſhop, was ſtruck
down in the ſtreet, and inſtantly expired. On the 20th of September 1787, the inhabitants were alarmed by a tremendous
peal. Every perſon trembled, while he inquired after the fate
of his children and his domeſtics. The melancholy tidings were
inſtantly ſpread over the town, that four men had been killed
in the old correction houſe, at that time uſed as a wright's ſhop.
Two of the four, though ſeverely ſtunned and wounded, gradually recovered. The other two were found without any remains of life.

dences on which they are made to reſt, newſpapers and other periodical publications, are by no means entitled to the attention and belief of a ſincere inquirer after truth. Even the great Lord Verulam, when writing on this ſubject, loſes that acuteneſs, ſagacity, and ſtrength of mind, which he uſually diſplays, and deſcends to the level of the weakeſt, the moſt ſanguine and credulous, of the ſpeculating philoſophic tribe. He ſeems to give credit to the accounts recorded by Pliny, in his natural hiſtory, of 124 perſons, who, in the reign of Veſpaſian, were found in that diſtrict of Italy, lying between the Appenine mountains and the river Po, who had all lived beyond the age of 100, and many of them to their hundred and thirtieth, or hundred and fortieth year. Notwithſtanding the many amuſing hiſtories, which have been given to the public, of the vigour and feats of thoſe who are now alive in this country, and who have paſſed the hundredth year of their age, yet ſhould any one undertake to produce ſatisfying evidence, that there are *two* perſons only in the county in which he reſides, who have reached this extreme age, he would find himſelf engaged in a difficult, and probably fruitleſs, attempt *. The annexed inſtances

---

* In the regiſter of burials belonging to the pariſh of Cupar, the following entry is made: " Buried, 21ſt December 1757, " Lady Denbrae, aged 107 years." It was the general belief of the town and neighbourhood, that this lady, whoſe maiden name was Fletcher, and who had been married to —— Preſton, Eſq; of Denbrae, was, at the time of her death, 106 or 107 years old. Her friends, when talking of the length of days to which ſhe had attained, never failed to boaſt, that ſhe was one of the celebrated beauties who graced the Court of the Duke of York, when he reſided in the palace of Holyrood-houſe, in the reign of his brother Charles II. Upon the moſt accurate inveſtigation, however, of every circumſtance that could be traced, relating to the age of this female, who had long ſurvived all her cotemporaries, it has been found, that ſhe had but juſt completed her 99th year.

ftances of longevity, however, in the parifh of Cupar, may be relied on as perfectly authentic *.

Antiquities.

* JAMES WEMYSS, Efq; of Winthank, who was born in the beginning of 1696, died in the month of March laft, (1793) in his 98th year. This gentleman, whofe ftature did not exceed the common fize, but who was handfome and well made, poffef-fed a very uncommon degree both of bodily and mental vigour. Through the whole of life, he never failed to rife in the morning at an early hour; was frequently on horfe-back; was no enemy to the free circulation of the glafs, though, upon the whole, he might juftly be faid to be regular and temperate. He poffeffed, in an eminent degree, the politenefs peculiar to the laft age, and long remained a venerable fpecimen of the antient fchool of manners. He was the only perfon, the writer of thefe ftatements ever knew, who retained, in extreme old age, the fame ufe of all the mental faculties, which had been the poffef-fion and enjoyment of youth and manhood. When he was upwards of 90, he not only regularly amufed himfelf, feveral hours every day, with reading, particularly hiftory, but could give a diftinct account of the fubject to which he was directing his attention. He had never, in the courfe of his long life, been confined to his bed a fingle day by ficknefs. And even when he began to feel the gradual approaches of age, and decays of nature, he was in a great meafure exempted from the weakneffes and fufferings incidental to this mournful period. Though he was born in one century, and lived to fee almoft the conclufion of the next, and thus ought to have paffed through the feven ages of human life marked by the Poet, yet the defcription of the laft ftage, given by the bard of nature, was by no means applicable to the concluding period of his exiftence. He never, indeed, reached the " laft fcene of all, that ends the " ftrange, eventful hiftory of man, fecond childifhnefs, and mere " oblivion." Attacked at laft by the refiftlefs power of fever, he retired to his apartment, and, after a confinement of 4 days, yielded to the univerfal law of nature.

The venerable Sir ROBERT PRESTON, late minifter in the firft charge at Cupar, died in September 1791, having nearly completed the fixty-firft year of his miniftry. He was firft admitted a minifter of the church at Arbirlot, in the county of Angus, and out-lived, during the courfe of feveral years, all the members

Antiquities.—The parish of Cupar affords little to interest or to gratify the antiquarian *.—Cairns of stones, or *tumuli*, containing the remains of human bodies, are frequent in this district,

members of the synod of Angus and Mearns, though they amounted to no less a number than 80.—Mr William Miller of Star, and Mr Alexander Melvil of Kilmaron, were born in Cupar in the course of the same year, and lately died in it, at no great distance of time from each other, about the age of 90. The union of the last of these two with his wife had subsisted upwards of 60 years.—David Brown weaver, and his wife, who both lately died, had lived in the married state during the same uncommon length of time.—There were living, about 10 years ago, 5 men in the town of Cupar, all considerably upwards of 90, and who all died nearly about the same time, viz Walter Douglas, musician, 96 years old ; David Brugh, gardner, 95 ; John Lorimer, weaver, 94 ; James Anderson, wright, 91 ; and ——— Lumisdain, day-labourer, 92. The first of these, Walter Douglas, who died in his 97th year, was town-drummer, had served the corporation in that capacity 74 years, and, at the time of his death, might perhaps have been justly accounted the oldest office-bearer in the kingdom. He was of low stature, but broad chested and well built. Through the whole of life, he could only command coarse and scanty fare, and knew none of the advantages of warm and comfortable lodging. Angling was his favourite amusement, and he continued to fish on the river till within a little of his death. He was of a family in the town, who had long been noted for their longevity. His brother John died nearly of the same age with himself, after having buried a son upwards of 72. Some of the same name still reside in the town, who preserve a striking likeness to the family, who possess the same robust appearance and vigorous frame, and who bid fair to equal the age of their fathers.

* In levelling a piece of ground, in order to form the turnpike road that leads from Cupar to the east, there were lately found, in the vicinity of the Castle-hill, several stone coffins containing human skeletons. The coffins were adorned with the figures of warriors, rudely sculptured, and covered with unknown characters. English and French coins, of considerable antiquity, have been dug up, in removing the rubbish from the ground where the Castle once stood.

diftrict, fimilar to thofe found in many different parts of the country *.

Carflogie Houfe.—The houfe of Carflogie, diftant about a mile from Cupar, on the road that leads to the weft, is the moft antient family feat in the parifh. It had been originally intended for a place of fecurity and ftrength. Colonel Clephane, the prefent proprietor of Carflogie, is the 20th of that name, who, in regular defcent, has poffeffed the eftate †. In a field adjoining to the houfe of Carflogie, and near to the public road which leads from Cupar to the weft,

the

* One of thefe was lately opened on the heights of Middle-field, about an Englifh mile to the north eaft of Cupar, in which were found feveral urns of baked clay, inclofing the afhes of the warriors of a diftant age. That the urns were not Roman, appeared from the nature of the inftruments of war, placed by the fide of them The heads of the battle-axes were formed of a very hard ftone, of a white colour, neatly fhaped, and nicely carved and polifhed. Thefe arms muft have been employed by a rude people, ftrangers to the ufe of iron. Two of thefe battle-axes are in the poffeffion of a gentleman in Cupar. The fpot where thefe tumuli had been formed, from the remains of ramparts that had furrounded it, feems to have been, in fome remote period, a military ftation of confiderable importance; and to have been a height well adapted for that purpofe, commanding a very extenfive profpect to the ocean on the eaft, and to the Ochil hills on the weft.

† The CLEPHANES, who for many ages have been proprietors of the Caftle and the furrounding grounds, in times of barbarifm, confufion, and diforder, often leagued with the neighbouring ancient family of the Scots of Scotftarvet, who inhabited a ftrong tower, (Scotftarvet Tower), which is ftill entire, fituated about two Englifh miles fouth from Carflogie. On the appearance of an enemy, *horns.* from the battlements of the caftle from which the hoftile force was firft defcried, announced its approach, and the quarter from whence it was advancing; and both families, with their dependents, were inftantly

under

the ſtately and venerable remains of an aſh, which for ſeveral centuries has retained the name of the *Jug Tree**, ſtrikes the eye of the traveller.

Garlie Bank.—The Garlie Bank, the property of James Wemyſs, Eſq; of Winthank, ſituated to the ſouth of Cupar, and the higheſt ground in the pariſh, has been rendered famous by the treaty ſigned there, on the 13th of June 1559, betwixt the Duke of Chattelrault, and Monſieur D'Oyſel, commanding the army of the Queen regent, and the Earl of Argyle,

under arms. There is a charter belonging to the family, bearing that " DUNCANUS, *Comes de* FYFE, *confirmat* JOHANNI de
" CLEPHANE, *et haeredibus, totam terram de Cleſclogie, et de Eri-*
" *therrogewale,* (Uthrogyle), *adeo libere, ſicut* DAVID de CLE-
" PHANE, *pater ejus, et predeceſſores, eas ienuerunt. Teſtibus Domi-*
" *no Alexandro de Abernethy, Michael et David de Vemys,* Hugone
" *de Lochor, Johanne de Ramſey, cum multis aliis.*" From the aera at which theſe witneſſes lived, the charter muſt have been given, at the lateſt, in the beginning of the reign of Robert I. The family have been in poſſeſſion, time immemorial, of a hand made in exaçt imitation of that of a man, and curiouſly formed of ſteel. This is ſaid to have been conferred by one of the kings of Scotland, along with other more valuable marks of his favour, on the Laird of Carſlogie, who had loſt his hand in the ſervice of his country.

* The iron jugs, in which the offenders on the domains of Carſlogie ſuffered the puniſhments, to which they were doomed by their lords, fell from the hollow body of this tree, in which they had been infixed, only about 3 years ago. During the courſe of the greater part of this century, ſuſpended in the view of every paſſenger, they ſilently, but impreſſively, reminded him, to rejoice that he lived in a happy and meliorated period, in which the oppreſſive juriſdiçtions, and capricious and cruel puniſhments, to which his fathers were long ſubjeçted, are entirely annihilated, and mild, equal, and powerful law, hath extended its proteçting arm to the meaneſt individual, in the moſt diſtant cot, in this free and favoured land.

Argyll, and Lord James, prior of St. Andrews, leading the forces of the Congregation *.

Mote-hill, Temple Tenements, &c.—A mound of earth rifing confiderably above the adjoining grounds, extends to a great length on the north fide of Cupar, called *the Mote*, or, as fome write it, the *Moat-hill* †.—The Knights Templars

* The hoftile camps were only feparated by the river Eden. The morning of the day had been employed by the generals of both armies, in making the neceffary arrangements for a deci-five engagement. The advanced parties were now about to clofe, when the Duke fent a meffenger to the Lords of the Con-gregation, to demand a conference. They, equally unwilling to rifk a general action, complied with the requeft. The prin-cipal man in both armies repaired to the higheft eminence of the Garlie Bank, a fpot known by the name of the *Howlet*, or *Owl Hill*, and which commanded a full view of the whole plain wherein the troops were now drawn up in order of battle, and there adjufted and figned that truce, in confequence of which the forces of the Queen retired to Falkland, from whence they had that morning advanced ; and thofe of the Congregation to Cupar, St. Andrew's, and Dundee. The violent reformer, KNOX, having completely deftroyed the religious houfes at Perth, Cupar, Crail, and St. Andrew's, had repaired to the camp at Cupar Muir, and by his rude, but impreffive eloquence, inflamed the zeal of the Lords of the Congregation. He details, in his Hiftory, (pages 141. 142.), the events of the morning of the 13th of June, with all the minutenefs and ardour natural to one who had fo deep an intereft in every important public tranf-action, and who had ftaked his reputation and his fortunes on the fuccefs of Argyll, and the party who adhered to him.

† They who ufe the latter orthography contend, that this rampart is formed of artificial earth ; that it originally exten-ded as far as the Caftle ; and was conftructed to defend the town from any fudden attack from the north, as the river, in fome meafure, fecured it on the fouth. There is no doubt, however, that it ought to be ftiled the *Mote Hill*, as it was pro-bably the place where, in early times, the Jufticiary of Fife held his courts, and publifhed his enactments, for the regulation of
the

plars had conſiderable poſſeſſions in land adjoining to Cupar
on the ſouth.   There are ſtill two houſes, in different parts
of the town, called *Temple Tenements*, which belonged to
that order.   They now hold of the Earl of Hadington, and
enjoy all the privileges and exemptions uſually attached to
the poſſeſſions of the Templars.—The only religious houſe
which exiſted in Cupar, at the time of the Reformation, was
a convent of Dominican, or Black Friars.   It was ſituated
at the foot of the Caſtlehill, and connected with the Caſtle *.
A conſiderable part of the chapel, built of cut free-ſtone,
ſtill ſtands.

Playfield,

the country.   The Latin name, by which this hill is ſometimes
mentioned, muſt decide the controverſy, if with any plauſibility
it could ever have been maintained ;—" *Mons placiti*," which
may be tranſlated " *Statute-hill*."

* No part of the Caſtle now remains.   Though long the reſidence of the Earls of Fife, it had at laſt become a national
fortreſs.   It had been a place of conſiderable ſtrength.   Buchanan ſtiles it *Arx munitiſſima Cuprenſis*.   The Engliſh were in
poſſeſſion of it anno 1297.   In the courſe of that year, it was
recovered by the bravery of Wallace.   [*Buchan. Hiſt. book* viii.]
—Robert Wiſhart, biſhop of Glaſgow, who had joined the party of Bruce, after the murder of Comyn, held the Caſtle of Cupar againſt the Engliſh.   He was made priſoner there, arrayed
in armour, and, in that uncanonical garb, was conducted to the
Caſtle of Nottingham   This happened anno 1306.   [*Dalrymple's Annals*, vol. II.]—Edward Baliol, aſſiſted by Edward III. of
England, reviving his pretenſions to the crown of Scotland,
defeated the Scotch at Halidon, *anno Dom.* 1333, during the
minority of David II ; upon which the greater part of the
kingdom ſubmitted to him.   Upon this occaſion, we find the
Caſtle of Cupar entruſted to William Bullock, an eccleſiaſtic of
eminent abilities, chamberlain of Scotland, in whom Baliol placed his chief confidence.   [*Dalrymple*.]—The king was again
put in poſſeſſion of this fortreſs, by the ſucceſsful valour of William Douglas, and ſoon after he cauſed it to be entirely demoliſhed.

Playfield, &c.—During the dark ages, theatrical reprefen-
tations, called *myfleries* or *moralities*, (the perfons allegorical,
fuch as Sin, Death, &c.) were frequently exhibited The
place, where thefe entertainments were prefented, was called
the Playfield *. " Few towns of note," fays Arnot, in his
History

* The pieces prefented in the Playfield of Cupar, however,
feem not, at the aera of the Reformation, to have had any connection with religious fubjects, but were calculated to intereft
and amufe, by exhibiting every variety of character, and every
fpecies of humour. To illuftrate the manners which prevailed
in Scotland in the 16th century, and as a fpecimen of the dra-
matic compofitions which pleafed our fathers, Arnot, in the
appendix to his Hiftory, gives a curious excerpt from a manufcript comedy, which bears to have been exhibited in the Playfield at Cupar, and which had been in the poffeffion of the late
Mr Garrick.

That part of the excerpt only, which relates to the place
where the play was prefented, is here tranfcribed.

" Here begins the proclamation of the play, made by DAVID
LINDSAY of the Mount ‡, Knight, in the Playfield, in the month
of   , the year of God 1555 years."

" Proclamation made in Cupar of Fife.

" Our purpofe is on the feventh day of June,
    " If weather ferve, and we have reft and peace,
    " We fhall be feen into our playing place,
" In good array about the hour of feven.
    " Of thriftinefs that day, I pray you ceafe ;
" But ordain us good drink againft allevin §.
    " Fail not to be upon the Caftlehill,
" Befide the place where we purpofe to play ;
    " With gude ftark wine your flaggons fee you fill,
" And had yourfelves the merrieft that you may.

" *Cottager.* I fhall be there, with God's grace,
        " Tho' there were never fo great a price,
            " And foremoft in the fair :
        " And drink a quart in Cupar town,
        " With my goffip John Williamfon,
            " Tho' all the nolt fhould rair," &c.

‡ *The* MOUNT, *formerly the eftate of Sir* DAVID LINDSAY, *lies
in the immediate neighbourhood of Cupar.*

§ *i. e. Eleven.*

Hiſtory of Edinburgh, " were without one. That of
" Edinburgh was at the Greenſide-well ; that of Cupar in
" Fife was on their *Caſtle-hill.*"

Agriculture.—Fife, though poſſeſſing natural advantages
ſuperior to thoſe enjoyed by many neighbouring counties,
was, till of late, far behind them in the important knowledge, and valuable improvements of agriculture.— The herring fiſhery, the making of ſalt, the burning of lime, and
working of coal mines, circumſtances which might naturally
have been expected to accelerate a meliorated huſbandry,
contributed long to retard its progreſs. Occupied entirely
in the purſuit of theſe objects, the great landholders in Fife
were unhappily diverted from paying that attention to the
ſurface of the ground, which would not have failed to have
made a more certain and valuable return for the expence
which they often incurred, and the activity and induſtry
they exerted. During the laſt 15 years, however, in many
diſtricts of the county, the landholders and farmers have
adopted and proſecuted every plan of modern improvement,
with a degree of eagerneſs, perſeverance, and ſucceſs, not
ſurpaſſed in any corner of the iſland. That part of the county, in particular, which lies between the Eden and the Tay,
naturally fertile, has been ſubjected to a new and better mode
of cultivation. The farmers in this diſtrict, with a liberality which does them honour, readily acknowledge, that they
are indebted for many eſſential improvements, which are
now general among them. to the example of thoſe who have
come to ſettle in Fife, from the oppoſite country of the Carſe
of Gowrie.

Improvements.—The grounds adjoining to Cupar, on the
north,

north, having lately paffed into the hands of new mafters, who have fpared no expence to drain and inclofe them, who have enriched them with abundance of manure, and employed them in a proper rotation of crops, have entirely changed their appearance, and now afford a pleafing proof of the power of cultivation. From the improvements which have been mentioned, the erection of handfome houfes, by the different proprietors, and the plantations which have been formed, the whole prefents to the eye the appearance of what the French call *ferme ornè.*

Hills, Plantations, &c.—The country around Cupar cannot be faid to be level, as the grounds, in general, rife to a confiderable height on both fides of the Eden ; yet there are no hills in the parifh, except thofe of Wemyis-hall and Kilmaron, both of which are cultivated to the top. There are extenfive and thriving plantations on Cupar Muir, but no trees of age or fize, except at Carflogie and Tarvet, the family feat of Patrick Rigg, Efq; of Morton. At the laft mentioned place, the pleafure grounds, laid out with tafte, around the fpacious and elegant houfe lately built there, derive much of their beauty from the appearance of the antient and lofty trees fcattered through the lawn.

Soil.—The foil, on the north fide of the Eden, is in general of an excellent quality, black and deep, on a dry whinftone bottom. The foil on the fouth fide of Eden, as foon as you leave the valley, is cold and thin, and, in general, on a bottom of till.

Farms, Crops, &c.—The farms contain from 100 to 300 acres. The rotation of crops, on the beft black land, is the following:

following: 1. Clover and rye-grafs; 2. Wheat with dung; 3. Barley; 4. Drilled beans, with dung; 5. Wheat; 6. Turnips or potatoes; 7. Barley; 8. Oats, with grafs feeds. Thus, in the courfe of the 8 years, we have one eighth clover, two eighths wheat, two eighths barley, one eighth drilled beans, one eighth turnips or potatoes, and one eighth oats. —The following rotation is obferved in clay land: 1. Summer fallow; 2. Wheat, with lime and dung; 3. Peafe and beans; 4. Barley, with grafs feeds; 5. Hay, cut green; 6. Wheat, with dung; 7. Barley; 8. Oats; 9. Summer fallow, &c.—The rotation followed in grounds chiefly employed for pafture: 1. Oats; 2. Barley or flax; 3 Oats, with grafs feeds; 4. Hay; 5. Pafture.—Artificial graffes, chiefly rye-grafs, and red and white clover, are cultivated to a great extent, and with abundant fuccefs. Turnips have only been introduced of late years, and as yet a fmaller number of acres, in proportion to the extent of the parifh, are occupied with this crop, than in the eaftern parts of the county —The feed time extends from the middle of March to the middle of May. Harveft begins in the middle of Auguft, and commonly ends about the middle of October.

Potatoes.—No fpecies of culture has fo amply rewarded the labour beftowed on it, by the inhabitants of Cupar, as that of the potatoe. They have good reafon to join with thofe who affirm, that the potatoe is the richeft prefent, which the new world ever made to Europe. The produce of an acre is from 40 to 100 bolls. The average crop, on good ground, 60 bolls. The difeafe peculiar to this plant, known by the name of *the curl*, has not yet materially affected the crops in the neighbourhood of Cupar. The kinds commonly planted are, for the table, the *long kidney*, and the *London dropper*. For cattle, a large red potatoe, known by the name of *the*

Tartar,

Tartar, and extremely prolific. The moſt ſuccefsful farmers plant them in drills, at the diſtance of 50 inches from
each other. They clean them chiefly with drill harrows
and ploughs.

Horſes, Black Cattle, &c. *—Horſes are principally employed in every ſpecies of labour. The breed has been greatly improved within the laſt 15 years. The farmer ſeldom yokes a
pair in his plough, or in his cart, for which he could not
draw, in the market, 50 l. This diſtrict of the country, and
indeed the whole of what is commonly called *the Laigh of
Fife,* has long been famous for its excellent breed of black
cattle †.—The inſtruments of huſbandry, uſed in the pariſh,
are all of the neweſt and beſt conſtruction ; and the farmers
begin to build, at their own expence, mills for threſhing out
their corns.

Inclofures, Minerals, &c.—There is not an acre of common or waſte ground in the pariſh, the whole being either
planted or employed in tillage, except one large field, the
property of the town, kept for the purpoſe of paſturing the
cows belonging to the inhabitants. A conſiderable proportion of the grounds are incloſed. As there are inexhauſtible
quarries

* For the number of cattle, &c. ſee the Table. About 20
years ago, there were 12 or 13 flocks of ſheep in the pariſh ; for
ſeveral years paſt, there has not been one.

† James Wemyss, Eſq; of Winthank, a few years ago, ſold,
to an Engliſh drover, two bullocks, bred on his farm of
Wemyſs-hall, among the largeſt which the county of Fife has
ever produced. They were exhibited on account of their ſtu-
pendous ſize, during many months, in different parts of England, to the eye of public curioſity ; and when killed at Smith-
field, were found to be among the heavieſt ever brought to that
market.

quarries of excellent free-ftone in the parifh, the inclofures are chiefly formed by ftone dykes, the expence of building which is from 30 s. to 40 s. per rood of 36 yards.

Rents and Mills.—The grounds, to the diftance of an Englifh mile round the town, let at an average of 3 l. per acre. Fields under fown grafs, let for 6 l. per acre, fometimes as high as 8 l. There are no lefs than 11,000 bolls of grain annually made into meal, at the 4 different ftations in the parifh, where mills are erected.

Roads, &c.—Turnpike roads began to be formed in the parifh of Cupar, only within thefe few years. The meafure met, at firft, with almoft univerfal oppofition from the adjacent country. The farmers, however, have already entirely changed their opinion with refpect to turnpikes; they pay chearfully at the toll-bars, and feem, in general, to be convinced of the vaft importance and utility of the roads that have been formed. The turnpikes, in the neighbourhood of Cupar, are made on an excellent plan, are formed of the beft materials, and contain a hard and foft, or fummer and winter road.—The crofs roads in the parifh are, in general, exceedingly ill kept; nor is it likely, that by the ftatute labour, as at prefent applied, they will ever be in better order. As improvements of every kind have advanced fo rapidly, during the laft 7 years, it muft appear an unaccountable defect, that fo very common, and fo very ufeful a machine, as that of a *ftill-yard* for weighing hay, coals, &c. has never yet been erected in the town of Cupar, nor on any of the roads leading to it.

Wages and Prices of Provifions.—A labourer earns per day, in fummer, from 1 s. to 1 s. 6 d. In winter, from 10 d. to 1 s.

The

The prices of provisions vary little, in the countries adjoining to Edinburgh, Perth, Dundee, &c. The vicinity of these great towns did not contribute, in any great degree, to raise the price of provisions, till within the last 30 years. An increased population, and new modes of life, have of late occasioned an immense additional consumption of fish, poultry, &c.—In the Cupar market, beef, mutton, pork, and veal, sell at an average at 4 d. per lib. Dutch weight; hens, 13 d. each; geese, 3 s. each; rabbits, 6 d. per pair; pigeons, 3 d. per pair; butter, 9 d. per lib.; best cheese, 5 d.; coarse cheese, 3 d. tron weight; oat meal, 13 d. per peck; potatoes, 4¼ d.; eggs, 4 d. per dozen; salmon, 5 d. per lib.— Though the price of provisions is thus high, and though there has been also a great rise on the necessary articles of leather, soap, salt, candles, &c. yet the labourer at present is better lodged, better fed and clothed, and can give a more decent education to his children, than his father, who paid only 6 d. or 7 d. for a peck of oat meal; 1½ d. for beef and mutton per lib.; who bought eggs at 1 d. per dozen; butter at 5 d. per lib.; cheese at 1½ d.; and haddocks in abundance at 1 d. or 2 d. per dozen. This improvement in the situation of the labourer is owing chiefly to these causes: 1*st*, The proportion of the price of his own labour, and that of his family, to the price of provisions, is more in his favour than at any preceding period. 2*dly*, The introduction of the potatoe, which has been long in general cultivation, affords a vast additional supply of food to the labourer and his family, and enables him, at the same time, to rear pigs and poultry. 3*dly*, He can depend on being employed during the course of the whole year, an advantage which his father, who received only 5 d. or 6 d. for his day's work, could not always command.

Character

Character of the People.—The labourer and the mechanic are in general able, by the exertions of their induſtry, to make a decent livelihood for themſelves and their families; they poſſeſs more foreſight and economy than thoſe of the ſame rank in the neighbouring kingdom. They cheriſh the laudable pride of not being indebted for their ſupport to the parochial fund, or to the humanity of the charitable. They are in general contented with their humble ſituation; friends to that government which extends protection and ſecurity to their dwellings; and have had the good ſenſe to reſiſt and to deſpiſe the attempts of thoſe, who have endeavoured to make them believe, in oppoſition to their own happy experience, that they are burdened, oppreſſed, and wretched.

Manners.—The manners of the inhabitants of Cupar, of better rank, are, in general, correct and polite. Gentlemen of the military profeſſion, having ſpent their youth in the ſervice of their country, frequently fix their reſidence here, in the decline of life. Formed in that ſchool, which has long been diſtinguiſhed by the eaſe and politeneſs which it communicates, they have contributed to diffuſe an elegance of manners. To this circumſtance alſo, perhaps, it is in ſome meaſure owing, that families reſiding in Cupar, and enjoying only a limited and narrow income, make a decent and reſpectable appearance; and are enabled, by habits of attention and economy, frequently to exerciſe an elegant hoſpitality.

STATIS-

STATISTICAL TABLE OF THE PARISH OF CUPAR OF
FIFE.

CONDITIONS AND PROFESSIONS, &c.

Principal refiding heritors *	7		Mafons	-	21
Ditto non-refiding †	9		Wrights	-	48
Attorneys or writers	12		Smiths	-	24
Clerks and apprentices to			Shoemakers	-	35
ditto	20		Glovers	-	5
Medical practitioners	5		Hatters	-	2
Clergymen	3		Barbers	-	7
School-mafters	3		Saddlers	-	5
Private teachers	4		Candle-makers	-	2
Mantua-makers	10		Linen-merchants	-	6
Milliners	6		Shop-keepers	-	31
Houfe painters	3		Midwives	-	4
Stationers	2		Watch-makers	-	3
Bakers and fervants	19		Excife officers	-	3
Butchers and ditto	16		Carriers	-	4
Brewers	5		Meffengers	-	3
Tailors	29		Footmen	-	20
Dyers	5				

Valued

* Viz. Patrick Rigg, Efq; of Morton, James Wemyfs, Efq;
of Wemyfshail, Henry Stark, Efq; of Teaffes, Charles Bell, Efq;
of Pitbladdo, William Robertfon, Efq; of Middlefield, Peter
Walker, Efq; of Kingafk, and John Swan, Efq; of Prefton-
hall.

† Viz. the Earl of Crawfurd, Colonel Clephane of Carflogie,
James Robertfon, Efq; of Balgarvie, Oliver Gourlay, Efq; of
Kilmoran, George M'Gill, Efq; of Kemback, Charles Mait-
land, Efq; of Rankeillor, Henry Weft Efq; of Foxtown, Mifs
Bell of Hillton, and Alexander Low, Efq; of Pittencrieff.

Valued rent in Scotch money - L. 5331
Bank offices   -   -   -   -   2
Tan-works   -   -   -   -   2
Weaver's looms   -   -   -   223
Licenſed ale-houſes   -   -   -   43
Ditto in the county of Fife   -   -   784

CATTLE, &c.

Horſes - -	338	Coach - -	1
Cows and young cattle	722	Chaiſes - -	8
Ploughs - -	68	Pack of fox hounds	1
Carts - -	137	Ditto of harriers -	1

PARISH OF DAIRSIE.

(*County of Fife.*)

By the Rev. Mr ROBERT M'CULLOCH,

Situation and Surface.

THIS pariſh is ſituated in the county and ſynod of Fife, and in the preſbytery of Cupar. It is of an irregular form, extending from the ſouth-eaſt, to the north-weſt, two Scots miles, and from the ſouth-weſt, to the north-eaſt, nearly as much. Its general appearance is that of a gently riſing ground. There are in it two hills of a moderate height, from which are very extenſive proſpects. The one is called *Foodie*, the other *Craigfoodie*, and both of them are remarkable for bearing good crops nearly to their tops. The ſoil in this pariſh is for the moſt part fertile, and in many places rich and deep. The air is generally dry and healthy. There are no conſiderable rivers in this diſtrict, except the Eden, which forms its boundary to the ſouth and ſouth-eaſt, and, a little farther on, runs into the Eaſtern ocean. It abounds with excellent trout, and a few ſalmon are ſometimes caught in it. The fiſh are moſtly taken by the rod, and very few are ever ſent to market.

Population.—This pariſh contains 540 perſons. In Dr Webſter's report, the number of ſouls is 469. There are 11

farms

farms-here of different extent, from 330 down to 60 acres. The pariſh is laboured by about 24 ploughs. Every two ploughs employs at leaſt three men, two for the ploughs, and one for the barn and other work. A farmer having two ploughs of land, commonly keeps two boys for taking care of the cattle, and two women, chiefly for harveſt work. The population of this pariſh is not materially different from what it was 18 years ago. There are, upon an average, five marriages, and 13 births.

Cattle and Productions.—There are no ſheep in this pariſh. There are about 110 horſes, 400 cows, oxen, and young cattle. Of wheat there are ſown about 190 acres. Sowing artificial graſſes, and the cultivation of potatoes and turnips, have of late exceedingly increaſed. About 20 acres or more are annually ſown with flax ſeed.

Church and Poor.—The ſtipend of this pariſh is five and a half chalders of victual, and about L. 28 in money, with a manſe and a glebe of ſix acres. The church was built by Archbiſhop Spottiſwood, in 1622, when he was proprietor of the eſtate of Dairſie. In the old houſe near the church, it is ſaid, that he wrote his hiſtory. The church is a remarkably neat and well proportioned building, having a flat lead roof, and a ſpire on the ſouth-weſt corner. Its ſituation is beautiful and picturesque. The manſe was built in 1749. Beſides Miſs Scot, who is proprietor of a great part of this pariſh, there are four other heritors, none of whom, except a minor, reſide in the place. There are four or five perſons ſupported by the poor's funds. The contributions for the relief of the poor on the Lord's day are from 3 s. to 3 s. 6 d. weekly.

Miſcellaneous Obſervations.—In this pariſh are ſeveral good
whin-

whin ſtone quarries, which are eaſily got at, and good free
ſtone is to be had, at different places not far diſtant. Excellent cattle are bred in the neighbourhood, which, when
three or four years old, bring, in the market, from ſix
to ten guineas. This pariſh derives conſiderable advantage
from its ſituation, being about four computed miles from the
Frith of Tay, and nearly the ſame diſtance from St Andrews,
to both which the farmers ſend a great deal of grain. Coal
is the fuel generally uſed here, and coſts 2 s. 8 d. at the pit,
for the double horſe cart. The ploughs formerly uſed here,
were drawn by four oxen and two horſes; now they are
made much lighter, and drawn by two horſes only. There
is nothing peculiar either in the ſtrength, ſize, or ſtature of
the inhabitants, who in general live eaſy, and are diſpoſed to
be induſtrious. They are a plain and frugal people, and enjoy, in a reaſonable degree, the comforts and advantages of
ſociety. There is a good bridge here over the Eden, conſiſting of three arches, ſaid to have been built by Archbiſhop
Spottiſwood. The roads in this neighbourhood are as yet in
bad repair. The ſtatute work is commuted. Turnpike roads
are juſt beginning to be made. Some of the beſt land in
this pariſh has been lately let at about 40 s. the acre; other
farms rent from 15 s. to 20 s. The pariſh in general is un-
incloſed. There is hardly any alteration in this place more
remarkable, than the change in the people's dreſs, which,
within theſe 20 years, has become much gayer than formerly.

PARISH of DALGETY,

(Presbytery of Dunfermline, Synod of Fife, County of Fife.)

By the Rev. Mr Peter Primrose.

Situation and Extent.

THE pariſh of Dalgety is ſituated in the county of Fife, and in the preſbytery of Dunfermline. It is bounded by the pariſh of Aberdour on the Eaſt and North, by Inverkeithing on the Weſt, and by a ſmall part of the pariſh of Dunfermline on the North Weſt: On the South, it is bounded by the Frith of Forth, along which it extends in a ſtraight line about three miles; but as the coaſt in this place is interſected by many bays, its circuitous extent is conſiderably more. It is of an irregular form, but approaches neareſt to the triangular, being about four miles long from South to North, but its breadth gradually diminiſhes towards the North, and in ſome places it ſcarcely exceeds half-a-mile.

Soil, Surface, and Produce.—The ſoil is various. In ſome places it conſiſts of a light loam, and is dry; but the greater

part

part of the parish confifts of a deep ftrong loam, mixed with clay, naturally wet and ftiff, but productive in general of fertile crops. The ground, in moft places, rifes confiderably above the level of the coaft ; but there are few hills in the parish, and thefe are neither high, nor much covered with rocks. The furface in fome places is covered with heath, and a few little hills with furze : there are alfo fome fmall moffes and fwampy ground ; but the fpace which thefe occupy is of fo little extent, that there is not above a fixth part of the parish which is not arable. The principal crops raifed in the parish are wheat, barley, oats, peafe, and beans. Potatoes too are cultivated in confiderable quantities, and, in fome places, partly ufed for feeding cattle. Turnips are alfo raifed for this purpofe, and grow to a confiderable fize ; but, on account of the wetnefs of the furface, and the injury which the land might fuftain in winter, by being cut with horfes and carts when they are carried off, they are not generally ufed. Tares are fometimes fown, and produce abundant crops : Flax is feldom raifed but for private ufe. A great part of the parish confifts of grafs grounds, which have been laid down in good order, and, when let to graziers, yield confiderable rents. From fome inclofures, a proprietor has been known to draw 2l. 5s. per acre ; but the average rent of the land in grafs may be from 1l. 5s. to 1l. 10s. annually, per acre. A confiderable number of black-cattle, and about 900 fheep, are ufually grazed in the parish.

Prices of Grain and Provifions.—The price of wheat and barley is frequently regulated by the fiars of Mid Lothian. Some farmers get the higheft fiars for their grain, and others in the Northern part of the parish, where the land is ufually of an inferior quality, fell fomewhat lower. Few oats are fold in the parish, and the price of oat meal is generally the

fame

fame with that of the Edinburgh market. Though the number of inhabitants is not large in proportion to the extent of the pariſh, yet, on account of the great quantity of land in graſs, beſides what is allotted to the production of other crops, the oats raiſed in the pariſh are far from being ſufficient to ſupply the conſumption of meal. The average price of beef, mutton, and veal, is 4d. the pound, Dutch weight. The price of a hen is from 1s. to 1s. 3d. and chickens are ſold from 8d. to 10d. the pair. Butter is uſually at 9d. the pound Tron weight. Cheeſe varies according to its quality ; but the ordinary kind is 3d. the pound. Eggs are ſold at 4d. and in the ſeaſon of ſcarcity, at 6d. the dozen. During theſe two laſt winters, herrings have been caught in great plenty upon this coaſt, and the fiſhermen are encouraged to bring very conſiderable quantities of them to St David's, a harbour in the pariſh, both for the purpoſe of curing, and of ſupplying the people in the neighbourhood. They prove a very beneficial article of food to this part of the country, and are ſold at an eaſy rate, being frequently at 6d. the hundred of ſix ſcore. It is thought by many, that ſhoals of herrings have, for a long time paſt, come into this Frith in winter, without being generally diſcovered or looked after ; whether they were in ſuch great quantities as they have been theſe two years, it is impoſſible to aſcertain : but a fiſherman in the neighbourhood, has, for many years, caught ſome during the ſpring ſeaſon, in a net little accommodated for the purpoſe, from the wideneſs of its interſtices, and which he had ſpread out near the coaſt, where there were runs of freſh water, in order to catch ſalmon trouts. It is therefore much to be wiſhed, that fiſhermen would be diligent in ſearching the Frith occaſionally every winter, to diſcover if there are any herrings in it, and upon what part of the coaſt they principally lie, that they may loſe no opportunity of being
ing

ing employed in a fifhery at once fo profitable to themfelves, and fo beneficial to the community. Perhaps the offer of a ftanding premium or bounty to the crews of the firft boats, who fhall, after a particular feafon every year, carry a certain quantity caught in the Frith to the Edinburgh market, might prove an ufeful incentive to their diligence in this refpect.

Number of Proprietors, Tenants, Amount of Rent, &c—There are three proprietors who poffefs all the land in the parifh, and have houfes in it, where fome of them ufually, and others of them occafionally, refide, viz. the Earl of Moray at Donibriftle, Sir John Henderfon at Fordel, and Dr Robert Moubray at Cockairny. The two firft of thefe retain in their own hands a confiderable part of their eftates in the parifh, and they have of late highly improved their grounds, and adorned them with thriving plantations. The farm Cockairny is the largeft that is let in the parifh; and there are eleven others of fmaller extent. The are about 190 inhabited houfes in the parifh, of which only 12 are feus, the reft belonging to the proprietors; and by far the greateft number to Sir John Henderfon, for the accommodation of the people employed in working his coal. As a great part of the land in the parifh is not at prefent let, the real rent cannot be afcertained; but its annual value, it is fuppofed, would amount to 2,000l. Streling, or upwards. The valued rent, as ftated in the cefs-roll, amounts, according to the old valuation, to 5394l. Scots.

Population.—In 1755 the numbers were rated at 761. By an enumeration lately made, there were 869 perfons in this parifh, of whom there were

Under

Under	10	years of age	202
Between	10	and 20	163
Above	20	unmarried	180
Married perfons			276
Widowers or widows			48
			869
	Number of fouls in 1755		761
	Increafe		108

There are no particular inftances of longevity in the parifh at prefent. A few of the oldeft inhabitants may be about 80 years of age, and fome have lately died, who were fuppofed to be upwards of 90. In the year 1770, James Spital Efq; of Leuchart died in this parifh, reported by fome to have arrived at the age of 102 : he had been in the Scotch Parliament; and, for a confiderable time before his death, was fuppofed to be the only furviving member.

Climate and Diseases.—In the lower part of the parifh, which is upon the coaft, it is confiderably warmer and milder than in the upper, and the difference is very perceptible when the wind blows from any northern direction ; but during the Eafterly winds, which particularly prevail in the fpring feafon, it is fharp and cold, almoft over the whole parifh. The air however is generally dry, and, during the continuance of the Eaft wind, is ufually more free from fogs or damp than the fhore on the oppofite fide. There are no difeafes that can be faid to be peculiar to the inhabitants, or that prevail here more than in the neighbouring parifhes. I have obferved indeed a few more inftances of rheumatifm, and other complaints arifing from cold, among the colliers, than among the other parifhioncrs, but thefe are to be attributed, not fo much to the climate, as to the damp fituations in which they have fome times to work. An epidemical diftemper

temper, which made its firſt appearance in the village of A-
berdour in ſummer 1790, and created no ſmall alarm, got into this pariſh in the autumn, and two or three people died
of it ; but as the weather turned colder, it became leſs fatal
and infectious, and in the winter it altogether abated. The
ſmall-pox ſometimes makes great ravages ; and it is to be lamented, that the prejudices againſt inoculation are ſo ſtrong
among the generality of people in this part of the country,
that no perſuaſion can remove them ; nor can the evident inſtances of its ſalutary effects, often exhibited by the medical
gentlemen in this quarter, reconcile them to the practice, e-
ven when the diſeaſe is gathering ground, and proving very
fatal in the natural way.

Language and Etmology of Names.—The language commonly ſpoken in the pariſh is the Old Scotch dialect, and
there ſeem to be no peculiar words or phraſes which are not
in general uſe throughout moſt parts of the kingdom. The
words are pronounced with a broad accent ; and I have often
heard in this part of the country a ſound given to the diphthong oi, which is not, I believe, ſo uſual in other places : it
is frequently pronounced as if it conſiſted of the letters ou,
as for *boul* boil, *pount* for point, *vouce* for voice, &c. Many
of the names of places are derived from the Engliſh, and are
expreſſive of their particular or relative ſituations, as Hilland,
Seafield, Bankhead, Broomſide, Boghead, Croſsgate, &c. O-
thers are probably derived from the Gaelic, and denote greater antiquity in regard to their names, as Donibriſtle, Fordel,
Cockairny, Lethem, &c.

Character of the People.—The people are in general ſober
and induſtrious ; and, with a few exceptions, regular in attending, and paying reſpect to the public inſtitutions of religion.

ligion. Though, in regard to the doctrines of Chriſtianity,
many of them, as in other places, are yet perhaps too fond
of hearing ſpeculative propoſitions, and abſtract reaſoning ;
they alſo liſten with attention to diſcourſes which repreſent
religion as a moral ſcience, whoſe doctrines and precepts are
all calculated for the improvement of the character. It is
pleaſing to obſerve that the colliers, who compoſe a conſiderable part of the inhabitants of the pariſh, and who, in former times, were leſs enlightened and civilized, have, for a long
while, been making progreſs in religious knowledge and moral improvement ; and ſo attentive are they to give education
to their children, a duty formerly among this claſs of people
too much neglected, that for many years they have mantain-
ed a teacher by ſubſcription, as they are at a great diſtance
from the parochial ſchool.

Eccleſiaſtical State of the Pariſh.—There is no church but
the eſtabliſhed one in the pariſh. The Seceders who reſide
in it are moſtly Burghers, and attend a meeting houſe in Inverkeithing. The church is an old building, very much out
of repair, and not well adapted, either in reſpect of conſtruction or ſituation, as a place of worſhip for the pariſh ; the
ſituation is peculiarly inconvenient, being upon the coaſt, and
the moſt populous part of the pariſh almoſt at the other extremity. The manſe is about a quarter of a mile Weſt from
the church: it is alſo an old houſe, but there is a proſpect
that another one will ſoon be built. The following is a liſt
of the miniſters of this pariſh, as far back as the Seſſion records give information. Mr Andrew Donaldſon was ſettled
in 1644. Upon the introduction of Epiſcopacy into this
country, he was obliged to retire, and Mr John Corſar was
ſettled in 1669 ; Mr John Lumſdaine in 1680, and Mr George
Gray in 1687. After the Revolution, Mr Donaldſon, though

at

at an advanced àge, was called to refume his paftoral charge, and continued to officiate as minifter here till the time of his death. It is reported, that during the time he was laid afide, which might be about twenty years, he lived in a building on the Weft end of the church, which is now partly ufed as a feffion room, fupported by prefents from the parifhioners, and undifturbed by the above mentioned Epifcopal clergymen, which does credit to the fteady attachment of the former, and to the liberality and forbearing fpirit of the latter, in thofe times of intolerance and perfecution. Mr Archibald Campbell was fettled in 1696; Mr William Henderfon in 1717; Mr James Bathgate in 1738; Mr John Hoyes in 1778; and, upon his tranflation to another parifh, the prefent incumbent was fettled in 1787. The ftipend, by a decreet granted in the year 1650, confifted of 67 bolls, 2 firlots, 3 pecks, and 1 lippie of grain, and 37l. 6s. 5 $\frac{4}{12}$ d. Sterling. By an augmentation lately obtained, the ftipend is now raifed to 115 bolls, 2 firlots, 3 pecks, and 1 lippie of grain, and 42l. 6s. 5 $\frac{4}{12}$ d. Sterling. The glebe confifts of about 12 acres. The Earl of Moray is patron. There are two fchools in the parifh, one eftablifhed and provided with a falary, the other, as formerly obferved, maintained by fubfcription. With refpect to the parochial fchool, the falary, as in moft other places, is too fmall, being fomewhat below 7l. There is indeed a profpect of its being a little increafed here, from a voluntary offer lately made; but there is much need of a general increafe, not only in humanity, and it may be faid juftice to fuch as are engaged in the practice of teaching, but for the fake of thofe who are to be benefited by their inftructions. It muft be admitted, that the defire of acquiring in independence and fame operates chiefly on the minds of men in regard to the choice of their purfuits in life; and in the improved and improving ftate of things in this country, where

where ſo many paths lie open to theſe by following the various arts, it is eaſy to foreſee, that, while the proviſion allotted to ſuch an uſeful claſs of men as ſchool-maſters, is in general ſo ſmall, and inadequate to the purpoſes of a decent maintainance, few perſons of liberal education, and poſſeſſed of that ſpirit which a mind enlarged with knowledge has a tendency to inſpire, will turn their views to a profeſſion that may reduce them to ſtraits, and of courſe ſink them into contempt. The difficulty of obtaining proper teachers in country ſchools begins already to be felt ; and it is much to be feared that learning will ſoon come to decline, if encouragement be not given to fit perſons to diffuſe and promote its growth. Many who at preſent ſubmit to this laborious taſk, cannot earn more than a daily labourer ; and muſt not the riſing generation and poſterity ſuffer in an education conducted by thoſe, who may hereafter turn their thoughts to ſuch an ungainful profeſſion ? Ignorance, among the bulk of the people, would certainly be attended with the moſt pernicious effects, and it is to be hoped that all who are intereſted in the honour and welfare of their country, will have diſcernment to foreſee, and patriotiſm to guard againſt, ſuch an evil before it comes to any alarming height : and what can contribute more ſucceſsfully to this beneficial purpoſe, than to encourage the diffuſion of knowledge by competent rewards ?

State of the Poor.—There have been uſually, of late, 10 or 12 perſons upon the poors roll, who receive aid from the weekly collections, and from the intereſt of 130l. ariſing from legacies appropriated for their ſupport. In the year 1783, the heritors and ſeſſion bought 60 bolls of oatmeal, part of which was given to families in indigent circumſtances, and the reſt fold to others that were leſs needy, at reduced

duced prices, which contributed much to the relief of the parifh, during the fcarcity which then prevailed.

Mifcellaneous Ofervations.—The parifh, as was before obferved, extends along the Forth about three miles; and the banks are in many places fo beautifully fkirted with trees, and diverfified with fuch a variety of profpects, both of nature and art, as prefent many fcenes truly picturefque and fublime. There is alfo a fmall loch at Otterfton, about a mile from the coaft, which for its fituation is univerfally admired; on its banks ftand three gentlemen's houfes, two of which are ftill inhabited; and it is fo furrounded with rifing ground and trees, as to furnifh a pleafing miniature fcene. There are few antiquities in the parifh, and concerning thofe which are, fuch as the remains of what is fuppofed to have been a camp, a Druidical temple, and one of thofe marks commonly called a *Standing Stone,* there is no confiftent tradition, nor certain account. The houfe of Donibriftle was formerly the refidence of the Abbot of St Combe, but it has fince been greatly enlarged and improved. Oppofite to the eaftern extremity of the parifh, and within a mile of the fhore, is the ifland of St Combe, the defcription of which, and of the monaftery upon it, have been given in the Statiftical Accouut of the parifh of Aberdour. The Earl of Dunfermline's feat formerly ftood at a little diftance from the church of Dalgety, but little of it now remains. The church itfelf is a very ancient building. The exact period of its erection cannot be afcertained; but there are documents which fhow that a grant of the ground on which it ftands, was made to the Abbot of St Combe, as far back as the 14th century. Additions however have been made to it, which bear the marks of a later date.

Trade.

Trade.—There is no particular branch of trade in the parish, except what arises from the coal and salt works, carried on to a considerable extent on the property of Sir John Henderson. The various branches of these works afford maintenance to several hundred people of one description or other. The greatest part of the coal and salt is exported from St Davids, a spacious harbour situated at the Western extremity of the parish in Inverkeithing bay, where vessels of any burthen, not exceeding 500 or 600 tons, can load in safety. The distance from the pits to the shore is near 4 miles, along which the coals are carried in waggons that contain 48 cwt. It is well ascertained, that this coal has been known and wrought for upwards of 200 years, and a considerable field of it still remains. The surrounding district, lying in the parishes of Dunfermline and Aberdour, contains also many seams of coal of an excellent quality, sufficient it is thought, to supply the usual demand for centuries to come.

PARISH OF DENINO.

(County and Synod of Fife—Presbytery of St. Andrews.)

By Mr. WILLIAM WEST, *Session Clerk and Schoolmaster.*

Origin of the Name.

SOME persons, little less fanciful, perhaps, than intelligent, think that Denino derives its origin from the Gaelic word *Dunynach*, whose first constituent signifies *a hill*, and the two last *young women*. This feminine original seems, in their judgments, to be deducible from the apparent similitude of the Gaelic word to the name *Denino*. They infer, therefore, that *Denino* and the *Hill of Virgins* are terms perfectly equivalent. But times, and manners too, are doubtless much changed since the primary imposition of this so very pure and endearing title of our parish. Unfortunately, there is not the least circumstance, either in tradition or record, tending to establish the authenticity of this derivation. Indeed no circumstance appears so decisive of the matter as the local situation of Denino. The simple consideration of its standing in the immediate vicinity of a large and deep *den*, where, in right opposition to it,

it, two huge rocks feem to threaten an embrace over the per-
ennial ftream below, appears to have naturally fuggefted the
name, *Denino;* or, in other words, the *Village on the Den.*
And, when it is further known, that, unlefs in cafes of inaccuracy, or of inadvertency, the ancient and modern ortho-
graphies of Denino are uniformly the fame, the latter opinion, with regard to its original, muft appear the more cre-
dible. The firft fyllable of the word being attended with no
difficulty, by only admitting a common tranfpofition, as to
the two remaining ones, *Denino* and the Village ON THE DEN,
will appear plainly fynonymous.

Situation and Extent.—The parifh lies among the eaftern
diftricts of the county of Fife, on the road between St. Andrews and Anftruther. The extent of Denino is uncommonly
circumfcribed, being fcarcely 3 miles in length, and little more
than half as much in breadth.

Figure, Surface, Rivulets and Fiſh.—The form of the parifh
is pretty regular; diftinguifhed by no interfections from other
parifhes ; to a good degree paralellogramical ; with a large
extent of its centre furrounded by circularly rifing ground,
which, being generally but barren, produces a fingular conca-
vity of very confiderable fertility. It is beautifully interfperfed with a variety of fmall rivers, abounding with trout
of various fpecies and of moderate fize, but of fuperior flavour. The wild and protuberant banks of thefe rivulets, if
fuitably decorated with thofe diverfities of plantation, with
which, to the honour, and, eventually, to the emolument of
their proprietors, they now begin to be occupied, muft prefent fcenes highly picturefque and gratifying.

Soil

Soil, &c.————This pariſh, though ſurrounded on every
hand, almoſt, by extenſive moor, deſtitute nearly of what
might, at a very trifling expence, compared with future returns, contribute to general gratification and indulgence, in
addition to the more intimate advantage and pleaſure of individuals, is far from being barren. Though, from the ſmallneſs of the extent, no perceptible variation of air, or of climate, can be naturally expected ; yet this is not the caſe reſpecting its ſoil, which is confiderably diverſified. Some of the
ground confiſts of a black and light, but tolerably fertile loam,
reſting upon a gravelly bottom ; while a large proportion of
it diſplays a ſoil of a deep and ſtiff clay, with a bed of white
and light ſand. The moſt juſt idea of it, however, will be
had from the information, that the ſoil, in general, is, in a
great meaſure, wet and ſpungy ; in moſt of the farms of the
pariſh, frequently broken by large ſwamps and fens ; and,
though pretty well adapted for producing corn, is principally
remarkable for crops of artificial graſs and natural paſturage.
Some of the proprietors, therefore, availing themſelves of this
obvious property of their eſtates in this diſtrict, have, with
much ſucceſs, converted them into thoſe ſpecies of farms, for
which their lands are thus ſo very well calculated.

Climate and Diſeaſes.—Denino, ſheltered from no quarter
by any confiderable planting or eminences, except by ſome
riſing ground towards the S. W., is often expoſed to great
winds from the ſea, which, blowing with great force and
ſharpneſs, concur with the natural coldneſs of the ſoil, in ren-
dering the frequent humidity and bleakneſs of the climate,
the more ſenſibly felt. The air and climate are, however, of
ſuch a nature and temperature, as to occaſion but few interruptions in the health and native gaiety of the people, the
rheumatiſm and hyſteric complaints being the chief diſorders
which

which occur. The inhabitants, though commonly healthy, and many of them long-lived, furnish no inftances of remarkable longevity.

Minerals and Mineral Waters.—Coal feems, from the vaft number of old pits in various places of the parifh, to have, fome time ago, been a very plentiful article here. There is ftill, it is faid, plenty of it in feveral eftates of this diftrict ; but it is uncertain when any of its proprietors will open thefe mines, or rather, whether their future gains would compenfate the expenditure neceffary for that purpofe. Free-ftone is alfo found in much abundance ; but, though of an eafy accefs, and of a tolerable good quality, it is feldom called for beyond the limits of the parifh. The erection and reparation of enclofures, particularly on Sir William Erfkine's eftate of Denino, and the building of his tenants fubftantial premifes, are the chief ufes to which it has hitherto been, and is ftill occafionally applied. There is an uncommon variety of places in the parifh, where ochre is found, particularly at a number of chalybeate fprings. Between 30 and 40 years ago, thefe were much reforted to, for relief in diforders, chiefly fcorbutic ; but of late they have loft much of their former celebrity, though, to all appearance, very undefervedly.

Curiofities.—Towards the S. W. end of the parifh of Denino, there is a moft remarkable fall of water, of probably near 20 feet, from the fhelve of the rock to the common furface of the very deep pond, into which, among a vaft number of the finny race, (and which, according to the conjectures of the inhabitants, forms the boundary of their journeying upwards,) it pours almoft perpendicularly. This fall, from fome ludicrous, but perhaps natural, analogies, has, for time immemorial,

memorial, been conſtantly known by a very mark'd appellation. To the pond below there is no acceſs, but up either ſide of the headlong current, overhung by rocks, ſome of them imminent and dreadful ; while the immediate entrance to the pond is narrowed, by the ſeemingly artificial and mutual projection of two rocks, erected in the form of poſts, deſtined for doors and hinges! The only artificial curioſity, is a ſubterraneous canal, of nearly 30 yards in length, of between 4 and 5 feet of an average breadth and height, and dug from the one end to the other, under a ſolid and continued rock of freeſtone, about 20 yards from the ſurface of a large piece of arable ground, actually peninſular. This very ingenious conduit, which forms the peculiar haunt of a few otters, was, about 60 years ago, effectuated by one of the then reſiding heritors, with an intention of conducting, through below the foundations of this iſthmus, an increaſe of water to his mill, in its remote vicinity. The expence, attending the atchievement of ſuch an aſtoniſhing piece of work, was no leſs than *three pounds Sterling*, and a *boll of meal!* and for the damage occaſioned by the *intake*, as it is ironically called, there is ſtill an yearly allowance of 2s. and 3 firlots of oats, made by the tenant of the above mill, to a tenant of another, through whoſe farm the water runs, before its diſappearance in the mouth of its inviſible receiver. There are two or three echoes to be met with in the pariſh, which merit no deſcription.

Population.—The pariſh records of Denino extend back only to a little before the middle of laſt century ; and it is ſomething curious to obſerve, that the ſtate of population was then very little above what it is at preſent. From 1771 till towards 1778, the population of the diſtrict of Denino appears gradually to have decreaſed, till it aſſumed its preſent ſeemingly

ingly fettled ftate *. The total amount of fouls, with various other circumftances relating to the ftate of the parifh, according to a very recent and exact calculation, are as under :

STATISTICAL TABLE of the Parifh of DENINO.

Length in Englifh miles,	-	3	Aver. ditto, from 1742 to 1752,	23
Breadth, not quite	-	2	—— ditto, from 1761 to 1771,	16
Population in 1755,	-	598	—— marriages, from do. to do.	3
———— anno 1793,	-	383	—— deaths, - ————————	† 7
		——	—— births from 1780 to 1790,	10
Decreafe,	-	215	—— marriages, from do. to do.	‡ 2
Aver. births, from 1643 to 1653,	8		—— deaths, from do. to do. -	6

Inhabitants

* For fome time preceding the middle of the prefent century, the principal part, if not the whole, of the parifh hufbandry was performed by cottagers; who enjoyed, as a material perquifite of their fervices, a fmall portion of land.— The parifh alfo abounded with *pendiclers*, or inferior tenants. Thefe, therefore and the cottagers, together with a confiderable number of families employed in the coal mines, but moft of all, the divifion of farms, and employing of hired fervants in their cultivation, contributed much to the multiplication of the inhabitants; and hence it is eafy to perceive the caufes of fo remarkable a depopulation; which is a natural confequence of the union of farms. More than 30 inhabited houfes exifted in the parifh, about half a century ago, of which fcarcely a fingle veftige now remains. It may be remarked farther, that the converfion of a very large extent of the diftrict into grafs farms, has operated very materially to the decreafe of the people, by employing a much fmaller number of fervants of either fex.

† This is the average, after making a proportional deduction, for the many burials from other parifhes, that take place here, on account, it is faid, of the fuperiority of our burial-ground. In the above averages, the baptifms, marriages, and burials of the inhabitants of Kings Muir are included; it being found impoffible, from the connection they neceffarily had with Denino, to make any exact difcrimination from the records.

‡ The number of births, marriages, and deaths, for 10 years immediately preceding 1790, are as follows :

Years

Inhabitants in Denino, - 230

—————— Kings Muir, - 153

Number of males in Denino, - 107

———— females, - 123

———— persons under 10 years of age - 65

———— between 10 and 20, 57

———— —— 20 and 50, 73

———— —— 50 and 70, 31

———— —— 70 and 100, 4

———— houses inhabited, about - 38

Aver. of persons in each, nearly 6

Number of houses uninhabited, 6

———— new houses lately built, - 1

———— married persons, - 88

———— children, at an average, from each marriage, - 4

———— married women above 45, - 4

Number of widows, 6

———— members of the Established Church, - 151

———— Burgher Seceders, 11

———— Relief ditto, - 3

———— persons born out of the parish, - 144

———— proprietors, - 5

———— feuers, - 4

———— clergymen, - 1

———— schoolmasters, - 1

———— farmers, at 200l. per annum, - 1

———— do. at 50l. and upwards, - 6

———— do. between 20l. and 50l., - 5

———— shopkeepers, - 2

———— innkeepers, - 1

———— smiths, - 1

———— carpenters, - 2

Number

Year.	BIRTHS.	MARRIAGES	DEATHS.
1780	11	3	7
1781	10	4	4
1782	18	2	7
1783	9	2	7
1784	12	1	11
1785	8	0	3
1786	10	3	5
1787	10	1	6
1788	14	1	2
1789	4	1	5
Total within 10 years, -	106	18	57
Average, nearly, -	11	2	6

Number of weavers,	-	4
————— tailors*,	-	3
————— millers,	- -	4
————— male fervants,	-	24
————— female ditto,	-	11
————— flax-dreffers,	-	1
————— apprentices,	-	2
————— day-labourers,	-	2
————— poor,	- -	3
Capital of their funds,	-	120l.
Annual income,	- -	12l.

Number of young perfons taught		
English, writing, &c.		40
————— acres, in English mea-		
fure,	-	2280
————— carts,	- -	24
————— ploughs,	-	20
Valued rent, in Scotch		
money,	-	2324l. 6s. 8d.
Real rent, anno 1793,		
in Sterling,	-	1157l. os. od:

Proprietors, Rents, and Improvements.—None of the proprietors refide in the parifh. A few remains of the very ancient and venerable feats of their progenitors lie in it, in the
wildeft ftate of ravage and of Gothic defolation ; and which,
whether reftored according to their former conftitution, or
after a modern and more refined plan, muft, at any rate, afford but indifferent accommodation for their more illuftrious
fucceffors. There is a fmall farm in this parifh, of 17 acres,
belonging to the kirk-feffion of Ely, a confiderable village
about 5 miles S. of this ; and there are 4 feuers in it, whofe
feu-duty, to Mifs Scott of Scotftarvet, for about 12 acres
of pretty good ground, is 5l. 2s. 4¼d. Within lefs than 30
years, the landed property of the diftrict of Denino has undergone frequent changes, and has always been attended with
confiderable augmentations in the purchafe. The whole rental
of a confiderable eftate in it, little more than 20 years ago,
was only 196l. per annum, though now it draws no lefs than
500l.

---

* It is fomewhat remarkable, that there neither are, nor have been, for an
unknown time paft, any *fhoemakers* in the parifh of Denino, notwithftanding of
the inceffant demand for their fervices in every other place. To remedy as
much as poffible, however, this inconvenience, the parifhioners are far from being defpicable *menders* of fhoes. The circumftance of being, at the neareft, 3
miles diftant from any *makers*, has taught them this article of ingenuity.

500l. a year. The average price of the whole parish is nearly
10s. 6d. an acre ; good farms letting at about 15s. per acre,
at an average. The very best may be about 2l. ; the second
about 12s.; while the inferior kind is not worth more than
5s. an acre. Last year, a considerable estate here, though almost wholly uninclosed at the time, was sold for 5,000 guineas, which was no less than 35 years purchase. What has
chiefly contributed, to raise the price of land to such a degree,
is the now general practice of inclosing, which only commenced in this district about 20 years ago, but ever since has
made the most rapid advances. Most of the inclosures of the
parish consist of dry stone dikes, topped with a stony layer,
of stones placed upon their edges, and the whole cast with
lime. Inclosures, consisting of ditch and hedge, likewise go
fast forward, and are paving the way for an universal emulation on those grounds, which best agree with such kinds of
inclosures.—The valued and real rents of the whole district
are stated in the table. In calculating the latter, the feus are
not included.

Agriculture.—There is only a small proportion of the parish under grain; but that small part is well cultivated. During the short space of 20 years past, the state of our cultivation has undergone very considerable improvement; insomuch,
that the ground, which formerly was let for about 2s. 6d. an
acre, on an average, is now rented at near 14s. an acre ; and,
even at this rate, it is thought sufficiently cheap. There is
perhaps something in the management of the grass farms in
the parish worthy of remark : Of such small portions of them,
as are solely occupied by oats and barley, the species of grain
for which their soil is naturally adapted, the tenants are prohibited from taking any more than two crops running ; and
of these farms also, which are almost all arable, about a sixth
part

pàrt is annually under the above fpecies of crops ; the one half, or near it, is to be yearly fown down with clover and rye-grafs. This fingular rotation muft be uniformly and punctually obferved. There being fcarcely any cattle ufed in hufbandry here, and only 5 cottagers employed in it, who have portions of land for part of their labour, the hired fervant cultivates his fields with 2 middle fized horfes yoked in a plough, which is almoft uniformly of the English conftruction.

ANNUAL PRODUCE*.

Crops.	Num. of Acres un- der each.	Produc per Acre Bolls.	Price per Boll. l.　s.　d.	Total Produce. Bolls.	Total Value. l.　s.　d.
Oats,	3–9	5	0 12 0	1945	1167 0 0
Barley,	113	6	0 14 6	678	491 11 0
Peafe,	33	3	0 12 6	99	61 17 6
Wheat,	28	7	1 1 0	196	205 16 0
Potatoes,	9	27	0 5 0	243	60 15 0
Flax,	12	*St.* 15	0 10 0	*St.* 180	90 0 0
Turnips,	18	-	3 15 0	-	65 10 0
Sown Grafs, Hay, }	109	200	0 0 5 *per St.*	21,800	454 3 4
	711				2590 12 10
Straw, 2s. per boll of corn, }	-	-	-	*B.* 2918	291 16 0
Pafture, at 3l. per horfe, 2l. per cow, }	-	-	-	{ £273 £528	801 0 0
					3689 8 10

VALUE

* The above fketch of the annual produce of the parifh may be of fervice, in helping to form a conception of fimilar articles in thofe diftricts, from which no fpecimens of the kind may have been given in.

VALUE OF STOCK.

Number of draught horſes,	- 62,	valued at	L. 15 each, is	L. 930
———— ſaddle ditto,	٭ 3,	————	15 ————	45
———— young ditto,	- 26,	————	9 ————	234
———— beſt cattle,	- 92,	————	6 ————	552
———— inferior ditto	- 172,	————	4 ————	688
———— ſwine,	- 18,	————	1 10s.————	27

Total value of ſtock, - - - - L. 2476

Paſturage, Sheep, &c.—From a ſurvey of the above tables, it appears, that there are only about 711 acres of the pariſh of Denino under real crops. There are fully 180 acres of perfect moor in it, of no uſe, unleſs perhaps for planting, of which it is hitherto deſtitute. The pariſh is, however, adorned with nearly 60 acres of planting, conſiſting, in a great degree, of ſtripes, as they are called, and judiciouſly enough deſigned for cheriſhing the cold grounds, where they flouriſh in beautiful and plentiful variety. There are, in the laſt place, generally about 40 acres of fallow in the pariſh ; ſo that, if from 2280 acres, which the whole diſtrict of Denino contains, we deduct 991, the number under corn, fallow, &c. &c. there will appear a balance of 1289 acres of natural and artificial paſturage ; upon the laſt diviſion of which, great numbers of excellent cattle are fed, during the ſummer, by the graziers, and either occaſionally diſpoſed of, to the itinerant merchant, or driven to the country markets. The number of ſheep in the pariſh does not exceed 20 ; they are kept and fed by ſome of the farmers, for their own uſe only, during the ſummer.

Prices of Labour and Proviſions.—From a view of the table of the annual produce, it appears, that the pariſh muſt do conſiderably more than maintain its inhabitants. The average prices of the ſeveral ſpecies of grain, therein ſpecified, are

are ſtated as regulated by the county fiars ; or rather, by the general ſtate of the market.—The yearly wages of a labouring man-ſervant, are 7l. ; and thoſe of a woman, 3l. The day-labourer has 1s. a day, without meat ; 2s. 2d. per acre, for hay cutting; and for making ditto, or for turnip hoeing, either by males or females, 6d., and ſometimes 7d. per day. The price of a gooſe here is commonly 3s. ; a hen, 1s.; and eggs, 3½d. a dozen ; butter ſells at 8d., and cheeſe from 3d. to 6d. per pound ; pigeons, 3d. a pair ; chickens at 4d. each; rabbits, (animals very common in the pariſh of Denino), at 6d. a pair, without the ſkin ; and butcher meat, univerſally, at 4d. per pound.

Eccleſiaſtical State.—The manſe, almoſt thrown down from the foundation, and rebuilt, on a durable conſtruction, about the year 1741, is a tolerably decent houſe, 2 ſtories high, and contains 6 moderately good rooms, with a kitchen, and ſome other apartments. Since its laſt erection, it has undergone very many repairs. The glebe contains little more than 4½ acres of Engliſh meaſure, worth about 1l. 10s. per acre, if duly cultivated. The ſtipend conſiſts of 24l. in money, with 5 chalders, or 80 bolls of victual ; the one half meal, and the other bear. The whole annual income, excluſive of the manſe, and a tolerably good garden, is about 90l. Sterling. The church is one of the ſmalleſt of country churches, perhaps, with an aile, and a ſmall porch by one of its front doors. It is uncertain when it was built; but *ſome* perſons are perfectly ſure of its having been very lately and very materially repaired. Mr. JAMES BROWN, ordained 13th May 1790, is the preſent miniſter of Denino.

School.—The ſchool-houſe is a very ſhort, low, thatched houſe, and, though not very old, a very crazy edifice. The ſchool,

ſchool, very fortunately for the health of the teacher, as well
as of thoſe who are taught, is large, and capable of containing
a few more ſcholars, beſides the parochial ones; a great number of whom commonly attend it. Beſides a very good garden, of 8 by 12 paces, there is a ſalary of 100 merks
(5l. 11s. 0¼d. Sterling), and the ſeſſion-clerk's fees, which
amount to 2l. 15s. 8d.; with an occaſional gratuity of 5s.
Sterling, at the diſpenſation of the Lord's Supper, for extraordinary ſinging. The fees for teaching are, for Engliſh, 1s. 3d.;
for reading and writing, 1s. 6d.; for arithmetic, 2s.; and for
Latin, 2s. 6d. Other branches of education are ſeldom deſired; and even the laſt not very frequently. Moſt of the
people have a laudable ambition to have their children educated; and the payment of the quarter fees is ſcarcely ever
grudged, though often paid with a good degree of tardineſs,
ariſing from the actual penury of ſome of the parents. The
dues on a proclamation of marriage, are 2s. 6d. when regular, one third whereof goes to the beadle; and, when irregular, or performed in ſhorter time than the church ſtandards
dictate, an additional gratuity is commonly given by the
employers. The dues on each baptiſm are 1s., of which the
beadle gets 3½d.; and thoſe on certificates are 6d. each, of
which the beadle has no ſhare. The ſeſſion-clerk has alſo
4d. each for regiſtrating burials. His annual income, altogether, does not exceed 22l., at an average, one year with another. Such, however, is the *liberal* proviſion allotted for the
far greater part of thoſe members of ſociety, from whoſe ſervices muſt ever, fundamentally, proceed whatever is elegant
and reſpectable in the lives and manners of their fellow
citizens.

Poor.—The large contributions formerly made for the poor
here, and the ſmall diſburſements, have raiſed the preſent ca-

pital

pital of their funds to 120l.; which is lodged partly in the hands of a landed proprietor, partly in fome of the Banks, and draws intereſt, commonly at 4¼ per cent. per annum. This, with the weekly collections at church, which are about 2s. each Sabbath, at an average, and the dues ariſing from the two palls, (the one of which produces 5s. and the other 1s. 6d. from the funerals at which they are uſed), may raiſe the annual income of the poor to about 12l. Each of the poor has nearly 7½d. every week; but their penſions are proportioned, notwithſtanding, to their occaſional neceſſities. What of their yearly income remains thus unexhauſted, is expended in the payment of ſalaries; fuch as, the ſeſſion-clerk's, the beadle's, the preſbytery clerk's, &c. &c.; with various repairs about the church, the ſchool, and ſchool-houſe; and even about the public bridges of the pariſh. Theſe repairs, however, devolve upon the kirk-ſeſſion, who defray theſe expences only in fuch caſes as they judge unworthy of an application to the heritors of the pariſh. But, at any rate, thoſe who have their ſalaries as above, paid from the poor's funds, are perhaps equally neceſſitous with thoſe for whom they were originally deſtined. Upwards of 15l. was expended lately in the purchaſe of a new pall, without touching the poor's capital.

Antiquities, &c.—It is affirmed, that there are fome relics of antiquity in the pariſh, but they happen to exiſt more in the imaginations of the credulous antiquary, aided by ſuperſtitious report, than otherwiſe. There are only two even of theſe: the one is a Druidical temple, which is faid to have ſtood in the vicinity of a place called *Balkethly*; from which, (in the opinion that *Baal*, the Sidonian deity, and the God of *Jezebel*, was worſhippd there), it is aſſerted to have derived its name. Of this Druidical temple not the moſt ſmalleſt veſtige

veſtige can now be ſeen.——The other ſuppoſed antiquity
is a Roman camp ; which is ſaid to give name to a place near
it, called *Cheſtus*.   There are, it is true, ſome very viſible
marks of this ancient entrenchment ; but inſtead of being
what it is vulgarly believed to be, it appears, on a proper
view of circumſtances, to be in reality no more than a homely drain from a number of old coal-pits !   The ſeeming con-
formity of *Cheſtus* to certain Engliſh names, ſuch as, *Cheſter*,
Colcheſter, *&c.* lays a foundation for the ingenious conjectures
of ſeveral learned antiquaries.   Many of the names of places,
however, in the pariſh of Denino, are evidently of Celtic derivation ; ſuch as, *Bely*, *Kinaldy*, *Stravithy*, *&c.*   Moſt of
them, however, are obviouſly of Engliſh origin, and ſignificant of their local ſituations ; as, *Bonnyfield*, *Primroſe*, *Four-
ſtone-fold*, and the like.

Diſadvantages.——The leading ſubject of complaint, with the
inferior claſſes of our pariſhioners, is the ſcarcity of coals,
(the only article of the pariſh fuel), even in the *land of coal.*
By the ſelfiſhneſs of individuals, the people here ſeem to be,
in a great meaſure, excluded from thoſe ineſtimable and neceſſary favours, ſo liberally poured around them, by the be-
nignity and wiſdom of the Almighty.   For, notwithſtanding
the great quantity of coals formerly raiſed in our immediate
neighbourhood, the ſpirit of monopoly has for many years
paſt deprived us of this bounty of Providence; and it is hard
to ſay how long the ſame ſpirit may continue to afflict the
poor of this pariſh ; the principal proprietor of the coal-mines
here having entered into an agreement with the proprietor of
an adjoining colliery, to keep his own coal-works ſhut till
thoſe of the other ſhall be completely exhauſted ; in return
for which the other has bound himſelf, and his heirs, &c. to
pay him an annuity of 20 l. a-year !   Thus the poor of this
pariſh,

parifh, as well as the adjacent country, are deprived of a bleffing evidently intended for them by Providence ; and obliged to purchafe fuel from a confiderable diftance, at a higher
price, and of a worfe quality. To this effential, and feem-
ingly irremediable grievance, may be added, *mill thirlages,*
which, however, are not fo much felt in this as in other
places.

KING'S MUIR.

Name, Privileges, &c. This is a very extenfive tract of
ground, containing more than 1000 acres. It is called *King's
Muir*, on account of its being, fome time after the reftoration of
Charles II. conferred by that Prince upon one Col. Borthwick,
who had attended him in his adventures and exile, previoufly to
his attainment of the throne, as a reward for his attachment
and fervices. This is the account given of its origin by Mr.
Hanno, the prefent proprietor. Moft of the ground of this
ancient royal donation is, as its name infinuates, extremely
wild in appearance ; though, upon the whole, much lefs un-
fertile than might be expected. The proprietor, however,
is of opinion, that, taking all of it together, it is not worth
more than 1s. 6d. an acre ; while others rate it much higher.
It is wholly exempt from affeffment ; and the circumftance of
its not yielding either minifter's ftipend or fchoolmafter's falary, feems, in the conjectures of many, to have claffed it
with no parifh whatever. Its inhabitants have, neverthelefs,
either from their vicinity to our church, or the popularity of
its minifters, always confidered themfelves as parifhioners of
Denino, in the moft decided preference to Crail ; in whofe
parifh they are afferted, by a few, to be legally included. As
the prefent laird of King's Muir has not his charter by him,
we

we ſhall leave the determination of this controverſy, to thoſe who may think it worth the inveſtigation. It may not be amiſs to obſerve, however, that although the people of King's Muir have, for time immemorial, connected themſelves with the diſtrict of Denino, *quoad ſacra* ; yet there is a little farm, ſituated between this pariſh and it, which pays ſtipend to the miniſter of Crail, as he himſelf ſays, though perfectly uncon‑ nected with King's Muir, and belonging to a different pro‑ prietor. The moſt fertile parts of King's Muir are parcelled out into ſmall farms, let by the lump, to perſons, moſt of whom are either tradeſmen, or work, during a great part of the year, by day-labour. The population of it is as un‑ der :

POPULATION TABLE OF KING's MUIR.

Males, above 10 years of age,	59	Families,	- -	25
Females, - - -	75	Widows, - - -		7
Children, under 10, -	19—153	Widower, - - -		1
Between 10 and 20, -	42	Natives, either of King's Muir,		
———20 and 50, - -	57	or Denino, - -		78
———50 and 70, -	30	Burgher Seceders, - -		4
———70 and 100, -	- 5—153			

Proprietor, Rent, Minerals, &c.—The eſtate of King's Muir is now entailed on the name of *Hanno*, the ſurname of its preſent laird, whoſe whole yearly rental amounts to 100l. There is nothing remarkable in the King's Muir, beſides its containing the coal-mine above mentioned, and one of the two mines that convey the water from the links, which was dug nearly 50 years ago, being more than 300 fathoms in length ; in moſt places 9 ditto from the ſurface of the earth ; originally 18 inches wide, and 3½ feet high. The coal here was hitherto wrought by a wind-mill, no veſtige of which remains ; but will in future be wrought by a different ele‑ ment;

ment, and by different machinery. The eſtate of King's Muir is wholly devoid of planting, and no leſs deſtitute of encloſures, or any kind of fence. This large piece of ground, apparently an *outcaſt* from all pariſhes, as its inhabitants are ſometimes humourouſly told, by thoſe of the adjacent diſtriəts, would, with that extenſive part of *this* pariſh, which went to complete the vicarage of Cameron, but which ought ſtill to pay ſome proportion to Denino, form a pariſh of a very re-ſpeətable extent.

General Charaəter.—Of the inhabitants of this pariſh it may juſtly be aſſerted, that induſtry and hoſpitality, ſincerity and an obliging behaviour, are their general charaəteriſtics. They are alſo noted for moderation and ſobriety, generoſity and candour. From theſe virtues there may be, however, as is but too natural, not a few deviations. The bulk of the people, though poor, are contented and reſigned. The mi-nority, whoſe circumſtances are more affluent, appear to in-dulge as much in the luxuries of the table, and of dreſs, as the ſuperiority of their fortunes can well countenance. The inferior claſſes ſeem to be uncommonly fond of perſonal de-coration ; and rather than (as they imagine) diſgrace the back, they will often ſtarve its ſupporter. This remark is, perhaps, not more applicable to the one ſex than to the other; or to this diſtriət more than to other pariſhes. Spiritous li-quors produce, at preſent, fewer unpleaſant ſcenes than ſome time ago. Notwithſtanding the general penury of the di-ſtriət, the inhabitants are proof againſt the ſordid invaſions of avarice. As a ſpecimen, both of the morals and natural tempers of ſome of the individuals in the pariſh, let the fol-lowing faət ſuffice : Two men in the pariſh of Denino have, for nearly 30 years, held a conſiderable farm and mill in con-junəion ; preſerving every article, regarding their external property,

property, in perfect community, their wives and private
property only excepted. The people in general are humane ;
and, as far as means will allow, more than ordinarily charitable to the poor.

Language.—Reſpecting this article there is nothing at all
ſtriking, except that the vulgar dialect is remarkably exempted from the corruptions that abound on the coaſt, as well as
from many of thoſe Scotticiſms, and uncouth phraſes, ſo peculiar to many other places, whoſe inhabitants lay claim to a
higher degree of refinement. This bit of *lingo-eminence* may
have ariſen from the vicinity of Denino, in common with
many other adjacent diſtricts, to *Alma Mater !* Agreeably
to the general practice of the county, the inhabitants here
diſplay a ſingular hollowneſs in the accentuation of their
words, with an unuſual prolongation of the final tone of
their ſentences ; all aided at leaſt by the antique manner of
enunciating ſome of the vowels and diphthongs,

PARISH of DUNBOG,

(COUNTY OF FIFE.)

By Dr GREENLAW, *Minifter of Criech.*

Name, Situation, Soil, &c.

THIS parifh lies low, between 2 hills, and has a pretty large bog or morafs, one mile long, and about half a mile broad, at the W. end of it, from which the name *Dunbog* has probably arifen. It is bounded by Monimail on the S. and E.; by Abdie on the W.; by Flifk on the N.; by Criech on the E.; and is fituated in the prefbytery of Cupar, and Synod of Fife. Its length is about 3 miles, breadth 2. The greateft part of the lands is arable, but much of them wettifh. They produce good barley.; great part is capable of bearing wheat; and the tenants are improving in their mode of culture. There is only 1 flock of fheep, of about 13 fcore, of a pretty large fize, brought hither from the fouthern parts of Scotland.

Population.

Population.—Souls, - - - 235
Males, - - - 115
Females, - - - 120
Aged below 10, - - 48
Between 10 and 20, - 56
20 and 50, - 100
50 and 70, - 26
70 and 100, - 5

Wages, Cottagers, &c.—A ploughman's uſual wages are from L. 4, 10 s. to L. 8, according to his character for care and ſkill; thoſe of women ſervants, L. 2, 10 s. or L. 3; a good wright or maſon's wages, in ſummer, are 1 s. 6 d. in winter, 1 s. 2 d.; a tailor's, 6 d. or 8 d. with victuals. The people are induſtrious, and there is only 1 ale-houſe. Cottagers generally hold the farmers ploughs, get livery meal, have an acre of land, a houſe, and ſmall garden, and furniſh 2 reapers in harveſt. There are ſeveral threſhing machines here; but they ſeem, as yet, to ſave only a *lot-man*, as he is called, who threſhes for ſo much the boll. Theſe machines are uſeful, when a merchant offers for barley or wheat, and who would not wait the ſlow progreſs of a lot-man; for the machines can threſh 40 bolls in a day.

Church, Stipend, School, Poor, &c.—The church and manſe are in pretty good order. The ſtipend is between L. 70 and L. 80, with 4 acres of a good glebe. The Crown is patron. There are 3 heritors, none of whom reſide. The ſchoolmaſter's ſalary is only about 100 merks. The poor are ſupplied by the weekly collections, and intereſt of poors money.

Remarks on the State of the Clergy and Schoolmaſters.—Unleſs a general augmentation of ſtipends becomes an object to
perſons

perfons of influence, the clergy of Scotland muſt degenerate. If they become objeĉts of compaſſion, their weight muſt be leſſened, and no reſpeĉtability of charaĉter will counterbalance that evil. Should the teachers of religion become meanly thought of, on account of their poverty, religion will ſuffer; and if good morals decline, induſtry, which requires regularity and ſobriety of conduĉt, muſt decline alſo. The very ſmall encouragement alſo given to ſchoolmaſters, is one of the greateſt evils; for it is not only an unſpeakable loſs to the poor men who teach, but to the riſing generation. There are not a few pariſhes in this neighbourhood, where the ſalary is only 100 merks. Some have L. 100 Scots. But what man fit to teach can live upon this? What knowledge can he communicate? A common tradeſman can live more at his eaſe. Were the encouragement increaſed, though but a little, it would do more good than can be expreſſed. Imperfeĉt teaching of youth is like bad plowing in ſpring, which muſt of neceſſity produce a bad crop in harveſt. The poorer ſort of people are left without a remedy, and muſt ſend their children to the pariſh ſchoolmaſters, ſuch as they are.

PARISH of DUNFERMLINE,

(County and Synod of Fife, Presbytery of Dunfermline,)

By the Rev. Mr Allan Maclean, *and the Rev. Mr* John Fernie.

Name, Extent, Situation, &c.

DUNFERMLINE is faid to derive its name from the Gaelic, and to fignify in that language " The hill of " the crooked pool or water *." According to this ety- mology, the name is fufficiently defcriptive of the prefent fituation of the town, which ftill, for the moft part, ftands on a hill, bounded on the weft by a winding rivulet, running

---

* Dunferlin, from *Dun*, a hill, *Fiar*, crooked. and *Lin*, a pool or water ; if we fuppofe the name to be Dunfermlin, the fignification will vary a little; *Dun*, a hill, and *Foirm*, a murmuring noife, *i. e.* " The hill of the noify pool or water.

ning through a deep and narrow glen *. The parish is extenfive ; of an irregular form ; at an average it may be
reckoned 8 miles in length from S. to N. and 5 in breadth
from E. to W. It is bounded by the parishes of Beath,
Dalgety, and Inverkeithing on the E.; of Carnock and
Torryburn on the W; of Cliesh and Saline on the N.; and
on the S. by the frith of Forth. The air in general is dry
and falubrious, but there is a very perceptible difference as
to climate in the parish, being much milder in the fouthern
part, which flopes gently to the fea, than towards the N.
where the ground continues to rife, and is more hilly and
expofed. The parish contains a variety of foils : In general towards the S. of the town, called the laigh land, the
foil is fertile, moftly in tillage, and in many places in a
ftate of high cultivation ; towards the N. the foil is greatly
inferior in quality, in many places covered with heath, and
containing moffes of confiderable extent, though many fpots
are well cultivated, yet the land in general is chiefly adapted to pafturage.

Borough, Profpeƈt, Conftitution, &c.—Dunfermline is a
Royal Borough, the feat of the Prefbytery, and one of the
moft confiderable manufaƈturing towns in Fife. It is 3 miles
from the fea, and about 190 feet above its level ; the great_
er part of the town is fituated on a hill or rifing ground,
having a pretty bold declivity towards the S. ; the ground,
however, foon flattens, fo that what is called the Nether
town

* The fituation muft have accorded ftill more exaƈtly with the name, if
we fuppofe, as feems highly probable, that Dunfermline owes its appellation to a little peninfulated hill fituated in the glen ; from this hill the
borough has borrowed its arms ; it is of fmall circumference, but of confiderable height, very rugged and fteep towards the N., and appears to
have been anciently a place of ftrength ; a tower built upon it was the
refidence of Malcolm Canmore.

town ſtands on a plain. The town is moſt pleaſantly ſituated, and the proſpeƈt it commands remarkably various,
beautiful, and extenſive. There is an excellent view of
Edinburgh, the Caſtle, Arthur-ſeat, and the elevated
grounds in the vicinity of the metropolis ; in clear weather
different ſpires of the city can be counted with the naked
eye ; immediately in view are the oppoſite and fertile banks
of the Forth, comprehending a part of Mid and Weſt Lothians, Binnylaw, the pleaſure-grounds northward of Hopetoun, and the borough of Queensferry. The frith is a moſt
pleaſant objeƈt, and in its courſe from near the North Ferry
up towards Culroſs, ſometimes concealed by an elevated
ſhore, but here and there breaking forth in varied openings,
greatly enlivens and diverſifies the beauty of the ſcene.
From the church-ſteeple there is a grandeur, a variety, and
extent of proſpeƈt, of which it is believed few towns in
Scotland can boaſt. Here is ſeen a part of 14 different
counties ; the moſt diſtant and remarkable places are Soutra-
hill in the ſhire of Berwick, Tintock in Lanark, Ben-
lomond in Dunbarton, Benlady in Perth, Lammermoor
in Haddington, Campſie and Logie-hills in Stirling, and
the Pentland-hills in Mid-Lothian ; Hopetoun-houſe, the
Caſtle of Blackneſs, Port of Borrowſtounneſs, the borough
of Culroſs, and the beautiful windings of the Forth from
Leith near to Stirling Caſtle. The borough, it appears,
held of the monaſtery for near two centuries. It became
Royal by a charter from James VI. dated 24th May 1588.
In this charter, called a charter of confirmation, the King
ratifies ſundry charters, donations, and indentures by John
and Robert, Abbots of Dunfermline ; and particularly, an
indenture made at Dunfermline, 10th Oƈtober 1395, between John, Abbot of the Monaſtery, and the Eldermen
and Community of the Borough ; by this deed the Abbot
and Convent renounce, in favour of the Eldermen and Community,

munity, the whole income of the borough belonging to their
revenue, with the fmall cuftoms, profits of court, &c. re-
ferving, however, the yearly penfions payable to the monaftery from the lands of the borough, and the correction
of the bailies, as often as they, or any of them, fhould be
guilty of injuftice in the exercife of their office *. By the
fet or conftitution, the government of the borough is lodged
in a council of 22; confifting of 12 guildry or merchant-
councillors, 8 deacons of incorporations †, and 2 trades-councillors; the magiftrates are, a provoft, 2 bailies, and dean
of guild. The town-council are annually elected after the
following manner. On the Thurfday preceding Michaelmas each incorporation elects a leet, or lift of four of their
members. Thefe leets are prefented to the council on
Friday, who elect two out of each leet of four, and fend
down this leet of two to each incorporation, with orders to
elect one of them as their deacon. The new deacons are
prefented to the council on Saturday, when the old deacons
and other members of council elect two new guild, and two
new trades-councillors; the old deacons are then removed
out of council; and upon Monday, the eight deacons, and
four new councillors, and other members, elect a provoft,
two bailies, dean of guild, and other office-bearers in council; then two of the guildry, and the two old trades-councillors, who now are fupernumeraries, are removed from
the ordinary council, but continue to act as extraordinary
councillors

* Salvis dictis dominis Abbati et Conventui, terris in dicto burgo, &c.
ac correctione balivorum quoties contigerit, eos aut eorum quemlibet
in jure, feu in jufticia facienda feu exiquenda delinquere.

† Smiths, wrights, weavers, tailors, fhoemakers, mafons, bakers, and
flefhers.

councillors till the next election.—The armorial-bearing of the borough is a tower, or fort, ſupported by two lions, en-cloſed in circles ; round the exterior circle is written, *Sigillum Civitatis Fermeloduni* ; and round the interior one, *Eſto Rupes Inacceſſa* ; on the reverſe, is a female figure with a ſceptre in her hand, and on each ſide an inverted ſword, point upwards, and round *Margaretta Regina Scotorum.* The annual revenue of the borough is conſiderably above L. 500 Sterling. Eight public fairs are held through the year *, and two days in the week, Wedneſday and Friday, are appointed for markets ; the market on Wedneſday has for ſome time fallen into diſuſe.

Manufactures.—This town has long been diſtinguiſhed for the manufacture of diaper or table linen : For many years paſt, no other cloth has been woven in the pariſh to any conſiderable extent. In the infancy of the trade, it was the cuſtom to weave diaper only during the ſummer, the winter being employed in weaving ticks and checks. This practice continued till about the year 1749, when the manufacture of ticks and checks was in a great meaſure relinquiſhed †. Since the above period the diaper trade has been gradually increaſing ; in 1788 there were about 900, and laſt year (1792) no leſs than 1200 looms employed in the trade ; of this number, above 800 belonged to the pariſh. The value of goods annually manufactured has for ſome

---

* January, 3d Wedneſday O. S. ; March, 2d Wedneſday ; April, 4th Wedneſday ; July, 1ſt Wedneſday ; Auguſt, 1ſt Tueſday ; September, 4th Friday ; October, laſt Thurſday ; November, 4th Wedneſday.

† About 7 or 8 years ago when the diaper trade was low, ſome of the manufacturers had recourſe to the making ticks and checks ; but the tradeſmen being unaccuſtomed to the work, engaged in it with diſlike, and it was given up as ſoon as the diaper trade revived.

fome time paſt been from L. 50,000 to L. 60,000 Sterling, and the trade was on the increaſe. Aſtoniſhing improvements have been made within leſs than half a century in the art of weaving, and in the manufacture of table-linen : By the introduction of machinery labour has been greatly abridged. Formerly, in weaving diaper, two, and ſometimes three perſons, were requiſite for one web ; now, by means of the fly-ſhuttle, and what is called a frame for raiſing the figure, a ſingle weaver can work a web $2\frac{1}{2}$ yards broad without the leaſt aſſiſtance. Many of the tradeſmen in this place diſcover conſiderable genius in drawing figures for the diaper, and ſeveral of them have obtained premiums for their draughts. Table cloths can be furniſhed of any deſired breadth, length, and fineneſs ; and noblemen and gentlemen may have their coats of arms and mottos wrought into any table linen they chooſe to commiſſion. In the cheſt of the incorporation there is preſerved a very curious ſpecimen of the weaving art : It is a man's ſhirt wrought in the loom about 100 years ago, by a weaver of this place of the name of Ingles. The ſhirt is without ſeam, and was finiſhed by the ingenious artiſan without the leaſt aſſiſtance from the needle ; the only neceſſary part he could not accompliſh was a button for the neck *.

Town-Improvements.—In ſpeaking of theſe, it would be injuſtice to paſs over in ſilence the name of Mr George Chalmers, late of Pittencrieff. To the enlightened and ſpirited exertions of this gentleman, in order to promote the feuing out of his lands, Dunfermline is indebted for one of its
                                                            greateſt

---

* Mr Stark has lately erected at Brucefield, near Dunfermline, a mill for ſpinning yarn from flax, hemp, tow, and wool. The yarn ſpun from flax has given great ſatisfaction.

greateſt improvements; we mean the bridge built by him over the glen, by which an eaſy and healthful communication has been opened up to the town on the W. immediately oppoſite to the principal ſtreet. Formerly, the only road from the W. was by the bridge at Malcolm's Tower, running eaſtward, cloſe by the Queen's Houſe, and then N. to the town by a confined narrow lane. The bridge was a work of great labour and expenſe *. Within theſe 30 years the trade and population of this place have rapidly increaſed. On the S. the Abbey Park has been feued, and ſeveral ſtreets built upon it, and immediately on the W. additions are daily making to the extenſive feus on the lands of Pittencrieff: The population on this eſtate at preſent exceeds 1200 ſouls. It is but juſtice to obſerve, that the police of the borough has within theſe few years been much improved : A laudable attention has been paid to the paving of the ſtreets, and furniſhing them with additional lamps; and much greater care has of late been taken to keep the ſtreets clean, a practice highly worthy of imitation. Nothing is more neceſſary to the health of the inhabitants than cleanlineſs, eſpecially where the ſtreets of a town are narrow, which is the caſe with moſt of our Scotch boroughs : This conſideration, and the high price which

may

---

* The bridge is of a peculiar ſtructure. An arch 297 feet long, 12 broad, and 15 feet 5 inches high, was thrown over the burn, in the bottom of the glen, and the remaining hollow filled up by a mound of earth 68 feet 6 inches thick at the centre, having a gradual ſlope on both ſides to the extremities of the ſtone arch below. On the top is the road now almoſt completely encloſed on both ſides by houſes forming a very neat ſtreet. On the ſides or ſlopes of the mound, and at the back of the houſes, are very convenient hanging gardens. The whole was finiſhed by Mr Chalmers at his own expenſe, the town only allowing a ſmall piece of ground neceſſary for carrying on the undertaking. Mr Chalmers ſubjected 12 acres of his eſtate to the payment of ceſs to the town, and they burdened 3 of their acres with the payment of 1 d. to Pittencrieff.

may be eafily got for ftreet-dung, muft render the conduct of magiftrates inexcufable when they do not attend to this moft neceffary branch of police *. As another very commendable improvement, we may mention the removal of the butchers (formerly fcattered through different parts of the town) into one public flefh-market, and the obliging them to kill their cattle in a flaughter-houfe built for the purpofe, at fome diftance from the market, and entirely removed out of the town. An officer has lately been appointed, whofe conftant employment is to overfee the police of the borough : He fuperintends the cleaning of the ftreets, attends the fifh and butter markets, and examines the weights, feizing on what he finds deficient ; thus an immediate and conftant check is given to impofitions on the public : He likewife difmiffes all vagrants found begging in the town. Formerly the inhabitants were very much haraffed with ftranger poor, but are now effectually delivered from that burden. The officer of police has L. 25 a-year ; and from his care and diligence he well deferves it.

Advantages and Difadvantages of the Town.—The great abundance of coals in the parifh, the fhort carriage, and comparatively eafy rate at which they can be purchafed, render Dunfermline highly favourable for carrying on extenfive manufactures. Coals may be had at half a mile's diftance †. Plenty of good water is not ufually to be got

in

---

* It was formerly the practice here for the magiftrates to let the ftreet-dung, and the tackfman engaged to clean the ftreets : As long as this practice continued, the ftreets were fhamefully dirty, and not above L 10 was got for the dung. The magiftrates now employ ftreet-rakers, &c. and fell the dung when collected, and gain from L. 40 to L. 50 a-year, exclufive of all neceffary expenfes.

† The inhabitants have the privilege of being ferved with coals at a hill belonging to the town at a cheaper rate, than they are fold to the country

at

in the neighbourhood of coals, and the inhabitants of this place have but a ſcanty ſupply, eſpecially in ſummer. Water is brought in pipes from about a mile's diſtance, but the fountain is not ſufficiently abundant. The greateſt diſadvantage felt by the manufacturers and ſhop-keepers is their diſtance from the ſea ; the land-carriage they are obliged to employ being expenſive. A canal from the Nethertown to run S. W. about two miles, and join the ſea near Lord Elgin's lime-works at Charleſtown is ſaid to be eaſily practicable, and that only a few locks would be neceſſary. Should ſuch a canal be formed, many advantages might accrue to Dunfermline as a place of trade, and much expenſe be ſaved in the conveyance of coals for exportation : Foreign wood likewiſe might be brought at an eaſy rate to Dunfermline, and the neighbouring pariſhes ſupplied with that commodity at conſiderably leſs expenſe.

Population 1791-2.

Families,	-	-	-	2131
Souls,	-	-	-	9550*
Males,	-	-	-	4740
Females,	-	-	-	4810
Under 10 years of age,		-	-	2481
Between 10 and 20,		-	-	2020
—— 20 and 50,		-	-	3951
—— 50 and 70,		-	-	914
—— 70 and 100,		-	-	184

In

at large ; at preſent they may have $400\frac{1}{2}$ cwt. of coal on the hill for 7 d. or laid down at their doors for 1 s. the carriage being 5 d. But it is to be regretted that the road to this coal is bad, and that it is worked in ſuch a. way that carts are often obliged to wait long on the hill before they are ſerved.

* The North Ferry is legally in this pariſh. but its population is not included. The population of the eſtates of Urquhart and Logie, near Dunfermline, but which are legally in the pariſh of Inverkeithing, is included.

In the town and fuburbs, and neighbouring
   feus, &c. of Pittencrieff,   - - 5192
In the village of Limekilns,   - - 658
In the village of Charleftown,   - - 487

In the prefbytery records 1713, when it was propofed to
have a 3d minifter, the parifhioners are ftated to be 5000.
According to the return to Dr Webfter 1755, the population was 8552. There are feveral people in the parifh
above 80, and a confiderable number above 70 years of
age. In the town there died lately a woman above 90,
who was the youngeft of 21 children of the fame parents;
and there is now living another woman, alfo above 90
years of age, who is the youngeft of 25 children, all of the
fame marriage; fhe has been almoft blind thefe fix years,
and partly fupports herfelf by fpinning on the rock.

Abſtract of the Baptiſms and Marriages for the laſt ten years.

Years.	Baptiſms.	Marriages.
1783,	280	63
1784,	267	73
1785,	292	74
1786,	282	68
1787,	244	57
1788,	284	74
1789,	305	70
1790,	283	71
1791,	278	82
1792,	292	92

No regifter of burials has been kept for a confiderable
period back till within thefe four years.

Account of Burials for the laſt three years.

Years.	Males.	Females.	Under 12 years.	Total.
1790,	47	55	141	243
1791,	38	53	93	184
1792,	50	51	108	209

From

From the preceding table the number of burials cannot be exactly afcertained, as many of the inhabitants in the S. part of the parifh bury in a church-yard in the parifh of Inverkeithing.

Divifion of the Inhabitants.

Heritors and feuars liable in ftipend, - -		78
Clergy connected with the Eftablifhment,		3
Clergy Seceders, -		5
Phyficians, - -		2
Surgeons, - -		4
Merchants, - -		15
Writers, - -		7
Manufacturers, -		21
Shop-keepers, -		43
Brewers, - -		10
Diftiller, - -		1
Officers of Excife, -		7
Meffengers, -		2
Smiths, - -		40
Wrights, - -		96
Weavers, - -		862
Tailors, - -		93
Shoemakers, -		54

Mafons, - -		37
Bakers, - -		29
Flefhers, - -		13
Gardeners, - . -		11
Sailors, - -		109
Colliers, - -		184
Ale Sellers, -		101
Belonging to the Relief, children included, about		600
Belonging to the Burgher Seceders, - -		4223
Belonging to the Anti-burghers, about -		320
Epifcopalians, -		44
Independents, -		7
Baptifts, - -		6
Cameronians about		12
Berean, -		1
Roman Catholic, -		1

Ale-Houfes.—Of thefe there are 101 in the parifh, including a very commodious inn, and two or three of an inferior kind. There is alfo a number of fhops where fpirits are fold in fmall quantities. It is not 25 years ago, when almoft nothing but the ale brewed in the town was drunk by the trades people ; not only at home, but even in the public-houfe, they fought no better cheer : but this
formerly !

formerly healthy and invigorating liquor, from additional duty, and other caufes, is now fadly degenerated, and become fo weak and infipid a beverage, that whifky is too often fubftituted in its place. The general ufe of whifky is arrived at an alarming height among many in the lower ranks of life. This is a growing evil, and loudly demands the ferious and fpeedy attention of the Legiflature *.

Poor.—There is no legal affeffment for the fupport of the poor. Few beg in the parifh, but the indigent who receive charity from different funds are numerous. No vagrants have been permitted for fome time paft to afk alms in the borough. The poor belonging to the fectaries are not admitted on the parifh funds; the money collected at fome of their meetings is not, it is faid, wholly given to their poor, but converted to the fupport of their minifters. The number of poor on the roll of the kirk-feffion is variable, but for

fome

---

* To furnifh the people with good and cheap malt liquor by a reduction of the duty, feems to be the moft effectual method of preventing the general and pernicious practice of ufing fpirits. It is unqueftionably criminal, and a direct breach of morality, to defraud the revenue; but many feem to think that there is nothing very finful in the practice. If the inclination to evade taxes be too common, furely the opportunities and temptations to fmuggle ought to be as few as poffible. Were the duty taken entirely off the ale, and laid wholly on the malt, this would not only prevent the brewer from defrauding the revenue, but meliorate the quality of the ale. In difcuffing this fubject, " The only people," fays an intelligent writer, " likely to fuffer by the change of fyftem here propofed, are thofe who brew for their own private ufe. But the exemption which this fuperior rank of people at prefent enjoy, from very heavy taxes, which are paid by the poor labourer and artificer, is furely moft unjuft and unequal, and ought to be taken away, even though this change was never to take place. It has probably been the intereft of this fuperior order of people, however, which has hitherto prevented a change of fyftem that could not well fail to increafe the revenue, and to relieve the people." Dr SMITH's Wealth of Nations, III. 370.

fome time paft has very much increafed. In December
1792 the number was 49; at prefent there are 45 on the
roll. The funds for their fupport are, collections at the
Church and Chapel of Eafe, money paid for burying
grounds, &c. and the intereft of a capital arifing from donations *, and former favings. From the increafed number of poor, the kirk-feffion have been obliged to encroach
on their capital.—The following is a ftate of their funds
from 7th April 1792, to 7th May 1793:

To intereft of money, - - L. 15 5 8
To collections, money for burying-grounds, &c. 51 0 0
                                            ———————
                                      L. 66 5 8
Difburfements, feffion-clerk's falary, &c. included, about L. 30 of principal being up-
  lifted, - - - - L. 96 5 8

There is no fcheme refpecting the poor to which objec-
tions may not be ftated. It is, however, a primary object,
and of great importance, to difcourage vagrants, and to
confine beggars to their refpective parifhes, who ought to
fupport their own poor; thus the worthlefs and fturdy beggar will be difcovered, and the public no longer impofed
upon by pretended objects of charity. With regard to the
beft mode of fupporting the poor, there is a variety of opinions. It is no doubt unreafonable that the burden fhould
fall chiefly on thofe who are leaft able to bear it, and that
non-refiding heritors, though they draw confiderable rents
from a parifh, fhould contribute little or nothing towards
the fupport of its poor; on the other hand, poors rates are
                                                  found

* The Rev. Mr James Thomfon, minifter of this parifh, left to the
poor of the Eftablifhed Church L. 100 Sterling, the intereft thereof to be
diftributed yearly on the 31ft December, by the kirk-feffion, to the poor
on the weekly roll.

found from experience to be moſt hoſtile to induſtry a-
mong the lower ranks, and to have the moſt pernicious
influence on their morals. One thing however is certain,
that whatever may be for the public good, it muſt be for
the intereſt of heritors to contribute voluntarily, in order
to prevent kirk-ſeſſions from being obliged to exhauſt the
funds in their hands, and recourſe being had to aſſeſſments.
Where there are no poors rates eſtabliſhed, non-reſiding
heritors may eaſily perceive, that it is but reaſonable that
they ſhould contribute voluntarily, in proportion to the value of their eſtates. Kirk-ſeſſions, it is well known, have
a good deal of trouble, but derive no pecuniary advantage
from the poors funds entruſted to their management *.

                                                        Schools.

* *Charitable Inſtitutions.*—The moſt ancient of theſe is St Leonard's
Hoſpital. It is not certainly known who was the original founder. The
account-books reſpecting the management of the hoſpital from 1594 to
the preſent time, are ſtill extant. The object of the inſtitution is the
maintenance of 8 widows. Each widow is entitled to 4 bolls of meal,
4 bolls of malt, 8 loads of coal, 14 loads of turf, 8 lippies of fine wheat,
8 lippies of groats yearly, and a chamber in the hoſpital, with a ſmall
garden; and to ſome of them 2 s. ſilver yearly for pin-money. The a-
bove proviſion for 8 widows, is payable out of 64 acres of land, lying
near Dunfermline, and immediately adjacent to the place where the hoſpital once ſtood; the houſes in the vicinity are called the Spittal. The
patronage of this hoſpital has long been exerciſed by the Marquis of
Tweeddale.

Pitreavie's Hoſpital.—In the year 1676, Sir Henry Wardlaw of Pitreavie, " for implement and fulfilling of ſeveral vows, promiſes and engagements made by him before God, after great mercies received, and
for certain other good cauſes, motives and conſiderations," inſtituted an
hoſpital at Maſtertown in favour of 4 widows, " women of honeſt fame,
relicts of honeſt men who live in the ground of Pitreavie, or other land
belonging to him and his ſucceſſors," who are declared to be patrons;
failing widows of the above deſcription, ſuch other honeſt women as the
                                                          patron

Schools.—There is no parochial ſchool. The original foundation of the grammar-ſchool here is not certainly known

patron chooſes, are to be preferred. Each widow is to have a chamber or houſe, and 6 bolls of meal yearly; or 3 bolls of oats, and 3 bolls of bear at the option of the patron *.

Graham's Mortification.—In the year 1710, 600 merks Scots, (being the money found in the poors-box at the death of the Reverend Mr Graham, laſt Epiſcopal miniſter of Dunfermline), was by the Juſtices of the Peace, heritors, and town-council, mortified in the hands of the town for the uſe of the poor. By the bond, the council are obliged to pay the intereſt of the above ſum yearly ; the one half to the poor of the borough, conform to a liſt, to be yearly ſubſcribed by the Magiſtrates and Town-council, and the other half to the poor of the landward part of the pariſh, conform to a liſt to be yearly ſubſcribed by the Juſtices of Peace, and heritors, or a quorum of them.

Reid's Mortification.—John Reid, a ſhopkeeper in Dunfermline, who, from ſmall beginnings, had acquired a conſiderable property, mortified the whole (a few legacies excepted) to the poor of this pariſh, eſpecially to poor houſeholders, and perſons who have once been in better circumſtances. He committed the management to the Provoſt, two Bailies, and Dean of Guild of the burgh, the miniſters, and two elders of the Eſtabliſhed Church, the miniſter, and three elders of the Relief, and the miniſter, and three elders of the Burgher Congregation. By the deed of mortification, the managers are accountable to the heritors of the pariſh ; and it is provided, that in the event of a Poor's Houſe or Orphan's Houſe being built in the pariſh, the whole of the eſtate mortified ſhall be applied to the ſupport of ſaid Poor's or Orphan's Houſe. The revenue ariſing

* *In the year* 1764, *the Preſbytery, in conſequence of an application from the heritors, miniſters, kirk-ſeſſion, and Magiſtrates of Dunfermline, inquired into the management of Pitreavie Hoſpital. The patron diſputed the juriſdiction of the Preſbytery. The cauſe came at laſt before the Court of Seſſion ; and that Court, (notwithſtanding in the deed of mortification, all judges or miniſters, civil or eccleſiaſtic, are diſcharged from meddling therewith in any ſort), found, that the patron was accountable to the Preſbytery for the management of the mortification, and ordained him to account for* 40 *years backward.*

known *; it appears, however, that Queen Anne of Denmark mortified L. 2000 Scots in the hands of the town, chiefly for settling an yearly falary to the fchoolmafter of the borough. The rector, on the recommendation of the Town-council, is prefented by the Marquis of Tweeddale, as heritable bailie of regality. His falary, arifing from the Queen's mortification, and what is paid him by the town, (part of which is voluntary), amounts to L. 17, 7 s. 6 d.

arifing from faid mortification amounts to L. 70 Sterling a-year. The number of poor at laft diftribution was 151. Befides the poor's funds belonging to the feveral incorporations; to the Society of Gardeners, and to the Guildry, who have confiderable property, there are 12 Friendly Societies in the parifh. Thefe have different defignations, but their rules refpecting the admiffion of members, entry-money, quarterly payments, &c. are on the whole pretty fimilar. The object of all them, is moft laudable, to afford relief and affiftance to the members, when by ficknefs or accident, difabled from purfuing their ordinary occupations; a certain allowance when death happens in their families, and a weekly penfion, when unable to work, through infirmities or old age. Upon the death of any of the members, their widows, and alfo their children below 12 years of age, have a certain allowance. All thefe focieties have been inftituted within thefe 11 years, except that of the Weaver Lads †, which began about the year 1739 or 1740.

* *The entry-money to this fociety is 2 s. 6 d. with 6 d. to the clerk; and the quarterly payment 1 s. When difabled from working, each member is entitled to 2 s. 6 d. weekly. If through old age or infirmities, unable to follow his employment as formerly, 1 s. 6 d.; and if through old age or infirmities, totally unfit for his bufinefs, 2 s. 6 d. a-week. On the death of his wife, 30 s. and of a child under 12 years, 10 s. His widow to have 20 s. a-year, and if in diftrefs, 1 s. a-week, and 1 s. 3 d. for every child below 9 years. Children, when their parents are both dead, to have 6 d. weekly, till they are 12 years of age; 30 s. allowed for the funeral charges of members.*

† The prefent fchool and fchool-houfe are faid to be a donation by a Mr Ged, a Romifh clergyman, to the mafters of the grammar-fchool, and by which donation they were obliged to put up prayers for an eafy paffage through purgatory to their benefactor.

6 d. Sterling. The doctor, or uſher to the grammar-ſchool, is elected by the town-council and kirk-ſeſſion, and has a ſalary of L. 12 : 7 : 6 Sterling. The maſter of the Song, (an office inſtituted by Queen Anne), is preſented by the Marquis of Tweeddale, on the recommendation of the town-council. He officiates as precentor in the church, receives the dues for baptiſms and marriages, and keeps a ſchool for muſic, Engliſh, and arithmetic. His ſalary is L. 5 Sterling. There are a number of private ſchools in the pariſh.

Eccleſiaſtical State.—In this pariſh, there are 8 clergy-men, two on the Eſtabliſhment, one who officiates in a Chapel of Eaſe, one of the Relief, three of the Burgher, and one of the Antiburgher perſuaſion. The Chapel of Eaſe being in the town, does not contribute in the ſmalleſt degree to the accommodation of the pariſhioners at a di-ſtance from the church. The miniſter is ordained, but has no particular diſtrict of the pariſh aſſigned him. He is choſen by popular election, and has a bond for L. 50 Ster-ling of ſtipend. Upon the death of Mr Gilleſpie, (who, after his depoſition in 1752, ſet up a Relief meeting in Dunfermline), his congregation ſplit into two parties ; the party moſt numerous were for continuing in connexion with the Relief, the other, though few in number, but to whom the greateſt ſhare of the property of the meeting-houſe belonged, applied by petition to the preſbytery for having their houſe converted into a Chapel of Eaſe. This was oppoſed by the miniſters of the pariſh ; the chapel how-ever, after 5 years litigation, was at laſt granted by the General Aſſembly in 1779. The congregation is not nu-merous, it conſiſts of ſome who were Mr Gilleſpie's hear-ers, and people who formerly attended the pariſh church ; ſeveral likewiſe from neighbouring pariſhes have ſeats,

and

and attend worſhip in the chapel. There are two Burgher meeting-houſes, one in the town, and the other in the village of Limekilns. The meeting houſe in the town was built in 1740, for Mr Ralph Erſkine, and is one of the largeſt in Scotland, and has for a conſiderable time been a collegiate charge. Their ſenior miniſter's ſtipend is L. 80, with a houſe and garden, and that of his colleague, L. 70 Sterling. The preſent Relief meeting houſe was built in 1775. Their miniſter has L. 60, and L. 5 for a houſe. The Antiburgher houſe was erected in 1790. Their miniſter's ſtipend is ſaid to be L. 45 or L. 50 Sterling. The preſent eſtabliſhed miniſters are two in number. The firſt miniſter's ſtipend conſiſts of 8 chalders of victual, half meal and half bear, and L. 50 Sterling. He has alſo by decreet, L. 3 : 6 : 8 for manſe-rent, L. 1 : 13 : 4 for foggage, and L. 10 Sterling for communion-elements. His glebe is arable, and conſiſts of 4 acres, which are let at preſent for L. 14 Sterling a-year. The ſecond miniſter has at preſent a proceſs of augmentation of ſtipend before the Court of Teinds. He has neither manſe nor glebe *.

Antiquities.

* The Preſbyterian miniſters of this pariſh, ſince the Revolution, were Meſſrs Kemp, Buchanan, Erſkine Wardlaw, Thomſon and Fernie. The laſt incumbents, Meſſrs Thomſon and Fernie, were colleagues for very near 44 years. Mr Fernie died 5th April 1788, in the 74th year of his age, and 44th of his miniſtry. He publiſhed a volume of ſermons in 1786. Mr Thomſon died 19th October 1790, in the 92d year of his age, and 52d of his miniſtry. Before his ſettlement in this pariſh, he had been 14 years a miniſter in the army. Within 3 years of his death, he preached regularly in his turn, and in his 90th year, adminiſtred the Sacrament of the Lord's Supper, preaching an action ſermon of 2 hours. There is preſerved in the Advocates Library, " *Ane Sermon Preichit befoir* the Regent and Nobilitie, upon a part of the third chapter of the Prophet Malachi, in the Kirk of Leith, at the tyme of the Generall Aſſemblie on Sonday the 13. of Januarie. Anno Do. 1571. Be David Ferguſſone, miniſter of the Evangell at Dunfermline. In this diſcourſe, Mr Ferguſſon loudly

Antiquities.—Dunfermline became at an early period a royal reſidence. Malcolm III. ſurnamed Canmore or Great Head, uſually reſided in a tower or caſtle, erected on

loudly complains of the miſapplication of the tithes, the ſcanty proviſion made for the Preſbyterian clergy, the neglect of the poor, and the little attention paid to ſchools and churches. In the dedication to the Earl of Marr Regent, Mr Ferguſſon mentions his reaſons for publiſhing this ſermon, and his having laid it before the General Aſſembly, who by a Committee approved of the ſame." *Albeit*, (ſays he), my mynd nor purpois was not (richt Nobill and werthie Lord), to have publiſhed this ſermō at ony time, zit becaus it did not fructifie as I ſuppoſit it ſuld have done, being, (as ſayis Ezechiel), lyke a tone or pleaſant ſang to the heirers for a ſeaſon, thair hartis in the meane time ſtill going efter their covetouſnes, provokit alſo be the malitious toungis of ſū, and eirneſtly requeiſtit be utheris. At length I was compellit, (for farther inſtructioun of the negligent heirers, the ſtopping of the mouthis of evill ſpeikers, and the ſatisfactioon of the inceſſant requeiſtis of gude and godlie men), to beſtow and ſpend ſum time and travel, to put it in that ſame forme and ordour, that it was ſpokin and preichit in befoir zour Grace. Quhilk quhē I had faithfully performit, (as all tha that heard it, quhen thay ſall reid it agane I trow will teſtifie), diſtruſting myne awin judgement, I preſentit it to the kirk now laſtly aſſemblit in Perth, the ſext of Auguſt, that they qha (for the maiſt part) wer heireris of it micht judge aſweil of the foundnes of the doctrine contenit into it, as of my ſinceritie in the wryting thairof, and ſa micht allow, or diſallow it, as it meritit, unto the quhilk beſines the kirk appointit Johne Erſkin of Dun, ſuperintendent of Angus, M. Johne Dowglas, Biſchop of Sanctandrois, M. Johne Winram, ſuperintendent of Stratherne, M. Knox, miniſter of Edinburgh, and Williame Chriſtiſon, miniſter of Dundie, qha diligently red and approvit the ſame, ſubſcriving it with thair handis, in the name of the haill kirk, as a ſermon conſonant and aggreabill to Goddis word" . . . . . Zour humanitie and gentilnes, qhairof not only I, bot almaiſt all uther men, have experience, muiſis me to be ſa hamely as to offer and dedicate ſa ſmall a wark unto zour Grace, &c. From Dunfermlyne, the 20th day of Auguſt, Anno 1572. Be zour Grace's humbill ſubject and daylie Oratour David Ferguſſone, Miniſter of Chriſtis Evangell."—A ſhort ſpecimen of the ſermon itſelf will not it is preſumed be unacceptable.— "Brethren, for my part I wald ze had Angelis to zour miniſteris, gif ze wer worthy of thame, or that it wer the will of God, bot ſeeing that

God's

on the peninfulated hill in the glen *. A palace was afterward built a little S. E. of the tower in a moft romantick

God's will is not fo, bot that ze fal be zervit be the minifterie of men, it behouvis zow to tak thame as thay ar, with all thingis yt. of neceffitie belangis unto thame, or lawfully dependis on thame, fic as are wyfes, childrē and familiē, quhilk not only muft be honeftly reulit, and the children haldin under obedience with all honeftie, (as Paul teachis), bot alfo muft be provydit for hofpitalitie, quhilk all men knawis requyris baith foirficht and expenfis . . . . For this day Chrift is fpulfeit amang us, quhil yt. quhilk aucht to mantene the minifterie of the kirk and the pure, is gevin to prophane men, flattereris in Court, Ruffianes and Hyrelingis. The pure in the meane tyme oppreffit with hounger, the kirkis and tempilis decaying for lack of minifteris and uphalding, and the fchuilis utterlie neglectit and overfene . . . And as for the minifters of the word, they ar utterly neglectit and cū in manifeft cōtempt amang zow, ze raill upon thame at zour pleafure, of thair doctrine, (gif it ferve not zour turne, and aggre not with zour appetytis), ze ar becum impatient, and to be fchort, we ar now made zour tabill talk quhom ze mock in zour mifferies, and threatin in zour anger. I am compellit to fpeik this, thocht I be as plane as pleafant, and appeir to zow as the greiteft fule of ye reft to ftand up heir to utter that quhilk uther men thinkis, weil, let me be coūted a fule for fpeiking the treuth. Langer at this prefent, feeing that the tyme faillis me, I will not hald zow, bot befeikis zow all, and principallie zow maift nobill and worthie perfonages, to prēt thir thingis in zour myndis to zour profite, to fuffer the wordis of exhortation patiently, and tak in gude worth yt. quhilk is fpokin, albeit it have bene fumquhat rudely and fchairply utterit, confiddering that it procedit from the hart of him that luifis and favouris baith zow and zowr caus, remembring the faying of Salomon, Oppin rebuke is better then fecreit lufe, and the woundis of a lufer mair faithfull then the kiffis of ane enemie thocht they be plef āt. . . . . — The following note is added to the fermon : " This fermon was prefentit to the kirk, red and approvit be the perfounis underwrittin, appointit thairunto be ye Affēblie halden at Perth 6. Augufti. Anno 1572. *J. Sanctandrois. Jhone Erfkyn. M. Johne Wynram.* William Cryftefone, M. of Dundie. John Knox with my dead hand, but glaid heart, praifing God that of his mercy he levis fuche light to his kirk in this defolatioun."

* A fmall fragment of Malcolm's tower is ftill to be feen.

tick situation, close on the verge of the glen, but at what particular period is not now known. The S. W. wall of the palace still remains a monument of the magnificent fabric, of which it is a part, and tradition continues to point out the chimney of the apartment where that unfortunate monarch Charles I. was born. The palace is said to have been rebuilt * by Queen Anne of Denmark, but of this there is no tradition in this place, nor as far as we know any authentic proof whatever. It appears to be a mistake, arising from the words of an inscription found on a house built for Queen Anne of Denmark, and adjoining to the palace. The Queen's house continued in good repair long after the palace was in ruins. About 40 years ago, it was occupied as an accademy by a Mr Moir, now a teacher in Edinburgh. Within these 15 years, part of it was inhabited, but no attention being paid to keep it in repair, it gradually became ruinous, and was lately sold, and made a quarry for stones, and is to be entirely removed †. Within these 30 years, there was to be seen in the bed-chamber of an inn at Dunfermline, the nuptial bed of Queen Anne, which she is said to have brought along with her from Denmark. For this piece of royal furniture, the innkeeper, Mrs Walker, a zealous Jacobite, entertained a very high veneration. Bishop Pocock of Ireland, happening to be in her house, and having seen the bed, offered her 50 guineas for it, which she refused, telling him, " that she still re- " tained so great reverence for the two royal personages
                                                             " whose

* Grose's Antiquities.

† On the front of this house was the following inscription—" Propy- læum et superstructas, ædes vetustate et injuriis temporum collapsas, di- rutasque a fundamentis in hanc ampliorem formam, restituit et instauravit Anna Regina Frederici Danorum Regis Augustissimæ Filia, Anno Salutis, 1600."

" whofe property it was, and who flept in it when they
" refided here, and to their pofterity, all the gold and fil-
" ver in Ireland was not fit to buy it." Some time before
her death, Mrs Walker made a prefent of the Queen's bed
to the Earl of Elgin, an heritor in this parifh. The bed
is of walnut-tree, of curious workmanfhip, and ornamented
with feveral very antique figures neatly carved. Another
piece of furniture which belonged to Queen Anne is at
prefent in the poffeffion of a private family of this place.
It is a kind of cabinet, what the people ufed to call the
Queen's *ambrie*, of very curious workmanfhip, finely polifhed and ornamented with a variety of figures, fome of
which indicate a very ftrange fancy. One figure has the
head and neck of a man, the wings of an eagle, and the
body of a lion ; from the profufion of ornament, it muft
have coft the artift much time and labour. This cabinet,
like the bed, is of the walnut-tree, and is f id likewife to
have been brought by the Queen from Denmark. It is
ftill perfectly entire, excepting only the original feet on
which it ftood, which have been loft.

The *Monaftery* was one of the moft ancient in Scotland,
founded by Malcolm Canmore for the Monks of the order
of St Benedict ; the building being left unfinifhed by Malcolm, was completed by his fon Alexander I. The monaftery and its church were dedicated to the Holy Trinity,
and St Margaret, Malcolm's Queen. In fome old manu-
fcripts, it is called Monafterium de monte infirmorum ;
hence fome have conjectured, that it was originally intended for an hofpital or firmary. It continued to be governed by a prior till the reign of David I. who raifed it
to the dignity of an abbey, and in 1124 tranflated thither
13 monks from Canterbury ; before the diffolution, however
the

the fraternity had increaſed to 26 *. Some of the grants to the abbey were of a ſingular nature, and on that account may not be unworthy of particular notice. David I. † grants to the abbey, omnem decimam de auro quod mihi eveniet de Fif et Fothrif, *i. e.* the tenth part of all the gold he ſhould derive from Fife and Fothrif ‡. By a charter

* The abbey was richly endowed, and derived part of its extenſive revenue from places at a conſiderable diſtance. Kirkaldy, Kinghorn, and Burntiſland, called of old Weſter Kinghorn ; likewiſe Muſſelburgh and Invereſk belonged to this abbey. According to a rental given up at the time of the Reformation by Allan Couts, in name of George Durie Abbot, the yearly revenue was as follows.—Money, L. 2513 : 10 : 8 Scots ; wheat, 28 c. 11 b. 1 f.—bear, 102 c. 15 b. 1 f. 3 p.—meal, 15 c.—oats, 61 c. 6 b. 2 f.—horſe-corn, 29 c. 1 b. 1 f. 2½ p.—butter, 34 ſt.—'ime, 19 c. 15 b.—ſalt, 11 c. 8 b.——According to another rental by the ſame perſon :—Money, L. 2404, 4 s.—wheat, 27 c. 4 b. 3 f.—bear, 83 c. 11 b. 2 f. 2 p.—oats, 158 c. 5 b. 2 f. whereof 84 c. white oats.—lime, 20 c.—ſalt, 11 c. 8 b.—capons, 374.—poultry 746.

† James I. is reported to have ſaid of David. " He was an ſoir Sanct for the Croun." Had James I. (ſays Lord Hailes), been poſſeſſed of the revenues which his predeceſſors beſtowed on the clergy, he would have employed them in augmenting the influence of the Crown, and to ſpeak in the dialect of Bellendin, *have kythed an ſoir King for the Lordis.* Hailes's Ann.

‡ *Fothrif* is called *Forthrick, in Chart. Cambuſkenneth.* Sir Robert Sibbald, *Hiſtory of Fife*, c. 2. ſays, that Mr Robert Maule, the antiquary, derived *Fothrick* from *Veachric, i. e.* " the painted kingdom," or " the kingdom of the Picts." Lord Hailes ſays, that *Fothrick* is compounded of *Forth* and *rick, i. e.* the kingdom or territory at the Forth ; and ſuppoſes that it means that country on the northern bank of the Forth, from the neighbourhood of Stirling to where the river is loſt in the ſalt water. Hailes's Ann. In Hay's Scotia Sacra, the monaſtery of Dunfermline is ſaid to be in Fothrick moor, and on the north ſide of this pariſh there is a moor which ſtill retains the name of Fatrick moor. Lord Hailes's derivation of the word Fothrick appears extremely natural ; but it ſhould ſeem that the country ſo denominated, extended farther eaſt than he ſuppoſes.

charter of confirmation, the fame monarch grants to the abbey the feventh, (after the tithe,) of all the feals caught at Kinghorn *. Baftards, it would appear, were in general excluded from monafteries ; Pope Innocent †, at the requeft of the abbot of Dunfermline, grants him permiffion to admit one baftard into the number of his monks with this exception, " dummodo non fit de adulterio, vel inceftuofo coitu procreatus." The firft abbot of this monaftery was Gosfridus, formerly prior of Canterbury, ordained in the year 1128. The laft abbot was George Durie, commendator and arch-dean of St Andrew's. The abbey was a magnificent and very extenfive building, but fell an early facrifice to the barbarous policy of the Englifh, being almoft entirely burnt down by them, in the beginning of the 14th century. Edward I. of England wintered at Dunfermline in 1303. " In that place there was an abbey of the Benedictine order, a building fo fpacious, that according to an Englifh hiftorian, three fovereign princes, with all their retinue, might have been lodged conveniently

---

* Malcolm IV. grants to the abbot and monks the heads, (the tongues excepted), of certain fifhes, fuppo'ed to be a fmall kind of whales caught in fome particular diftrict of the Forth, near the abbey church. The words of the grant are, " Pro falute animæ predecefforis mei Davidis Regis, capita pifcium qui dicuntur crefpeis præter linguam, qui in meo Dominio ex illa parte Scottwater applicuerint, in qua parte illorum Ecclefia fita eft." Malcolm IV. likewife gave them a grant of the half of the blubber (dimidium fagiminis) of the crefpeis, or fmall whales, which fhould be taken between the Tay and Forth for the ufe of the church, " ad luminaria coram altaribus prenominatæ Ecclefiæ."—Several indulgences granted by different pontiffs are recorded in the chartulary of this abbey. As oil of olives could not be procured within the diocefe of St Andrew's, Pope Nicholas, by bull in 1459, grants a free indulgence to make ufe of butter, (et aliis lacticiniis) during Lent, and on all other days when animal food was forbidden.

† It does not appear which of the pontiffs of that name.

conveniently within its precincts. Here the Scottiſh Nobles ſometimes held their aſſemblies. The Engliſh ſoldiers utterly deſtroyed this magnificent fabrick. M. Weſtminſter juſtifies this brutal extravagance. The Scots, (ſays he,) had converted the Houſe of the Lord into a den of thieves, by holding their rebellious parliaments *there*. The church, however, and a few manſions *fit for monks*, were graciouſly ſpared by the Engliſh reformers *." The cells belonging to the abbey, which were ſpared by the Engliſh, and likewiſe, it is probable, the principal part of the church, were demoliſhed at the Reformation in 1560 †. The ruins of the abbey are now but inconſiderable. There ſtill remains a window which belonged to the Frater-hall, remarkable for its ſize and beauty ‡. At the general diſſolution of monaſteries in 1560, Mr Robert Pitcairn was appointed commendator of Dunfermline. The abbey was erected into a temporal Lordſhip in 1593, and beſtowed on Queen Anne of Denmark, James VI's Queen. This Lordſhip included all the lands which belonged to the monaſtery on this ſide the Forth, except the barony of Burntiſland and New Birne, in which Sir Robert Melvil of Murdocamy, and Andrew Wood of Largo were infeft. Muſſelburgh, which alſo belonged to this monaſtery, was erected

* Hailes's Annals.

† Robert Lindſay, in his Hiſtory of Scotland, ſays, that the abbey of Dunfermline was deſtroyed by the Reformers on the 28th March 1560.

‡ In the Maygate, immediately adjacent to the monaſtery, is a houſe which belonged to the laſt commendator, and which tradition ſays was inhabited by his miſtreſs. Over the ſtreet door of this houſe is the following curious inſcription.

Sen Vord is Thrall and That is Fre
Keep Veill Thy Tonge I coinſell The.

erected into a temporal Lordſhip, and given to Lord Chancellor Thirleſtone. In 1641, Charles I. granted a leaſe of the Lordſhip for three 19 years, to Charles Seton, Earl of Dunfermline. To this leaſe the Marquis of Tweeddale obtained a right in payment of a debt due to him by the Earl of Dunfermline, and afterward got the leaſe renewed in his own name. The laſt grant to the Tweeddale family having expired in 1780, the Counteſs of Rothes, Lord Elgin, and others, obtained a tack of the teinds of the Lordſhip, for behoof of the heritors of the pariſh, for payment of L. 100 Sterling yearly *.

In the middle of the church-yard, there was, till within theſe 3 years, a moſt venerable thorn, ſaid to have been 400 years old; at the foot of this tree, in Popiſh times, the people are ſaid to have held a market on Sabbath, before aſſembling for public worſhip †.

Church and Tombs.—The church is of great antiquity, being a part of that large and magnificent edifice built by Malcolm

---

* There is to be ſeen in the Advocate's Library at Edinburgh, a very elegant copy of St Jerom's Latin Bible in MS. beautifully illuminated. This Bible, (according to a note annexed), is ſaid to have been uſed in the great church at Dunfermline in the reign of David I.; and at the time of the Reformation, to have been carried over to France, (along with many other things belonging to the church and abbacy), where it became the property of the famous Monſ. Foucault, as appears from his coat of arms affixed, at the ſale of whoſe books, it was purchaſed by a Scotch gentleman, by whom it was brought back to this country.

† On a piece of level ground, a little ſouth of the monaſtery, is a hillock about 15 feet high, and 300 in circumference, which, according to tradition, was formed of ſand, brought by people on their backs from the ſea, as a penance enjoined by the church in the days of Popery. The name of the hillock, Pardieus, *i. e.* Par Dieu, ſeems to favour the ſtory of its origin, at leaſt to prove its being ſomehow connected with religion. On Craigluſcar-hill, in this pariſh, there are the remains of an ancient fortification, ſaid to be Pictiſh.

Malcolm Canmore. In its ſtructure it is ſaid to reſemble the cathedral at Durham. It is very capacious, and fit for containing ſo numerous an auditory, as few ordinary voices can reach, ſo as to be diſtinctly heard ; ſuſceptible of much improvement, and of being made, if not a neat and comfortable, at leaſt a dignified looking place of worſhip. It is much to be regretted, that far from any attempts being made to beautify ſo venerable a ſtructure, very little attention has been paid to have it ſeated, and fitted up with becoming decency ; the whole is cold and dirty, and wears rather a gloomy appearance. A ſtranger may well be ſurpriſed, to find the church of a town ſo populous and thriving, and which externally has ſo grand an appearance, ſo miſerably fitted up within. This may be accounted for, from the church having never been legally divided among the heritors, the non-reſidence of ſome of the moſt conſiderable property, and ſeveral of them being of the Seceſſion principles ; from the inattention of the town-council, and from the diſpoſition very prevalent among heritors, to be at as little expenſe as poſſible, in what regards either churches, or thoſe who officiate in them. To theſe cauſes may be added the want of the interference of ſome ſpirited and generous individual, from whoſe exertions, improvements in general are often found to originate.

After the famous Iona or Icolmkill, in the Hebrides, the church of Dunfermline became the common cemetery of the kings of Scotland. Here Malcolm Canmore, and his Queen St Margaret, and other 7 of our Scottiſh kings were interred *. The reader, fond of antiquities, might
naturally

---

* According to Sir Robert Sibbald, in his Hiſtory of Fife, there were interred at Dunfermline, Malcolm III. with St Margaret his Queen, and King Edgar their ſon. Alexander I. with Sibilla his Queen. David I.
with

naturally expect, that the royal tombs would furnish us
with something worthy of his attention ; but it is little in
our power to gratify the antiquary ; were it not that the
page of hiftory affures us, that with us are the fepulchres
of kings, it could not now be otherwife difcovered. The
principal part of the church appears to have been demolifhed at the time of the Reformation, and to have buried
the royal monuments in its ruins. The area of this part
of the church is covered with rubbifh to the depth of 3 or
4 feet ; it has long been ufed as burying ground, and on
that account cannot now be explored. In digging a grave
lately, there was difcovered a ftone-coffin 6 feet in length,
containing human bones ; at the fame time were found feveral fragments of a marble monument, which had been
finely carved and gilt. Here is fhown what is faid to have
been the tomb-ftone of St Margaret, and 6 flat ftones, each
9 feet in length, where as many kings are faid to lie *.

Eminent

with his two wives. Malcolm IV. Alexander III. and his Queen Margaret. Robert I. and Ifobel his Queen. Edmond II. fon to King Malcolm III and his brother Etheldrade, Earl of Fife. Macduff, Earl of
Fife. Conftantine, Earl of Fife. William Ramfay, Earl of Fife. Thomas Randel, Earl of Murray, Governor of Scotland.

* In this church-yard, a handfome monument has been erected to the
memory of the late Earl of Elgin, a Nobleman whofe memory is dear
to thofe who had the happinefs of being known to him. Seldom has a
perfon in any rank of life been more generally beloved, feldom has high
rank been diftinguifhed for fo many virtues, fuch amiable and conde-
fcending manners. Refpected and beloved in life, his death was the
caufe of fincere and general forrow and regret in this parifh. We fhall
tranfcribe the following elegant tribute to his memory.

Sacred

Sacred to the memory of
Charles Earl of Elgin and Kincardine,
who died the 14th of May 1771, aged 39 years.
By the goodneſs of his heart, and the virtues of his life,
He adorn'd the high rank which he poſſeſſed ;
In his manners amiable and gentle,
In his affections warm and glowing ;
In his temper, modeſt, candid and chearful,
In his conduct, manly, and truly honourable,
In his character of huſband, father, friend and maſter,
As far as human imperfection admits,
Unblemiſhed.
Pious without fuperſtition,
Charitable without oſtentation.
While he lived,
The bleſſing of them that were ready to periſh came upon him.
Now
Their tears embalm his memory.

Reader,
Beholding here laid in duſt
The remains,
Which once ſo much virtue animated,
Think of the vanity of life,
Look forward to its end,
And prepare as he did for eternity.

In the preſent church are the tombs of Mr Robert Pitcairn, Commendator of Dunfermline, and of Mr William Shaw, Architect to King
James VI. King Robert the Bruce is ſaid to lie here. His interment
at Dunfermline is thus deſcribed by one of our ancient Scottiſh Bards :

They have him had to Dumfermline,
And him folemnly erded fyne,
In a fair tomb into the Quire.
Biſhops and Prelate that there were,
Aſſoilzied him, when the ſervice
Was done, as they beſt could deviſe.
And fyne, upon the other day,
Sorry and wo they went their way,
And he debowelled was cleanly,
And als balmed fyne full richly.

And the worthy Lord of Dowglas
His heart, as it forefpoken was,
Received has in great daintie,
With great and fair folemnitie *.

In the porch of the church, is a neat Monument, erected to the memory of Mr Rolland, late of Gafk, father of Adam Rolland, Efq; Advocate, with the following excellent character of him, written in elegant Latin.

M.   S.

Adami Rolland de Gafk,
Viri non uno nomine celebrandi,
Utpote non paucis virtutibus ornati,
Ob pietatem erga Deum,
Amorem in patriam,
Benevolentiam in genus humanum,
Amabilis ;
Ob vitæ integritatem,
Morum comitatem,
Affectuum temperantiam,
Spectabilis ;
Quifvos paterno, probos quofvis fraterno
Omnes benigno animo amplexus;
In publicis, privatifque officiis
Prudens, fidus, diligens ;
Mente et manu munificus,
Futurorum providus,
Fortunæ femper fecurus :
Ita volente
D.   O.   M.
XII. Calend. Auguft M,DCC,XLIII.
Ætat. LVII.
Animam Creatori, exuvias terræ,
Reddidit ;
Trifte fui defiderium, amicis relinquens.

* Life and Acts of Robert Bruce by John Barbour.

Eminent

Eminent Perſons.—Dunfermline was the birth place of the Princeſs Elizabeth from whom his preſent Majeſty is deſcended. As Dunfermline was the uſual reſidence of Malcolm Canmore and his illuſtrious Queen, ſome ſhort notice of theſe perſonages will not, it is preſumed, be improper. Malcolm Canmore was the eldeſt ſon of Duncan, King of Scotland, who was aſſaſſinated by Macbeth. Upon the uſurpation of Macbeth, Malcolm fled into England, and during his exile in that country, reſided a conſiderable time at the court of Edward the Confeſſor; through the exertions of Macduff, Thane of Fife, and Siward, Earl of Northumberland, the uſurper was ſlain, and Malcolm aſcended the throne of his father in 1057. About 1070 Malcolm eſpouſed the celebrated Margaret *. Malcolm, (ſays Lord Hailes), " was a prince utterly illiterate, of intrepid courage, but of no diſtinguiſhed abilities." With reſpect to the internal polity of his kingdom, he appears to have been guided by Queen Margaret. An incident is related of Malcolm, which is highly deſcriptive of his character. Having received intelligence that one of his nobles

* Margaret was the daughter of Edward, ſon of Edmund Ironſide, King of England. Upon William the Conqueror aſcending the Engliſh throne, Edgar, ſon of Edward, with his mother Agatha, and two ſiſters, Margaret and Chriſtian, retired into Scotland. Some authors ſay, that being on a voyage to Hungary, they were accidentally driven thither by a ſtorm. The place in the Frith where the ſhip anchored is a ſmall bay, about a mile N. W. of the N. Queensferry, near the preſent toll-bar. This bay is called St Margaret's Hope. On a ſtair-caſe in the houſe of Pennycuik, in Mid Lothian, there is a painting which repreſents the landing of Margaret at the Hope, the proceſſion from thence to Dunfermline, and the King and Queen, the day after their marriage, entertaining a number of mendicants. The proceſſion is ſaid to have been on foot. On the ſide of the preſent road, near Pitreavie, about two miles from Dunfermline, is a large ſtone called St Margaret's ſtone. Here ſhe is ſaid to have reſted leaning on this ſtone. N. and S. Queensferry derive their name from St Margaret.

nobles had formed a defign againft his life, he fought an opportunity of meeting the traitor in a folitary place. " Now, faid he, unfheathing his fword, we are all alone, and armed' alike, you feek my life, take it." The peni- tent threw himfelf at the King's feet, implored forgivenefs, and obtained it. At the earneft requeft of Margaret, Malcolm is faid to have abolifhed an abominable law of King Evenus or Eugenius. " Uxoris etiarh precibus de- diffe fertur, ut primam novæ nuptæ noctem, quæ proceri- bus per gradus quofdam lege Regis Eugenii debebatur ; fponfus dimidiata argenti marca redimeri poffet : quam penfionem adhuc Marchetas mulierum vocant." Buch. lib. 7. 21.

Malcolm was flain at the fiege of Alnwick in Northum- berland 13th September 1093, his body was depofited at Tinmouth, and afterward brought to Dunfermline.

The character of Queen Margaret is fully and elegantly delineated by Lord Hailes in his Annals. " She reftored (fays he) the religious obfervance of Sunday, an inftitu- tion no lefs admirable in a political than in a religious light. In the adminiftration of her houfehold, fhe fo blended feverity of manners with complacency, that fhe was equally revered and loved by all who approached her. She entertained many ladies about her perfon, employed their leifure hours in the amufements of the needle, and gave ftrict attention to the decency of their conduct. In her prefence, fays Turgot, nothing unfeemly was ever done or uttered. On the education of her children, fhe beftow-, ed the moft confcientious care. She enjoined their pre- ceptors to chaftife them as oft as they needed chaftifement. On them fhe beftowed her tendereft thoughts in her dying moments. Turgot pathetically defcribes his laft interview with this affectionate mother. After long difcourfe on her fpiritual ftate, fhe thus addreffed him, " Farewell, my life draws

draws to a cloſe, but you may ſurvive me long. To you
I cᴏmmit the charge of my children, teach them above all
things to love and fear God ; and whenever you ſee any
of them attain to the height of earthly grandeur, Oh !
then, in an eſpecial manner be to them as a father and a
guide. Admoniſh, and if need be, reprove them, left they
be ſwelled with the pride of momentary glory, through
avarice offend God, or by reaſon of the proſperity of this
world, become careleſs of eternal life. This in the preſence of *Him*, who is now our only witneſs, I beſeech you
to promiſe and to perform *."

Springs,

* By a tedious and painful indiſpoſition, endured with exemplary pa-
tience, ſhe was brought very low. During a ſhort interval of eaſe, ſhe
devoutly received the communion; ſoon after her anguiſh of body returned with redoubled violence, ſhe ſtretched herſelf on her couch, and
calmly waited for the moment of her diſſolution. Cold, and in the ago-
nies of death, ſhe ceaſed not to put up her ſupplications to heaven.
Theſe were ſome of her words : " Have mercy upon me, O God ; according to the multitude of thy tender mercies, blᴏt out my iniquities, make
me to hear joy and gladneſs, that the bones which thou haſt broken may
rejoice. Caſt me not away from thy preſence, and take not thy holy Spirit
from me, reſtore unto me the joy of thy ſalvation. The ſacrifices of God
are a broken ſpirit ; a broken and a contrite ſpirit, O God, thou wilt
noʈ deſpiſe. Do good, in thy good pleaſure, unto Zion, build the walls
of Jeruſalem." At that moment, her ſon Edgar, returning from the
army, approached her couch. " How fares it with the King and my
Edward ?" The youth ſtood ſilent, " I know all," cried ſhe, I know
all : By this holy croſs, by your filial affeꞔtion, I adjure you, tell me the
truth. " He anſwered, your huſband and your ſon are both ſlain."
Lifting her eyes and hands towards heaven, ſhe ſaid, " Praiſe and bleſſing be to thee, Almighty God, that thou haſt been pleaſed to make me
endure ſo bitter anguiſh in the hour of my departure, thereby, as I truſt
to purify me in ſome meaſure from the corruption of my ſins ; and thou
Lord Jeſus Chriſt, who, through the will of the Father, haſt enlivened
the

Springs, Lakes, Coasts, &c.—Some springs are mineral, and suppofed to be medicinal. The fprings from which the water is conveyed to the town, in lead pipes, are rather inferior to fome others, and infufficient for fupplying the inhabitants; but it is believed, that endeavours will foon be ufed for meliorating the quality, and increafing the quantity of this neceffary article. The Lyne is the only brook deferving attention in the parifh. Its fource is near the eaftern extremity of it. Having received various acceffions, it becomes confiderable below the town, frequently overflows its banks, and lays the rich fields of Pittencrieff, Loggie, Cavil, and Pitliver under water. After running towards the weftern extremity of the parifh, it unites with another fmall brook, and takes a fouthern direction towards the frith of Forth. There are feveral lakes of confiderable depth and extent, in which perch, pike, and eel are found. Two of them may be drained at no great expenfe.—The fouthern extremity of the parifh extends about a mile and a half along the coaft of the frith

of

the world by thy death, Oh! deliver me." While pronouncing *deliver me*, fhe expired *.

* *She died 16th November* 1093, *and was buried at Dunfermline. In the* 1250 *or* 1251, *her bones were removed, and placed in a more honourable place in the Church of the Trinity of Dunfermline,* Hailes's Ann. " *Alexander III. caufed her bones to be put into a cheft of filver, enriched with precious ftones, after many prayers and folemn proceffions, and placed it in the nobleft part of the church. During the troubles of the Reformation, the coffer wherein her head and hair were inclofed, was carried to the caftle of Edinburgh, and from thence tranfported to the manor-houfe of the Laird of* Dury, *who was a Reverend Father, Prieft and Monk of Dunfermline. After he had kept this religious pledge fome years, it was in* 1597 *delivered into the hands of the Jefuits, miffionaries in Scotland, who feeing it was in danger to be loft or prophaned, tranfported it to Antwerp. Her relics are kept in the Scots College at* Doway *in a buft of filver.*" Hay's Scotia Sacra.

of Forth. The coaft here is partly flat, and partly high and bold. The fifh found on the other coafts of Scotland are fometimes caught. No rocks, banks, nor iflands, within the Frith, are off this part of the coaft. The fea-weed is ufed as manure. Kelp is occafionally made in fmall quantities. Salt is alfo made, which is reckoned of an excellent quality. Soap is manufactured in fmaller quantities than formerly. There are two excellent harbours. The one is fituated at the village of Limekilns, and the other at Charleftown. They admit veffels at ftream tides, from 200 to 300 tons. Many of the articles imported into the country are conveyed to thefe harbours; and from them, a great deal of its valuable productions are exported to other parts.

Agriculture, &c.—The foil is various. The low ground is a deep, ftrong, black loam, which gradually becomes lighter towards the N. Clay is found in every field, at no great diftance from the furface. In fome places it is covered with earth that is brown and gravelly, and in other places with what is dark, extremely rich, and fertile. Above the town, the foil is much inferior to the foil below it. Though greatly improved of late years, yet many acres of moor and morafs ftill remain in a wild and uncultivated ftate, of which the one half is improvable. In this, as in the other diftricts of Scotland, hufbandry was in a languid ftate till about the middle of this century. Inattention, indolence, fervitudes, bad roads, the want of wheel carriages, and other neceffary implements of hufbandry, prevented all improvements. The land is divided among 80 proprietors, of whom the Earl of Elgin is the principal. His Lordfhip lately gave new leafes of moft of his farms, and built excellent farm-houfes and offices upon them. His lands are fufficiently enclofed, and regularly fubdivided, with fences

of

of ftone and lime, or ditches and hedge-rows of various
kinds, in a profperous condition. His Lordfhip is alfo
planting all the uncultivated fpots, and confpicuous places
of his eftate, with belts and clumps of trees, which, in a few
years hence, will have a fine effect in ornamenting this part
of the country. George Chalmers, Efq; late of Pittencrieff, about 1760, began improving his lands after the
Englifh mode. Regardlefs of the ancient cuftoms and
prejudices of the people, he perfevered in his expenfive improvements, which for many ages will probably remain as
monuments of his ingenuity. Much about the above mentioned period, or foon after it, the late Sir John Halket of
Pitferran began his judicious improvements. Unlike many
thoughtlefs landholders, who repair to populous cities to
fpend their time, health, and fortunes in fafhionable amufements, extravagance, and folly, this Honourable Baronet refided on his eftate, infpected his operations, and influenced
his neighbours to cultivate the ground. Accordingly, it
foon affumed a new appearance. Agriculture became an
object of importance. Every landholder began to ftudy
what kind of culture might ultimately become moft beneficial. A great deal of wafte land was drained, levelled,
and enclofed. In fome places, the fences confift of ftone
and lime, and in other places, of fingle or double ditches,
hedges, and plantation. On the barren and unimproveable
parts of the country, many hundred thoufand trees are
planted, which are profpering, enriching the foil, and becoming a fource of wealth to the proprietors. The moft
numerous and thriving are, the Scotch fir, beech, elm,
plane, larix, fpruce, afh, and oak. With thefe, the town of
Dunfermline lately planted 170 acres of its wafte land,
which was not worth 6 d. the acre, but in 50 years hence
may bring L. 200 Sterling the acre. The climate and foil
in the foutbern parts of the parifh, being extremely different

ferent from the northern, the mode of cultivating and cropping is alſo different. The arable land on the S. is ploughed
with Small's chain-plough, drawn by two horſes. In ſome
places on the N. the Scotch plough, drawn by four horſes,
is uſed, and the ancient diſtinction between croft and outfield preſerved. The whole manure is laid upon the croft,
which is conſtantly in tillage, while the outfield is occaſionally ploughed, and afterwards left to reſt. But this
mode of culture prevails only in a very few places, where
manure cannot be obtained without great expenſe. On the
S. of the town, the land is highly cultivated, and produces
as luxuriant crops as any in the kingdom. Farms are uſually divided into different portions, and the crops are in the
following order: After ſummer fallow, wheat is ſown, the
next year, barley, the following year, graſs, and laſt of all,
oats; ſome, after ſummer-fallow or potatoes, ſow wheat,
peaſe and beans, barley, graſs, and oats, in their order.
Wheat is generally ſown in September and October; peaſe,
beans, and oats, from the middle of February to the end of
April; and barley, from the middle of March to the end
of May. Potatoes are planted after the plough, about the
beginning or middle of April. Hay is made from the
middle of June to the end of July. The other crops are
uſually reaped from the middle of Auguſt to the middle of
October; ſometimes the harveſt is earlier, and ſometimes it
is later. Flour, oats, oatmeal, and barley, are imported;
wheat is exported.

Rent.—The valued rent of the pariſh is L. 22,127 Scotch.
It is difficult to aſcertain the real rent, as many of the landholders poſſeſs their own lands. In general, it is valued
according to its quality, and diſtance from the town of Dunfermline. In the immediate vicinity, it is feued from L. 8
to L. 20; and lets annually from L. 3 to L. 5 Sterling the
acre,

acre. On the S. of the town, it lets annually from L. 1 to
L. 3, and on the N. from 5 s. to L. 2 Sterling the acre.
One third of the furface would let at L. 1, 5 s. and two-
thirds at 10 s. Sterling the acre. Valuing the land in this
manner, the whole furface, confifting of 36 fquare miles, or
23,040 fquare acres, would let at L. 17,280 Sterling a-year.
Of this yearly rent, the fourth part may perhaps be fpent
in the parifh. The value of farms is various. Many have
fmall portions of land. About 50 farmers pay annually
from L. 50 to L. 100 ; 30 from L. 100 to L. 200 ; 10 from
L. 200 to L. 300 ; and 6 from L. 300 to L. 400 Sterling.
A farm which prefently lets at L. 320 annually was lately
bought for L. 17,500 Sterling.

Value of Stock.

1000 draught-horfes, valued at L. 12 each,	L. 12,000
64 faddle and carriage horfes, at L. 20,	1280
800 beft cattle, at L. 8, - - -	6400
1600 inferior ditto, at L. 4, - -	6400
2000 beft fheep, at L. 1, - - -	2000
1000 interior ditto, at 10 s. - - -	500
200 fwine, at L. 1, 10 s. - -	300
Total value of ftock, -	L. 28,880

ANNUAL

ANNUAL PRODUCE.

Crops.	Acres.	Produce the acre. Bolls.	Price the boll.	Total price the acre.	Total produce. Bolls.	Total value.
Oats, - - -	6500	7	L. 0 16 0	L. 5 12 0	45.500	L. 36,400 0 0
Bear and barley, -	3300	7	0 18 0	6 6 0	23.100	20,740 0 0
Wheat, - - -	1000	10	1 3 0	11 10 0	10.000	11,500 0 0
Peas and beans, -	2000	6	0 17 0	5 2 0	12.000	10,200 0 0
Potatoes, - -	400	50	0 5 0	12 10 0	20.000	5,000 0 0
Turnips, - -	200			5 0 0		1,000 0 0
Pasture, - -	6000			0 10 0		3,000 0 0
Waste land, lakes, rivers,	400			0 1 0		20 0 0
Gardens, orchards,	200			8 0 0		1,600 0 0
Woods and plantations,	550					300 0 0
Flax, - -	50	*Stones.* 22	*The stone.* L. 0 10 6	11 0 0	*Stones.* 1,100	550 0 0
Meadow hay, or natural grass,	140	100	0 0 6	2 10 0	14,000	350 0 0
Sown grass, -	2000	200	0 0 7	5 16 8	320,000	9,333 6 8
Ditto fold, the acre,	300	—	—	6 0 0	—	1,800 0 0
Straw at 2 s. the boll of corn,						9,200 0 0
Pasture at L. 5 the horse, L. 3 the cow, 8 s. the sheep,						36,500 0 0
Mines, -						—
Total value of annual produce,						L. 147,493 6 8

Minerals.—This parish abounds with valuable mines and minerals. In many places there are prodigious rocks of freestone, extremely white, durable, and susceptible of a fine polish. Granite, or blue whin, is also found in great quantities, and of an excellent quality for paving streets, making roads, and other useful purposes. Limestone is found in various parts of the parish, near the surface. This valuable fossil has lately been wrought to a great extent. Several seams are quarried, and manufactured in the lands of Craiglufcar, belonging to Charles Dury, Esq; and also in the lands of South Fod, belonging to Mr John Stenhoufe. Besides supplying the interior parts of the country in the immediate neighbourhood, the lime is carried to a considerable distance for manure and building. But the most extensive limeworks in this parish, or even in Britain, belonging to any particular person, are those of the Earl of Elgin, situated on the coast of the frith of Forth. From the vestiges of limekilns along the shore, the village of Limekilns derives its name; and it appears from these ancient ruins, that the limeworks were carried on at a very remote period. The seam of limestone is opposite to the Forth. It is a mile long from E. to W. from 20 to 50 feet thick, and dips to the E. and W. from about the centre. The late Earl, his Lordship's father, who was no less distinguished for his intellectual than his moral qualities, conceived the idea of extending his limeworks on a larger scale than had ever been attempted by any of his ancestors. Accordingly, in the years 1777 and 1778, his Lordship began to build nine large draw-kilns, a harbour, waggon-ways, for drawing the stone from the quarry to the kilnheads, and a village for accommodating his work people, which, after himself, was called Charlestown. As the works were great, the expense was proportionable; before they were finished, the necessary utensils for quarrying procured, and the difficulties inseparable from new and great

undertakings

undertakings ſurmounted, it is ſaid they coſt above L. 14,000 Sterling. But great as this expenſe was, it has been repaid. By prudent arrangements, and conſtant attention, the works have ſucceeded beyond expectation. Their ſucceſs was partly owing to the fidelity and diſcretion of the managers, and party to the valuable qualities of the lime, which ſecured for it a ready and an extenſive ſale. Ever ſince their commencement, the public has progreſſively increaſed its demands. From 80,000 to 90,000 tons of limeſtone are quarried annually. It is partly manufactured into lime at the works; and partly ſold in the unburnt ſtone. Of the manufactured lime, about 200,000 bolls of ſhells, or unflocked lime; and from 30,000 to 40,000 chalders, at 18 bolls the chalder, of flocked lime, are annually ſold in 1300 ſeparate cargoes. The total annual value is above L. 10,000 Sterling. Lime ſhells, including all expenſe at ſhipping, are ſold at L. 4 Sterling the hundred bolls; flacked lime at 5 s. 3 d. the chalder, or 3½ d. the boll; and limeſtone at 1 s. 8 d. the ton. The principal market for the lime is along the coaſts of the frith of Forth and Tay, and the N. of Scotland. From 30 to 50 veſſels are uſually lying at Charleſtown, waiting their turns of loading limeſhells during the ſummer months *.—From the very liberal credit that has always been given at theſe works, it is obvious, that a large capital is neceſſary for carrying them on. But neither the money ſunk in erecting nor conducting them has been loſt. While they have amply rewarded their noble proprietor, they have occaſioned an extenſive circulation of money; retained in their native land,

---

* Above 200 men are employed in quarrying, and other neceſſary operations. They work moſtly by the piece, and during the limeburning months, earn from 1 s. 6 d. to 2 s. the day. About 4000 chalders, or 12,000 tons of coal, are annually conſumed in burning the lime.

land, and supported many thousand people ; greatly promoted improvements in agriculture; and may be considered among the moſt laudable, important, and beneficial works for the good of the country, that have ever been undertaken in this part of the kingdom.—Ironſtone is found in the lands belonging to Sir Charles Halket, Baronet. Of this mineral there are two ſeams at a ſmall diſtance from each other. The uppermoſt is 4 inches, and the lowermoſt 2¼ inches thick. Being above a ſeam of coal, they are wrought along with it. They are of an excellent quality for making cannon, and have been exported to the Carron Company for that purpoſe. The ironſtone began to be wrought by that Company in 1771, and in 1773 and 1774, there were 60 miners, and as many bearers employed in the mines. Since that period, the ironſtone has been wrought by the tackſmen of the coal.—Coal is alſo found in great abundance in almoſt every part of this pariſh. The coal mines of this pariſh are the moſt ancient in Scotland. The earlieſt account of coal uſed as fuel, is a charter of William de Oberwill, in which he granted liberty to the Abbot and Convent of Dunfermline to open a coal-pit wherever they inclined, excepting on his arable land, and permitted them to take as much as was neceſſary for their own uſe, and to open a new mine whenever the old was exhauſted ; but not to ſell any part of it to others. The charter is dated at Dunfermline, on the Tüeſday immediately before the feaſt of St Ambroſe 1291*. But at that early period

---

* Carta de Pethyncreff de dono Willielmi de Oberwill, 1291.

Omnibus has literas viſuris vel audituris Willielmus de Oberwill, dominus de Pethyncreff, eternam in Domino ſalutem ; noveritis me, ex mera gracia nixa et propria voluntate, conceſſiſſe religioſis viris Abbatti et Conventui de Dunfermlyn, unam carbonariam in terra nixa de Pethyncreff ubicunque voluerint, excepta terra arabili, ita quod ſufficientiam ad uſus

suos

period it does not appear that coal was wrought to a great extent. It was only used in the abbey, and by persons of distinction in the country. In progress of time it was more generally used as fuel; and when trade began to flourish, it was exported to foreign parts. Although it was worked by crop levels ever since the above mentioned period, there was little exported till about the middle of this century. Even so late as 1763, the annual value of exported coal was only L. 200; and in 1771, it did not exceed L. 500 Sterling. The coal-mines, since 1771, have been sources of great wealth to many of the proprietors.

Description of the Subterraneous Coal Strata.—The first appearance of coal on the S. W. extremity of the parish, is a seam about 2 feet thick, situated under the Earl of Elgin's lime-rock at Charlestown. Northward, near broad-hills, there is another seam, from 4 to 6 feet thick, which dips very rapidly towards the N. E. the crop of which has been wrought by a level in the same direction. Advancing still northward, about 3 miles from the Frith, through a fine level country, we again find various seams of excellent coal in the lands of Sir Charles Halket of Pit-ferran, immediately above the village of Crosford. From a remote period, the family of Pitferran, obtained from Government, the privilege of exporting these coals to foreign parts, free of all duty whatever. The original privilege was renewed by Queen Anne on December 21. 1706,

suos inde percipiant, et aliis vendere non presumant, una vero deficiente aliam pro voluntate sua facientes quoties viderint expediri sibi, &c. &c. In cujus rei testimonium presentibus sigillum meum apposui, una cum sigillo officialis domini Episcopi Sancti Andræ, et sigillo Roberti de Ma-lavilla, qui sigilla sua ad instantiam meam presentibus apposuerunt. Datum apud Dunfermlyn die Martis proxima ante festum Sancti Ambrosii Episcopi et Confessoris, anno Gratiæ millio ducentesimo nonagesimo primo.

1706, and ratified in Parliament on March 21. 1707. The family continued to enjoy the privilege till 1788, when it was purchafed by Government for L. 40,000 Sterling, when the property that could injure the revenue was nearly exhaufted.

The moft remarkable, in thefe lands, are the feams, confifting of 5 feet, 2 feet, and 4 feet each. They are all found within the fpace of 14 yards, at the diftance of 3 fathoms and a half from each other, and in their natural ftate, they dip from one foot in four, to one in fix towards the N. E. Immediately above the two feet feam, are the ftrata of iron-ftone already mentioned. The furface being irregular, the pits are from 10 to 80 yards in depth. Eaftward from the mines of Pitferran, are thofe of Urquhart and Pittencrieff, which are nearly exhaufted, until deeper levels are made or engines erected.

Northward from thefe are the numerous feams of coal that appear above each other, (as *per* fection), fituated under the lands of Weft and Midbalbridge, Clune, Lufcar, and Rofebank. They are the property of the Earl of Elgin *. They contain immenfe quantities of coal, of various qualities, within 30 fathoms from the furface of the uppermoft

---

* The difficulty of finding a regular fupply of coals to burn his lime, lately induced his Lordfhip to purchafe this extenfive field of coal. It confifts of more than 900 fquare acres, and contains valuable feams of all the various kinds that are found in the country. From thefe coal-mines, his Lordfhip is making a waggon way, of 4 miles extent, to his lime works. It is faid he intends to make a new harbour, a little weft from his harbour at Charleftown, for exporting his coals, which will have 20 feet of water at ftream tides, and be one of the beft in Scotland. A harbour fo fafe and convenient will be extremely advantageous for the town of Dunfermline, whenever the canal, which has been propofed, fhall be made from the town to the Frith. Nor will it be lefs advantageous for the country in general than for his Lordfhip.

uppermoſt ſeam, which is covered with other 4 fathoms of earth. None of them are at a greater diſtance from each other than 5 fathoms.

	Feet.	Inch.
The 1ſt ſeam near the ſurface, is	4	thick.
—— 2d, - -	7	
—— 3d, - -	6	3
—— 4th, - -	2	6
—— 5th, - -	2	
—— 6th, - -	5	
—— 7th, - -	3	

Theſe 7 ſeams contain　　29　9 inch. of excellent coal.

The next colliery deſerving attention is Roſebank : It contains the following ſeams :

	Feet.	Inch.
The 1ſt ſeam is,	4	6 thick.
—— 2d, -	3	4
—— 3d, -	4	
—— 4th, -	4	
—— 5th, -	3	

Making altogether, 18 10 of coal under thoſe lands. There are found in theſe collieries belonging to the Earl of Elgin, a kind of allum rock, and alſo ſoft ſulphur, which would make green vitriol. Detached pieces of ironſtone ſometimes appear. This is the only colliery in the pariſh in which inflammable air is found.

The next in the ſame direction is the colliery of Balmule, which comprehends the coal lying under the lands of Lochhead, Coalton, Lochend, and Balmule. In number
ber

ber of feams, thicknefs, depth, and quality, it refembles Rofebank.

Having mentioned the collieries in the northern direction, it may be proper to return to thofe in the middle of the parifh. Of thefe middle, Baldridge colliery, the property of Robert Wellwood, Efq; of Garvoch, deferves attention. It is in many refpects fimilar to that of Pittencrieff, and the other mines in the fame direction. The loweft feam is a fine fplint coal. This colliery has been worked for many years, and been extremely advantageous to the proprietor. Eaftward, in the fame line, are the collieries of Venterfair, Dunfermline town coal, and Whitefield. They are worked level free, and contain an immenfe quantity of excellent coal, which is moftly fold in the country. The town fupplies its inhabitants with this important article at a reduced price, which makes the fuel cheaper than in any other town in Scotland.

To the eaft of thefe is the colliery of Halbeath. It contains 8 or 9 feams of good workable coal, amounting in all to upwards of 30 feet. The loweft or fplint feam is the fame as in the other collieries, and is in high repute. Some of the other feams on the north of a large dike *, which

---

* Dikes are confufed maffes of metals, that in fome places feem to interfect the earth from the furface to the centre. They are of different thicknefs. They generally alter the fituation of the ftrata, by cutting them off entirely, and fubftituting other ftrata in the place of them, or by elevating or depreffing them beyond their natural fituation. Sometimes they raife the coal to the very furface, and at other times, fink it to an unapproachable depth. Befides throwing up the coal, they are often of great ufe in keeping off the water from the neighbouring mines. The dikes with which the coal of this parifh is troubled run in different directions, but moft generally towards the S. E. and N. W. †. Their courfe is however very uncertain. Their elevation is generally from 40 to 80 degrees, and they are compofed of every kind of fubftance, from hard green whin and white fpar, to blue clay.

† (See the annexed fketch).

which has a S. E. direction, have been wrought many
years ago, by crop levels. The coal dips nearly in the
ſame manner and direction as in the weſt of the pariſh,
but is freer of dikes. This colliery was purchaſed in ſummer 1785 by Meſſrs Campbell, Moriſon and Company.
They have built two large engines. The one is erected
on ſtone, and the other on a frame of wood. From this
colliery vaſt quantities of coal are at preſent exported.
The ſame ſeams are found in the lands of Praithouſe, and
run eaſtward to the croſſgates into the neighbouring pariſh.

Sinking pits is not difficult in this pariſh. The cover
generally conſiſts of a few fathoms of earth, and afterward
freeſtone and blue metals.

Explanation of the Eye Sketch.—Were the ſeams of coal
and dikes in the pariſh of Dunfermline viſible, they would
appear as they are exhibited on the annexed ſketch.

The letters a. b. c. denote the three ſeams of coal in
the eſtate of Pitferran, &c.

D. The two bands of iron-ſtone, above the two feet or ſecond ſeam.

E. E. E. The loweſt level mine driven from the ſouth of
  Pitferran, to the face where it is ſtanding in
  Lord Elgin's property.

E. E. E. In dotted lines, ſhow how the ſaid level, if continued, would interſect and drain the uppermoſt ſeams of coal to the depth of the level.

A. A. A croſs level, by which the crop of all the north
  ſeams have been worked.

B. B. B. A level brought up from the lower grounds,
  farther ſouth, which is a few fathoms deeper
  than the one above.

M.

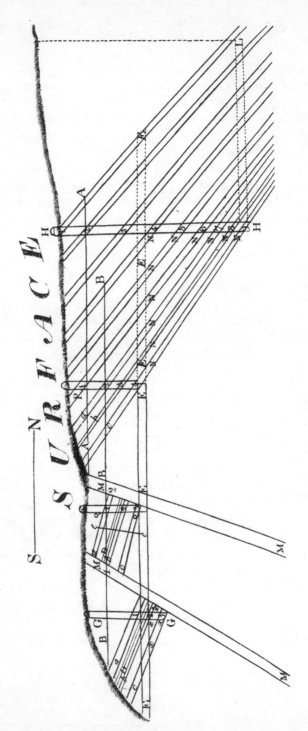

SKETCH of the situation of the seams of COAL and DYKES in the Parish of DUNFERMLINE.

Engraved for SIR JOHN SINCLAIRS Statistical Account of SCOTLAND.

M. M. 1*st*, An upcaft dike to the north.

a. b. c. D (between two dikes). The three feams of coal, and two of iron-ftone, reprefented on the fouth of faid dike, which are caft up by it into the north, all above, and drained by the loweft level.

Q. Q. A coal pit, by which the faid three feams are wrought and raifed level free.

e. e. A kind of dike, or rather ftage, which is fometimes met with in the level courfe of the coal, nearly perpendicular, without cafting the coal up or down on either fide of it.

M. M. 2*d*, Another large dike, which throws up the feams of coal confiderably to the north, and in fome parts they dip more rapidly after- ward.

G. G. An engine pit on the fouth fide of the firft dike, to drain the coaft from x. to x. that is below the level.

H. H. Another engine pit to the north of all the dikes, to drain the coal from N. to N. in all the feams below the level.

P. E. A level free pit, on the four loweft feams on the north fide of the north dike.

1. 2. 3. 4. 5. 6. 7. 8. 9. Nine feams of coal on the north fide of the fecond dike, from two to five feet thick each, making in all, upwards of 30 feet of coal under the furface, in fome parts of this parifh. The three loweft of thofe nine feams are fuppofed to be the three feams a. b. c. on the fouth. The other fix appear to be upper feams that come on from the north. Thofe nine feams are mark- ed where they are interfected by the north engine pit, and are continued downward, to fhow, that if there were no

dikes

dikes to caſt up the coal to the north, it would ſoon get
below the ſurface level, and be loſt without the aſſiſtance
of the engine, which wins from N. to N. in all the ſeams
to the ſouth of it.

If a level mine were driven from the bottom of the pit,
at H. to L. it would win the upper ſeams to the north of
it, between the levels E. E. and H. It alſo ſhows, that
if it were not for ſuch dikes, the coal would ſoon run too
deep to be raiſed to any advantage. Suppoſing the loweſt
ſeam to be 100 fathoms deep at the north engine pit, then
the uppermoſt ſeam will be 100 fathoms deep at L, and
conſequently the loweſt ſeam will be 200 fathoms deep at
that point.

The proportion will always be, according to the dip of
the coal, and the elevation of the ſurface towards the
north.

The level E. E. E. would be about 40 fathoms from
the ſurface at the north engine pit, ſo that the engine
would have to lift the water about 60 fathoms, and deliver it into the ſaid level, where it would diſcharge itſelf
at the loweſt ſouth point.

Numbers employed.—At the above mentioned coal mines
of this pariſh, there are about,

  180 colliers.
  140 bearers.
  300 perſons above ground employed at the works,
      repairing roads, driving and ſhipping coals,
      &c.
  400 women and children, w o occaſionally work,
      and are ſupported by the mines.

Total, 1020 employed and ſupported. Beſides, there are
alſo 200 horſes employed above and below the ſurface, in performing various operations. There are about

50 waggons conftantly employed in carrying coal from the mines to the fhips. Having excellent waggon ways, the waggons contain from two to three tons each.

Annual produce and value of Coal.—The annual quantity of coal raifed from the various mines of the parifh amounts to 90,000 tons. Of thefe, 60,000 tons are exported from Lime-kilns, Brucehaven, and Inverkeithing. The remaining 30,000 tons are confumed in the town and parifh of Dunfermline, and the immediate neighbourhood. The great coal is fold at from 6 s. to 7 s. the ton ; the chows from 5 s. to 6 s.; and the fmall at 3 s. the ton ; valuing the whole at 5 s. the ton, the total annual value of coal amounts to L 22,650 Sterling. Of this fum, there are L. 3000 annually expended on timber, iron, ropes, incidents, &c. &c. and L. 13,000 for labour.

Price of Labour and Provifions.—The miners in the horfe-pits, without bearers, make about from 1 s. 6 d. to 2 s. 6 d. a-day ; with bearers, from 2 s. 6 d. to 3 s. 6 d.; and the people above ground, from 1 s. 4 d. to 1 s. 6 d. a day *.

Villages.—There are 8 villages in the parifh. The populous villages of Lime kilns and Charleftown are pleafently fituated on the coaft of the frith of Forth.

Crofsford,

* The wages of men fervants employed in hufbandry, are from L. 6 to L. 9, and women from L. 3 to L. 4 Sterling a-year. Gentlemens domeftick men-fervants, get from L. 12 to L. 20, and women from L. 4 to L. 6 Sterling a-year. A day-labourer, in hufbandry, and other work, gets 1 s. 2 d.; a carpenter, 1 s. 6 d.; a mafon, 1 s. 8 d.; and a tailor, 10 d. with his meat a-day.

As the price of labour is double of what it was 30 years ago, fo the price of provifions is alfo double. Beef, veal, mutton, lamb, and pork, are from 3 d. to 5 d. the lb.; a pig is 6 d.; a duck, 1 s.; a hen, from 1 s. to 1 s. 6 d.; a chicken, from 3 d. to 5 d.; eggs, from 4 d. to 6 d. the doz.; butter, 11 d.; and cheefe from 3 d. to 5 d. the lb.

Crofsford, Halbeath, and Croffgates, are fituated on the great turnpike road, which paffes through the town and parifh of Dunfermline, from the weftern to the eaftern extremity. Maftertown, Petimuir, and Pitliver, are fituated on the fouthern divifion of the parifh.

Mifcellaneous Obfervations.—The advantages of this parifh are various. It abounds with lime. Coal is comparatively cheap. Houfe rents are moderate. There is a regular poft-office, which annually brings to the revenue upwards of L. 400 Sterling. There is a ready market for the various productions of the land; and there are feaports, with convenient harbours, for exporting or importing by water, all the neceffaries of life.

In this, as in every other parifh, there are fome difadvantages. Owing to the numerous mines and fubterraneous levels which, have lately been opened, the water is greatly drained from the furface, and in fome places it is fcarce, and but indifferent. The roads are often in difrepair. Within thefe few years, fince turnpikes were raifed, they are however greatly improved, and it is expected they will be ftill better, when the ftatute-labour fhall be paid in money, and properly expended. The removal of the Sheriff-fubftitute from this diftrict is another difadvantage deferving attention. Being near 30 miles from Cupar, the inhabitants are expofed to much trouble and expenfe, before they obtain decifions in litigated queftions.

The language is a mixture of Scotch and Englifh. The voice is raifed, and the emphafis frequently laid on the laft word of the fentence. Many of the names of places are derived from the Celtic.

There are about 200 ploughs, almoft all of the Englifh or lately improved kind; about 300 carts; 8 gentlemens wheel-

wheel-carriages, 400 male-fervants, and 300 female-fer-
vants employed in hufbandry. From 6000 to 10,000 bolls
of barley are annually manufactured into fpirits, porter,
ftrong, and fmall beer.

In general, the people are ftrong, and abundantly quick
in learning mechanical employments. Many are remarkably ingenious, induftrious, and frugal. Such perfons enjoy the neceffaries and comforts of life, and are happy in
their prefent fituation. It muft be acknowledged, that
there are alfo many idle, factious, difcontented perfons,
who are greatly divided in their political, moral, and religious fentiments. In gratifying their capricious humours,
and fupporting their refpective parties, they fometimes involve themfelves in unneceffary expenfe, and defraud their
juft creditors. Their expenfe in drefs, furniture, and living, too often exceeds their income. Increafing trade,
manufactures, and the rapid circulation of money, have
had an unhappy influence on their morals.—At public
works, nothing is required but labour. Education is too
often neglected. Many cannot read. Proprietors are not
fufficiently attentive to the inftruction of youth, and providing them with teachers. Many come to the parifh,
and go from it, whofe characters are never attefted. The
profligate repair to thefe works, where they are under no
reftraint, and their infectious example is as hurtful to the
morals of unguarded youth, as their unfeafonable labour is
hurtful to their conftitutions. Being too early removed
from the watchful eye, and faithful admonitions of their
parents and teachers, the young and the thoughtlefs frequently become grofsly ignorant, and openly profane.
With regard to the religious fentiments of the people, it
may be obferved, that in general, they are more mild than
they were about the middle of this century. The rigid
                                              feverity

ſeverity, that then generally prevailed, is now found only
amongſt a few. The violence of party ſpirit ſeldom appears. The ſectaries have ſubdivided, weakened their
own influence, and ſeen the folly of their former diſputes.
Many of them are now peaceable, ſocial, and friendly in
their diſpoſitions. Various denominations of Chriſtians
converſe freely with each other, enjoy mutual intercourſe
in buſineſs, as well as in all the ſocial, relative, and domeſtic walks of life. Upon the whole, the people are in
general ſober, induſtrious, and religious. They have juſt
views of religion and morality. All attend public worſhip, and are apparently decent and devout, excepting a
few of the wealthy, and a few of the ignorant and the
profligate, who neglect the ordinances of religion.

*⁂ Since the greater part of this Account was printed, the fol-
lowing Particulars were tranſmitted by the Miniſters of the
Pariſh.*

Mr Chalmers's bridge was begun in 1767. finiſhed in 1770, and coſt
about L 5000 Sterling.—The value of the cloth annually manufactured
when trade was flouriſhing, amounted to between L 60.000 and L 70,000
Sterling.—Mr Fernie's ſtipend is L. 71 Sterling, and 5 chalders of grain;
viz. 2 of bear, 2 of meal, and 1 of oats.—Mr Chriſtie's ſalary amounts to
L. 11 : 3 : 4 Sterling.

PARISH OF DYSART,

(COUNTY AND SYNOD OF FIFE, PRESBYTERY OF KIRK-CALDY.)

By the Rev. Mr. GEORGE MUIRHEAD.

Name, Extent, Surface, Soil, Climate, &c.

THE name is of Gaelic origin, fignifying the Temple of the Moft High *. The form is irregular. It is about 10 miles in circuit. Its extreme length is about 4 miles; its greateft breadth near to 3. It contains 3054 acres. The ground rifes gradually from the fea above a mile northward; and then flopes down to the river Orr, which forms the boundary on the N. E. The foil is generally light : near the coaft it is well cultivated, and the harveft early. In the N. W. of the parifh, a track of land between the Orr and the rivulet

Lochty,

---

* The parifh of Glenurchay was formerly called Clachan Dyfart, or the church of the High God. Clachan fignifies ftone or building, Dy, (ΘΕΟΣ) God, art, high.

Lochty, which there forms the boundary, is wet and very ſtony. In the ſpring, E. winds prevail, and bring miſts from the ſea, which are unfavourable to pulmonic complaints: at other times, the climate is not unhealthy *. The ſea coaſt extends about 2 miles. It is high and rocky: but the rocks do not projeĉt far into the ſea; and in ſome places there is a ſandy beach below them. Sea-ware thrown aſhore by ſtorms, is occaſionally uſed as manure with ſuccefs. The ware upon the rocks is cut once in 3 years, and produces a few tons of kelp. The courſe of the tides is regular, high-water being two hours after the moon comes to the meridian. But in ſhore, the current ſets down the Frith 2 hours before high-water, and up the Frith, 2 hours before low-water. The harbour is much expoſed to ſtorms from the E., which, in winter are ſometimes very violent. It may contain 12 large veſſels at a time. The depth at a ſtream, 12¼ feet.

Minerals.—There is plenty of good freeſtone at no great diſtance from the ſurface. Limeſtone has been found of an inferior quality, and is not quarried, as there is plenty of good limeſtone in the neighbourhood. The mines are coal and ironſtone. There are 14 beds of coal in the Sinclair eſtate.

---

* Epidemics are not frequent · when they come, they prove moſt fatal in Pathhead, not from the ſituation of the town, which is high, on rock or ſand; but from the houſes being crowded with inhabitants, and from want of ſufficient attention to cleanlineſs. More attention is paid to this than formerly; but there is ſtill room for improvement, in this reſpeĉt, throughout the pariſh. It is a pity, that what tends ſo materially to promote health and comfort, ſhould not be confidered of great importance. There are two mineral ſprings. The one, impregnated with vitriol, had once ſome reputation for its medicinal qualities; but has for many years been entirely negleĉted. The other, impregnated with iron, was much reſorted to about 12 years ago; but is now generally abandoned. Both are from coal mines, and come to the ſurface on the ſea-ſhore.

eftate. Moft of them are thin, and have been wrought out
above the level of the fea. Three of the thickeft of thefe
beds, which are near one another, are now working. The
uppermoft bed is 5 feet thick. The diftance between it and
the fecond bed, is 18 inches, being a foot of coal, with 3
inches of till above and under it. The 2d bed of coal is 8
feet thick ; under it, is a bed of ftone and till 2 feet 3 inches;
and under it the 3d bed of coal, 5 feet thick *. They are now
working thefe beds of coal 60 fathoms below the furface.
The water is raifed by 2 fteam engines : the coals are raifed
by 3 horfe gins. Horfes are employed under ground to bring
the coals to the pit bottoms. The average quantity of coals
raifed annually for 7 years preceding 1791, is 15,267 tons,
value 4000l., and 7000 tons of culm, value 583l. ; 105 perfons are employed †. There are 5 beds of ironftone, which
being

* The metals cut through in getting to the coal, are, 1ft, next the furface,
2 fathom brownifh ftone ; 2d, 14¼ fathom till, very clofe ; 3d, 8 fathom brownifh ftone, porous, and mixed with iron veins ; 4th, 7 fathom till, mixed with
thin beds of freeftone, hard; 5th, 2 fathom blueifh ftone, very hard, muft be
wrought with gunpowder ; 6th, 6 fathom till, mixed with thin beds freeftone ;
7th, ½ fathom, a hard coarfe coal, mixed with ftone, which is immediately a-
bove the beds of coal that are wrought, and is left for a roof.

† Dyfart coal was amongft the firft wrought in Scotland, having been begun
more than 300 years ago. It was on fire nearly as far back. It is faid to have
had periodic eruptions once in 40 years ; a remarkable one in 1662. This fire
is fuppofed to have been occafioned by pyrites, which is found in this coal. It
is defcribed by Buchanan,

" Vicini deferta vocant : ibi faxea fubter
" Antra tegunt nigras vulcantia femina cautes."
BUCH. FRANCISCANUS.

The effects of it may ftill be traced by the calcined rocks from the harbour,
more than a mile up the country. The road from the harbour is called Hot
Pot Wynd, and another near it, the Burning. In the beginning of this century, the flames were feen at night coming out of the pit mouths. In 1741,
the

being near each other, are wrought at the same time. They lie below the coal ; and as they dip the same way, are wrought to the W. of it, where they come nearer the surface : 24 men are employed in this work, who raise 2080 tons annually. A ton of stone yields about 1200 weight of iron.

Population, &c.—According to Dr. Webster's report, the number of souls in 1755, was 2367. Little is known of the ancient state of Dysart. Trade is said to have flourished there in the end of the 15th century ; 50 sail, probably small vessels then belonging to the town. Many of the inhabitants, particularly sailors, accompanied Lord Sinclair to the battle of Flodden, who were mostly cut off. This gave a great shock to their trade *. The shipping has increased considerably

the coal was set on fire by a lime kiln, which had been placed too near it. It did not burn violently : but was not extinguished for some years. In 1790, it again took fire, from what cause is unknown. It did not burn with fury ; but occasioned much smoke and bad air. The colliers were prevented from working for some months. It is now extinguished. The means used, were to exclude the air as much as possible, and to allow the water to rise by stopping the engines. Dysart coal has a strong heat : but being slow in kindling, and having much ashes, is not so pleasant for rooms as some lighter coals. It dips to the S. E. (most of the metals on the sea coast of this parish dip the same way) 1 fathom in 3 near the shore ; but is flatter as it goes north.

* It was made a royal burgh in the beginning of the 16th century : but the original charter, and old records are lost. In 1546, it is mentioned as one of the principal trading towns on the Fife coast. In the beginning of the present century, its trade was much decayed : but from the number of well built houses in it then, it had the appearance of having been in a flourishing state. At that time much salt was made there ; and their trade consisted chiefly in exporting coal and salt to Holland. At that time too, malting and brewing were carried on to a great extent. In 1756, foreign trade revived. Severals commenced wine merchants, and imported wine and spirits in their own vessels. This trade, supported partly by defrauding the revenue, is now happily done away. Individuals might gain by it : but the town was much hurt. Its effects on the morals

ably of late years ; manufactures have been introduced ; and the town may be pronounced in a thriving ſtate. In 1756, the number of inhabitants was 1378. In 1792, 1827. The revenues of the town are ſmall, ariſing from ſome landed property and the harbour dues.

Pathhead is named from its ſituatian near a ſteep deſcent called the Path. It is divided into Pathhead Proper, or Duni-keer, ſituated on Dunikeer eſtate, and Sinclairton ſituated on Sinclair eſtate. Dunikeer is the old town : the greateſt part of Sinclairton has been built within theſe 40 years. The chief employment in Pathhead was, for a long time, the mak-ing of nails. They ſent great quantities to Edinburgh, to Glaſgow, and to the north of Scotland. Two things favour-ed this trade, plenty of good coal near them, and the facility of getting old iron, by the ſhips trading from Dyſart to Hol-land. But when other places came to have the ſame advan-tages, and nail factories were erected in different quarters, the profits of this trade were diminiſhed. Manufactures have been introduced ſince that time. Many bred ſmiths have be-come weavers : the women too are beginning to handle the ſhuttle with ſucceſs. Several manufacturers of ſubſtance now reſide there, who have raiſed themſelves by ſober induſtry : and the town is in a fair way of flouriſhing, if the ſudden riſe of wages do not lead the young men into habits of diſſi-pation. Symptoms of this have appeared of late : but the practice is as yet happily not general ; and we hope the inha-bitants, in general, will continue to ſhow that regard to the laws of the land, and that reſpect for the precepts of the goſpel, without which they cannot hope to proſper. In 1756, Pathhead,

morals of the people are not yet entirely effaced. New laws and greater vi-gilance on the part of government rendered the trade very hazardous ; and it is now ſeldom attempted. A fair trade has ſucceeded it, where the profits may be leſs, but the ſecurity is greater.

Pathhead, including Sinclairton, contained 1107 inhabitants : in 1792, 2089.

There are two villages, Galaton and Borland. In the former, nailing was the chief buſineſs ; and is ſtill carried on. But many weavers now reſide there, who are employed by the manufacturers in Dyſart and Pathhead. In 1756, it contained 203 inhabitants ; in 1792, 432. Borland was begun in 1756, for accommodating the colliers, and has been ſince increaſed. It contains 196 inhabitants.

In 1756, the numbers in the country were 241 ; in 1792, 409. This increaſe is not from more farmers reſiding than formerly, but from a number of weavers and ſome ſmiths having from time to time built houſes along the high road, and in other places of the country.

TABLE of the Population of Dyſart Pariſh.

	Fami-lies.	Numbers in the Families.			Increaſed ſince 1756.	Houſes.	Of theſe built ſince 1781.
		Male.	Female.	Total.			
Dyſart,	451	819	917	1736	358	224	10
Pathhead,	581	1062	1027	2089	982	320	100
Galaton,	137	227	205	432	227	70	12
Borland,	41	87	109	196	127	30	6
Country,	84	190	219	409	168	80	8
	1294	2385	2477	4862	1862	724	126

The cauſes of this increaſe of population are, an Antiburgher meeting-houſe being erected at Pathhead, which drew thoſe of that perſuaſion near it ; the advantage of being near coal, and the encouragement for labour about the coal-works ; and what has contributed much more than either, the rapid increaſe of the manufactures.

Improvements

Improvements by Proprietors.—In the Sinclair eſtate, there was originally an extenſive moor, burdened with feal, divot, turf, &c. to the burgh of Dyſart. Servitudes of this kind are a great bar to improvements : and, in eſtates where coal is an objeçt, the attention paid to it, too often prevents the cultivation of the ſurface. When the inhabitants of Dyſart came to give up the uſe of turf, either for burning, or other purpoſes, their privileges on the moor could not be of great importance. An agreement concerning them ſeemed evidently for the advantage of all concerned. This was accompliſhed at different periods. As a compenſation to the town, above 100 acres were conveyed to them in property : and the family of St. Clair were at liberty to cultivate what remained. In the beginning of this century, a few years after the firſt tranſaçtion with the town, Lord St. Clair began to plant and encloſe near the Orr. His example was followed by his ſucceſſors : and what ſtill retains the name of Dyſart moor, now conſiſts of good encloſures, chiefly in paſture, ſurrounded with belts of plantation. Within theſe 50 years, between 300 and 400 acres have been planted and improved, no more remaining in its original ſtate, than what is neceſſary for ſuch of the feuars as uſe divot for a covering to their houſes. The whole eſtate, a few acres excepted, is encloſed with ſtone and lime, or ditch and hedge. The laſt is preferred as a cheaper, warmer, and more beautiful fence. The eſtate is ſtill capable of improvement.

The proprietor of W. Strathorr, while he is buſied in carrying on an extenſive manufaçture in a neighbouring pariſh, dedicates his leiſure hours to the improvement of his eſtate in this. The ground has been cleared of ſtones, which almoſt covered the ſurface : the fields have been encloſed, drained, and manured : belts have been planted to ſcreen it ; it aſſumes a very different appearance from what it did a few

years

years ago. It already makes some return for the money laid out upon it ; and will soon repay it with interest.

Farms in the Hands of Tenants.—These are 15 in number, containing from 30 to 280 acres each. Upon these, are 51 men, including the farmers and their servants ; 94 horses ; 350 cattle ; 24 ploughs * ; 38 carts. They breed annually 16 horses, 79 calves. There are several extensive enclosures in pasture, on which 100 cattle are fed annually ; 339 bolls of oats are annually sown, which produce 1824 bolls ; 101 bolls of barley, which produce 589 bolls ; 43 bolls of wheat, which produce 351 bolls ; 70 bolls of pease, which produce 271 bolls. Potatoes, turnips, hay, and flax †, are also raised in no great quantities ; and the proportions cannot be easily ascertained. The rent of the best grass-ground in the burgh acres is, 2 l. 15 s. the acre : of the best arable land, 3 l. In the farms, there is little above 1 l. an acre ; and much below it. There is a considerable extent of ground not above 7 s. 6 d. the acre. The leases being only for 19 years, is against these farms. Had the farmers a lease of double that time, they would be encouraged to improve by the hope of a return ; or, were the proprietors to take them for some time into their own hands, and improve them, they would afterward get more than double the rent, and do an important service to the publick. The produce of the parish goes but a little way to supply its consumption. Meal and flour are imported from Lothian ; meal, wheat, barley, and hay, from the neighbouring parishes. Little manure can be got but lime, which is used in considerable quantities. For some time,

---

* Small's ploughs are now generally used.

† More flax was formerly cultivated ; but in the late leases, the farmers have been restricted in this article, from some mistaken notion of its being too scourging.

time, servants were preferred to cottagers : but since the late rise of wages, and great demand for labour about the roads and manufactures, they feel the want of them, particularly in harvest, when hands are with difficulty procured. Men-servants wages are 6 l. a-year. Our farming cannot be said to be in a very advanced state : but there has been great improvement within these 20 years. The advantages of enclosing and laying down in grass are now felt : the distinction between infield and outfield is doing away : * balks are disappearing ; and green crops are substituted in the place of summer fallow. The soil is none of the best ; but might be made much better than what it is at present.

Burgh Acres.—About Dysart, Pathhead, and Galaton, numbers who keep cows and horses, find it necessary to farm a few acres at a high rent. Where farming is only a secondary object, perfection cannot be expected. They have the advantage of the country farmers in more easily procuring dung ; and accordingly the soil near the towns appears richer than in the country. They often sow too thick ; and are seldom at pains to keep their fields clear of weeds. Drilling was introduced about 40 years ago. Wheat, barley, beans, and oats, are sometimes sown in this way ; turnips and potatoes always. Where the ground is over-run with weeds, as is the case with the burgh acres, from their being almost constantly in tillage, the drilling is surely a great advantage ; seed is saved ; the crop is generally more vigorous, and more easily kept clean. There are a few of those who have the burgh acres, who push the farming with vigour, and have their grounds

* In stony ground, the stones used to be thrown into the hollow between the ridges, by which one-third of the ground lost these ridges called balks.

grounds well dreſſed.   Such examples are needed, and are
worthy of imitation *.

Manufactures.—The number of looms in the pariſh, is from
700 to 750, employed in making checks and ticks.   The
quantity of cloth made annually, is about 795,000 yards,
which being, at a medium, about 11¼d. the yard, makes the
annual value of this manufacture 38,093 l. 15 s.   About half
the cloth is ſold in London; a fourth, chiefly the coarſe kinds,
in Glaſgow; the other fourth in Mancheſter, Liverpool, Nottingham, Leeds, and ſome other towns in Yorkſhire.   In the
linen trade, 10 hands are reckoned to be employed by each
loom ; but as three-fourths of the flax conſumed in this trade
are foreign, 7 to a loom may be a proper medium, which, for
725 looms, is † 5075 people employed.   Seven-eights of the
flax uſed in making white or bleached yarns, are imported from
Riga, and ſpun in Fife.   What is uſed for the blue and dyed
yarns, is chiefly made from home grown flax : but, as a ſufficient quantity cannot be got, Dutch flax is imported and
ſpun to make up the deficiency.   Of late years, a conſiderable quantity of coarſe yarn has been imported from Bremen
and Hamburgh.   Not above a fourth of the yarn uſed in the
pariſh is ſpun in it.   The greateſt inconveniency the trade labours under, is a ſcarcity of good weavers.   People not qualified to teach, take apprentices for 2 or 3 years, inſtead of a
longer period.   The apprentices, not attended to, get into
                                                      bad

* From being in ſuch variety of hands, it was difficult to form any calculation of the produce of theſe acres.   More wheat, and potatoes, and turnips, in
proportion, than in the country farms.

† That is more people than the pariſh contains, becauſe a great proportion
of the flax is dreſſed and ſpun out of the pariſh.   The number of hands employed in this pariſh in this manufacture, is between 2000 and 3000, beginning at
the flax-dreſſers.

bad habits; and many of them never can make a piece of good cloth.

This manufacture began in this parifh between 1710 and 1720, and increafed flowly till 1776, when it did not exceed, in value, 8500 l. annually. About that time, 2 or 3 of the eftablifhed manufacturers got into the Englifh trade, and making goods fuitable to that trade, increafed their demand beyond what their capitals were equal to ; or, though they had had funds beyond what they could find hands to execute. They of courfe gave their orders for coarfe goods to manufacturers in the neighbourhood, who employed from 2 to 8 looms. Thefe, by economy and induftry, faved money from the orders they got ; and foon increafed the number of their looms. But the value of the goods made, has increafed much more rapidly than the capital of the manufacturers, owing chiefly to the many branches of the banks, by which credit is got too eafily. On this foundation, about a third of the goods is at prefent made, and of an inferior quality to what is made by thofe of character and capital. Thofe who began this manufacture here, had to work with the fweat of their brow for 8 or 10 years, ere they gained the firft 100 l. of their capital : now, a weaver * without 10 l. capital, will get credit for 200 l. or 300 l. value of yarn, or cafh for a bill, with 2 or 3 names upon it, to the fame amount. To retire thefe bills, the goods muft be expeditioufly manufactured. To effect this, they feduce by drink, and offers of extravagant wages, the workmen of eftablifhed manufacturers : the
consequences

---

* Since the above account of the cloth manufacture was fent me, a ftagnation has taken place ; and fcarcely any money can be procured at the banks. As yet, this parifh has been lefs affected by it than many other places. But few hands have been difmiffed : the wages have been lowered, but are ftill good. But unlefs there come a favourable turn foon, manufacturers cannot afford to make goods, when the fales are fo low.

&onfequences muft be obvious. The fales of the parifh of late, are not under from 48,000l. to 50,000l. a-year *. It muft be obferved, to the honour of the Englifh, that in the trade with them, there are very few bad debts.

Ships.—A fhip-carpenter employing about 6 men, fettled here in 1764. His bufinefs gradually increafed, till he found employment for upwards of 30 men. He has built here, 43 veffels meafuring 5189 tons. Of thefe, 15 were for Dyfart; 6 for Greenork; the reft chiefly for the neighbouring ports. In 1778, another carpenter bred under the former, began to build, and has had very good encouragement. He has built 31 † veffels meafuring 3445 tons. About 45 men are at prefent employed, including both. At an average, for 15 years back, 501 tons have been built annually, which at 5l. the ton, makes the annual value of this manufacture 2505l. The crooked timber is imported from Hamburgh and Bremen, and the oak plank from Dantzick. The foreign timber, after paying duty, is cheaper than what can be brought from any place in Britain. A confiderable proportion, however, of Englifh oak is ufed, where it is moft ufeful. The feparation of the American Colonies from Britain, and the amendment of the navigation act in 1786, have contributed much to the rapid progrefs of fhip-building in this country. The employment which this bufinefs gives to fhipping in importing the materials; the numbers employed in building, manufacturing fails, cordage, iron work, &c.; and the duties paid

on

---

* The fales of the parifh exceed the produce, becaufe our manufacturers buy cloth from other parifhes, and employ weavers there. It may be obferved, too, that a number of the weavers in this parifh are employed by the Kirkcaldy manufacturers.

† Only one of thefe veffels is yet known to be loft; 11 were for Dyfart, the reft chiefly for the neighbouring ports.

on importing the foreign articles, render it of importance ; and it muft be confidered as a valuable acquifition to commerce. It is but juftice to fay, that the improvements in this art, have kept pace with the other improvements of the country. It is thought a boat-builder might find encouragement here.

Nails.—In Pathhead there are 43 fmiths, who make about 6 million of nails annually, value about 1000 l. They are fold in the country round, and confiderable quantities carried to Edinburgh, and fome to the north country. In Galaton there are alfo 43 fmiths, they do not make the fame number of nails, as feveral of them are far advanced in life, and a number of them make nails of a larger fize for fhip-building. The value of their manufacture, alfo about 1000 l. Their nails are fold in the neighbourhood, and quantities carried to Perth, Montrofe, and Aberdeen. The nails are made of old iron imported from Holland : and the merchants who furnifh the fmiths with old iron, take their nails and fend them to market.

Salt.—Salt was made here, at leaft fome time before 1483, as appears by an agreement with the family of St. Clair, of that date. The works were more extenfive than at prefent. There are veftiges of many falt-pans, which have been demolifhed long ago. Much falt was exported to Holland ; but none of late years. Seven pans are now going, and employ 14 falters, befides 2 or 3 other hands occafionally to carry the falt to the granaries. About 17,100 bufhels are made annually, value 1200 l. The fuel employed is chiefly culm. 120 loads are required to make 100 bufhels of falt. The bittern has been fometimes fought after by the chymifts ; but is generally allowed to go to wafte.

Brewery

Brewery and Ropery.—In the former, about 1000 bolls of barley are malted annually, moftly the growth of this county. About 2500 barrels of ale and beer are brewed, from 10 s. to 36 s. the barrel, value 2150 l. A confiderable quantity of this is fold in * Kirkcaldy, to which the brewery pays 40 l. annually, impoft. A manager and 4 labouring fervants are employed. An addition is now making to the works, to carry on a diftillery there. In the latter, about 6 men are employed in making fmall ropes.

Domeftick Commerce.—There are 4 annual fairs in Dyfart, one for linfeed, one for white cloth, one for white cloth and wool, and one for black cattle. In Pathhead, one for white cloth and wool. In Galaton, one for white cloth. About 50 years ago, great quantities of cloth were expofed at thefe fairs, and bought by merchants from Edinburgh, Glafgow, and Stirling. This trade has gradually fallen off.; and very little bufinefs is now done at any of the fairs, except that for black cattle. Lefs white cloth is made in Fife than formerly, fo many of the weavers being taken up in the check and tick manufacture: and the merchants choofe rather to pick up the cloth at the bleachfield, than after it has been dreffed for the market. The wool market too is entirely gone. Formerly many families fpun wool, and made cloth for their own wearing : now Englifh cloth is generally worn. And fince enclofing became general, very few fheep are kept in Fife. The eafy intercourfe by means of pofts and carriers, and fhops being eftablifhed in every little village, render fairs lefs neceffary. Bufinefs is thus better managed. When every body reforted to the fairs, they were generally a fcene of diffipation. Whatever day the fair began on, no bufinefs was done

that

* It is fituated juft on the boundary of the Kirkcaldy parifh.

that week. There is a weekly market in Dyſart during the ſummer, for the articles of the couptry produce : and a fleſh-market in Dyſart and Pathhead, in which about 300 cattle are killed annually, beſides mutton, and veal, and lamb, in their ſeaſon. Mutton is often brought from Perth. The land ſale of coal annually, is 7100 tons ; and of ſalt 2000 buſhels. There are alſo conſiderable ſales of meal and of wood *.

Maritime Commerce.—Twenty-three ſquare rigged veſſels, and two ſloops belong to Dyſart, meaſuring, by regiſter, 4075 tons, value 30,000 l.; and employing 249 men. There is not trade from this port to employ this ſhipping. They are moſt-ly in the carrying trade, going out in ballaſt, or loaded with coals, and bringing home wood and other articles from the Baltick to Leith, Sealock, Dundee, Perth, and other ports. A few of them trade from London, Liverpool, and other Engliſh ports, to the Mediterranean, Weſt Indies, and Ame-rica. Three of them are at preſent in Government ſervice, as armed ſhips, and one as a tender. As to foreign exports and imports from and to Dyſart annually, there were export-ed 4584 tons of coal, chiefly to Copenhagen, Gottenburgh, and

---

* *Prices.*—Beef from 4 d. to 5 d. the pound tron ; veal and mutton the ſame ; mutton, when ſcarce, 5½d. and 6 d. ; lamb from 1 s. to 1 s. 8 d. the quarter ; ſalmon from 5 d. to 8 d. the pound ; fowls from 2 s. to 2 s. 6 d. the pair ; chick-ens from 8 d. to 1 s. 4 d. the pair ; eggs from 4 d. to 6 d. the dozen : fowls and eggs very ſcarce, from our vicinity to the capital ; butter from 8 d. to 10 d. the pound tron; cheeſe from 3 s. 4 d. to 4 s. the ſtone tron ; Engliſh cheeſe 5½ d., or 6 d. the pound Engliſh. Maid ſervants from 2 l. to 3 l. 10 s. a-year ; day-labour-ers from 1 s. to 1 s. 2 d. a-day; journeymen maſons 1 s. 6 d. a-day; ſhip car-penters from 10 s. to 12 s. a-week ; houſe carpenters 1 s. 8 d. a-day ; ſhoemakers from 7 s. to 8 s. a-week ; tailors 6 d. a-day and their victuals ; weavers from 2 s. to 2 s. 6 d. a-day; gardeners 1 s. 6 d. a-day ; ſailors from 2 l. to 2 l. 10 s. a-month ; a ſalter, with his ſervant, from 1 l. to 1 l. 4 s a-week.

Many of the above articles are double in price of what they were 40 years ago.

and the ports of Holland. Imported from Memel, Eafterizer, Chriftianfand, Dantzick, Hamburgh, and Bremen, about 14 cargoes of wood. From Rotterdam, Campvere, Hamburgh, Memel, and Dantzick, 2 or 3 cargoes of other goods *. Goods fent coaftways annually, are, 2080 tons iron-ftone to Carron-works; 3583 tons coal to Dundee, Perth, Montrofe, Aberdeen, &c.; 15,100 bufhels falt to Aberdeen and Inver-nefs; 160 bales cloth to Leith. Imported from Leith, 1000 bolls oatmeal †, 160 bolls flour, 130 bolls oats, and a variety of other articles ‡. From Aberdeen, tiles, bricks, cheefe, and butter. From John's-haven, fome cargoes of dried fifh. This coafting trade is carried on in fmall veffels.

The people are fond of a feafaring life : but generally a-verfe to go into the navy, owing partly to the horror with which, from their infancy, they are taught to look upon a prefs-gang. Many of the feafaring people think, that were the failors in Government fervice, to get 30 s. a-month, and fome fmall allowance to their widows and families, in cafe of death,

* The detail of wood, and other articles imported from thefe places laft year, is as follows : 2614 fir baulks, 1344 fir deals, 687 oak plank, 1961 pieces of oak, 74 fpars, 300 deal ends, 230 plank ends, 5600 tree nails, 1500 clap-boards, 112 pailing boards, 2 fathom, and 90 pieces lath-wood, 48 bundles hazle rungs, 244 handfpikes, 900 ftaves, 148,000 hoops. Other goods; 17 pipes Geneva, 2 cafks 14 tons and 17 cwt. old iron, 499 matts flax, 682 hogfheads linfeed, 78 bags and 7 hogfheads clover feed, 94 cafks tallow, 40 bags rags, 2 cafks pearl afhes, 156 bufhels apples, 20 barrels onions, 265 kegs fpruce bear, 3 cafes books, 39 tons oak-bark, 2 bales linen, 5 bales yarn, imported in 17 veffels, 3 Danifh, the reft belonging to Dyfart, and the neighbouring parts.

† More than double that quantity of meal is brought over to the parifh; but as what comes to Pathhead is generally imported at Kirkcaldy, it does not ap-pear with the Dyfart imports.

‡ Such as 25 barrels falt herring, 30 ankers fpirits, a few pipes of wine, 15 hogfheads porter, 48 cafks afhes, 15 barrels tar, 200 mats flax and tow, 16 bales yarn, 4 bales leather, cordage, &c. for the fhips built here. Thefe Leith im-ports are in a paffage-boat that goes twice a-week from Dyfart to Leith.

death, the navy might, at any time be manned, without having recourse to a practice, not strictly conformable to the spirit of the British Constitution, and which is often cruel in its operation, upon a brave and hardy race of men, who, in war, have spread the terrors of the British arms, to the most distant parts of the earth, and who, in peace, convey to us, from every quarter, the comforts, conveniences, and luxuries of life. The expense attending the impress service, it is thought, would go far to defray the necessary addition to the seamen's wages. The subject certainly deserves the attention of every politician, of every patriot: and any hints, however imperfect they may be, and from whatever quarter they may come, in a matter of such importance, should not be entirely overlooked.

Stipend, Schools, Poor, &c.—The charge is collegiate. The first minister has a commodious manse, built in 1779, and a garden, but no glebe. His stipend is 5 chalders meal, 5 chalders barley, and 16 l. 13 s. 4 d., two load of coals a-week, and a chalder of salt annually, while the coal and salt-works are carried on: the teind of fish caught and sold in the parish, and half teind of fish brought for sale from other parishes. The second minister has neither manse nor glebe, nor any allowance for them. His stipend is 55 l. 11 s., two chalders of meal, and two of barley, and a load of coals a-week, while the works are carried on. The heritors are, Sir James Erskine St. Clair of Sinclair, Bart., who is patron of both charges, and titular of the teinds ; James Townshend Oswald of Dunikeer, Esq. the Countess of Rothes, Walter Fergus of Strathorr, Esq. Major St. Clair of Skeddoway, the Town of Dysart, and 4 others who have each a few acres. None of the principal heritors reside, except Sir James St. Clair occasionally. The church is old ; its date unknown ; tradition

tion ſays it was built by the Picts. The architect, if he intended it for preaching, cannot be praiſed for his contrivance.
It is dark, the ſide walls low, and the incumbrances of pillars, &c. ſo many, that it is difficult to make the voice reach
it. It does not ſeat above half the congregation *.—The
ſchool-houſe belongs to the town. They elect the ſchoolmaſter, and pay his ſalary. The preſent maſter is alſo ſeſſion-clerk. His ſalary, perquiſites, and wages, amount to
50 l. He teaches latin, engliſh, book-keeping, arithmetic,
and navigation. About 70 at preſent attend his ſchool. There
are ſeveral private ſchools in Dyſart and Pathhead, and one
in Galaton. The maſters have no ſalary nor ſchool-houſes,
but depend entirely on the ſmall wages they get from their
ſcholars, which are often but ill paid. About 230 attend
theſe ſchools †.—Twelve perſons go from door to door once
a-week,

---

* About a year ago, the kirk-ſeſſion applied to the heritors to make it more
commodious. An architect was deſired to inſpect it, who gave in ſome plans
of alteration, and there the matter reſts: but it is to be hoped the heritors will
ſee the neceſſity of doing ſomething ſoon. Numbers are obliged to take ſeats
in neighbouring congregations; ſome go to the ſectaries; others, it is to be
feared, take advantage of this circumſtance, to forſake public worſhip altogether. Were heritors eager to promote religion by their influence and example,
they would do much to ſupport government and good order, and would have
leſs cauſe to complain of the corruption of the lower ranks, at leaſt they might
do it with a better grace. Almoſt the only ſectaries in the pariſh are Burghers, Antiburghers, and Relief, amounting in all to 552 families. The two laſt
mentioned ſects have churches in this pariſh; the former attend worſhip in
Kirkcaldy pariſh. The animoſity between the church and ſeceſſion, is now happily much abated. The people, in general, attend church regularly; but a
few are beginning to be ſo faſhionable as to attend only occaſionally.

† It is much to be wiſhed ſome better proviſion could be made for the education of youth. Dyſart and Pathhead would require each two eſtabliſhed maſters, Galaton and Borland each one. A Sunday ſchool was begun in Dyſart two
years ago, ſupported by ſubſcription. At firſt, upwards of 100 attended; but
afterward, many who had come from novelty, gradually dropped off. At preſent,

a-week, and receive alms in meal or money. Few have recourse to this mode; and such seldom get from the funds. The
funds are:

Collected at the church-door annually,   -   L. 46 6 0
Interest of stock,   -   -   -   9 4 0
Seat rents,   -   -   -   6 6 0

                                       L. 61 16 0

51 persons are now upon the roll, who receive from 1 s. to
5 s. monthly. Few of the industrious born and bred in the
parish, come to be a burden on the funds. But numbers in
the decline of life, come into the parish, and in a few years
must of course be supported; others who have been idle and
thoughtless in youth, when distress or age come, are cast upon the public *.

Advantages

sent, about 40 attend. It has had good effects: the children are regular in attending church, and attentive when there; but those parents are much to blame,
who, wanting ability or inclination to instruct their children in the principles
of religion, do not avail themselves of the assistance they might have, by sending them to the Sunday school. As the funds raised for this school were more
than equal to its support, they are partly applied to purchase bibles, and put
poor children to the weekly school.

   * There are several private funds of great use. In Dysart, the sailors, the
maltmen, the bakers, have each their boxes for assisting their members in distress. In Pathhead, there are two associations of weavers, and one of smiths:
In Galaton one: In Borland one. In 1782, the poor were in great straits. The
patron (then Colonel James St. Clair) bought quantities of meal and pease, to
be sold at reduced prices for their behoof, and gave money to be distributed to
the most needy. In Dysart and Pathhead, money was raised by subscription, to
purchase meal for them. When, by any unforeseen accident, a person or family is reduced to great distress, the neighbours frequently procure a temporary
supply, by a contribution among themselves. None, I believe, get from the
funds who do not stand in need: but the supply afforded is rather scanty. Sooner or later, it is supposed the heritors will be brought in: as few of them reside,
they by no means pay their proportion. The kirk-session at present manage
the funds: but are always ready to allow the heritors to inspect their books,
and take a share in the management.

Advantages and Difadvantages.—The firft advantage is, plenty of coal; but pofterity will not thank us for wafting it fo faft by exportation. 2d, Its vicinity to the fea, convenient for commerce and fifhing. Little attention is paid to the laft. We have only one family of fifhers. The town is fupplied with fifh from Wemyfs parifh. They are carried on women's backs. The fifh caught here, are, cod, whiting, flounder, mackerel, baggety, fand-eel, crabs, and lobfters. The lobfters are fent to Edinburgh. 3d, A good public road through the parifh. So much cannot be faid for the crofs roads, which are next to impaffable. When the public roads are finifhed, it is to be hoped attention will be paid to them. Tolls have been erected in the neighbourhood, and one in the parifh, not without grumbling. It is generally thought they were neceffary; and few will grudge to pay them, when the roads are well made. The chief difadvantage is, a fcarcity of good water, particularly in the town of Dyfart; the furface is much drained by the working of the coal.

Improvements fuggefted.—1. It would be of great importance to the trade of the place, to have the harbour deepened, and rendered more fecure. The town can do very little in this way from their own funds; but as upwards of 3000 l. are annually paid to Government from goods exported and imported at this harbour, and a great value of fhipping is there annually expofed to danger, they think they have a claim for fome aid from Government, for carrying on fo neceffary and fo ufeful a work. 2. A dry dock might be eafily made in the W. fide of the harbour. The ftones are daily quarried for building: at fome additional expenfe, they might be fo quarried as to form a dock in the folid rock. 3. Ground might be gained from the fea, near the harbour, which is much wanted to contain the wood ufed in fhip-building. Some
thoufand

thoufand carts of ballaft are annually caft upon the fhore, at the back of the harbour. Were proper means ufed to prevent the fea from wafhing it away, it would foon accumulate and become folid. 4. Our trade is chiefly to the Baltic, which is frozen in the winter, of courfe the failors are at home 3 or 4 months in the year. It is a pity they were not employed during that time; fo much labour is thus loft to the community, and fo much comfort to the individual. They would be happier employed than idle. Thofe who are bred weavers or fmiths have an advantage in this refpect: they fometimes follow thefe employments when at home. 5. The engines and falt pans occafion much fmoke, which is very difagreeable, deftroying vegetation in the gardens, and penetrating the inmoft receffes of the houfes. By erecting the proper apparatus on the chimney tops, it might be converted into tar. Thus the nuifance would be prevented, and a manufacture eftablifhed, peculiarly adapted to a fea-port town.

Remarkable Events.—On the 7th of January 1740, a number of boys, according to cuftom, on 1ft Monday of the year, were diverting themfelves on the fands below Pathhead.; 13 had gone into a cave, when the roof fuddenly fell in; 3 only were taken out alive, and one of thefe died foon after. The friends of thofe who met this untimely fate, for many years kept the firft Monday of the year as a faft. An inftance of 3 at a birth has happened 5 times during the incumbency of the prefent minifter. Few of them furvived long *.

General

* *Antiquities.*—There was a priory of Black Friars in the town of Dyfart. Their chapel, called St. Dennis, was long in a ruinous ftate, but was lately converted into a forge. The Romans had a ftation here. A high rock, commanding the harbour, is called the Fort, and is faid to have been fortified by Oliver Cromwell. No remains of any works there appear. There is a ftone erected in a field to the N. of the town. The tradition is, that a battle with the Danes had

General Observations.—The people are well clothed, have good houses, and live comfortably. They ought to be, and it is to be hoped, are, contented with their lot. No doubt complaints are heard, and not altogether without reafon, from fome in the lower ranks, of the hardnefs of the times. Women, efpecially in the decline of life, find it hard to gain a livelihood by fpinning, which is almoft their only employment. Farmers too complain of the difficulty of getting hands for their work. And it is to be regretted, that agricu ture, ufeful to health, favourable to morals, and indifpenfably neceffary to the well-being of a ftate, fhould be fo much neglected. But we cannot expect every thing to our wifh in this world : and if the above account of this parifh be juft, it will appear they have their own fhare of the comforts of this life. May they never forget the obligations they are under to Him from whom their bleffings flow ; and that godlinefs is the only fure foundation they can lay for lafting profperity and true enjoyment. " It is profitable for all things, having

had been fought there. A rivulet running through that field is called Kingslaw-burn. The caftle of Ravenfcraig is fituated on a rock, projecting into the fea, at the E. end of Pathhead. It was given by James III. to William St. Clair Earl of Orkney, with the lands adjoining to it, when he refigned the title of Orkney. It has been ever fince poffeffed by the family of St. Clair. It was inhabited in Oliver Cromwell's time, and was fixed upon by a party of his troops. It has, for many years, been uninhabited, and in a ruinous ftate. Three old trees ftood together near the road from Dyfart to Pathhead. Two traditions were handed down concerning them ; the one, that three brothers of the St. Clair family had encountered there, during the night, miftaking one another for robbers, and had fallen by each others hands ; that they were buried there, and three trees planted on their graves. The other is, that all the ground on the neighbourhood of Dyfart had been originally in wood ; and that when the wood was cleared away, thefe three trees were left as a memorial of its former ftate. They were much decayed, and three young ones have been planted in their place. The arms of the town of Dyfart bear one tree : and it has long been a proverb here, As old as the three trees of Dyfart.

ing the promife of the life that now is, and of that which
is to come." To fee religion profper among them, would
gratify the higheft wifh of their paftor, who, having the comfort
to be fettled in the place of his nativity, and being called
to be a fellow labourer with his father in the fame charge,
could not poffibly defire a more eligible fituation for the exercife
of his minifterial functions. He cannot but be interefted
in every thing that relates to them, and efpecially in what
concerns their eternal welfare ; and his joy would be great, to
perceive, from their conduct, that his labours among them
have not been in vain.

PARISH OF ELY.

(COUNTY AND SYNOD OF FIFE.—PRESBYTERY OF ST.
ANDREWS.)

By Mr WILLIAM PAIRMAN, *Minister.*

Name, Situation, &c.

ELY, the modern name, ELIE or ELLIE, the old name,
is so called from *A Liche*, in Gaelic, " Out of the sea,
" or out of the water," the town being built so near the
sea, that it washes the walls in some places. The houses
are preserved with great difficulty by sea dykes, notwithstanding which, the sea is yearly making great incroach-
ments. If this derivation is a just one, and if it was built out
of the sea, the sea is fast resuming what it gave.

Ely has a most pleasant, dry, and healthy situation. The
shore is sandy, and shelving gradually; is remarkably well
adapted for sea-bathing ; and is, of late, much resorted to for
that purpose. It is a mile and a half long, and about a mile
broad. It is bounded by the parish of Newburn, on the west ;
by the parish of Kilconquhar, on the north ; the parish of St
Monance, on the east ; and the sea, on the south. It was
disjoined from the extensive parish of Kilconquhar about the
year 1640.

Population.

Population.—The number of families in this parish is 152; of souls 620, which is nearly 4 to each family. The incumbent took an accurate list of the inhabitants about the year 1790, which may be relied on. The population in 1755 amounted to 642, consequently there is a decrease of 22.

The following is an abstract of Births, Burials, and Marriages, for 7 years, from October 1. 1783, being the time when the act commenced, granting to his Majesty a duty of 3 d. on each of these articles, which has since been repealed.

	Births.			Burials.			Marriages.
	Males.	Fem.	Total.	Males.	Fem.	Total	
From Oct. 1. 1783 to Ditto 1784	6	14	20	4	10	14	7
From 1784 to 1785	19	11	30	17	13	30	5
—— 1785 to 1786	15	13	28	13	6	19	6
—— 1786 to 1787	7	14	21	9	11	20	4
—— 1787 to 1788	8	12	20	4	9	13	4
—— 1788 to 1789	11	10	21	5	6	11	9
—— 1789 to 1790	9	9	18	5	3	8	5
Total for 7 years	75	83	158	57	58	115	40
Average for each year	$10\frac{5}{7}$	$11\frac{6}{7}$	$22\frac{4}{7}$	$8\frac{1}{7}$	$8\frac{2}{7}$	$16\frac{3}{7}$	$7\frac{5}{7}$

From 158, the total number of births,

Take 115, the total burials,

Rem. 43, the total increase in 7 years; which, on an average, is only one more than 6 to a year.

Proprietors, &c.—Sir John Anstruther is patron of the church, and sole proprietor of the parish, one single farm excepted,

excepted, lately purchafed by Captain Chriftie of Bal-
chriftie.

Fifheries.—There are 8 fifhermen belonging to this parifh.
They have houfes, rent free, from Sir John Anftruther, fuperior of this place, on condition of their fupplying the town
of Ely with fifh, at leaft three times a week. They are well
fituated for carrying on the fifheries, and, on the whole, are
pretty fuccefsful.

Lake.—There is a beautiful lake, called Kilconquhar Loch,
bounded by that parifh and Ely. In it there are plenty of
pikes and eels. The fifhing, however, is of no great value,
and will naturally be more fully defcribed in the Statiftical
Account of Kilconquhar.

Poor.—The feffion here maintains all its poor. No beggars belong to the parifh. There are about 20 regular penfioners, who receive a fmall fum monthly, befides others
who get charity occafionally, as their wants require. The
funds for their fupport amount to about 50 l. *per annum.*

Inclofures.—The whole parifh was inclofed with ditch and
hedge by Sir John Anftruther. The inclofures are kept in
great order, and are very flourifhing. The burgh acres,
near the town, anno 1790, let at about 40 s. and the large
farms at 30 s. per acre, but have fince rifen. Burgh acres
now (anno 1795) let at between 50 s. and 60 s. the acre; and
large farms between 40 s. and 50 s. Sir John Anftruther
lately let a farm, of near 100 acres, at 3 l. per acre.

Fuel.—Coal is the only fuel ufed here. There is an excellent coalwork, belonging to Sir John Anftruther, 3 miles
from

from this pariſh. The price of coals, independent of carriage, in 1790, was 3 s. for 75 ſtones, and 4 s. 4 d. for 75 ſtones of a better quality, but is now 4 s. for 75 ſtones of the firſt ſort, and 5 s. for the other.

Wages.—Men ſervants wages, beſides maintenance, were from 5 l. to 6 l. *per annum,* and women from 1 l. to 2 l. the half year. Day labourers got 10 d. and 1 s. per day, and carpenters 2 s. and 2 s. 6 d. Now, (anno 1795,) men ſervants are 7 l. and 8 l. yearly. Women 30 s. and 2 l. and no labourers are to be found under 1 s.

Harbour, &c.—There is an excellent harbour at Ely. It is the deepeſt in the Frith of Forth, Bruntiſland excepted. It has remarkably eaſy acceſs, and is perfectly ſafe. It is the reſort of more wind-bound veſſels, than any other harbour, perhaps, in Scotland. It has alſo been the means of ſaving many a ſhip, cargo, and ſeaman, that would otherwiſe have been driven out of the Frith; many of them being ſo poorly manned and proviſioned, that they never would have been able to regain the coaſt. This uſeful harbour, however, is going faſt to ruin. It were much to be wiſhed, that ſome public ſpirited perſon would recommend it to the attention of the Chamber of Commerce, or the Convention of Royal Burghs, to obtain ſome aid to put it in a better ſtate. An inconſiderable expence, in proportion to the importance and utility of the object, would completely repair it. It may be remarked, alſo, that the value of the ſhipping brought in, bears but a ſmall proportion to that of their cargoes, which are often grain and other periſhable commodities, that might ſuffer by being expoſed to a ſtorm, even though the ſhip were to weather it. There are, belonging to this place, ſeven ſquare rigged veſſels, carrying 1000 or 1100 tons, all employ-

ed

ed in foreign trade, and one floop ufed as a coafter. Veffels, of a confiderable fize, are built here. There is a manufacture of check and bed tikes, and alfo of ropes, by the Meffrs Wood.

Ecclefiaftic State.—Sir John Anftruther is fole patron of the church of Ely. There are a few Seceders, Independents, and Bereans; but the great body of the people belong to the Eftablifhed Church. The ftipend of Ely is 80 l. old ftipend, and 20 l. lately given voluntarily by Sir John Anftruther, in all 100 l. The fchoolmafter's falary is 11 l. Part of the parifh lies in the very heart of Kilconquhar parifh, owing to this, that at the disjunction, the proprietor of Ely wifhed all belonging to that barony to be in the parifh.

Mifcellaneous Obfervations.—Near the town of Ely, is the cave of M'Duff, Thane of Fife, a ftupendous arch, in the face of Kincraig rocks, fronting the fea. In this place, Macduff hid and defended himfelf, by a fortification, againft his purfuers, when he was flying from M'Beath, to the King's fon, Malcolm, in England. The inhabitants of Earlsferry, (fo called from Earl M'Duff,) ferried him over to North Berwick; and out of gratitude, when the King's fon was reftored, he got the town made a Royal Borough, which it ftill is, and retains all its privileges, but that of fending a member to Parliament, which privilege it loft, owing to its being unable to maintain its member, and its having petitioned to be relieved from the burden. It is in the fame fituation with Falkland, Newburgh, and fome other towns in Scotland. Tradition fays, that, among other things, Macduff obtained this privilege from the King, that, on the application of a criminal, the town is obliged to ferry him over immediately, and dare not ferry over his purfuers, till he is half way over the Frith. This, it is faid, was claimed and

granted

granted in the case of Carnegie and Douglas of Finhaven.
A tumulus was opened here some years ago. In it were
found several bones of a remarkably large size. They were
sent to the Musaeum of the Society of Scottish Antiquaries.
Real rubies have been got on the shore, which were gradually washed from the rocks. Some of them were sent to Dr
Black, Professor of Chemistry in the University of Edinburgh.

To the east end of the harbour of Ely, and at a small
distance from it, Wadehaven is situated; so named, it is said,
from General Wade, who recommended it to government
as proper for a harbour. Others call it Wadd's Haven.
How it got that name, if the right one, is not known. It is
very large, and has deep water, in so much that it would
contain the largest Men of War, drawing from 20 to 22
feet water.

PARISH of FALKLAND,

(COUNTY OF FIFE.)

By the Rev. Mr ANDREW BROWN.

Name, Situation, Soil, Surface, &c.

THE ancient name of the parish was *Kilgour;* in the Gaelic language, *Cul-gawn* is the ' hill of goats.' Its modern name is evidently taken from that of the town, or burgh, and probably took place in that year in which the church was transferred from Kilgour to Falkland.—It is fituated in the prefbytery of Cupar, and Synod of Fife. The contiguous parifhes are, on the W. Strathmiglo, which alfo, by a narrow ftrip of land ftretching along the fouth fide of the water of Eden, feparates it from Auchtermuchty, and bounds it on the N.; on the E. Kettle and Markinch; and on the S. Leflie and Portmoak. It is of a regular form, and approaches nearly to a fquare of about 10,000 acres. Its general afpect is not unpleafant. On the N. there is a confiderable plain or flat, called the Park of Falkland, extending about a mile and an half fquare, from which the furface gradually rifes to that hilly ridge which forms the Lomonds. That ridge, which is the fteepeft, a little weft of the town, is fkirted with furze, above which it prefents

a

a beautiful verdure at all ſeaſons, and riſes into a conical
ſummit, called the eaſtern Lomond. On the eaſtern ſide of
this hill the ridge gradually ſlopes, and is partly verdant
and partly heathy. On the weſt the deſcent is ſteeper, to
the gap or opening which ſeparates it from the weſtern Lomond, and which extends above a mile nearly on a level.
Upon the northern front of this intermediate ſpace, the
eaſtern part of it, which ſwells beyond the line of the ridge,
riſes in 4 tires of hills, reſembling ſo many ſegments of a
circle. The loweſt is totally covered with a ſhort heath,
interſperſed here and there with abrupt and rugged maſſes
of freeſtone rock. It is well named the Black Hill. From
its ſummit, as you approach the foot of the ſecond, the ſurface becomes verdant; but the face of the hill, which is
called the Stony Fold, is covered with looſe heaps of blue
moor-ſtone, very hard, and of the fineſt grit. They are
found in various ſhapes and ſizes, from that of the ſmalleſt
pinnings, to the moſt ſolid binding maſſes employed in
building. The ſides and top of this hill are clothed with
a cloſe and beautiful verdure, from which it is named the
Green Hill, and is reckoned ſuperior, as a ſheep walk, to
all the ſurrounding paſture. Of ſimilar form, but leſs magnitude, are the two remaining hills, by which you riſe to
the common ridge which divides the Lomonds. Their
graſs, too, is of coarſer quality than that of the Green Hill,
but ſtill very fit for paſture. The weſtern part of this intermediate ſpace, and which is divided from the eaſtern by
a deep ravine, ſtretches from the circular into the rectuli-
neal appearance; and from the firſt aſcent, which is higher,
more abrupt and broken, runs to the ſummit of the ridge,
by three different aſcents, bearing ſome reſemblance to ter-
race walks in a hanging garden. From the ſummit of the
hill and ridge, the ſouthern aſpect has little variety, but a
gradual and uniform deſcent, till it joins the pariſhes of
Leſlie

Leſlie and Portmoak.—The ſoil, as well as the ſurface, is conſiderably diverſified. Part is of a light brown loam, upon a red bottom, part a light black ſand, with a mixture of moſs, and in the plain or flat of Falkland Park, already mentioned, part of it is barren ſand and gravel, covered with ſhort heath and furze, but a greater part of it deep black moſs, generated from the oak and other timber which grew there, when it was incloſed for a hunting park to royal ſportſmen, ſome of which hath been cultivated at great expence, and the reſt is lying in its natural ſtate. That track of land which extends almoſt the whole length of the pariſh, from weſt to eaſt, between the plain and the foot of the eaſtern Lomond, is generally of deep loam, and needs only proper culture to produce both ſure and luxuriant crops. On the ſouth ſide of the hill and ridge, the ſoil is ſpungy and wet, more fit for paſture than for the plough. About one half of the pariſh may be conſidered as paſture-ground, in which is included the eaſter Lomond, and that part of the weſtern which lies within the pariſh, both of which are a commonty to the contiguous heritors, and the town of Falkland.—The air is of a middle temperature, rather dry than moiſt, particularly about the town of Falkland, and that track which ſtretches along the foot of the hill, both to the eaſt and weſt. For, on the one hand, the Lomonds attract the moiſt vapours floating in the ſurrounding atmoſphere, and either collect them in fogs about their head and ſhoulders, or conduct them along their range in ſhowers. On the other hand, the creeping fogs which ſet in from the eaſt, more frequently in ſpring and autumn, attracted by the water of Eden, interſecting the valley between Falkland and Auchtermuchty, and by the planting and marſhy ground, ſettle there, and leave the air more dry and pure on the riſing ground, or that part of the pariſh which is moſt populous. In general, therefore, the inhabitants

tants are very healthy. Formerly, thofe who lived on the low grounds are faid to have been' fubject to aguifh complaints, which, no doubt, arofe from their vicinity to mofs and marfh, and the ftagnation of water from the overflowing of the Eden, which fometimes covered a great part of the valley. But of late years, the moffes and marfhes have been much drained, and in this neighbourhood the Eden confined within its banks, by a new ftraight cut or channel, and the aguifh complaints are lefs frequent. From the Lomonds, on all fides, iffue fprings and fmall ftreams of the pureft and moft wholfome water, fo that the inhabitants enjoy in great perfection that neceffary of life, and moft falutary beverage.

The Lomonds are the only hills which deferve notice, and that not from their natural magnitude, but their relative fituation and appearance. As being the higheft ground of the county, they command a very extenfive and variegated profpect into many neighbouring and diftant counties, and are feen by travellers, in fome directions, at a very great diftance. The eaftern, which is the moft regular and beautiful, is faid to be about 550 yards above the level of the plain already mentioned; and where it is moft acceffible, feems to have been fortified near the top, with a deep trench, for what purpofe, there is no record or tradition. Very near the higheft part of the hill, there is a fmall cavity, about a foot and an half diameter, which, in rainy weather, collects fome water, and is called by the common people a fpring or well, but by fome travellers a volcanic crater; and the ftones immediately under the northern fummit, though common to the whole ridge, and without any appearance of calcination or vitrification, are carried away in triumph, and exhibited as fpecimens of volcanic lava found in the eaftern Lomond. The weftern hill is confiderably higher, and has on its top a large heap of loofe ftones, or a cairn, fuch as is found on many hills

and

and mountains of Scotland. On the eaftern Lomond is plenty of limeftone rock, a few feet below, and in fome places very near the furface, and eafily wrought. There are alfo ftrata of coal of very good quality, but not yet dif-covered in fuch quantity as to be thought worth the dig-ging, efpecially in a country where there is abundance of fine coal, at a reafonable rate, in the neighbouring parifhes of Leflie and Markinch. On the .fouth fide of the fame hill, too, was formerly difcovered a lead-mine of very rich ore ; but either through unfkilfulnefs, or neceffity of circum-ftances, given up. It is now opened again, and with hope of fuccefs. There is alfo in the parifh, particularly on the Lomond hills, plenty of fand, and moorftone of good qua-lity for building, and eafily got at. Marl and fuller's earth have been difcovered, but in fmall quantities.

Population.—According to Dr Webfter's reports, the numbers were 1795. In the parifh at prefent are 2198 fouls. Of thefe 937 are in the town of Falkland, 120 in Ballinblae, a contiguous village, 193 in Newton, another village, 476 in Freuchie, another village, and 472 in what is properly the country part of the parifh.

Of thefe 287 Males, 265 Fem. from 1 to 10 years of age.

235 ——	210 ——	from 10 to 20
374 ——	447 ——	from 20 to 50
139 ——	156 ——	from 50 to 70
33 ——	52 ——	from 70 to 100
1068 ——	1130	

In a ftate of celibacy, including that of widowhood, are 304, of whom 91 are males, and 213 females, reckoning the ftate of celibacy from 25 years of age and upwards. ,The prefent number of the married, and of thofe in a ftate of widowhood, who have had children, is 464. Of thefe have
been

been born 2373 children, fecond marriages included, which is 5 to each family. The proportion of barren to prolific marriages, is as 1 to 31. Of the Eftablifhed Church 1860, Seceders 338.

The annual births, marriages and deaths, for the preceding 7 years, from 1784 to 1790 inclufive, are as follows, *viz.*

	Males.	Females.	Tot. Births.	Mar.	Deaths.
In 1784	28	21	49	14	36
1785	26	24	50	18	29
1786	33	22	55	21	33
1787	25	24	49	16	29
1788	32	22	54	12	48
1789	30	26	56	11	32
1790	41	28	69	20	30

The annual average of births for the preceding 7 years, is, of males 30, of females 24, of marriages 16, and of deaths 34. The proportion between the annual births and the whole population, is as 3 to 122; between the annual marriages and the whole population, as 1 to 131, and between the annual deaths and the whole population, as 1 to 61. Thefe calculations and proportions are founded on the parifh regifter, and according to it, as near the truth as whole numbers will admit. But the regifter of annual deaths is not pretended to be nearly accurate, as is evident from the proportion between them and the whole population, which, it is believed, falls confiderably fhort of the annual proportion of mankind that die, even in the moft favourable of the common circumftances of human life. For many years the parifh of Falkland has been confidered as very ftationary, in refpect of population, manufacture and agriculture. Of late it has made fome progrefs, though flow and gradual. The increafe of population in the laft 7

years

years is 168, and arises more from the increase in the families, than from that of their number.

Manufacture.—In the parish are 337 tradesmen, of whom 50 are apprentices. Of these 231 are weavers, 45 shoemakers, 22 tailors, 12 masons, 16 wrights, including wheel, plough, cart, wrights, and cabinet-makers, of the last very few, and 11 blacksmiths, each trade including its proportion of apprentices.—The weaving of coarse linen is the principal branch of manufacture, and that is principally carried on in the town and villages. Supposing the number of looms well employed, and it is the utmost that can be supposed, 200, the quantity of yarn annually manufactured, at 300 spindles to each loom, is 60,000. The value of the above yarn, manufactured and brought to market, at 3 s. 9 d. the spindle, is   L. 11,250 0 0

A complete tradesman will weave 400 spindle in the year, which at 9 d. the spindle, the highest price given, is   -   -   L. 15 0 0

Deduct for winding 200 spindles woof, at 1½ d.
the spindle,   -   -   1 5 0

The weaver's wages are   -   -   L. 13 15 0

The markets for their green cloth are Auchtermuchty and Cupar. The other trades do little more than supply the demands of the inhabitants. There are also cloth-merchants and grocers, fully adequate to the demands of the place.

Agriculture.—Agriculture, from its long rude state, has of late years made some progress, and the arable part of the parish is considerably improved, both in beauty and richness. Still, however, there is much room for improvement. That greater progress has not been made, may be
accounted

accounted for from the particular state of the parish. The great body of the inhabitants live in the town and villages. Of these there are a number of small proprietors, and others who farm from 1 to 2, 3 or 4 acres, for convenience, generally tradesmen, who depend upon their trade for the subsistence of their families, and by consequence have neither leisure nor skill to manage their little farms to the best advantage. From this division of the land, about the town and villages, into small portions, it lies uninclosed and naked, and from the want of a more skilful ploughing and rotation of crops, though well manured, it has neither that beauty nor richness, to which its soil and situation are both naturally disposed. There are a few farms of from 2 to 3 and 4 ploughs in the parish, of which that of Falkland Wood or Park is the most extensive. There are some inclosures, and a taste for them is prevailing; but, in general, the land is very naked. Oats and barley are the prevailing crops. Peas and turnip are raised in small proportions. Artificial grass, as clover and rye-grass, begins to be cultivated with more attention. Flax too is raised, and in some years in considerable quantities. The whole produce, however, is not sufficient for the consumption of the inhabitants. The old valuation of the parish, as it stands in the cess-books, is L. 5824. The present bears a proportion to the increased value of land. The farms, from the various quality of the soil, are very differently rented; but, it is believed, in general moderately, considering the late rise of rents. That of the land immediately about the town is from L. 2 to L. 2, 10 s. the acre. The price of labour and servants wages are, as in the country in general, high. The day-labourer has 10 d. in winter, and 1 s. or 1 s. 2 d. in summer. Men servants have from L. 5 to L. 7, women from L. 2 to L. 3 wages.

Burgh

Burgh of Falkland.—Falkland was erected into a burgh by King James II. in the year 1458. The preamble to the charter of erection states, as reasons of granting it, the frequent residence of the Royal Family at the manor of Falkland, and the damage and inconvenience sustained by the many prelates, peers, barons, nobles, and others of their subjects, who came to their country seat, for want of innkeepers and victuallers. This charter was renewed by King James VI. in the year 1595. In this charter is mentioned the right of holding a weekly market, and 4 public markets or fairs, yearly. To these last have been added other 2 markets, 1 in April, called the Lintseed-market, and 1 in September, called the Harvest-market. The 4 old markets are the most frequented, and very considerable numbers of both horses and black cattle are sold and bought at them. What is commonly called the set of the burgh, is as follows. There are 3 bailies, 15 councillors, of whom 1 is treasurer, and a clerk. The councillors elect themselves annually, and generally continue councillors till chosen bailies. The bailies are chosen by a majority of the councillors, and may continue as long as that majority pleases. No old bailie is ever chosen a councillor, and can come into council again only as bailie. The revenue of the burgh arises from custom at markets, landed property, and a mill, and is, *communibus annis,* from L. 100 to L. 110, exclusive of public burdens : A sum which, in the hands of patriotism and œconomy, might be turned to much public good in so small a town. It has not altogether been misapplied. There is one monument of public spirit in the town, a plentiful supply of fine water. It was brought into it in the year 1781. The expence amounted to near L. 400. Partiality for the place of his residence, and that share of credit which every individual naturally assumes to himself, from connection with a famed public, would na-

turally

turally lead a writer to wiſh, that he could add more inſtances of public ſpirit and beneficence, or that, by a courſe
of ſtrict and judicious œconomy, the means of doing good
were accumulating. In this reſpect, Falkland claims no
diſtinguiſhed ſuperiority to ſimilarly circumſtanced burghs,
nor is it perhaps juſtly chargeable with greater degeneracy.
It only adds to that maſs of conſiderations which calls aloud
for borough reformation. Great as the evil is of the want
of œconomy, or the miſmanagement of public revenue, it
is ſmall, compared to the neglect or miſmanagement of public authority and power. Magiſtracy is highly reſpectable,
and will always be reſpected by every man of ſenſe, and
friend to the public weal. It is more particularly ſo when
it is contemplated, as deſcending from the ſupreme, to every ſubordinate magiſtrate, inveſted with the ſacred majeſty
of public law, and circumſcribed by the rules of equal juſtice. But where office is not decently ſupported, it were
better not to exiſt. There are not wanting, in our country,
many inſtances in which the vigilance, activity, and patriotiſm of magiſtrates do them great honour, and mark them
out to public reſpect, as public bleſſings; at the ſame time,
it cannot eſcape the obſervation of partiality itſelf, that
there is ſometimes little or nothing of its ſpirit to be found
in thoſe who are inveſted with the office. There is a natural diſpoſition in mankind, to reſpect and reverence official authority; but when it is degraded by office-bearers,
the contempt and irreverence which naturally fall upon
them, deſcend to their office, and are productive of the
moſt pernicious conſequences to the great body of the
people.

Stipend, School, Poor, &c.—The ſtipend is 4 chalders of
bear, 2 chalders of meal, and 600 merks. Beſides, there
is allowed for communion-elements 100 merks, and in lieu
of

of a manfe and glebe, only a chalder of bear.   Mr Sandilands of Nuthill is patron.—There is no houfe nor garden
for the fchoolmafter, in hiring of which, his legal falary of
about L. 6, 10 s. is nearly exhaufted.   The average number
of his fcholars is about 80, of whom the fmall proportion
that read Latin and arithmetic, pay only 2 s. 6 d. the quarter, and the Englifh fcholars 1 s. 6 d.   Thefe, with the perquifites arifing from the offices of feffion-clerk and precentor, conftitute the whole of his emolument, on which he depends for his own and the fubfiftence of his family.   His
emoluments not admitting of an affiftant, both limits the
number of his fcholars, within what the populoufnefs of the
parifh might afford, and render it neceffary to employ o-
ther teachers in different parts of the parifh.   To thofe who
have any regard for the education and right principling of
the common people, it muft appear evident, that no clafs
of men are of more importance to fociety, or more deferving of patronage than fchoolmafters.   The legal provifion
made for them, was, at the time, adequate to the objeĉt in
view, and the happy effeĉts of it foon were, and ftill are,
confpicuous in our country.   Education was univerfally
diffufed.   The loweft claffes of the people were taught to
read the fcriptures, inftruĉted in the firft principles of religion and morality, and thus prepared in fchools for being
further enlightened and improved by the theological and moral leĉtures of churches.   Hence the diftinguifhed fuperiority
of the common people of Scotland in knowledge and fobriety.   Parifh fchools have hitherto been the great nur-
feries for the church, and many other learned profeffions.
There many men of ufefulnefs and eminence in the different departments of fociety, have received thofe rudiments of literature which they could not otherwife have
obtained, but to the great lofs of fociety and of their country, muft have continued blinded with the common mafs,
                                                     and,

and, like the deſert roſe, waſted, in vain, their uncultivated ſweetneſs. All who value theſe advantages, and wiſh
to ſecure them to their country, will ſee the neceſſity of in-
terpoſing, for the greater encouragement of that order of
men, on whoſe abilities and fidelity they ſo much depend.—
Conſidering the populouſneſs of the pariſh, and the town
and villages which are in it, the proportion of poor is
as ſmall as in the generality of pariſhes ſimilarly circumſtanced. Of thoſe who receive regular ſupply, the annual
average is about 15, and of thoſe who are occaſionally aſſiſted about 22. The funds for this ſupply are, the weekly collections at the church-door, the yearly rent of ſome
land, the intereſt of a ſmall ſum of money, perquiſites at
marriages, when the bride is of the pariſh, and at burials,
for the uſe of the mortcloth or pall. Theſe, at an average
of the laſt 7 years, amount annually to about L. 44, of
which the annual collection is L. 24.

Inns and Ale-houſes.—The market for every thing generally bears a proportion to the demand. The unfrequency
of travellers by the way of Falkland, eſpecially ſince the
great north road was made by Kinroſs and Queensferry,
has greatly diminiſhed the demand for inns. Still, however, there are 2 houſes in it that go by the name of inns.
—Of ale-houſes, for which there is a greater demand from
the populouſneſs of the town and neighbourhood, there is a
greater number. There are 10 in the town of Falkland,
1 in Newton, and 3 in Freuchie. Theſe generally belong
to brewers; and though ſtill more than are favourable to
either the health or morals of the inhabitants, are ſaid not
to exceed half the number of what have ſometimes been
known in the pariſh. This diminution of inns and ale-
houſes has ariſen from the increaſed demand for ſpirituous
liquors. It were injuſtice to the generally ſober and induſtrious

ftrious character of the parifhioners, to fay, that they are
either idle or prodigal; but where there are temptations,
fome will always be tempted.

Antiquities.—Of this parifh, the moft memorable antiquity is the ruinous palace of Falkland, which, for many
years, was the occafional refidence of the Royal Family of
Scotland.—On the S. fide of the Eden, directly between
Falkland and Auchtermuchty, are the remains of what is
called a Danifh camp. That it was fo, is probable from
the name of a neighbouring village, Dunfhelt, fuppofed to
be a corruption of Danes-halt, and to have derived its
name from the circumftance of the Danes having formed
an encampment in its vicinity. Another circumftance adds
to the probability of the tradition, that it is of a circular
form. The remains of this camp confift of five concentric
circular trenches, nearly equidiftant from one another, and
feem to have been feparated only by the bank of earth
thrown up from each. The centrical fpot inclofed by the
firft trench is about 22 feet diameter, and where they are
not demolifhed, the trenches are at prefent from 10 to 15
feet wide.—On the E. of Nuthill, and nearly half a mile
W. from the houfe, are 4 parallel trenches, in the form of
inverted wedges, of from 250 to 300 yards in length, evidently the work of art.—And the fame is to be faid of
what is called the Maiden Caftle, on the fame eftate, fituated above half a mile diftant, on the S. fide of the green
hill already mentioned. It is an oblong circular mound,
gradually rifing from a level on the E. to a fteep and abrupt termination on the W. of nearly 400 yards in circumference, and, except the fteep part on the W. and the
level on the E. where are the remains of a ftone wall, is
furrounded with a ditch of 12 feet wide.

PARISH OF FERRY-PORT-ON-CRAIG.

(County and Synod of Fife.—Presbytery of St. Andrew's.)

By the Rev. ROBERT DALGLEISH *of Scotscraig*, D. D.
Minister of the said Parish.

Erection and Name.

THIS parish was erected by an act of the 18th parliament of King James VI. in the year 1606. There is a tradition, that the village Ferry-Port-on-Craig belonged to the neighbouring parish of Leuchars, previous to that period, and had a chapel of ease, though no record can be found old enough to authenticate this fact. So strongly is the tradition thereof impressed on the minds of the people, that the supposed foundation of this chapel, ever since that distant period, has to this day remained unplowed, in the midst of a well cultivated field, named *the Chapel.*—The parish has its name from its local situation. There is a public passage over the Tay, from the village of Ferry-Port-on-Craig on the south, to Broughty Castle, which stands opposite, on the north bank of the river. This passage was named *Ferry-Port-on-Craig*, to distinguish it from the many other ferries in this part of Scotland. There being at that time no pier, or quay, on either

side

fide of the river, where the paffage boats might fhip paffengers
or horfes, it was the cuftom to boat horfes at the point of a
craig, or rock, whence the name *Ferry-Port-on-Craig.*

Ferry.—Before the bridge was built over the Tay at Perth,
this paffage was much frequented by perfons of all ranks;
but fince that period, fewer people travel this way, and the
road has become almoft deferted. The drovers, however, ftill
frequently pafs here, having good conveniency for their cattle on both fides of the river. It is, indeed, efteemed one
of the fafeft paffages over the Tay, there being no inftance
(in the memory of the oldeft man alive), of a paffage boat
being caft away croffing from the village of Ferry-Port-on-
Craig to Bruchty Caftle; though the river at this paffage
is reckoned two miles broad. The prefent freight for a man
is 2d.; and for a horfe 4d., when they go in the birth boat*.
It was often found fo inconvenient and dangerous to boat
horfes from a ragged craig, that the Legiflature interpofed
their authority, ordaining the ferriers to make *Brigges* to their
boats, (by which is meant a kind of timber platform, to be
laid from the moft proper part of the craig, to the gunwale of
the boat); for fhipping horfes with more eafe and fafety.
Thefe briggs were always ufed at this paffage, till fome time
ago, that piers were built for the convenience of paffengers,
and fecurity of horfes; but the brigges are ftill kept, and
ufed occafionally at times, when high winds and tides oblige
the

* There is an act of the 7th parliament of King James III. held at Edinburgh, May 9th 1474, regulating other paffages, and extended to this in thefe
words: " And at the *Port-in-Craige*, ane penny for the man, and the horfe ane
" penny : And quhat ferriers that dois in the contrarie, fall pay fourty fhillings
" to the King, and his perfon prifoned at the will of the King : And that the
" ferriers make brigges to their boates, after the forme of the acts maid of be-
" fore, under the paine conteined in the famin."

the boatmen to ſhip horſes at a rock or craig. This paſſage is 4 miles farther eaſtward, and nearer the ocean and mouth of the river, than the paſſage at Dundee. It is private property, being part of the eſtate of Scotſcraig.

Situation, Surface, Village, &c.—This pariſh is ſituated on the ſouth ſide of the river Tay, and ſtretches along the ſouth bank of the river, from its mouth, where it empties itſelf into the German ocean, 5 ſtatute miles from E. to W. It is irregular as to its breadth from N. to S., being in ſome places one mile, and at other places not above half a mile broad. On the E. the ſurface is flat and low. Though there are no remarkable mountains, yet towards the W. it is high and rocky, where the hills have not ſoil enough for cultivation. They are moſtly covered with whins and ſhort graſs, the bare rocks appearing but in few places. Where the pariſh is bounded by the German ocean, the ſhore is ſandy ; but where it is bounded by the river, it varies, being in ſome places ſandy, in others covered with ſea gravel. At the village it is a rocky ſhore. The pariſh contains the houſe of Scotſcraig, (where the family reſides), four farms, with their cottaries, and the village of Ferry-Port-on-Craig, from whence the pariſh has its name. The greateſt number of the pariſhioners live in the Ferry, where the church and manſe are both ſituated, and are very centrical for the pariſhioners.

Extent, Soil, and Produce.—From a map of the pariſh, it appears there are in it 2,026 Scotch acres. The ſoil is of various kinds, conſiſting of clay, ſtrong and light loam, ſand, and links. The crops that are beſt adapted for the clay, to produce the greateſt profit, are, wheat, beans, barley, graſs, and oats. Flax is ſown to very good advantage; but, on the whole, it is rather an uncertain crop ; it likewiſe pro

duces

duces potatoes, but the quality is generally not fo good as in light foils. The ftrong loam ftands on a whin rock; and, where there is fufficiency of foil, it produces wheat, oats, beans, barley, grafs and potatoes, in great perfection. Flax is fometimes fown on this foil, but feldom proves a good crop. The light loam is founded on fand, and produces barley, grafs, oats, potatoes, turnips and flax. This foil produces the two laft articles, in a moift feafon, very abundantly; but when long tracts of dry weather take place, they prove but poor crops. The fand produces barley, grafs, oats, rye, turnips and flax; all which crops, in a favourable feafon, turn out far beyond what a ftranger to the nature of the foil could imagine. The flax in particular, turns out to be a very lucrative crop. The links produce a kind of pafture for cattle and fheep, and afford accommodation for the grey rabbits, which, within thefe few years, have turned out very valuable to the poffeffors, on account of the extraordinary demand for their fkins, which fold at 8s. Sterling per dozen laft year.

Cultivation, Cattle, Exports and Imports, &c.—All the tenants now ufe only ploughs drawn by two horfes; one man both holds the plough, and drives the horfes with a pair of long reins. In driving their corn and dung, they ufe carts drawn by two horfes. The farmers in the country employ 17 ploughs. Cultivating the acres occupied by the feuars in the Ferry, gives fufficient employment to 3 more, which makes the number of ploughs ufed in the whole parifh amount to 20.—There are 61 working horfes. The greatnefs of their number is owing to the villagers in the Ferry, keeping more horfes than would be fufficient for the cultivation of the land they poffefs, were they always employed in agriculture; but they frequently ufe them in driving coals for hire, and fuch like work.—Only 1 farmer keeps a flock; they are of the fmall white

white faced breed, and weigh at an average 22 pounds the whole carcaſe. The ſame breed has been kept in that farm for many years paſt, without any change. The farmers have in all about 240 ſheep; they produce excellent wool, which is ſold to the people in the neighbourhood at about 15s. Sterling the ſtone weight. The pariſh exports barley, and imports oat-meal *.

Climate and Diſeaſes.—The air is reckoned very wholeſome. The people are generally healthy. Epidemical diſtempers ſeldom rage here; the beſt evidence of the ſalubrity of the air is, that during the incumbency of the preſent miniſter, there have always been in the village ſome old people of 80 years and upwards. There are ſeveral of that age alive juſt now (October 5th 1792). About 20 years ago, the ague was ſo frequent, that few people eſcaped it, in a greater or leſs degree at ſome period of life; but for ſome years paſt, it has ſcarcely made its appearance. Rheumatiſms and nervous diſorders are now moſt prevalent.

Fiſheries.—There are conſiderable ſalmon fiſhings in the river Tay, oppoſite to this pariſh. The ſalmon is eſteemed of a good quality, being taken ſo near the ocean. They are ſold to the Perth merchants, who ſend them to the London market. Theſe fiſhings afford ſummer employment for ſeveral hands, and often yield them great returns for their labour, and the expence laid out in preparing their nets and other apparatus

* In ordinary ſeaſons, the wheat ſeed continues from the middle of September to the end of October; the rye is ſown from about the 15th to the 25th of November; oats, peaſe, and beans, from the 12th March to the end of April; potatoes are planted from the 15th to the end of April; barley is ſown during the month of May; turnips during the month of June. The harveſt is rather early; but in wet ſeaſons, the harveſt is both late, and very uncertain.

paratus for the fishing; but they are not equally productive
every season. They do not begin to fish for salmon, in
this part of the river, till about the end of April; and they
give over the 26th of August. There is only one boat's
crew engaged in the white fishery. The fishing ground for
white fish is mostly without the river. The fishermen carry
their fish to Dundee; so that the price of the small quantity
sold here, is regulated by the market there; but this fishing
has failed much for some years past. In the summer months,
great numbers of small flounders are caught in this part of
the river, as any person is permitted to use hand lines in that
fishing. It is very useful to the poor people, who have an opportunity of supplying their families with these fish, at no
expence. On the fouth side of this part of the Tay, there is
a *scalp* of a small kind of muffels, efteemed good bait for the
white fish; they are purchafed for that purpofe by the fifhermen in the neighbourhood. In the fands there is alfo plenty of
fea worms, which the fifhermen call *Lugg*, and prefer them
even to muffels for bait in the fummer feafon; but thefe
worms fink fo deep in the fand in winter, that they cannot
be got. Thefe fmall muffels are, therefore, the only bait ufed
for the white fifhing, in winter.

Migratory Birds.—Several kinds of fea fowls frequent the
fhore during winter. Every year, about the month of April,
they leave the coaft, to go and hatch their young. They return again in the month of Auguft, and continue in this
country till April, when they take their annual flight. They
are immediately fucceeded by other fea fowls, that make their
appearance here in the fpring, remain during the fummer
months, and hatch about the fhore. In the month of Auguft
or September, they remove from this to their winter habitations. Next feafon, at the ufual time, they pay their annual
                                                    vifit

viſit to this country. Thus they follow each other in conſtant ſucceſſion every year.

Population.—It appears from the pariſh roll taken up this
year, compared with a liſt made out in the year 1762, that
the village has had an increaſe of 84 families, and the country of 4, within theſe 30 years, in all 88 families; that the
former has increaſed 194 examinable perſons, and the latter
11; and that the whole pariſh has increaſed to the number of
205 perſons, above 7 years of age, within that period. The
following table exhibits the preſent ſtate of the pariſh, and the
total increaſe, within theſe 40 years.

	In the village.	In the country.	Total.
Number of families, - -	208 -	32 -	240
Perſons above 7 years of age, -	569 -	131 -	700
———— below ————— -	135 -	40 -	175
Total, -	704 -	171 -	875
The return to Dr. Webſter in 1755, was - - -			621
Increaſe, -			254
Number of males above 7 years of age, - - -			310
———— females above ditto, - - - -			390
Majority of females, -			80

Number of ſailors * about -	35	Number of ale ſellers, who are	
———— weavers, 67 - 9 -	76	brewers, -	3
———— wrights, - -	9	———— male labouring ſervants	
———— tailors, - -	9	about - -	35
———— ſmiths, - -	3	Annual average of births within	
———— ſhoemakers, - -	5	the laſt 9 years, -	$27\frac{1}{3}$
———— bakers, - -	3	———— ditto, marriages, -	$6\frac{1}{3}$
———— ale ſellers in the vil-		———— ditto, deaths, nearly -	18
lage, - -	6		

The

* Theſe are moſtly employed in the Dundee merchantmen.

The increafe in population, which is chiefly in the village, is owing partly to the neighbouring farmers not inclining to keep fuch large cottaries as formerly : This has obliged feveral families to come into the Ferry, where they hire fmall houfes, and fupport themfelves by their induftry, either as tradefmen or day labourers. The great increafe of manufactures, has alfo encouraged many young men to follow that line of life, who continue to refide as tradefmen within the town.

Abftract of Baptifms, Marriages, and Deaths, as entered in the Parifh Regifter, for the laft nine years.

Years.	Baptifms.	Marriages.	Deaths.
1783	18	7	21
1784	24	6	18
1785	25	6	10
1786	31	8	26
1787	26	7	18
1788	38	5	13
1789	28	6	15
1790	29	5	12
1791	27	7	28
In all	246	57	161

Manufactures.—The principal manufacture, is weaving coarfe brown linens, of different fabrics. The weavers are chiefly employed by the merchants of Dundee in manufacturing thefe linens. They fometimes weave other cloth for country ufe. The women's work is generally fpinning the yarn for thefe brown linens. So great is the prefent demand for fuch linens, that both the weavers and fpinners have more work offered them, than they are able to undertake ; and the
wages

wages are conſiderably higher than formerly *.—The other
artiſts work principally for the uſe of the people in the pariſh
and neighbourhood ; and ſometimes manufacture articles for
ſale.

Church and School.—The King is patron. The preſent incumbent is the 8th miniſter ſince the Revolution, and has
been 32 years in the pariſh.—The value of the living varies
according to the prices of grain. It conſiſts of 39 bolls 2
firlots of bear, 40 bolls of oats by the decreet, but by uſe
and wont of payment, 4 bolls 1 firlot of theſe 40 bolls of oats,
are paid in oat-meal : 10 bolls of peaſe ; and in money the
ſum of 17l. 11s. 8d. Sterling ; 10s. of that ſum is paid by
the proprietor of Leuchars for a ſalmon fiſhing. The proprietor of Scotſcraig pays the whole ſtipend, except the 10s.
juſt mentioned, and holds up the kirk, manſe and ſchool. Out
of the teinds of this pariſh, 5 bolls bear, 7 bolls 3 firlots of
white

---

* A common day-labourer, from Candlemas to Martinmas, will, at an average, earn from 12d. to 14d. a-day ; an ordinary tradeſman, who works on day's
wages, from 15d. to 18d. ; but maſons have higher wages than ordinary tradeſmen, owing to the great increaſe of manufactures, which have excited ſuch an
uncommon ſpirit for building, that they get from 20d. to 22d. a-day in ſummer ;
but from Martinmas to Candlemas, maſons have only about 14d., and the labourers about 10d. a-day. During the whole year, they all furniſh themſelves
with proviſions out of their wages. The greatneſs of the wages depends much
on the demand at the time. Tailors get 6d. a-day, and their meat, throughout
the year. It is cuſtomary for both tradeſmen and ſpinſters, to hire themſelves
to the neighbouring farmers, at fixed wages, for the whole harveſt, without
reſtriction to any number of days. At an average, the farmer will hire a tradeſman, for the whole harveſt, at 1l. 3s. Sterling, and a woman at 17s. 6d.
Both ſexes have their victuals from the farmer, beſides their wages. When a
man is occaſionally hired per day, he receives 1s., and a woman 10d., beſides
their maintenance. The hire of labourers and ſervants wages are ſtill on the
increaſe.

white oats are paid yearly to the minifter of Dull, in Athol;
and 1s. 8d. Sterling of vicarage to the minifter of Leuchars. The
glebe confifts of 4 acres of arable land, let at prefent for 2
bolls 2 firlots of barley each acre; the foggage, being all inclofed, is let for 4l. 7s. Sterling, for which the minifter pays
10s. Sterling yearly to the tenant of the Mains of Scotfcraig;
the ground taken off that farm for foggage, being eftimated
in value to that amount above the legal allowance. The glebe
adds to the value of the living 10 bolls of barley, and 3l. 17s.
Sterling of money; making the living, with the glebe, amount
to 99 bolls 2 firlots of victual, and 21l. 8s. 8d. Sterling of
money.—The church was built in the year 1607, the year
after the erection of the parifh, the date being cut in the kirk:
The family aifle, by Sir John Buchanan, then of Scotfcraig,
in the year 1644. Under it there is a large vault, where the
feveral proprietors of the eftate have been buried, ever fince the
manfe was built, about the year 1727.—The falary of the parifh fchool is 100 merks Scotch money, paid by the proprietor of Scotfcraig. The fchoolmafter is alfo feffion-clerk.

Poor.—The poor's fund arifes from the intereft of a fmall
fum of money appropriated to them, the profits of the mort-
cloth, and the very liberal weekly collection made by the parifhioners. The feffion has no act fixing any certain weekly
penfion on any of the poor; but varies the fum given to them,
enlarging or diminifhing their allowance, according to the difference of their fituation; but they always give them fuch ample
occafional fupplies, as enable the poor, with their own induftry,
to fubfift comfortably in their own houfes; none having been
allowed to beg from door to door for many years paft, either
within or without the parifh. The parifh funds have fupported the poor, without any affeffment, thefe 50 years. The
number of the poor varies as circumftances occur. The pre-

ſent number, of thoſe that receive aid from the public
pariſh fund, is about 16. Upon ſetting forth, that, from
extraordinary loſs, accidental misfortune, or ſudden and ſevere
diſtreſs in their family, any are reduced to ſuch a ſituation as
to require a greater interim ſupply, than the ordinary ſeſſion
funds are able to afford to one family, then, by order of the
ſeſſion, an extraordinary collection is intimated from the pulpit, to be made for their benefit, either at the church doors,
or from houſe to houſe within the pariſh, as circumſtances may
require. Whatever is collected is given to them, that they
may have aſſiſtance ſuitable to their preſent urgent neceſſity.
Upon a favourable change of circumſtances, they again ſupport themſelves by their induſtry, without having recourſe to
ſeſſional aid. When they are in ſuch indigence as not to be
able to educate their children, the ſeſſion always pays the
ſchool fees, for teaching them at leaſt to read the holy ſcrip-
tures ; as they judge it their duty to ſee the children of the
poor well educated, and conſider that the beſt beſtowed charity, which procures for them the means of education.

Heritor and Rent.—There is but one heritor, the preſent
miniſter, who is proprietor of the whole pariſh. The villagers in the Ferry are all his feuers, for their houſes and
ſmall gardens : The farms are his property lands.—The valued rent of the pariſh is 2183l. Scotch money. The value
of the rental cannot, with accuracy, be eaſily aſcertained : a
great part of it being paid in victual, the value muſt vary, according to the prices of grain, every year.

Scotſcraig Mains.—The farm of the mains of Scotſcraig
was originally church land, belonging to the archbiſhopric
of St. Andrew's. The Pope, by his bull, allowed the archbiſhop to feu out ſaid farm at the ſum of 132l. 18s. 8d.
Scotch,

Scotch, and 4 bolls of peafe. The yearly value of the peafe, with the faid fum of money, is annually paid to the collector of the bifhop's rents. It is handed down by tradition, that a Mr. Scott, a fon of the family of Balwirie, in Fife, was the feuer; and, to diftinguifh it from other farms called *Craig*, he prefixed his own name to it; hence Scotfcraig. This eftate was formerly the property, and the houfe the country refidence, of *Archbifhop* JAMES SHARP, for many years before his death; and belonged to his fon Sir William Sharp feveral years after the death of the bifhop. His arms are ftill on the outer gate, dated 1667.

Antiquity.—The only antiquity in the parifh is the remains of an old caftle, in which there are feveral vaults quite entire. We are greatly at a lofs to know by whom, or at what period it was built, as there is no record to determine, nor even any traditional account handed down concerning it; but it muft have been after the invention of fire arms, embrafures being fo placed, as to carry a line of fire round the fort. The top of one of the hills is furrounded with the foundation of an old wall. As, from the top of this hill, there is an extenfive profpect along the banks of the Tay, and the country around, it is fuppofed to have been the place of fire fignal, in the time of the Danifh incurfions into Scotland; but there is no record about it.

Fuel.—There being neither coals, peats, nor wood, found for fuel, the dependence of the parifhioners for firing, is upon coals brought from a diftance, either from the frith of Forth, or by fea, at a confiderable expence. What is called the boll, which weighs 8 cwt., or 56 ftone Englifh, is fold here at prefent at 6s. the boll. Though we pay no duty for Scotch coals, they are confiderably dearer this feafon, than ever they were remembered to have been, which bears hard upon the

people

people in the lower ranks of life. Some drive coals from the coal-works in this country, at the diſtance of 9 or 10 ſtatute miles, which they ſell at 7s. the cart load. Some of the cottagers, in the country pariſh, burn dryed turf and whins ; but they all uſe coal as the principal part of their fuel. The villagers in the Ferry uſe coal only, which they purchaſe at the above prices.

Charaɛter.—The people are peaceably diſpoſed, and firmly attached to the preſent happy civil conſtitution of their country. They all adhere to the principles of the eſtabliſhed church of Scotland ; and regulatly attend divine worſhip in the pariſh kirk, excepting one Unitarian, (who, however, frequently hears ſermon with the other pariſhioners), and one Seceder ; both of whom came lately into this pariſh from Dundee.

Miſcellaneous Obſervations.—There are no lime-ſtone quarries ; but lime is brought by ſea from Sunderland. It is ſold at the Ferry at 1s. 6d. Sterling the boll of wheat meaſure, or 2s. 4d. Sterling the barley meaſure. Some drive lime by land carriage, at the diſtance of 10 and 15 miles, which can be afforded at 3s. 1d. the boll, barley meaſure. The only ſtone, got in this ground, is a hard whin ſtone, which makes ſtrong and laſting work when built with good lime.—There are two mills for grinding meal, to which the pariſhioners are thirled only for what meal they make, or what malt is brewed within the pariſh ; but not for the whole crop of corn growing on the ſeveral farms.—As there is a conſtant weekly demand for all kinds of country vivres in Dundee, ſome perſons make it their buſineſs to go through this part of the country, and gather them up for the Dundee market. The prices here are, therefore, always regulated by what they fetch there.—

there.—This Ferry is a cuftom-houfe creek, within the pre-
cints of the cuftom-houfe at Dundee. As it is the loweft
creek in the river, a King's boat, with 6 boatmen, under the
command of a tide furveyor, is ftationed here, to board all
veffels coming up the river from a foreign port, for the fecurity of the public revenue. It is alfo the refidence, appointed
for the excife officer of the *St. Andrew's fecond ride*, the whole
parifh being in that divifion.

PARISH OF FLISK.

(*County of Fife.*)

By the Rev. Mr WILLIAM GOURLAY.

***

Situation and Extent.

THIS parish is situated on the river Tay, opposite to that beautiful, fertile country, the Carse of Gowry. It is bounded by Birkhill on the east, and the castle of Ballinbrieck on the west, along the Tay. This castle is an old edifice, approaching fast to ruin, and which was long the residence of the Rothes family. It has been a place of good accommodation as well as strength. The extent of this parish is about three miles in length, and more than a mile in breadth, in many places.

	Males.	Females.	Total.
Population.—Under 10 years	42	42	84
from 10 to 20	40	31	71
from 20 to 50	52	69	121
from 50 to 70	24	22	46
from 70 to 100	5	4	9
Total	163	168	331

In Dr Webster's report, the number is 318.

Productions.

Productions.—The farmers fow a good deal of wheat. About 12 or 15 years ago, there was very little wheat fown; but now they fow, one year with another, 150 bolls, in the extent of one or two and twenty ploughs of land. As the barony lands in this parifh are upon the Tay, the farmers have their barley, which is efteemed very good, fhipped off in cargoes to other places; but, before the demand from the diftilleries, &c. they often found it difficult to procure a market for their grain. They have now got threfhing-mills introduced, which will forward their operations not a little.

Hills.—There is a very large hill, called *Norman's Law,* which rifes from the level of the Tay, upon two eminences, one above another. From this hill there is a moft extenfive profpect. The common opinion, as to the origin of the name *Norman,* is, that the Norwegians, in their piratical incurfions, did, for fome time, encamp upon this hill. This traditional account is favoured by the appearance of an intrenchment round the fummit.

Sheep.—There is not a fheep in this parifh, nor indeed, from the prefent mode of farming, can fheep be kept, unlefs the low lands, as well as the hilly grounds, of which there is a vaft extent, were inclofed.

PARISH OF FORGAN,

(COUNTY AND SYNOD OF FIFE, PRESBYTERY OF ST ANDREW'S.)

By the Rev. Mr JAMES BURN, *Miniſter.*

Origin of the Name.

FORGAN, *alias* ST PHILLANS, is the name of the pariſh. On the communion cups, made in the year 1652, it is ſpelled *Forgon.* The derivation of the name is uncertain. From ſome old charters it would ſeem to ſig-nify *Fore Ground.* Indeed, a good part of it has a gentle deſcent towards the ſouth. The name, however, is not uncommon. In Angus-ſhire, there is a pariſh named *Long-Forgan;* in the county of Perth, there is another called *Forgan-Denny.* The other name, *St Phillans,* ſeems to have been derived from a Popiſh ſaint of that name, of ſome renown in the days of antiquity. About an Engliſh mile weſt from the manſe is the ſeat of ROBERT STEWART, Eſq; which bears the name of *St Fort.* This was probably in ancient times the dwelling of the ſaint. It ſtands upon

a

a rifing ground, and might perhaps be then confidered as a place of ftrength. There is alfo towards the eaft of St Fort, the *Upper* and *Nether Friartown*, which, no doubt, were formerly inhabited by Popifh friars.

Extent, Soil and Climate.—This parifh is about 4 Englifh miles in length, but not above 2 in breadth. A part of it is a ftrath from E. to W. the ground rifing gently on each fide. Much of it is of a fouthern expofure. Another part of it lies bending towards the N. on the fide of the river Tay. The foil is for the moft part light, but is rendered fertile by the ufe of lime. Some of it is black; other parts of a mixed nature. There is little clay foil in the parifh. The climate is healthy; few epidemic diftempers prevail much here, except the fever, which now and then proves fatal to many. Some are now alive betwixt 80 and 90 years of age. One is faid to be above 90. He lives on the ground of St Fort *.

River, Ferries, Coaft, Harbours, Fifh, &c.—The river Tay runs along the northern fide of the parifh. On the oppofite fide of the river, which is about 2 miles in breadth, ftands the populous and flourifhing town of Dundee. There are two ferries on this fide of the river, Woodhaven and

---

* Colonel Lindfay, brother to Mr Lindfay, who was then proprietor of that eftate, one day having met this old man, afked him, how many *Lairds of St Fort* he had feen ? he anfwered, he had feen *fix*, and hoped he might live to fee the *feventh*. What, faid the Colonel, do you wifh to fee a change of the Laird ? I fuppofe, faid the old man, you will have no objection againft the coming home of the young Laird. The proprietor was at that time lately married. The Colonel was fo much pleafed with the good humour of the old man, that he gave him half a crown, which made him very happy, as it is more than probable he had feldom before been poffeffed of fo large a fum at one time. This man has lived to fee another, who is the *feventh* proprietor of the eftate of St Fort.

and Newport, both of which are in this parish. There is a number of boats employed, some of a larger, others of a lesser size, some of which, when the weather permits, cross at all tides. The tide is about half an hour later here than at Leith. These ferries were much more frequented before the bridge was built over the Tay at Perth, than they have been since. Some of the ferrymen are sober and discreet; others of them borrow the language and behaviour of those who frequent the passage, especially of such whom they look on as their superiors in rank and station. How much is it to be regretted, that from so many of these they often learn to be rude and profane. The coast extends along the north side of the parish. It is for the most part rocky. The harbours at Woodhaven and Newport are very inconsiderable, fit only for their boats, and a few sloops, which are sometimes employed in importing coals, and exporting corn. On the banks of the river there are several salmon fishings *, some of which have of late increased, in value. They are for the most part carried on by means of what is called *a Yair*. But by some, the long net with a boat is made use of. The salmon are sometimes disposed of at the rate of 4 d. and even 6 d. *per* lb. to the people of Perth, who export them to London, and sell them at high prices. By others they are sent to the neighbouring towns of Dundee and Cupar in Fife, distant about 6 computed miles.

Cultivation.

* A process before the Court of Session was lately commenced respecting one of these, and most keenly agitated on both sides. Several hundred pounds were expended by each of the contending parties, one of whom, the Rev. Dr Dalgleish of Scotscraig, not only prevailed, but obtained his expences.

Cultivation.—The improvement of the ground has, of late years, made confiderable progrefs, chiefly from the ufe of lime, which, on our light and dry foil, has the moft happy effects. The lime is driven in carts from the diftance of 8 or 10 computed miles; fome of the tenants bring it from Northumberland by fea. Their crops are by it enriched when the feafon is not too dry. Some lands that are marfhy have of late been greatly meliorated by draining. ROBERT STEWART, Efq; of St Fort, who is very active and induftrious, befides other improvements which he has made, has drained a piece of ground, which, during the winter, was almoft covered with water. It was fit for nothing but feeding a few young cattle in fummer; and, though confifting of 52 acres, was fometimes let for about L. 5 or L. 6. It is more than probable, that in a few years it will fet for upwards of L. 50 Sterling. What a blefling is it to the country, when proprietors of land, inftead of debauching their neighbours by examples of intemperance, fet them patterns of activity and honeft induftry! How is the blefling enhanced, when, by their example, the people under them are led to fear God, and to reverence his fanctuary! The neglect of this feldom fails to ruin the morals of the people, and to deftroy their induftry.

Produce.—The farmers raife a pretty large quantity of wheat, although it is reckoned to fcourge the ground; but they are tempted to prefer this crop by the high prices, which are generally from L. 1 to L. 1, 5 s. *per* boll. It is meafured with the fmall firlot, which is a great deal lefs than that ufed for oats and barley. They commonly have good crops of barley, and generally get a good price, from 15 s. to 18 s. Sterling *per* boll. They have alfo tolerable crops of oats and peafe. The oats fell at from 12 s. to 14 s.

per

per boll. Peafe are by no means a lucrative crop, but they ferve to meliorate the ground when the crop is rank, and the ftraw is excellent fodder for horfes. It is chiefly on thefe accounts that the farmers continue to fow them, for the price of peafe is generally low, and their returns very inconfiderable. The foil is very much adapted to the culture of turnips; of thefe they raife good crops, with which, during the winter, they feed their cows and cattle, fome of which they fatten for flaughter, and for which they fometimes draw good prices. They have alfo good crops of potatoes, from the light and dry foil. Thefe yield a falutary fupport to the poor people, when they do not ufe them to excefs. To this, however, they are ftrongly tempted, when the meal is high priced. On fuch occafions they feed upon them *thrice a day*, by which their health is fometimes hurt. With the refufe, and the fmaller potatoes, they commonly feed fwine, which they falt up for winter provifion. This practice is become fo common of late, that the price of a young pig of a few weeks old is generally 7 s.

Rents.—Their rents are from L. 100 to L. 400 *per annum*, and upwards. The tenants are all in eafy circumftances, and fome of them are opulent. All of them are fober, active, and induftrious. Thofe of them that have lately got new tacks pay double, and fome almoft triple their old rents. Several of the tenants have fubfet fome acres of their ground, lying at a diftance from the farm houfes. They who enjoy thefe fmall poffeffions are called *Pendiclers.* Some of them have 10 or 12 acres, fome more, fome lefs.

The valued rent of the parifh in Scotch money
is, - - - - L. 5145 5 7
The real rent, in Sterling, is fuppofed to be
about, - - - L. 2873 0 0
Black

Black Cattle.—Of thefe a confiderable number is annually reared. Till of late years, they were employed in drawing the plough, but they are now feldom or never ufed. Inftead of two horfes and two oxen in the plough, which required a man fervant and a boy to drive them, two horfes only are ufed, and one man manages both them and the plough at the fame time. This is a confiderable faving to the farmer, now when the wages are fo high ; and as the horfe plough moves quicker, more ground is ploughed in the fame time. It is the new plough that is ufed in this part of the country.

Sheep.—Several flocks of thefe were formerly in the parifh ; now there is but one. The tenants found the fheep very hurtful to their fown grafs, which, in the winter, they tore up by the roots. Their *Sheep Walks* are now, by means of lime, turned into good corn-fields, which they find to be more profitable. They may, however, at length be compelled to return to their former practice of feeding flocks of fheep, to meliorate thofe fields which are at too great a diftance for driving dung to them ; when the ftrength of the lime is fpent, and they become unfit for producing crops of corn, the tedding of the fheep may be found neceffary to recruit thefe fields.

Minerals.—There is abundance of rock, fome of a more hard, fome of a fofter nature. The firft is very proper for common buildings, the latter for the making of roads ; to improve which there is fuch an uncommon fpirit now happily prevailing in this part of the nation. There is alfo much channel, well adapted to the fame purpofe. But there is no free ftone : this is brought from the other fide of the Tay in boats, from a noted quarry in Angus-fhire, commonly known by the name of Millfield Quarry.

Fuel.

Fuel.—There were formerly ſome peats dug out of the moſſes in the pariſh ; but the proprietors have prohibited this practice for many years paſt. There are ſome muirs that abound with whins ; from theſe the poor people get a part of their fuel. Coals are both ſcarce and high priced. The land coal is driven from the diſtance of 8 or 10 computed miles. A quantity ſuch as two horſes can conveniently draw, coſts about 7 s. 6 d. ; an equal quantity, or rather larger, but of a much better quality, brought from Alloa and other places by ſea, will coſt 12 s. weighing about 112 ſtone weight. This makes the fuel coſtly to the poor, many of whom, during the cold of winter, aggravated to them by their meagre diet, are not a little injured by the want of it. But amidſt all their ſtraits, it is truly pleaſant to ſee them poſſeſſing that cheerfulneſs and contentment which Chriſtianity is ſo much fitted to inſpire.

Population.—The population is on the increaſe. Several feus have been made on the banks of the river Tay, and ſeveral new buildings have been of late erected on them. The number of examinable perſons in the pariſh at preſent (1793) is about - - - 700
Allowing the uſual proportion of $\frac{1}{4}$ for children, 175

The total number of ſouls may be ſtated at 875
The return to Dr Webſter, in 1755, was only 751

The increaſe ſince that period is therefore not leſs than 124

A

A Lift of Marriages, Baptisms, *and* Burials, *for* 10 *years, extracted from the Parish Records of Forgan.*

	Marriages.	Baptifms.	Burials.
1780,	5	25	15
1781,	9	14	8
1782,	7	19	29
1783,	7	19	13
1784,	12	25	21
1785,	15	24	17
1786,	5	16	35
1787,	9	16	17
1788,	5	23	8
1789,	10	21	10
Total,	84	202	173

Prolific Births.—In the fpace of 4 or 5 years, twins have been born at four feveral births. Since I came to the parifh, one of the boatmen's wives was at one birth delivered of three fine children. They all lived till they were weaned, and two of them arrived at manhood.

Conditions and Professions.

No. of Heritors, refident, 7	No. of tailors, - 6
—— Ditto non-refident, 4	—— fhoe-makers, 3
—— Minifter, - 1	—— wrights, 3
—— fchool-mafter, 1	—— mafons, 4
—— tenants, - 9	—— weavers, 14
—— pendiclers, or fub-tenants, - 16	—— poor on the roll, 6

Villages, Occupations of Women, &c.—There are feveral villages in the parifh. The female inhabitants are generally

ally employed in ſpinning coarſe yarn, of which a kind of
cloth is made that gets the name of *Oſnaburgh*. Of this
the merchants in Dundee export large quantities; but in
this, as in moſt other manufactures, there is a very great
ſtagnation ſince the commencement of the preſent war.
They got 1 s. 6 d. for ſpinning a ſpindle of this yarn; but
ſince the war it has been ſo low as 1 s. and ſometimes 10 d.
While the encouragement for ſpinning was high, it was
ſometimes difficult for the tenants, and others, to get maid
ſervants. But though their gain was conſiderable, yet the
conſtant ſitting at the wheel, and the immoderate waſte of
ſaliva, was by no means favourable to their health. Many
of theſe people are employed in cutting down the corns in
harveſt. During this ſeaſon they are uncommonly chearful and healthy; but as this exerciſe in the field is an extreme entirely oppoſite to the ſedentary life they generally lead through the reſt of the year, diſagreeable effects
are ſometimes felt after the harveſt; however, the danger of this is not a little abated by their preſent manner of living during this ſeaſon, which is upon oat bread
and ale, which, when freſh and good, is a moſt wholeſome
diet. How much preferable to that which was uſed ſome years
ago, *viz.* ſalt meat and ſalt broth, and ſometimes, it is ſaid,
milk and ſalt herring? This, with their exceſſive labour,
could not fail to excite a moſt painful thirſt; to quench
which, as ſoon as they came to the *Land's End*, as they call
it, they went in queſt of cold water; of which, when within
their reach, having taken a plentiful ſhare, they ſat down
to reſt, without reflecting on the danger they were in, which
it is ſaid, has in ſome inſtances proved fatal.

Prices of Labour and Proviſions.—A maſon commonly
gets 1 s. a day; a carpenter, or common wright, the ſame,
ſometimes rather more; a tailor, 8 d.; a weaver gets ſo
much

much a yard, fometimes more, fometimes lefs. A common labourer, when he works by the piece, will fometimes earn 1 s. 6 d. or 1 s. 8 d. a-day ; maid fervants get about L. 3 Sterling a-year ; men fervants get from L. 6 to L. 10 Sterling ; the men fhearing in harveft get 1 s. *per* day; the women 10 d. : but the generality of them are hired for a certain fum during the harveft ; the men from L. 1, 1 s. to L. 1, 5 s. and a lippie of lintfeed ; the women 16 s. or 17 s. and a lippie of ditto, fometimes half a peck.—The beft beef is for the moft part 4 d. *per* lb. (16 ounces); the mutton fells ufually at the fame rate ; the veal, early in the feafon, fells at 6 d. *per* lb. when plenty at 4 d. fometimes at 3 d.; a hen 1 s.; a goofe at 3 s. ; eggs 4 d. *per* dozen ; rabbits, when fkinned, fell at 5 d. *per* pair ; their fkins fell from 7 s. to 9 s. or 10 s. *per* dozen ; cheefe at 5 s. *per* ftone ; pigeons at 5 d. the pair. Within thefe 20 years, or even lefs, provifions are almoft doubled in their price.

Church.—The King is the patron. The prefent incumbent, Mr JAMES BURN *, is faid to have been the firft prefentee in Scotland of his prefent Majefty King GEORGE the III. having been admitted to this parifh in May 1761. He has a ftipend, *communibus annis*, about L. 80 Sterling, befides a manfe and glebe of about 6 acres. An augmentation of ftipend is in procefs. The church and manfe were repaired in 1771.

Religious

* His predeceffors were Meffrs Wedderburn, Nairn, Ruffell, Gellatly, and Beat : and it is remarkable, that they were all minifters of this parifh for much the fame fpace of time, about 13 or 14 years, and that all of them, fave one, were tranflated to other parifhes. The prefent incumbent had it in his choice oftener than once to have followed their example, but preferred his prefent fituation.

Religious Sects.—There are not many Diſſenters in the pariſh; only two Epiſcopalians, and a few Antiburgher Seceders, moſt of whom had left the Eſtabliſhed Church before the preſent incumbent was ſettled here. Some of them left the Seceſſion, and came to the pariſh church; but when the new mode of ſinging without reading the line was introduced, they again withdrew, and carried two or three individuals along with them. They are ſober and induſtrious, not at all ſo bigotted as are many of that ſect; they are very uſeful members of ſociety.

Poor.—There are no begging poor belonging to the pariſh, but many ſuch from Perth and other places. By theſe, and travelling tinkers, this part of the country is not a little oppreſſed. It is much to be regretted that each pariſh does not take care of its own poor, and hinder them from travelling abroad to other pariſhes. Beſides the number of penſioners on the poors roll, which ſometimes does not exceed 4, there are not a few who obtain a temporary ſupply of 10 s. 15 s. or L. 1, at a time when ſickneſs is in the family, or the head of it unable to work. Parents who are not able to pay for the education of their children, have them educated upon the poors funds, which are made up from the weekly collections on Sabbath, to which the ſeafaring people, of all others, contribute moſt liberally. The annual amount of the collections is above L. 14 Sterling. A farmer in the pariſh, at his death, ſome few years ago, left a legacy of L. 20 Sterling. This made a conſiderable addition to the fund, which has been more than doubled within theſe 30 years. It is managed by the kirk-ſeſſion with care and attention, without the leaſt expence to the fund.

Character.

Character.—They are generally fober and induftrious. A few years ago a fpirit of fmuggling too much prevailed in this corner, than which nothing is more ruinous to the health and morals of thofe who are addicted to it *. There is reafon to believe that little or no gain was made by that moft mifchievous traffic, of the effects of which the minifter, from time to time, did not fail to remind them from the pulpit. This ruinous traffic is now nearly annihilated among us ; and happy were it for the nation that the temptations to it were lefs frequent and powerful than they fometimes are. None of the people of this parifh have been the fubject of a criminal procefs, nor have any of them emigrated.

* One young man, a tenant in the parifh, was moft unhappily addicted to it ; in a few years he hurt many others, and ruined himfelf. The laft time he called at the manfe, he expreffed his wifh that he had followed the advice the minifter had often given him.—Had he done this, he had probably fucceeded as a tenant, and efcaped thofe miferies which, by fmuggling, he unhappily brought upon himfelf. He lay in a prifon for feveral months, reduced to great indigence. This is mentioned as a warning to others, who by fmuggling hope to be made rich, but are far more likely to become ruined, and to entail mifery and mifchief on themfelves and others.

PARISH OF INVERKEITHING.

(Prefbytery of Dunfermline.—County and Synod of Fife.)

By the Reverend Mr ANDREW ROBERTSON, *Minifter.*

Name, Situation, and Extent.

INVERKEITHING, or Innerkeithing, is fuppofed to be derived from the Gaelic word Inver or Inner, which fig-nifies the Mouth, and Keith, faid to be the name of the running water at the eaft end of the town. It is of a very irre-gular figure. The North Ferry hills form a peninfula; the weft part, formerly the parifh of Rofyth, extends about three miles, and the north part about three miles and an half, from the town. Thefe refemble two arms ftretched out almoft at right angles, and each of them does not much exceed a mile in breadth; the one lies between the Frith and the parifh of Dunfermline, and the other between Dunfermline and Dal-gety parifhes.

Town, Conftitution of the Burgh, &c.—Inverkeithing is pleafantly fituated upon a rifing ground above the bay of the harbour; it confifts of one ftreet, with another fmaller turn-ing off near the middle, befides fome wynds. It has many good gardens. It is a very ancient royal burgh. King Wil-liam, furnamed the Lyon, gave them the firft charter. Several

veral Kings of Scotland granted them charters at different
periods; and King James the VI. by a charter, dated 4th
May 1598, ratifies and confirms them all, and declares their
rights and privileges, to extend from the water of Dovan to
that of Leven, and as far north as Kinroſs. It it is ſaid to
have been a very conſiderable burgh, of large extent, populous,
and paid to government great taxes. The ſet of this burgh
is uncommon in ſome things. The provoſt, the two bailies,
the dean of guild, and treaſurer, are annually elected by the
counſellors and deacons of the trades. The counſellors are
choſen from among the burgeſs inhabitants, the guildry, and
even the members of the incorporated trades, who ſtill retain
a vote in their reſpective incorporations. The five incorporated trades elect their deacons yearly as their repreſenta-
tives. The town council, including the magiſtrates, cannot
be under 20; but it is not limited to any number above it;
ſo that the whole burgeſs inhabitants might be made counſellors. What is very ſingular, the counſellors continue in office during life and reſidence. There is a good town-houſe,
built in the year 1770, containing, beſides a priſon, ſome convenient rooms for holding the bailie-courts, the meetings of
council, and public entertainments. The yearly revenue a-
mounts to 200 l. Sterling and upwards; many of their extenſive rights and dues have been ſold and diſpoſed of at
different times. The ſtreets were once lighted with lamps
during the winter ſeaſons; but this has been diſcontinued
for a long time. The preſent magiſtrates are very attentive
and active in making improvements, and doing whatever is
in their power for the advantage and convenience of the inhabitants. There are ſeveral markets or fairs in the year
for horſes, cattle, and different kind of goods, ſuch as
coarſe linens, checks, ſhoes, &c. This burgh is repreſented

in

in Parliament, and fends a member along with Queensferry, Stirling, Culrofs, and Dunfermline.

Population, &c.—The population, by an accurate furvey in the beginning of the prefent year 1793, amounts to, Souls, - - - - - 2210
The return to Dr Webfter in 1755 was - - 1694

Increafe - - - - - 516

In the town	1330	Between 10 and 20	362
In the North Ferry	312	——— 20 and 50	932
In the country parifh	568	——— 50 and 70	306
Number of males	1056	——— 70 and above	30
——— of females	1154	The number of families	
Under 10 years of age	580	is about -	550

Many have arrived at advanced periods of life. There are feveral perfons here between 80 and 90, and fome of them going about their ordinary bufinefs. There is a man living here, but moftly confined to his bed, whofe age, from authentic accounts, is 94: He was by trade a gardener, and has had five wives. The annual average of births from the parifh records is about 50, and of marriages 15. There is no regifter of deaths kept here. The number of births and marriages cannot be exactly afcertained, as there are many diffenters from the eftablifhed church, who do not infert their names in the parifh regifter. The population has greatly increafed within thefe few years, owing to the flourifhing ftate of the coal trade brought from Halbeath and fhipped here, to a confiderable diftillery and brewery in the neighbourhood of the town, and a branch of the iron foundery bufinefs lately introduced.

Proprietors

Proprietors and Value.—The parifh belongs to the Earls of Hopetoun and Morton, Sir William Erfkine and Sir John Henderfon, Mr Cunningham and a few fmall heritors. The laft gentleman is the only one of any confequence refiding in it. The valued rent in the cefs books is 6956 l. 16 s. 8 d. Scots. The real rent amounts to near about 3000 l. Sterling, and upon new leafes would rife confiderably above it.

Appearance, Soil, and Agriculture.—The parifh, in general, excepting the Ferry hills, and a few others, is either flat or gently rifing ground, the greateft part of which is ftrong, rich, or clay foil, and yields plentiful crops; even among thefe hills many places are arable, and produce moderately good crops. Towards the extremity, upon the north, the foil is cold, and a fmall part is muir. Some of the farms are extenfive, and others of an ordinary fize. The farmers are, in general, wealthy, induftrious, and active: They improve and cultivate their lands to great perfection and advantage: They moftly ufe the new conftructed ploughs, drawn by two good horfes without a driver: They manure and enrich their field with dung, lime, and earth, mixed together, with fea-weed, when they can obtain it, and by fummer fallow. From the goodnefs of the ground, and the moft proper mode and means of cultivation, they raife grain of all kinds, equal in quantity and quality to many parts in Scotland. The farms are not yet all inclofed and properly fenced; but, from the difpofition of the proprietors, and the improvements now carrying on in that way, it is expected this will foon be the cafe. There is a fociety formed here, called the Farmer Club, the members of it belong alfo to moft of the neighbouring parifhes, and feveral gentlemen of landed property have joined and patronife it. The great object of it is to confider and improve the different modes of agriculture. At ftated meetings

meetings they have ploughing matches ; the competitors are
their fervants, each man takes his ridge. When the work
is done, it is examined by proper judges, and a fuitable premium is given to the beft, and two or three more of the
ploughmen. This practice has been attended with very beneficial effects.

Harbour, Shipping, and Ferry.—Before the entrance of the
harbour, there is a large and fafe bay, which affords excellent fhelter for fhips in all winds. Here his Majefty's fhips
of war fometimes come from Leith roads, and ride at anchor
to avoid the winter ftorms ; and merchant fhips from the
Mediterranean formerly ufed to perform quarantine here.
The harbour itfelf is a fmall bay ; at the mouth of which,
upon the weft fide, there lies a large Dutch built veffel as a
lazaretto, where, inftead of detaining fhips from foreign
ports, the particular goods, in which any infection may be
fuppofed to lodge, are immediately received, aired under the
infpection of a proper officer, and delivered, within a limited
time, to the owners, by the exprefs orders of the cuftom-
houfe. At the head of the bay is the quay, the proper place
for landing and receiving goods. The depth of water at
fpring tides is 13 and fometimes 15 feet. It was deepened
within thefe few years ; and a narrow channel cut farther
down to admit fhips up to it. This is kept pretty clear by
the rivulet that runs through it at low tide. Another
quay is now building, with great improvements, to accomo-
date the fhipping. There are here fometimes between 40
and 50 veffels from different places waiting for coals, efpecially in the winter feafon. Several fhips belong to this
place ; but none of any confiderable burden. Some of them
fail to foreign ports, and the reft are chiefly employed in the
coal and coafting trade. Between the North Ferry and Rofyth

ſyth Caſtle is St. Margaret's Bay or Hope, ſo called from the
Princeſs of that name, afterwards Queen of Malcolm III.
having in her flight from England landed there. On her
account, the Ferry is called the Queensferry, being her conſtant paſſage to and from her favourite reſidence at Dunfermline. This paſſage is well known to every traveller; the
diſtance is near two miles. All the boatmen reſide in the
North Ferry. There are four boats and four yawls employed upon it; theſe belong to certain proprietors of land on
each ſide of the Frith, who claim an excluſive right to the
paſſage, and for which the tackſmen, beſides keeping the
boats in repair, pay annually about 280 l. Sterling. The
common freight is by far too low, being only a penny each
paſſenger. There are ſeveral landing places on each ſide,
and it is propoſed to build more. This paſſage is ſafe and expe-
ditious, and may be had at all times, excepting in a very few
caſes; and this only happens from high winds, together with
particular and unfavourable times of the tide. There was
a large boat overſet ſome years ago, occaſioned by a ſudden
ſquall, and its being fully loaded with black cattle; the boatmen were loſt, and alſo the paſſengers. Upon the weſtern
boundary of the pariſh, is a ſmall harbour, called Brucehaven; ſhips ſometimes take in coals, but no other trade is
carried on there.

Manufactures and Trade.—There is but little trade carried
on here. Some ſmall merchants, for the moſt part, ſupply
the inhabitants with neceſſary articles; and there is a near and
eaſy acceſs to Dunfermline and Edinburgh. This is a very
convenient ſituation for ſhip-builders. Some time ago, they
met with great encouragement, but at preſent there is little
doing in that line. A conſiderable whiſky diſtillery is erected here: It belongs to a Company, and is managed by one

of the partners. The spirits are said to be of a fine, and even superior quality; they are sold at the common current prices; and the sale of them is very extensive. It seems to be in a prosperous and flourishing state. There is likewise a brewery, carried on to no great extent, and serving chiefly for the consumpt of the inhabitants. There is a Company who import annually from the Baltic large quantities of wood; they have extensive and rapid sales, and are very successful in that trade. The coal shipped here is by far the greatest article of trade. The colliery is at Halbeath, in the parish of Dunfermline: It once belonged to a Dutch Company; but, being attended with no advantage, they disposed of it. It is now worked by a Company of our own countrymen, who carry it on with spirit, and have brought it to a flourishing state. There is a proper waggon road laid with timber, for the distance of five miles, and kept in good repair at a great expence. Twenty-four waggons are employed; they are drawn, some by one and others by two horses, and bring down two tons each time. The coals are good, burn well, and have great heat and force; they are sold at 15 s. *per* waggon, the great coal; and 11 s. 6 d. the chows or small coal: The burgess inhabitants buy them, by a particular agreement, at a cheaper rate. Twenty-five thousand tons and upwards are shipped annually; the demand is greater than can be answered; and ships frequently wait 5 and 6 weeks. There are a few salt-pans that make annually from twelve to fifteen thousand bushels. An iron foundery was lately set up. Several experienced workmen are employed in it: They make beautiful chimney grates, waggon wheels, and all kind of cast iron work for machinery and house utensils. This seems to be a convenient and advantageous situation; the metal can be brought by sea; it is near to coal; and the manufactured goods can be transported ve-

ry

ry cheap, and in small quantities, by means of the coal ships, to many parts in Scotland, and by the vicinity to Leith, to any foreign port. There is a branch of the Borrowstounnefs custom-house established here for the convenience of the coasting trade carried on from this port, and from St. Davids, the property of Sir John Henderson, Baronet, of Fordel, and the shipping place of his great coal works.

Ecclesiastical State, School, &c.—Sir William Erskine, Baronet, of Torry, is the patron, having lately purchased the estate of Spencerfield, to which is annexed the right of patronage. The church was repaired and partly rebuilt within these 20 years. It is large enough to contain the parishioners. It is a little singular in outward appearance, being covered with three roofs of equal dimensions, which are supported by two rows of arches within, and the two side walls. It could easily be made a handsome, commodious, and elegant church. Upon the west side, adjoining to it, is the steeple, which seems to be very ancient, from the appearance of the stones and the form of the building. The stipend at present consists of 5 chalders victual, and 500 merks Scots, besides 4 l. Sterling, of what is called vicarage. The free teinds are considerable : There has been no augmentation since the year 1636, and a procefs is now carrying on for that purpose. There is no manse or garden, but an allowance for house rent is paid by the town and some of the heritors. A small house and garden at Rosyth goes by that name. There are two glebes and a small park by itself, making in all eight acres of excellent ground. The one is the glebe of Rosyth, which was annexed to this parish, and lies adjacent to that old church now in ruins ; but it is proposed to have it exchanged and placed with the other, which is near the town.

There

There is a tolerable fchoolhoufe, with a fufficient garden. The prefent fchoolmafter *, who is a very good fcholar, has been here upwards of 40 years ; he draws an annual falary of 200 merks Scots, paid by the town and heritors. He is alfo precentor and feffion clerk, for which he receives 28 l. Scots, with the ordinary emoluments and dues belonging to that office. He teaches, befides the common branches of education, the languages, navigation, and the other parts of mathematics. The number of fcholars is about 50, being commonly 40 in fummer and 60 in winter. There are feveral private teachers befides. The fchool wages are too low, and by no means adequate to the teachers abilities and labours ; although as much as can be well afforded by the poor part of the inhabitants. The number of poor receiving public charity, is not confiderable. Their funds were much diminifhed by the failure of a perfon who had their money in his hands ; and they now chiefly arife from the weekly collections at the church doors, which at prefent anfwer the demands.

Religious Perfuafions.—Rather more than the half of the inhabitants in the town and parifh adhere to the eftablifhed church ; the reft are Burghers, Antiburgers, Relief, and Cameronians. A Burgher meeting houfe was built here about 40 years ago, occafioned by the fettlement of the late incumbent, who, it feems, though a moft worthy and refpectable character, was difagreeable to a great number of the parifhioners ; it is moftly attended by the loweft part of the people, and many of them come from the neighbouring parifhes. The Antiburghers and Relief are not numerous, and attend their meeting houfes in Dunfermline. The Cameronians,

* Mr Robert Duncan, tranflator of Boethius on the Confolation of Philofophy.

meronians, in this place, took their rise, a few years ago, from a difference among the Burghers, many of whom, along with their minister, at that time, joined themselves with this sect: They have no proper meeting house, and are occasionally supplied with sermons, though but seldom, by their itinerant preachers. It is remarkable, that all these differences arose about church politics, they are maintained and kept up with the same spirit and zeal, and the leaders of each sect use the utmost endeavours to retain their adherents and followers, which, among such a class of hearers, are frequently attended with considerable success.

Eminent Men.—This parish has given birth to several persons who have distinguished themselves in their professional line. Commodore Roxburgh, born in this town, was promoted to that rank in the Russian service, and was very active and attentive to its interests before he quitted it. The famous Admiral Greig was a native of this town, was educated under the present schoolmaster, and went, at an early period of life, into the British service. While in the navy of Great Britain, he distinguished himself at the defeat of Conflans by Admiral Hawke, the taking of the Havannah, and several other engagements in that successful war. After the peace of 1762, he entered into the Russian service; and there, at the battle of Chio, contributed principally, by his advice and exertions, to the destruction of the whole Turkish fleet. Sensible of his great professional merit, her Imperial Majesty promoted him (though a foreigner) to the chief command of the Russian navy, which he raised to a degree of respectability and importance it never before had attained. In reward of his great services, the Empress bestowed on him many honourable marks of distinction, and an estate in Livonia which his family now enjoy. In the last war, between the Russians
and

and Turks, which laft were joined by the Swedes, he, in the
Baltic, defeated the Swedifh fleet, and had not a part of his
fquadron, through cowardice, refufed to come into action, he
probably had captured or funk the moft of them. Soon after
this, he was feized with a fever, and died at Revel, on the
26th October 1788. He was no lefs illuftrious for courage
and naval fkill, than for piety, benevolence, and every private virtue *.

Character.

* *Antiquities.*—Upon the top of Lethem hill, there are fome
large ftones, placed in a circular form, faid to have been a Druidical temple. King David the I. frequently refided in this place.
Some perfons remember to have feen the ruins of a houfe at the
north end of the town, which commonly went by the name of
King David's Houfe, but there remains not the fmalleft veftige.
At the North Ferry, there are the ruins of a chapel, which was
liberally endowed by King Robert the I. and ferved by the
Monks of Dunfermline. The Francifcans and the Dominicans,
or the black and grey Friars, had both of them convents in this
town. There is a houfe called the Inns, which ftill has peculiar privileges and exemptions, not being within the jurifdiction
of the magiftrates, and appears to have been one of them, from
its form, vaults, high garden walls, and other buildings. Towards the north part of the parifh, there is a ftone fet up about
10 feet high, 2½ broad, and 1 thick, commonly called the ftanding ftone. Many rude figures feems to have been cut upon it,
but are much defaced by the weather and length of time; however, two armed men on horfeback, the one behind the other,
appear pretty difcernible on the eaft fide. It is fuppofed, that
after fome battle between the Scots and Danes, fought near this
place, fome Dane of diftinction had fallen, and been buried there,
and this ftone, as was then very commonly done, raifed as a
monument over his grave. In this parifh is the caftle of Rofyth, almoft oppofite to Hopeton Houfe; it is built upon rock,
and furrounded by the fea at full tide; it confifts of a large
fquare tower, and fome low ruinous walls adjoining to it, but
there is the appearance of larger and more extended buildings.
It cannot now be afcertained by whom it was built, or at what
time. Above a door, upon the north fide, there is a coat of
arms with a crofs, a crown, &c. and M. R. 1561. Upon the
ftone bars of windows in the fquare tower, there is T. * S. and
M.

Charaƈter.—The people in general are ſober, induſtrious, and attentive; they follow their ſeveral employments with aſſiduity and care, and earn a comfortable livelihood for themſelves and families. They ſeem to be contented and happy with their ſituation in life. The better ſort are kind and hoſpitable, diligent and aƈtive in proſecuting their buſineſs and purſuits, and are much given to company and entertainments in each others houſes, but it is to be remarked, that the parties, who aſſociate much, are united in the ſame political ſentiments and views. Burgh politics, and the eleƈtion of members of parliament, have an unhappy influence upon the morals of the people. They carry on theſe conteſts with the greateſt animoſity and keenneſs, and exert their utmoſt endeavours to promote the intereſt and cauſe of the favourite candidate.

M. * N. *anno* 1639. Upon the ſouth ſide, near the door, is this inſcription, pretty entire and legible,

IN DEV TIME DRAV YIS CORD YE BEL TO CLINK
QVHAIS MERY VOCE VARNIS TO MEAT & DRINK.

This caſtle was the ancient ſeat of the Stuarts of Roſyth, lineally deſcended from James Stuart, brother german to Walter the great Stuart of Scotland, and father to King Robert. The laſt laird of that name, having no near relations, diſpoſed of the eſtate to a ſtranger ; it afterwards became the poſſeſſion of Lord Roſeberry ; and is now the property of the Earl of Hopeton. There is a tradition, however unfounded it may be, that Oliver Cromwell's mother, being a daughter of the family of Stuart of Roſyth, was born in this caſtle, and that the proteƈtor viſited it, during the time he commanded the army in Scotland. It is ſaid; there is a record in the Advocate's Library at Edinburgh, which gives an account of the ſtruggle, the ancient Culdees maintained for their rights, lands, &c. which contains alſo the cenſure pronounced againſt them by the Romiſh clergy, in theſe words: Aƈta in eccleſia parochiali de Innerkethyn, anno ſecundo regni regis Alexandri, gratiae anno 1250, &c. and mentions the probability that this ſevere procedure and ſentence obliged them to ſubmit to the biſhop of St. Andrew's, who by degrees ſuppreſſed their order, and eſtabliſhed the Popiſh Clergy in their place.

candidate. It is much to be lamented, that religion is made fubfervient to thefe purpofes, and the fettlement of its minif- ters connected with the politics and the factions of the burgh. Here the inhabitants have fupported or oppofed, according as the promotion of the perfon was fuitable or inimical to their political views; and they now ftand diftinguifhed in the records of the church, for two fucceffive oppofitions, in the laft of which, and that but lately, many of the people declared againft their political leaders, and would no longer obey their unreafonable and unchriftian orders. However, upon the whole, the people, with a few exceptions, are religious and devout, peaceable and ufeful members of fociety, and attached to their king and country, its civil conftitution, and its mild, equitable, and falutary laws.

Mifcellaneous Obfervations.—The fituation of this parifh is healthy and chearful: There are no difeafes peculiar to it, the fmall-pox raged laft fummer with great violence, and car- ried off great numbers of children. Inoculation is much ne- glected by the lower fort of the people, and many of them have an infuperable prejudice and averfion againft the practice of it. Provifions of all kinds are good and plenty, but fome of them dearer than in Edinburgh. The roads are well made: There is a toll bar, a mile from the North Ferry, the produce of which, with the commuted ftatute labour, keeps them in good repair. Near the North Ferry, there are large quarries; the ftone is very hard and durable, and generally dug out in perpendicular rows. Some time ago great quantities were prepared and fhipped, to pave the ftreets of London, but none has been carried there for fome years. The Frith gradually contracts from Kinghorn; here the fhore, which is high and rocky, fuddenly ftretches out towards the fouth, and brings it within a narrow compafs. The water is deep, and the tides rapid, owing to the widenefs and length

of

of the Frith above. There was a battery erected, upon this point of land to the eaſt of the Ferry, after Paul Jones appeared, with his ſmall ſquadron, and alarmed the coaſts. There is a higher and a lower battery, mounting, together, 8 iron guns, 20 pounders, and 8 field pieces. In the middle of the Frith, and right oppoſite, ſtands Inch-Garvie, the old fortifications of which were repaired at that time; and 4 iron guns, 20 pounders, mounted upon them. Each gun has 100 rounds of amunition. One man belonging to the corps of artillery lives here, to notice the works, and take care of the ſtores. There is no account of any remarkable battle within the pariſh. There was a ſmall ſkirmiſh upon the Ferry hills, between the Scots and Engliſh in Oliver Cromwell's time. The great and ſevere engagement upon the following day, which was maintained with ſo much obſtinacy and ſlaughter on both ſides, and terminated in the defeat of the Scots, was indeed begun near this town, upon a place called Hillfield; but the Scots retreating, it was chiefly fought upon the oppoſite bank of Maſterton, which, though not far diſtant, lies in the pariſh of Dunfermline. Upon the top of the Ferry hills the proſpect is beautiful, extenſive, and pictureſque to the higheſt degree. There is a view from the Iſland of May to Stirling, and far beyond it, of a rich country diverſified with towns, villages, caſtles, and noblemen's and gentlemen's ſeats, and bounded by the diſtant hills, with numerous objects, and variegated ſcenes on each ſide; the coaſts of Lothian and Fife, with their fertile fields; the ſeveral little iſlands of Garvie, Comb, Cramond, and Keith; ſhips ſailing in all directions, and ſome of them lying at anchor in Leith Roads and other places; and to complete the whole, there is a magnificent view of Edinburgh, its majeſtic caſtle and lofty buildings, together with the New Town, which is perhaps one of the moſt handſome and elegant in Europe.

☞ The

☞ The following additional particulars were received since the preceding account went to the press.

In the grounds of *Castland Hill*, the property of the Earl of MORTON, a lead mine was accidentally discovered about 30 years ago. The ore is said to have been of an extraordinary fine quality. The stratum was found to be very irregular, and of unequal thickness. After being wrought for some time, it totally disappeared. A considerable sum was expended, and the working of it attended with some loss. It is, however, thought, that there is plenty of lead ore in these lands, and that it might be wrought out to great advantage.

In the beginning of last winter, a considerable shoal of *herrings* came into this bay ; and, about the North Ferry, they were caught in great quantities, and the fishing continued for a long time. In the beginning of this winter, there came a still greater shoal, extending all the way from *Inch-Comb* to *Inch-Garvie*. A great number of boats, from the east coasts of Fife, well manned, and supplied with proper nets, are now employed in this herring fishing, and meet with ample success. The herrings are pretty large, and very good. They are sold at different prices, and sometimes so very low as 6 d. *per* hundred. They are carried to Edinburgh, and many other places, in a fresh state. Some merchants have sent up several vessels to take them in, properly salted in barrels ; and, it is said, propose to send them to the London and foreign markets. They still continue * in the greatest plenty, and may probably do so during a great part of the winter season. Some young *whales*, one of which has been caught, disturb the fishing, and sometimes destroy the nets.

In

* December 9th, 1793,

In this town, there is a *tan work*. The fituation is convenient for carrying on that bufinefs. The raw hides can be got in great quantities, this being the market where the adjacent parts of the country and the fhipping, both in this and the neighbouring ports, are fupplied with provifions. The prefent work is but fmall; the leather made is faid to be of an ordinary quality, and meets with a ready fale.

PARISH of KEMBACK.

(COUNTY AND SYNOD OF FIFE, PRESBYTERY OF ST.
ANDREW'S.

By the Rev. Mr. JAMES M'DONALD.

Extent, Soil, Surface, Climate, &c.

ABOUT the origin of the name of the parifh, there
does not exift even a probable conjecture. It
ftretches in length from E. to W. about 4 miles, and its
greateft breadth from S. to N. is about a mile. Its
eaftern extremity is diftant about 4¼ miles from St. Andrew's, and its weftern approaches within half a mile
of Cupar. It contains about 1850 acres, of which more
than 1500 are arable. Of the remainder, fome part was
planted feveral years ago ; and the plantations, confifting
principally of Scotch fir, are in fo thriving a ftate, that
they afford a ftrong inducement to the feveral proprietors to appropriate the reft of their moorifh ground to
the fame ufe. Almoft all the varieties of foil are to be
found here, clay, black loam, light fandy foil, with a
dry

dry bottom, and thin gravel, with a wet clay bottom.
Of theſe, all, except the laſt, are tolerably fertile, and
produce, by proper management, good crops of all the
plants commonly raiſed by farmers in this country.
The ſurface of the ground, on the W. ſide of the pariſh,
is nearly level, ſloping gently from S. to N.; but on the
E. ſide, Nature, in the formation of its ſurface, ſeems
to have indulged herſelf in a ſportive mood, by throwing it into a variety of the moſt irregular and fantaſtic
ſhapes : it riſes above the level of the W. ſide about 70
or 80 feet ; and the elevations in ſeveral places are ſo
ſudden and abrupt, as to render the cultivation of the
fields very expenſive, and even dangerous, and the roads,
from one part of the pariſh to the other, almoſt inacceſſible. The air and climate are favourable to health.
Endemic diſeaſes are unknown. The people in general
are healthy, and ſometimes reach extreme old age.
There are at preſent ſeveral perſons in the pariſh between 80 and 90 years of age.

Character of the People, &c.—The inhabitants of this
pariſh are not diſtinguiſhed from their neighbours, by
any peculiarity of character. In general, they are ſober minded, induſtrious, and temperate ; decent in their
manners, attending to their own buſineſs, living in peace
with one another, and giving regular attendance upon
the public ordinances of religion. During the incumbency of the preſent miniſter, which comprehends a period of nearly 13 years, there has not occurred a ſingle
inſtance of any perſon belonging to this pariſh ſuffering
the ſlighteſt puniſhment from a civil judge.

Population.—The return to Dr. Webſter in 1755 was
                                                    420

420 fouls. According to an account taken about half a year ago, the number of inhabitants is as follows :

Belonging to the Eſtabliſhed Church,	540
Burgher Seceders, - - -	13
Antiburgher Seceders, - -	28
Of the Preſbytery of Relief, -	3
Epiſcopalian, - - -	1
Anabaptiſt, - - -	1
Unitarians, - - -	2
In all,	588

Of the 540 belonging to the Eſtabliſhed Church, 300 are females, and 240 males ; ſo that the proportion of males to females is exaɛtly as 4 to 5. There are among them 7 widowers, and 15 widows.

State of Agriculture, &c.—Agriculture hath been held in high eſtimation in all ages, by thoſe perſons whoſe ſplendid talents and eminent virtues have entitled them to be regarded as inſtructors and patterns to the reſt of mankind. The Romans, who attained a pitch of grandeur which hath ſeldom been equalled in the hiſtory of nations, paid the moſt particular attention, from the earlieſt times, to this delightful and uſeful art. It was the occupation of their wiſeſt ſtateſmen and braveſt generals, when they were not neceſſarily engaged in the deliberations of the ſenate, or exploits of the field. Cincinnatus was found at the plough, when he was called upon by his countrymen to aſſume the ſupreme adminiſtration of public affairs. And though that high-ſpirited and warlike people engaged in the ſervice of the ſtate with the prompteſt alacrity, and marched out to meet
their

their enemies with the moſt heroic ardour, yet they gladly exchanged the fatigues of war for the pure and healthful pleaſures of a country life. When it was no longer neceſſary to bear arms, they beat their ſwords into plough-ſhares, and their ſpears into pruning hooks; and ſolaced their minds, after the horrors of war, with the delightful contemplation of that variety of natural beauty which, from time to time, the fields preſent to the eye of the induſtrious and enlightened huſbandman. And as the greateſt of their heroes dignified this profeſ- ſion, by ſharing in its toils, the ſublimeſt of their poets made it the ſubject of the moſt finiſhed work, perhaps, of which antiquity can boaſt, that he might entice his countrymen to the ſtudy of agriculture, by adorning it with all the graces and beauties of the moſt exquiſite poetry. In Scotland, conſiderable attention has of late been applied to the improvement of this important art. Many excellent treatiſes have been written upon the ſubject, by men of eminence in the literary world, who, by devoting a portion of their time and talents to the ſtudy of agriculture, are no doubt entitled to the grati- tude of their countrymen. Of theſe, none ſeem deſerv- ing of higher praiſe than the celebrated Author of Ele- ments of Criticiſm, who, in his Gentleman Farmer, hath brought together a collection of facts and obſerva- tions, which, to the judicious farmer, are of ineſtimable value, and will ſtand the teſt of ages. And it muſt af- ford every ſincere lover of his country very high ſatis- faction, to ſee that Board of Agriculture, which Lord Kames ſo ſtrongly recommends, actually eſtabliſhed by Government, with ſuch a proſpect of its anſwering the important purpoſes for which it was inſtituted *.

In

* Before, however, books on farming can operate as means of general

im-

In this parish, till very lately, the capital improvements which farming has received during the course of the present century, have not been generally adopted. Within the recent period of 12 years, neither turnips nor artificial grasses of any kind were sown in the largest farm in the parish. The fields, after being exhausted by cropping, were resigned in succession to pasture, and remained in that condition several years, producing scanty crops of natural grasses, till it became necessary to break them up again for corn; and the instruments of husbandry corresponded in clumsiness with the rudeness of the mode of cultivation. Of late, however, things have assumed a very different appearance. Turnips are raised in every farm. The rotation of crops is sometimes such as the best writers on husbandry recommend; the fields are laid down with a plentiful allowance of clover and rye grass, and the ploughs, and harrows, and carts, &c. are generally of the best construction. Still, however, to an accurate and judicious observer, there may perhaps appear room for much future improvement, both in the formation and in the execution of the plans adopted by farmers here for the management of their grounds.

improvement, before a person can be qualified for reading such books with advantage, it would be necessary for him to go through a more complete course of education, than can be commonly obtained at a country parish school. A considerable acquaintance with the English language, arithmetick, book-keeping, and mensuration, are qualifications without which a farmer can neither make himself master of the improvements made in the art, nor prosecute these improvements in a manner either beneficial to himself or his country. This, by the way, shows the necessity of giving greater encouragement to public teachers, than is at present done; as there is not, perhaps, any single circumstance that would conduce so much to the advancement of agriculture in Scotland, as making provision for the proper education of that class of men by whom the art is to be carried on.

grounds. Of the improvements above mentioned, the caufes are no doubt various. One of the principal of them, however, certainly is, the attention which feveral of the gentlemen who refide on their eſtates have themfelves paid to huſbandry. By introducing into the ſmall farms in their own poſſeſſion the moſt approved ſyſtem of management for the different kinds of ſoil, they have exhibited an example to their tenants, which, confpiring with other caufes, has produced the change of culture mentioned above, a change no leſs beneficial to the proprietor and tenant, than delightful to the judicious fpectator.

For 2 or 3 years paſt, it has been the cuſtom, in different parts of the pariſh, to raiſe potatoes from ſeed, in order to prevent degeneracy, to procure greater variety of kinds, and more abundant crops ; and there is little doubt, that in this way thefe defirable ends will be attained. There is another article of improvement, which has been lately introduced, which promifes to be a fubſtantial and permanent benefit. I mean, the uſe of rutabaga, or Swediſh turnip. This plant is either ſown in the field, like common turnip, and treated in the ſame manner, or ſown in a ſeed bed like cabbage, and tranfplanted at the diſtance of 10 or 12 inches in the drill. In point of taſte and flavour, it is greatly fuperior even to yellow turnip ; and though in many refpects fimilar to turnip, it poſſeſſes fome peculiar qualities which ſeem to render it well calculated to ſerve in ſpring as a fuccedaneum to turnip, and to afford green food for cattle till they can be put to graſs. It is confiderably more folid than common turnip. Its fpecific gravity to that of common turnip being nearly as 1013 to 878 ; (it may be proper to mention, however, that the accuracy of this

this proportion refts on a fingle experiment). It refifts froft better than turnip ; after fhooting in the fpring, the root ftill remains juicy and fucculent, and even after the feed is ripened upon the ftalk, a confiderable part of the root remains fit for the ufe of cattle.

Threfhing machines have been lately introduced here, and though there has not been time for them to receive the fanction of experience in their favour, yet as they perform a great quantity of work in a very fhort time, and cut off almoft every opportunity of embezzlement, they promife to conftitute a valuable improvement upon an extenfive farm.

There are no fewer than 3 corn mills in the parifh ; but, from this circumftance, little or no benefit accrues to the inhabitants in the way of competition, as almoft all the lands are bound thirle to one or other of them. The multure exacted by thefe mills, is, I believe, almoft precifely the fame. It cannot be expreffed in general terms, becaufe it is drawn in grain, and partly in meal. By a calculation upon oats, I found, that when the boll of oats produces a boll of meal, the multure is 1-13th, and when the boll produces only 3 firlots of meal, the multure is 1-12th of the quantity fent to the mill. This fuggefts an inducement, which, along with many others, fhould difpofe farmers to pay attention to raife grain of the beft quality, as the multure is always lefs in propor- tion as the quality is finer.

The rents of farms are various. Of late, there has ap- peared in this neighbourhood a tendency to offer higher rents for farms, than the average prices of corn and cattle, and the improvements of the art feemed to juftify. The fame fpirit of unfounded fpeculation, which had per- vaded feveral other orders of fociety, feized upon farm- ers.

ers. This ſpirit in farming, however, as well as in trade and manufactures, has received a check from the ſtate or the times : Had it proceeded much farther, it would have produced the moſt fatal conſequences. It would have proved an effectual bar to every ſpecies of agricultural improvement, becauſe the farmers bound to pay more than the land could produce, would ſoon have found themſelves in a ſtate of bankruptcy and ruin ; and it would have neceſſarily foſtered in the country that ſpirit of diſſatisfaction, which almoſt invariably accompanies the feeling of diſtreſs.

In this pariſh, the rent of land ſtill continues moderate ; there is only 1 or 2 ſmall farms which let ſo high as 20s. the acre, and the beſt land in the pariſh is, at preſent, let conſiderably under that rate. The largeſt farm in the pariſh conſiſts of about 270 acres. There are in the pariſh about 122 horſes, 437 cattle, and from 80 to 100 ſwine. Every cottager almoſt feeds a pig for the uſe of his family.

Rivers.—The river Eden is the northern boundary of the pariſh. Of this ſtream the courſe is not ſtraight, but forms many beautiful ſerpentine windings, the banks ſometimes almoſt level with the ſurface of the water, and ſometimes riſing above it to the height of 40 or 50 feet ; and at the eaſtern extremity of the pariſh, the river forms a curve of ſo curious a kind, that it ſhapes about an acre of land, which it nearly ſurrounds, into the figure of a guitar, with the broad end oppoſed to the water on the E. ſide.

The portion of the Eden belonging to this pariſh, abounds both with river and ſea trout. The river trout are of two kinds, red and white. They begin to be in

ſeaſon

feafon in March, but are in higheft perfection in April and May. The largeft will weigh about 2 lbs. Eng-lifh weight; the middle fize from ¼ lb. to a lb. The fea trout are alfo of 2 kinds, red and white. They begin to come up from the fea in May. The largeft are about 3 lbs., and the common fize about 1 lb.

There is a fmall falmon-fifhing too upon the Eden in this parifh. The falmon begin to appear in the river in May, but are generally more frequent in June and Ju-ly. They are commonly fold at 4d. the lb, Englifh. About 30 years ago, the average number of falmon caught, was 3 fcore; and the average number caught in the part of the river belonging to Nyddie, which borders with this parifh, was 12 fcore. For feveral years paft, both fifhings have been occupied by the fame perfons; and though no exertion of induftry and fkill has been ne-glected, the average number of both hath not exceeded 4 fcore. The caufe of this deficiency, however, it does not feem eafy to afcertain with any degree of probabi-lity.

Mines and Minerals.—Of free ftone, there are vaft quantities in the parifh. Veins, both of coal and lime, have been alfo found in it; but of thefe laft, the expenfe of working has been hitherto fo great, that though feve-ral attempts have been made at different times, they have always proved unprofitable fpeculations. In the year 1722, a difcovery was made at the foot of a pretty high hill at Myretown of Blebo of a quantity of metal in large pieces, which, upon trial, proved to be rich lead ore. This circumftance induced the proprietor, Mr. John Bethune of Blebo, with fome of his friends, to form themfelves into a company, to work, dig, and fearch

for

for the whole metals and minerals upon the lands of Blebo.

In the course of their trials, they found at Myretown, a little below the place where the ore was discovered, a vein in the solid rock, about 2 feet wide, containing spar, and other vein stuff, mixed with large spots or flowers of fine ore; and in another place, about half a mile W. from the former, they discovered a nest of the purest lead ore, containing large lumps, one of 24 stones, and several of 10 or 12 stones, and the rest smaller ; and a little below the nest, a vein of about a foot wide, in working of which, in a small level, they came to a rib of pure metal of about 3 inches, which increased to 6 inches. But as the levels to both lay through rocks so excessively hard, as could only be wrought with gunpowder, the expense of the work became so great, that it was thought proper to dissolve the company. About 2 tons of lead were manufactured, and exported to Holland *.

Curiosities.—The parish is interfected from S. to N.

by

* Afterward, in the year 1748, a gentleman, from the county of Mid-Lothian, Captain William Thynne, took a lease of the mines and minerals in the lands of Blebo, and came with a few workmen, and made a trial at Myretown, where the vein appears in the solid rock. Both he and his workmen thought the appearance promising; but, in a few weeks after the commencement of the work, Captain Thynne received an offer of going to the West Indies, to superintend some work there, which he accepted ; and since that time, no new trials have been made. A few years ago, however, all the discoveries above stated, were communicated to a gentleman of great professional knowledge and experience in these matters ; and he gave it as his opinion, that, very probably, something of importance may be stumbled upon in the neighbourhood ; and that, therefore, it would be proper to open up and examine the old works, especially as the expense of such an examination would not exceed the sum of 200l. Sterling.

by a fmall rivulet called Ceres burn, which falls into the
Eden a little below Kemback mill. The banks of this
ftream on both fides rife to a great height, in a great variety of inclinations, forming a den, called the Den of
Dura, which prefents an affemblage of wild grandeur
and natural beauty, fuch as is very rarely to be met
with. Of this den, the windings are about a mile in
length; and, on both fides, the eye is delighted with a
rich variety of picturefque and romantic fcenery. The
banks in fome parts flope gently towards the water, and
are covered with a beautiful verdure of grafs, affording
pafture for fheep; in other parts, they are perpendicular, or overhang the ftream at an elevation of 50 or 60
feet; and in one place, the bank on the W. fide, forms itfelf into the figure of a very extenfive amphitheatre. Here
and there we meet with fmall plantations of afh and oak,
and fir, and gean; and where the banks are fteepeft, they
prefent a furface of broken faced rocks towards the bottom, and higher up, are covered with large thickets of
wild hazles, which produce great quantities of nuts. It
is not eafy to conceive a fcene more beautiful, or more
highly diverfified than this den exhibits in the fummer
months. The murmuring noife of the ftream, running
along its rocky channel, the mufic of birds, the fragrance
of woodbine and eglantine, the beautiful bloffoms of the
furze and the broom, and the gean interfperfed with the
different fhades of verdure of the oak, the afh and the
fir, joined to the wild variety of views, which every ftep
almoft prefents, confpire to render it one of the moft delicious fpots, which nature, without the affiftance of art,
can form.

School, &c.—In this parifh, for 30 years paft, the inhabitants

habitants have ſuffered a great hardſhip from the want of a proper public teacher for their children *. The ſalary is only 100 merks Scots. And here I cannot help remarking again, that a proper proviſion for the education of youth in the country pariſhes of Scotland, ſo as to give them an opportunity of acquiring at home the principles of grammar and a conſiderable knowledge of arithmetick, book-keeping, and menſuration, is a national object of much greater magnitude than is generally ſuppoſed : It is certainly eſſentially neceſſary to general improvement in the art of agriculture, an art upon the advancement of which the happineſs of individuals, and the proſperity of the nation, in a great meaſure, depend. At preſent, the ſalaries and perquiſites of eſtabliſhed ſchoolmaſters in the country, are, in general, ſo exceedingly ſmall, that they do not exceed, and often hardly equal, the wages of an ordinary mechanick ; and it can ſcarcely be expected, that a perſon, properly qualified for communicating the neceſſary branches of education, will devote himſelf for ſuch an income to the moſt laborious of all profeſ- ſions.

Heritors, Poors Funds, &c.—There are in this pariſh, 5 heritors

* The perſon who ſupplied the charge, though a man of blameleſs character and inoffenſive manners, was not qualified for inſtructing youth in any ſingle branch of education. The bad effects of ſpending in vain the few years that ſhould have been devoted to the acquirement of uſeful knowledge, may eaſily be conceived, and will be felt for many years to come. About a twelvemonth ago, the heritors generouſly a- greed to give the old ſchoolmaſter an annuity of 11l. 10s. Sterling, du- ring life, and his wife an annuity of 4l. Sterling during her life, after her huſband's death ; upon condition of his reſigning his office, which theſe annuities enabled him to do, without loſs either to himſelf or fa- mily. He accepted the offer, and his place is now ſupplied by a ſtudent of divinity, a very deſerving young man, and an excellent teacher.

5 heritors, 4 of whom reside. The valued rent of the parish is 2312l. 13s. 4d. Scotch money. The stipend is about 90l. a year, including communion elements. The church and manse are both old buildings. The school and school-house is a new building. The glebe consists of about 5 acres of good dry flat land, upon a sandy bottom, and is enclosed. The principal and professors of the united college of St. Andrew's, are patrons of the parish, and titulars of the teinds. The fund for the maintenance of the poor arises from the interest of 220l. Sterling, at 5 per cent. ; the rent of 1¼th acres of land, and of several seats in the church, mortcloth-money, fees of proclamation, and collections at the church door on Sunday, and may amount to about 20l. or 25l. a year. The money at interest, and that with which the 1¼th acres of land was purchased, seems to have arisen from the gradual accumulation of a long course of careful management. The only donation that appears to have been made to the session, is a legacy left about 2 years ago by Mrs. Margaret Bethune of Blebo, a lady whose beneficence to the poor during her lifetime, was most extensive and exemplary, and who, at her death, bequeathed to them the sum of 50l. Sterling. Of this legacy, however, only 30l. were added to the session funds ; the other 20l. were immediately distributed among the poor, to alleviate, in some measure, their grief for the loss of one of their greatest benefactors. With this small fund, the session is enabled to relieve the pressing necessities of several families of well disposed Christians, whom it hath pleased Providence to reduce to circumstances of distress, to soothe, in a small degree, the affliction of the widow and the fatherless, and to afford some little consolation to the infirmities and distresses

of

of old age. But the ſmallneſs of the funds, and a virtuous feeling of decent pride, prevent many from applying and receiving aſſiſtance, who yet ſtand much in need of a ſmall addition to the income ariſing from the fruits of their own induſtry.

Whether it be practicable in an advanced ſtate of ſociety, to introduce ſuch meliorations into the ſituation of the labouring poor, as to enable them to rear a family of children, without ſuffering the extremes of hunger and nakedneſs, and to lay up a ſmall pittance for their ſupport in ſickneſs and old age,—whether this be a practicable improvement, is a political queſtion which it is not perhaps eaſy to reſolve; but it is a certain fact, which often affects, with unavailing melancholy, the minds of thoſe who are called by their profeſſion to viſit the poor, that common labourers, in the time of their ſtrength, cannot afford to purchaſe for a numerous family of children, the bare neceſſaries of life; and after 40, when the vigour of life is over, they generally languiſh and decay for want of the more delicate nouriſhment, which declining nature then ſeems to require. In the preſent ſtate of things, it ſeems to be the intention of Providence, that even the induſtrious poor ſhould depend, for a conſiderable ſhare of their comfort in life, upon the generoſity and beneficence of the rich among whom they live; and the rich are, in this way, furniſhed with an opportunity of gratifying the moſt amiable feelings of the human heart, and of practiſing virtues from which the mind derives at once the higheſt improvement and ſweeteſt delight.

PARISH of KENNOWAY,

(COUNTY AND SYNOD OF FIFE, PRESBYTERY OF KIRKCALDIE.)

By the Rev. Mr PATRICK WRIGHT.

Name, Extent, &c.

KENNOWAY is faid to take its name from its fituation. The church and village are built along the top
or height of a very beautiful and romantic den; the fides
of which are fteep and rocky, and contain fome caves,
which the feuars and inhabitants ufe as pigeon-houfes. Of
this particular fituation, the name is faid to be expreffive,
Kennoway fignifying in the Gaelic, " The town above the
" cave." Its form is nearly an oblong fquare; its length
from E. to W. about 3 miles; its breadth about 2. The
church and village are placed in the S. E. corner of the
fquare.

fquare. The whole parifh lies on a bank, afcending from
S. to N.: the profpect from almoft every part is extenfive
and beautiful, commanding a diftinct view of the ifland of
May, of the Bafs, of Inch Keith, of the fhipping on the
Forth, from which it is diftant about 2 miles; of the coaft
S. of the Forth from Dunbar, to the W. of Edinburgh; of
the Lammer moor hills, &c. From the N. part of the
parifh, which reaches the top of the bank, there is one of
the moft extenfive views imaginable, taking in not only
the forementioned profpect to the S. but comprehending almoft all Fife, and a great part of the counties of Angus,
Perth, Stirling, the Grampian mountains, &c.

Soil, Climate.—The foil is all arable, and generally fertile, confifting on the S. of a light loam, which in fome
places approaches to fand and gravel, and on the N. of
loam and clay; the crops are both rich and early, particularly on the S. The air is dry and wholefome, and many
inftances of longevity have occurred of late. A woman
died 14 years ago, who remembered to have feen Archbifhop Sharp at the manfe of Kennoway, the day before he
was murdered, Within thefe 7 years, one died whofe family believed him to be above 100.; another of 94 for
certain, and feveral of 90. In the 2 houfes next to the
manfe, there are 2 men living, the one born in May 1695,
the other in July 1700, the oldeft of the two ftill enjoys
great health and ftrength *.

Minerals.—The village is built of freeftone, taken from
the neighbouring-den, but it is coarfe and foft, and foon
moulders down with the froft. The fcarcity of good ftone,

is

* They are both alive at prefent, May 1793.

is one of the difadvantages under which this, and fome of the neighbouring parifhes labour. There are appearances of coal in feveral parts. Some of it was lately wrought ; but as the quality was not very good, nor the feam thick, and as there is great plenty of excellent coal in feveral of the neighbouring parifhes, the mines that had been opened, were foon abandoned. After this it is unneceffary to add, that the only fuel ufed in the parifh is coal, and that the great plenty of this moft neceffary article, with which the neighbourhood abounds, is one of thofe advantages which it enjoys in common with all the S. coaft of Fife.

Population, &c.—According to Dr Webfter's report, the population then was 1240. The number of the people and houfes, feems to have been nearly the fame for centuries. In 1785, the whole inhabitants of the parifh, (of whom the village contains about one half), amounted, from the age of going to fchool, to 1200, of whom 800 atttended the Eftablifhed Church, and 400 were Seceders. A Burgher meeting houfe was erected in the village, about 40 years ago, and all that do not belong to the Eftablifhment, attend that meeting, except a very few of the Relief party, for there is not a fingle perfon of another perfuafion in the parifh. All the houfes are inhabited, none are allowed to go to ruin, and very few are known to have been built on a new foundation. About 20 yeas ago, and for fome time before, the village exhibited a very ruinous appearance. A confiderable malting bufinefs was formerly carried on in it ; the great road, too, between the ferries of Dundee and Kinghorn, paffed through it ; but about 40 years ago, that bufinefs failed, and the road was carried 3 miles to the weftward. In confequence of thefe events, the malt and brew fteadings, which amounted to 15 or 16 in the village,

befides

beſides two or three in its near neighbourhood, became uſeleſs, and ſoon fell into ruin : the whole, however, have been repaired or rebuilt of late, and are now inhabited by weavers and other trades people. There are at preſent, but two brewers in the pariſh, keeping ale-houſes, none of which can well be termed an inn. A turnpike-road is making in the old line through the village.

Agriculture, &c.—After what was ſaid of the nature of the ſoil, little need be ſaid of the crops it produces. The greateſt part is encloſed or encloſing, and every farm bears wheat, barley, oats, peaſe, beans, potato, and turnip. The ſoil of the greateſt part is particularly adapted to pototo. That root is therefore generally and carefully cultivated. Nearly the whole graſs is ſown. The valued rent is L. 4442 : 13 : 2 Scots. The real rent of land, about L. 2400 Sterling. The rent of land roſe to a great height here ſeveral years ago: about 125 acres, that lie contiguous to the village, and had for ages been let to the inhabitants, at from 14 s. to L. 1, 8 s. the acre, were let 8 years ago at L. 2 and L. 3, and the greateſt part at upwards of L. 4 the acre. For ſome years paſt, the form and faſhion of the plough has been perpetually changing. The wright and ſmith ſeem now to underſtand their intereſt juſt as well as the button and buckle maker. The principles of this uſeful inſtrument ſeem to be but imperfectly underſtood as yet ; and till they be underſtood, the operation of taſte and faſhion, and art cannot be excluded. The plough in uſe at preſent is ſaid to be Small's, ſomewhat improved, *i. e.* altered. It was lately introduced from the coaſt of Angus, into the north ſide of Fife, and has become pretty general over the county. It is drawn by two horſes, and held and managed by one man ; the beam and handles are ſhort,

the

the head and mould-board are made of iron; its value about 2 guineas *.

Stipend, School, Poor.—The ftipend confifts of 80 bolls meal and bear, and 500 merks money, amounting, with a glebe of 6 acres, to about L. 80 Sterling. The church and manfe are old, but were lately repaired. The King is patron. —The fchool was rebuilt, and the fchoolmafter's houfe repaired, 6 years ago. His falary, including a donation of L. 20 Scots, is L. 8 : 6 : 4 Sterling. His perquifites about as much. He values the whole of his income at about L. 40 Sterling.—Only 6 poor perfons receive alms at prefent, and the only fund provided for their maintenance, is the weekly collections at the church-door, which are very fmall; there is not however, a travelling beggar in the parifh.

Mifcellaneous Obfervations.—Every perfon almoft that is not engaged in the labours of the field is employed at the loom. A confiderable quantity of coarfe linen is made in the parifh, which is fold brown, and fome alfo of a better quality, which is bleached and fold at the fummer markets in the neighbourhood, to merchants from Edinburgh, Stirling, &c. at from 1 s. 6d. to 3 s. the yard. All are remarkably fober, induftrious, and economical, fo that even the dearth of 1783 had no vifible effect upon the pooreft and

* *Prices and Wages.*—The price of butcher meat is from 5 d. to 6 d. a pound tron, at different feafons of the year; of a hen, from 1 s. 2 d. to 1 s. 4 d; of butter, from 8 d. to 9 d. The wages of farm-fervants are from 7 to 8 guineas for a man, and from L. 3 to L. 4 for a woman. The wages of a fufficient day-labourer, 1 s. 3 d.; of a gardener, 1 s. 6 d.; of a wright and mafon, 2 s. 8 d.

and lowest of the people; nothing was done for them by the heritors, yet all fupported themfelves in their ufual manner.—Only one inftance of fuicide has occurred within the laft 20 years, and not a perfon belonging to the parifh has been punifhed for any crime or even been imprifoned, on any account whatever, during that period.

PARISH OF KETTLE.

By the Rev. Mr PETER BARCLAY.

Name, Situation, and Extent.

KING'S KETTLE, formerly called Catul, or Katul, is situated in the county of Fife; in the presbytery of Cupar, and synod of Fife. The origin of the name is uncertain. It is, however, proved by authentic records, that the lands of Kettle were once the property of the crown, and were afterwards fued in 8 divisions, in perpetual tacks, at the rents then received; which are still paid to the King, under the name of Crown Rents. Kettle is bounded by Falkland on the West; by Markinch, Kennoway, and Scoonie, on the south; by Ceres, Cult, and Colleffie, on the east; and by Aughtermuchty on the north. The parish contains somewhat more than 9 square miles. It is of a curved oblong figure, narrowest towards the west; in length, from east to west, nearly 8 miles; and in its greatest breadth a little more than 2 miles. The village of Kettle is situated in the flat of the strath, rather low and wet, on the south side of the Eden; the floods of which reach to the skirts of the village. Balmalcolm is situated about a furlong south-east, at the foot of the rising ground; and the road by Cupar, between the Forth

and

and Tay, runs through it. Coalton is on the brae head above it, and is clayey.

Soil, and Surface.—The largest and most valuable part of the parish lies in the course of that strath which extends from Kinrofs to St Andrews. Here the furface is level; but towards the fouth, fouth-eaft, and fouth-weft of the village, which is nearly in the center of the parifh, it becomes bleak and hilly, including the higher grounds which run eaftward from the Lomonds. The hills are in general covered with verdure, and in fummer afford excellent pafture for all forts of cattle; yet, in fome places, there are many large rugged ftones projecting confiderably above the furface. Woods are only wanting in this part of the parifh to realife the poets defcription :

Juffit et extendi campos, fubfidere valles
Fronde tegi fylvas, lapidofos furgere montes.

The nature of the foil is various. In many places on the banks of the Eden, which nearly bounds the parifh towards the north, there are excellent carfe foils; yet, at a fmall di-ftance from them, extenfive beds of fand, with a moorifh, or moffy furface, are frequently found. The ftratum of fand is in many places covered with a ftrong ftiff clay, in others with a light friable mould. Even in the hilly part of the country, the foil is in general excellent, and of a dark co-lour.

Climate and Difeafes.—The climate is, for the moft part, dry and healthy. It is not fubject to any local difeafes. Some years ago the ague was frequent in the lower parts of the parifh; but, for the laft 20 years, it has almoft entirely difappeared;

appeared; owing, moft probably, to the many drains that have been made in this and the neighbouring parifhes. The common people are now peculiarly liable to dropfical fwellings of the limbs. During the above mentioned period potatoes have been introduced, and now form the principal part of the fuftenance of the poorer houfeholders. It may perhaps be fufpected, that this change of diet has produced fome alteration in the conftitutions of the inhabitants.

Rivers, Springs, &c.—There are no confiderable lakes or rivers in the parifh. The Eden, whofe ftream in fummer is fcarcely fufficient for a corn mill, abounds with excellent red and white trout, pike, and eels. There are feveral fprings, fome of which are fuppofed to be impregnated with minerals. The courfe of the Eden being down a low ftrath, bordered on each fide by hills for a confiderable diftance above Kettle, and the river having very little fall, frequently overflowed its banks, fo that the crops on its carfe haughs were always precarious, a plan was projected of making a cut fo deep as to confine the water; but it was never executed, owing to the difagreement of the proprietors of the lands which lye on the oppofite fides of the river. About 10 years ago Mr Johnfton purchafed the whole, and formed the projected cut on an enlarged plan. A fpacious canal was made for the water, 12 feet wide at the bottom, and 30 at the top, fecured on the fides by raifed banks and hedges, which include a fpace of 70 feet in breadth, and ferve to confine the water at high floods. This cut has been carried on a confiderable way, but not with equal effect, as the direction of the ftream was obliged to be accommodated to the convenience of perfons with whofe property it interferred. Mr Johnfton, fince his refidence at Lathrifk in 1783, has built an elegant houfe on the eftate. He has alfo got feveral of the farms in-

to

to his own hand, and has improved them; subdivided them mostly with ditch and hedge, and belts of planting; adorned them with clumps of trees, and elegant farm houses of two stories and garrets, covered with blue slate, and rigged with lead; all which give more vivacity and beauty to this part of the country than it had before, and will, when the planting is grown up, enliven it much more.

Minerals.—In the farm of Barntark there is a quarry of free-stone. It is covered by a stratum of earth 4 feet thick. When this is removed, we observe upon the surface of the rock numerous impressions of vegetable bodies, apparenily formed by branches of trees, of various diameters, curiously ramified and interwoven. The stone is of the same nature with that below, but of a darker colour. A large piece of petrified wood, and a petrified horn, were lately found here. About a furlong to the eastward of this quarry, on the declivity of the hill, some persons searching for minerals discovered a large mass of petrified shells of various kinds, some of which were completely filled with transparent concretions. The mass is situated at the lower extremity of a lime-stone rock. The forms of the shells are most distinct on the surface. There are not any petrifying springs in the parish; but, in some places, stalactites are formed by the oozings of coal water. There is no marble or slate here; but an almost inexhaustible abundance of moor-stone and free-stone, which are of an excellent quality, and much employed in dyking and building. Lime-stone of the best kind is also abundant: One quarry at Forthar, belonging to Dr Pitcairn, physician in London, and farmed by James Blythe, Esq; employs, on an average, 60 persons throughout the year, in the different processes of digging, wheeling away the earth, blowing, and breaking the stones, and filling the kilns. A great number of men and

and horfes are alfo engaged in conveying the lime to New-burgh port, for the Carfe of Gowrie, and other parts of Perthfhire, &c. The coals with which it is burnt are brought from Balbirnie and Balgonie, about 3 miles diftant. A large quantity of iron-ftone, excellent in quality, is found on feve-ral parts of thefe eftates.

In Barntark Muir, the furface of which is a common, and covered with heath, coals have long been procured. For want of proper contrivances to carry off the water, they have not as yet been wrought far below the furface. Thefe mines, which are the property of Alexander Murray, Efq; of Ayton, have been let, for the laft 40 years, to Alexander Low, Efq; who is now ferioufly engaged in attempting to obviate thofe inconveniencies which have hitherto impeded the working. The coals are of a fuperior quality, moft of them refembling the oily Newcaftle coal. There is another ftratum of coal, but inferior in quality, at Dovan, belonging to Dr Pitcairn. Coals have alfo been procured at Clothie, en eftate belong-ing to Mr Balfour. Some time fince, when finking a fhaft to difcover the extent of the coals, fome metallic ores were difcovered, which have not as yet been effayed. When thrown into the fire, they emit a fulphureous fmell, and in appearance refemble pyrites. The price of coals at Balgonie and Balbirnie Hill is 7 d. per 18 ftone Dutch weight.

Church.—The annual value of the living, including L.3 : 6 : 8 for providing the communion-elements, and L. 2 : 3 : 4 for pafturage, is L. 52 : 3 : 4 in money, 24 bolls of barley, and 41 bolls of meal. The glebe is one of the pooreft in Scotland, its yearly rent not exceeding L. 2. The King is patron. The number of heritors is 28 ; but only the half of them are fuperiors, the others being feuers. The prefent

minifter

minister is Mr Peter Barclay, who was settled in May 1778. He is married, and has four sons and one daughter. The church appears, by a date on it, to have been built in 1636. It has been twice repaired since, and is in good condition. The manse is at present in such bad order, that it is intended to move for a new one in the spring.

Poor.—There are at present about 14 persons who receive alms constantly or occasionally, being almost all infirm old people. The collection for the poor has been, for the last 12 years, L. 16 *per annum ;* and there is L. 300 out at interest at 4½ *per cent.*

School.—The school and master's house are in good repair. The master is rather too old for much activity ; but he has an assistant of considerable abilities. The salary, with the house and session-clerkship, is about L. 22 a year, beside the school-dues, which are, for English, 1 s. 3 d. ; writing, 1 s. 8d.; arithmetic, 2 s. ; Latin, 2 s. 6 d.

Price of Provisions and Labour.—From the vicinity to Edinburgh, and many coast towns, provisions are commonly kept at the Edinburgh prices. The grain is always lower than the lowest Edinburgh or Lothian grain. A day-labourer is paid 10 d. a day, on an average ; a carpenter or mason 1 s. 6 d. ; a taylor 1 s. ; but the common way of charging is by the piece. Labourers generally earn about 13 guineas a year ; and their wives, if industrious, about L. 7 or L. 8 by spinning, when not otherwise engaged. The women always spin with both hands. Domestic men-servants wages, at an average, L. 6 ; female servants L. 2 : 15 : o.

Population.

Population.—Number of inhabitants by Dr Web-
ster's account in 1755 . . . 1621
By furvey in 1778 1643
Males in the parifh in Dec. 1790, above 8 years old 639
under 8 years old 187
Females . . . above 8 years old 753
under 8 years old 180
Total inhabitants in Dec. 1790 . . 1759
Increafe in 12 years . . . 116
Houfeholders 414
Separatifts from the eftablifhment above 8 years 587
Of the eftablifhment above 8 years . . 805
Children under 8 years old . . . 367
Males born in 12 years, from 1778 to 1790 . 323
Females 328
Total born from May 14. 1778 to May 14. 1790 651
Males dead in the fame 12 years . . . 200
Females 178
Total deaths in 12 years . . . 378
Increafe of population from births and deaths . 273
Increafe in fact 116
Perfons who have left the parifh in 12 years . 157
Average of males married in 12 years . $14\frac{1}{6}$
Of females . . . . . $12\frac{1}{6}$
Total average of marriages . . . . $26\frac{1}{3}$

The higher average of males marrying muft be owing to a
greater number of them getting wives from other parifhes
than females hufbands. More males are twice, or even thrice,
married than females. Women are better qualified, at leaft,
according to the manners of this country, for living fingle
than men.

Average

Average of males born in 12 years   .   . $26\frac{1}{12}$

Females   .   .   .   .   . $27\frac{1}{3}$

Total average of births   .   .   . $54\frac{1}{4}$

Average of males dead in 12 years   .   . $16\frac{2}{3}$

Females   .   .   .   .   . $14\frac{5}{8}$

Total average of deaths   .   .   . $31\frac{1}{2}$

Average of a family nearly   .   .   .   . $4\frac{1}{4}$

30 families confift only of one individual.

Kettle village contains of inhabitants   .   .   516

Balmalcolm   81

Coalton   78

Country part of the parifh   .   .   .   1084

The mean population may be nearly had by multiplying the average of births by $31\frac{1}{3}$; or the average of deaths by 54; or the average of marriages by $64\frac{1}{3}$; or the average of a family by the number of families. The mean or average population, for any time, is the real population increafed or diminifhed by half the decreafe or increafe in that time: Thus, the real population 1759, diminifhed by 58, half the increafe is 1701. But this can only be true on the fuppofition that the increafe or decreafe is uniform. The true mean population muft be deduced from the following Table, which poffeffes many more important ufes than merely determining the population.

A

A Table, ſhewing the number dead in 20 years, viz. 625, and the number who have died at each age.

Age,	dead.	Age,	dead.	Age,	dead.	Age,	dead.	Age,	dead.
0	20	20	7	40	3	60	10	80	4
1	40	21	7	41	3	61	10	81	4
2	35	22	7	42	3	62	10	82	4
3	20	23	6	43	3	63	10	83	4
4	15	24	6	44	3	64	10	84	3
5	10	25	6	45	3	65	10	85	3
6	8	26	5	46	3	66	10	86	3
7	6	27	5	47	3	67	10	87	2
8	4	28	5	48	4	68	10	88	2
9	3	29	4	49	5	69	10	89	2
10	3	30	4	50	6	70	10	90	2
11	3	31	4	51	6	71	10	91	2
12	3	32	4	52	6	72	10	92	2
13	4	33	4	53	6	73	9	93	2
14	4	34	4	54	6	74	8	94	1
15	5	35	4	55	7	75	7	95	1
16	5	36	4	56	8	76	6	—	
17	6	37	4	57	9	77	5	625	
18	6	38	4	58	9	78	5		
19	7	39	4	59	9	79	4		

$625 \div 20 = 31.25$ medium deaths in the pariſh. This Table, upon trial, is found to anſwer better for Scotland than any yet publiſhed by Mr Wilkie.

By this Table, there will be found living together 25392 ſouls; ſo that, ſuppoſing the number of deaths and births equal, viz. 625 yearly, the population would be 25392. Hence 1 birth and 1 death would give a population of 40.6;

or

or the expectation of life for a child in Kettle parish is 40.6 years. Thus, 625 : 25392 :: 1 : 40.6. Kettle population, by this rule, would be 31.5+54.25 (i. e. medium deaths and births), ÷2=42.87, which ×40.1 (—.5 deduced for the time of the year in which an infant may be born),=1719, the medium population of 12 years.

Beside the people employed in a manufacture, to be mentioned afterwards, there are,

Blacksmiths, including 3 apprentices . .	7
Shoemakers, including 2 apprentices . .	8
Taylors, including 4 apprentices . . .	10
Butchers	2
Bakers	2
Carpenters and wheelwrights . . .	8
Lint-dressers	5
Masons	12
Clockmaker	1
Colliers, about	12
Hired servants, exclusive of apprentices . .	130
Day-labourers, who have families, about . .	90
Gardeners	4
Students at college	4
Shop-keepers	3
Gentlemen's families	6
Clergy, 1 established and 1 relief . .	2
Batchelors, not including domestic servants, and children who have not left their father's house .	10

Manufacture.—A considerable quantity of linen, from 7 d. to 2 s. 6 d. a yard is made in the parish ; a small part of it is bleached ; but the most of it is sold as it comes out of the loom in Cupar or Auchtermuchty, and thence sent to Glaf-

gow,

gow, Leeds, and London. There are about 170 looms, which are wrought or fuperintended by about 60 mafter-weavers; the number of apprentices is 18, and the reft of the workmen are journeymen. During their apprenticefhip, or ftay in their mafter's houfes as journeymen, they pay 2 s. a week for board, and live wonderfully well. The average grofs produce of a loom, including apprentices and old men who do little work, is about L. 60 a year, (a good hand will fetch confiderably above L. 100); and the average grofs expence to the mafter in lint, fpinning, boiling, working, &c. is about L. 46 : 15 : 0, moft of which is laid out in the parifh and near neighbourhood. The looms find employment for women and children; and hence, a family being advantageous, the men marry early; and hence one of the principal caufes of the increafed population. This manufacture circulates above L. 10,000 annually; the greateft part of which is brought into the parifh, as all the work is performed by the inhabitants; and the greateft part of the raw-material is home produce. Of the flax ufed, about $\frac{1}{8}$ is Dutch, and $\frac{1}{8}$ Riga; the reft is the produce of Kettle.

Agriculture, Produce, &c.—The farms in the parifh are 32, and the average of fervants on each is 5, viz. 3 men and 2 women. Moft of the farms have cottages, whence they obtain affiftance in hay-time and harveft. Befides thefe, there are many pendicles (*prædiola*), partly let off the farms, and partly let immediately by the proprietor; and a great number of fmall feus, from 1 to 5 acres. The farms are very unequal, both in fize and rent. The rent of pafture grounds is from 4 s. to L. 1 : 5 : 0, and of arable land from 5 s. to L. 1 : 11 : 6 an acre. About a fourth part of the arable ground is inclofed; and the advantages of inclofures is now fo univerfally acknowledged, that all new leafes are let on inclofing plans. The fences are ditch and hedge, or ftone-walls,

walls, as is moſt convenient or ſuitable.   Three commons lie
on the confines of this and the adjoining pariſhes, and are
now under the procefs of diviſion.

                                                    Scotch acres *.
Contents of the pariſh   .   .   .   5668
   Of which there are, in
Wheat   64
Barley   360
Oats   756
Flax   100
Green crop   100
Fallow   40
Paſture not arable   160
Graſs for hay   400
Arable paſture after hay   .   .   .   2870
Planting   160
Common yet undivided   .   .   .   650
Black cattle in the pariſh   .   .   .   1050
Horſes   260
Sheep of the common kind   .   .   500
Ploughs   76
Carts   128
Valued rent in Scots money   .   L. 6965 : 13 : 4.

The pariſh produces both more corn and cattle than is fufficient for its own maintenance, and of courſe brings the ſurplus to market.   Wheat is ſown, from the middle of September to the end of November ; peaſe and beans in the beginning of March ; oats from the middle of March to the
end of April ; and barley in the month of May.   The harveſt generally laſts during September and October.

Roads.—Statute-labour for the roads is partly exacted in
                                                    kind,

* To convert Scotch acres into Engliſh multiply by 1.270773.

kind, and partly commuted. A turnpike bill for the county was obtained last session, and the gentlemen of the county are using every exertion for putting it in execution.

Antiquities, &c.—On Banden Hill, which overlooks Coalton from the eastward, and commands an extensive view of the Strath of Eden, from Kinross to St Andrews Bay, are some remains of a circumvallation and rampart, of which tradition is silent. It is of a circular form, and nearly 200 yards in diameter. About half a mile to the eastward is another eminence, with ruins of the same kind on its summit. It is called Down Hill; is the highest in the parish; and commands the whole Strath of Leven, the Firth, and the Lothians. From the situation of these buildings, they were probably used as places of observation. The Knock of Clathe is a beautiful hill, rising smoothly without any appearance of fortifications. A regular coffin, of six stones, was found here some time ago, by men who were digging for gravel. Within it were human bones, and several trinkets; among which was the brass head of a spear, now in the possession of the Earl of Leven. There are at least 8 barrows in the parish, 3 of which have names: Pandler's Know, and Lowrie's Know, in Forthar ground; and Liquorich Stone in Kettle ground. Bones have been found in the rest. There is a tradition about the first, that, when dissensions arose between families in different parts of the country, they met there to decide their contention by arms, and those who fell were buried in the tumulus. The barrow in Forthar is said to have been a regular place of burial, and to have had a church or chapel near it. But of this no vestiges are now extant.

The lands of Clatto, which constitute the east end of the

parish of Kettle, and through which lay the old road from
Cupar to Kinghorn, belonged to a family of Setons, who are
celebrated in tradition for the most cruel robberies and murders. The grounds about Clatto Den are still desert. In the
face of the brae, which forms one side of the den, is a cave,
that is said to communicate with the old castle or tower of
Clatto, a furlong distant, the remains of which are still visible. The same cave is said to have had another opening to
the road, at which the assailant rushed out on the heedless
passengers, and dragged them into the cavern, whence there
was no return. All appearance of a cave is now obliterated,
by the breaking down of the banks. A similar cavern was
found, not many years ago, at Craighall in Ceres parish. Of
these Seatons many stories, replete with the superstitions of
preceding ages, are still current among the country people.
One may suffice. One of the Scottish Kings, said to be
James IV. passing that way alone, as was common in those
days, was attacked by a son of Seaton's. The King having a
hanger concealed under his garment, drew it, and with a
blow cut off the right hand that seized his horse's bridle.
This hand he took up, and rode off. Next day, attended
by a proper retinue, he visited the Castle of Clatto, wishing
to see Seaton and his sons, who were noted as hardy enter-
prising men, fitted to shine in a more public station. The
old man conducted his family into the King's presence. One
son alone was absent: It was said, that he had been hurt by
an accident, and was confined in bed. The King insisted on
seeing him, and desired to feel his pulse. The young man
held out his left hand. The King would feel the other also.
After many ineffectual excuses, he was obliged to confess that
he had lost his right hand. The King told him that he had
a hand in his pocket, which was at his service if it would fit
him. Upon this they were all seized and executed.

Miscellaneous

Miscellaneous Observations.—The people are in general charitable, and well difpofed. Both living and drefs have undergone a remarkable change within thefe 20 years, owing to the influx of wealth, and rife of wages. Few, however, have proved infolvent. Property has, in confequence, increafed in value, and is now rated at 29 years purchafe. A martial fpirit feems to pervade the lower ranks, who can fcarcely be prevented from entering into the army or navy on the report of a war. Their condition might perhaps be meliorated by improving the lands ftill farther, and encouraging the loom; but, on the whole, few diftricts in the country have more reafon to be fatisfied with their prefent ftate.

Kettle poffeffes very material advantages in its coal and lime works. Marl is eafily procured. The lands are improved and drained with facility, from their floping direction, and plenty of water. It affords employment and fubfiftence for the whole of its inhabitants. The language commonly fpoken is Englifh, with a provincial accent. The names of places are faid to be derived from the Gaelic.

No effential hurt was felt from the fevere years 1782 nor 1783 in this parifh. Some individuals, perhaps, might be a little diftreffed; but, in general, the farmers made money in thofe years. The crops being early, and tolerably reaped, yielded much meal, and fupplied feveral places with good feed. Whatever degree of improvement this parifh has yet attained, has almoft all been given it (excepting the eftate of Wefter Lathrifk) within thefe 12 years. Much, however, yet remains to be done, both in acquiring fyftem and execution.

There are 7 or 8 public houfes in the parifh, but they produce

produce no bad effects : Moſt of them are places of accommodation, and could not be wanted. The inhabitants of this pariſh are neither chargeable with the vice of drunkenneſs, nor of waſting their time or money. Several new houſes have lately been built. Few cottages have been built, and as few allowed to become ruinous. There is no jail in the pariſh. Feudal ſervices are wholly obliterated.

PARISH of KILCONQUHAR,

(County and Synod of Fife, Presbytery of St Andrew's.)

By the Rev. Mr Alexander Small.

Name, Extent, Surface, Soil, &c.

*K*ILCONQUHAR is derived probably either from *Cella*, the cell or chapel of a faint or monk, called *Conachar;* or from the Gaelic *Kil*, a place of worſhip or interment, and Conachar. From S. to N. that is, from the ſea to the borders of the pariſh of Ceres, it is about 8 Engliſh miles in length; and, in general, about 2 in breadth. It is ſituated in that part of the county of Fife, which, on account of the narrowneſs of the land, jutting out into the German Sea, and waſhed by the friths of the Forth and the Tay, is called the Eaſt Nook of Fife. Its ſurface is ſomewhat irregular, being flat in the ſouth for $1\frac{1}{2}$ miles from the ſea; riſing gently towards the north for about 2 miles; then, after a ſmall declivity, aſcending again towards the north for more than $\frac{3}{4}$ of a mile, on the north of which the ground is is partly flat, but, for the moſt part, declining towards the north. The ſoil in the ſouthern part is light and ſandy, but by proper culture, bears rich crops; in the higher ground of the very beautiful and fertile bank that faces the ſea, it is deep black loam; in ſome places, very rich clay. In the northern parts, though it is in ſome places abundantly rich, the climate is leſs favourable; the ſoil too, in many places, being a clay bottom mixed with ſand, is of inferior quality, and leſs productive; it is now arable in general; not long ſince, a great part of it was taken from moors; in dry ſeaſons, however, it yields good crops; much wheat and barley of excellent quality is raiſed in the ſouthern parts; peaſe and beans alſo, and every kind of grain that is uſual in this country, ſucceed well here.

Agriculture, &c.—Though the farmers are not attached to any particular mode of farming, the following is a rotation of crops frequently obſerved here, wheat, turnip, or any green crop, barley. and clover *. There are few oats raiſed in the lower part of the pariſh, but they are much uſed in the higher grounds. Sometimes we ſtand in need of importation of oats and oat-meal; while we export conſiderable quantities of wheat, barley, peaſe and beans, and ſome potatoes. The late Earl of Balcarras, about 40 years ago, introduced field turnip into his plan of farming, and fed oxen with them to a great extent; the uſe of that valuable root was not perhaps ſooner known in this part of the country; his Lordſhip's example was but little follow-

ed,

* Wheat is ſown in September, October, November, ſome even in January and February; which laſt is ſometimes found to anſwer well: It is reaped commonly in Auguſt and September. Peaſe and beans are ſown in February, March, and beginning of April; barley generally in May: And reaped in Auguſt, September, or ſometimes beginning of October.

ed, if at all, till within thefe 25 years; the practice is now become very general, to the great benefit of the country. —When the turnip appears above ground, it is often much hurt from a caufe that feems not to be well underftood, fome imputing it to a fly that eats the tender leaves; an ingenious gentleman in this neighbourhood, who has beftowed much attention on this fubject, imputes it to froft, and is confident the turnip fuffers nothing from the fly. The *Ruta baga* or Swedifh turnip, was introduced into this parifh about 4 years ago. Its leaves refemble the rib kail plants, the root refembles field turnip, not fo large in general, but heavier in proportion to its fize, and of much firmer texture. It is believed, that as great weight of this root may be raifed on an acre, as of field turnip; this plant feems to be gaining ground here; it is proof againft the moft intenfe froft; the feafon for fowing it is from the 1ft to the 20th May; it may either be tranfplanted as cabbage, or managed as field turnip. Potatoes were fcarcely known in this country 40 years ago; they now afford the poor half their fuftenance, and generally appear at the tables of the rich; they are well known to be very proper food for horfes and other animals, and are fometimes diftilled into whifky. Peafe and beans are much ufed, and generally fown in drills; they are hoed with the plough, and afterwards with hand hoes, which renders them meliorating crops. The number of horfes in the parifh is about 239; of cattle, 624; of affes, 22; of wheel-carriages, 3. The plough generally ufed is that of Small's conftruction, with a broad fock and mold board of Carron metal. Twenty or 30 years ago, the almoft univerfal practice of the farmers of this parifh was, to yoke 2 horfes and 4 oxen in a plough; now, ploughs are generally drawn by 2 horfes, one ploughman managing them; fcarcely are any oxen feen in a plough.—There are between 70 and 80 ploughs, and about the fame number of

carts;

carts; about 40 years ago, few carts were ufed in this country ; coals, victual and other articles, were at that period, and perhaps later, carried on horfeback; corn, hay, manure, &c. were driven with wains, drawn by 2 horfes and 2 oxen. The parifh contains 63½ ploughgates, confifting of between 40 and 50 acres each, fo that the whole parifh may be computed at upwards of 3000 acres arable, befides 280 acres of links or fandy plains, the haunts of rabbits, a fpecies of animals, which, though deftructive to corn, bring no fmall profit to the proprietors ; they are extremely prolific, being faid to have young 5 or 6 times in the year, 3 or 4 of the firft litter, 5, 6, or 7, of the following ones. Property in land has changed much in this parifh of late years. The value of land is rapidly increafing ; farms let for 19 or more years, are generally raifed one third, and the rents of fome are doubled within thefe few years; a farm of good land uninclofed, fit for the higheft culture, is let from 40 s. to 50 s. a-acre; the beft pafture, inclofures, &c. from L. 2 to L. 3 the acre. Thirty or 40 years ago, there was fcarce a large farm in this country that had not a flock of fheep ; now there are very few fheep in the country, excepting thofe in gentlemens inclofures, for family ufe; fince fummer fallow, for the culture of wheat, and the clover and turnip fyftem for feeding cattle, were introduced, the farmers difcontinued keeping flocks of fheep *. The valued rent of the parifh is L. 9509 Scots.—The real rent is
increafed

---

* Servants wages are gradually increafing in this parifh. The wages of a common labourer 6 or 7 years ago, were from 7 d. to 10 d. a-day; now they are from 10 d. to 15 d. The wages of men-fervants hired for the year at the above period, were from L. 4 to L. 5; now they are from L. 6 to L. 8, and their victuals. The wages of maid-fervants at the fame period, were from L. 1, 10 s. to L. 2 Sterling, for the year; now they are in general from L. 2, 10 s. to L. 3. The wages of wrights or carpenters a-day, are 1 s. 6 d. in fummer, and 1 s, 3 d. in winter. Of mafons the fame.

increafed in proportion to that of other parifhes in the neighbourhood. The air is wholefome in general, though damp in fome places ; the people live to a good age ; there are many who live beyond 80, and fome beyond 90 years. There is a poor woman in this parifh, who avers, that fhe is more than 100 years old. This, however, is not authenticated by our records.

Population.—At the time of Dr Webfter's report, the number of fouls was 2131 ; the number of the inhabitants at prefent is about 2013*. There are 4 villages or fmall towns. Colinfburgh contains about 357 inhabitants; Earlf-ferry, about 350 ; Kilconquhar, about 258 ; Barnyards, about 198 ; the country part of the parifh, about 850. There are 2 clergymen, one of the Eftablifhed Church, the other of the Relief Congregation. There are between 600 and 700 fectaries, adhering chiefly to the Prefbytery of Relief, with fome Burgher-feceders and ,Independents ; few of the Epifcopal profeffion, and no Roman Catholics. There are 13 proprietors of land, 5 refiding, and 8 non-refident ; 1 writer, 11 merchants, 20 farmers above L. 50 rent, 10 innkeepers and brewers, 8 fmiths, 89 weavers, 23 tailors, 18 mafons, 21 failors, 3 butchers, 12 gardeners, 46 fhoemakers, 8 bakers including apprentices, 4 flax-dref-fers, 2 coopers, 5 millers, 2 tanners, with 1 clerk, and a currier, 6 faddlers, who are employed occafionally in fhoe-making. The apprentices and journeymen are included in the numbers of the refpective trades.

Stipend,

* Years.	Baptifms.	Marriages.	Deaths.
1788	52	20	30
1789	52	20	35
1790	59	20	26
1791	46	16	64

Stipend, School, Poor.—The ſtipend is 10 chalders 3 ſir-
lots 3 pecks and 2 lippies barley, and L. 17 : 13 : 9⅓ Sterling,
with a glebe ſaid to be more than 7 acres.—There is one eſtabliſhed ſchoolmaſter with 200 merks of ſalary, a good
ſchool-houſe, dwelling-houſe, garden, and a ſmall croft of land.
The ſcholars are commonly between 30 and 40 in number ; 4 of whom are at preſent learning Latin.   Two and
ſometimes 3 teachers are employed by the inhabitants of
diſtant parts of this extenſive pariſh.—The number of poor
at preſent is 26.—They receive a monthly allowance, and
ſometimes oftener, from our public funds, according to
their reſpective neceſſities.   For theſe purpoſes and accidental caſes that occur, our weekly collections, and the liberal aid of the heritors, with the intereſt of our ſtock, are
generally ſufficient, without affecting the principal.   There
are but 3 travelling poor in the pariſh.

Annual income in	1790,	-	L. 45	2	5¾
——————————	1791,	-	34	2	4
——————————	1792,	-	58	17	5¾

Annual expenditure in	1790,	-	L. 31	13	7
———————————	1791,	-	32	8	0¼
———————————	1792,	-	51	13	10¼

The ſmall income in 1791 was owing to the vacancy in
that year.

Royal Borough.—There is one Royal borough, Earl's
Ferry*.   From a copy of a charter in the poſſeſſion of the
magiſtrates, renewed in the year 1589 by King James,
it

* There is a tradition, that on account of the generous and obliging
attentions of the inhabitants of this town to the Earl of Fife, when he
lay concealed in a cave in their neighbourhood, and particularly for fer-
rying

it appears, its erection into a royal borough, is of very ancient date. The original charter is loft, having been deftroyed by a fire of the borough of Edinburgh, as fpecified
in the copy above mentioned. In this borough there are 3 magiftrates, 15 councillors and a treafurer, the oldeft magiftrate
acting as provoft. The election is annual and by poll. They
forfeited their right of voting in the election of members of
Parliament, in common with fome other towns in this country, through their inability to pay their proportion of the
fums neceffary for defraying the expenfes of a commiffioner in Parliament fome centuries ago; when ' the anxiety
of

rying him over the frith, at the hazard of their lives and liberties, while
he was efcaping from the cruelty of Macbeth, the Earl obtained from
King Malcolm the following privilege in their favour, *viz.* That the perfons of all who pafs the frith from Earl's Ferry in a veffel belonging to
the town, were declared inviolable, or fafe from their purfuers, till they
were half fea over. This, it would appear, is the origin of the name of
Earl's Ferry. There is one floop, and a few fmall fifhing-boats, belonging to Earl's Ferry. Formerly there were 18 fifhermen; but fince the
year 1766, when 7 of them were loft in a ftorm in one boat, only a very
few are employed in fifhing occafionally.— There is in our records a copy
of the infcription on Macduff's crofs, written in a language unknown
in this part of the country, as follows:

     Maldraradrum dragos, maleria largia largos,
     Spalando fpados, five nig fig gnippite gnaros,
     Lauria laurifcos lauringen, lauria lufcos,
     Et Columburtos, et fic tibi curcia cortos
     Exitus et baradrum, five lim, five lam, five labrum;
     Propter magidrum et hoc oblatum,
     Ampi fmileridum, fuper limpide, lampide, labrum.

Part of the above infcription has been tranflated as follows:

' I King Malcolm Kenmore, grant to thee Macduff Earl of Fife, free
liberty to punifh all traytors that defert, and troublers of the peace, and
free indemnity to thy own kin; thou paying to the King nine cows
and a heifer.'

of our anceftors to obtain an exemption, was almoft equal to the eagernefs with which our contemporaries folicit admiffion into Parliament *.'

Rocks, Caves and Lakes—On the weft of the Earl's Ferry is Kincraig-rock, remarkable for caves, which, though fome of them refemble the works of art, are probably excavations caufed by the influx of the fea. In one of them, Macduff's cave, are fome remains of a wall, which tradition fays, was built by Macduff, Earl of Fife, to defend him from Macbeth, who, having murdered his coufin King Duncan, afcended the throne of Scotland, and treated his fubjects with the cruelty of a tyrant. Macduff afterward fled into England, and encouraged Malcolm, fon to the late king, to return to Scotland and recover the throne of his anceftors.—Macduff's cave penetrates into the rock about 200 feet, and the roof, being the fummit of the rock, is fuppofed to be at leaft 160 feet high, forming a grand alcove, projecting over the cave and the fea at full tide.— The ftone of this rock is of excellent quality, fufceptible of fine polifh, refembling granite, or perhaps a fpecies of it. Mr Gourlay, the late proprietor, had high offers made him, for liberty to quarry in it fome years ago, when the ftreets of London were paving ; but apprehenfive of the fall of fome parts of the rock, and the lofs of fome of the rich foil behind, which he fufpected might be the confequence, he declined the offers. Coal is found in this rock too, which cannot be worked, as the fea comes fo clofe upon it. There is a fpecies of ftone in this rock, which is fuppofed to be marble of the bafaltic kind ; a fpecimen of which is to be feen in Mrs Gourlay of Kincraig's cuftody ; its colour is white, variegated with blue, and it is finely polifhed. There is a beautiful piece of water on the fouth of the village of
Kilconquhar,

* Dr ROBERTSON's Hiftory of Scotland.

Kilconquhar, commonly called Kilconquhar Loch, almoſt
¼ of a mile in length, and about ¼ of a mile in breadth.
This loch was originally called Redmire, from which much
fuel was got, as peat and turf. It had a drain weſtward to
the ſea. There is a tradition here, that in the year 1624 or
1625, the drain was filled up with ſand driven by a violent
guſt of wind from the ſea, and that the water, thus ſtopped in
its courſe, became a lake. Between 60 and 70 ſwans uſed
greatly to enliven and adorn this loch; but they deſerted
it about 20 years ago. There are 9 at preſent. In the
loch are ſeveral ſmall iſlands planted with ſhrubs, formed
for the uſe of the ſwans: they hatch in the month of May*.

Country Seats.—There is a variety of beautiful country
ſeats in this pariſh, among which Balcarras is conſpicous,
ſituated on an eminence, with a gentle declivity to the
ſouth,

---

* A ſpecies of birds called bald coots, are alſo on the loch in great
numbers, reſembling crows, but have longer legs; they make their neſts
on the flags, and hatch in May; and feed upon vermin in the mud.
They left the loch, it is reported, about 40 years ago, and did not return
again for ten years. Here are wild ducks; herald ducks, as they are called here, (perhaps heron ducks), ſmaller than wild ducks, with a ſhorter
wing, red head, and gray variegated feathers; a ſpecies of duck called
widgeon, ſomewhat leſs than the herald duck; and teals, ſmaller than
theſe ducks. Theſe ducks appear on the loch in great abundance in
ſummer, but leave it in winter. In the evening, they fly off in a body
to the ſea, as is ſuppoſed, and return through the night. The only fiſhes
in the loch are pikes and eels; of the former ſome weigh 14 lb. ſome
16 lb. and are, ſome 36, ſome 38 inches long. There is a drain in the
loch to the ſouth, where the eels are taken in an ark; they go to the ſea
in autumn. Perches have been ſeen in the loch, but they are deſtroyed,
it is thought, by the pikes.—The gray plover and fieldfare come hither
in October, and leave us the beginning of March; the green plover, as
it were by concert, comes to us in March, and leaves us in October.
The lark, blackbird, thruſh, with birds of almoſt every note and every
feather, haunt a pleaſant wood of Sir John Anſtruther's on the ſouth of
Kilconquhar loch, where there are charming walks, adorned with flowers
and ſhrubs, and lovely bowers.

ſouth, commanding a noble view of the coaſt, and of the frith of Forth ; a pleaſant and grand object, beautifully winding round the coaſt, almoſt in a ſemicircular direction, often agreeably diverſified with ſhips of various burdens, and ſometimes with fleets ; North Berwick law, the Baſs, and the iſland of May, are alſo pleaſing and grand objects from this charming villa, appearing as ſo many floating iſlands and caſtles in the ſea. Balcarras commands an ex- tenſive proſpect on the ſouth of the frith likewiſe, com- prehending Edinburgh, with a great part of the counties of Lothian, Haddington, Berwick, &c. There is a beautiful craig on the Eaſt of Balcarras-Houſe, riſing in the midſt of rich fields, from which the objects above mentioned are ſeen to great advantage. Here alſo is an excellent quarry for building. On the eaſt of the craig is a delightful den, about an Engliſh mile in length, enlivened by a ſtream of water paſſing through the middle, whoſe riſing banks are adorned with thriving trees of various kinds. The feather- ed tribes ſeem proud of pouring forth their various melody in this pleaſant retreat, not inferior perhaps to the Tempe of ancient Theſſaly. Balcarras is no leſs fertile than beauti- ful, the fields are properly divided and incloſed, and in the higheſt ſtate of cultivation. The late Earl of Balcarras, a nobleman diſtinguiſhed by the benevolence of his heart, the liberality of his ſentiments, and the uncommon extent of his knowledge, particularly in hiſtory and agriculture, was among the firſt that brought farming to any degree of perfection in this country.

Hic, ———— Ridet inter omnes
Angulus terræ.

It would exceed the bounds proper for an account of this kind to dwell on the beautiful ſituation, and elegant manſion houſes of Kilconquhar, Newton, Lathallan, Kincraig,

oraig and Grange; the castle of Rires merits particular notice, situated on a high eminence, commanding a most extensive view, and intended, it would appear, for a place of defence; it is surrounded by a ditch 70 feet wide, whose depth cannot now be ascertained with accuracy, by reason of the alterations time has made on the ground: No planting remains about it, excepting one remarkable tree, called ' the Bicker tree,' measuring 14 feet round, and its branches extending about 75 feet; that part of the tree where the great branches separate from the trunk, affords a very agreeable seat, and shade in summer; and tradition says, that one of the hospitable proprietors, after liberally entertaining his guests in the castle, was wont to conduct them to this tree, and give them an additional bicker there: In those days, it was usual with people of rank, to drink out of wooden cups or bickers tipped with silver.

Miscellaneous Observations.—There are 4 dumb people in this parish. One became dumb after he was 4 years of age, in consequence of a stroke on the head: He enjoys the faculty of hearing in perfection, and is abundantly intelligent and active. Another articulates a little, and is quite deaf, occasioned by a fever; two of one family have been both deaf and dumb from their birth: All the 4 are abundantly sensible and active, and attend public worship regularly.—The common people in this and the neighbouring parishes, pronounce the diphthong *oi* with a long and broad accent, giving it the sound of *ow*, for instance, they make no distinction of sound, between *boil* and *bowl*. They use the Scots dialect; some names of places are derived from Gaelic, as *Balcarres*, ' the town of sheep,' *Kincraig* ' the ' end of a rock,' &c.

Advantages

Advantages and Diſadvantages, &c.—There is a confiderable number of coal fields in this pariſh, which have, in
great meaſure, ſerved the adjacent country for ſome centuries paſt, and afford coal of various kinds, as hard, ſplent,
parret, and ſoft, known here by the name of cherry ; and
of a mixed nature, in many places ; all generally good of
their kinds : The ſtrata are ſubject to many interruptions,
as is the caſe with moſt of the coal in the inland parts of
Fife, being often broken off, or thrown into different directions, by hitches as they are called, which are of very
different thickneſſes, compoſed variouſly of heterogeneous
materials ; the coal ſtrata themſelves alſo differing in thickneſs, quality, ſtricking, and declivity ; ſeldom found to go
much deeper than 30 fathoms from the ſurface ; whereas
the coal ſtrata, cloſe by the ſea, both here, and in many o-
ther parts of our iſland, are ſaid to run for miles, almoſt in
the ſame direction, and of the ſame dimenſions. The
coal fields in this pariſh that have been worked are Balcarres coal.—Kilbrackmont coal, the property of Miſs Scott
of Scotſtarvet.—South Falfield coal, the property of Mr
Bethune of Blebo. The above mentioned coals are not worked at preſent, but might afford more coal, were engines
erected, or mines driven deeper than formerly to carry off
the water.—Reres coal, the property of Mr Bayne of
Reres, worked by a mine, employs 6 men, a grieve, and
overſman. The price of a cart load, 75 ſtone weight, is
2 s. 6 d.—Lathallan coal, the property of Major Lumſdaine
of Lathallan, worked by a mine, affords both hard and ſoft
coal, frequently of good quality ; employs at preſent 8 colliers, 2 windlace-men, and a ſuperintendent. The price of
a cart load 75 ſtone weight, is 2 s. 2 d.—Largo-Ward coal,
the property of James Calderwood Durham, Eſq; of Largo,
conſiſts of many ſhort ſtrata, lying in tranſverſe directions,

worked

worked by a mine of 3540 yards, upwards of 2 miles long, produces hard and foft coal, generally of good quality, employs at prefent 37 people for the various purpofes, with 2 grieves, and one overfman.—North Falfield coal, the property of the above defigned Mr Durham, worked by a fteam engine, erected in 1784, which drains two diftinct coal fields, each confifting of 2 ftrata, one of a mixed nature, about 5 feet thick, the other fine parret, in great requeft for the clear light it affords, and other properties : of thefe ftrata the one is 9 feet thick for 60 yards, then gradually diminifhing for about 60 yards, till it comes to 5 feet thick, where fplent becomes perceptible, united to the parret on the pavement, the fplent increafing in an uniform progreffive manner, and the parret diminifhing in the fame proportion, till its thicknefs becomes 4 feet, where the coal is cut off by a hitch of confiderable thicknefs, and leaves the parifh. The other ftratum is excellent parret, in fome places 9 feet thick, but not uniform ; the coal is always beft where it is thickeft This colliery employs feldom lefs than 40, fometimes more than 50 men, with one as grieve and accountant, and another as engineer and overfman.— Confumption of one year, at an average for 7 years paft, is as follows :

Coals at 18 ftone the load of the various kinds,

Loads,   -   47,572

Yearly returns,   -   -   L. 1553 : 17 : $11\frac{1}{4}$.

The pits by which the greater part of the coal is put out, are 54 or 56 yards deep. This muft have been a colliery for a confiderable time, as an account is to be feen in Largo houfe of fo many loads of parret coal, driven yearly from Falfield to Falkland, a diftance not lefs than 10 miles, for the ufe of King James VI. his own chamber. The

colliers

colliers of this pariſh are tolerably regular and induſtri-- ous.

Fiſh.—Cod, ſkate, ling, turbot, and ſhell-fiſh of variou̶s kinds are in great plenty on the coaſt in all the ſeaſons. Be- ſides the great quantities ſold here, many are ſent to the Edinburgh market ; haddocks, for which our coaſt is fa- mous, have deſerted us for ſome years paſt. Whales and grampuſes are ſometimes ſeen here. The length of coaſt waſhed by the ſea, belonging to this pariſh, is about 2 miles, all rock and ſand. The farmers next the coaſt have acceſs to ſea-ware, which is excellent manure for raiſing barley, and to ſome kelp. The ſcarcity of growing timber for farming utenſils, is a diſadvantage to the farmers.

Manners.—The gentlemen who reſide on their eſtates, contribute not a little to the good order and happineſs of their tenants, and the other inhabitants of the pariſh ; being affable, humane, and hoſpitable to all around them, they ſe- cure the affection, eſteem, and attachment of their depen- dents, and by employing a variety of tradeſmen and labour- ers in the field, they are benefactors to many. They are abundantly active, and public ſpirited likewiſe with reſpect to the improvement of roads. The farmers are intelligent ſenſible men in general, who, by means of their knowledge and induſtry, live comfortably, and ſeveral of them genteelly, notwithſtanding the high rents. The manufacturers and tradeſmen are generally induſtrious and regular. The peo- ple of this pariſh are much improved in point of ſobriety ; they are ſeldom ſeen in clubs in public houſes, and inſtances of drunkenneſs are very rare ; 30 or 40 years ago, public houſes were much frequented here by people of all ranks ; in theſe days they drank much brandy, and other ſpiritous liquors,

liquors, which were not only deftructive to health, but proved fertile caufes of intoxication and quarrels ; now, not only gentlemen and farmers, but people of almoft every defcription, entertain their friends and acquaintances in their
own houfes, where they drink milder and lefs intoxicating
liquors, and in greater moderation ; the fociety of the female fex, fecuring decency, politenefs, and agreeable con-
viviality.—The tradefmen of the village of Kilconquhar
make a fine apperance on his Majefty's birth-day ; fo many
handfome, genteel, well dreffed young men, can hardly be
muftered in any other place of equal extent and population
in the country : Perfect order, decorum, and loyalty, are
manifeft in every expreffion, motion and countenance, during the whole proceffion and feftivity.—Notwithftanding
the confufions and diforders we hear of in other parts of the
country, it muft afford high pleafure to all lovers of order
and of their country, to obferve the inhabitants of this
parifh in general, fenfible of the unparalleled happinefs we
enjoy as members of a community, under the protection of
the wife laws of our moft excellent conftitution, and the
mild adminiftration of our moft gracious Sovereign, dwelling
in peace and fafety, in full and fecure poffeffion of liberty
and property, with none to make us afraid ; while we continue, (according to the injunction of the wifeft of men,
under the direction of Divine infpiration) to fear God, to
honour the King, and not to meddle with them that are given to change.

NOTE.

Difeafes.——1. Febrile Difeafes.—Inflammation of the throat and
breaft, rheumatifm, croup, eryfipelas, fpitting of blood, confumption of the
lungs, catarrh, very common and frequent. Inflammation of the brain,
bowels, liver and kidneys, not frequent. Gout and dyfentery, very uncommon. Intermittent fever, very frequent formerly in the village of
Kilconquhar.

Kilconquhar. Continued fever, frequently endemic. Natural ſmall-pox and meaſles, epidemic from time to time. Inoculated ſmall-pox, few inſtances.——2. Nervous Diſeaſes.—Apoplexy, epilepſy, cholera morbus, not frequent. Palſy, fainting, not unfrequent. Locked jaw, diabetes canine madneſs, no inſtance for 20 years paſt. Hooping cough, epidemic from time to time. Diarrhœa, very frequent. Inſanity, one inſtance at preſent.——3. Cachectical Diſeaſes.—General dropſy, dropſy of the belly. ſcrofula, very frequent. Tympany, jaundice, not unfrequent. Dropſy of the brain and breaſt, rickets, uncommon. Atrophy, lues venerea, ſcurvy, no inſtances.——4. Local Diſeaſes.—Iliac paſſion, ſuppreſſion of urine, not frequent Hernia, abortion, not uncommon. Flooding, frequent. Gangrene, rare. Cancer, very rare. Aneuriſm, no inſtance. ——5. Anomalous Diſeaſes.—Caſualties, drunkenneſs, few inſtances. Dentition, frequent. Gravel and ſtone, pretty frequent. Worms, very common.

PARISH OF KILMANY,

(County and Synod of Fife, Presbytery of Cupar),

By the Rev. Mr John Cook, *Minister.*

Name, &c.

THE parish of Kilmany has the same name with that by which the most considerable village it possesses is distinguished. From a small burying-ground * which surrounds the church, the name has probably been derived.

This village, which the name, the number of people it contains, and the vicinity of the church, distinguish above every other in the parish, is about 5 miles distant from

Cupar,

* Kilmany is, according to common opinion, of Celtic origin. If only that part of the word which signifies a burying-ground be Celtic, it will not be a singular instance of such composition in our mixed language. The other villages in the parish have, in general, either names descriptive of their situation, or those of former possessors.

Cupar, the county town, and the feat of the prefbytery. It
is fcattered along the fhallow and narrow water of Motray *, which unites, in the weftern extremity of the parifh,
two fmall ftreams, iffuing from different fides of Norman's
Law, and which, after a fhort and gentle courfe, falls into
the river Eden, not far from the bay of St Andrew's.
A little attention to the pleafing irregularities in the ground
on which Kilmany is fituated, and through which the rivulet flows, might have made it a beautiful picture of rural
fcenery. But how feldom has fuch attention either chofen
the fituations, or arranged the forms, of the largeft towns!
Accident, or the idea of conveniency, which can feldom be
hurt by a regard to beauty, is allowed to have in thefe matters too powerful an influence; and in the pofition of the
ftraggling huts of this village, as in that of many other
places, we have to lament the careleffnefs which can build
in a beautiful place of refidence, and yet neglect to take
advantage of the aids which the fcenery at once furnifhes
and fuggefts, to decorate the dwellings of men, and from
thefe thus decorated, to derive ornaments in addition to its
own.

The church † ftands on a beautiful bank, rifing gradually
from the ftream, which flows paft it on the S.; is fkirted on
the W. by fome tall afhes; and fronts the hill of Forrit,
once covered with firs, but now ftript of the whole. No
little clump has been left upon any of its brows; not even

a

* The water could not float any kind of veffel for tranfporting corn.

† So late as the year 1768, the church was renewed. The building is
fimple and neat : but unfortunately, the long narrow form in which almoft
all the old churches in this part of the country are conftructed, has been too
much retained. It feems ftrange, that there fhould have been fo prevalent
a partiality to a form of building, of all others leaft fitted for public
fpeaking.

a ſolitary tree to ſhow of what it could have boaſted formerly, in a country very deſtitute of ſuch riches.

Extent of the Pariſh.—The grounds of the pariſh ſtretch
from W. to E. about 6 Engliſh miles, chiefly in that fertile tract of country, which runs almoſt without interruption, from the barren plain betwixt the mouths of the
Eden and the Tay, to the town of Newburgh and Loch
Lindores. Where the valley is confined, the pariſh is
ſcarcely a mile in breadth ; but to the W. beyond the village of Rathillet, it widens with the valley, riſes on each
hand over the adjacent heights, and gains an extent of about
four miles. The greateſt part of the pariſh, however, is
contained between one continued branch of the Ochil mountains, and ſome hills, of different ſizes, and of various forms,
which are ſcattered to the S.

Kilmany is diſtant from the river Tay, and from the
port of Balmerino, about 3 Engliſh miles ; but is ſeparated
from them by the branch of the Ochil Hills which ſtretches
along the N. of Fife, and gradually diminiſhes in ſize, till
it ſhoots down into the river near Scot's-craig.

Wood and Scenery.—This range of hilly ground, which
diverſifies in the moſt ſtriking manner the ſouthern ſhore
of the Tay, which in ſome places ſwells in full unbroken
maſſes, with variegated colouring, in others, raiſes ſuddenly upwards rugged fragments of uncovered rock, might,
were the hand of improvement to perform its office, make
this part of Fife a ſcene of the moſt luxuriant beauty.
There are brows on theſe hills which the plough cannot
reach, or where its labour would not be rewarded ; which
equally by their ſituation and their ſoil are fitted to rear
timber. This is ſo obviouſly the only uſe to which they
can be put, that the traveller who takes time to look around
him,

him, muſt lament the nakedneſs they diſplay. He will lament it the more in a ſcene, where the hand of nature, and
the toils of the huſbandman, have done ſo much to admini-
ſter to his delight ; where the contraſt of broken rocks and
ſwelling hills, with plains in the richeſt cultivation; and
where the cultivation, breaking with irregular ſteps the
bleakneſs of the hills, ſometimes left at their baſe, ſometimes climbing on their ſides, concur to form an exquiſitely
varied landſcape. How much would it add to the ſcene,
were the rich corn fields to riſe into the boſom of woods
ſtretching with various length down towards the plain ;
were ſome of the bareſt ſummits to eſcape above their
verdure ; and were the beautiful waters of the Tay ſeen
through openings made thus picturesque ?

Neither would ſuch exertions in improving the country
be unprofitable ; nor is the idea of making them viſionary.
Independently of the value of the wood, (and it is well
known how ſoon it does become valuable), it tends, by
affording a warm ſhelter, to meliorate the adjacent land in
a ſtate of tillage. From every appearance it is alſo probable that the ſoil, which cannot be ploughed, might bear
a rich covering of wood. From experience, indeed, little
can be ſaid, for the pariſh can boaſt of few attempts to plant
trees ; but where ſagacity and taſte have made the attempt,
and continued the ſmall attention neceſſary for ſucceſs, they
have been in general rewarded with a conſiderable recompenſe
for the labour, and a rich addition to the beauty of the ſurrounding ſcene. The hill of Forrit, in the pariſh of Logie,
was, till ſome years ago, covered with firs; 21 acres on the
eſtate of Lochmalony, bear them in great perfection, and
we may ſee them ſcaling ſome of the ſteepeſt hills in the
neighbourhood *. In as far, indeed, as the beauty of the
country

---

* It is but juſt to obſerve, that the ſpirit of raiſing wood ſeems now to
awaken : ſeveral plantations have been of late made, and are ſtill making
in

country is concerned, it would be rather defirable that in fome fpots they fhould fail entirely. The irregularity thus produced, the wandering inartificial line in which the foliage would then appear, would give an eafe to the fcenery, which the formal fquares and circles, ufed with fuch partiality by cuftom to bound plantations, effectually deftroy.

Even were the trees not to rife to a great height, the proprietor, though he could not be otherwife enriched by them, would be indebted to the fhelter they afforded to his arable lands; and the country would wear almoft as rich an afpect, with its hills thus covered, as if they were crowned with lofty wood. On a rugged country this is peculiarly beautiful. A little diftance always gives a fine effect, even to the pooreft plantations; the fhortnefs of the wood the eye cannot then accurately meafure; while, at the fame time, the foliage feems deep, and the boldnefs of the ground towers above its fhade.

Antiquities.—No ruins of any abbey or chapel, not even the fragments of any remarkable building, give folemnity to the fcenery of the parifh. A few pretty large ftones, funk in the top of one of its hills, have excited curiofity; and the genius of antiquarianifm, unaided by the information which the country can afford, would probably find in them the remnant of fome camp or caftle. The lefs fplendid, but the more juft account of the inhabitants, makes them part of fome common decayed fence.

Scarcely a mile to the N. of Kilmany, there is a romantic rocky den, cut deep in the face of the mountain. It has probably been gradually worn down by the fucceffive torrents, which the heavy rains in winter throw from the
higher

in the parifh, and its neighbourhood; and if the exertions are vigoroufly continued, in 20 years the face of this part of the country will be completely changed.

higher ground, daſhing amongſt its rocks. The name it
has received in the country is, Goule's Den. By thoſe who
live near it, no explanation of the name is given. The
manner in which it is written here would lead any one, acquainted with the Arabian Nights Entertainments, to imagine, that ſuperſtitious terrors had peopled it with the de-
ſtroying demons mentioned in one of theſe ſtories. The
fact is, that diſmal reports, of what had been ſeen and heard
there, were in other days circulated; reports which have had
often leſs to gain them credit, than the diſmal gloom which
the ſhades of night muſt draw over that rugged unfrequent-
ed ſcene.

Number of Acres, and Nature of the Soil.—The irregular
extent of the lands in the pariſh, already mentioned, includes, (beſides a glebe of 9), 3963 Scotch acres. Of theſe,
the ſoil differs according to their local ſituation. In ſome
of the acres, which are fartheſt ſouth, the ſoil is a ſtrong
clay; in thoſe forming the flat banks of the Motray, which
runs through the whole length of the pariſh, the ſoil is a
rich black loam, continued beneath the ſurface, beyond the
reach of the plough; in thoſe which are extended on the
gentle acclivities, it is loam, with a gravelly and ſometimes
a rocky bottom; and in the reſt, the ground is cold moor,
on ſome ſpots covered with furze *.

Agriculture.—A very great proportion of the lands in
the pariſh is in a ſtate of high cultivation.—Of 3963 acres,
3216 are arable, the moſt of which commonly produce good
crops. In raiſing theſe crops, there is no particular rotation
uniformly

---

* There is alſo in the eaſter. corner of the pariſh a piece of light ſandy
ſoil, which carries broom to the height of 6 or 8 feet; a produce of very
great beauty, and of ſome utility as fuel, but which takes ſuch poſſeſſion of
the ground, that to extirpate it is a very difficult taſk.

uniformly obferved throughout the parifh ; but the one moft approved, is that which the ingenious Lord Kames has recommended. The arable land is laboured by 55 ploughs, drawn each by two horfes, which are driven by the ploughman. Though the ufe of cattle in tilling the ground, and even in dragging carriages, be entirely exploded here, it may be computed that 139 are raifed annually within the parifh, and fold when from betwixt 3 to 4 years old. There are no more horfes bred than what are neceffary for the purpofes of hufbandry, and for preventing the places of thofe which fail from being fupplied out of the public markets *.

Of the land which at prefent lies wafte, a confiderable extent may be brought into a ftate of cultivation. The meadows, in particular, on the banks of the Motray, and which the water often overflows, might be made the moft productive ground in the parifh. Activity has already converted a part of thefe into the moft luxuriant corn-fields; but to the improvement of the whole an obftacle is oppofed, which perhaps may not fpeedily be removed. The water of Motray turns four mills in its courfe through the parifh. The accumulation of water which hence muft be made at each, renders it impoffible to drain the meadows fo thoroughly as otherwife might be done ; and the proprietors of thefe mills have not as yet been difpofed to give up for any equivalent the privilege they poffefs. This privilege was undoubtedly acquired, when ignorance of agriculture fuppofed thefe meadows to be ufelefs ; but notwithftanding this ignorance of the nature of the compact, it was fairly acquired, and the enjoyment of it has now become a right. Though it would be abfurd to think that it might be facrificed to benevolence, it would not be unnatural to expect, that for a proper equivalent it would be yielded to promote the public good. But the proprietors of thefe

mills

* The parifh feeds alfo two flocks of fheep, amounting in number to about 240, moftly of the Englifh breed.

mills have a much weightier reafon, in the eftimation of the world, to induce them to make fuch a conceffion. Their own intereft, independently of all equivalent given them, would be thus advanced, for the removal of the mills * would make way for the improvement both of the meadows of their neighbours, and of thofe which belong to themfelves. Till this change take place, the rich meadows will be overflowed with water, and the country denied the corn which in great abundance they would produce †.

Wood.—Of all the ground which might be planted with wood, only about 74 acres bear trees grown to a vifible fize. Except a few afhes, which clufter in the villages, or run out in hedge-rows; and fome trees of different kinds, which are fcattered round the family-feats, on the grounds of Rathillet, Lochmalony, and Mountwhannie, the plantations have, chequered with two or three ftraggling birches, the

---

* Thefe four mills, one of which is ufed for dreffing flax, are all that remain in the parifh of a much greater number. The fmall decreafe in the confumption of oats, peafe, and barley, (they were corn-mills), can hardly be confidered a reafon of this diminution. A better will be found in the fuperior fize and mechanifm of thofe that remain. Thirlage, a fpecies of monopoly, which, like all others that are privileged, arofe from a fear, that can exift only in the infancy of the arts, impofes here no heavier burden on the farmer, than to make him grind the corn ufed in his family at the neareft mill.

† In eftimating the improvements in agriculture, which have been made within the parifh, it will not be fafe to follow as a guide the increafe of cultivated land. This increafe has by no means correfponded to the fuperior order into which greater fkill in hufbandry has brought fields which have been long under the plough; and unlefs the quantity of grain now raifed could be compared with what was raifed formerly, a comparifon which cannot be made, it will not be known what have been the improvements in agriculture, nor what praife the farmers deferve. The amazing rife of rents may be fome rule of judging.

the deep gloom of the Scotch, or the gayer verdure of the larch-fir. The ſmall proportion of wooded ground, in comparison of what may be wooded, has been in part removed by conſiderable plantations lately made on the eſtates of Lochmalony, Mountwhannie, and Myre Cairnie; and it is to be hoped, that a few years will fill the melancholy blank, which the eye, in wandering over this pariſh *, finds upon its mountains.

Tithes.—The tithes of the pariſh, with the right of preſentation to the living, were given to the College of St Salvator, in the Univerſity of St Andrews, by Biſhop Kennedy, the founder of that college. They were intended to be a valuable donation; and would have been ſo in a high degree, from a pariſh in ſuch a ſtate of cultivation, had they been allowed to keep pace with the progreſs of agriculture and the price of corn. This was not allowed; and they have now ſhrunk out of all proportion to the real rent. The Principal and Profeſſors of the United College, ſince the union of St Salvator's and St Leonard's, have received them, and are titulars of the tithes, and patrons of the pariſh.

Fuel, &c.—In the ordinary articles conſumed for the ſupport, or for the comfort of life, the inhabitants of this pariſh may be abundantly ſupplied. But the ſupply cannot be procured at low prices. Coals, in particular, muſt both be purchaſed at a high rate, and brought into the pariſh by tedious or difficult roads. In the county of Fife, no coal pits have as yet been opened to the north of the river Eden; hence no coals of any kind can be brought hither over land by a ſhorter road than ſix miles, and none good by one leſs than 16! and it is no eaſy matter to convey them from the

Tay,

* Eleven proprietors poſſeſs at preſent, in different proportions, the lands of the pariſh. For planting, the larch is in a ſpecial manner recommended to their attention.

Tay, by the rugged road which croſſes the ſteep hills ſepa-
rating Balmerino from Kilmany *. From the vicinity of
the pariſh to the towns of Cupar and Dundee, it feels the
price of ſuch proviſions as the country produces in abundance, affected by the conſtant demand of theſe large markets. Hence cheeſe, butter, fowls, eggs, are bought at a
higher price at Kilmany, becauſe, from the progreſs of
luxury, they are ſought with greater avidity than beef or
mutton, and from the wealth of the inhabitants, are purchaſed at an enormous rate at Dundee. Out of the markets of the towns juſt mentioned, thoſe who do not kill their
own meat are ſupplied. It was once eaſy to bring, at all
hours, ſuch ſupplies to Kilmany ; for the high road betwixt
Cupar and Dundee run through the village. Some years
ago, (for it is but of late that Fife can boaſt of having a
turnpike-road), the courſe of this road was turned eaſtwards,
three miles from Kilmany. The public profited by the
change, for they travel by a ſmooth inſtead of a hilly road ;
but the village ſuffered ; for it no longer enjoys the wonted
frequent opportunities of conveyance betwixt Cupar and
Dundee.

Population.—The pariſh is the reſidence of huſbandmen.
Agriculture is the univerſal employment ; it is the ſource
and the ſubſtance of its few commercial tranſactions. It
gives ſubſiſtence to almoſt every individual in the pariſh ;
to the farmers, to their ſervants, to the families of theſe
ſervants, who are the great body of inhabitants ; and to the
few mechanics, whoſe offices are neceſſary for carrying on
country

---

* It muſt ſurely be deſired by all who have grain to export, that the
road to Balmerino were better made.

country affairs, or for promoting the comforts of life *.
From the occupations of the inhabitants, it is evident that
they cannot be numerous. Agriculture, however capable
of affording the means of ſubſiſtence, never collects within
the ſame bounds ſuch numbers, as do the various branches
of manufactures cultivated throughout the iſland. Fewer
hands can conduct its operations. One great object, too,
which in its preſent ſtate it ſeems to have in view, is to take
from theſe hands as many as poſſible. In many places, proprietor and tenant have united to accompliſh this object.
To have a large and eaſily collected rent is naturally deſired
by the former, and this has effected the annihilation of the
little tenants ſcattered over the country; to ſave as many
ſervants as poſſible in the management of country affairs,
the latter has imagined it to be important economy, and
this has often ſubſtituted unmarried men in the place of numerous families. The healthieſt and the pureſt nurſery, of
the moſt vigorous and innocent claſs of our countrymen, has
hence been much depopulated. However true it may appear, that a numerous claſs of tenantry are incapable of
keeping the ground in order, or of paying the proper rent,
there are bounds, beyond which the idea muſt prove fatal
to the country in which it is put in practice; and it is evidently full of danger, whatever elſe it be, to turn away the
cottagers who have been wont to reſide on a farm. The
natural conſequences are, that ſervants of that kind are
ſcarce,

---

* There is no baker in the pariſh. The greateſt part of the bread conſumed is prepared by the families who eat it. The increaſe in the conſumption of wheaten bread has of late been conſiderable, but that it bears no
proportion to the uſe made of oaten and peaſe meal in baking bread, is apparent, from the circumſtance of the pariſh having no baker of its own.
May it not be inferred from thence, that in times of ſcarcity it is no alle-
viation to the wants of the poor, when the rich give up the uſe of flour.
The caſe is different in large towns. There is no flour preferred by bakers,
nor barley by brewers, to that which this pariſh raiſes.

scarce, and their wages great; and that a corn country depends upon foreign aid for cutting down its crops. So long as this aid can be eafily procured, the helpleffnefs of the fituation does not appear; but it would be feverely felt, were any happy change to meliorate the condition of thofe regions of poverty from whence the aid is derived.

There is no fuch dependence in this parifh. Its population, though from the fituation mentioned it cannot be great, has not, as far as can be afcertained, diminifhed within the laft 20 years. The number in 1755 was 785 *. There are now living in the parifh 396 males, and 473 females; in all, 869 †.

Poor.—The funds of the feffion, for the affiftance of the poor, are adequate to afford the common fupplies. They confift of the intereft of about L. 200 Sterling; upon which capital no encroachment has been found neceffary; of the money paid for the ufe of the mortcloth; and of the collections at the church-door.

There are in the parifh no ftated poor, who receive weekly from the feffion. More or lefs is given to them, according to their wants ‡. They very feldom, and with much hefitation, afk; their wants muft be noticed and fupplied. Thefe two happy confequences, happy for the virtue of mankind,

* The baptifms have been, at a medium for 20 years paft, 21. Thofe buried in the church-yard, 14. There is no feparate lift kept of the parifhioners buried, as they are fometimes carried elfewhere, and ftrangers brought to Kilmany. The average number of marriages is 8; but of thefe one of the parties frequently belongs to another diftrict.

† Several families are Seceders from the Eftablifhed Church, and affemble at a place of worfhip within the parifh.

‡ Their number may be ftated about 4 at an average, and their annual income L. 24, 10 s.

mankind arife from hence. The rich are roufed to take
that care of their brethren, which anticipates the wifhes of
the needy, which is man's beſt acquifition, and a fource of
pure enjoyment; while the poor lofe not that withdraw-
ing, declining modeſty, to which it is fo pleafant to afford
affiſtance. Of both, fuch is the prefent ſtate of feelings and
manners, there are here frequent inſtances. The more
wealthy (for the parifh may be divided into feveral large
families under the immediate care of the different farmers)
take a kindly charge of thofe who live under them, and
near them, affifting them very liberally when ficknefs or
age has unfitted them for their fervice. On the other
hand, the reluctance, not merely to folicit, but often even
to receive aid, fhews that delicate fenfe of dignity, which
poverty may fo keenly feel; of which nothing can diveſt a
man but the meannefs of his own foul; and which is much
defiderated amongſt the lazy, diffipated, importunate beggars of large towns.

Religion, &c.—It cannot be foreign from the object of a
Statiſtical Account to mention the influence which religious
principle has within the parifh. Notice of individuals is
often improper and undignified; a general ſtatement of a
point, which, whatever public opinion or practice may pronounce, is of infinite confequence to the ſtability and to
the happinefs of fociety, no man, whatever the ſtatement
might be, fhould be afhamed or afraid to make. It is
grateful to give a favourable ſtatement. Religion will be
found here to be much more than mere fpeculation; it has
great influence on the conduct; it concurs, with unfeducing
fituation, to preferve the manners fimple, and to make the
morals pure; and it yields fupport in the hour of diſtrefs,
which the ſtouteſt hearts might wifh to have. Calm, placid refignation, in the certain profpect of approaching diffolution,

folution, affords an example of true heroifm, which philofophy might be proud to reach. But it is heroifm, arifing
from a caufe that well accounts for it, in minds which have
no incitement, from vanity, of the poor defire of impofing
on the world, to affume the appearance of fortitude which
they do not feel. It is the confequence of religion; of
their firm belief of a better ftate of exiftence; and of their
hope of what a good man will in that ftate enjoy for ever.
Patriotifm furely cannot wifh for a more fubftantial trea-
fure to the country, the intereft of whofe inhabitants fhe is
defirous to promote, than that the purifying influence of
true religion fhould prevail amongft them; nor deprecate a
greater evil, than the petulant prefumptuous licentioufnefs,
which tolerates no reafonable, no virtuous reftraints, which
holds thefe up to ridicule, and labours to make them difre-
garded.

PARISH OF KILRENNEY.

By the Rev. Mr WILLIAM BEAT.

Name, Situation, Extent, and Soil.

THE name of this parish seems to be derived from the saint to whom the church was dedicated, viz. St Irenaeus, Bishop of Lyons, whose fame for piety was at that time great throughout Christendom. What serves to confirm this origin of the name is, that the fishermen, who have marked out the steeple of this church for a meath or mark to direct them at sea, call it St Irnie to this day; and the estate which lies close by the church is called Irniehill; but, by the transposition of the letter i, Rinnie-hill. What adds to the probability of this interpretation, is a tradition still existing here, that the devotees at Anstruther, who could not see the church of Kilrenney till they travelled up the rising ground to what they called the Hill, then pulled off their bonnets, fell on their knees, crossed themselves, and prayed to St Irnie.

This parish lies in the county and synod of Fife, and presbytery of St Andrews. It is about 2 miles long, and 2 broad, almost in the form of a circle, somewhat elliptical on the coast. It is bounded by Crail on the east; Anstruther on the west;

Deninno

Deninno on the north; and one continued ridge of black rocks, that ſet bounds to the ſea, on the ſouth. The ground riſes gradually from ſouth to north, and forms ſuch a declivity as is a barrier to inundation. After a ſtorm, abundance of ſea weeds are thrown on the ſhore, which ſerve for manure. The land, at an average, lets at 40 s. an acre.

Fiſh.—The incumbent was born, and has ſpent the greateſt part of his life, in this pariſh ; and, within his remembrance, vaſt quantities of large cod, ling, haddocks, herrings, holibut, turbot, and mackarel, have been caught here; but the fiſheries are now miſerably decayed. He can remember, when he was a young man, that he numbered no leſs than 50 large fiſhing boats, that required 6 men each, belonging to the town of Cellardykes, all employed in the herring fiſhery in the ſummer ſeaſon. He can recollect that he ſaw ſuch a number of boats throwing their nets at one time as he could not number, but heard that the Collector of the Cuſtoms at Anſtruther at that time, who kept an account of them, ſaid they amounted to 500, being gathered together from all quarters to this ſhore; and the winter fiſhery was proportionally great. He has ſeen 10 or 12 large boats come into the harbour in one day, ſwiming to the brim with large cod, beſides 30, 40, or 50, ſtrung upon a rope faſtened to the ſtern, which they took in tow ; and, what will hardly be credited, many a large cod's head lying for dung on the land. At that time, a gentleman in Dunbar had the largeſt cod in tack for 4 d. each, on this proviſo, that every inhabitant of the pariſh ſhould be at liberty to pick the beſt fiſh for their own uſe at his price; and of all the thouſands he ever ſaw, the largeſt were bought for 4 d. At that time, he remembered no leſs than 24 ſmall brewers in the town of Cellardykes, probably ſo called from a range of cellars along the
ſhore,

shore, built for preparing fish for exportation, but now they are reduced to two or three, owing to the decay of the fishery. So strong is the contrast between that time and this, that not only few or no fish are caught, but, to the amazement of every body, the haddocks seem to have deserted this coast; and for two years past it has become a rarity to see one.

Population.—The population of this parish has considerably decreased within these 30 years. According to Dr Webster's state of the population, the number of inhabitants was 1348. The numbers have been diminished by the decay of the fishery and the union of farms.

33 families consist of	1 person	33
49	2	98
46	3	138
44	4	176
29	5	145
19	6	114
10	7	70
11	8	88
4	9	36
6	10	60
1	11	11
5	12	60
1	13	13
2	14	28
1	16	16

261 families   inhabitants 1086

Annual

Annual average of births from 1770 to 1790   .   34
Males born in the preceding period   . .   331
Females 350
Annual average of deaths during the ſame period   . 20
Males who died   177
Females   235

Prices of Proviſions. — The incumbent remembers, that, when the fiſhermen uſed to lay up their winter proviſions, they bought beef for a merk Scots a ſtone ; a good hen was got for 4 d. ; a pound of butter for 3½ d. ; and other victuals in proportion : Now, 4 d. a pound is paid at all ſeaſons of the year for beef, mutton, veal, lamb, and pork ; a pound of butter coſts 8 d. ; a hen 1 s. ; and the price of geeſe, ducks, &c. is proportionally raiſed.

Stipend, &c. — The value of the ſtipend, including the glebe, amounts to L. 100 Sterling. Sir John Anſtruther of Anſtruther is patron. Of 9 heritors only 3 reſide. The manſe was originally built by Mr James Melvil, an eminent reformer. On the lower lentile of the higheſt window, which directly overlooks the town, he ordered this inſcription to be made, " The Watch Tower," which remains diſtinct to this day.

Rent. — The valued rent is L. 8470 Scots. The real rent is difficult to be preciſely aſcertained ; but it may be ſtated at L. 2195 Sterling.

School. — The ſchoolmaſter is accommodated with a neat little houſe, fronting the public ſtreet, containing a ſchool room and kitchen on the ground floor, 2 rooms and a cloſet above, with a garret, and a ſmall piece of ground before the
door,

door, inclosed for a garden. His salary, as schoolmaster, and perquisites as precentor and session-clerk, amount to about L. 11 Sterling, besides what he can make of school fees, which are here very small. The number of scholars is about 50 or 60, at 1s. 2d. a quarter for English ; writing 1s. 6d.; writing and arithmetic 2s. 6d.; Latin 3s. which few are disposed to learn.

Antiquities.—On the eastern extremity of the parish, at the very verge of the sea mark, is a cave, which seems to have been the habitation of some solitary saint in the days of old. The successive tenants of this mansion have left figures of crosses, rudely cut, here and there. It has been converted into a barn, and is large enough to admit two threshers at a time.

TOWN AND PARISH OF KINGHORN.

(COUNTY AND SYNOD OF FIFE, PRESBYTERY OF KIRKCALDY.)

By the Rev. Mr. JOHN USHER.

Situation, Name, Extent, Soil, &c.

THE town of Kinghorn, is pleafantly fituated upon a declivity on the N. fide of the Frith of Forth, nearly oppofite to the town of Leith, and diftant from it about 7 miles. At what time this town was firft built, it is perhaps, impoffible for us, at prefent, to determine. It is not improbable, that the aborigines of the country, would fettle here, at a very early period, for the conveniency of fifhing *, even before either commerce, or agriculture, or pafturage, had become objects of attention to their uncultivated minds. However this may be, it is next to certain, that when Edinburgh began to rife into a capital, and to become a place of refort, fifhermen

---

* There was formerly a confiderable quantity of fifh caught between the town of Kinghorn and the ifland of Inch-Keith ; but of late the fifh have retired nearer to the mouth of the Frith.

fiſhermen and ſailors would naturally be induced to build and take up their reſidence here for the ſake of ſerving the paſſage between Fife and Leith, the port of Edinburgh *. With reſpeĉt to the origin of the name of this town, we have not been able to diſcover any thing certain, and will therefore venture to offer a conjeĉture. Upon a riſing ground, immediately behind the town, overlooking it, and commanding a view of the whole Frith of Forth, from Kinghorn downwards, and of all the oppoſite coaſt, there formerly ſtood a caſtle, the ruins of which were very lately to be ſeen, which was one of the ordinary ſeats of our ancient Kings. This place of reſidence was probably choſen by the Scottiſh Monarchs, not only for the ſake of the proſpeĉt which it commands, and the ſalubrity of the air, but for the conveniency and pleaſure of hunting. For, tradition ſays, and the names of places in the neighbourhood confirm it (ſuch as Woodfieldpark, and Kingſwood-end †) that the ground behind the town, and to the weſtward, was once covered with wood. From the winding, therefore, of the King's horn, when ſallying out with his attendants to take the diverſion of the chaſe;

---

* In confirmation of this, we may obſerve, that the part of the town which ſtands upon the ſea-ſhore, and neareſt to the harbour, is evidently the oldeſt. So early, as about the middle of the 11th century, in the reign of Duncan I. we are informed that Canutus King of Norway, ſent a large fleet with 9000 men, commanded by his brother, who landing at Kinghorn, over-ran and ravaged the adjacent country; but that M'Beath, Thane of Fife (with whoſe charaĉter and hiſtory every admirer of the inimitable Shakeſpeare muſt be in ſome meaſure acquainted) attacked and defeated them with great ſlaughter, forcing the ſurvivors to retire to their ſhips. It was not, however, till near a century after this, that the town of Kinghorn was inveſted with the privileges of a royal burgh, by King David I.

† Woodfield-park, Kingſwood-end. The former of theſe is a farm about a mile to the W. of the town, the latter is a high and rugged rock, at much about the ſame diſtance from the town, and on the ſame ſide of it, where King Alexander III. was killed by a fall from his horſe when hunting in this foreſt.

chafe, the town of Kinghorn may have derived the name which it ftill bears.

The parifh of Kinghorn is about 4 miles in length, and 3½ in breadth. It is bounded by the Frith of Forth on the S. and E. *. Few places are more beautifully diverfified than the face of this parifh. It exhibits, it is true, neither lofty mountains nor deep valleys; neither high hills, nor extenfive plains; but there is a variety of foil and of furface, and an undulation of ground, which is very feldom to be met with. The long extended fides of little hills covered with furze, ever-green, and almoft always in bloom, or planted with young and thriving trees of different kinds; the rich and fertile land that lies between the great number of gentlemen's feats and farmer's houfes, with trees and enclofures around them, and with here and there a ruin interfperfed, as mementos of the viciffitude of human things, prefent to the eye a moft picturefque and fanciful fcene, and produce upon the imagination the fineft effect. The foil is, in general, very good, being moftly a·rich black earth upon a rotten rock. Along the fea-coaft, for upwards of 2 miles, it is deep, ftrong, and fertile in the higheft degree. As you retire from the fea, it gradually becomes more and more light and fhallow, for about a mile, as the ground rifes. Behind this, the ground begins to fall, and the nature of the foil becomes more variable, being fome of it inclined to clay, upon a whin-ftone bottom, but moft of it, thin and light upon a dry gravel. Almoft every where throughout the whole parifh, it is fharp and very fertile, when properly managed.

Antiquities, Natural Curiofities, and Mineral Waters.— There can fcarcely be faid to be any antiquities within the
bounds

---

* The extent of fea-coaft is about 3 Englifh miles, the greater part of it is high and rocky, and produces very little kelp.

bounds of this parish, unless perhaps the ruinous tower of Seafield, the ancient seat of the Moutrays, which stands upon the sea-shore, about a mile to the eastward of Kinghorn; and St. Leonard's tower, which stands in the middle of the town, which in times of Popery was a place of worship, but is now converted into a town-house and common prison, deserve to be so called. Glammis tower, a seat of our ancient kings, already alluded to, is now no more; and as for the monastery which stood somewhere about the bottom of the town, there is not so much as a vestige of it to be seen, and even the place where once it was, cannot be ascertained. At a little distance from the ruins of Seafield tower, there is a large cave, which appears either to have been formed by some violent concussion of the earth, or to have been excavated by the sea, which has since retired. There is the appearance of some kind of building having been once at its entrance; but whether it had been thus fortified and secured as a place of refuge from the sudden descents of the Danes and Norwegians, with which this coast was formerly so much infested, or, as a den for thieves and robbers, and as a place for concealing their ill-got booty, we have not been able to discover. About half way between Kinghorn and the Petty-cur *, close by the sea, there is a specimen of the Basaltes, which well deserves the attention of the curious, who may not have had an opportunity of surveying those more stupendous works of nature of the same kind, the Giants Causeway, in the county of Antrim in Ireland, or the rock Pereneire near St. Sandoux in Auvergne, in France. The Basaltic columns are of different diameters, with between 4, 5, 6, 7, faces. They are, in general, about 12 or 14 feet in height,

---

* Petty-cur, a small harbour for the passage-boats at the distance of about ¼ of a mile from the town, to the S. W.

height, with a few joints or cracks in each, all parallel to one another, and inclining towards the fea, to the E. The ſtream of lava, of which this maſs' of matter is compoſed, appears to have flowed from W. to E., and pouring into the fea, in this direction, from its impulſe and refiſtance, to have cooled, and chryſtalized, and taken the eaſterly inclination which it holds. At a little diſtance from the Petty-cur, there is a medicinal ſpring, commonly called the Kinghorn Spa *.

Upon Inch-Keith, a ſmall iſland about half way between Kinghorn and Leith, and which is confidered as belonging to this pariſh, there are the ruins of a fort which was in repair in the reign of Mary Queen of Scotland, and which was then garriſoned with French ſoldiers.

Population.—Upon comparing the late with the preſent ſtate of the population of this pariſh, the number of inhabitants appears to have decreaſed to a confiderable degree. According to the returns made to Dr. Webſter in the 1755, the number of ſouls within the bounds of this pariſh, was 2389. It now amounts to no more than 1768, including perſons of

every

* In the year 1618, the celebrated Dr. Anderſon, inventor of the pills that ſtill go by his name, wrote a Treatiſe upon the nature and properties of this water, with directions for uſing it.

It is impregnated, he ſays, with chryſtal, gypſum, and nitre; is a powerful diuretic, gives vigour and ſtrength to debilitated conſtitutions, relieves ſuch as are troubled with a difficulty of breathing, and allayeth all inflammations internal and external; that it ought to be taken in the morning faſting, and taken at the rock from which it iſſues.

But, for farther particulars, both with reſpect to the nature and properties of this water, and the way of uſing it, we muſt refer the reader to the foreſaid Treatiſe. We ſhall only add, that Dr. Anderſon concludes his account of it, with informing us, that in his time, " this fair ſpring" was much frequented; and that he himſelf had many opportunities of obſerving its ſalutary effects, from his attending patients that were drinking the water.

every age and denomination *. Of the preſent inhabitants of
this pariſh, there are 1118, that reſide in the town, and 650
that dwell in the country, and in a village called the Bridgetown, about 2 miles N. E. from Kinghorn. Of theſe, there
are 1237 that adhere to the Eſtabliſhed Church, the remaining 531, are Seceders of different denominations, but moſtly
Burghers. Of the whole body of the people, both in the
town and country, there are, under 10 years of age, 401 ;
between 10 and 20, 321 ; between 20 and 50, 778 ; between
50 and 70, 240 : and between 70 and 100, 28. The number
of married people amounts to 610 ; of bachelors, to 295 ; of
unmarried women from the age of 15 and upwards, to 323 ;
of widows, to 102 ; and of widowers, to 33. The number
of marriages for the laſt 10 years, amounts, at an average,
to 13 ; and that of births, to 30 annually. To account for
the ſeeming diſproportion between the marriages and births,
and the population of this pariſh, we may obſerve, that there
are annually, ſeveral irregular marriages, and ſeveral baptiſms (particularly among the Seceders) that are not entered
in the pariſh regiſter. The inhabitants of the town, and of
the village called Bridgetown, are moſtly ſailors, weavers,
tradeſmen,

---

* As we do not find, that by the return given in to Dr. Webſter, above men_
tioned, a diſtinction was made between the population of the town, and of the
country, it is impoſſible for us now to diſcover with certainty, where the deficiency lies ; whether in the one, or in the other ; or ſuppoſing it in both, in
what proportion it has taken place. We are diſpoſed to think that it is principally in the latter ; and that it may be accounted for, from the following
cauſes :—1ſt, From the diminution of landed proprietors reſiding in the pariſh ;
ſeveral ſmall eſtates having been ſwallowed up by the larger. 2dly, From the
union of farms. 3dly, And principally from the expulſion of cottagers, and
from the employing of hired ſervants in their ſtead, for carrying on the operations of huſbandry. What the town may have loſt in reſpect of population, from
the decay of its trade, we conſider as compenſated by the growth of manufactures, as will afterward appear under the article of commerce.

tradefmen, innkeepers, and horfe-hirers ; thofe of the country, farmers, their children, and fervants, who are employed
in agriculture.

Ecclefiaftical State, Stipend, Poor, &c.—There are two places of public worfhip in the town of Kinghorn ; the parifh
church, and a Burgher-feceder meeting-houfe. The Earl of
Strathmore is patron of the parifh. The ftipend confifts of 3
chalders of victual, half meal, half bear, and 58 l. 6 s. 8 d. in
money, together with 4 loads of coal, deliverable at the manfe,
and the teind of the fifh: The laft of thefe articles has failed entirely, as there is no more at prefent, but one family of
fifhers in the town, and the quantity of fifh caught fo fmall,
that the teind thereof is not worth the trouble or expenfe of
collecting it.

There is alfo mentioned in the decreet of modification and
locality of the ftipend of Kinghorn, 14¼ loads of coal at the
pit of Carden ; but as this pit is not now wrought, this part
of the living has likewife failed. The glebe confifts of very
little more than 3¼ acres of arable ground, with 10 s. a-year
to compenfate for the deficiency of meafure ; and about an a-
cre of grafs, which lets at 16 s. 8 d. The manfe is old, but
got a thorough repair about 3 years ago, at a very confiderable expenfe. The church was rebuilt in 1774. The fhell
of the houfe is refpectable enough ; but within, it has rather
an awkward and paltry appearance, from its not being as yet
completely feated, and from the mixture of new, and of old
pews and forms *.

The

---

* The Burgher meeting-houfe was built about 16 years ago, partly by diffa-
tisfied and difcontented Seeeders ; and partly by people belonging to the Eftablifhed Church in this place, who did not think that the late incumbent, Dr.
Webfter, was fufficiently warm in his zeal againft the Popifh bill, which raifed
fuch a noife and clamour in this part of the country at that period.

This

The number of poor is great, and the funds for supporting them are, comparatively, but small. There are commonly between 60 and 80 upon the poor's roll; and for maintaining these, the whole sum to be distributed annually by the church-session, does not amount to 40 l. This sum arises partly from the interest of legacies left for the behoof of the poor; and partly from the collections that are made for them at the door of the parish church. The legacies amount to 500 l., 400 l. of which was bequeathed by the Rev. Mr. Henry, minister of this parish, before the late Dr. Webster; and 100 l. by a gentleman of the name of Shanks, who lived in Kinghorn; for both which, the church-session receives annually (at the rate of 4 per cent. interest) the sum of 20 l. The yearly collections do not come to quite so much; and of this the landed proprietors contribute but a very small proportion, as the greatest part of them do not reside in the parish, and as most of those that do, dwell at a distance from the parish church. The most which any pauper in the parish receives, (and indeed which the church-session have it in their power to give, as the heritors have not as yet agreed to assess themselves for the maintenance of the poor) is 1 s. a-month; and perhaps 3 s. 6 d. more at each of the quarterly distributions. This scanty

---

This house was at first connected with what is called the Presbytery of Relief; upon which footing it stood, till within these few years, when the proprietors of the house, finding their meeting upon the decline, and the seat-rents and collections unequal to the expense of supporting a clergyman, and of paying the interest of the money which they had advanced, they very prudently agreed to change their ground, to join themselves to the Burgher Seceders, and to give a call to a licentiate of that denomination. The bulk of what remained of their scattered congregation went along with them, and they were joined by others of the same class or sect, residing in the town and its neighbourhood. Amidst all these manoeuvres of their leaders, however, the name of a patron was not heard of. And it was all very well.

scanty supply is evidently inadequate to the exigencies of such as are unable to work ; the consequence of which is, that they must either beg, or steal, or starve. What others receive is proportionally less; and thus, even the labour of such as could do a little, were the deficiency of their earnings to be made up to them by regular supplies, is lost to the community, from their being forced by necessity to have recourse to begging; after which, every idea of labour and industry is at an end *.

Commerce and Manufactures.—The town of Kinghorn has 2 harbours ; one at the bottom of the town, which is called the Kirk-harbour, from its vicinity to the church, which stands upon a point of land close by it ; and another called the Petty-cur, at about half a mile's distance from the town to the S. W. The former of these is of very ancient date : How

old

* And here, by the way, we cannot help observing, that legacies left for the behoof of the poor, at least in parishes, where the law, with respect to the maintenance of the poor is not enforced, have a tendency to defeat the very end for which they were bequeathed. For that, trusting to these, the heritors of such parishes, are apt to neglect what the law, what reason, what religion and humanity so loudly call upon them for, viz. " to consider the cause of the poor." We would not be understood, from what we have here said, either to condemn, or discourage the donations of the charitable at the time of their death, to the poor of parishes to which they may belong, or to which they may be attached; only let them be left in such a way, as to be distributed immediately, and not be hung up, so as to intercept that provision which the wisdom and benevolence of our Legislature has made for them. Having had occasion to mention legacies, we may here observe, that the foresaid Mr. Henry bequeathed the sum of 300 l. for the purpose of founding a bursary, to assist young men, in the prosecution of their studies, at the University of St. Andrew's. The nomination of the bursar is vested in 3 bodies of men; the magistrates and town-council of Kinghorn, the kirk-session of Kinghorn, and the presbytery of Kirkcaldy. Each of these 3 bodies choose a delegate out of their own number; the delegates meet by appointment of the minister of Kinghorn, and, after having examined the qualifications of the candidates, proceed to the election. The bursar enjoys his benefice for 4 years.

old it is, we cannot certainly ſay. The latter was built about 30 years ago, as being a more convenient ſituation than that of the former, for the paſſage over to Leith. This harbour was lately very much choked up, and in danger of being loſt, from the great quantity of ſand continually drifting from the W. at low water, with the weſterly winds, and accumulating within it. But by means of 2 baſons, the largeſt of which was only finiſhed within theſe few months, (the former having been found inſufficient for the purpoſe), it is now thought that this bank of ſand will be completely removed, and the harbour be kept clear of it, and open for the future. Within theſe few months alſo, there has been a light-houſe erected upon the end of this key, for the benefit of the paſſage-boats. It is, however, the opinion of many, that had the money which has been expended upon the Petty-cur, and its baſons, been laid out upon the extending of the key, and upon the otherwiſe improving of the old harbour, not only all the purpoſes of the Ferry might have been equally well anſwered, but a ſafe and capacious baſon might have been formed, for the admiſſion of ſhips of conſiderable burthen. As they are at preſent, neither the one nor the other will admit veſſels of above 150 tons. Should ever Kinghorn become a great manufacturing and commercial town, this plan might ſtill be put in execution. Hitherto, it cannot be ſaid to have ever been either. Formerly, indeed, there were a few brigs, and ſeveral ſloops belonging to this town ; but theſe were generally either freighted by merchants reſiding in other places, or engaged in ſmuggling. At preſent there are only two ſmall ſloops employed in the coaſting trade, that ſail from this port, with 9 paſſage-boats, of about 50 or 60 tons each, and a few pinnaces that ply the ferry. As for manufactures, though till of late, ſince the introduction of ſtocking-frames, there was, for a long time, a conſiderable quantity of thread-ſtock-

ings

ings, manufactured annually by the women, with the kitting-needle, yet it was always but an unprofitable, and poor employment. Within thefe few years, however, a manufacture has fprung up, which promifes fair at prefent to render Kinghorn one of the moft flourifhing towns upon the coaft of Fife; this is, the teafing, and rolling, and fpinning of cotton and flax, by means of the Arkwright and Darlington machinery.

Through the middle of the town there runs a ftream of water, which iffues from a lake called the loch of Kinghorn, and diftant from it only about half a mile. Upon this ftream there have already been erected, and fet a-going, 4 mills for the purpofes above mentioned; a fifth is to be built this fummer, and there might ftill be falls of water found for 1 or 2 more. The number of hands which thefe mills will employ, muft amount to fome hundreds; but the 2 largeft of them, which were built laft feafon, owing to the fhock which has been lately given to public credit, and the confequent ftagnation of all bufinefs, have not as yet been completely fitted up, and filled with machinery by the proprietors. Before adventuring too far, they wifh to fee what turn affairs may take. Already, however, the beneficial effects of thefe works are to be feen by all; and they are fenfibly felt by almoft every defcription of people in the place.

Young women, who before were not able to earn by the needle, or by the knitting of ftockings, or by the fpinning of flax, above 1 s. 6 d. or 2 s. in the week, can now eafily earn between 5 s. and 7 s. 6 d. in the fame fpace of time. Little girls, between 8 and 12 years of age, who before were a burthen to their fathers and mothers, by engaging at thefe works, are not only able to fupport themfelves, but to affift their aged and indigent parents. The boys, who before thought of nothing but the fea, or of running about idle, or, which was little better, of running about the country at the horfes's heels,

as

as horſe-hirers ſervants, have now generally turned their attention to the loom, and bind themſelves as apprentices to the
weaver. Such are the effects of capital well employed ! Such
are the effects of regular and well directed induſtry ! But the
command of water for working machinery, is not the only
advantage which Kinghorn enjoys : Beſides the ſtream already mentioned, there are two other rivulets, one at each end
of the town, by means of which bleachfields might be formed,
and, it is to be hoped, will in a little time be formed, for farther facilitating the operations of the manufacturer.

As a beginning has now been fairly made ; as a ſpirit of
induſtry and of enterpriſe has now been rouſed, by the exertions of a few active individuals, it is to be hoped, that it
will continue to ſpread, and will ſoon begin to operate in o-
ther directions. The cheapneſs of coal for fuel, and of lime
for building ; its vicinity to the ſea, and to the capital of this
part [of the kingdom, might alſo have been mentioned among
the advantages which Kinghorn derives from its local ſituation.

Landholders, Rent and Diviſion of Land.—The number of
landed proprietors in this pariſh is 13 ; but by far the greater
part of them do not reſide in it. There is no map of the pariſh ; by conſequence, the number of acres which it contains
cannot be exactly aſcertained. But they amount to nearly
3050 arable, and 340 inarable. The greateſt part of the latter is hill-ground, either covered with furze, or planted with
trees. Of the former, there are, at an average, 170 acres annually employed in raiſing wheat, 397 in barley, 212 in peaſe
and beans, which are commonly ſown in drills ; 749 in oats,
148 in potatoes, 110 in turnip, 328 in hay, 836 in paſture,
and 100 lying in ſummer fallow. The quantity of flax ſown
is ſo inconſiderable, as not to be worth the mentioning. A
great

great part of the land of this parish is now enclosed, either with hedge and ditch, or, what is called Galloway-dike. The farms are, in general, from 80 l. to 200 l. a-year, consisting of between 60 and 150 or 200 acres. The best arable ground in the neighbourhood of the town, has, of late, let at 3 l., and some of it at 3 l. 10 s. an acre. At a distance from the town, the average rent is about 1 l. 10 s. The best pasturage lets at 2 l. 5 s., and the inferior kind, from 15 s. to 1 l. 1 s the acre. The valued rent of the whole parish is 13,280 l. 18 s. 2 d. Scotch; the real rent about 5000 l. Sterling.

Horses, Black Cattle, Ploughs and Carts.—There are in this parish 250 horses, including young horses reared by the farmers in the country. About 70 of these horses are kept by people in the town for post-chaises, for letting out to hire, for carrying coals, and for labouring a few acres of ground, which most of them endeavour to get in the neighbourhood. There are 651 cows, and young cattle (exclusive of cattle grazed in parks during the summer), 99 carts and 91 ploughs, almost all of the Small-construction, and drawn by 2 horses; the old Scottish plough having now fallen into general disuse*.

School.

---

* *Wages.*—From the rapid increase of manufactures in this, and some neighbouring parishes, the price of labour of every kind has risen to an uncommon height. The wages of a male servant kept in the house, are from 8 l. to 10 l. a-year; those of female servants are generally 3 l. A labourer, for the day, gets from 1 s. to 1 s. 6 d., finding his own provisions: For mowing and reaping, from 1 s. 4 d. to 2 s., and sometimes 2 s. 6 d. Or, with breakfast and dinner, from 1 s. to 1 s. 6 d.: And women from 9 d. to 1 s., with the same provisions.

Effects of discontinuing Cottagers in Agriculture.—One bad effect of this has been already alluded to; the decrease of the population of the country. This effect begins now to be felt, and lamented by the farmer, particularly in the neighbourhood of manufacturing towns. In this whole parish, where this description

School.—The ſchoolmaſter's ſalary, paid wholly by the town, is 100 merks Scotch ; the number of ſcholars is about 60 ; the fees for teaching to read Engliſh, 1 s. 6 d. a quarter, reading and writing, 2 s., Latin, 2 s. 6 d., arithmetic, 2 s. 6 d. The ſchoolmaſter has alſo an official houſe, with a ſmall garden, provided for him by the town. And here, we cannot help obſerving with regret, that a body of men, ſo highly uſeful to the community as country ſchoolmaſters, that a body of men, from whoſe ſucceſsful labours Scotland has derived that reputation for literature which ſhe ſo deſervedly enjoys ; and upon whoſe future labours, the preſervation of this reputation, and the proſperity of her ſons, in every quarter of the globe, muſt in a great meaſure depend, ſhould be, in general, ſo poorly provided for by the country.—" Sic vos, non vobis."

Character of the People.—The general character of a people commonly takes its complexion from their local ſituation, their engagements and their purſuits. The public ferry may juſtly be conſidered as having been hitherto the ruin of Kinghorn, both in reſpect of induſtry and morals. It opens, it is true, an eaſy road to an immediate ſubſiſtence, but it introduces, at the ſame time, all thoſe vices and miſeries to which people are expoſed, whoſe time is not half occupied, whoſe thoughts are never

turned

ſcription of innocent and uſeful people was once ſo numerous, there is only 1 farmer, who, patriarch-like, has continued this practice of employing and cheriſhing the cottager, in its full extent ; and in this, he is now become the envy of all his neighbours around him ; eſpecialy in bad harveſts, ſuch as we have lately had, when reapers could not be tempted to come from the towns even for high wages. There are other effects, which might likewiſe be ſtated, as ariſing from the ſubſtitution of hired ſervants in the place of Cottagers, viz. the diminution of the quantity, and conſequently the riſe of the price of ſeveral uſeful article of life, ſuch as butter, eggs, and poultry.

turned towards the acquisition of capital, and whose ldom look beyond the present moment. Drunkenness, dissipation, and debauchery in youth, poverty and wretchedness in old age ; and, besides this, to say nothing of the tendency of burgh-politics, the scum of the creation continually floating here, cannot fail to taint whatever it touches. All the banditti and vagabonds of the country continually passing and repassing through this great thorough-fair, and occasionally stopping, and lodging for days and weeks together, cannot fail to poison the principles, and to corrupt the morals of those with whom they mingle, and among whom they nestle. Not but that there are exceptions to be found, even among those that are the most exposed to these temptations. Not but that there are many here, as sober, as industrious, and as respectable in their several stations as in any other place. Even where the plague rages with the greatest virulence, there are always some that escape the fatal infection. And here we must do justice to a class of men, whom we have frequently had occasion to hear represented as drunken, rude, and insolent to a proverb ; we mean the boatmen. That some such there are, we readily admit ; but at the same time we will venture to affirm, that there is not in the island, nor perhaps in Europe, a public ferry, where the watermen are, in general, more active, more civil, and more obliging. If to the rough and insolent, they sometimes behave with rudeness, the fault, surely, is not entirely theirs. To their skill and activity, and even general sobriety, it may, in some measure, be attributed, that there is not an instance of so much as one of these boats having been lost, within the memory of man, or even upon record. With respect to the inhabitants of the country parish, who are mostly employed in the cultivation of land, we may observe, that they are, in general, a sober, industrious, and charitable people,

ple, ſeveral of them intelligent and ſkilful in their profeſſion, and that, amidſt all the corruption of rotten and rotting burghs in the neighbourhood, they ſtill retain much of that ſimplicity of life, and purity of manners, which renders paſtoral deſcription ſo pleaſing to contemplate.

PARISH of KINGLASSIE,

(COUNTY OF FIFE.)

By the Rev. Mr JAMES REID.

Name, Situation, Surface, Soil, &c.

IT is the opinion of fome, that the name is originally
Gaelic, and expreffive of the fituation ; others trace it
from a faint, whofe name was *Glafs*, and point out a well
of fine water, called St Glafs's well. The parifh is fituated in the prefbytery of Kirkaldy, and Synod of Fife.
The extent from W. to E. is about 4 computed miles, and
2 from N. to S. Its form is nearly a parallelogram, and
it is bounded on the W. by part of Portmoak, Ballingry,
and Auchterderran ; on the E. by part of Markinch and
Dyfart ; on the N. by the river of Leven, and part of
Portmoak and Leflie ; on the S. by part of Dyfart and
Auchterderran. The diftrict is partly flat on the banks of
Lochty and Ore, two fmall rivulets ; at a fmall diftance
from which, the ground has a regular afcent, and forms 2
ridges. The foil is partly light loam, and partly ftrong
clay, with rich meadows on the banks of the rivers. The
ftreams would abound with excellent trout, were the people reftrained from watering their flax in them. The Leven

ven produces trout of the ſame quality with thoſe in Loch-leven, with pike and ſome ſalmon. The air in the flat part of the pariſh is damp, and often occaſions rheuma-tiſms. There are many ſtone quarries and coal mines. Coal is the only fuel. The mine preſently worked is eſteemed the beſt burning coal in Fife. The coals are ſold on the hill at 6 d. the load, each load weighing 22 ſtone Dutch weight. There are 2 moors, both covered with ſtones, heath, and furze; but being commonties, no attempt is made to divide or bring them into a better ſtate, which might be done at ſmall expence.

Population.—At the time of Dr Webſter's report, the numbers were 998. Population has not varied much theſe 20 years. The number of ſouls was then about 1200, and does not at this day exceed it. Though the inhabitants of the village have increaſed from 150 to 250, the other parts of the pariſh have ſuffered a proportionable decreaſe, from a number of the ſmall farms being thrown into one. Births are nearly 25 or 30 annually ; but as the half of the heads of families adhere to ſome or other of the Sectaries, the births of their children cannot be well aſcertained ; as few of them are inclined to have their names recorded in the pariſh regiſter, which ſubjects them to a ſmall expence. There are 34 farms in this pariſh, beſides cottagers and feuers. The trades are weavers, employed by the manu-facturers in the coaſt towns, with maſons, &c.

Agriculture, &c.—Plantations are in a very proſperous ſtate in many places. The extent of the pariſh is about 6000 acres nearly. The whole rent in money and victual is about L. 3000 yearly. There is ſcarcely one-third of the land in tillage. Above two-thirds in paſturage. The pariſh is ſuffi-cient to ſupply itſelf in proviſions, and can ſend to maket about

about 200 black cattle, and 40 horfes annually, befides wheat, barley, and oat-meal to a confiderable amount. The breed of cattle is greatly improved in fize and quality. Oxen, after ploughing is over, fell at L. 20, and fome at L. 24 the yoke, for putting on grafs-fields. The breed of draught horfes is alfo much improved within thefe 20 years, owing to the particular attention of Major Aytoun of Inchdairnie, who fent down from England the beft ftallions and Flanders mares ever feen in this part of the country. Formerly each farmer kept or bred fheep; but now there are none, except a few ewes and lambs for the ufe of families, owing to the general practice of inclofing with ditch and hedge and Galloway dikes, and laying down the inclofed fields with grafs-feeds. Nearly 1800 cattle, including horfes, are paftured here annually. There are fown with lintfeed from 80 to 100 acres; with oats and barley about 1200; with wheat above 120. Potatoes, turnip and fummer fallow, occupy 200. Oats and peas are fown in March, lintfeed in middle of April, barley from end of April to end of May.

Stipend, Poor, &c.—The living is 6 chalders victual, 3 bear, and 3 meal, with L. 40 money. The Countefs of Rothes has the patronage. The church was repaired in 1773, and the manfe rebuilt in 1774. There are 23 heritors who pay ftipend; of this number 6 are feuers. The feuers only refide.—The ufual number of poor, including their children, are between 30 and 40. They are not allowed to beg, the parifh funds being fufficient for their fubfiftence, and amount in whole to near L. 40 yearly, in land, money and collections.

Prices and Wages.—During fpring and fummer, good beef is fold at 5 d. the pound, veal, mutton and lamb,
from

from 4½ d. to 5 d. and 6 d. all Tron weight, within the bounds of the preſbytery of Kirkaldy. The lower claſs uſe no animal food, but live on meal, potatoes, milk and ſmall beer, with kail.—A common labourer earns 1 s. a-day. Servants wages are of late greatly increaſed. A man ſervant's wages for the plough and cart are from L. 5, 5 s. to L. 7, 7 s. yearly. Maid ſervants from L. 2, 10 s. to L. 3.

Miſcellaneous Obſervations.—There is only one village in this pariſh.—Toll-bars are lately erected.—Rent of land varies with the ſoil and crops. Some acres are let at 5 s. each, others at 15 s. and L. 1, 10 s. ; and when let for lintſeed or potatoes, at L. 3, L. 4, and L. 5. There is a hill called Goat-milk Hill, let 20 years ago at L. 25, for ſome years paſt it rents at L. 120 ; it is 24 acres. The rents of farms are from L. 20 to L. 200, and the higheſt rent is for the moſt part the cheapeſt bargain. Twenty years ago, few farms in this pariſh were incloſed ; now every farm is either incloſed in whole, or in part, to which the people are now perfectly reconciled.—Civilization of manners has made a little progreſs among farmers and the better ſort of inhabitants. The lower claſs ſeem, in a great meaſure, to retain the rough manners and barbarous cuſtoms of their anceſtors, while each vie with the other in expenſive dreſs, often above their ſtation, or what they can ſeldom afford ; which may be occaſioned by their high wages, and reduced prices of home manufactures, as well as a taſte for that ſpecies of luxury.

PARISH of KINGSBARNS,

(COUNTY OF FIFE.)

By the Rev. Mr JAMES BEATSON.

Name, Situation, Soil, Air, &c.

THE pariſh of Kingſbarns originally belonged to Crail, till 1631, when it became a ſeparate cure. I have not been able to obtain any deciſive information as to the origin of the name. The tradition is, that King John uſed frequently to live in a large building called the Caſtle, placed on a ſmall eminence above the beach, and at a quarter of a mile's diſtance, (where the village is now built), had his ſtore-houſes for grain. The remains of the caſtle were taken down ſeveral years ago, and the ſtones were of an immenſe ſize. The pariſh is in the preſbytery of St Andrew's, and Synod of Fife. It lies about 6 Engliſh miles E. of St Andrew's, and is nearly ſquare, being fully 4 Engliſh miles each way. It is bounded on the N. by St Andrew's pariſh; on the W. by Deninno; and on the S. and E. by Crail. The ſoil upon the coaſt is light and ſandy, but now, from proper culture, it bears the ſame grain with the higher grounds, and of equal quality; although the higher grounds are in general deep, ſtrong, black

clay.

clay. Being fo near the fea-coaft, it is natural to imagine
the air is pure, and upon the whole healthy; though I
have often thought the water which comes from the higher
grounds, and ftagnates in the village, occafions nervous fevers, efpecially among young people, and makes epidemical diftempers to rage feverely among us. This eafily might
be prevented, as there is a beautiful and gradual defcent
from the fummit of the higher grounds to the fea-fhore,
and conduits for the water, at little expence, could be
made. The only fpring worthy of notice, is a fteel mineral, which, about 30 or 40 years ago, was reforted to by
many diftreffed with various complaints. Its tafte and
ftrength are the fame with the Peterhead water, fo juftly
famed, but the fpring much greater; fo that, at one period,
what flowed from it, afforded a fufficient quantity of water
for driving a meal-mill.

Population.—At the time of Dr Webfter's report, the
numbers were 871. From the laft ftate of the rolls, the
numbers amounted to 807, of whom 467 refide in the village, and the remaining 340 inhabit the country part of
the parifh. For 30 years back, the annual averages have
been 16 deaths, 22 baptifms, and 6 marriages. There are
about 24 extenfive farmers, whofe families amount to 192
fouls. There are only 11 Seceders.

Wages, Manufactures, Agriculture, &c.—Male fervants
wages, able to hold a plough, are not under L. 5, 10 s. or
L. 6, 6 s.; the overfeer is allowed from L. 10 to L. 12 a-
year. Maid fervants wages are from L. 2 to L 2, 10 s. or
L. 3. The wages given to labourers hired by the day, in
fummer, are 10 d. or 1 s.; in winter 8 d.—The Ofnaburgh
fheeting, and fhirting, is the manufacture carried on in the
village, which is moftly bought by the Dundee merchants.
The

The number of weavers is from 20 to 30; and thefe are the people, at certain feafons of the year, who are alfo employed in the different fifhings. They have greatly the advantage over the fifhers in the coaft towns to the weftward, who, as they are not bred to bufinefs, confequently in ftormy weather, not only are they idle, but half ftarved, while the people here are occupied at their looms, and can earn wages fufficient to maintain their familes.—The people in general are induftrious, much difpofed to humane generous actions, and are well contented with the lot affigned them by Almighty God. The feafaring is preferred to the military life; and there is feldom a feafon but fome of the young men are employed in the Greenland whale-fifhing.—The cattle annually reared will amount to 480; 5 or 6 yoke of thefe were conftantly employed in agriculture by each farmer fome years ago, but horfes are now more generally ufed. At 3 years old, thefe cattle are put upon turnips, and fattened for the butcher; the price they bring varies according to their fize, from L. 11 to L. 12 or L. 14 each. There is no feparate map of the parifh, but multiplying the number of ploughs, which are 50 by 50, the arable acres accurately may be afcertained; 16 of thefe plough-gates furround the village, and each of them pay an annual feu of 9 bolls wheat, 11 bolls of bear, and 8 s. 4 d. The beft arable land is let from L. 1, 15 s. to L. 2, 2 s. the acre, and the inferior from 15 s. to L. 1. The valued rent of the parifh is L. 6353 : 6 : 8 Scots.

Stipend, Poor, &c.—The ftipend, including L. 5 allowed for glebe and foggage, amounts to about L. 85 yearly. The manfe was rebuilt about 28 years ago, and fince that time, has been once and again repaired. The Earl of Crawford is patron.—The average number of poor who receive weekly from the feffion is 12; befides thefe, many indigent

gent families receive occasionally; and the annual sum expended for their relief will amount to L. 22, some years L. 27 Sterling. These weekly poor are all maintained in their own houses, and are not allowed to beg from door to door. The kirk-session is extremely attentive to give them relief, according to their necessities. They provide medical aid for them when sick, and pay the schoolmaster for teaching their children reading, writing, and the common rules of arithmetic. Besides these advantages, their children have an opportunity of attending the Sunday's school, (established about 2 years ago), where the young ones are instructed in the principles of the Christian faith, and are taught to read and write.

Miscellaneous Observations.—Some years ago vast quantities of haddocks were caught, and sold at moderate prices; but few have appeared for these 3 years. Still a few large and small cod, skait and ling, are got, but not in plenty. At certain seasons the lobster-fishing is worthy of attention, and these all go to the London market. The poor suffer much from the want of herring, as they were the chief part of their winter's provision. Early in spring and autumn are the seasons when the herring appear; but such as are caught are bought at exorbitant prices by merchants, who cure them, and send them up the Mediterranean. —There is no account of any battle or sea engagements. Upon the shore, graves are found lined with stones, after the same construction they are met with in many places of Scotland, and supposed to be Danish.—The only remarkable wreck upon this coast happened in October 1761. After a severe storm from N. E. a three masted vessel, Danish built, was driven ashore, and soon went to pieces; not a human creature was found on board.—On the confines of
the

the pariſh, limeſtone has been found in abundance. The quarry belongs to the Honourable Henry Erſkine of New-hall, which he has taken into his own hands, and intends working to a conſiderable extent.

STATISTICAL ACCOUNT

OF

SCOTLAND.

PARISH OF KIRKALDY.

(COUNTY OF FIFE.)

By the Rev. Mr THOMAS FLEMING.

Name, Situation.

THE *town* of Kirkaldy has been called by its prefent name, as far back as there are any records of it. It is fuppofed to have derived its name from the Culdees, (the Keldei as they are often called in the Old Charters), of whom it is faid to have been a cell *. It is fituated in the county of Fife,

---

* This is Sir Robert Sibbald's derivation, in his hiftory of Fife. The word might, with the ufual licence of etymology, be derived from the Gaelic; to which language, a great proportion of the names of places in the neighbourhood, and indeed through the whole of Fife, may unqueftionably be traced. All names of places beginning with Bal, Col, or Cul, Dal, Drum, Dun, Inch, Inner, Auchter, Kil, Kin, Glen, Mon, and Strath, are of Gaelic origin. Thofe beginning with Aber, and Pit, are fuppofed to be Pictifh names, and do not occur beyond the territory which the Picts are thought to have inhabited.

Fife, on the Frith of Forth, about 10 miles north of Edinburgh. It is the feat of one of the four prefbyteries which compofe the provincial fynod of Fife*; and, alternately with Cupar, the ordinary feat of the fynod,

Extent.—The *parifh* of Kirkaldy,. fo called from the town, is a kind of irregular oblong, extending from S. E. to N. W. between 2 and 3 miles, and from N. E. to S. W. about one mile. It is bounded on the S. E. by the Frith, on the N. E, by the parifh of Dyfart, on the N. W. by the parifhes of Dyfart and Achterderran, and on the S. W. by the parifh of Abbotfhall.

This laft parifh, with the exception of 3 farms which belonged to Kinghorn †, was originally a part of the parfonage of Kirkaldy. In 1649, the prefbytery on an application from the heritors, found that a new kirk fhould be erected in the parifh of Kirkaldy, for the accommodation of the parifhioners; and recommended to the Commiffioners of the Parliament for furrenders and tythes, to carry the erection into effect. The next year, the new parifh of Kirkaldy, fince called *Abbotfhall* was erected; and the parifh of Kirkaldy proper, has from that time been confined nearly to the burgh, the burgh acres, and the common land and moor; comprehending, in all, an extent of about 870 Scotch acres.

Afpect of the town.—The town of Kirkaldy is fituated at the foot of a bank, on the fea-fhore, along which it ftretches the whole breadth of the parifh. It is properly but one long ftreet, with a few lanes of fmall extent opening on each fide of it. The principal part of the ftreet appears to have been originally wider than it is now, many of the houfes on both fides

* The other three are, Cupar, St. Andrews, and Dunfermling.
† Eafter and Wefter Touchs, and Weft Bogie.

fides of it fhewing *internal evidence* *, that they have at fome time or other been extended beyond their firft limits, and that the property of individuals has been enlarged by encroachments on that of the community. At prefent, the ftreet is narrow, in fome places inconveniently fo ; winding and irregular ; deformed by the frequent projection of contiguous houfes and ftairs ; and as the traveller daily feels, wretchedly paved †. The houfes are in general mean, aukwardly placed with their ends to the ftreets, and conftructed without any regard to order or uniformity. Of late, however, a better ftile of building has begun to be introduced ; and different fpecimens have been given of an improving tafte in architecture.

Public Buildings, Town-houfe.—The only public buildings worthy of notice are, the town-houfe and the church. The town-houfe, which was rebuilt in 1678, ftands near the middle of the town, and contains the hall in which the magiftrates and council affemble for conducting the ordinary bufinefs of the burgh. Here too the baillies hold a weekly court for judging in queftions between the burgeffes ; and the juftices of the peace have occafional meetings for determining queftions of revenue, and difcuffing petty caufes that are brought before them from the furrounding diftrict. Over the town houfe is the prifon, with feparate apartments for debtors and criminals ; and under it the guard-houfe, the meal-market, and the public weigh-houfe. The whole forms a plain building of hewn-ftone, ornamented with a tower and fpire.

* Strong beams run along the roofs of the rooms, to fupport the place of the front wall, which has been brought forward to increafe the width of the houfes.

† The ftatute labour of the town is now converted, and the produce left to accumulate for new paving the ftreets. Ruinous houfes are in fome inftances rebuilding at fuch a diftance from the ftreet, as to leave it of a decent width.

ſpire. The tower contains the town-clock and bell, and ſerves as a repoſitory for the archives of the burgh.

The Church.—The church ſtands on an elevated ſituation, on the top of the bank, which riſes immediately behind the town. It is a large unſhapely pile, that ſeems to have been reared at different times, to ſuit the growing population of the pariſh, and in the conſtruction of which convenience has been more conſulted than unity of deſign or beauty. The nave or body of the church, is in the antient Gothic, or rather the Norman ſtile of architecture ; without buttreſſes ; with low ſemicircular arches, ſupported by ſhort thick columns, and having aiſles behind them. The choir is fitted up in common with the nave for the reception of the pariſhioners ; and a large wing has been added for their farther accommodation. Cloſe to one end of the church ſtands the ſteeple ; which in its original form was a plain, and not unhandſome ſquare tower with a cornice, above which it was covered with a roof. But it has been raiſed beyond its original height, by the addition of a ſmaller, and a very diſproportionate tower, terminating in a pyramid.

The Sands.—On the one ſide of the town, the ſea is ſeparated from it by a beach of firm and level ſand ; on which the inhabitants have always, excepting at the height of the tide, a ſafe and agreeable walk; and by which the traveller may generally avoid the uneaſy jolting of a long and rugged pavement. As the ſand continues firm and ſmooth, and the ground ſhelves gradually for a great way into the ſea, this place is peculiarly favourable for ſea bathing; for which purpoſe there has been for ſome years an increaſing reſort to it, during the months of ſummer and harveſt.

Aſpect

Aſpect of the Pariſh.——On the other ſide of the town, the
country immediately joins it, and riſes by a gentle but varied
aſcent, almoſt to the oppoſite extremity of the pariſh.——
Taking the pariſh by itſelf, the face of it preſents little to the
view that claims particular notice. In the vicinity of the
town, where the ſoil is light and dry, and very ſuſceptible of
cultivation, the fields are in general incloſed, and in a regular courſe of tillage; and exhibit an appearance in no ſmall
degree pleaſing.——Farther back, the ground has been more
recently brought into culture; and the ſoil appears to be
leſs kindly in its nature, and leſs ſuſceptible of improvement. But an extenſive proprietor, Mr Oſwald of Dunnikeer, having now built a manſion houſe on a fine commanding ſite, in the center of the grounds which are at preſent
the leaſt cultivated *, the plan of cultivation and of ornament
which he has begun, will ſoon improve the appearance of
that part of the pariſh. In the proſpect of building, that
gentleman ſometime ago incloſed and planted a romantic valley, which ſtretches from the eaſt end of Kirkaldy towards
the ſite of his new houſe. This valley is now beginning to
be cloſely and beautifully wooded: Fanciful walks, partly of
turf, and partly of gravel, are cut through it in different directions. To theſe the more reſpectable inhabitants of the
town are indulged with acceſs; and enjoy in this reſpect
an advantage which the vicinity of few towns can furniſh.

Relative Situation.—If this pariſh, taken by itſelf, affords
but little to admire in its general appearance, the defect is
abundantly ſupplied by its relative ſituation.—Commanding
from different points, a full proſpect of the adjacent country, from Dyſart on the eaſt, to the green-toped hills of
Glaſsmount

* The Burgh moor.

Glafsmount on the weft ; and the eye embracing within that
range the profperous town of Path-head, with the once royal
caftle of Ravenfheugh *, feated on a cliff overhanging the
fea ; the town and harbour of Kirkaldy ; the induftrious
town of Linktown, with the modern church of Abbotfhall;
the high-placed manfion, the picturefque grounds, and the
extenfive improvements, of Mr Fergufon of Raith ;—and
having extended before it the Frith of Forth, fkirted by
the coaft of Lothian from Edinburgh to North-Berwick,
diverfified by the iflands of Inch-Keith, Bafs, and May, and
enlivened by a conftant fucceffion of fhips of all burdens,
paffing and repaffing on their deftined voyages:—The parifh
of Kirkaldy thus fituated, forms part of a fcene, in which
the beauties of external nature, and interefting difplays of
the operation of mind, are in no ordinary degree united.

Air and Climate.—Afcending N. W. from the head of the
bay which is called by its name, this parifh lies much expofed
to the eafterly winds. Thefe, efpecially during the latter
part of fpring, blow frequently, and bring up from the fea,
a thick difagreeable haze, that renders the air moift and pier-
cingly cold. But as the wefterly winds prevail, during at
leaft two thirds of the year, the air is upon the whole dry,
kindly and wholefome.

Difeafes.—It may be owing partly to this caufe, that there
are few difeafes which can properly be faid to prevail here ;
and that even thefe few are feldom marked with any peculiar
fymptoms of violence. The moft prevalent difeafe is the
chronic rheumatifm, which chiefly affects the aged, and even
thefe chiefly among thofe claffes which are expofed to hard
labour

---

* Or Ravenfcraig.——See account of Dyfart.

labour in the open air. A fpecies of fever with nervous fymptoms, but of no diftinct or regular type, has fome years been
frequent, particularly in the beginning of winter, and in fpring.
Children have been more fubject to it than adults. Children are
frequently and fatally affected by the difeafe which is called the
croup. Inftances of confumptions now and then occur, chiefly
in young females. The palfy, which not long ago was fo rare,
as to have been vulgarly accounted a fpecial vifitation of God,
is now by no means uncommon. Scrophulous taints are not
much known here; and the meafles, fmall-pox, and other
epidemical eruptives are obferved to be ufually milder than
even in the neighbouring parifhes. Innoculation for the
fmall-pox is practifed with the happieft effect. The religious
fcruples, which long prevented the general ufe of this falutary
invention, are every day diminifhing; the body of the people yielding to the impreffion of that convincing atteftation in
favour of it, which Divine Providence has given in its fignal
fuccefs.

Longevity.—The inhabitants in general are healthy; and
many of them attain a good old age. It is no unfatisfying
proof of this, that in four years preceeding 1793, there lived
in the parifh 47 perfons who reached the age of 80, the full
half of which number were alive at one time; that in five
years preceding 1791, four inftances occurred in which the
marriage relation had fubfifted above half a century; and
that on an average of 14 years preceding 1788, the annual
burials were but as 1 to 59 of the population.

Population.—On the firft day of January 1790, there were
in the town of Kirkaldy 646 families, containing 2607 fouls;
in the country parifh, 15 families, containing 66 fouls; in
the

the whole parish, 661 families, containing 2673 souls * : of whom 521 were under, and 2152 above, 8 years of age.— Of those who were above that age, 908 were males, and 1244 females. The proportion of souls to a family was $4\frac{1}{64}$ in the town, $4\frac{3}{5}$ in the country, $4\frac{5}{8}$ in the whole parish.

Division of the Inhabitants in 1790.—The inhabitants, reckoning those only who had families, or who did business on their own account, were in general divided in the following manner :

Proprietors residing	7	Saddler	1
———— non residing *	4	Candlemaker	1
Ministers	2	Sellers of stone ware	4
Preachers	2	Keepers of inns and licen-	
Merchants, traders, and		sed houses for ale and	
shopkeepers	36	spirits	31
Seafaring men	34	Brewers	2
Farmers, who have no other		Smiths and founders	10
employment	2	Watchmakers	3
Medical men	5	Masons and plasterers	19
Officers who have served in		House carpenters	25
the navy	5	Ship carpenters	7
Do. who have served in the		Coopers	2
army	4	Painters	2
Officers of the customs and		Weavers	56
salt office	11	Stocking weavers	4
Officers of excise	3	Dyers	4
Writers	4	Hecklers	9
Bookseller	1	Tanners and curriers	8
Schoolmasters	3	Shoemakers	13
			Taylors

---

* The return . Dr. Webster in 1755 made the population 2296.

† Besides there are 3 corporate bodies which have property.

Tailors	10	Male farm servants	14
Salters	2	Female do.	3
Glover	1	Female teachers	5
Butchers	4	Mantua-makers	4
Bakers	12	Milleners	4
Barbers	4	Midwives	3
Cork-cutters	2	Widows with families	73
Gardeners	7	Single householders, chiefly	
Carters, many of whom oc-		females	70
cupy a few acres of land	30	Young persons of both sexes	
Carriers	3	at school, about	250
Land labourers and hired		——at the university	2
servants with families	61	Merchants clerks, not ap-	
Male domestic servants	8	prentices	9
Female do.	217		

In this table, the distinctions are not always precise. The class of merchants includes the principal manufacturers. Some of the shop-keepers have other employments, and are introduced under other names. The farmers inserted are those only who have no other specific character.

State of Husbandry.—Of those who are more or less engaged in husbandry, the whole number, including 5 proprietors, is 25. Many of these occupy but a few acres, which they cultivate for the sake of accommodation more than of gain. This circumstance is not favourable to good husbandry. The spring of interest is too slightly touched, to produce that regular exertion which is necessary to success.

Some other object engages the first care; and the few acres are neglected. At any rate, if they answer the purpose of convenience for which they are held, the melioration of them is little attended to. This, however, is not always the case. Some who occupy small portions of land, have been

at

at pains to improve them. And the land which is poſſeſſed
in any conſiderable quantity, is in general cultivated with attention and ſucceſs.

Means of cultivation.—The means of cultivation are here
obtained with little difficulty. The ſtables and ſtreets of the
town afford a regular ſupply of manure ; but what is collected
from the ſtreets is leſs valuable, on account of a mixture of
ſand which it receives from the houſes of the ordinary claſs of
inhabitants, whoſe floors are frequently covered with it.——
Lime is to be had at a ſhort diſtance, and at a moderate expence ; but it has hitherto been ſparingly uſed, particularly
on the lands lying neareſt to the town ; in the idea that the
ſoil is too light and warm to permit it to be uſed with ſafety.
Sea-weeds furniſh an occaſional acceſſion of valuable manure,
but in a quantity that bears no proportion to the extenſive demand for it.

Improvements in Huſbandry.—The mode of culture has of
late undergone ſome important alterations. The *tillage* is
improved ; to which drilling and hoeing, now much uſed in
all crops, have not a little contributed. Green crops are introduced ; and the proportion of land employed in them is
every year increaſing. The *rotation* of crops is better regulated ; the alternate ſucceſſion of culmiferous and leguminous
crops being pretty generally attended to. The *implements* of
huſbandry are improved ; particularly the plough. Of this
valuable inſtrument, two kinds are employed ; the common
Scotch plough, which begins to be better conſtructed than
formerly, and the chain-plough introduced by Small of Black
adder-mount. The former is ſtill the moſt prevalent ; for of
24 ploughs uſed in the pariſh, 17 are of this kind, and 7 of
the other. The ploughs are all drawn by horſes, generally
two

two in each, guided by the ploughman. Oxen, though e-
qually adapted to the purpofes of hufbandry when managed
with fkill, though lefs .expenfive in the purchafe and the
maintenance, though equally, if not more durable, and though
vaftly more valuable, when unfit for work, are here in total
difufe; and nearly fo in the whole furrounding diftrict.

Cattle and Carriages.—The number of horfes employed in
the parifh is 139; of which 94 are kept for work, 28 for the
faddle, and 17 for carriages. The carriages are 9 in number *, 2 coaches and 7 poft-chaifes. Of thefe a coach, and 5
chaifes are kept for hire. The number of carts is 73. The
number of milk-cows is 98. Some individuals have been at
pains to improve their breed of cows, and with good fuccefs.
But cows are here kept lefs for breeding than for their milk,
which is fold in the town with great advantage. They
are commonly fed in the houfe; the land near the town
being too valuable to permit much of it to be employed in
pafture.

Rent.—The rent of land, fituated near the town, runs from
three to four pounds the acre; and decreafes, with the diftance, down to half a guinea. As the greater part of the
parifh is cultivated by proprietors, the rent of the whole cannot
be certainly known: but it is computed at L. 1250 fterling;
which is to L. 1320 Scots, the valued rent, nearly as 11¼ to
1. There is no map of the parifh; but moft of it has been
furveyed: and the whole, exclufive of the ground covered by
the town, extends to about 830 acres. Of thefe about 10
acres

* Since the above was written, the number of carriages has diminifhed two
thirds.

acres are mofs, 11 wafte-land and roads, 130 planted, 327 fown out in pafture, 32 garden ground, and 270 in tillage.

Crops, and times of Sowing and Reaping.—The crops ufually raifed on the land in tillage are; *wheat*, fown from the beginning of October to the end of November, and reaped from the 12th to the end of Auguft ;—*barley*, fown from the 1ft to the 20th May, and reaped from the middle of Auguft to the beginning of October ;—*oats*, fown from the 20th March to the 20th April, and reaped from the 20th Auguft to the beginning of October ;—*beans*, fown from the 10th to the 20th March, and reaped from the 12th September to the 12th of October ;—*potatoes*, planted from the 20th April to the beginning of May, and dug up from the 12th to the end of October ;—*turnips*, commonly fown about the 20th June ;—*clover*, and generally a fmall proportion of rye-grafs with it, fown from the 20th April to the end of May ; and always fown with grain, which is fometimes wheat, fometimes oats, but oftenest barley.

Produce and Value.——The following table will fhew the proportions in which thefe feveral crops were raifed in 1792, with the value of the produce, eftimated on the average of the feven preceeding years.

TABLE

TABLE of Crops in 1792.

Crops.	Acres under each crop.	Bolls produced per acre.	Average value of the boll.	Total value per acre.	Total bolls produced.	Total value.
			L. s. d.	L. s. d.		L. s.
Wheat,	13	10	1 1	10 10	130	136 10
Barley,	72	9	0 15	6 15	648	486 0
Oats,	54	8	0 12	4 16	432	259 4
Beans,	24	9	0 12 6	6	216	135 0
Potatoes,	35	50	0 5 0	12 10	1750	137 10
Turnip,	25			8		200 0
Clover,	47			3		376 0

327 Acres of fown grafs ufed in pafture at L. 1 per acre.	327
Many of the inhabitants have fmall gardens adjoining to their houfes. Thefe may amount together to 20 acres, and the annual produce of them may be eftimated at L. 10 per acre ; the whole,	200
There are 12 acres of garden ground cultivated for fale, the produce of which may be eftimated at L. 20 per acre.	240
Total grofs value of the annual produce of the ground	2497 4
From which deduce ¼ for the expence of feed, labour, and manures,	936 9
Free produce, including the rent,	1560 15

Minerals.—Befides the produce of the furface of the ground, this parifh yields free-ftone, iron-ftone, and pit-coal. At prefent, however, there is little or no increafe of value derived from thefe fources. The *free-ftone* is dug merely for the ufe of the parifh *. The *iron ftone* is found in the coal-pits, and the working of it depends on that of the coal. Different

feams

* The parifh does not furnifh all the ftones that are employed in uilding. The beft houfes are built from the quarries of Bruntifland, Long-Annet, or Culello ;—which laft, though but lately opened, promifes, on account of its fuperior texture, colour, and folidity, to be in much requeft.

ſeams of coal from 2¼ to 4¼ feet thick were formerly wrought; but they have for ſometime been exhauſted above the draining level. They continue, and are ſuppoſed to be more valuable, below the level; but the expence of machinery, for draining, has hitherto prevented the working of them.——At preſent, the inhabitants are ſupplied from the coaleries of Dyſart, belonging to Sir James St. Clair Erſkine, or of Cluny, belonging to Mr Ferguſon of Raith. The former is diſtant from Kirkaldy about 2 miles, the latter about 4. At the former, 2 *metes*, about 9¼ cwt of ſmall coals or *chews*, the kind generally uſed for home conſumption, are ſold for 2s. 1d. and the expence of carriage to Kirkaldy is 1s: At the latter, 3 *loads*, weighing about 9¾ cwt. are ſold at 1s. 6d. and the expence of carriage is 2s. There is a depot of Cluny coals kept at Kirkaldy for exportation; from which about 600 tons have been annually ſhipped during the laſt 5 or 6 years, partly for Hamburgh, but chiefly for Middleburg, where the Cluny *ſplint* is ſaid to have the preference of every other ſpecies of Scotch coal. As there is now a turnpike road from Cluny to this place, it is probable that the quantity of coal exported from it will increaſe.

Turnpikes.—Turnpikes begin to be generally introduced in this part of the county. The erection of toll-bars, and the impoſition of the higheſt toll which the law permits to be exacted before a foot of road was made, excited at firſt, a prejudice againſt them. But in proportion as the roads have been put in repair, the prejudice has abated: And there can be no doubt, that if the intereſt of the public is ſufficiently conſulted in fixing the courſes of the roads, the introduction of turnpikes will, on the whole, be beneficial *.

Hiſtory

* By an act of Parliament, for making and repairing roads in the county of Fife, the truſtees appointed to carry it into execution are impowered, inter

alia,

Hiſtory of the Burgh.—It is probable that the local advantages of vicinity to fuel, to land capable of producing grain,
and above all to the ſea, ſo favourable to ſubſiſtence and ſo
neceſſary to commerce, brought men at firſt to ſettle at this
place. It is not known, however, at what particular time
the town was built; nor are there any traces of its hiſtory before it became one of the regality burghs of the lordſhip of
Dunfermling. It was mortified A. D. 1334, by David II. to
the

alia, " to widen the roads to any breadth they ſhall think proper, not exceed-
" ing 40 feet; and for that purpoſe to pull down and demoliſh any houſe or
" building, as well *within* royal burghs as without the ſame; paying ſuch da-
" mages to the owners or occupiers, as the *ſaid truſtees* ſhall judge reaſonable."
Theſe powers are complained of : 1ſt, As unprecedented and unknown in
the other counties : 2d, As trenching on the chartered rights of royal burghs;
the internal government of which is, by charters ratified by parliament, veſted
in their own proper magiſtrates : 3d, As affecting the ſecurity of private property, which is thus left, in certain circumſtances, to be ſeized without the
conſent of the owner, and without any other compenſation to him, than
what the very perſons who are to ſeize on it *judge reaſonable*. It is true, there
lies an appeal on the value of the property to the Juſtices of the Peace in
their general ſeſſions. But as the Juſtices are truſtees, and in point of influence, the principal truſtees under the road act, the appeal is nearly from
one deſcription to another deſcription of the ſame perſons. If the public convenience at times require that the property of individuals ſhould be ſacrificed
to it; juſtice ſurely requires that thoſe, whoſe property is affected, ſhould be
fully indemnified, and that too in the way in which they are moſt likely to be
ſatisfied that the indemnification is adequate,——the verdict of a jury.
The conſideration of the effect which the powers conveyed by the act alluded to might, if exerciſed to their full extent, produce on Kirkaldy, has given
riſe to theſe reflections. Kirkaldy is properly but one long ſtreet, through which
the great county road at preſent paſſes. As the greater part of this ſtreet is
under 40 feet broad, the truſtees have it in their power, if *they ſhall think proper*, to bring it to the full ſtatutory breadth, at the expence of half a mile of
demoliſhed houſes; the owners of which would be obliged to reſt ſatisfied with
what damages the truſtees, or in the laſt reſort, the juſtices, ſhould think reaſonable.

the abbots of Dunfermling ſucceſſively ; in whoſe poſſeſſion it continued till A. D. 1450, when the commendator and convent, by indentures made with the baillies and community of Kirkaldy, diſponed to them and their ſucceſſors for ever, the burgh and harbour, burgh acres, the ſmall cuſtoms, common paſture in the moor, courts, &c.

Chartered Privileges.——It was ſoon after erected into a royal burgh, with the cuſtomary privileges : And theſe were ſpecifically ratified by a charter of confirmation granted by Charles I. in 1644 ; and the burgh, *for good and gratuitous ſervice* done by it, erected *de novo* into a free royal burgh and free port, and new and larger immunities granted it. Among its privileges were enumerated, the powers expreſsly given to the baillies, counſellors and community, of electing and conſtituting annual magiſtrates for the adminiſtration of juſtice and the government of the burgh; of uplifting cuſtoms and applying them to the public good ; of holding courts ; of ſeizing and incarcerating, and puniſhing delinquents ; with which were conjoined various other privileges expreſſed in the barbarous language, and ſome of them conceived in the barbarous ſpirit of the times ; ſuch as herezelds, bludewits, merchetæ mulierum, fork, foſs, ſok, ſak, thoill, thame, wraick, vert, weth, wair, venyſon, infangtheif, outfangtheif, pit and gallows, &c. *.

Though there be no authentic record of the ſtate of Kirkaldy, at the time it was disjoined from the lordſhip of Dunfermling, or firſt erected unto a royal burgh, it may be warrantably ſuppoſed, that before either of theſe events could happen, the place muſt have attained to ſome importance. Previous to the union of Scotland with England, its commerce

and

* Charter of confirmation.

and navigation were in a great meafure confined to the towns which lay on both fides of the Frith of Forth. Thefe had early applied themfelves to the bufinefs of fifhing *, which their favourable fituation enabled them to profecute with vigour and fuccefs. And fo diftinguifhed were thofe of them efpecially which lay on the north fide of the frith, that when James VI. in 1602 planted a colony in Lewis, to introduce the fifhing trade among the Weftern iflands, the colony was drawn from the coafts of Fife †. The towns on the Frith of Forth too had almoft the exclufive poffeffion of the trade with the Low Countries, at that time the only branch of commerce of any importance, and were carriers for nearly the whole of the northern part of the United Kingdom.

State in 1644.——Of the advantages derived from both thefe branches of commerce, Kirkaldy appears to have enjoyed a principal fhare. Tradition relates that, when Charles I. erected it anew into a royal burgh in 1644, it had an hundred fail of fhips belonging to it. And the tradition is fupported, by an authentic account, preferved among the records of the burgh, of loffes fuftained betwixt that time and the Reftoration. From this account, in which the mafter's name, and the feparate value of each fhip are particularly fpecified, it appears, that 94 fhips belonging to this port, were during that period either loft at fea, or taken by the enemy.

There are other circumftances too, which ferve to fhew that,

---

* As early as the ninth century, the inhabitants of the Netherlands reforted to the coafts of Scotland, to purchafe falted fifh from the natives; of whom they learned the trade, which the Dutch have fince purfued with fo much national advantage.——Anderfon's Hiftory of Commerce.

† Robertfon's Hiftory of Scotland.

that, during a confiderable part of the laft century, Kirkaldy was in a very flourifhing ftate.

Early Population.——1. The population of the parifh was equal, or moft probably fuperior, to what it is at prefent. During a period of 14 years, commencing with 1616, the yearly average of regiftered births was 121 ; which would make the population, computing it as 26 to 1 of the births, to have been 3146. For fome time after, the numbers appear to have increafed rapidly. In 1643 the accommodation of the parifh required a new wing to be added to the church ; and in 1650 it was found neceffary to make a new erection *. The annual average of births, for 10 years immediately preceding the date of that erection, was 174$\frac{1}{10}$, which made the whole population about 4540; and for the fame fpace of time immediately following it, 115; which made the population 2990. From this ftatement it appears, that, fuppofing the whole inhabitants to be as 26 to 1 of the births, the parifh of Kirkaldy was more populous, for fome time after its firft reduction to its prefent limits, than it is at this day. And were the eftimate to be made by the proportion which the prefent number of inhabitants actually bears to the annual births, the difference in the population of that time would appear to have been very confiderable †.

2. The

* See page 2d.

† The above rule for computing the population of a parifh or diftrict from the births, is fuggefted in " Queries for the purpofe of elucidating the Natu-" ral Hiftory and Political State of Scotland, circulated by Sir John Sinclair." In this parifh, however, the computation falls fhort of the real proportion. The number of regiftered births in 179: was 60 ; and on an average of the 20 preceding years, 50. But, as the regiftration of births has for fome time

paft

2. The contributions which were then made for purposes of charity, and still more for the support of the state, shew the place to have been respectable. In 1622, when the General Assembly of the protestant churches in France deputed Basnage to the King of Great Britain, to sollicit aid for resisting the oppression of Lewis XIII. the town and parish of Kirkaldy contributed, *according to the gudewill and permission of the King,* a pecuniary aid of 1030 merks *. During a period of 12 years, from 1634 to 1645, at which time money was so valuable as to bear interest at 9 per cent. the weekly collections at the church doors were greater than they are at present; the average amounting to L. 73 : 10 ; while that of the same number of years preceding 1791 does not exceed L. 63 9s. 4d.

Public Assessments.——In all public assessments, the town was rated as the sixth burgh, and assessed in the proportion of 1 to 40 of the whole supplies levied from the burghs of Scotland †. For several years before and after 1650, the monthly assessments laid on it, for the maintenance of troops, exceeded

ed

past been much neglected, let one half more be added for births not entered, and the whole annual births will, on an average of 20 years, be 75 ; which, compared with the actual numbers, is nearly in the proportion of 1 to 35. Estimated by this proportion, the population from 1650 to 1660 would exceed 4000.

There is no public register of burials. But by a very exact list kept by the grave-digger for his own use, it appears, that the average of burials for 14 years preceding 1788 was 44¼, which is to the population nearly as 1 to 59.

* Basnage's receipt is engrossed in the minutes of the kirk-sessions.

† See the acts of the Convention of Estates from 1665 to 1678, and subsequent acts of Parliament. The burghs which were rated higher were Edinburgh, Dundee, Aberdeen, Glasgow, Perth, and at first St. Andrews; but the assessment of that burgh gradually fell to a fourth part of that of Kirkaldy.

ed at an average L. 400 *. In 1667, the Convention of
Eſtates aſſeſſed it, for defraying the expence of the war which
Charles II. had declared againſt the Dutch, in the ſum of
L. 228 monthly for 12 months ; over and above its proportion of the ſupply of L. 480,000 which the Parliament had
granted to the King for life, and of the further ſupply of
L. 133,000, which a former Convention had granted him
for 5 years. And the ſame ſum of L. 228, it continued to
pay monthly, ſometimes for 5 months, ſometimes for 8
months in the year, as the exigencies of the ſtate required.

Effects of the Civil War.——About the middle of the century, indeed, the proſperity of this place received a conſiderable check. The quarrel of the Parliament of England with
Charles I. having in 1643 extended to Scotland, the inhabitants of Kirkaldy had taken a decided part in it.——Feeling
that love of independence which the commercial ſpirit gene-
rates, and intereſted in having the fruits of their induſtry
ſecured from the gripe of arbitrary power, they had early eſpouſed the ſide of liberty : And notwithſtanding the conci-
liating exerciſe of the royal prerogative, in renewing and extending their charter in 1644, they had entered warmly into
the views of the Parliament. The Solemn League and Covenant was publicly ſworn, and ſubſcribed. And numbers, eſpecially of the ſeamen, joined the army of the Covenanters,
and were preſent at the battle of Kilſyth †, in the event of
which

---

* Collectors liſts ſtill exiſting.

† A. D. 1645. The records of the kirk-ſeſſion about this time, contain
many facts, that ſerve to ſhew how deeply this pariſh was intereſted in the
cauſe of the Parliament. Public prayers were offered up for its ſucceſs ; and
every advantage gained to it was celebrated with thankſgiving. The families
of

which this place suffered the loss of many of its most active inhabitants.——That unhappy event was followed by a succession of misfortunes. No less than 58 ships, belonging to this port, were either taken or lost at sea, before the English invasion in 1650; and from that time to the Restoration, 36 ships more were taken, many of them with cargoes; making in all (as stated in page 17.) 94 ships, the value of which is ascertained, by a particular appretiation contained in the account of losses already mentioned, to have amounted to the sum of L. 53,791 sterling. A considerable number of these ships were taken in the harbour of Dundee, when that town was stormed and sacked by General Monk; at which time, too, effects belonging to the inhabitants of Kirkaldy which had been deposited at Dundee as a place of security, were carried away or destroyed, to the value nearly of L. 5000 *. Besides this, different individuals suffered the loss of money, which they had lent to the Committee of Estates for the public service, but which on the establishment of the Commonwealth it was impossible to recover †. In consequence of these heavy losses, and the still greater loss of 480 men killed in

the

of those who had joined the army, were many of them assisted by public contributions. Deserters were cited before the kirk-session : there is an instance of nine of them being called before it in one day, and ordained to return to their colours under pain of excommunication. A person was summoned before the presbytery, for *calling the cause of God presently in hand, the Devil's cause, as he trowed.* Different persons who, during the success of Montrose at Perth, had been induced to declare for the King, appeared before the kirk-session, and professed their sorrow for their conduct. After the battle of Kilsyth, the date of which, and of Philiphaugh, is marked on the margin of the record, horses for transporting the wounded, necessaries, medicines, and attendance, were at different times paid for out of the parish funds.

* A particular account of its loss is preserved among the burgh records.

† Both these facts are annexed to the account of losses at sea.

the courſe of the war *, the commerce and ſhipping of Kirkaldy were deeply affected. And through the ſubſequent interruption of the trade with Holland, during three ſucceſſive wars with that country, aided perhaps by the unfriendly influence of an arbitrary government on the general ſpirit and exertions of the people, the place continued to languiſh during the uſurpation of Cromwell, and the deſpotic reigns of Charles II. and his ſucceſſor James. In 1673 the number of ſhips belonging to it had fallen to 25. And in 1682 its diſtreſs was ſo great, that application was made to the Convention of burghs to conſider its poverty, and to take methods for eaſing it as to its public burdens. But the burgh having fallen under the diſpleaſure of the Court, on account of the oppoſition given by its repreſentative to the arbitrary meaſures which were then carrying on, the inhabitants were not only denied relief, but further burdened by an addition of 2000 merks to their annual aſſeſſment †. The application to the Convention was however renewed in 1687, when a viſitation of the burgh was ordered. A committee appointed for that purpoſe met at Kirkaldy the following year; and, on the evidence of the books and declarations both of the magiſtrates of the burgh and the officers of the cuſtoms, reported, *inter alia*, to the Convention, " that the cuſtoms payable " to his Majeſty were not the half of what they had been ſome " years before: that this was occaſioned by the death of many " ſubſtantial merchants and ſkippers, and loſs of ſhips and " decay of trade: that many of the inhabitants, ſome of " whom were magiſtrates of the burgh, had fled from and " deſerted the ſame: that ſo great was the poverty of the in-
" habitants,

---

* It is ſaid that the battle of Kilſyth alone left 200 widows in Kirkaldy.

† Stated in a petition to King William.

" habitants, that all the taxations impofed on the town could
" do no more than pay the eight months cefs payable to the
" king yearly, and that with difficulty, &c. *"

Revolution in 1688.—Before the effect of this reprefentation
could be known, the Revolution took place ; an event highly
grateful to the Scots in general, and particularly to the *whigs
of Fife.* The inhabitants of Kirkaldy, entering warmly into
the fpirit of it, and anxious to diftinguifh themfelves in the
fupport of it, found means to apprehend the Earl of Perth,
who was Lord Chancellor, and had managed the affairs of
Scotland under James; and who knowing that he was generally
obnoxious on account of the cruelties which he had practifed
on the Prefbyterians, withdrew himfelf as foon as the public mind had declared in favour of the Prince of Orange,
After detaining that nobleman in prifon 5 days and 5 nights,
under a conftant guard of 300 men, they fent him under a
convoy of 3 boats manned with 200 hands to Alloa, where
they delivered him *on receipt* into the cuftody of the Earl of
Mar. The guard of 300 men they found it neceffary to
keep up for 4 months, on receiving information that a force
was coming from the Highlands to burn the town, in re-
venge for Perth's apprehenfion.——Thefe facts, and a particular account of their loffes, having been ftated in a petition to King William in 1689 †, they obtained an abatement
of L.'1000 Scots of their annual affeffments. And the Revolution having happily diffufed eafe and freedom and fecurity,
and with thefe a fpirit of induftry and commercial exertion,

through

---

* Copy of the report of the commiffion of vifitation *penes* town-council.

† In this petition, the inhabitants offered to inftruct, that their loffes during the diftracted ftate of the country amounted to L. 800,000 Scots, or
L. 66,666 : 13 : 4 Sterling.

through the country in general, the languiſhing trade of Kirkaldy revived, and wealth began again to circulate among the inhabitants. As one indication of this, the public collections at the church doors, which, on an average of 10 years preceding 1688, amounted only to L. 58 : 3 : 1, and on that year fell to L. 42 : 18 : 7¼, produced annually for 4 years, commencing with 1693, L. 125 : 7 : 10 ; and L. 110 8s. 2d. on an average of 15 years from 1693 to the Union.

Effects of the Union.—This laſt event, whatever advantages have been ultimately derived from it'to the nation at large, was long conſidered as an æra of miſfortune and diſtreſs to the trade of Scotland. Taxes, which by the treaty of union were laid on many of the neceſſaries of life, the duties and cuſtoms which were impoſed on various articles of merchandiſe, and the numerous reſtrictions with which the Engliſh contrived, in the narrow ſpirit of commercial monopoly, to fetter the trade of Scotland in general, were quickly and ſeverely felt over the whole of this part of the united kingdom. Commerce every where declined ; in ſpite of the attempts which were made to ſupport it by the wretched reſource of ſmuggling. It ſuffered particularly in the towns on the Frith of Forth ; many of which were quickly reduced to diſtreſs, and all of them languiſhed. This town was involved in the common fate. Its ſhipping, on which it had till then entirely depended, fell rapidly into decay ; and the ſeveral wars, which followed each other with little intermiſſion for more than half a century, having continued the effect which the diſadvantageous terms of the Union had begun, the trade of this place was at laſt ſo much reduced, that in

I   1760,

1760, it employed no more than one coafter of 50 tons, and two ferry-boats, each of 30 *.

On the return of peace in 1763, the fhipping immediately revived. By the year 1772, it had increafed to 11 veffels, carrying 515 tons and 49 men; and although its progrefs was retarded by the war with America, it amounted, at the clofe of that war, to 12 veffels, carrying 750 tons and 59 men. ——From that time, it has made conftant and rapid advances.

Prefent State of the Shipping.——At prefent †, it confifts of 26 fquare rigged veffels ‡, 1 floop, and 2 ferry-boats, carrying by the regifter 3700 tons, about 5000 tons dead weight, employing 225 men to navigate them; and worth, when clear to fail, about L. 30,000. One or two of the fmalleft veffels are employed as coafters, and trade either to Aberdeen or London; carrying to the former, falt and coals; to the latter, the manufactures of the diftrict; and returning from both with goods, chiefly for this port and Leith. All the other fhips are employed either in the foreign trade for home confumption, or in the carrying trade. Some of the largeft of them are employed in the trade to the Mediterranean, the Weft Indies, and America; and of thefe fome have been occafionally abfent from this place for 3 or 4 years. But the greater number is employed in the trade to Holland and the Baltic. To thefe the only article of export is coals, fhipped here, at Dyfart, Wemyfs, and other ports on the Frith; and the chief articles imported from them are corn, flax, flax-feed, linen-

yarn,

* Copy Report of the cuftom-houfe here to the Board of cuftoms, A. F. 1760.

† A. D. 1792.

‡ One of the fhips was built in 1713.

yarn, wood, iron, afhes, bark, hides, tallow, clover-feed apples, cheefe, geñeva, &c.

Cuftom-Houfe.—The duties payable on exports and imports in all the towns on the north fide of the Frith of Forth, from Aberdour to Largo inclufive *, are under the management of the cuftom-houfe at this port ; the bufinefs of which is conducted by a collector with principal and junior clerks, a comptroller, a land furveyor, 3 land waiters and 14 tidefmen. The office has alfo the management of the falt duties within the fame diftrict ; the collection of which employs 1 fupervifor, 7 officers, and 20 watchmen. - In 1792, 101 veffels were cleared out at the cuftom-houfe, and 92 entered ; 13 of the fhips cleared out, and 43 of thofe entered, belonged to Kirkaldy.

Duties.——The whole duties paid on exports in that year, amounted to L. 2570 : 10 : 4¼ ; on imports to L. 2227 : 3 : 7½ ;

on

* The whole fhipping of the above diftrict, ftood as in the following table at the different periods referred to.

Ports.	In 1760.			In 1772.			In 1782.			In 1792.		
	Ships.	*Tons.*	*Men.*	*Ships.*	*Tons.*	*Men.*	*Ships.*	*Tons.*	*Men.*	*Ships.*	*Tons.*	*Men.*
Kirkaldy,	3	110	11	11	515	49	12	750	59	29	3700	225
Dyfart,	7	580	50	14	1365	115	10	1210	84	25	3926	231
Wemyfs,	1	130	9	2	200	17	6	315	26	6	752	49
Methel & Leven,	6	460	38	8	540	53	1	100	7	8	655	48
Kinghorn, including ferry boats,	15	760	80	18	805	86	12	405	48	15	663	57
Burntifland,	10	1135	93	10	615	63	3	100	11	6	257	21
Aberdour,	18	940	88	4	215	20	4	150	12	5	349	21
	60	4115	369	67	4255	403	48	3030	247	94	10,302	652

on both to L. 4797 : 14; of this fum, the exports from Kirkaldy produced L. 244 : 18; the imports into it L. 1187 : 3 : 7¼;
total L. 1432 : 1 : 7½. The duties on falt for the fame year
amounted to L. 5542 : 10 : 6; which, added to the duties on
exports and imports, made the whole revenue paid at this cuftom-houfe for that year L. 10,340 : 4 : 6.

Linen Manufactures.—The profperity of this place, which was
at firft begun, and for a long time entirely fupported by fhipping and commerce, has of late been greatly promoted by
manufactures; and particularly by the manufacture of linen.
The kinds of linen manufactured here are bed-ticks, chec-
quered and ftriped linens, with a mixture of cotton in fome
of them, and a low-priced fpecies of plain linen. Thefe appear to have been taken from the models of Holland and Flanders; the names which fome of the fabrics ftill bear, fuch as,
ftriped Hollands, Dutch checks, Dutch ticks, Flanders checks
and ticks, pointing their origin to the Low Countries. The
particular time at which the manufacture of thefe articles was
introduced, is not exactly known; but they can be traced
back to the commencement of this century. And probability feems to fupport the opinion that they were introduced earlier; perhaps between the middle of the laft
century and the Revolution, when the declenfion of their
navigation and trade, forced the inhabitants to have
recourfe to new ways of employing their induftry.

Manufactures, however, made but little progrefs here, till
the foreign trade had again declined in confequence of the
Union. In 1733, the whole amount of cloth ftamped at
Kirkaldy *, was no more than 177,740 yards. In 1743, it
had

* By an act of Parliament in 1727, no linen cloth can be fold or expofed
to fale, till it has been infpected and ftamped,—under the penalty of L. 5 on
the

had increaſed to 316,550, the computed value of which a-mounted to nearly L. 11,000 *. And, although during the commotions of 1745 and 1746, the ſale of manufactures was in a great degree ſuſpended, yet that circumſtance did not much affect their progreſs. They continued to be diligently proſecuted, and gradually to increaſe, till the war of 1755 interrupted the communication with America and the Weſt Indies, at that time, almoſt the only market for the goods of this diſtrict. The effects of that interruption, the interval of peace that ſucceeded was not ſufficient entirely to remove. From the value of L. 22,000, to which the manufactures of the diſtrict had in ſome former years riſen, they fell in 1773 to L. 15,000 ; and the next year ſtill lower. Such indeed

was

the ſeller, and the ſame ſum on the buyer. For the convenience of dealers in linen, public offices are eſtabliſhed in different diſtricts, under the authority of *truſtees*, whom his Majeſty is impowered by the ſame act to appoint for *overſeeing, directing, and improving, the linen manufacture in Scotland.* And theſe truſtees have in ſome inſtances authoriſed manufacturers to ſtamp their own cloth according to the directions of the act.

Although the law requiring the ſtamping of linen, was founded on apparent views of public utility, it is doubtful whether any advantage has been derived from it ſufficient to compenſate the expence and loſs of time, to which the manufacturer is ſubjected by it. The approbation of the ſtampmaſter is never found to have any influence on the judgement of the merchant : Nor is it to be ſuppoſed, that a perſon, who has no connection with the trade, and whoſe emoluments depend on the quantity which he ſtamps, will be equally ſcrupulous of affixing the ſeal of his approbation, as if his intereſt depended on the quality. If ſtamping be found a neceſſary political regulation, the ends of utility appear to be beſt attained, by giving the power of ſtamping his own cloth to the manufacturer ; whoſe credit and intereſt, operate as a joint ſecurity to the truſtees ; and to the public, that no improper goods are ſent into the market.

† At that time the whole cloth manufactured in the diſtrict, including the pariſhes of Kirkaldy, Abbotſhall, Dyſart, Leſlie, &c. was ſtamped here, and is included in the computation.

was their ſtate about that time, and ſo unpromiſing had the proſpect become; firſt, through the non-importation agreement of America, and afterwards, through the commencement of hoſtilities with that country, that ſome of the manufacturers thought of turning their capital into a different channel.

One of them *, however, previouſly reſolved on an attempt to introduce the manufactures of this place into the internal comſumption of England. The attempt was made, and immediately ſucceeded; and the manufacture of checks and ticks having been of late reſigned in many parts of that country, for finer and more profitable articles, and the difference in the price of labour too, enabling the Scots manufacturer to furniſh them at a lower rate, the demand from England has increaſed; and the trade has in conſequence been progreſſively advancing for 15 years, without ſuffering any other interruption, than that periodical ſtagnation, which is produced in times of proſperity by *over-trading*

At preſent the manufactures of Kirkaldy employ about 810 looms †; of which about 250 are in the pariſh ‡, about 300

in

---

* The late Mr. James Fergus, of the houſe of John Fergus and Sons; to whoſe diſcernment and ſpirit, the manufacturers of this diſtrict owe their introduction to a market which of all others yields the quickeſt and ſureſt returns,——the inland market of England

† This number is aſcertained from liſts furniſhed by the manufacturers individually. The whole diſtrict employs about 2000 looms; the produce of which for the year ending 1ſt November 1793, when the returns from the ſtamp-office to the truſtees are made up, may be eſtimated at L. 110,000.

‡ The whole looms in the pariſh, which are triple the number that they were 4 years ago, amount to 266. But of theſe from 10 to 16 are employed by inhabitants of the neighbouring pariſhes; two of whom have ſhops here for the purchaſe of goods, but are not ranked among the manufacturers of the pariſh.

in the parifh of Abbotfhall, about 100 in the parifh of Dyfart, about 60 in the parifh of Largo, and the reft fcattered
over the neighbouring parifhes. The annual amount of a
weaver's work (allowing for the variations of age, ability, and
habits of application, among the whole weavers employed) is
found to be at a medium from 10 to 12 pieces, meafuring
one with another, about 110 yards. On this computation,
the annual produce of a loom runs from 1100 to 1320 yards,
worth on the loweft eftimate of yards, and at the average
price of 1s. each *, L. 55: And the annual produce of the
whole looms employed amounts, on the fame eftimate, nearly
to 900,000 yards †, worth at the fame average about L. 45,000.
Reckoning 22 *fpindles* as the average quantity of yarn to
a piece, 178,200 *fpindles* are annually manufactured into
cloth. Of this quantity about a ninth part is cotton yarn;
which is fpun here, and in the neighbourhood, with the affiftance of machinery; as mentioned formerly. The flax-yarn
has hitherto been fpun with the hand ‡. After the flax is
heckled, the manufacturer fends it to undertakers in different
parts of the country, who give it out to be fpun; and receive
a certain commiffion on the quantity of yarn returned by them.
The expence of fpinning, when commiffion and carriage are
included, amounts at an average to 1s. 3d. the *fpindle*. Befides

* The prices of checks run from 6d. to 1s. 6d. per yard; of ticks, from 7d.
to 2s. 6d. The proportion of plain linen is very inconfiderable, perhaps not
as 1 to 500 of the whole, and the price is low. As the cheaper fabrics prevail, a low average is taken.

† This is nearly as 1 to 5½ of the whole linen made in the county of Fife,
the amount of which for the year ending the 1ft, November 1793, was
5,013,089 yards.

‡ A mill for fpinning flax, on the Darlington model, is erecting in the neighbourhood by a manufacturer of this place; from which fpecimens of good
work have already been produced.

fides the yarn fpun on the manufacturers account, a confiderable quantity is regularly bought in from the neighbourhood; and frequently from Montrofe, Brechin, Cupar-Angus, &c. Of the whole linen yarn manufactured, about a feventh part is fpun from flax produced in the country; and the reft from flax imported, chiefly from Riga, at the average price of L. 45, per ton. For fome years a confiderable quantity of yarn has been brought into this port from Bremen and Hamburgh. The quantity has in one year amounted to 441,400 lbs; which at 3 lbs. to the fpindle, made 147,133 fpindles. Of this, however, but a fmall proportion is commonly ufed in the parifh; and no great proportion in the neighbourhood. The far greater part of it is fent to Perth, Dunfermling, Falkland, Auchtermuchty, and fome other inland towns, in which coarfe linen is manufactured.

Of the yarn ufed in making checks and ticks, about threefourths are whitened, and the remaining fourth dyed. Moft of the principal manufacturers whiten and dye for themfelves; the reft employ public bleachers and dyers. The different operations of heckling, fpinning, dyeing, bleaching, warping, winding, and weaving, may be computed to employ 5¼ hands to every loom; which makes the whole hands employed in carrying on the manufacture of the place; reckoning men, women, and children, 4455. Deducing the price of materials, (flax, cotton, foap, afhes, indigo, &c.) which, when thofe of the beft quality are ufed, will be about one third of the value of the cloth, there remains L. 30,000 as the price of labour and the manufacturers profit. And this being divided among the whole number of productive hands, each is found to produce annually to the community about L. 7 Sterling.

The manufacturers of Kirkaldy, befides the cloth made by them

them, purchase annually a considerable quantity from the neighbouring district. The value of the cloth purchased by manufacturers or merchants in the course of last year, exceeded L. 30,000. Of the whole cloth, made or purchased, about three fourths are sold in England ; from which a small proportion is exported to the West Indies and America. Of the remaining fourth, about one half of it is sold in Glasgow for exportation ; the other half is consumed in the country *.

The

* The above was the state of the manufactures of Kirkaldy, before the distresses which commerce and manufactures in general have suffered of late began to extend to them. Through the operation of particular circumstances, those distresses were prevented for a while from having any considerable effect on this district.——An engagement with a navy contractor, which enabled one of the principal manufacturers of the place, to purchase considerable more than the usual quantity of checks, contributed to keep the trade alive there for some months, after it had suffered in other places. The manufacturers too, calculating on the prosperity of the former year, had prepared a large stock of materials for the probable consumption of the succeeding year : And these materials, many of them were under the necessity of working up and selling, although with loss, to retire their bills as they fell due. This brought the usual quantity of cloth, and perhaps a greater quantity than usual to the market, during the first part of the year 1793. But the causes which produced this effect were temporary, and have now ceased to operate. The engagement with the contractor has been for some months at an end. The materials provided in the former year have been generally wrought up. And while the profits on the sale of the manufacture have not been sufficient to replace them, the want of ready money cannot now be supplied, at least with the same facility as formerly, by negotiating bills. Hence there is already an increasing stagnation. The number of looms employed *without* the place is fast diminishing. The prices of spinning and weaving have been twice reduced within the compass of a few months. On some fabrics, the price of weaving has fallen $\frac{1}{12}$, on others $\frac{1}{6}$ and $\frac{1}{4}$, and on a great proportion of the coarser goods, $\frac{3}{7}$ of the former prices. An industrious weaver can still earn from 8s. to 12s. in the week. But the actual earning of all the weavers employed,

ployed,

Leather.—The next, both in ftanding and importance to the manufacture of cloth, is leather. This branch was eftablifhed on a fmall fcale in 1723 ; but it has fince been much extended. At prefent, it employs 16 hands ; who manufacture annually from 3200 to 4000 hides of oxen, and cows, about the fame number of calf-fkins, and a fmall proportion

of

ployed, and for all kinds of work, do not now exceed the weekly average of five fhillings.

Much has of late been faid of the bad effects of high wages on the induftry and profperity of the people. It may be doubted, however, whether fuch reflections are founded on liberal or juft views of the intereft of the community. High wages, it is true, like high profits on trade, or high rents of land, increafe the means of diffipation to thofe who are addicted to it, and abate the neceffity of *their* application to induftrious habits. But when the mind hath candidly diftinguifhed between things themfelves, and the abufe of them, it will unqueftionably be found, that liberal wages are on the whole attended with important advantages. The liberal reward of labour, inftead of abating induftry, ferves in general to increafe it ; that quality, in the opinion of one of the moft competent judges *, " *improving like every other, in* " *proportion to the encouragement which it receives.*" As high wages facilitate the fupport of a family, labourers when they receive them are enouraged to marry young ; and population increafes. The induftrious are enabled, not only to fupport their families comfortably, but in many inftances to fave a little, which they generally apply to the purchafe of ftock, and begin to work for themfelves. In this way, a number of operative weavers have been of late coming forward into the rank of manufacturers, and, by widening the foundations of the trade, were contributing to increafe the fecurity of its continuance. By the fall of wages, a ftop is put to this gradual advancement. And by the ftagnation of trade, which is radically the caufe of that fall, many of thofe who were advancing beyond the ftate of workmen, are thrown back into it ; with earnings that are hardly fufficient to maintain their families. In this fituation, if they happen to have apprentices, their diftrefs is often increafed by them, The ordinary plan on which apprentices are taught here is rational and liberal. The time of apprenticefhip is fhort, ufually 3 years. No premium is required for inftructing them : But the mafter receives in lieu of it

one

* Dr. Smith, Wealth of Nations, book i. chap 8.

of ſeal-ſkins. The raw hides and ſkins are collected chiefly
from the county of Fife.   But as that range is not ſufficient
to ſupply the conſumption, a conſiderable quantity is imported from the North of Scotland, from Ireland, and ſometimes
from Holland. For ſome years back, the price of raw hides
has been about 7s. per ſtone of 22 lbs; but the preſent
ſtagnation of trade has reduced it under 5s.

From 220 to 240 tons of oak bark are annually conſumed
in this manufacture. For many years the bark was brought
wholly from England; excepting only a ſmall proportion
from

ône half of the apprentice's earnings, while the other goes to his own ſupport.
In favourable times, an induſtrious apprentice, over and above the ſhare
which goes to his maſter, earns conſiderably more than is neceſſary for his ſupport. And as the ſurplus is his own, his induſtry is conſtantly ſtimulated by
partaking of its fruits. But when the wages of labour fall ſo low, that an apprentice cannot maintain himſelf with the half of his earnings,—which is the
caſe at preſent with the young, the weakly, and the inexpert, he muſt become a burden upon his maſter, or upon his friends, or abandon the trade.

If things continue long in their preſent ſtate, the conſequences will in this
view, be extenſively injurious to this community. The number of apprentices
is very great; the demand for weavers, and the high wages of labour for two
or three years paſt, having increaſed far beyond the ordinary proportion. Not
only was every hand that could be ſpared from the neighbourhood determined
to the loom ; but plans were formed for procuring ſupplies from a diſtance.
Advantageous propoſals were circulated through different diſtricts of the Highlands, in conſequence of which about 50 young men, chiefly from Sutherland
and Caithneſs came to this place as apprentices to the buſineſs of weaving, and
many more were preparing to follow. Thoſe who came had ſcarcely begun to
feel the advantages of their ſituation, when a reduction of wages took place.
Diſcouraged by this circumſtance on the one hand, and tempted on the other,
by large bounties to enter into the army, moſt of them have run off, and en-
liſted.——And this is a ſcheme likely to be fruſtrated, which promiſed to
bring large ſupplies of productive labourers to this diſtrict; and, in the event,
perhaps to carry manufactures and induſtry into diſtricts of Scotland, where
they are at preſent almoſt entirely unknown.

from the Highlands of Scotland. At that time the average price, including freight and carriage, was about L. 5 : 10 per ton. But British bark having within the last 3 or 4 years advanced almost to double the former price, (from L. 8 to L. 10) it has since been found neceſſary to import a great proportion of what is uſed here, from Germany and the Netherlands. The leather, which is of all the uſual denominations, viz. bend, crop, ſhoe-hides, cordovan, ſaddler's leather, &c. is ſold in the neighbouring towns and country, in the north of Scotland, in Perth, Glaſgow, Edinburgh, and occaſionally in London. The annual ſales have for ſome years produced at an average from L. 7000 to L. 8000. The duties paid on this branch produce annually about L. 470. The wages of a tanner, which are nearly double to what they were 30 years ago, run in the week from 6s. to 10s; thoſe of an induſtrious currier will average 15s.

Cotton ſpinning.—The ſpinning of cotton, chiefly for woof, has been carried on here for 8 or 9 years; and till this year with conſiderable ſucceſs. In 1792, 110 hands, reckoning men, women, and children, were employed in the town; beſides thoſe who were employed by manufacturers of this pariſh, in the neighbourhood.——At preſent, the number is reduced to 75. Theſe prepare and ſpin about 1100 lbs. of cotton in the week, or about 57,000 lbs. in the year. This quantity is ſpun into 32,000 ſpindles of yarn; which at the average price of 4s. per ſpindle, yields L. 6400. The yarn is ſpun on the common *jenny;* of which inſtrument 29 are employed. The carding is performed on cylinder cards, moved by horſes. The weekly wages paid to the whole hands employed amount to L. 12.

Before this year, a conſiderable quantity of the yarn ſpun here was ſent to Perth, to be wrought into callicoes. At

preſent,

present, almost the whole of it is consumed in the manufactures of the district. And to supply these, about as much more is spun by manufacturers of this place in a neighbouring parish *, where the convenience of water has induced them to erect machinery.

Ship-building.—Ship-building was introduced here in 1778. Previous to that time, a great proportion of the ships employed in the trade of Great Britain, was built in America; the contiguity of navigable rivers to immense forests making the constuction of ships less expensive in that country than in any other. But since the separation of America, and especially since the register act of 1785, excluded all ships not British-built from the trade of this country, ship-building has generally increased in it. 38 Vessels carrying about 3000 tons, carpenters measure (about 4500 dead weight) have been built here in 15 years; most of them for the ports of the Frith; but some of them also for Glasgow, Dundee, Aberdeen, &c. One of the largest of them for the capital of Zealand. The ordinary contract-price for building with oak plank, is from L. 4 : 5. to L. 6 per ton of the burden, and the hull is usually from $\frac{1}{4}$ to $\frac{2}{3}$ of the price of the ship when clear to sail. The ship timber used here is partly brought from England, and partly imported from Hamburgh. The number of carpenters employed varies from 10 to 30. The average of their daily wages is about 1s. 8d.

Manufacture of Stockings.—The manufacturing of stockings has been carried on here since the 1773. 11 Looms are at present employed in it; 7 in what is called *customer-work*, i. e. in working materials which families or individuals prepare for their own comsumption, and 4 in manufacturing for sale.

* Kinghorn.

fale. Calculating on the average of all fizes and qualities of ftockings, every loom employed for fale produces annually about 520 pairs, worth from 2s. to 4s. each, or about L. 70 the whole produce. The average of the earnings of an induftrious ftocking maker is about 8s. in the week.

Sea Salt.——The making of fea falt was once a manufacture here, and a long eftablifhed one. In the town's charter of confirmation (1644), the falt pans are mentioned as part of the defcription of the burgh. But little or no falt has been made fince coal ceafed to be wrought in the parifh *.

Bank.—The general profperity of this place has been much promoted by the eftablifhment of a branch of the bank of Scotland in 1785. As moft of the bufinefs of the neighbouring diftrict is tranfacted through the medium of this branch, its annual operations in the way of cafh accounts, difcounting bills, and circulating the paper of the company, are very confiderable. And it is worth while to remark, that notwithftanding the increafed facility of obtaining credit which has been produced by it, yet no failure of any confequence has happened here; nor has the bank, or their agent, who guarantees to them all the bills which he difcounts, fuffered any lofs, fince the office was eftablifhed.

About two years ago, the banking company of Dundee attempted to fhare this profitable trade with the bank of Scotland

---

* Since the above was written, the making of falt has again begun, and is likely to be carried on with fuccefs : a late advance on the price of falt being more than fufficient to balance the extra expence of bringing coals from a diftance.

land. But owing to the circumſtances of the times, the at‑
tempt has not ſucceeded.

Diſadvantages.——While different circumſtances conſpire
to render this town an advantageous ſituation for commerce
and manufactures, there are obvious diſadvantages un‑
der which it labours. 1. The harbour is narrow, incommo‑
dious, and ſo much expoſed to an heavy ſea from the eaſt,
as to ſuffer frequent injury. This, it is poſſible in ſome
degree to remedy; but at an expence to which the funds of
the town are at preſent inadequate. 2. The pariſh affords
no water for the neceſſary operation of bleaching, or for
driving the machinery by which the ſpinning both of cotton
and flax is now beginning to be performed. 3. The vicinity
of the capital contributes to increaſe the prices of labour and
proviſions, and perhaps too, to produce ſome effect on the
general habits of living : Add to all this, 4. The unfriendly
influence of corporation and burgh privileges. The corpo‑
ration ſpirit, limiting to a few, advantages to which all have a
natural claim, and making the *freedom of the trade*, as it is
called, paramount both to ſkill and induſtry, cannot in the
nature of the thing, but operate unfavourably on the proſpe‑
rity of the community. It is probably owing to the operation
of this ſpirit, that although free burgage tenure be every way
ſuperior to that of burghs of regality and barony, yet the
adjacent towns of Linktown and Pathhead, which are of the
laſt kind, have for 30 years back increaſed in more than a
double proportion to the royal burgh of Kirkaldy. The *politics*
of burghs, too, generally affect the public induſtry and the
public morals : Or if they ſhould not, at any rate they tend
to abate the public happineſs and proſperity. The colliſion
of political opinions and political intereſts, dividing the in‑
habitants

habitants into *parties* or *fets*, not only diminifhes the freedom
of intercourfe and familiar fociety, but prevents the application of the public ftrength *entire*, to the profecution of the
public good.

Although this place has fuffered in common with others
from that unhappy caufe, it is but juftice to fay, that there is
perhaps none of the burghs of Scotland, of which the conftitution is more liberal, or of which the government is lefs
appropriated.

Conftitution of the Burgh.——At the time that the oldeft
exifting records of the burgh commence (A. D. 1586,) the
form of its government was popular, and extremely fimple.
The whole adminiftration was vefted in two baillies, annually
elected *by the inhabitants, nybors and freemen at large,* who as
the minute of election bears, *gave them commiffion, and promifed them fubjection and affiftance.* The baillies, after taking
an oath of fidelity, named what was called the *head court* or
annual affife. This court immediately fat, and *ordained acts
and ftatutes for the public weil;* which were inftantly recorded
as the baillies guide for their year of office. In 1595 a council was added to affift the baillies. This council, two or
three years after, affumed the power of naming a *leet,* from
which the inhabitants were to choofe the magiftrates; and
after the preparation of a year or two more, took the election wholly into its own hands, and excluded the community.
In the charter of confirmation, however, the right of electing
their magiftrates was refolved to the community in common
with the council. And when the burgh was in 1652 incorporated with the commonwealth of England, that right was
exprefsly recognifed and continued to them : And " the
" neighbours and inhabitants of the town were authorifed and
" appointed, according to their former rites and cuftoms, from
" time

" time to time to nominate and chooſetheir magiſtrates and o-
" ther officers for the government of the burgh *". The Reſtoration produced a new conſtitution ; the formation of which
was a ſource of violent diſſenſions among the inhabitants.
Theſe were, however, at length compoſed by the arbitration
of the Earl of Rothes, then Preſident of the Privy Council ;
who by his decreet arbitral pronounced in 1662, eſtabliſhed
the *ſet* or *conſtitution* which ſtill ſubſiſts ; and which has continued ſince that time without interruption, ſave only during
the reign of James II. who by his organ, the Privy council,
expreſsly nominated and appointed to the magiſtracy, &c.
ſuch perſons as he judged moſt *loyal and ready to promote his
ſervice* †. By this conſtitution the government of the burgh
is veſted in a council annually choſen from three claſſes of
inhabitants, mariners, merchants, and craftſmen. The council conſiſts of 21 members ; of whom 10 muſt be mariners, 8
merchants, and 3 craftſmen. The old council elect their
ſucceſſors ; to whom, however, they do not wholly reſign
their places, till they have voted along with them and with
the deacons ‡ of the incorporated trades in the election of the
new magiſtrates. Theſe are taken from the new council ; and
conſiſt of a provoſt, 2 baillies, a dean of guild, and a treaſurer. The incorporated trades are 7 in number ; and rank
in the following order ; ſmiths, wrights and maſons, weavers, ſhoemakers, taylors, bakers, and fleſhers. Here as in
　　　　　　　　　　　　　　　　　　　　　　　　other

* Commiſſion from the Parliament of the Commonwealth of England, to
the inhabitants of Kirkaldy, to chooſe their own magiſtrates, *penes* Town
Council.

† Act of the Privy Council in 1687, appointing the Earl of Balcarras, and
others, magiſtrates of Kirkaldy. *penes* Town Council.

‡ The Deacons have a vote in the Council in all caſes, excepting the formation of the new Council.

other burghs, the privilege of exercising their several trades is enjoyed exclusively by the members of the incorporation ; excepting in the case of weavers and fleshers. The exclusive privileges of the former were reduced by an act of the legislature in 1751 ; by which weavers in flax and hemp are permitted to settle and exercise their trades any where in Scotland, free of all corporation dues. And the injurious consequences of the corporation privilege are guarded against, in the case of the latter, by an act of the first Parliament of Queen Anne, (sess. 1. ch. 7.) ; which declares it to be leisume to all persons whatsomever, to sell and break all sorts of fleshes on every lawful day of the week, and that in all towns and burghs of this kingdom, free of any imposition whatsomever, the petty custom of burghs excepted.

Parliamentary Representation.—Since the Union of the two kingdoms, this burgh joins with the neighbouring burghs of Dysart, Kinghorn, and Burntisland, in sending a representative to the British Parliament. Delegates, nominated by the councils of the several burghs, elect the representative. The return of the representative is made by the burghs in rotation ; and in case of an equality, the delegate of the returning burgh has a double voice. The greatest number of those who vote for the delegate is 28 ; and the choice is determined by a majority. The delegate, when chosen, is not merely the legal organ by which the sense of his constituents is expressed. He acts in the matter of election, without limitation or controul ; and his principles are their only security for his conveying their sentiments.

Revenue.——The revenue of this burgh is but inconsiderable. It arises partly from feu-duties on land. By the original

nal charter of erection *, 52 acres of adjacent land, which, together with the burgh, had been conveyed to the abbey of Dunfermling in 1450, were disjoined from the regality of the abbey, and annexed to the burgh, to be held of the crown. Some time after, the right of paſturage in the moor, which had alſo been conveyed to the burgh in 1450, was by a new conveyance from the abbey, converted into property †. The moor and burgh acres extended to full three fourths of the preſent pariſh. The burgh acres were early alienated. The moor continued long in the poſſeſſion of the community. In 1648, at which time the parts of it that lay neareſt the town were begun to be converted into arable land, it was let at L. 72 : 6 : 8 ‡. In 1688, the moor and common loan were let at L. 68 : 10 §. Since that time the whole property of the town has been feued out, and it now yields L. 40 : 12,

to

---

* This charter, which is referred to in the Charter of Confirmation, but without ſpecifying its date, is not now to be found. It is probable that the papers which related to the erection of the burgh, were either deſtroyed in 1560, when the French, whom the Queen Regent brought into Scotland to aſſiſt in ſuppreſſing the Proteſtants, plundered and burnt Kirkaldy in their deſtructive progreſs along the coaſt of Fife, or loſt in 1651 at the taking of Dundee, to which place they had, on Cromwell's invaſion, been removed for ſecurity, with other valuable effects, as mentioned in page 21ſt. One or other of theſe is ſtated in a memorial from the town in 1678; as the reaſon why they could not be produced in a proceſs before the Court of Seſſion, in which an exhibiton of them had been ordered. The facts ſtated above are taken from different papers in poſſeſſion of the burgh.

† This conveyance is mentioned in an inventory of writs belonging to the burgh in 1722.

‡ Renounciation and diſcharge Henry Boſwell to the town.

§ Report of the Commiſſion of Viſitation, appointed by the Convention of Burghs.

to the community *. In this fum all public burdens are included; the community having become bound, when their lands were feued, to relieve the feuars of all public burdens in all time coming; thus leaving to pofterity one incontrovertible proof, at leaft, that they once had property.

The reft of the revenue is drawn from a port duty on goods landed at the harbour, from the petty cuftoms on goods interchanged with the neighbouring country, and from an impoft of 2 pennies Scots on the pint of ale brewed in the town for fale, or fold into it from the neighbourhood. This laft is a parliamentary grant, which was firft given for a limited period, in 1707, with the burden of L. 10 annually, to the profeffor of mathematics in the King's College of Aberdeen; and which has, fince that time, been again and again renewed, without any burden. The whole revenue produced laft year L. 317 †, but it does not average above L. 260. The ordinary purpofes to which the revenue is applied, are: 1. The difcharge of public burdens, amounting annually to about L. 60. 2. The payment of intereft on a debt of L. 2430 ‡. 3. The reparation of the harbour. 4. The payment of clerks, officers, and all the incidental expences incurred in conducting the bufinefs of the community.

The annual cefs paid to government from this burgh is L. 80:9:8; to which it was reduced on a reprefentation

to

---

* Above 400 acres of the moor were feued to the late Mr Ofwald of Dunikeer, at the yearly feu-duty of L. 45 : 10. But, in confequence of a referve to the feuar, to buy up the feu-duty at leaft to a certain extent, at 20 years purchafe, it has been lately reduced to L. 20 : 18 : 4; fo that the whole feu duties now payable to the town, are as above ftated.

† Feu duties L. 40 : 12 ; petty cuftom L. 28 : 10 ; fhore-dues L. 135 ; impoft L. 105 ; meal market, weigh-houfe, &c. L. 8. Total L. 317 : 2.

‡ At the Revolution, the debt of the town was 60,000 merks, or L. 3333 6s. 8d. Sterling, as afcertained by the Commiffion of Vifitation.

to the convention of royal burghs in 1770, after having ſtood at L. 94 : 15 : 9, ſince the Union. Part of the ceſs is levied from the traders, according to the trade of each, aſcertained by a jury of 5 mariners, 5 merchants and 5 craftsmen ; who are nominated by the council, but who cannot at the time be members of the council. Part of it is levied from the burgh acres. But three fourths of it are raiſed by a poundage on houſe rents. Theſe have been progreſſively advancing for 30 years. In 1763, they were eſtimated at L. 729 ; in 1783 at L. 1050 ; in 1793 at L. 1654. As houſes in the poſſeſſion of proprietors are always rated below the real value, the whole houſe rents may be eſtimated at L. 2000 ; which is about the proportion of L. 3 of rent for each family.

The window tax amounts nearly to as much as the ceſs. The whole duties paid to the tax-office for the year ending 5th April 1793, amounted to L. 171 *. The whole duties paid to the exciſe-office †, for the year ending 6th July 1793, amounted to L. 2250 : 15 : 6¼. The poſt office produced in 1793 ; L. 528 ; the diſtribution of ſtamps L. 433. When to theſe branches the cuſtoms are added, the whole revenue drawn

---

* Window duty, old and new, L. 76 : 19 : 10 ; inhabited houſes L. 6 : 12 : 3 ; wheel-carriages L. 48 : 8 ; male ſervants L. 23 : 18 : 6 ; horſes L. 15 : 2 : 6. Total L. 171 : 1 : 1.

† This is properly the reſidence of the collector of exciſe for the county of Fife. It is alſo the reſidence of a ſupervisor, and of ――― officers of exciſe. The detail of the exciſe-duties ſtated above, is as follows : Ale, L. 259 : 13 ; candle, L. 59 : 2 ; leather, L. 471 : 14 : 10¼ ; malt, L. 174 : 11 ; wine and ſpirits imported, excluſive of the cuſtom-houſe duty, L. 1130 : 15 : 8 ; wine licences, L. 12 ; foreign ſpirit do. L. 71 : 8 ; plain aquavitæ do. L. 46 ; tea do. L. 9 : 7 ; tobacco do. L. 5 : 5 ; licences for brewers, candlemakers, tanners, and curriers, L. 11 : 10. Total, L. 2250 : 15 : 6¼.

drawn from this parish for one year will amount to
L. 4814 : 18 : 3; which is nearly in the proportion of
£. 1 : 16, for every perfon, man, woman, and child in the
parish *.

Ecclefiaftical State.——The ecclefiaftical eftablifhment of
this parifh has, through the low ftate of the burgh funds,
fuffered a temporary reduction. In 1614, the date of the
oldeft ecclefiaftical record, the church appears to have been
collegiate; the duty of it having been conducted by two minifters, exercifing equal powers, and having nearly an equal
provifion †. At that time the ftipend of the fecond minifter
was 800 merks, paid the one half by the heritors, the other
by the town council ‡; while that of the firft minifter in 1630,
was no more than 480 merks, a chalder of bear, a chalder of
oats, and 4 bolls of wheat §. Both charges continued to be
regularly fupplied, and both minifters to fit as conftituent
members of all the ecclefiaftical judicatures ||, till 1759; when
a vacancy happening in the fecond charge, the minifter of the
firft undertook to do the duty of the whole parifh, on condition of receiving, together with his own ftipend, the half of

that

* Of the articles which pay duty in this parifh, a great proportion is confumed out of it. This, however, may be confidered as balanced by other
articles confumed in the parifh, which pay duty, but of which the duty is
either not paid in the parifh, or not included in the above ftatement. Articles
of the firft kind, are tea, coffee, fugar, rum, porter, vinegar, home-made
fpirits. tobacco, glafs, paper, filk, printed cloth, fail-cloth and cordage,
foap, ftarch, pins, newfpapers and almanacks, cards, and dice, &c. Articles
of the laft kind, are, falt, hats, drugs, perfumery, &c.

† Seffion records, *paffim.*

‡ The amount of the ftipend and the mode of payment, is written on a
leaf at the beginning of the oldeft volume of the Seffion records.

§ This is recorded in a volume of the Prefbytery records of the above date.

|| Records of Prefbytery, Synod, and General Affembly,

that which had been enjoyed by his colleague. This arrangement, the oſtenſible reaſon of which was the poverty of the
burgh, (which after the disjunction of Abbotſhall, paid the
whole of the ſecond miniſter's ſtipend); the preſbytery were
prevailed on to allow for a time. And although the town-
council have, ever ſince the death of the incumbent with
whom the arrangement was made, appropriated that ſtipend to their own uſe, the charge to this day continues
vacant.

Stipend.—The crown preſents to the firſt charge; the town
council were in uſe of ſupplying the ſecond. The ſtipend of
the ſecond charge in 1759, was 1000 merks Scots. The
preſent ſtipend of the firſt charge is 120$\frac{14}{64}$ bolls of bear, 79$\frac{3}{4}$
bolls of oats, and 100 merks of vicarage. The laſt decreet
of augmentation (which, was paſſed in 1737) gives alſo the
tiend of fiſh *according to uſe and wont*. But as almoſt the
whole of the fiſh ſold here, is carried over land, and the uſe
and wont is underſtood to confine the miniſter's right to fiſh
carried into the pariſh by water, no advantage is at preſent
derived to him from this part of his decreet. The firſt miniſter has a manſe; a glebe of about 2$\frac{1}{4}$ acres, and about the
ſame quantity of land, *independent of the glebe*, enjoyed ſince
1678 by a private mortification. By a recent judgement of the
preſbytery, the miniſter is found intitled to have this glebe
enlarged to the legal ſtandard, and to have ground aſſigned
to him for paſture. This judgement has, however, been
ſuſpended, and is now under the review of the Court of
Seſſion.

Church.——The church is old, how old is not exactly
known. It is ſaid to have been dedicated to St. Briſſe; who

in

in the days of fuperftition appears to have been the tutelar faint of the place *, and who has entailed his name on a fmall divifion of the burgh lands, which is called in the regifter of fafines St. Briffe or *St. Bryce's Deal.* The church is but in indifferent repair ; nor could it well be otherwife, when neither the heritors nor town-council have for more than 180 years taken any charge of it. What repairs it has received during that time have been paid for by the kirk-feffion. On the recommendation of the heritors and council, the collections made at the church doors before the afternoon fervice were for a while employed for this purpofe. But the prefbytery having inhibited that application of the collections, the church has for more than a century been kept in repair out of a part of the feat-rents, which are under the management of the kirk-feffion.

Seats.——Originally the whole area of the church was in their hands : And their records fhew that all the incorporations, and fuch of the heritors as have feats, (more than the half of them have none) derived their rights from the kirkfeffion. They ftill retain about a fourth part of the church ; from which they draw annually from L. 18 to L. 20. The neceffary repairs are defrayed from this fund, the remainder of which goes to the maintenance of the poor in common with the collections. Some of the heritors of Abbotfhall retain their feats in the church of Kirkaldy ; and by a decreet of the Court of Seffion in 1685, are found liable
in

* The arms of the burgh appear to have been framed in compliment to this faint. Thefe are a Gate of a Church, with the Saint ftanding in it, having a Mitre on his head, fomething refembling a Crofs in his hand, a Moon and Star, as emblems of night round him ; and the motto under, *Vigilando munio.*

in their proportion of the repairs. The tiends of Abbot-shall are, by the fame decreet, liable for the repairs of the quire of Kirkaldy.

Diffenters.——There is no place for public worfhip in the parifh, but the parifh church; if a mafon lodge be excepted, which is employed for that purpofe by an handful of independents. Moft of the other diffenters attend at different places in the neighbouring parifhes. On the firft of January 790, the diffenters, taking the whole number of fouls, were 595; which was to the eftablifhment nearly in the proportion of 1 to 3½, and of 1 to 4½ of the whole population. Thefe were divided among the different denominations of diffenters in the following proportions, viz. Burghers 304, antiburghers 206, prefbytery of relief 51, independents 11, epifcopals 10, reformed prefbytery 9, Bereans 2, baptift 1, Roman catholic 1.

The diffenters of this place, and particularly thofe of them who retain the ftandards of the church, are diftinguifhed for moderation and liberality. Of that forbidding afperity, which for fome time after their firft feparation characterized the conduct of feceders towards the members of the church, there is fcarcely a trace remaining. Good men of the feceffion and of the eftablifhment, dwell together as brethren in the exercife of mutual charity and of mutual efteem. And in one of their congregations, the minifter of which refides in Kirkaldy and takes his official defignation from it, the eftablifhed congregation of the place, has not unfrequently by name, a friendly intereft in the public prayers.

School.——The public fchool is under the care of two mafters; who teach in feparate rooms, and without any dependence one on the other. The firft mafter teaches Latin,

French,

French, Arithmetic, Book-keeping, &c.; the fecond, Englifh and Writing. The firft has a yearly falary of L. 20; which, with the fchool-fees, and the emoluments of the office of feffion-clerk which he holds at prefent, makes his living a-bout L. 60. The fecond has a falary of L. 10 * ; which, with the emolument of his fchool and private teaching, makes his living about L. 40. The ftated falaries of both are paid by the town-council. There are feveral private fchools in the place. In all the fchools there are about 250 children in the ordinary courfe of attendance.

The Poor.—The poor of this parifh are chiefly fupplied from the collections at the church doors. Thefe, notwith-ftanding the increafe of money, which the profperity of the country has of late produced, are not fo great as they were an hundred years ago †. This may be partly a confequence of the Seceffion, which has diminifhed the numbers of the eftablifhed congregation. But it may be partly attributed alfo, to a feceffion of a different kind, the feceffion of too many of thofe, who are called " the better fort," from the public ordinances of religion.—The Seceders of this clafs are unhappily fo numerous in moft parts of the country, that a plain man, who fhould judge from the general conduct, might be apt to conclude, that the poffeffion of a little land, a commiffion in the army or navy, or any diftinction pro-feffional or official, which allows a man to add Efquire to his name, were confidered as a charter, entitling the poffeffor to " hold blanch" of Heaven, on paying an occafional duty ; and

---

* Since the above was written, the falary of the fecond mafter has been augmented to L. 16.

† Vide pages 523, and 528.

and that, perhaps, only when demanded by royal proclamation. This is " a ſore evil," of which the country at large is at preſent eating the bitter fruits ; no one cauſe perhaps having contributed more; if not to excite, at leaſt to foment that ſpirit of " inſubordination," which has of late occaſioned ſuch general alarm. Not only does the irreligion of the higher ranks abate their perſonal reſpeſctability and influence; but, as the common people, by a proceſs of mind of which the meaneſt are capable, transfer the charaſcter of their ſuperiors whom they know, to thoſe whom they know not, it has the effeſct of inducing an unfavourable opinion of the holders of place and power in general. And, what is ſtill more injurious to the intereſts of ſociety, it operates in the way of example, gradually to weaken and deſtroy the reſtraints of religion on the public mind, and ſo to leave it open, and without a guard to the impreſſions of the ill-diſpoſed and deſigning.

Were men of rank and fortune to ſee their duty, or even their intereſt, in the proper light, and to cultivate and maintain the religious charaſcter; beſides the advantage which they would derive to themſelves, in reſpeſct of improvement and comfort, they would ſecure at once, a perſonal influence, and an acceſſion of ſtrength to the ſtate, which, ſo long as they ſet up independant of religion, all their exertions will be inſufficient to gain.

Through the irregular attendance of many of the upper ranks, the public ſupplies for the poor are here drawn chiefly from that claſs of inhabitants on which they ought to fall lighteſt, thoſe whoſe perſonal labour is generally no more than ſufficient for the comfortable maintenance of their own families. It is not ſurpriſing, therefore, that notwithſtanding the populouſneſs of the pariſh, the ordinary collections for 12 years preceding 1791, produced no more
than

than L. 63 : 10. Since that time, by difpenfing the facrament twice in the year, and by making an extraordinary collection at the new year, they have averaged L. 85. When to this is added, the furplus of feat rents *, the donations which are cuftomary among the more opulent on occafion of marriages and the death of friends, and the intereft of an accumulated fum of L. 290, the whole funds, under the management of the kirk-feffion, have for 2 or 3 years amounted to about L. 110; or about L. 100 clear, after deducing (the only expence incurred in the management), fmall falaries to a treafurer and diftributor, a clerk, and an officer. Out of this fum above 40 perfons are regularly fupplied ; 8 or 9 of the moft deftitute of whom have the additional benefit of lodging, in a houfe purchafed for the poor, about 50 years ago. Befides the regular penfioners, above 40 more are fupplied occafionally †. That the whole muft be inadequately fupplied, any one may fee who compares their number with the funds to be divided among them. Although no man, who has the welfare of his country at heart, would wifh to fee poor's rates eftablifhed here on the fame footing on which they are in England, yet the friend of humanity muft regret, that fome equitable plan is not generally adopted for fecuring more effectually to the indigent, the neceffary aid of their more fortunate brethren. Perhaps the time is not very remote, when fomething of this kind muft be done. When

fo

---

* See page 551.

† Since the above was written, the poor have become fo numerous, and their neceffities fo urgent, that befides extraordinary and liberal contributions made by the inhabitants, the kirk feffion have been obliged to encroach on their capital. Upwards of 170 perfons, a confiderable proportion of them with families, have been fupplied at one public diftribution.

ſo many of thoſe on whom the law reſts the burden of the poor, beſtow neither time, nor thought, nor money, to provide for them, it is not improbable that kirk ſeſſions, whoſe attention to the poor is merely " a labour of love"; to which they are no otherwiſe bound, than by the common obligations of humanity, will find themſelves conſtrained to do in general, what ſome of them already threaten, give up collecting at the church doors, and leave it to the civil magiſtrate to make proviſion for the poor, by putting the laws for their ſupport in execution.

It is fortunate for the poor of this pariſh that they do not all depend upon the public funds. The ſociety of ſeamen, the company of merchants, the incorporated trades, the maltmen, the carters, have all of them ſeparate boxes for aſſiſting the poor of their reſpective ſocieties. The ſeamen, in particular, have funds, ariſing partly from rents and feu-duties, and partly from a poundage on the wages of ſailors, which enable them to pay annually to indigent members of their ſociety, or to their widows and families, about L. 40, beſides furniſhing ten of them with a houſe to lodge in.

Charitable Aſſociations.—Three different aſſociations have of late been formed here, for the purpoſe of aſſiſting the members, when their ordinary labour is ſuſpended by diſtreſs. Theſe are all conſtituted on the ſame general plan. Each member, beſides a ſmall ſum paid on his admiſſion, contributes at the rate of one penny in the week, and receives weekly, when confined, 3 ſhillings. To thoſe, whoſe daily ſubſiſtence depends on their perſonal induſtry, this is often a ſeaſonable ſupply; and the meaneſt labourer can without difficulty afford the contribution which entitles him to receive it.

Means

Means of Subsistence, and Wages.—The inhabitants of this parish, upon the whole, enjoy the means of subsistence in an equal degree with those of the same level in any other part of the country. The late successful exertions of the trader and manufacturer, have, by increasing the demand for all kinds of labour, and of course increasing their price, contributed to improve the circumstances of the community in general. And, although the cause of this improvement does not at present operate with the same force, yet weaving, the price of which was the first increased, is perhaps the only species of labour of which the wages have yet suffered any considerable diminution. Wrights and masons still earn from 9s. to 10s. 6d. in the week; smiths from 7s. to 10s.; shoemakers from 5s. to 10s.; taylors from 6s. to 8s.; hacklers from 9s. to 15s.; gardeners from 8s. to 12s.; day-labourers from 6s. to 7s. in all seasons; and during the time of harvest, and of weeding and hoeing, which, since drilled crops have become so frequent, continue through a great part of the summer, their earnings are still higher. Male farm servants, and female servants, whether for house or farm, are commonly hired by the half-year; and receive of wages, the former from L. 3 : 10s. to L. 4. the latter from 25s. to 40s. exclusive of their subsistence.

Provisions.—While such is the rate of wages, and labourers in general are fully employed, provisions are obtained easily, and upon the whole at a moderate price. Oat meal, now less used than formerly, but still a chief article of food among the working classes, sells, on an average of seven years, at 1s. the peck; flour at 1s. 4d.; pease and barley meal at 8d. When oat meal is cheap, the consumption of it is to that of flour, nearly in the proportion of two thirds, when dear, of one half. Two thirds of the oat meal consumed here is

brought

brought from a diftance, chiefly from Mid-Lothian. The flour is chiefly furnifhed by the county of Fife, though there is occafionally a fupply from England.

The flefh market is well fupplied in all feafons, and the confumption of butcher-meat very confiderable, probably three times what it was twenty years ago. The average of the number, weight, and value of the different kinds of cattle which have been annually killed, and fold here for fome years, is as follows.

Kinds.	Number.	Weight of each in tron ftones.	Total weight of each kind.	Medium price, per lib. of 22 oz.	Total value.
Beeves	600	24	14.000	$3^{d}\frac{3}{4}$	L.3.500
Calves	550	3	1.650	4 $\frac{1}{2}$	495
Sheep	1500	2	3.000	4 $\frac{1}{2}$	900
Lambs	900	$1\frac{1}{4}$	1.125	4 $\frac{1}{2}$	337
Hogs	60	8	480	4 $\frac{1}{2}$	144
	3610		20.255 ftones or 445 6ro lb. Engl.		L.5.376

Of this quantity, a full third goes into the confumption of the neighbouring parifhes: About 700 ftones are bought for fea-ftores, by the fhipmafters of the place; whofe principal fupplies of falt-beef are from Ireland: The remainder (about 12.530 ftones *tron*; or 275.660 lib. Englifh), is confumed in the parifh; and is nearly in the proportion of 4 ftones, 11 lib. or 103 lib. Englifh, to every man, woman, and child in it.

The fupply of fifh is leffened, and the price raifed, by the nearnefs of the metropolis. There are no fifhers that belong to this parifh: About the beginning of fummer, a family or two ufually come from Buck-haven, the principal fifhing ftation on the fouth coaft of Fife, and refide here for a few months, for the convenience of fupplying the inhabitants. But the chief fupply is carried from Buck-haven and Wemyfs,

over

over land, on the backs, fometimes of horfes, but more commonly of women. In this way, moft kinds of fifh that are caught in the Frith, are pretty regularly brought to Kirkaldy in their feafons, haddocks excepted; which have for feveral years, been extremely rare, and have been fold at enormous prices. A fhilling has been paid for a fingle haddock, that 15 years ago would have fold for a halfpenny.

The vicinity of Edinburgh has an effect alfo on the prices of eggs, poultry, and butter. Eggs fell from 4d. to 7d. the dozen, hens from 1s. to 1s 6d. each, chickens from 8d. to 1s 4d. the pair, butter from 8d. to 11d. the pound, green cheefe made of fkimmed milk, from 2d. to 3d. the pound *. All thefe articles, (together with the yarn that is fpun in the neighbourhood with the hand), are regularly expofed to fale, in the weekly market, which holds here on Saturday, and has this peculiarity, that it begins between 3 and 4 o'clock in the morning, and is generally over by 6 o'clock. This cuftom was probably introduced at firft, to evade the law which prohibits Saturday and Monday markets †. And the convenience of attending the market in the morning, and returning home in time for the ordinary labour of the day, has induced the country people to continue the cuftom, notwithftanding that frequent attempts have been made to alter it. By the Charter of Charles, the Burgh had the privilege of holding two annual fairs; one on the third Wednefday of July, another on the laft Wednefday of September. For a long time, thefe were regularly kept; but as the conftant trade of the place advanced, the fairs gradually diminifhed; and for many years, there has not been a veftige of them.

The

---

* Cheefe and butter, as well as butcher meat, are here fold by the tron or heavy pound of 22 ounces.

† Charles II. Par. i. fefl. 3. cap. 19.

Manners and Charaƈer.—The inhabitants of this pariſh ſeem in general to enjoy the advantages of their ſituation, and live comfortably. Among the upper claſſes, the ſtile of living is genteel, but not luxurious or expenſive. Allowing for the diverſity of circumſtances, all claſſes dreſs well, and are generally civil in their manners, and decent in their external deportment. Although a conſiderable proportion of them have been bred to the ſea, there is nothing of the roughneſs which common opinion has attached to that profeſſion. The claſs of ſeamen is not leſs reſpeƈable in character than in numbers. The great body of the people are induſtrious and ſober : but 31 houſes and 19 ſhops licenſed to retail ſpirits,—a number that is in the proportion of 1 to 13 of all the families in the place,—furniſh room to ſuſpeƈ, that from this part of the public character there muſt be exceptions. Strong drink appears to have been long a conſiderable article in the conſumption of Kirkaldy. A temporary impoſt on wines and foreign ſpirits *vented* within the burgh, having, by a charter of Charles II. been granted to the magiſtrates and council for the payment of their public debts, the *deficiencies* of that impoſt for *one* year ending November 1671, are ſtated in a proceſs for recovering them, brought againſt the vintners, to have been 60 pieces, (hogſheads) French wine, 6 butts Sack, 60 pints Rheniſh, 80 pints Tent, and 80 pints * brandy. Far down in the preſent century, it was the practice, even among citizens of ſome character, to take a regular *whet* in the forenoon, and moſt commonly to ſpend the evening in the public houſe. For a conſiderable time this practice has been given up ; and the habit of drinking ſpirits to exceſs is confined to a few, and theſe generally of the very

loweſt

---

* Scotch pints, two of which are about $\frac{1}{10}$ leſs than the Engliſh wine gallon.

loweft order. It is remarkable, however, that no lefs than 8 perfons, and fome of them ranking above the loweft order, have in little more than 4 years vifibly fallen victims to this deftructive habit. With fome exceptions, among the two extremes, the higher ranks, and the very loweft and moft worthlefs, the inhabitants are regular in attending the ordinances of religion, and generally obfervant of its moral duties. Although petty thefts, and other breaches of law that call for correction, may be fuppofed to happen at times in fo large a community, yet the public character has been rarely ftained by the commiffion of great crimes. One or two inftances of child-murder have occurred within the remembrance of the prefent generation. But no inhabitant of Kirkaldy has fuffered the punifhment of death fince the commencement of the laft century; a man and his wife excepted, who were burnt here in 1633, for the fuppofed crime of witchcraft *.

Eminent Men.—In refpect of intellectual abilities, the inhabitants of Kirkaldy are not beneath the ordinary level; and the parifh has at different times produced men that rofe far beyond it. The firft, and not the leaft diftinguifhed, whofe name has reached us, is MICHAEL SCOT, the Friar Bacon of Scotland;

---

* At that time the belief of witchcraft prevailed, and trials and executions on account of it were frequent in all the kingdoms of Europe. It was in 1634 that the famous Urban Grandier was, at the inftigation of Cardinal Richelieu, whom he had fatirifed, tried and condemned to the ftake, for exercifing the black art on fome nuns of Loudun, who were fuppofed to be poffeffed. And it was much about the fame time, that the wife of the Marechal D'Ancre was burnt for a witch, at the Place de Greve at Paris.

Scotland *; who, in the 13th century, contributed, by his at-
tainments in ſcience, to break the gloom of that benighted
age. After purſuing with unuſual ſucceſs the ſtudy of languages, belles lettres, and mathematics, at home, Mr Scot
travelled into France, where he reſided ſeveral years. From
France he removed into Germany, and lived for a while at
the court of the Emperor Frederick II. a prince the moſt e-
minent of his time, both for his own learning, and for the encouragement which he gave to learned men. But that prince
being then engaged in war, Mr Scot withdrew from the court,
to proſecute with more advantage in retirement his favourite ſtudies of medicine and chemiſtry. After ſome years he
returned through England, (where he was well received by Edward I.) into his own country, and there died in 1291.

The extraordinary diſcoveries of this man, particularly in
chemiſtry, made him paſs in that ignorant and ſuperſtitious
age, for a magician ; and a thouſand popular ſtories are in
different parts of Scotland told to this day, of his commerce
with evil ſpirits, and of the wonders which he atchieved
through their agency. He is alſo ſaid to have been a prophet, and among other events to have foretold the union of
Scotland and England †. He left behind him. 1, A tran-
ſlation of Avicena's book on animals from the Arabic into
Latin : 2. A Commentary on the works of Ariſtotle : 3. A
Treatiſe on the Secrets of Nature, on the principles of the A-
riſtotelian Philoſophy. In this book he treats at large of a
ſcience, to which a modern author ‡ has applied much ingenuity,

* He was born at his family ſeat of Balweary, now the property of Mr.
Ferguſon of Raith, and ſince 1650 part of the pariſh of Abbotſhall.

† Belſour's Hiſtory of Scotland.

‡ Lavater.

nuity, Phyfiognomy : 4. A book on Alchymy, entitled, the Nature of the Sun and Moon : 5. A book entitled Menfa Philofophica.

Sir George M'Kenzie calls him one of the greateft Philofophers, Mathematicians, Phyficians, and Linguifts, of the times in which he lived ; and fays, that had he not been fo much addicted to aftrology, alchymy, phyfiognomy, and chiromancy, he would have deferved well of the republic of letters.

Towards the middle of the 17th century, Meffrs George and Patrick Gillefpie, natives of this place, and Mr. Robert Douglas, who, with Patrick Gillefpie, was fome time minifter of Kirkaldy, diftinguifhed themfelves by their writings and their conduct, in the ecclefiaftical hiftory of thofe difficult times. All the three were zealoufly attached to the caufe of Prefbytery, which was then confidered in Scotland as intimately connected with the caufe of general liberty. Two of them, Mr George Gillefpie, and Mr Douglas, having been previoufly tranflated to Edinburgh, were in 1643 nominated by the General Affembly of the church of Scotland, Commiffioners to the Affembly of Divines at Weftminfter ; in the proceedings of which, Mr Gillefpie in particular conducted himfelf with much ability and prudence. He was one of the firft characters at that time in the church. He wrote Mifcellanies, &c. He died in 1649, at the age of 36. A marble monument, which was infcribed to his memory, (it is believed at the public expence), and which, as an appended infcription bears, was pulled down through the " malign in- " fluence of Archbifhop Sharp," but afterwards repaired by the relations of Mr Gillefpie, is ftill ftanding in this church yard.

After the death of Charles I. Mr Douglas and Mr Patrick Gillefpie took different fides. The former efpoufed the interefts of Charles II. at whofe coronation at Scone in 1651

he

he preached, and conducted the religious part of that cere-
mony *. The latter favoured the views of the commonwealth of England, by whoſe commiſſioners he was made
Principal of the Univerſity of Glaſgow ; but was ejected at
the Reſtoration. The counſels and pens of both were employed to ſupport the ſides to which they ſeverally attached
themſelves.

During the preſent century this pariſh has produced different perſons, who have attracted public notice. Dr. John
Dryſdale, late one of the miniſters of Edinburgh, and author
of two volumes of poſthumous ſermons, was a native of it,
and received the rudiments of his education at what his
learned biographer calls, The obſcure ſchool of Kirkaldy.
He was born in 1718, and died in 1788.

Kirkaldy was the birth-place of that diſtinguiſhed ſtateſman, Mr Oſwald of Dunnikeer. Mr Oſwald was originally
bred to the bar.— But having in 1741 been choſen to ſerve in
parliament for the diſtrict of burghs, of which this is one, he
bent the whole force of his mind to his parliamentary duty ;
in the proſecution of which, his abilities, integrity, and laborious attention to the intereſts, particularly the commercial
intereſts, of his country, raiſed him from the level of a citizen
of Kirkaldy, to the firſt offices and honours of the ſtate. He
was ſucceſſively a commiſſioner of trade and plantations, a
lord of the treaſury, and vice-treaſurer of Ireland. He was
alſo a privy counſellor. After repreſenting this diſtrict of
burghs in three parliaments, and the county of Fife in a fourth,
he, in 1768, retired from public buſineſs, on account of ill-
health induced by too intenſe an application to it. He died
in 1769 at the age of 54.

Kirkaldy has alſo the ſignal honour to have given birth to
that

---

* His ſermon on that occaſion was publiſhed, and is ſtill extant.

that eminent benefactor to fociety, Dr Adam Smith, the enlightened author of the " Inquiry into the Nature and Caufes
" of the Wealth of Nations," and to have been the place of his
refidence during moft of the time that he was employed in
writing that incomparable book. Dr Smith was born in
1723. He publifhed his Inquiry in 1776 ; and before his
death, which happened in 1789, he had the fingular good fortune to fee it tranflated into the languages, and the principles
of political economy contained in it, adopted into the fyftems,
of almoft all the commercial nations of Eurcpe. He wrote
alfo "The Theory of Moral Sentiments."—Thofe who would
know more of this great man, may confult a memoir of his
life and character publifhed in the fecond volume of " The
" Tranfactions of the Royal Society of Edinburgh."

In the more retired, though not the leaft ufeful or refpectable fphere of private citizens, Kirkaldy could reckon different perfons, who would have been diftinguifhed as citizens
of the firft clafs in any community.

E R R A T A.

Page 511. l. 7. *from the bottom, for* four *read* five.
 512. *laft line, infert* thefe *after* befides.
  524. To the money ftated in this page, *fupply* Scots.
  525. l. 2 *from the bottom, for* its *read* this.
  534. l. 17 *for* formerly *read* afterwards.
  536. l. 7. *dele* of it. l. 17 *for* there *read* here.
  536. l. 15. *for* confiderable *read* confiderably.
  538. l. 4. *from the bottom, for* this *read* thus.
  540. l. 18. *for* . One *read* ; and one.
  545. l. 8 *from the bottom, after* delegate *infert* of this burgh.
  546. l. 6. *from the bottom, infert* the *before* poffeffion.

PARISH of LARGO,

(COUNTY OF FIFE.)

By the Rev. Mr SPENCE OLIPHANT.

Situation, Soil, Air, &c.

THIS parifh is fituated in the prefbytery of St Andrew's, and Synod of Fife; bounded on the W. by the parifh of Scoonie, on the N. by Ceres, on the E. by Newburn, and on the S. by Largo Bay. It is of an irregular figure, extending from S. W. to N. E. nearly 6 miles. Its breadth is very unequal. The area of the whole contains 5469 acres. To the traveller, the fouth part of this parifh muft afford a picturefque and delightful fcene of elegant country-feats, fkirted with well laid out and thriving plantations, populous villages, furrounded with fertile fields, hill and dale, wood and water. The foil on the W. towards the fea, is light, bordered with link ground; the northern parts in general are of a thin black mould, on a wet bottom; in the fouthern, of a black loam, partly on a dry, and partly on a wet bottom, interfperfed with fields of light land. Rich breaking clay is peculiar to the S. E. part of the parifh, and there are fome tracks in different directions, to the weftward of the hill, confifting of clays

of

of a more obdurate nature, and on a wet bottom.—From
our vicinity to the German Ocean, we are frequently vifited with cold and damp winds from the E. accompanied
fometimes with much rain. During the fpring and fummer months, when the fun has had influence to rarify the
air in the firft part of the day, we may look for a very
cooling fea-breeze by three in the afternoon. But this is
common upon all the coaft. We are indeed more fheltered
from its influence, than many of our neighbours, from our
local fituation, and the plantations that furround. To the
above circumftances, our prevailing difeafes may be attributed; for, from the effect of cold and wet, coughs are
very general, rheumatifm and other inflammatory complaints are not unfrequent. Epidemic diforders fometimes
appear, of which the nervous fever prevails chiefly among
thofe who are much expofed in the fpring and autumn, and
who live at the fame time upon a low and fpare diet. Few
children are now cut off by the fmall pox, as inoculation
is generally introduced with remarkable fuccefs. During
20 years practice, our furgeon has not loft one patient.

Agriculture, &c.—In improvements, it may be juftly
faid that this parifh has led the way to all the neighbourhood. An open field is fcarcely to be met with. All is
inclofed, either with ftone, or with ditch and hedge. Draining has not been neglected. Not only the fpouts in the
wet bottomed land have difappeared, but even the ufelefs
marfh and the deceitful bog, by draining, paring, and
burning, have been turned into fruitful fields. The implements of hufbandry are much improved. A light well
contrived plough is introduced. The brake and roller are
in common ufe. The diminution of the expence of culture is no fmall improvement. In place of 6 cattle and 2
horfes, that feemed to be yoked for fhow, 20 or 30 years
ago,

ago, and theſe driven by a ſtout lad or 2 boys, 2 horſes, reined by the ploughman, now perform the work to much better purpoſe, and with greater ſpeed. Hand and horſe hoeing are practiſed. When the crop is gathered, it is preſerved in the barn-yard from vermin, by being placed upon pillars of ſtone, 2 feet high. Machines for threſhing have been introduced, but do not come up to expectation; from their very complex conſtruction, they are apt to go wrong; the horſes have a dead draught, and are made giddy by the circular motion. Wherever they can be erected upon a fall of water, all the purpoſes deſired will be anſwered.—In the northern parts of the pariſh, there are conſiderable plantations of fir. Places covered with thorns, briars, and furze, 30 years ago, are now filled with all kinds of foreſt-trees, the annual thinning of which already produces a conſiderable ſum. In 30 or 40 years, wood of different kinds will be a moſt profitable production.—The value of land is in a high proportion increaſed. What brought from 16 s. to L. 1 the acre, 20 years ago, now lets at L. 2 and L. 2, 10 s. and feus at L. 4 Sterling. —Except on the north ſkirts of the pariſh, where bear, oats, flax, and a few wretched potatoes, are the chief productions, every perſon poſſeſſing from 500, down to 1 acre of land, raiſes wheat almoſt as good as the beſt in Lothian. Thoſe only who poſſeſs farms can afford to fallow for their wheat; but even theſe, as well as the ſmalleſt tenants, raiſe the greateſt proportion of their wheat after clover, beans, and potatoes. Upon the beſt ſoil, barley is conſidered a profitable crop, and oats the leaſt advantageous, unleſs after paſture. Turnips and cabbage are raiſed with ſucceſs, for the cattles winter-proviſion. The carrot, the Swediſh turnip, and root of ſcarcity, have not anſwered expectation. The Swediſh turnip, it is ſuppoſed, will become very uſeful, when, by experiment, the proper mode

of

of cultivating it fhall be afcertained, and generally under-
flood.—Cattle are reared in confiderable numbers; much
attention is paid to the breed. The confequence of which
is well known, as our cattle have been diftinguifhed for
beauty and fize even in the London market. Horfes are
bred, both for draught and faddle. Sheep are fed, not produced here. Every family has fwine.—In our quarries
are found hard and freeftone. Limeftone is wrought in
2 different places. There is an extenfive field of marl;
and coal may be wrought to advantage. On the eftate of
Lundin, the coal has been cropped; but by erecting an engine near to the fea, a deep feam, which ftretches over upon the eftate of Largo, would be opened. This would amply fupply the neighbourhood, and afford befides a confiderable exportation.

Sea-coaft, Fifheries, &c.—The fouth boundary of this parifh is about $2\frac{1}{2}$ miles of fea-coaft. Largo Bay extends from
Kingcraig Point to that of the Methul, making a diameter
of near 7 miles in length, and marked by a ridge of fand.
The included bay forms a femicircle of about 10 miles
fea-coaft. The above ridge is called by fifhermen the
Dike. Of this there is a tradition, although probably not
well founded, among the oldeft inhabitants of Largo, that
there was formerly a wall or mound running from Kingcraig Point to that of the Methul, containing within it a
vaft foreft, called the Wood of Forth.—About 10 years
ago, fifh abounded on this coaft, particularly haddock, of a
very delicate kind. But fince that period, fifh of every
kind have become fcarce, infomuch that there is not a
haddock in the bay. All that remain, are a few fmall
cod, podlies, and flounders. The fifhermen have alfo difappeared, who, 20 years ago, conftituted the chief part of
the inhabitants of Largo and Drumochy. At prefent there

is

is not a fiſherman in Largo, and only 1 in Drumochy, who fiſhes in ſummer, and catches rabbits in winter.—The harbour of Largo is formed by the influx of the water Keil. There is a ſtone key, where veſſels of 200 ton may receive or diſcharge their cargoes ; but at no great expence it might be made to admit of ſhips of greater burden. The whole bay forms a ſafe road-ſtead for ſhips of every deſcription, being ſheltered from all winds, except the S. and S. W. ; and were it better known, might be a mean of preſerving many lives, particularly when ſhips are forced into the Forth by ſtorms from the N. E.

Mountains.—There is but 1 large hill, well known by the name of Largo Law. It is of a conical form, and riſes about 800 feet above the level of the ſea. Perhaps the name Law was given to this and many other hills of ſimilar form, from the flame that did, or was ſuppoſed to have iſſued from their tops. The Swedes call flame, 'loa ;' and the Danes, ' lue ;' which reſemble in ſound our Scotch word ' low ;' a flame. In ſupport of this conjecture, there are, in the poſſeſſion of Mr James Calderwood-Durham of Largo, ſeveral proclamations from the Privy-council of Scotland, ordering fires to be kindled on Largo Law, and that of North Berwick, as ſignals for the appearance of any ſhips of the enemy.—Beſides this, there are 2 other Laws. But it is evident that theſe have been artificial. When the cairn was removed from one of theſe, a few years ago, a ſtone coffin was found at the bottom. From the poſition of the bones, it appeared that the perſon had been buried in a ſingular manner. The legs and arms had been carefully ſevered from the trunk, and laid diagonally acroſs it.

Manufactures

Manufactures and Trade.—The principal manufacture is weaving. No woollen cloth indeed is wrought, but for a partial supply to the lower ranks of people. Linen and checks are the great articles. Almost every weaver, and a good number of others, have their bleaching ground, where they prepare linen, from the value of 9 d. to 4 s. the yard. Those who can afford to purchase yarn, work check and green linen, which they sell in Dysart, Kirkaldy, Cupar, and Dundee. Others, of less stock, are employed in these branches by manufacturers in the above towns. The greatest proportion of flax is imported; much of it is dressed and spun in the parish. A woman commonly spins 2 hanks a-day, and she is paid from 1 s. to 1 s. 2 d. the spindle.—The farmers deal considerably in cattle, which go to the shambles in the surrounding country, and not a few to Edinburgh; the remainder are bought for the most part by English drovers. Wheat, barley, oats, beans, and sometimes potatoes, are shipped for Leith and the West country; salt, for Dundee and Perth. Wood and iron are imported from Norway. There are 3 corn-mills, having thirlage; 2 barley, and 3 lint mills; 2 salt-pans, supplied with coals from the distance of 4 miles.

Population.—At the time of Dr Webster's report, the numbers were 1396. At present (1791) 1913.

Under 5 years of age,	212
Under 10 years,	226
Under 20,	361
Under 30,	272
Under 40,	245
Under 50,	177
Under 60,	226
Under 70,	136

Under

Under 80,   -   -   -   49
Under 90,   -   -   -   7
Under 100,   -   -   -   2
In the year 1754, the number of people
    was about   -   -   -   1400

Marriages, Baptiſms, and Burials, for the laſt ten years.

Years.	Marriages.	Baptiſms.	Burials.
1781	13	29	41
1782	24	48	42
1783	16	42	56
1784	23	43	33
1785	17	39	35
1786	17	48	35
1787	16	33	15
1788	14	45	48
1789	16	26	23
1790	12	42	24
	168	395	352
Yearly average,	17	39	35

Some deduction ought to be made from the average of
burials, on account of an hoſpital in the pariſh for old
men, amounting to 14 in number, who are ſeldom admitted
under 60 years. There are commonly 2 vacancies every
year; ſometimes 3, 4, and 5.

Stipend, School, Poor, &c.—The ſtipend conſiſts of 6 chalders of victual, L. 36 : 6 : 4, L. 20 Scots for foggage, 5 acres
of glebe, manſe and garden. The manſe was rebuilt 20
years ago, and is among the beſt in the preſbytery. Since
the demiſſion of Mr Ferrier, who, in conjunction with a Mr
Smith, miniſter at Newburn, formed a ſect of Independents,

a

a spirit of schism has prevailed in this and all the adjacent parishes. Clergy abound here. There being 1 of the Establishment, 1 of the Relief, 1 of the Independents, and 2 of the Anabaptists. The number of souls belonging to the Establishment is 1211; belonging to Separatists, including 3 of the Episcopal persuasion, 702. There are 9 heritors. —The funds for the public school amount to about L. 30 a-year. A man of ability and application may look to this place as an object, as he would have a numerous school from the parish, and the safe and healthy situation of the place would attract boarders from all quarters.—At an average, the number of regular poor is 25, each of whom receives from 2 s. to 4 s. and 5 s. a-month. The funds amount to from L. 40 to L. 50 a-year, arising from money at interest, collections at the church-door, and mortcloths. From this state of the poor, and their provision, it may be justly observed, that the heritors and tenants, upon whom the legal support of the poor depends, save annually a considerable sum, on account of the management being vested in the kirk-session. Were the heritors to appoint a factor or treasurer for supplying the poor, were the poor to know that they are entitled to a legal support, they would soon discover either their real or fictitious wants, and boldly demand a supply; whereas the present mode of supporting them is attended with an opposite effect. By daily seeing and hearing of collections for the poor, the needy will suffer much, and work hard, before they can think of being classed among the number; and should this spirit be at last vanquished, either by distress or poverty, their children and friends will exert their utmost, to preserve their needy relation from what they think a reproach. If any at last become beggars, their monthly allowance is immediately withdrawn, with a view to induce them to return to some usefulness in society.

Wages,

Wages, Living, &c.—Working by contraƈt is now much praƈtiſed, the gain ariſing from which muſt be according to the bargain they make, and the induſtry with which they purſue their work. The wages of common labourers and hired ſervants can be eaſily aſcertained, the general run being from 9 d. to 1 s. a-day; hired ſervants L. 13 a-year. This is to be underſtood of the man's earnings; and if a wife and children be concerned, it is but rare, that any addition can be ſtated to his income. Female ſervants have from L. 2 to L. 4, excluſive of their board, &c. Labourers and hired ſervants who have families, from the above account, cannot live ſumptuouſly. Except at a birth or marriage, or ſome other feſtival, they do not in general taſte butcher-meat. Meagre broth, potatoes, cheeſe, butter in ſmall quantities, and a preparation of meal in different forms, make up their conſtant fare. All things conſidered, it is aſtoniſhing to ſee man, wife and children, in their Sunday's clothes; all are clean and neat, with faces expreſſive of contentment.—With reſpeƈt to the general rank of people, their mode of living is undoubtedly improved, both as to lodging and diet.—Notwithſtanding the jarring opinions in matters of religion, which may ſometimes occaſion a diſtant and reſerved behaviour, the people in general have a kind and obliging turn. They are honeſt, ſober and induſtrious; more forward to ſympathiſe with their neighbour in diſtreſs, than to rejoice with him in his proſperity. Tenacious of the peculiar doƈtrines of Chriſtianity, they do not pervert them to encourage licentiouſneſs, being convinced, that purity of heart and life cannot be ſeparated from the exalted hope which the goſpel inſpires.

Hoſpital.—In 1659, an hoſpital for old men of the name of Wood was founded by a Mr John Wood, who was a conneƈtion connection of the famous Sir Andrew Wood of Largo. As hofpitallers, there are 12 old men of the above name, who, with their wives (if they have any) are accommodated with a room and clofet, with an annuity of L. 100 Scots. There is a large garden, which fupplies them with vegetables of all kinds. There is alfo a porter, who, among other parts of his office, calls them to morning and evening prayers, which are given by a chaplain appointed for that purpofe. The furgeon in the parifh receives fo much a-year for his attendance and advice. The funds arife from money at intereft, and an excellent farm adjacent to the hofpital. The gentlemen who poffefs the eftates of Largo, Lundin, Wemyfs and Balfour, with the minifter of Largo, are patrons. Thefe meet on the firft Tuefday of September, in the hall of the hofpital, to examine the accounts of their factor, to fill up vacancies, &c. A dinner is allowed by the founder. Of this dinner we lately found an old bill of fare, which fhewed the tafte of former times. There was charged for wine 3 s. and ale 10 s. The charge now is entirely reverfed.

Eminent and Notable Men.—1. The faithful and brave Sir Andrew Wood, who flourifhed in the reigns of James III. and IV. of Scotland, was a native of this parifh. Under James III. he poffeffed the barony of Largo in tack. But James IV. invefted him in the property of it, on account of two fignal victories he had obtained at fea, over the Englifh, about the beginning of his reign. It appears that Sir Andrew, like Commodore Trunnion, brought on fhore his nautical ideas and manners. From his houfe, down almoft as far as the church, he formed a canal, upon which he ufed to fail in his barge to the church every Sunday in great ftate.—2. After Sir Andrew Wood, the barony of Largo came into the poffeffion of the family of Durham,

ham, to which the celebrated Mr James Durham belonged,
being brother to Sir Alexander Durham of Largo. This
gentleman was diſtinguiſhed both as a ſoldier and divine,
being firſt a captain of dragoons, and then miniſter of the
High Church of Glaſgow. He was ſolicited to become profeſſor of divinity in the college there ; but being eminent-
ly diſtinguiſhed among his brethren, he was by them appointed to the honourable office of chaplain at court.
While at Glaſgow, he had an opportunity of preaching before Oliver Cromwell, when he took occaſion to ſpeak with
freedom of the injuſtice of Oliver's invaſion. Being afterwards ſeverely challenged by the Uſurper, he calmly anſwered, that he thought it incumbent upon him to ſpeak
his mind freely upon that ſubjeƈt, eſpecially as he had an
opportunity of doing it in his own hearing.—3. Alexander
Selkirk, who was rendered famous by Monſ. de Foe, under
the name of Robinſon Cruſoe. His hiſtory, diveſted of fable,
is as follows : He was born in Largo in 1676. Having
gone to ſea in his youth, and in the year 1703, being ſailing maſter of the ſhip Cinque Ports, Captain Stradling,
bound for the South Seas, he was put on ſhore, on the
iſland of Juan Fernandez, as a puniſhment for mutiny. In
that ſolitude he remained 4 years and 4 months, from
which he was at laſt relieved, and brought to England by
Captain Woods Rogers. He had with him in the iſland
his clothes and bedding, with a firelock, ſome powder, bul-
lets and tobacco, a hatchet, knife, kettle, his mathematical
inſtruments and Bible. He built 2 huts of Piemento trees,
and covered them with long graſs, and, in a ſhort time,
lined them with ſkins of goats, which he killed with his
muſket, ſo long as his powder laſted, (which at firſt was
but a pound) ; when that was ſpent, he caught them by
ſpeed of foot. Having learned to produce fire, by rubbing
two pieces of wood together, he dreſſed his viƈtuals in one

of

of his huts, and flept in the other, which was at fome diftance from his kitchen. A multitude of rats often difturb-
ed his repofe, by gnawing his feet, and other parts of his
body, which induced him to feed a number of cats for his
protection. In a fhort time, thefe became fo tame, that
they would lie about him in hundreds, and foon delivered
him from the rats, his enemies. Upon his return, he declared to his friends, that nothing gave him fo much un-
eafinefs, as the thoughts, that when he died, his body would
be devoured by thofe very cats he had with fo much care
tamed and fed. To divert his mind from fuch melancholy
thoughts, he would fometimes dance and fing among his
kids and goats, at other times retire to his devotion. His
clothes and fhoes were foon worn, by running through the
woods. In the want of fhoes he found little inconvenience,
as the foles of his feet became fo hard, that he could run
every where without difficulty. As for clothes, he made
for himfelf a coat and cap of goats fkins, fewed with little
thongs of the fame, cut into proper form with his knife.
His only needle was a nail. When his knife was worn to
the back, he made others as well as he could, of fome iron
hoops that had been left on fhore, by beating them thin,
and grinding them on ftones. By his long feclufion from
intercourfe with men, he had fo far forgot the ufe of fpeech,
that the people on board Captain Rogers's fhip could fcarce
underftand him, for he feemed to fpeak his words by
halves. The cheft and mufket which Selkirk had with
him on the ifland, are now in the poffeffion of his grand-
nephew, John Selkirk, weaver in Largo.

Antiquities.—On the bank of the water Keil, are the
ruins of the ancient caftle of Balcruvie, a place once of confiderable ftrength, occupied of old by the family of Crawford.

ford. There is a ſquare tower pretty entire. Of the old houſe of Largo, one round tower remains. A little ſouth-wards, in a large park, there is now an elegant modern houſe, commanding one of the fineſt and moſt extenſive proſpects in Scotland. About a mile to the weſtward, is the ancient tower of Lundin, which now conſtitutes a part of a modern building, with a Gothic front.—Near to this, in the middle of a plain, are 3 remarkable ſtones, ſtanding upright in the ground, each meaſuring 6 yards above, and as much it is ſuppoſed below the ground. There are alſo fragments of a fourth, which ſeems to have been of equal magnitude with the other three. There is no inſcription, nor the leaſt veſtige of any character to be found upon them. But the tradition is, that they are the grave-ſtones of ſome Daniſh chiefs, who fell in battle with the Scots near this place.

PARISH OF LESLIE.

(PRESBYTERY OF KIRKCALDY, SYNOD AND COUNTY OF FIFE.)

By the Rev. MR. GEORGE WILLIS.

Name.

THE original name of this parish was Fetkill ; but when the family of Leslie, Earls of Rothes, became the principal proprietors, they gave their own name to their possessions here, and the whole district came at last to be known by the same appellation.

Surface, Soil, Rent, &c.—The parish is in general flat, but rises gently from the banks of the river Leven, which forms the southern boundary. It is almost wholly an arable district. The soil is in general good——The real rent is not known. The valued rent is L. 4561 Scotch.—The parks of Leslie are let annually by auction, and generally taken by the town's people of Leslie, who pay, at an average, from L. 1 : 15 to L. 2 per acre. As they are pastured by milch cows, and as

about

about L. 2 is paid for a cow's grafs, it is neceffary to keep as good cows as poffible; and, indeed, more good ones are to be feen in Leflie, than perhaps in any town of its fize. They commonly bring from L. 7 to L. 10, and are all of the Fife breed. Some Dutch cows were tried, and fome of the Irifh and Lancafhire breed; but they did not anfwer, as the firft were expenfive to keep up in winter, and the laft did not yield much milk. Almoft all the lands of the parifh have been cultivated; and by far the greateft part of them are either under crops of grain, potatoes, turnips, and flax, or in fown grafs. The farmers now deal more in rearing cattle, and in general plough lefs ground, but, at the fame time, raife more corn than formerly. While the farms were uninclofed, and little or no fown grafs raifed, the cattle gathered a miferable fubfiftence on bare leys; which, after refting feveral years, were broken up, and cropt, year after year, till they fcarce produced double the feed. The land is now plowed by one man commonly with a pair of horfes, inftead of four oxen with two horfes and a lad to drive them, as was formerly the cafe *.

Manufactures.——In the town of Leflie the weavers are the moft

---

* *Prices of Labour and Provisions.*—In 1759, a day labourer's wages were 8d. without victuals. If he was employed during the winter and fummer, he got only 6d. The yearly wages of a man fervant were then from L. 2 : 10, to L. 3, fter. and thofe of a maid fervant, from L. 1 : 10, to L. 2. But a fufficient man fervant cannot now be got under L. 5 : 10 or L. 6, nor a maid fervant under L. 2 : 10 or L. 3, a year. A common labourer now gets 1s. a day. In 1759, beef could have been bought, between Michaelmas and Martinmas, at 2s 8d. per ftone; it is now 5s 4d. The price of fowls and eggs is doubled. A good fowl is 1s, and a dozen of eggs, 4d.—— Butter was 5d. now it is 8d. a pound. Milk was 1d. a pint, now it is 2d. Coals were 4d. a load, now they are 7d. Salt was 4d. a peck, now 6d.

moft numerous fet of handicraftfmen, no other clafs of mechanics bearing any proportion to them. Their principal employment is weaving plain linen and cotton checks, by which
moft of them can earn from 14d. to 18d. or 20d. a day. The
chief employment of the women is fpinning lint and tow.
About 30 years ago, when they univerfally fpun with one
hand, a hefp or flip, which is the fourth part of a fpindle,
was thought a fufficient day's work for a woman; and miftref-
fes required no more of their maid-fervants when they fat the
whole day at the wheel. After they had fpun their hefp, the
reft of the time was their own. Before 1770, a wheel for fpinning with both hands was unknown in the parifh, now almoft
none elfe are to be feen it. The manufacturers ufed to give
only 10d. for fpinning a fpindle of yarn, fo that, at that rate,
a woman earned only 15d. a week; but now the manufacturers pay 1s. for fpinning a fpindle, and a woman can fpin 2½
fpindles a week, which makes 2s. 6d.

Stipend.——The ftipend confifts of 42 bolls of oat-meal, 8
Dutch ftones to the boll; 22 bolls of barley, Linlithgow
meafure; and L. 50 fterling in money. The manfe was
built in 1687, and repaired in 1789. The glebe is very indifferent. It is furprifing to fee fome minifters eftimating
their glebes, and adding their value to the livings; for there
is fcarcely a minifter who would not give his glebe to any
man that would drive his fuel, furnifh his family with milk,
and a horfe to ride on when he is neceffarily called from home:
and, if the minifter hath any tolerable fkill in arithmetic, he
might give the man, who would fupply him with the above
conveniencies, 5 guineas a year along with glebe; for in that
cafe he would fave the expence of a man fervant, which, as
times go, is at leaft L. 12 or L. 14, and the rifque of lofing a
horfe

horſe or a cow, which are fully as liable to mortality, in the
poſſeſſion of a clergyman, as in other hands *.

Poor,

* The following obſervations on the ſtate of the clergy, tranſmitted by Mr
Willis, tho' not immediately within the ſcope of this work, yet are here in-
ſerted, on account of their connection with the ſituation of ſo reſpectable
and ſo uſeful a part of the community.

Patriots, and friends to mankind would wiſh to know how to ameliorate the
condition of every uſeful claſs of men in the kingdom. With regard to the people at large, their condition and circumſtances are every day becoming more
comfortable and afluent ; while thoſe of the clergy are every day declining,
verging to poverty, and its uſual concomitant, contempt.
" Nil habet infelix pauperies durius in ſe,
" Quam quod ridiculos homines facit."
We all eaſily find out ways and means for the relief of the diſtreſſed, when
we ourſelves are well and at our eaſe. Some will ſay, that the clergy ſhould
return to that plain and homely fare and clothing, which their predeceſſoLs
uſed at the beginning of the century. Not to mention other anſwers to this
advice, even to live in that manner now, would coſt double of what it did then.
The boys in Heriot's Hoſpital live upon the ſame kind of food, and have the
ſame kind of cloths, as they had an hundred years ago ; and yet, I ſuppoſe,
it will be found, that the expence of their maintenance and clothing is now
double of what it was then. Others will ſay, that the clergy ſhould take
farms ; not conſidering how difficult they are to be got. Beſides, where one
miniſter will gain by farming, nineteen in twenty, or rather 99 in 100, would
probably loſe by it ; as they cannot always be at the head of their labouring
ſervants ; nor are they, in any way, a match for horſe-cowpers, cow-cowpers,
brewers, and butchers, the people that farmers have to deal with. Gentlemen farmers are on the ſame footing as a clergyman would be ; and ſure I am,
that there are not many inſtances of their meeting with much ſucceſs.
There are two difficulties in the way of applying for an augmentation of
ſtipends. The certain and almoſt unlimited expence of ſuch an application, (if
the heritors vigorouſly oppoſe the meaſure, as they often have done,) and the
abſolute uncertainty of obtaining it, as the courts of law are veſted with arbitrary powers to give or to refuſe. " Arbitria judicum pro legibus ſunt." If it
be ſaid, Is not the victual, of which part of our ſtipends often conſiſts, more
valuable

Poor, Funds, &c.——The collections at the church doors amount, on an average of the laft 10 years, to L. 18 *per annum;*

valuable in this century than in the laft? I fuppofe if you will pitch upon any 20 years of the laft century, and compare them with the 20 correfponding years in this, you will find the difference next to nothing; for befides, that from the improvements in agriculture, by which grain is raifed in greater quantities, and has become an article of commerce, it neither rifes fo high, nor falls fo low as formerly.

There feems to be but one way, in which the condition of the clergy can be ameliorated, with the leaft lofs to the public at large, and to the feweft individuals. In Scotland, the tithes of feveral parifhes, which belonged to religious houfes are vefted in the Crown, and are let in leafe for two or three lives; for which the tenant is bound to pay a certain annual fum to the Exchequer. At the firft eftablifhment of the Prefbyterian form of church government here, the bifhops rents alfo were vefted in the Crown, I have no doubt, from a counter-revolution being not only poffible but probable; and which actually took place. Again, at the Revolution, thefe were in like manner vefted in the Crown, and for the fame reafon: for if King William had been as well affured of the fupport of the Epifcopal clergy, as he was of the Prefbyterian, the form of church government had not been altered at that time. So that thefe unalienated tithes and bifhops rents are the patrimony of the church, and feem to have been vefted in the crown as a depofit; for they were never forfeited by rebellion or otherwife; and were lodged there, as a provifion againft an event, which now, by the treaty of union, and the king's coronation oath, never can take place. It is greatly to the honour of the legiflature, that it has reftored their family eftates to men whofe anceftors had forfeited them by rebellion; and hence, I fhould think it very unhandfome, upon a proper application, to refufe to their very beft and firmeft friends that part of their patrimony, from which they are excluded on account of no rebellion or forfeiture whatever. Suppofe this reftored, who would fuffer any lofs? As to the lofs to the Exchequer, what a trifle is it to an empire which has fuch revenues as ours? As to the lofs to the collectors, it would be a very ferious one, and a mighty hardfhip indeed, to extinguifh no lefs than about a dozen of finecure places. With regard to the tackfmen, whofe tacks are good for their term of years, would it make any difference to them, to pay the tack-duty to the church, in place of paying it to the exchequer?

I fhall mention but one confequence, if the incomes of the clergy be not ameliorated

num ; the hire of the mortcloths to L. 3 : 10 ; and the intereſt of principal ſums belonging to the pariſh to L. 25, making

meliorated, the decline of learning will follow. This muſt infallibly be the caſe
in any ſtate, where there is not a rank which requires a conſiderable degree of
learning, where there is not room for a conſiderable number of the learned to be
employed in it, and where that employment does not entitle them to a decent
degree both of profit and of reſpeЄt. Suppoſe the ſtipends of Scotland to fall as
much in their value for half a century to come, as for half a century paſt, how
few clergymen, who are enabled to give their ſons ſuch an expenſive education, as a miniſter ſhould have, would breed them to a profeſſion where they
cannot gain ſo comfortable a ſubſiſtence as many mechanics can earn ? With
what kind of young men would gentlemen be ſupplied as tutors in their families, and who are now ſo well ſupplied, by preachers and ſtudents in divinity ?
Though a Dionyſius might make it worth the while of a Pythagoras, to come
from Greece to Syracuſe, to inſtruЄt himſelf and his courtiers, I ſuſpeЄt, that
when Scottiſh lairds muſt ſend to Oxford and Cambridge for tutors to their
children, few will be ſent for, and fewer come to a country, where they can
look for no farther preferment. England, I think, will continue to be the
ſeat of learning ; till ſuch time as the livings of the dignified clergy of the
church there, ſhall be reduced to as low an ebb, as at preſent are the livings
of the dignified clergy in France.

I have ever been of opinion, that the downfall of the church will bury learning in its ruins ; and this ſeems to be warranted by the hiſtory of all nations.
That body of men, who are now ſneeringly called Prieſts, their office Prieſt-
hood, and their employment, Prieſtcraft, and which I ſhall call, the Clerical
order eſtabliſhed by law, have been in all ages and nations of the world, the
repoſitories of learning. In our own country, at the firſt appointment of the
Court of Seſſion, there was ſuch a penury of the learned laity, that they were
obliged to the church for one half of the judges. Wherever the clerical order
has been creditable and reſpeЄtable, light and learning have ſhone forth.
Whence proceeded the firſt birth of learning, but from the prieſts of Egypt ?
Whither did the Grecian ſages travel but into Egypt and the Eaſt ? Were not
the Brahmins, the Gentoo clergy, who were, and ſtill are, of high eſteem,
thoſe whom Pythagoras wiſhed, and travelled to learn from ? Were there not at
Rome a Caius Julius Cæſar Pontifex Maximus, and a Marcus Tullius Cicero
at the head of the college of Augurs ? Was ever virtue, and piety, and learning more nobly ſupported than in the writings of the divines of the church of
England ?

ing a total income of L. 46 : 10. Of which, L. 4 : 14 is paid for feffion clerk's and officer's falaries, quarter fees of poor fcholars, houfe rents and clothes for the poor. About L. 41, on an average, is diftributed among 33 penfioners, of whom 30 refide in the town of Leflie. The diftribution is made weekly; none get above 1s. nor any lefs than 6d. This is a much better mode than that followed by moft of the kirk-fef-fions in the neighbourhood, who make their diftributions monthly, thus occafioning the poor to live plentifully one week, and

England? I have not heard, indeed, whether the Hottentots, the Cherokees, the Chictaws, the Efquimaux, &c. ever had any clergy; and as little have I heard of the learned productions of thofe ornaments of human nature.

Upon the whole, I cannot help thinking, it would be bad policy in any ftate, to fuffer a body of men, who, firft and laft, have been of no fmall ufe to the interefts of learning and of virtue, to languifh in poverty, and dwindle into contempt. No doubt, the art of printing, and the eftablifhment of uni-verfities, have contributed, as well as the clergy, to the increafe, and to the diffufion of knowledge; but the clergy diffufe knowledge, and the beft kind of knowledge, to all men, high and low, to the cobler as well as to the king. While the fchools of the philofophers of old, thought it a profanation to enlighten the vulgar, the fifhermen of Galilee, and their fucceffors, have initiated the vulgar in the moft fublime doctrines, and the pureft morality; have fuggefted to them the moft noble confolations, and have drawn them forth to action, by the moft exalted hopes. And who are the men, who pro-vide fociety (I do not fay with the neceffaries and comforts of life only), but with all its elegancies, with all its fuperfluities, with all its luxuries? Who but the vulgar? They bear all its burdens, and I am forry to fay, fuffer all its hardfhips. And can juftice or gratitude, can humanity and compaffion, leave them to drudge in this world, like beafts of burden, cut them off from all confo-lation here, and leave them deftitute of all rational hopes of enjoying a better condition hereafter? That, however, muft be the cafe, if they are deprived alto-gether of the inftructions of their beft friends, and thrown into the hands of perfons who may be as ignorant as themfelves.

and beg or ſtarve the reſt of the month *. No diſtinction between the poor of the diſſenters, and the poor of the Eſtabliſhed Church is allowed.

For 17 years preceding 1781, the collections, on an average,
were L. 15 : 10 ; the hire of the mortcloths amounted to
L. 3 : 5 ; and the ſums diſtributed among the poor, to about
L. 30 annually.

Since 1759, no perſon in this pariſh hath periſhed by hunger, nakedneſs, or want of lodging ; nor have any taken to
begging. During this period, it muſt be mentioned, that
the heritors of the pariſh have not given one farthing to the
poor, offerings at the church door excepted; and even theſe came
only from one family, all the other proprietors being non-reſi-
dents †.

Population.

* The poor, ſays Mr Willis, ſhould be treated like young birds, give them
little at a time, but often.

† Many plans for the ſupport of the poor have been projected : this only
ſeems certain, that wherever poors rates have been adopted, they have generally
been found very expenſive. The philoſophers of the preſent day, inſtead of
thinking, " whatever is, is right," ſeem to think, " whatever is, is wrong."
Many new plans have been propoſed, and no one agreeing with another.
I have always thought, that it is better to begin with amending an old plan, that
has proved not to be very bad, than to take all at once a new one, however
finely ſpun. I will venture to ſay, with reſpect to our old plan, that, of all the
public funds of Europe, none are managed at ſo little expence to the fund itſelf, none ſo frugally; none ſo impartially, and none laid out more to the purpoſe for which they were raiſed, than the poors funds under the care of the
kirk-ſeſſions of Scotland. Never, perhaps, will Scotland find a more proper
jury to determine the objects of public charity, nor the quantum neceſſary for
their ſupply. Two amendments may be ſuggeſted : The firſt is, to protect
theſe funds againſt the burden of natural children being brought upon them,
which could be done by altering the preſent law, and making the oath of the
woman father all baſtards, as is the practice in England. The oath of that

3

party

Population.—When the returns were made to Dr Webſter, in 1755, the number of the inhabitants of this pariſh was ſaid to amount to - - - 1130

In 1756, the total number of ſouls was - - 1096

Of which in the town of Leſlie - 732

———— in the country part of the pariſh 364

In 1769, The number of ſouls in the whole pariſh 1165

———————— in the town - 786

——— ——.—— in the country - 379

In 1775, In the whole pariſh - - - 1189

In the town - - - - 786

———— males - - - - 344

———— females - - - - 442

In the country - - - - 403

————— males - - - 215

———— females - - - 188

In

party ſhould certainly be preferred who hath the leaſt temptation to perjury. The woman in all ordinary caſes of this kind has none : the man has a double temptation to perjury ; for firſt, he gets clear of the cenſure of the church, and next, which to him is a matter of greater conſequence, he frees himſelf of the expence of the maintenance of the child.

In the next place, it were to be wiſhed, that the gentlemen in Scotland, before it be too late, would voluntarily give leſs or more for ſupporting the kirk-ſeſſions, and enabling them to maintain the poor ; for ſhould kirk-ſeſſions give up their laborious and painful taſk, the gentry, who now give next to nothing, if they once came to be taxed by law for the maintenance of the poor, will find their rate operate pretty much in the ſame way as an heritable bond of the ſame extent, upon their lands. If every heritor, reſident, and non-reſident, were to give in as much to the kirk-ſeſſion, as it may reaſonably be ſuppoſed, his tenants and their families in that pariſh give, which may be 2d. or 3d. each Sunday, even that ſmall help would keep the poor from begging or ſtarving. Suppoſe the heritor has ſix tenants, it certainly would not be an exceſs of generoſity to give at the rate of a ſhilling each Sunday for the ſupport of the poor. The expence of maintaining the poor in England is well known.

In

In 1781, In the whole pariſh -   -   -   1211

In the town -   -   -   -   805

—————— males -   -   -   338

————— females -   -   -   -   467

In the country -   -   -   -   406

————— males -   -   -   202

————— females -   -   -   204

In 1785, In the whole pariſh -   -   -   1212

In the town -   -   -   -   806

————— males -   -   -   -   344

————— females -   -   -   462

In the country -   -   -   -   406

—————— males -   -   -   211

————— females -   -   -   195

Heritors

In London, in the pariſh of St. Martins in the Fields, the poor's rates, at 1s the pound upon the houſe rents, amouñts to L. 10,000 per ann. and many pariſhes in London pay more than 1s. the pound. Many particular inſtances might be mentioned. At Alnwick it is ſaid, the poor's rates amount to L. 600 per ann. while the pariſh of Alnwick is not more populous than ſome pariſhes in this neighbourhood, which have not L. 50 to ſupport the poor. Yet very many of the gentry of Scotland will contribute almoſt nothing, which may render a compulſary law at laſt neceſſary. Is it not a ſhame, that ſo many gentlemen (beſides never entering a church-door) never give a ſhilling from one end of the year to the other towards the ſupport of the poor? When the heart of an heritor is indeed ſoftened, and his hand opened, he may give once or twice in his life ſome carts of coals or bolls of meal to the poor ; but it is to them no more than a feaſt at the time, and is ſoon done ; whereas half the ſum delivered to the kirk-ſeſſion, and given out by them in ſhillings and ſix-pences would be of much greater ſervice to the poor, who, as I have ſaid above, can bear no wealth. Upon the whole, the proper way to maintain the poor, is to give them what is neceſſary to preſerve them from ſtarving, but not ſo much as to damp their induſtry, or encourage idleneſs; and even that little, they ought to receive, not as a right, but purely as charity ; and I am per-ſuaded, that all theſe purpoſes have been in general ſerved by the manage-ment of the kirk-ſeſſions.

Heritors	-	-	-	-	-	4
Houses in the country		-	-	-	-	84
Families in ditto.	-		-	-	-	84
Houses in the town of Leslie		-		-	-	129
Families in ditto	-	-	-	-	-	-	250

Since 1785, the population has not materially altered.

The great disproportion between the males and females in the town, and the difference in the country part of the parish, will appear strange, but may thus be accounted for : In the town, the number of maid-servants is greater than that of men-servants, and the reverse, in the country. Another reason may be, that the farmers in the neighbourhood purchase houses in Leslie for their wives to inhabit, after their death, and to which they come with their unmarried daughters. Besides, in the country part of the parish, the farmers have no more dwelling-houses than are sufficient for themselves and their servants : when, therefore, a cottager dies, his cottage must be let to another man to carry on the work of the farm, and the widow of the former, in that case, unless she hath a son to supply his father's place, or a married daughter to whom she might go to live with, rents a house in Leslie, that she may get coals driven for hire, and such other things to buy as are necessary for her subsistence : and, besides all these, some old women get houses in Leslie that they be near the church and the meeting-houses, of which there are two in town, one of the sect of Seceders, called Burghers, and the other Antiburghers. The town is choakfull of people, and has neither an empty nor ruinous house in it.

The increase of inhabitants in the country part of the parish, from 1759 to 1785, is probably occasioned by the establishment of two bleachfields; for the farmers in general keep fewer ſervants than formerly, owing to a greater proportion of their farms being incloſed, and laid down with ſown graſs, than heretofore.

From 1780 to 1789, both incluſive, 321 baptiſms are entered in the regiſter, whereof 168 were males, and 153 females; 231 were baptiſed by the eſtabliſhed miniſter, and 90 by Seceders. This, however, is no proper way of judging of the real number of births, as the regiſter of baptiſms is kept both inaccurately and irregularly, ſince 1732, when the Seceſſion began. Some poor people, to ſave the trifling expence of 10d. omit to regiſter the names of their children; and the Seceders, ſome through poverty and others out of ſuperſtition, do not regiſter theirs. Some of the latter carry their ſuperſtition ſo far as to pay the dues, and yet forbid the regiſtration.

Miſcellaneous Obſervations*.——The river Leven, which ſeparates

---

* *Antiquities.*——In the pariſh is the old caſtle of Strathendrie, which formerly belonged to a family of the ſame name, of no ſmall note in Fife. A battle has, probably, been fought near it, as 4 large ſtones, ſimilar to thoſe uſually ſet up at the graves of perſons of renown, who had fallen in battle, would ſeem to indicate. Near theſe ſtones ſtood a round hillock, called the Gallant Know; which, being ſuppoſed to conſiſt only of gravel, was made uſe of a few years ago to repair the roads: But in the center of it was found a piece of pavement, ſurrounded with large ſtones, containing ſome bones, and two ſpear heads of copper, the one like the head of an officer's ſpontoon, and the other, in the upper part, like a maſon's chiſel. A ſtone coffin and urn were found near the Gallant Know, beſide one of the 4 ſtones, about 1760. The old houſe of Pitcairn, which belonged to the well known Dr Pitcairn, is in this pariſh, but now in a ruinous ſtate. Near it ſtood a tumulus, in the center of which, about 1770, was found a ſtone cheſt, full of human bones, (in particular ſeveral entire jaw bones), ſtanding eaſt and weſt. At the eaſt end were found two urns of bluiſh clay, full of bones evidently calcined, and white as chalk.

parates this pariſh from that of Kinglaſſie, abounds with trout; and, about Michaelmas, great numbers of eels are taken in their paſſage from Lochleven to the ſea. On this account the lands of Strathendrie in this pariſh, were, before the Reformation, ſubject to an annual tax of ſome thouſands of eels to the abbey of Inchcolm.

There are in the pariſh quarries of whin-ſtone, but very hard, and expenſive to win; alſo ſome coal mines and limeworks.

The parochial ſchoolmaſter, beſides a houſe, has an annual ſalary of L. 5 : 11 : 1⅟₇. The ſcholars, at an average throughout the whole year, are 80 in number. The fees of teaching are very low.

There are 6 houſes where ale is ſold; but not one perſon or family ſupported by the profits of a public-houſe, all having ſome other employment.

Leſlie-houſe, a magnificent ſeat, built by the Duke of Rothes, round a court like the abbey of Holyroodhouſe, with a gallery three feet longer than that in the abbey, hung on one ſide with portraits of the connections of the Rothes family, and on the other ſide with thoſe of contemporaries and friends of the Duke, was burnt to the ground on the 28th December 1763. The fore-ſide of the ſquare was repaired by the late Earl of Rothes, in 1767.

Character of the People, and their Manner of Living.——
There is not, in Britain, a pariſh of the ſame extent, in which the people are more ſober, honeſt, and induſtrious, nor among whom there have been fewer groſs crimes committed, than that of Leſlie. Their manner of living is greatly altered: a remarkable inſtance of which is, that for ſeveral years after 1760, the preſent incumbent got all his wheaten bread from Edinburgh, and afterwards from Dyſart, rolls only being baked

ed at Leſlie; whereas now there are 3 bakers in this town alone. Their clothing and furniture are alſo much better than formerly. In the church of Leſlie no perſon is ever ſeen in rags. The young men wear coats of Engliſh cloth, fancy veſts, &c. and the young women, printed and white cottons, ſilk cloaks and bonnets, &c. The dreſs of the maid-ſervants makes no inconſiderable addition to the expence of a family in the article of waſhing. Their furniture alſo is much better. About 30 years ago, when the preſent incumbent was ſettled, there was not 6 clocks in the pariſh, and now there is not a houſe in Leſlie where there is not either a clock or watch.

PARISH OF LEUCHARS.

(COUNTY OF FIFE.)

By the Rev. Mr. KETTLE.

Name, Situation, Soil, &c.

LEUCHARS, if derived from the Celtic language, is said by some, to signify a wet flat; by others, a place abounding with rushes; either, or both interpretations faithfully describe the appearance which the surface made some years ago, a great way to the northeast, and a little to the southwest of this village. The district is of large extent from west to east, and from southwest to northeast, more than 9 statute miles, and more than 5 miles broad, at two different parts of the parish, considerably distant from each other. The measurement by Mr William Innes now lies before me.

The figure of the parish is completely irregular, being bounded on the northeast, east, and southeast, by the German ocean, and the various windings of the river Eden on the south, and southwest; on the other parts by the neighbouring parishes. It is affirmed with truth, that within the bounds of this district, every soil known in this country is to

be

be found: blue, white, and red clays, ftrong and weak, fharp lands, loam of various depth and ftrength; a mixture of loam and clay, light lands, mofs, heath and bent in no fmall quantities. Before Sir David Carnegie fold part of the lordfhip of Leuchars, he employed a number of workmen to cut a large drain of 3 miles long, paffing through the weft end of the village of Leuchars, that the furface on each fide of it might be turned into more important ufes. The Hon. Robert Lindfay bought this part of the lordfhip before the effect of the drain was fully proved. Mr Lindfay found himfelf under the neceffity, at no fmall expence, confiderably to enlarge the former drain, and thereby rendered it effectual for relieving the flat grounds of the water through which it paffed. Many acres formerly covered with coarfe grafs and rufhes, and about 36 acres fouth and weft of Leuchars, covered with water to a confiderable depth in the winter feafon, and not free from water in the fummer, are now producing abundant crops of all kinds of grain, clover, turnip, and cabbage. Thefe grounds are let from 14s to L. 1 : 16 per acre; yielding a profitable return to the generous landlord, and affording the labourers hope, that their expence and induftry may not be altogether unrewarded. Of the many remaining acres to the north and northeaft, fome are highly improved, and others in a ftate of preparation for fimilar crops. Thefe circumftances are motives which fhould prompt to exertion in all fimilar fituations in Scotland; but are by no means, to thofe who wifh well to mankind, the moft important motives for draining water from the neighbourhood of villages. Before the above drain (of 20 feet wide, and 14 deep, for a confiderable way above the outlet) was cut, the families who lived near the ftagnant water, were fubject in the fpring and end of autumn, to intermitting fevers of very long continuance; from 23 to 33, and fometimes to 39 days. Whole families were to be feen in
                                                           fuch

fuch diftrefs at the fame time, that no one could affift the others. They depended on the kind miniftrations of their neighbours, for the fupply of their neceffities. Often has the poor's fund been employed, to pay women to wait upon fuch diftreffed families; and it is hoped, it will not be looked upon as a proftitution of that facred fund. Since thefe ftagnant waters were completely drained, thofe difeafes and the fad train of complaints connected with them, have happily been unknown; meanwhile, it is fuppofeable, that the fame happy effects muft flow from the fame caufes in every part of the country, and fhould prove an irrefiftable motive to draining, independent of the profit or fatisfaction refulting from it. It is not eafy to defcribe the pleafure of viewing luxuriant crops, adorning the place where the eye had been accuftomed to fee ftagnant water and noxious vapour impregnated with difeafes and death.

Agriculture.—The culture of this parifh is conducted by a fober well informed perfevering and wealthy tenantry. No expence or labour is withheld. Every exertion is made to beftow whatever is thought neceffary, under the providence of a gracious God, to aid the fertility of the foil. All chilling moifture is led away, and the plough is made to return till the roots of every weed are deftroyed. Every meliorating crop has its due rotation. Lime, that genial pulverizer, that gives healthy fermentation, is brought by water from England and Scotland, and from lime-kilns in the neighbourhood by land carriage, and thrown with unfparing liberality upon the fertile bofom of the earth.

A very confiderable quantity of wheat is annually raifed in this diftrict, although feveral of the tenants have been unwilling to mention the exact number of bolls they fow; by their own account, there were 649 bolls fown in 1790; and in 1791,

670 bolls were sown. I believe that the sowing of wheat is upon the increase in this parish; and although I do not presume to be a judge, I have an apprehension, that it may be carried too far.

Considerable quantities of wheat, barley, pease, and beans, are annually exported from this district; several hundred bolls of oats, and sometimes of potatoes; but the exported potatoes as far as I know, never turn to great account, which has in some measure cooled the ardour of exporting this valuable part of the produce. Flax is also raised; but not in such quantities as to compete for premiums. It is thought a severe crop, and there is seldom more sown than what is necessary for the use of the families, or in order to induce labourers to engage for the harvest. The tenant gives 10 yards square to sow one lippy of lint-seed. Some tenants allow two lippies to each of their labourers. Formerly, the land here was ploughed by 4 and 6 oxen, and 2, sometimes 4 horses before them all, yoke fellows in a large Scots plough. The ground is now ploughed with 2 horses, in a chain plough made upon Small's construction. The horses are guided, and the plough directed by one man. Here may be one or two of the tenants who use 2 oxen and 2 horses in 1 plough, and one tenant who has 2 oxen without horses, in 1 or 2 of his ploughs. If it was proper for the writer of these facts to give his own opinion, he would be inclined to approve of and recommend the last practice, especially in large farms. Every tenant sows a considerable field of clover, in proportion to the extent of his farm, or the necessities of his stock. On every farm, turnips are raised in smaller or greater fields, as they are intended for the cows and young stock only, or for such as are fed for the knife. There is no great attention given to a peculiar breed of cattle in this district; because the cultivated lands are thought too valuable, and the weaker and

and uncultivated, infufficient for raifing cattle of bone. The Fife cattle, however, always bring good prices in the market; and I believe it will not be faid that the cattle of this parifh are inferior to thofe of the other parts of the country. Cabbages and greens are alfo planted in the fields, but in fmall quantities by the fide of the turnip, to be ufed when froft renders the turnip more difficult to be obtained. Potatoes, that make fo great a part of the food of the lower claffes of fociety, are cultivated by every one who rents land, for the ufe of his family, horfes, cows and hogs. They are in general ufed for the laft 3 animals without boiling. The tenants give 10 yards fquare or 12 for planting a peck of potatoes to the manufacturers and other labouring people, for fo many days work in harveft, or any other throng feafon; wifely thinking that this is preferable to money, as it procures them hands in the time of their need. Much ufeful information concerning the culture and prefervation of this invaluable root has been lately obtained, by means of the benevolent exertions of the Board of Agriculture.

I know not if the following obfervations have been made. Many caufes for the curle-top amongft potatoes have been affigned, that mankind might avoid this devourer of fo valuable a part of their food. When that part of the potatoe is cut for a fet which the former year adhered to its root, it invariably produces a curle-top. It would be of no fmall confequence, therefore, before the feed is cut into fets, that a careful hand fhould be employed to cut off this part of every potatoe, and keep it entirely feparate from the feed. When there is too little of the potatoe left at the bottom of the eye, that is feparated for a fet, it has the fame unhappy confequence. This year has led men of obfervation to conclude, that wet land produces the curle-top. There are two very long ridges in a field near this place, planted with the fame culture,

manure

.manure, and ſeed : the one ridge is rather lower and flatter than the other. In this ridge, there is not one plant of an hundred ſound. In the other ridge, the 4 rows lying neareſt the furrow on each ſide of the ridge, are curle-tops, with very few exceptions ; the 4 rows on the higheſt part of the ridge, are healthy vigorous plants. I know no way of accounting for this, but by ſaying that the exceſs of moiſture has produced it.

There were in this diſtrict in 1792, more than 1559 cattle young and old, male and female. There were 420 horſes of the above deſcription, and of ſheep, 1940. The tenants breed their own cows, and moſt of them their working horſes. There are in this pariſh 7 threſhing milns, and their number will ſoon be increaſed. One of theſe is ſet and kept in motion by water, a very conſiderable ſaving to the tenant ; and the machine, one would think, muſt move more ſteadily, and with greater effect, than thoſe worked with horſes. Some indeed have made uſe of oxen and horſes ; but theſe animals have ſo different a movement, that the practice has not become general. It is to be hoped, that oxen will be trained for this uſeful inſtrument of huſbandry ; and there can be little doubt, that in ſome ſituations and circumſtances, it might be worked by the force of wind. There are 4 meal milns in the diſtrict ; one lint and barley mill, moved by one water wheel ; and one belonging to a dyer for the purpoſes of his employment.

There are 3 bridges in the pariſh, all of them over the Multree burn ; one of them giving paſſage to travellers from Cupar to the north, and the other to travellers from the north to St Andrews : one end of the Guard bridge reſts on this pariſh ; the other on the pariſh of St Andrews.

On this end of the bridge is erected the only toll-gate within
the

the bounds of the diftrict. There are 50 tenants in the parifh. The extent of their farms is very different; from 10 to
500 acres. Thofe of the laft mentioned extent are in the
eaft part of the parifh. The land lets at from 10s to 50s an
acre, excepting thofe extenfive farms in the eaft part of
the parifh; which are rented at from L. 40 to between L. 60
and L. 70.

Heritors, Improvements, &c.—There are 16 heritors in the
diftrict, 14 of whom do not refide; a very material lofs to the
poor, and no fmall difadvantage to the inhabitants, as their
refidence would give real encouragement to the induftrious,
and a ferious check to thofe few who in every fociety are inclined to be diforderly in their manners and practice. In the
year 1782, we received no affiftance from the heritors for
the fupport of the poor, and were more than once obliged to
borrow from the members of the Seffion; being unwilling to
diminifh any little fum we had been enabled in more plentiful
years to lay up for the purpofe of increafing the poor's annual
income. For fome years paft indeed the heritors have attended with a fpirit of liberality to the neceffities of the poor;
and we cannot entertain a doubt, that their benevolence will
always be in proportion to the circumftances of the parifh.
On that part of the eftate of Leuchars, purchafed by the Hon.
Robert Lindfay, containing 3736 acres, ftands part of an old
houfe, commonly called the caftle of Leuchars, built upon a
forced bank of earth, on the edge of a fwamp, furrounded by
a deep and broad moat, inclofing about 3 acres of ground.
In the time of our forefathers, this muft have been a place of
defence, having no accefs but by a narrow bridge, till the
large drain was cut, which has rendered it acceffible on all
fides up to the moat. There is a draw-well in the middle of
the

the court, which, to the aſtoniſhment of thoſe who lived there ſome years ago, became dry when the water was let out of the moat, for the purpoſe of ſcouring it. The workmen came at laſt upon the mouth of a covered drain, which they found on a level with the bottom of the well; and upon going down into the well, they diſcovered the ſame drain open there; from which they were naturally led to think, that the inhabitants had been ſupplied with water from the moat without, when ſurrounded by an enemy.

On this eſtate, alſo are ſome fine old trees.

Mr Lindſay has planted 138 acres with various kinds of timber; the plantation is in the moſt thriving ſtate, and gives a moſt delightful reſt to the eye, where once there was nothing to be ſeen, but a moor producing ſome coarſe graſs, heath, and furze. The traveller too, is pleaſed with the variety of nature's luxuriant productions. Mr Lindſay has alſo incloſed ſeveral fields with ditch, hedge, and dyke; and hedge rows of trees. Theſe will in a ſhort time, ſhelter and beautify the diſtrict. In the meantime, they pleaſingly employ the imagination in anticipating what their maturity may produce. On the eſtate of Leuchars, have been built 5 farm ſteadings, ſuitable to, and convenient for the different farms, where the tenants are lodged, if not elegantly, yet with ſuitable conveniency. The proprietor has alſo feued ground to the manufacturers and others, for building a houſe, and a ſmall garden at the back of it, at the rate of L. 4 per acre. So that the village of Leuchars, in place of being literally the village built with turfs, is become a neat country village built with ſtones and mortar; the houſes at leaſt are commodious for manufacturers. There are more than 70 new houſes built in this village, within a few years; 8 of them have 2 floors, and 4 of them are covered with blue ſlates.

On

On the eftate of Earl's-hall, belonging to Robert Bruce Henderfon, Efq. Advocate, are a few old trees. On this eftate is built one of the moft extenfive farm fteadings in the parifh. Thefe two eftates, once were in what is called run-rig, two ridges belonging to Leuchars, one to Earl's-hall. This mode of divifion, while it may feem to fecure to each proprietor his proportion of good and bad land, muft be at-tended with the moft unhappy effects, as it drags the wheels of improvement, and expofes the labourers to no inconfide-rable temptations.

On the eftate of Pitcullo, belonging to Neil Fergufon, Efq. Advocate, are fome very fine old timber, and feveral fine thriving clumps of young trees. Here are more inclofures, both with ftones and lime, and a greater number of old hedges with rows of trees within, than on any eftate in the diftrict; here indeed were made the firft improvements in agriculture and inclofing. On this eftate alfo, are two fubftantial new farm tofts.

On the eftate of Ardit, the property of John Anftruther, Efq. Advocate, are alfo to be feen fome fine old trees, hedges and clumps rifing. Thefe two eftates on the weft fide of the parifh, as they rife above the flat ground on the eaft, afford an agreeable and pleafing variety to the traveller, from Cupar to St Andrews, from Cupar to Dundee; or from either of thefe burghs to Cupar.

On the eftate of Drone, belonging to Robert Meldrum Efq. of Clayton, there are more than 20 acres planted; fome 20, fome 7 years old: and within thefe 5 or 6 years, about 10 acres were planted with great tafte, in different di-rections, from the houfe of Clayton, that will greatly beautify the fituation of that building. Here alfo are two excellent farm fteads. There are 8 acres planted on the eftate of Pit-lethie, belonging to Thomas Lawfon, Efq.; befides fome old timber.

timber. This estate is inclosed with ditch and hedge, and hedge rows of different ages, which both give beauty and warmth to the fields.

In the garden belonging to Pitlethie, once stood one of the hunting seats of James the VI. King of Scotland; which had been taken down to a little below the surface, and thus rendered invisible. In digging this garden, the spade rung against a firm stone, and as stones are valuable here, upon removing the earth, the foundation of this hunting seat was discovered to a great depth and thickness. This was carefully raised, and a great part of Mr Lawson's house and offices was built from this quarry. Here too, were found the Royal Arms of Scotland, cut in a stone, which is still preserved, being placed in the front of one of the houses. In a field, near the house of Pitlethie, grows a venerable spreading thorn, where his Majesty's hawks after their toils, were accustomed to refresh themselves through the night.

Sheughy-dyke, or Tentsmuirs, is a very large flat part of the district on the east; about which many wonderful stories have been told, concerning the original inhabitants, and the peculiarity of their manners. After the most laborious enquiry, I find no reason to conclude, according to general report, that this part of the parish was peopled by the crews of a Danish fleet wrecked on the coast. I presume, that the greatest part of this flat, moory, benty, sandy ground, has been left by the gradual retiring of the sea. The sea has been making a gradual retreat from that part of the parish, for many years past, and has left what seems to me strong proofs of having once flowed and ebbed on those grounds. The name seems to have been founded in that caution and œconomy with which men take possession of property they are not sure of holding; for when the people took their station where the sea formerly made her furrowed bed, they must
have

have entertained a fear, that fhe would in fome future ftorm, return and occupy thofe parts fhe had been accuftomed to travel over. They did not at firft therefore build houfes, but erected tents on thofe parts that fwelled a little above the furrounding flats; and to make the fituation of their tents more comfortable and dry, they dug a fheugh or ditch, laying the fod, and cafting the earth inwards; hence feems to be derived the name Sheughy-dyke. The tent erected in the middle gave rife to the other name Tents-moors.

When thefe moors have been opened by digging, there has been found in feveral places, a greater variety of fhells, and fifh-bones, than could be reafonably fuppofed to fall from the tables of thofe tent-dwelling inhabitants; and feem to lead the mind to conclude, that the aged and ftorm-ftruck inhabitants of the ocean being wafhed to the fhore, obtained a grave by the next tide covering them with fand. There are like-wife in thefe moors 4 long beautiful canals. Thofe who efpoufe the idea of peopling this part of the diftrict with fhip-wrecked Danes, fay, that thefe canals were formed by thofe foreigners, to defend themfelves from the inhabitants of the furrounding country. I fhall not fay, how improbable this account appears. Thefe canals feem to give no countenance to fuch an affertion. The moft extended of them is not 2 miles long; and there is a great fpace of flat ground between the north end of them and the river Tay: the fouth end of them and the river Eden, confequently could form no defence. But, fuppofing they could have done fo, would it not have been eafy for the Scots, to fail from the Forth and Tay, dif-embark on their rear, while their land forces attacked them in front? Thefe canals do not poffefs depth of water to ren-der them the leaft defence. They feem to have been formed by the retiring ocean. There are 4 long, broad, beautiful, and almoft parallel canals; called Canal-loch, White-myre,

Toremont,

Toremont, and Tents-muir, or Big waters. I obferve this year, that the tenants are cutting drains, and letting the water out of thefe canals, to render the pafture more beneficial to their cattle. Strangers riding into this flat and not very fertile part of the parifh, are furprifed with finding this watery variety. I have feen their eyes return to it with pleafure. In the fummer, efpecially if it be a dry one, the greateft part of the water is carried away by the wind, and exhaled by the fun. When in this ftate, the canals furnifh a confiderable quantity of coarfe grafs for the horfes and cattle. In this part of the diftrict, there are cattle of a fmall fize reared, as may well be fuppofed, from the nature of their pafture ; and a few working horfes of a diminutive breed, to labour the fields, of no great extent, kept in tillage. One great difadvantage attending this fandy part of the parifh is, that after the fields are fown and harrowed, if the wind blows ftrong from the weft, or fouthweft, the mould is blown off the feed, and not infrequently, a confiderable part of the feed is blown from the fown ground.

This foil is favourable to turnips, barley, and clover ; good crops of oats and rye, are obtained here. The barley that grows in this fandy foil, is heavier in proportion to an equal quantity of the fame grain that is produced from good clay ; the former being thinner in the hufk than the latter. The crops of peafe, with a few beans among them, are not fo fure or productive.

There is in this part of the diftrict, a falmon fifhing of no inconfiderable value, oppofite to a fmall rivulet that runs into the ocean. From the entry of this rivulet, along the fhore to the river Eden, the people fometimes amufe themfelves by fifhing in the fummer feafon, in the following manner : Two of the people take a long net with weights upon the lower edge of it, go into the fea as far as they may with fafety, extend

tend their net, and drag it gently to the fhore: In this way, they are fometimes more, fometimes lefs fuccefsful in taking fea trout, flounders, and other kinds of fifh. They ufe the fame mode of fifhing alfo, in all the convenient pools in the river Eden, when it is low water. This they only do for amufement, or when they long for fifh. Is it not fuppofeable, that if thefe fifhings were properly attended to, they might fupply all the diftrict with this wholefome and agreeable article of food? There were two no way inconfiderable falmon fifhings in the river, one immediately below the Guard bridge, the other oppofite to the Coble-houfe; fo called, from a fmall boat being kept there, by which travellers from the fouth to the north, and from the north to the fouth, fhortened their way by 2 miles, in place of going round by the Guard-bridge. But fince the diftillery was erected upon the fouth fide of the river at Kincaple, upon a bank flopping towards the Eden, both thefe fifhings have been much injured by noxious water flowing from the diftillery which runs into the river. The one at the Coble-houfe is entirely given up, and the other greatly decreafed. When thefe were fifhed, falmon was bought here at $1d\frac{1}{4}$ and a $1d\frac{1}{2}$ per pound Dutch. No falmon can be purchafed now below 4d, or frequently 8d per pound. The Tents-moors, and many other farms in the parifh, abound with grey rabbits. It is allowed on all hands, that the fale of thefe animals with their furrs, yields more than L. 200 *per annum.* This part of the parifh is now almoft the only one where fheep are reared. It has been thought that the true breed of Scots fheep are to be found here: originally it might have been fo; but they have paffed through fo many crofs breeds, that they are greatly degenerated; yet there remain fome very fine-wooled fheep, which, if properly attended to, might again rival their neighbours for the finenefs of their fleeces. There has been a flock of 180 fheep lately added to
the

the former ſtock, making in all 2120. It is only in this part of the diſtrict, the numbers are kept up. They have been decreaſing in the weſt part of the pariſh, for many years, and now are reduced to one flock. In this flock, are a great proportion of long tailed ſheep without horns; their paſture is higher, and of courſe, more dry and nouriſhing; the ſheep of a larger ſize, and finer wool. But in the eaſt part of the pariſh, the graſs is of a coarſer nature, and the ſoil more ſubject to retain water from its flatneſs; the ſheep of a ſmaller ſize, the 4 quarters weighing from 20 to 26 pounds. The time was, when every farm in the diſtrict, had a flock belonging to it; till the culture of clover and rye-graſs became general, and every ſpot of graſs land was made to feel the pulveriſing effects of the plough and harrow, when it was thought more profitable to part with theſe meek, harmleſs, and uſeful creatures.

In the Tents moors, ſmuggling was carried on to a great extent, by thoſe men in the neighbourhood, who were determined to riſk their fortune and character on the events of a day; for the inhabitants of this corner, were only aſſiſting in concealing and tranſporting their unlawful imports. By the wiſe and vigorous interpoſition of the directors of our juſtly admired government, ſmuggling, that illicit traffic big with many evils to mankind, is now happily unknown over all our coaſts. The inhabitants of this remote corner have been blamed for cruelty to ſhip-wrecked ſailors. If the charge be juſt, it does not belong to them alone; they are but a handful; the place is thinly peopled. In the days of old, it might have been ſo; but I have ſeen much attention and kindneſs ſhewn to ſuch unhappy ſailors as were caſt upon our ſhore. I truſt, and believe, that every future period ſhall be marked with an increaſe of brotherly love to the unfortunate.

Church,

Church, Stipend, School and Poor.—The church of Leuchars is placed nearly in the middle of the parish. It is an ancient lofty building, part of it very ancient, situated on a rising ground. The building is more than sufficient to hold the parishioners. There is no record by which the time of its erection can be fixed, and there is even no tradition on the subject. The church was once the only one in Scotland whose steeple ascended on the east end of the building. The time was, when our forefathers worshipped here according to the forms of the Romish church. The door through which the organist entered to perform that part of the service allotted to him, is still seen in the east gable of the church; and the place where the holy water was kept to purify the worshippers on their entry into this temple is also visible. The iron hook on which was suspended the lever for weighing meal on the Lord's day, is batted into the key stone of an arch in the steeple; and in the place below, other merchant wares were sold on that holy day.

A very little west of the present church, once stood a chapel called St Bernard's chapel; no remains of this monument of antiquity are now visible, the stones of it having been used for common purposes. Round where it stood are to be seen many graves, constructed of 4, and some of 6 stones. Some of these graves have lately been looked into without affording any thing worthy of being recorded.

There is a most excellent well flowing with an abundant stream of soft water, near the west end of the village, (for the village is now extending westward,) called by the name of the Saint, to whom the chapel was no doubt consecrated. A little north of the east end of the village, to the convenience and comfort of the inhabitants, there is another well of equal excellence, called the Lady well, no doubt consecrated to the Blessed Virgin. Tradition says, there once stood

ſtood a houſe of worſhip on the eaſt ſide of the road, oppoſite to the houſe of Ardit; a ſmall field belonging to that eſtate retains the name of the glebe. There was alſo once a chapel and burying ground at eaſt Drone in this pariſh: The glebe is the name of a field there too, but the real hiſtory of theſe has not been tranſmitted to us. There is a tradition, according to the account by the Rev. Robert Dalgleiſh of Scots-craig, D. D. that the village of Ferry-Porton-craigs, before the 1606, belonged to this pariſh.

The ſtipend of this pariſh till the year 1791, was 64 bolls bear; 8 bolls wheat; 8 bolls oats; L. 330 : 10 : 9 Scots, and L. 36 : 16 : 8 Scots, vicarage, in which is included 40 merks for Communion elements. By an Interlocutor of the Court of Seſſion in 1791, their Lordſhips were pleaſed to give the following augmentation. Out of a part of the free tythes of the pariſh, 24 bolls bear; 24 bolls meal; and L. 42,: 15 : 11 Scots, in which is included, L. 42 Scots for Communion elements. The Sacrament of our Lord's Supper is annually diſpenſed in this congregation, in the beginning of March, and end of July, to between 700 and 800 communicants. The Kirk Seſſion received from the biſhop of St Andrew's, from funds belonging to himſelf, L. 28 Scots for Communion elements; the receipt of which, is entered for the laſt time in the Seſſion records, in the year 1728.

The legal ſalary of the pariſh ſchoolmaſter, is L. 6 : 13 : 4 ſterling. He has beſides, by a mortification, a houſe, garden, and croft; and 2 acres of light land, about half a mile northweſt of the village of Leuchars; and L. 4 : 10 : 6 ſter. left to thoſe who hold the office of ſchoolmaſter, by a late eminent and worthy clergyman of this pariſh, the Rev. Alexander Henderſon.

Leuchars is a pleaſant healthy country village, where boarders may be kept to advantage. The preſent incumbent,

got

got a few foon after he was elected, and has room for a greater number. The number of fcholars in the winter is from
80 to 100. The fchool fees are as low as any in Scotland.
Every man who is fenfible of the importance of educating the
youth, and underftands the true interefts of his country, muft
regret, that a body of men fo refpectable, and fo extenfively
ufeful as the parifh-fchoolmafters are, fhould have appointments fo very unequal to their labour and to the fituation of
their families.

The poor in this parifh are fupported in their own houfes.
The Kirk Seffion are enabled to provide for them by the
weekly collections at the church, and the money arifing from
the mort-cloths, which were originally purchafed from the
poor's funds; by the rent of 5 acres in the priory of St Andrews, purchafed in the fame way; and by the produce of a
few feats in the church, yielding about L. 1 fterling *per annum*.
I believe there is no fund managed with fuch care, or rendered fo extenfively ufeful, as the little funds in the hands of
the Kirk Seffions of Scotland. We do not allow any of our
poor to beg, though beggars pour in upon us from the north
and fouth, in greater numbers than the fituations of men in
moderate circumftances can enable them to fupply. There
are laws to prevent this; but of what ufe are laws, if they
are not put in execution? We have invariably found that
thofe who are moft unwilling to accept of aid from the parifh, are leaft eafily fatisfied, when they have begun to receive
it; whereas, thofe who modeftly intimate their wants and
receive affiftance, as foon as their circumftances become lefs
neceffitous, with hearts overflowing with gratitude to
Almighty God, inform us that they are able to fupport
themfelves, and thank the Seffion for the kindnefs fhewn
them while it was neceffary. Penfioners of this defcription,
we fupply with the greateft fatisfaction.

Population.—

Population, &c.—By the return to Dr Webſter in 1755, the numbers were 1691. By the laſt accurate ſurvey of the pariſh, the numbers were 1620. The decreaſe, which is 71, is to be accounted for in the following manner. There are 6 different farms in the pariſh, occupied by one tenant; formerly poſſeſſed by 3. There is indeed one farm divided into 3, but there are 3 other farms poſſ ſſed by one tenant, which were formerly occupied by 2. Every plough in the pariſh ſome years ago, had a man to hold, and a youth to drive it; the labour of the farms was chiefly carried on by married ſervants whoſe families reſided on them. It is more the cuſtom now to perform the labour by unmarried ſervants who have a houſe near the tenants, in which they ſleep, and prepare their food. After they retire from work, they are free from the reſpect due to the eye of their maſter, and if inclined to wander, are at full liberty. I believe that theſe circumſtances are not favourable to morals, and that the union of ſmall into large farms, is unfriendly to population.

Abſtract of Baptiſms and Marriages from 1750, to 1759 incluſive, (there being no record of burials kept at that period;) and from 1780, to 1789 incluſive, to which the liſt of funerals within that period is added. No calculation can however be made of the number of deaths from the funerals; as many from neighbouring pariſhes are buried here, and many of the people of this pariſh in the neighbouring church-yards.

Baptiſms.

	Baptifms.	Marriages.
1750 -	47 -	24
1751 -	55 -	20
1752 -	46 -	23
1753 -	51 -	10
1754 -	49 -	14
1755 -	58 -	19
1756 -	34 -	13
1757 -	45 -	14
1758 -	42 -	10
1759 -	51 -	18
	478	165

	Baptifms.	Marriages.	Burials.
1780 -	39 -	19 -	35
1781 -	41 -	12 -	30
1782 -	46 -	14 -	24
1783 -	36 -	14 -	25
1784 -	43 -	6 -	21
1785 -	57 -	6 -	41
1786 -	46 -	11 -	14
1787 -	18 -	4 -	42
1788 -	42 -	10 -	26
1789 -	43 -	13 -	25
	411	109	283

There are of fouls in the parifh, below 10 years, 322; from 10 to 80, 1288; and from 80 to 90, 10.

There

There are in the parish, 22 Antiburgher, and 13 Burgher
Seceders ; 1 Berean, and 1 member of the Episcopal church ;
37 Diffenters in all.   There are 13 wrights; 9 masons ; 9
smiths ; 8 shoemakers ; 6 taylors ; 3 wheel-wrights, 2 of these
are coopers ; 1 furgeon ; 1 brewer ; 1 baker, and 1 bee-hive
and basket maker. In the village of Leuchars, are 7 ale-houses,
and there are 2 others in the district. Two ale-houses in the
village of Leuchars, are certainly sufficient to supply all the
inhabitants ; and a greater number tends very much to destroy
the morals, and impair the health of the inhabitants.   There
are 90 looms in the parish, 34 of these in the village of Leuchars.   The weavers are employed in what is called household
work of various kinds ; but chiefly in brown linens, single
and double sail cloth, which they weave for the Dundee merchants.   Several of them buy yarn, weave it, and sell the
webs to merchants in Dundee and Cupar.   This kind of
manufacture is increasing, and it is thought will increase.
There is one of the weavers famous for working all kinds of
damask, and other table linens.   It is thought the population
will soon rise above the return made to Dr Webster : there
are 10 new houses built in the village of Leuchars this summer, to be inhabited at Martinmas next.   A great spirit for
building has discovered itself for several years past, especially
in the village : though building is carried on at a great expence, free stones have not been found in the district, except
on the southwest, by the side of the river Eden, below a most
valuable surface : The proprietors are unwilling to break more
of it than what is absolutely necessary for their own use, and
the use of their farms.   The cart load of free stones costs 2s,
the driving and toll, 3d.   On the west side of the parish
which is hilly, there are inexhaustible fields of fine hard blue
whin stones ; these cost 1s for driving the cart load, and 4d
for quarrying.   From the top of Lucklaw-hill, part of which

is

is in this district, there is a most extensive and delightful
prospect.

Advantages and Disadvantages.—It is no small advantage to
this district, that the river Eden is navigable nearly to what is
called the Inner-bridge; a little below which with the con-
currence and assistance of some of the heritors, the tenants
have built upon the north bank of the Mulltree-burn, commonly called Mothry water, a wall perpendicular on the side
of the water, and have filled up the ground behind the wall
in such a manner, as to make it easy for carts to approach the
wall where they may load and unload small vessels : This gives
opportunity of importing what the inhabitants stand in need
of, and exporting whatever they can spare. Carriers from St
Andrews to Dundee pass and repass twice every week through
the village of Leuchars. Carriers from all the towns of the
south coast, from Crail to the Ely, pass once in 14 days; perhaps oftener in summer. Carriers from Dundee and St Andrews to Edinburgh, going through Cupar the county town,
pass within a mile of the village. Thus, an easy and regular
intercourse is maintained between all those distant places,
and what we wish to send, or desire to have from them, is
conveyed at the ordinary expence of carriage, according to
the weight.

The inhabitants of this district derive no small advantage
from the shell-fish in the river Eden. They gather cockles
and muscles in their different seasons, sometimes eat them by
themselves, sometimes prepare them with potatoes, or onions;
and the high flavoured juice that is obtained from the fishes in
the boiling with a little seasoning, makes a truly wholesome
and delicious meal.

There was established by mutual consent, in the year 1792,
a society calling themselves the Brotherly Society of support,

in

in and about Leuchars, and members from the neighbouring parishes are admitted. The laws of the society are pious, benevolent, and well meant. Every member on his admiffion pays 2s 6d fter. and 8d quarterly, or 2s 6d annually. The intention of the fund is to relieve the members when under ficknefs or the infirmities of old age, or the widows and children of deceafed members; who, it is propofed, are to receive 3s 6d weekly, or if a nurfe fhould be neceffary, 4s 6d. If any of the members die whofe furviving relations are unable to defray their funeral expences, they are to receive L. 1 : 5 for that purpofe. (It is fubmitted, whether focieties of this nature in different parts of the country, may not be ufeful.) Their funds alfo enable them to buy quantities of meal, coals, or any other neceffary article to divide amongft them. There are 2 fairs held in Leuchars, the one on the fecond Wednefday of April old ftyle, for the fale of cattle, fheep, lint-feed, fhoes, and all other kinds of merchant goods, the other on the third Friday of October, old ftyle. The pit coal is at a great diftance, and from the throng in the fummer feafon, the fetching one cart containing 5 load, cofts 5s 2d¼, and is the work of a long day for one man and 2 horfes. The proprietors of coal, are threatening to raife the price.

Difeafes.—Epidemical difeafes are not known in this diftrict, fince the great drain was cut. I have known 3 perfons within thefe 20 years, affected with St Vitus's dance to a very high degree. It was defired that a fiddle fhould be played on in the prefence of the affected perfon. It was not regular mufic that gave relief, but the ftriking of certain ftrings, which the perfon under agitation, defired fhould be ftruck again. The effect was aftonifhing; the perfon affected, became quiet, fat down, and in a little, afked to be put

to

to bed, but ſtill called for the perſon to play, till the feelings
that produced the agitation were abated.

Some years ago, the people in this pariſh profeſſed a religious ſcruple againſt innoculating their children. They are
now come to look upon it as a religious duty to adopt the
practice ; and not a few of them, when a lancet loaded with
matter was procured for them, innoculated their own children. If the ſcruple could be got over throughout all parts
of the country, how many lives would it ſave, how many
ſore hearts to parents would it be the means under God of
preventing?

Character of the People.——They are in general ſober and
induſtrious ; regular attendants upon Divine worſhip on the
Lord's day ; and grateful to a kind providence for the bleſſings
they enjoy. They are remarkably ſteady in their attach-
ments, in their loyalty to Our Gracious Sovereign and happy
Conſtitution : 14 from this diſtrict entered to ſerve His
Majeſty when a late call for ſailors was made through the
counties.——With what pleaſure do I relate theſe facts, after
having read with horror in the Advertiſer, for Tueſday the
3d November 1795, the wicked and treaſonable attack made
upon the ſacred perſon of George the III. Thanks and
praiſe with my whole heart do I offer to the providence of
God, for preſerving the life of the beſt of Kings, who has
ever been the father of his people ; and pray moſt fervently,
that the crown may long, very long flouriſh on his ſacred
head, until it pleaſe the unerring Diſpoſer of all events, to
crown Our Gracious King with a crown that ſhall for ever
flouriſh in glory, and transfer his earthly crown to the head
of His Royal Highneſs George Prince of Wales.

PARISH OF LOGIE.

(Preſbytery of Cupar—Synod and County of Fife.)

By the Rev. Mr. ROBERT BOGIE.

Situation and Extent.

THE pariſh of Logie is ſituated about 3 miles from Cu_
par, (the principal town in the county of Fife, and the
ſeat of the preſbytery), and about an equal diſtance from the
water ſide, or Ferry, to Dundee. It extends about 2½ miles
in length from E. to W., and 1 in breadth from S. to N.,
though in ſome parts not quite ſo much. The general figure
of the pariſh, may be ſeen in Ainſlie's map of Fife.

Surface, Soil, Climate, &c.—The country is in general hilly,
but very fertile. The climate is pretty dry and healthy, excepting near the ſmall village of Logie, where there is a marſh,
which makes the air damp, eſpecially in winter.—There is a
conſiderable mountain in the pariſh, called *Luckla Hill*, upon
which, it is reported, that the kings of Scotland uſed to hunt,
and on which account it is called *the King's Park*. But of
this circumſtance, there is no authentic record extant.—From
the top of this hill, in a clear day, there is a very extenſive

five prospect, of Fife, Angus, the Mearns, and other counties.

Cultivation, Produce, Cattle, Wool, &c.—The ground commonly produces excellent crops of every kind of grain. The farmers sow a considerable quantity of grass and turnips, and have very good returns. They mostly plow their ground with horses ; and oxen are here very little used in husbandry. There are about 28 ploughs, with generally 2 horses to a plough, besides what the farmers bring up for their own use, or for sale. Most of them pay a good part of their rents by bringing up young cattle. There are two pretty considerable flocks of sheep in the parish. The mutton is small, but the wool they produce is of a tolerable quality, neither of the coarsest, nor the finest sort.

Population.—The inhabitants, it is said, are diminished in point of number, compared to what they were many years ago; and it is certain, that several cottages have been pulled down since the commencement of this century; but within these 40 years, there appears to be, upon the whole, very little variation. The population, at present, consists of 340 examinable persons ; which, allowing the usual proportion for children under 8 years of age, will make the number of souls   -   -   -   -   -   -   425
The return to Dr. Webster, in 1755, was only   -   413

Hence there appears to be an increase of   -   12

The average of annual births, is 10	Smiths, - - - 4
Ditto of marriages, - 2	Tailors, - - - 2
Ditto of burials, - 8	Retailer of spirits, - - 1
In the different professions there	Weavers, - - - 6
are, farmers, - - 9	And, Shoemakers, - - 3
Feuers, or small proprietors, - 2	

together

together with fome carpenters, mafons, day labourers, and fervants.

Proprietors and Rents.—Befides the three fmall heritors above mentioned, who refide in the parifh, and cultivate their own ground, there are fix greater proprietors, who do not re- fide, which is a confiderable lofs to the poor. The valued rent is 2916l. 6s. 8d. Scotch ; the real rent is not exactly known. The rent of farms, in general, run from 20s. to 40s. per acre. Some however, have their land on more reafonable terms.

Church, &c.—The manfe was built in 1736, and has fince got feveral partial reparations ; but it is ftill in a very in- different ftate. The ftipend amounts, on an average, to 80l. Sterling per annum. The glebe confifts of 4 acres arable, and 2 acres of a den for pafturage. The King is patron*. There are a good many Seceders, who attend a Burgher meeting houfe, in the neighbouring parifh of Kilmeny.

School and Poor.—A good fchool and fchool-houfe are now building, (1792) ; which, when completed, will be very com- modious. The falary is only 4l. 18s. 3½d., with 50 merks from a mortification, left in 1690, by Sir James Ramfay, Bart. of Eafter Logie.—The capital ftock belonging to the poor amounts to 120l. Serling. The collections at the church doors are but very inconfiderable. There are 3 ftated penfioners on the poor's funds, who get 1s. per week, and are paid at that rate

by

* In 1683, Sir David Balfour of Forret, one of the Senators of the College of Juftice, bequeathed a large folio Bible, for the ufe of the minifter on Sundays. It is ftill in tolerable condition, and was lately rebound.

by the treafurer every 5 weeks ; befides which, they get 5s.
in winter' to purchafe coals. The annnal collections, upon
an average, including what is drawn on facramental occafions,
do not much exceed 5l. Sterling.

Mifcellaneous Obfervations.—The people are in general healthy.
There are not a few of 60, 70, and 80 years of age : One
man died lately aged 87, and another 92.—The prices of all
kinds of provifions are nearly doubled within chefe 20 years,
or even lefs. Good beef, then, fold at 2d. and 2½d. per pound ;
mutton at 3d. and a good fowl at 6d.—Coals are the only
fuel ufed in this part of the country; but they have become
very high of late, which the poor feel very fenfibly.

PARISH of MARKINCH.

(County and Synod of Fife, Presbytery of Kirkcaldy.)

By the Rev. Mr. John Thomson.

Name, Extent, Surface, &c.

THE parish church and village of Markinch stand upon the southern declivity of an eminence, or little hill, surrounded on all sides by a marsh; and from this insular situation, the last part of the name is obviously derived. Mark, or Merk, according to the most ancient spelling, has probably been prefixed, from the valuation put upon this inch, or spot of ground. The greatest extent of the parish from N. to S., is five miles and a half; and, from E. to W., about five miles, which may contain about 7000 acres. The form of the parish is very irregular, being deeply indented in several places, by the adjacent parishes. The village of Dubieside, which con-

tains

tains near 200 inhabitants, and lies upon the Frith of Forth, on the W. side of the mouth of the Leven, forms a part of this parish, though totally detached by the intervention of the parish of Wemyss. Markinch consists of four straths, or valleys, running from W. to E., all of them approaching, and some of them joining one another on the E. These straths are separated by gently swelling hills, which rise to no great height, and which are usually called Laws. These hills, or laws, corresponding to the general rise of the country from S. to N., gradually rise above one another; the more northerly always overlooking those that lie towards the S. The hill on the northern boundary is in a line with the Lomond hills, and forms a part of that track of high ground, which, extending from W. to E., divides the northern from the southern part of the county.

Soil, Climate, and Diseases —The soil of this parish is various. A small part consists of strong clay, and deep loam. A larger proportion, of light loam, rich and fertile. There is also a good deal of dry, gravelly, sharp land, which, in moist seasons, yields plentiful crops. But the largest proportion is rather wet, and lies on a cold, tilly, or clayey bottom. Of this kind some is sufficiently deep, and, in warm springs and summers, abundantly productive. But other parts of it are thin, and, when allowed to lie untilled, apt to run into heath, or coarse benty grafs. The whole parish almost is arable, except a large mofs on the N. side, and some swampy ground, which has been planted with fir, and other kinds of barren timber. This parish has little shelter from the storm in any direction, but suffers most from the easterly winds, which, in the spring months especially, are exceedingly cold and penetrating. The climate, however, is tolerably mild and temperate, and the inhabitants generally healthy.

Rheumatism,

Rheumatifm, confumptions, and hyftericks, are the moft prevailing difeafes. . Nervous fevers are not uncommon, though feldom epidemical. During the incumbency of the prefent minifter, feveral inftances of fcrofula and cancer have occurred. The fmall-pox is frequently very fatal. Though a few individuals have been reconciled to the practice of inoculation, yet the prejudices of the bulk of the common people againft it continue fo ftrong, that it has not yet been generally introduced. Children from 4 to 10, or 12 years of age, feem peculiarly liable to worms, particularly that fpecies, called the teres, or long round worm. Some young people in this place, have been known to void, in the fpace of 24 hours, upwards of a fcore of thefe worms, fome of them 10, and 12 inches long.

Rivers.—The river Leven, which iffues from a large lake of the fame name, lying about 5 or 6 miles to the weftward, runs through this parifh, and empties itfelf into the Frith of Forth, at the town of Leven. The Orr is another confiderable river, rifing from a loch or lake, of the fame name, alfo to the weftward, and runs through the fouthern part of the parifh, joining the Leven about 2 miles below the parifh church. In both thefe rivers there is plenty of different kinds of fifh. Salmon, pikes, and burn trouts are the principal kinds. There is alfo to be found in them a fpecies of trout, of a tolerable fize, the flefh of which is red, refembling that of falmon, of a fine flavour, and very delicate. Thofe who are fond of the amufement of angling, can never mifs excellent fport in thefe rivers at the proper feafons.

Roads and Bridges.—The great road from Kinghorn to Cupar, and Dundee, runs through the weft part of the parifh ; and, fince the late turnpike act for this county was obtained,

has

has been moſtly put into excellent repair. On this road there are ſeveral bridges within the bounds of this pariſh ; but 3 only of ſuch conſequence as to deſerve notice ; one over the Orr, another over Lochty, a ſmall water, about a mile N. of the Orr ; and another over the Leven, near Balbirnie. The firſt of theſe is very old and narrow *. The other two have been lately rebuilt. There is another line of road, which leads from Kirkcaldy to Cupar, and paſſes through the eaſtern part of the pariſh. On this road there is an excellent bridge over the Leven at Cameron. There is alſo a public road, which leads from Kinroſs to Leven, Largo, and the eaſt coaſt, and nearly divides the pariſh in the middle. It is in tolerable order, though not yet in the ſame ſtate of repair with the two juſt now mentioned. On the W. road, there is a toll-bar near the northern extremity of the pariſh ; and another on the E. road, at Windygates, near Cameron bridge. Beſides the bridges already taken notice of, there is one over the Orr, about a mile and a half above its influx into the Leven ; and two over the Leven, one at Balgonie, and the other at Balfour. The by-roads are in a very bad condition. In winter, and in wet weather, even during the ſummer months, they are, in many places, almoſt impaſſable. This evil the pariſh of Markinch feels in common with the reſt of the county ; to remove which, ſome effectual remedy ought ſurely to be, as ſoon as poſſible, applied. Good toll roads are doubtleſs highly advantageous to a country : but the advantage will be almoſt entirely confined to paſſengers, and thoſe who live in the immediate neighbourhood, unleſs a ready communication with theſe be opened up for the remoter parts of the country, by putting the by-roads into a proper ſtate of repair.

Population.

* It was built about 260 years ago, by James Bethune, archbiſhop of St. Andrew's, ſon to the laird of Balfour in this pariſh.

Population.—Markinch is, perhaps, one of the moſt populous country pariſhes in Fife ; the number of ſouls amounting
to nearly 2800.' The return to Dr. Webſter in 1755, was
only 2188. Hence there is an increaſe of about 612. This
extraordinary population may be accounted for from the following circumſtances : There are 7 villages in the pariſh,
which contain about 400 families ; and two large collieries,
which employ a great number of hands. The feuars are very numerous, being about 120. There are a great many mills,
of different kinds, upon the Leven. · Every farm of any conſiderable extent has a cottage town upon it ; and there is a
great proportion of the heritors reſident, who, beſides the extraordinary number of ſervants they keep, employ a much
greater number of labouring people, than tenants could be
ſuppoſed to do *.

Heritors and Rent.—The principal heritors are the Earl of
Leven, Mr. Balfour of Balbirnie, Colonel Wemyſs of Wemyſs,
Mr. Bethune of Balfour, and the Counteſs of Rothes. Beſides theſe, there are ſeveral other reſpectable gentlemen, who
poſſeſs conſiderable property in the pariſh, and a number of
ſmall proprietors. The number of the whole is 21, of whom
11 are reſident. The valued rent amounts to 10,456 l. 5 s.
Scotch money. The real rent cannot be exactly aſcertained, as
many of the proprietors are reſident, and have a conſiderable
quantity

---

* Since the year 1785, when the preſent incumbent was admitted, the population of the pariſh has increaſed about 200, owing to the re-erection of Balgonie colliery, which had not been wrought for 40 years, and a great many new
feus, granted lately by the Earl of Leven. Within the laſt ſix or ſeven years,
about 80 new houſes have been built, and 8 rebuilt, beſides a great many more,
which are building. The expenſe of theſe buildings may amount to 4000 l.
Sterling. The diviſion of the inhabitants, and any other circumſtance relative
to the population of the pariſh, neceſſary to be remarked, will be ſeen in the Statiſtical Table hereto annexed.

quantity of their land in their own poſſeſſion. As nearly as it can be calculated, it may amount to upwards of 5000 l. a-year. Within the laſt 20 years, the rents have riſen above 2000 l. a-year; and they are daily advancing. The rent of land, let in large farms, is from 10 s. to 22 s. the acre. Small pieces of ground, if of ſuperior quality, or in the immediate neighbourhood of the villages, will bring from 30 s. to 40 s. the acre.

Agriculture.—Some years ago, the method of farming, in this pariſh, was extremely rude, ſlovenly, and unproductive. Excepting the pleaſure-ground around gentlemen's ſeats, and ſome encloſures, which the reſiding proprietors kept in their own hands, the whole pariſh almoſt lay open and unencloſed. Few turnips were ſown; and very little ground laid out in clover and rye-graſs. The land was ill tilled; no pains taken to make, or to keep it clean, and the ſcanty allowance of manure injudiciouſly applied. In conſequence of this, the grain was of an inferior quality, and brought a lower price at the market. But of late, by the example of the gentlemen, who begin to pay more attention to the improvement of their eſtates, by the regulations fixed in the new leaſes, and by the exertions of ſome intelligent, ſubſtantial, and enterpriſing farmers, agriculture begins to aſſume a more promiſing aſpect. Though much of the pariſh ſtill lies open, encloſing is going on very rapidly. The turnip huſbandry, becomes more and more extenſive every year. A great deal of land, is ſown with clover and rye-graſs. More attention is paid to fallowing, and cleaning; and more judgment ſhown in cropping the lands. The judicious farmer keeps more of his land for hay and paſture, and leſs in tillage than formerly; by theſe means, as well as by the quantity of turnips raiſed, and conſumed upon his farm, the quantity of manure is increaſed, and he enabled, to do

more

more juftice to his grounds. The ufe of lime too, as a manure, is becoming very general. One tenant lately laid upon his farm, upwards of 1500 bolls of fhells, or unflacked
lime, in one feafon. The Scots plough is ftill ufed by many,
but its conftruction has been much improved, by which
means it is rendered eafier for the horfes, and makes better
work, than formerly. However, the Englifh plough, with
the curved mould board, of caft metal, is coming faft into ufe.
Where the land is dry and clean, a couple of horfes are only
yoked into the plough, and the man who holds the plough,
drives the horfes : but in wet, deep, and ftrong land, cattle
are ftill ufed along with the horfes. This method is certainly very proper, for fuch a foil; as the fteady, deliberate ftep
of the cattle gives a due check to the hurry and impatient
ardour, natural to horfes, in wet deep ground *.

Produce.—Oats, and barley, or blanded bear, are the prevailing crops. Blanded bear, or rammel, as the country people here call it, is the produce of barley and common bear
fown in a mixed ftate. Thefe are diftinguifhed chiefly by the
form or ftructure of the ear ; the barley having only two
rows of grain, and the common bear fix. Barley is a ftronger and larger grain than the bear. It lies longer in the ground
before it fprings, and is later in ripening. And the fame difference

* Though improvements in agriculture are making confiderable advances,
yet there is one bar, which, unlefs removed, muft greatly retard their progrefs,
and prevent their ever coming to perfection ; I mean the difinclination of the
proprietors to give leafes of a fufficient length of time. To enclofe, and fub-
divide, and clean, and manure to purpofe, a farm of any confiderable extent,
would require from 500 l. to 1000 l. But there are few farmers who would
rifk fuch an expenfe upon a leafe of 19 years. To accelerate the improvement
of land, and to bring it to its higheft ftate of cultivation, the proprietors muft
either encourage the exertions of the farmer, by granting longer leafes, or take
the trouble and expenfes upon themfelves.

ference is obſervable, when they are made into malt. It is remarkable, however, that when barley and common bear have been cultivated, for ſome time, in a mixed ſtate, they ſpring, and ripen, and malten equally ; and little difference in point of ſtrength or ſize is diſcernible. This is probably owing to the pollen of the two ſpecies mixing and falling indiſcriminately upon both, when the plant is impregnated, and thereby producing a ſameneſs in the quality of the grain, whilſt the external form of the ear of each is preſerved diſtinct. Corrⷆſponding to this idea, the blanded bear holds a middle place, in point of quality, between barley and common bear. Though inferior to the former, it is of a better quality than the latter. This mixed kind of grain is wearing out, and the culture of clean barley becoming more general. Till lately, little wheat was ſown in this pariſh : at preſent, between 80 and 100 acres may be raiſed annually. It is doubtful, however, when the nature of the ſoil, in general, is conſidered, whether it would be advantageous to the farmers here, to puſh the cultivation of wheat to any conſiderable extent, at leaſt, till the improvement of the ground is brought to a higher degree of perfection than it is at preſent. Nearly as much land may be employed in raiſing peaſe and beans ; and upwards of 100 acres for flax. It may be proper to obſerve here, that whilſt improvements of other kinds have been attended to, the culture of flax ſtill continues to be conducted in a very injudicious and unprofitable manner. The farmers, beſides ſowing a quantity for themſelves, their ſervants, and harveſt reapers, let ſo much of their land to others, who either are adventurers in that article, and raiſe conſiderable quantities, or who raiſe it ſolely for the uſe of their own families. Little attention is paid either to the choice of the ſoil, or the preparation of the ground ; and of courſe, whilſt the product is ſmall, general-

ly

ly not above two, and fometimes not above one tron ftone, from the peck of feed, the land is fcourged, and a great deal of extraordinary labour and manure neceffary to fit it for a fucceeding crop. Potatoes too are raifed in large quantities. Befides what every farmer plants for his own ufe, all the cottagers upon the farm, and many of the inhabitants of the adjacent villages, take as much land for potatoes as they can plant with their afhes, and what dung they can procure; and for this, they either pay money, or labour in harveft. The rent at which land is let, for flax or potatoes, is generally from 3 l. to 4 l. the acre; and when let in fmaller quantities, it is from 15 d. to 18 d. the 100 fquare yards.

Cattle.—The breeding of horfes, and particularly of black cattle, has of late become an object of general attention. Moft of the principal farmers, befides rearing young cattle, graze in fummer, and feed upon turnips in winter, a confiderable number for the butcher. Formerly, every farmer, almoft, kept a quantity of fheep: but now they are totally banifhed, except a few, which fome of the refiding proprietors breed for their own ufe, and thefe are moftly of the large white faced kind. The farm fteads, with a few exceptions, are ample and commodious, and every farm of any confiderable extent, has a cottage town upon it. This is of great advantage to the farmer; as it enables him to furnifh a houfe and garden, or kail-yard, to fuch of his men fervants as are married; and the other houfes he can let upon fuch terms, as to fecure the labour of the cottagers in harveft, or at any other feafon, when extraordinary affiftance may be neceffary.

Mills and Multures.—There are a great many corn mills in the parifh; every heritor of any confiderable property, or who has the command of water, having a mill upon his eftate,

to

to which his tenants are usually thirled. The multures are very high, amounting to one 13th part of the value of the grain carried to the mill. For this, it is true, the mill master does a great deal of duty. He carries the grain from the farmer's barn, dries, and grinds it, and brings it home.

Manufactures.—On the Leven, near Balbirnie bridge, a manufacture of lintseed oil hath been established for a good many years, which hath been carried on to a considerable extent. This manufacture is not only profitable to the manufacturers themselves, but advantageous to the country around, as it furnishes a ready market, and ready money, for all the lintseed produced in the neighbourhood, which, being unfit for sowing, could not turn to account any other way.—There is also in this parish, a bleachfield, where a large quantity of cloth is whitened every year. It is under the best management, and gives general satisfaction. In the village of Markinch, a stocking manufacture has been set on foot lately, and promises to do well. Some time ago, a considerable quantity of brown linen was manufactured for sale. But of late, that kind of work has been mostly relinquished, and the weavers, not engaged in country work, have been employed by the great manufacturers on the coast, in making checks and ticks, and from the flourishing state of these manufactures, and the extraordinary rise of wages, the number of weavers hath greatly increased. There are a few who carry on business for themselves, on a small scale, and employ from 6 to 12 hands. Manufactures of different kinds, particularly of spinning and weaving, might be carried on in this parish with much advantage. The water of Leven affords many excellent situations for machinery. Coal is at hand, and abundant. There is great plenty of good freestone for building; and, therefore, should any man of ability and enterprise enterprife fet a bufinefs of this kind on foot, it might be highly beneficial to himfelf, and to the country around; and would be well worthy the countenance and encouragement of the gentlemen in the immediate neighbourhood; as, by employing a number of hands, it would furnifh a ready market for the produce of their eftates, and of courfe heighten their value.

Ecclefiaftical State.—The church of Markinch is a very ancient place of religious worfhip*. The King is patron. The living confifts of 128 bolls of victual, Linlithgow meafure, half meal and half barley, and 500 l. Scotch, in money; including 100 l. Scotch for communion elements, befides a manfe and 8 acres of glebe †. There are no Seceding meeting-houfes in this parifh. The great body of the people continue ftedfaftly attached to the Eftablifhed Church, about one 16th part only having joined the different fectaries.

Schools.

* It was given by Maldvinus, Bifhop of St. Andrew's, to the Culdees in the 10th century. Towards the end of the 12th century, it was mortified to the Priory of St. Andrew's, by Eugenius the fon of Hugo, a fecond fon of Gilli-michel M'Duff, the 4th Earl of Fife, which deed was confirmed by a charter of King William. From this Eugenius, the family of the Earl of Wemyfs is fuppofed to have fprung. About the beginning of the 17th century, the fmall parfonage of Kirkforthar, belonging to Lindfay of Kirkforthar, a cadet of the family of Crawford, was fuppreffed and annexed to Markinch. The ruins of the church of Kirkforthar are ftill to be feen: they ftand in the middle of the old church-yard, or burying-ground, which is enclofed by a wall; and there many of the people belonging to that diftrict ftill bury their dead.

† In the year 1636, the ftipend received a fmall augmentation on account of the annexation of Kirkforthar. Since that period, it has been but once augmented, and the augmentation got, was only 20 l. of money, and the converfion of fome oats into meal. Among the predeceffors of the prefent incumbent was Mr. Tullidelph, afterward Principal of the College of St. Andrew's.

Schools.—There is one established schoolmaster in this parish. He has a good house and garden, with a salary of 10 l. a-year. The school-fees are, 3 s. for teaching latin, 2 s. 6 d. for arithmetic, 2 s. for writing, and 1 s. 6 d. for english. And, as the village of Markinch, and the country in the immediate neighbourhood, are very populous, the emoluments are considerable. Including precentor's fees, and other perquisites, they may amount to 50 l. a-year. Besides the established school, there are 6 private schools in different parts of the parish, the most considerable of which, is fixed at the Coaltown of Balgonie. This is under the immediate patronage of Lady Balgonie, who has built, at her own expense, a school-house, and a house for the schoolmaster; and by the encouragement she ha afforded, and the perfonal attention she has paid to it, has greatly contributed to its prosperity and success. Her Ladyship has also established, at the same place, a school for teaching young girls to few; and has provided a house for the mistrefs, with an apartment for teaching, and has given such encouragement, as to induce a woman of character and abilities to undertake the management of it. At these different schools, upwards of 200 children are constantly taught, almost all of whom belong to the parish.

State of the Poor.—There are at present 20 poor people on the roll, who get regular supply every week; besides several others, who are affisted occafionally as their neceffities require. The sum expended annually for this purpose, is about 60 l. Sterling, arising from a fund of 320 l., the weekly collections at the church-door, and the dues of the mortcloths. There are no begging poor belonging to the parish.

Prices of Grain and Provisions.—For some years past, the average price of wheat has been 20 s., of barley 15 s. of

blanded

blanded bear 14 s., of common bear 13 s. 4 d., of oats 12 s., and of oatmeal 15 s. the boll. The wheat boll is nearly 4 Winchefter bufhels, the barley and oat boll 6 Winchefter bufhels, and the meal boll 8 Dutch ftone. Beef, mutton, pork, lamb, and veal, fell commonly at 4¼ d. the pound, of 22 ounces. At particular feafons, however, when thefe articles are plentiful, they fall to 3½ d., and at other times, when they are fcarce, rife to 5 d., or even to 6 d. the pound. The price of all kinds of poultry has advanced greatly of late. A fed goofe will fell at 3 s. 6 d., a turkey at 4 s., a hen at 1 s., and chickens at 6 d. or 8 d. the pair. Butter fells at 9 d., common cheefe at 3 d., and fweet milk cheefe at 4½ d. the pound. Butter and cheefe are fold by the fame weight with butcher meat. Some years ago, fifh of all kinds were abundant and cheap. But now the price is more than doubled. This extraordinary rife is owing partly to fcarcity, and partly to the increafed confumption of the Edinburgh market.

Prices of Labour.—The wages of day-labourers, from March to October, are from 1 s. to 1 s. 2 d., and for the reft of the year from 8 d. to 10 d., varying according to the nature of the work in which they are employed. In harveft, men get 10 d., and women 8 d. a-day, with their meat. When hired for the whole harveft, men have a guinea, and women 15 s. or 16 s. and their maintainance; and generally the privilege of fome lint fown. Men fervants, who eat in the houfe, get of wages from 5 l. to 7 l. a-year, and maid fervants from 2 l. to 3 l. Farm fervants, who furnifh their own provifions, get 6¼ bolls of meal, and an allowance for milk, befides their wages. Sometimes they have a houfe and kailyard, and a cow fed through the year, and, in that cafe, their wages are not fo high. Tailors get 8 d. a-day, with their meat; mafons have 1 s. 8 d.; and carpenters 1 s. 6 d. Within in thefe laft ten years, the price of labour, in general, has advanced in the proportion of 3 to 2.

Inns, and Ale-houfes.—Upon the W. road, there are two excellent inns, the New Inn at Pittillock-ford, and the Plafterers, near Balbirnie bridge. Thefe are fuperior to moft, and equal to any in the county. There are 10 ale-houfes in the parifh, which fell porter, whifky, and fmall-beer. Some of thefe brew, and the reft purchafe fmall-beer from brewers, partly for fale in the houfe, and partly to fupply private families with that article. Though ale-houfes are generally hurtful to the induftry and morals of the people, thefe bad effects have not been fenfibly felt in this parifh.

Minerals and Foffils.—In the eftate of Balbirnie, there is an extenfive bed of fhell marl. The fhells are moftly wilks (periwinkles) and mufcles. When expofed to the air, they fall in a fhort time to powder. The medium thicknefs of the bed is 3½ feet under a cover of 7 or 8 feet. This marl was difcovered a great many years ago ; and it is furprifing, that fuch a fund of manure fhould have been neglected for fo long a time, efpecially as there is level enough to drain it, at no great expenfe. There is abundance of freeftone in the parifh, and fome of it of excellent quality. On the N. fide of the parifh, there is a large mofs, from which a confiderable quantity of peats is dug every year. Thefe are partly ufed by the poorer people in the immediate neighbourhood, and partly carried to more diftant places, and fold for the purpofe of kindling fires.

But what chiefly deferves to be mentioned under this article, is the plentiful fupply of excellent coal, which this parifh enjoys. Balgonie coal * is within a mile and a half

S. E.

* Balgonie coal, the property of the Earl of Leven, was difcovered and
wrought

S. E. of the village, and Balbirnie coal within half that distance to the W. Both these collieries are too distant from a sea-port for exportation; but the whole inland part of Fife, for many miles round, and even N. to the river Tay, is supplied from them. The former has a water engine, with a wheel 26 feet diameter, which works two pumps to the depth of

wrought upwards of 300, some say 500 years ago. As far back as the year 1517, the Coaltown of Balgonie is mentioned in a scheme of division and valuation of the county of Fife, of that date. The name of the village evidently indicates, that it had been originally built for the accommodation of the colliers, or, because built on the ground where coal had been found and wrought. But since it had grown to such consideration at the above mentioned period, as to be taken notice of in the general description and valuation of the county, it must have existed, and, of course, the coal must have been wrought for a considerable time before. That this coal had been wrought at an early period, to a considerable extent, appears from the coal waste, which can yet be traced for upwards of 3 miles along the line of bearing, and which had been dried by a free level to the depth, at an average, of 14 fathoms. It would appear, however, that when the free level coal was wrought out, the workings ceased. How long ago this happened, it is impossible to say. The grandfather of the oldest man living on the spot 60 years ago, had neither seen it wrought, nor had he seen any person who could tell at what period it stopped. In the year 1731, it was again set a-going by Alexander Earl of Leven, who erected a water engine, which wrought two sets of pumps, with 9 inch working barrels, and which dried the coal to the depth of 30 fathoms. In the year 1732, this coal was let to tacksmen, who carried it on for some years, but meeting with large hitches yielding much water, their engine was overpowered, which obliged the tacksman to abandon this spot, and erect a wind-mill at a little distance on the crop, leaving a sufficient barrier to keep off the water, which drained a small breast of the coal. This mill wrought an 8 inch bore 14 fathoms deep, which enabled them to carry on a more extensive winning * farther on the dip than the old level free wastes. During this operation, George Balfour, Esq. of Balbirnie, wrought up a level to the coal in his estate, anno 1740, which enabled him to undersell the tacksman of this coal; by which means, in 1743, they were obliged to give it up, there not being demand for both. Nothing more was done till the year 1785, when Lord Balgonie erected it again, by fitting up the present engine.

* *Whatever extent of coal is dried, either by a free level, or an engine, it is called, in the language of the colliers, a winning, i. e. a gaining of the coal.*

of 30 fathoms, with 12¼ inch working barrels. What the late tackſman intended, is now carried into effect by the preſent winning, which commands a very fine breaſt of coal in both ſeams. The lowermoſt ſeam is yet untouched with this winning. The main ſeam, now working, conſiſts of

	Feet.	Inch.
A mixture of ſplint cherry coal and rough coal, -	3	0
Stone, - - - - -	0	4
Rough coal, which includes 9 inches of fine cherry,	3	0
Stone, - - - - -	0	4
Rough coal, - - . - -	1	2
Stone, - - - - -	0	3
Fine ſtrong ſplint, - - -	1	6
Fine Cherry, - - - -	0	4
Total between roof and pavement,	**9**	**11**

The roof conſiſts of hard blue till, about 10 feet thick, above which are ſtrong poſts of freeſtone, ſome of which are very hard. The other ſeam lies 10 fathoms deeper ; it is ſaid to be a very fine coal, 7 feet thick, but has ſome ſmall ribs of ſtone in it. The average out-put for the laſt four years is a-bout 30 tons a-day, and ſo much is the caſe altered ſince 1743, that there is a great demand, and the conſumption is daily increaſing. This coal dips to the E. at the engine, but to the S. E., after paſſing a large hitch about 500 yards from the engine pit, on the line of bearing at the crop, the dip, or declivity, is exactly a fathom in 3 ; but, in the dip workings, only one fathom in 4½ ; which gives ground to believe that it will at laſt flatten altogether, and even crop out at the oppoſite point of the compaſs, which, if the caſe, will make it a very productive colliery.

Balbirnie coal lies both in the Balbirnie eſtate, the property
ty

ty of John Balfour, Efq. and in Leflie eftate, the property of
the Counteſs of Rothes, being one and the fame feam : and is
called Leflie or Balbirnie coal, according to the eftate, in which
the works are for the time. But as almoft the whole of it,
level free, and more than half the under level are in Balbirnie
eftate, it is generally known by the name of Balbirnie coal *,
and confifts of two fpecies, called the little coal and the great
coal. The quality of the little coal is extremely good. It is
a cherry coal, has fomething of the caking quality, as it works
iron very well, and is the only coal in this part of Fife that
will do fo ; for which purpofe the very fmalleft particles of
it are fold to the fmiths on the coaft of Fife, from Dyfart to
St. Andrew's, and the whole inland part of the country, extending to 1000 tons annually, befides the quantity of great
coal, in the ftate aftermentioned. It varies in thicknefs from
6 feet to 4 feet. The diftance between roof and pavement is
generally the fame. When a ftone is found in the middle of the
feam, the coal diminifhes in thicknefs, as the ftone increafes,
till at laft, if the ftone be very thick, the coal is fo much thinned as to be hardly worth working. This field of coal is not
a regular

---

* When this coal was firft difcovered, cannot now be known, but it appears
to have been wrought at an early period near Balbirnie Burns, firft by a free
level, and afterward by fome fort of pumps, at a place called the Pump Sink,
to the northward of Balbirnie houfe. Old pits can be here traced along the
crop, but the period thefe were wrought, is unknown. About the year 1730,
George Balfour, Efquire of Balbirnie, a gentleman who had paid confiderable
attention to the ftudy of mineralogy, began firft to trace the ftrata by bores
and otherwife, from thefe old waftes, through great part of his eftate to the
river Leven, nearly one mile diftant;—then began at the river, and, by a ftone
mine acrofs the metals, wrought into the coal, and thus made it level free to a
great extent, about the year 1740. By this level, it was wrought from that
date, till the year 1780. In finking the firft pit on the level, a feam was found
18 inches thick of the little coal, and through the whole field it is exactly 21
feet above the main coal every where. The fame gentleman bored 12 fathoms
through the main coal in fearch of other feams, but found none above 3 inches
thick.

a regular one : it lies very nearly in the form of a horſe-ſhoe, ſuppoſing it 5 or 6 times broader than ordinary, and the open ſpace of the common ſize. At the place where firſt diſcovered, a little to the N. of the river Leven, the dip was directly S. In working forward, the field divided in two ; one level run toward the N. W., another to the N. E., and the crop was wrought till within 12 feet of the ſurface. The two branches of the level ſeparated further and further, and the two crops did the ſame, leaving a ſpace of many hundred fathoms between, in which was neither coal, nor appearance of it : this ſpace reſembled the open part of the horſe-ſhoe. The encreaſing conſumption of coal will appear from the following ſtate :

From 1740 to 1763, the quantity of coal ſold at Balbirnie appears to
    have been 42,135 loads, or 8,427 tons annually, which, in 23 years, is 192,811
From 1763 to 1777, both incluſive, the average ſales were 46,719
    loads, or 9,343 tons annually,   -   -   -   -   140,157
From 1778 to 1792, both incluſive, the average quantity was 54,660
    loads *, or 10,932 tons annually,   -   -   -   -   163,980
In 1784, owing to a ſcheme of lowering the price of the coal to all
    who were more than ten miles diſtant from the coal-works, there
    was an additional quantity ſold, not included in the foregoing aver-
    age, of   -   -   -   -   -   -   -   4,047
                                                                          ———
                Total number of tons ſold in 52 years,   500,995

On the ſuppoſition, that the demand for coal ſhould not increaſe above the average of the laſt 15 years, being 10,932 tons annually, but continue the ſame ; and although one half of the whole field of coal were yet entire (which certainly is not the caſe), an equal quantity would be entirely exhauſted in leſs than 46 years. But the increaſing conſumption muſt be immenſe, when it is conſidered, that during the firſt 40 years, there was no other coal-work, except this, to ſupply this

* The loads in the above computation contain 27 ſtone Dutch weight each, which is one third more than the ſale load, or load ſold to the country. The former is known by the name of the collier's load.

this part of Fife, and that during the laft feven years the coal
of Balgonie has alfo been wrought, and has fupplied the country with 9000 tons annually, notwithftanding of which, the
confumption of this coal is continually on the increafe *.

Antiquities,

* Since 1780, 3 water engines have been erected upon this coal. The firft
works 2 pumps, 14 inch working barrels; the fecond, 2 pumps of 11 inches diameter; the third, 2 pumps 15 inch diameter, of the working barrel; and a-
bout 20 fathoms left from the coal, to a mine in which the water is delivered
5 fathoms below the furface of the ground. Above the rock is gravel, which
admits the winter rains to pafs through the numerous cutters in the ftrata,
conveys it down to the coal, and is the great caufe of fuch powerful engines
being neceffary to drain the coal. It is a pretty general opinion, that all coals
are as good in quality, or better, in the dip than towards the crop. Alfo, that
any coal once difcovered, may be wrought to any depth from which it is poffible to draw the water. But what has recently happened in this very coal,
gives reafon to believe that opinion, however general, to be erroneous; for,
when the engines were firft erected, from the favourable appearance of the
furface of the ground, compofed of flat and gently rifing fields of vaft extent,
and from the extreme flatnefs of the coal, which did not dip above 1 in 12, often not above 1 foot in 20, it had the appearance of being almoft inexhauft-
able, or, at leaft, that the under level coal would be much more extenfive than
the crop already wrought; but the very reverfe of this was found to be the
cafe. An engine erected at the trifling depth of 20 fathoms, in the fhort fpace
of 10 years from its erection, was found not only deep enough, but actually
deeper than any coal in that field. In working up the engine level, it was
found to go deeper than any part of the coal; dead water was kept till the coal
was found entirely cut off in the dip by a gravel dike, compofed of gravel and
large bullet whin ftones, all of them rounded as if they had been long toffed
about in water. The level was pufhed on through this gravel, till it was found
impracticable to proceed with fafety to the workmen: the coal was, therefore,
wrought along the fide of this dike, as deep as there was any coal, and in the
progrefs of the work, the coal to the dip on the weft fide of the field, which
this engine was erected to drain, not only turned out to be of bad quality, but
its thicknefs was diminifhed by a hard ftone which divided the feam in two,
extending from 1 to 4 feet in thicknefs, fo hard as only to be wrought with
gunpowder; which added fo much to the expenfe, that the coal could not be
wrought with profit, and was therefore abandoned altogether, and the third
engine erected on the E. part of the fame coal where the feam was found 6

feet

Antiquities, &c.—Balgonie castle, one of the seats of the Earl of Leven, is a fabric of great antiquity, and confiderable

feet thick, without any stone at all. The proprietor wrought up a level along the side of the river Leven, about half a mile in length, which lessened the lift of the engine 5 fathoms. In working up this mine, about 150 fathoms from the place where he intended to erect his engine, he found the metals on edge perfect-ly perpendicular; a little further, he found them dip 1 fathom in 3, and that to the west, directly contrary to the dip of the coal, and there he found two seams of coal, with 7 fathoms of stone between them; the first, 2½ feet, and the other, 3 feet thick, dip 1 in 3. About 50 fathoms farther, he found flat metal rising to the west, the proper rise of the coal in that part of the field. These ap-pearances gave him reason to believe the main coal did not extend far to the dip, but was either cut off by these edge metals, or would be found on the dip separated by a stone into two seams, and suddenly thrown out to the surface in the form of the two seams he had discovered in his mine, by a rise of 1 fathom in 3, directly contrary to the ordinary crop of the coal. In order to discover this, as soon as the engine was erected, a level mine was pushed on to the eastward: The coal was found perfectly good till he approached within 50 fa-thoms of the edge metals, where a stone made its appearance in the middle of the coal, one inch thick, 6 fathoms farther, it increased to 18 inches thick, and continued to increase till it was found impracticable to be wrought, and appeared fairly to divide the seam of coal in two, corresponding in thickness to the two edge seams he had discovered in the said mine. The coal continues flat, but it can hardly be doubted, that if the level is driven 20 fathoms farther, it will rise the opposite way, 1 fathom in 3 *. Since this is the case upon the E. part of the field, it is not easy to account, why the same thing has not happened on the west part of the same field, where the gravel dike intervenes, and cuts off the coal in place of the edge metals: the probability is, that the edge metals are also there, and that the coal will terminate and be thrown out to the surface by them in the same way, though in this part the gravel dike seems to be thrust in, between the flat and the edge metals; and is of great thick-ness, as a trial was made at right angles, a hundred fathoms distant, and 17 fathoms

---

* *Since writing the above, an upset has been pushed forward, and the coal actually found to rise, as supposed above, 1 fathom in 5; and it will, no doubt, a little further on, rise 1 fathom in 3, and crop out at the surface; and the stone will increase in thickness, till it is found 7 fathoms at the surface, and the main coal is thrown out there, in the form of the two seams, above men-tioned.*

derable ftrength. The time when it was built cannot be exactly afcertained ; but from the beft information that can be

thom deep, where, in place of the rock and ordinary metals above the coal, nothing but gravel was found ; from which it may be concluded, that the dike exceeds 100 fathoms in thicknefs, how much more, it is hard to fay ; at the diftance of another 100 fathoms, the edge metals are feen in this part of the field alfo, which deftroys every hope of the main coal being again found beyond the dike. From what has appeared in the eaft part of the field, it feems pretty certain, that if the coal is found at all, it will be in the form of two feams on edge, thruft fuddenly up to the furface by thefe edge metals, and confequently of fmall extent and little value.

From what is above recited, it may be inferred, that it is not always fafe to truft to the dip fide of a feam of coal being of value, though the crop has been found good, which was the cafe here, the crop having been wrought for 40 years, and every where in the natural level found good, and yet the dip on the weft half of the field has been exhaufted in lefs than 12 years, at leaft, all that was found valuable in it ; how long the dip of the eaft part of the field now working may laft, it is hard to fay, though it is fcarce poffible, allowing the quality to be good through the whole extent of the known field, that any coal will remain to work 50 years hence.

From the foregoing hiftory of two valuable fields of coal, and facts above recited, fome very important conclufions may be drawn, viz.

1. The limited and fmall extent of coal fields.

2. The increafing confumption of the coal and its limited extent, gives reafon to apprehend its being totally exhaufted.

The limited extent of all coal, may be inferred from its being impoffible to trace any, very far in the line of bearing. Balgonie coal may be ranked among the regular ones, as the line of bearing is the fame with the general bearing of the ftrata in the greateft part of Britain, where they are not thrown out of their courfe by adventitious caufes, fuch as dikes, mountain rocks of a different fpecies from the ftrata that accompany coal, and fometimes by the waving and twifting of the coal metals themfelves, which frequently alter the line of bearing, as well as the dip of the coal, to all the points of the compafs. Such regular feams as this, with fo confiderable a dip, may be thrown out of their courfe by dikes and flips, but generally keep the fame line of bearing. The very flat feams, fuch as Balbirnie coal, being much more liable to wave and twift, till the dip and crop are in the oppofite direction from the regular courfe of bearing. It may be worth inquiry, why the moft regular feams of coal can be feldom purfued in the line of bearing above a few miles, for the

fact

be got, it appears to be of the fame age with the cathedral of St. Andrew's, which was built in the 12th century.

fact is, few or no feams in this part of Fife, reach above 2 or 3 miles in length at moft, and many not half that diftance ; for inftance, Dyfart coal which has the fame line of bearing with Balgonie, has been wrought from the fea-fide about 2 miles, where, near the water of Orr, it is entirely cut off and no more feen. About half a mile E., and 1 mile N., the S. extremity of Balgonie coal appears, and keeps the fame line of bearing, as well as refembles Dyfart coal fomewhat in quality, but not in thicknefs ; Dyfart coal being 22 feet, and Balgonie coal only 9 feet thick ; the declivity pretty much the fame. At the diftance of 3 miles, this coal, and all the ftrata accompanying it, is alfo cut off ; and not the leaft veftige or appearance of that coal, or any other, has been difcovered within fome miles of it. Wemyfs coal, Methel, and Durrie coal, are as regular feams as either Dyfart or Balgonie, but none of them can be traced farther in the line of bearing ; they are all cut off in the fame manner before they are 2 miles from the fea. The more inland coals diftant 8 or 10 miles from the Frith of Forth, fuch as Burnturk, Pitleffie, Divan, and Clatty, are fituated on the fides of hills of fmall extent, the metals of which have no continued line either of bearing or declivity ; and the coal in thefe fituations confequently fubject to all the irregularities ever found in coal works. Some of the feams are even feen to crop out quite round a fmall eminence. And even fmall as the extent of thefe fields is, the coal is found full of dikes, hitches, and all imaginable troubles ; which render them fcarce worth working. Beyond this, in the flat country, along the banks of the Eden, no coal has ever been difcovered. And from this to the Tay, there are no ftrata ever difcovered that indicate coal being there : nor are there fufficient fymptoms even to encourage trials for coal, with any rational hope of fuccefs.

The Fife coals, even the moft regular, being thus contracted in the line of bearing, are comparatively of very fmall extent, compared with the idea a ftranger has of them, on a flight view of the number of pits he fees at work on the various feams. Such a perfon, if unacquainted with the natural hiftory of coal and its ftrata, is apt to fuppofe the whole country full of coal ; the very dikes and interruptions in the bearing of the ftrata, increafes the deception, fhowing, as he fuppofes, a ftill greater number of feams and extent of coal. For inftance, a perfon unacquainted with the interruptions met with in coal fields, fees Dyfart coal and Balgonie both at work, he imagines the one may be wrought N. on the line of bearing, as far as the Lomonds, 6 miles diftant, and the other S. to the fea, and N. to the Eden, whenever the proprietors choofe to do fo ; and hence he concludes, both coals almoft inexhauftible : but inveftigate
the

tury.   This caftle is pleafantly fituated on the S. bank of the
Leven, elevated about 36 feet above the bed of the river.   It
is

the fubject thoroughly by proper judges, and they will declare the attempt
vain, to purfue the one further N., or the other either S. or N., than it has been
already done.   And what he imagined inexhauftible feams, may poffibly be
entirely wrought out in lefs than 100 years.   I fhall not attempt to account for
the frequent interruptions in the line of bearing of the coal, and all other ftrata.
I have only pointed out the fact, that neither coal nor any other ftrata whatever, can be traced to any confiderable diftance, without fuch interruptions being met with.   What actually happened in working the dip of Balbirny coal,
may happen in a hundred others, where the probability of the dip being both
good and extenfive, cannot poffibly be greater, than it was in that very coal,
till it was actually tried.   One fact feems to be eftablifhed by it, that fome
coals do not extend to any very great depth from the furface.   But after continuing to dip for fome time, they rife the contrary way, and crop out to the
furface on a point of the compafs diametrically oppofite to the former crop-
Many could be pointed out which actually do fo, though the greater part of
feams may reach to fo great a depth, and may at that depth be fo altered by
dikes and flips, as to throw the oppofite crop, or rife to fuch a diftance, as often
prevents its being perceived to be the fame feam, though it actually be fo.
This example, proves coal to be limited in extent in a different way.   And
that it is by no means certain that coal can be had in the dip, though good in
the crop, and wrought there above 40 years.

2. The increafing confumption of coal, and its limited extent, gives reafon to,
apprehend its being totally exhaufted.

It feems to be the opinion of the publick, that coal is inexhauftible.   Government appears to have adopted the fame opinion, in allowing fuch immenfe
quantities of coal to be exported to all the nations in Europe.   It is greatly to
be wifhed, that this opinion were well founded; but it is contradicted by incontrovertible facts.   It is not above 200 years fince coal came into common ufe,
and it is highly probable the firft 150 years of that period did not exhauft fo
much of it as the laft 50 years.   Examine all the coal fields, not in Fife only,
but through all Britain, and it will be found that every part of them near to a
fea-port, and many of the inland feams of coal, are not only exhaufted to the
depth of the natural level, but almoft all of them already wrought, and exhauft-
ing faft by fire and water engines, many of which are very deep.   It will alfo be
found, that the quantity already wrought is probably at leaft equal to the quantities yet to work of all the known feams of coal within the ifland.   It might, perhaps, be an object worthy of being invcftigated by Government : for if the iffue

is of a quadrangular form, and ftands upon an area of 135 feet by 105. The open court within, is 108 feet by 65. The tower,

fue of their refearch fhould be, as there is a high probability it would, that there was not a fufficient fund of coal unexhaufted in the ifland of Britain to fupply the prefent demand for 200 years to come, it is probable they would think it proper to interfere and prevent the too rapid confumption of an article indifpenfibly ne-ceffary to the very exiftence, not only of the capital and other great cities, but to almoft every fpecies of manufacture, and to the many thoufand artificers employed in them. Such could not even exift without a plentiful fupply of coal, in a country fo deftitute of wood as Great Britain is. The fuperiority which the poffeffion of coal gives to her manufactures, on the failure of that fupply, would be inftantly transferred to thofe nations in Europe, poffeffed of a fufficient quantity of wood for their confumption.

Is is not difficult to account how Government, and the nation at large, are lulled into fecurity on this point. The proprietors of coal have an intereft in a great and immediate confumption. No matter from what it arifes; immediate profit is the object, whether from the home or foreign market. The reft of mankind have little opportunity, and ftill lefs inclination to inveftigate a fubject of which the greater part have a very fuperficial knowledge. It is not the lefs neceffary that the alarm be given; the danger, upon candid inquiry, will not be found ideal. Great dependence is fometimes placed upon the difcovery of new feams of coal, never before known; but if it be confidered, that there is fcarcely a feam of coal of any confequence in Great Britain, which has not been known to exift for half a century, and that fcarce a new difcovery of coal has been heard of during that period, to what is this to be imputed? Not to the want of trials, for of thefe numbers have been made without fuccefs; but as it is an eftablifhed fact, that every feam of coal, as well as all other ftrata, rife and crop out, at or very near the furface of the ground, there is a high probability that few valuable feams of coal could remain fo long undifcovered. As in every extenfive field, the chance is, that fome part of the crop will approach fo near the furface, as to be laid open by rivers, canals, rivulets in little glens, and not feldom the rife or outburft of the coal, will be feen in the form of a black duft, mixed with fmall particles of coal, in common ditches, where nothing is meant but the enclofure of the ground. Such appearances fhould, and, I fuppofe, generally are examined. By fuch means the greater number of coals already known, have been difcovered. And though others may exift not yet difcovered, there is little reafon to fuppofe the number or extent of fuch undifcovered feams to be very confiderable.

The extent of the coal fields in Britain is very inconfiderable, when compared with

tower *, which ftands on the N. fide, and near the N. W. angle is 45 feet by 36 over the walls, and 80 feet high. The top is

with the immenfe tracks that have no coal metals (or ftrata that ufually accompany coal), nor any appearance to indicate coal being contained in them. But the coal fields themfelves are very far from containing coal every where. The county of Fife, for inftance, is a coal field, and has been held out in a late publication, on the caufes of the fcarcity of coal, as containing an almoft inexhauftible fund of that ufeful mineral, and as every where containing coal. No affertion could be more flenderly founded; it is probably much nearer the truth, that for every acre in Fife containing unwrought coal, there is not lefs than 50 that have no coal in them, nor any rational probability of any being found. That there is ftill much coal in Fife, is a certain fact; but if no other part of Britain is better ftored with it, it is equally certain, that more than one half of the whole quantity in the kingdom is already exhaufted. Add to this, that the remaining half muft be wrought with engines at a vaft expenfe; and it is not abfolutely certain whether, in quantity or quality, it may equal that part of the coals already exhaufted. To prove what is above alleged, would not, perhaps, be very difficult. Take all the coals in Fife, wrought out, or now working, one after another, examine confumption, and the quantity of ground wrought out within the laft ten years, and compare this with the quantity of ground which the proprietor fuppofes to contain coal as deep as there is a poffibility of working, it would immediately be known, fuppofing the confumption the fame, what number of years the remaining coal would fupply the demand, at the fame rate of confumption. Such an inquiry, I am afraid, would amount to a full proof that another century will confume the whole.

* Connected with the tower is a houfe of 3 ftories, built by General Sir Alexander Leflie, extending to the N. E. corner; and on the E. fide of the court is another houfe of the fame height, built by the prefent Earl of Leven's grandfather. From the vaults under thefe new buildings, and the thicknefs of the walls in the lower ftory, it appears probable that the old buildings had been equally extenfive, and that the new houfes had been raifed on the foundations of the old. On the S. and W. fides of the court, there is a high ftrong wall, which appears to be coeval with the tower: and without the wall there has been a large foffé, the remains of which are ftill to be feen. The gate-way is on the W. fide, befide which, and under the wall, there is a pit. There is alfo a dungeon, or dark cell in the bottom of the tower. This caftle ftands in the middle of an oblong fquare, inclufive of 300 acres, fenced by a ftone and lime wall. Near it there is a garden of about 7 acres, enclofed by a wall of 12 feet high, and a great deal of fine old trees around. Balgonie, which anciently belonged

is furrounded with battlements, projecting about a foot beyond the walls. The roof, which appears to have been repeatedly repaired fince it was firft built, is raifed in the middle, and between that and the battlements, it is flat, and covered with ftones. The walls of the two lower ftories, both
of which are vaulted, are 8¼ feet thick : but above that, they
are only 7 feet thick. There is an apartment in it called the
Chapel, and, in the wall on the oppofite fide of the court, the
ruins of a room are ftill to be feen, which was called the
Chaplain's Room. The architecture of this tower is ftill very perfect and entire, and the third ftory hath been lately repaired by the prefent Lord Balgonie. About half a mile to
E. of Balgonie, and on the fame fide of the Leven, is Balfour or Balor, an old building, ftanding in the middle of
fome fine enclofures, and furrounded with a good deal of old
plantations. This place gave the name of Balfour to a very
ancient family, from which the Balfours in Fife, of whom
there is a confiderable number, it is thought, moftly fprung *.
On the weft fide, and about half a mile from the parifh
church, ftands Balbirnie, which anciently belonged to Balbirnie

belonged to a family of the name of Sibbald, was purchafed in the reign of
Charles I., by General Leflie, who was created Earl of Leven by that monarch,
in 1641. Towards the end of the laft century, David, fecond fon of George
Earl of Melvill, married the Countefs and heirefs of Leven, in confequence of
which, the eftates and titles of the two Earldoms came to be united in the fame
family, as Lord Raith, the oldeft fon of the faid Earl of Melvill died without
iffue.

* In the 5th of the reign of Robert II., John, laird of Balfour, dying without
male iffue, Robert Bethune, alfo of an ancient family in Fife, married his daughter, the heirefs of Balfour, ftill, however, retaining the name of Bethune. From
this houfe, feveral refpectable families of the name of Bethune have defcended.
James Bethune, archbifhop of St. Andrew's, and Chancellor of Scotland, his nephew David Bethune, Cardinal and Chancellor of Scotland, and the Cardinal's
nephew, James Bethune, archbifhop of Glafgow, were all three of this houfe of
Balfour.

birnie of that ilk, but which, for fome generations back-
hath been in the poffeffion of a family of the name of Balfour.' A confiderable part of the old houfe ftill remains, and
is kept in good repair ; on the fouth fide of which, and connected with it, the prefent proprietor, hath built a neat commodious modern houfe. The fituation is rather low and concealed ; but delightfully romantick. In front, there is a
pretty extenfive lawn thinly and irregularly planted with different kinds of trees. The furrounding eminences, as well
as all the low marfhy ground near it, are covered with fine
thriving plantations of barren wood. Befides the attention
paid to the pleafure ground around the houfe, the prefent
proprietor has of late greatly beautified, as well as meliorated
his eftate in the neighbourhood, by enclofing regular fields
with belts of plantation ; and by placing clumps of trees on
the higher grounds, arranged and difpofed in fuch a manner,
as at once to pleafe the eye, and to afford fhelter to the adjacent fields.

The fteeple of Markinch is another ancient building, and
from the fimilarity of the workmanfhip, is probably of the
fame age with Balgonie caftle. It is about 15 feet fquare,
and preferves its thicknefs till it rifes to 80 feet high. From
that to the top, it is about 24 feet, drawing to a point, in a
pyramidical form. From its elevated fituation, it is feen at
a confiderable diftance in feveral directions ; and forms the
termination of a beautiful view from the houfe of Leflie, the
feat of the Countefs of Rothes, which ftands about 3 miles
to the weftward of Markinch. Markinch hill is a beautiful
object. It lies on the north fide of the village, and is of an
oblong oval form, and 200 yards in length. On the northern
declivity, there are 6 terraces of about 20 feet broad, and
which extend the whole length of the hill, winding round
the eaft end of it. They are evidently artificial ; but nothing
certain

certain can be learned as to their original use and design *.
The publick road from Markinch to the north, passes the
west end of this hill, and, on a rising ground, on the opposite
side of the road, stands a broad stone about 7 feet high, called
the Stobb Cross. It is a very coarse piece of work, without
any sculpture or characters on it, that can lead to the knowledge of the design of its erection †.

On the eastern extremity of the parish, in the farm of
Duniface, mortified to the United College of St. Andrew's,
by a gentleman of the name of Ramfay, for the education of
4 bursars at that college, there is a hill or eminence not unlike the one just now mentioned. On the north end of this
hill, there is a spot of ground which rises higher than the rest,
and is called the Maiden Castle, fenced on the south side by
ditches, the vestiges of which remain to this day ‡.

Character

* Two reports prevail; the one is, that these terraces were originally ditches,
intended to strengthen an encampment, or military post on the top of the hill;
but that they have been levelled since for the purpose of tillage. The other
report is, that they were made to accommodate spectators, assembled to behold
certain public games, performed in the plain below; which plain is called the
Play-fields to this day.

† Vulgar tradition says, that it was erected to the memory of a gentleman,
who fell on this spot, in a mortal rencounter with one of his neighbours. As this
cross stands upon the very edge of the road, and 8 or 10 feet above its level, it
has been in danger of tumbling down, by the earth's falling away from it. The
present Earl of Leven, therefore, caused it to be secured, by facing up the earth
with a wall of stone and lime.

‡ Boethius calls it " Arx septinalis totidem fossis munita, olim possessio Fife
Duffi, cujus posteritas, per multa secula, eam tenuere." Some pretend it was a
seat of M'Duff, Earl of Fife, and that there was anciently a subterraneous paffage from it to Brunton, which lies about a quarter of a mile to the E. of Markinch church, and where Malcolm, Earl of Fife, had a castle. It is said that the
entrance to this passage at Brunton was shut up so lately as in the time of the
late John Simpson of Brunton. Near the Maiden Castle a battle has been fought,
probably between the Scots and Danes, as a great many stone-coffins, with human bones in them, have been lately discovered in the immediate neighbourhood.

Chara&er of the People.—It would be facrificing truth to complaifance, to fay that there are no worthlefs or exceptionable chara&ers in this parifh. The number of fuch, however, is comparatively fmall. The great body of the people are fober, peaceable, and induftrious. Their attendance on the public ordinances of religion is pun&ual and exemplary, and their moral condu& correfpondent to their profeffion. It is worthy of notice, that the colliers of Markinch poffefs a refpe&ability in point of chara&er, to which few other colliers in the kingdom can pretend. In them you fee nothing of that grofs ignorance, that roughnefs and barbarity of manners, that extravagance and diforderly behaviour, but too generally chara&eriftical of this defcription of men. On the contrary, with a very few exceptions, they are remarkably intelligent, attentive to the duties of religion, civil and obliging in their manners, fober, frugal and diligent; in confequence of which, they and their families live comfortably, and make a decent appearance. It deferves alfo to be mentioned, to the honour of this parifh, that during the late ferment, when defigning, fa&ious, and turbulent men were endeavouring to difturb the public tranquillity, and to alienate the affe&ions of the people from the mild and equal government under which they live, their loyalty to their King, and attachment to the Conftitution remained uncorrupted. They joined no difcontented affociations; they imbibed no feditious principles; but every man attended to the duties of his ftation, and left the modelling and mending of conftitutions to others, as a bufinefs beyond their fphere, and above their abilities.

STATISTICAL

hood. In feveral other parts of the parifh, coffins of the fame kind have, at different times, been difcovered. One, in particular, was found about 7 years ago on the Headlaw, between Markinch and Balgonie. It was of a fquare form, made of four unhewn flabs of freeftone, fet edge-ways, and covered with a broad ftone of the fame kind, upon which was laid a large unformed mafs of ftone, and above all, a heap or cairn of fmall ftones. The bones enclofed in it were calcined.

STATISTICAL TABLE *of the* PARISH *of* MARKINCH.

Number of fouls,	-	2790	Number of wrights,	-	16
— males,	- -	1364	— fmiths,	- -	11
— females,	- -	1426	— fhoemakers,	- -	20
— families,	- -	653	— tailors,	- -	9
— married couples,		475	— brewers,	- -	4
— widowers,	- -	36	— gardeners,	- -	5
— widows,	- -	65	— midwives,	- -	2
— average of marriages			— colliers, including o-		
annually,	- -	20	verfeers, drawers,		
— of births *,	- -	63	&c.	- -	100
— under 2 years of age,		200	— coopers,	- -	2
— between 2 and 10,		538	— bakers,	- -	3
— ——— 10 and 20,		524	— wheelwrights,	- -	2
— ——— 20 and 30,		469	— flaxdreffers,	- -	8
— ——— 30 and 40,		393	— ftocking-makers,	-	2
— ——— 40 and 50,		272	— dyers,	- -	2
— ——— 50 and 60,		176	— turner,	- -	1
— ——— 60 and 70,		147	— fhopkeepers,	-	4
— ——— 70 and 80,		58	— male fervants,	-	136
— ——— 80 and 90,		13	— female fervants,		120
— heritors,	- -	21	— labourers,	- -	65
— refiding heritors,		11	— horfes above 1 year		
— feuars,	- -	120	old,	- -	383
— farmers,	- -	60	— black cattle above 1		
— teachers,	- -	7	year old,	- -	1540
— notary publicks,		2	— fheep,	- -	300
— plafterer,	- -	1	Valued rent, 871l. 7s. 1d.		
— weavers,	- -	160	Sterling.		
— mafons,	- -	24	Real rent of land belong-		
					ing

* There is no regifter of burials.

ing to the heritors, 500l. Sterling.

Rents of feuars property, 480l. Sterling.

Number of inns, - 2

— poft-chaifes, - - 5

— carts, - - - 100

— ale-houfes, - - 11

— bleachfield, - - 1

Number of corn-mills, 10

— lint-mills, - - 7

— barley-mills, - - 4

— wauk-mills, - - 2

— flour-mill, - - 1

— oil-mill, - - 1

— collieries, - - 2

— coal engines, - - 4

PARISH OF MONIMAIL.

(SHIRE OF FIFE.)

By the Rev. MR. SAMUEL MARTIN.

———————

Name.

BETWEEN Lindore's loch, in the parifh of Abdie, and the village of Monimail, where the church ftands, and from which the parifh is named, there is a hill, or rifing ground, over which lies the road between Perth and Cupar. The length of this hill is fuppofed to have given rife to the name, *Monimail*, " At the foot of a hill one mile over." It is often written and pronounced, *Money-Meal*, and ftrangers fuppofe, that it denotes, a " parifh of plenty," abounding in meal and money: but the number of Gaelic names in the neighbourhood, difcountenances this etymology.

Form, Extent, and Situation.——There is a large map of Fife, by Ainflie. The boundaries of the parifh of Monimail are not perfectly marked in it, though nearly exact. Its figure is fomewhat oval, about four feet by three.——Excepting on the north and eaft, the lands are flat and fertile. A marfh, of about 30 acres, (Lethem mire,) and the heights on the north and eaft are capable of little culture.——It is remarkable,

markable, that, in this neighbourhood, both to the north and
ſouth of the Eden, the ſoil, in riſing from the plain, becomes
richer; but is thin and ſandy in the low grounds.—The hills
are rather green than heathy. The Mount-hill is of conſiderable height, and has been planted for ſeveral years. Veſſels,
on making the land from the eaſt ſeas, are aſſiſted and directed by this mount, and by Monzie church, which ſtands
on the top of an eminence beneath it, as a land mark.———
The ſituation of the pariſh, in general, is dry and ſalubrious.
No peculiar epidemical diſtempers are known. The inhabitants are healthy; and there are ſeveral inſtances of conſiderable longevity.—About half a mile north of the church,
there is a ſpring, known by the name of Cardan's Well : It
is of no repute at preſent, but was highly eſteemed by the famous Cardan, who uſed it much; and, in particular, he is
ſaid, with this mineral water, to have cured Hamilton, Archbiſhop of St. Andrews, of a dropſy.—The pariſh is well watered; but its different brooks, or waters, as they are called,
are none of them conſiderable.

Thunder-Storms.———On the 27th October, 1733, Melvill-
houſe was ſtruck with a remarkable thunder ſtorm. The
whole houſe, on every ſide, and from top to bottom, was affected. The ſtream of lightning, it is ſuppoſed, was attracted by a long iron ſpike, on the top of a cupola covered with
lead. The effects of it were felt, and are ſtill viſible in almoſt
every part of the houſe : providentially no perſon was materially hurt. Profeſſor M'Claurin, at Lord Leven's deſire, examined the progreſs and veſtiges of the ſtorm *.———In a large
mirror, a piece, of the ſize of a crown, was melted, and no
crack

* See his letter to Sir Hans Sloan, in Pennant's Tour.

crack or flaw whatever appears in any other place. Many fplinters were torn out of the folid wainfcoting, particularly a thin one, about the breadth of a half foot joiner's rule, was beaten 14 feet from the top of the finifhing, on the floor, where it made a deep impreffion, which ftill remains. One of the chimney tops was thrown down, and fome of the ftones carried 100 yards into the garden. ——In July 1783, about fix o'clock in the morning, a girl and boy were killed with lightning. Peals of thunder, with vivid lightning, were that morning loud and frequent. The mother was a helplefs pal-fied woman, and had been carried from her bed to the fire-fide. The boy, who was much frightened with the thunder, was ftanding before the fire. The girl was feated oppofite to her mother, feeding the fire with brufh wood. On the def-cent of the lightning, the boy fell back, and was, for fome time, believed to be the only perfon affeeted: the girl retained her fitting pofture, and was not fuppofed to be injured. A dog lay motionlefs more than an hour, but on being thrown out as dead, revived and recovered entirely. The poor mo-ther faid, fhe thought the fire, that came down from the hea-vens, completely involved her with the reft. The fhock had no effect on her health, or conftitution, either favourable or unfavourable. What the minifter, who was fent for on the awful occafion, faw of the bodies of the children, was firm and well coloured, as in life.

Population.—Dr Webfter ftates the number of inhabitants to be 884. The regifters have been carefully examined, in order to afcertain the population, at different periods, but it is found, that they cannot be relied on. The inaccuracy of the records may be varioufly accounted for, in this, as well as in other parifhes. Vacancies, the negligence of parents, the carelefsnefs of feffion clerks, the illegal with-holding of

the

the dues by diſſenters, &c. each of theſe circumſtances may occaſion omiſſions. For ſome years back, (on which greater confidence may be placed,) the average is, births, 30,—marriages 9,—and deaths 8¾ yearly. In January 1791, there were,

	Males.	Females.	Total.
Above 70	23	20	43
—— 50	64	78	142
—— 20	200	236	436
—— 10	117	91	208
			—— 829
Below 10 of both ſexes	-	-	272

Total number of the inhabitants	-		1101
The number of families	-	-	241
Average number in each	-	-	4.5277

Of the different ranks in life, there are 2 noblemen, (of one of whom, the Earl of Leven and Melvill, it is remarkable, that the ſucceſſion canbe traced, in direct deſcent, from father to ſon, for 18 generations; the other, Lord Ruthven, is a minor); 8 heritors, reſident and non-reſident; 1 miniſter, 1 preacher, 1 ſtudent of theology; 1 public and 1 private teacher, 1 ſchool-miſtreſs; 30 farmers, 35 weavers, 7 ſhoemakers, 8 taylors, 11 carpenters, 3 brewers, 1 baker, 3 maſons, 4 ſhepherds, and 5 ſmiths.

With regard to religious opinions, there are 55 diſſenters; 27 of whom, are Antiburgher Seceders, 2 Independants, and the other 26 are Epiſcopals, Burgher Seceders, and members of the preſbytery of Relief.

Of married couples there are 172, bachelors 38, and widowers,

I

dowers, who are heads of families, and single women, in houfes of their own, 31.

There are three corn mills, and one lint-mill, driven by
water. Two threfhing-mills; one driven by horfes, one by
water. 5 fmall retail fhops. There is no occafion for any
lawyer, attorney, phyfician, or furgeon, in this parifh, as
the town of Cupar fupplies its environs, with legal and medical
aid.

Agriculture.—The mode of managing lands is the fame that
obtains in the low country in general: confifting of rotations
of crops, hay, turnips, inclofing, and draining. The face of the
parifh is confiderably changed of late, and improvements are ftill
going forward. The productions are the fame with thofe of the
reft of Fife and the Lothians. Confiderable quantities of wheat
and barley are annually exported, or otherwife fent away. The
raifing of black cattle is now more attended to, than formerly.
Of 8 fmall flocks of fheep, 3 have been very lately fold off,
chiefly becaufe fheep injure hedges and fown grafs, and becaufe it is faid, that more profit is reaped from black cattle.
There are 5 farms above L. 100 fterling, (one of them L. 300:)
the reft from L. 70 downwards. One pretty extenfive farm
rents at L. 1 : 10s per acre. The average rent of good farms is
below L. 1 per acre. Land of inferior quality is proportionally lower, 15s. 10s. &c. &c. Any eftates, which have been
lately fold in this parifh, and indeed in the neighbourhood,
have brought high prices.——Farm houfes are now built more
commodious and comfortable. The tenantry improve in their
manners, drefs, way of life, and form a refpectable body of
men.——The ploughs are 76 in number, made on different models: and new improvements are attended to, and tried, as they are fuggefted.

Church,

Church, Manſe, Stipend, &c.—The church is a long narrow building, rather old and incommodious *.

The manſe being very old, and inſufficient, a new and more commodious one is about to be erected.

In 1774, the rent roll of the pariſh was nearly L. 2500 ſterling.——The ſtipend is worth ſomewhat above L. 100. An augmentation was lately obtained.——The Earl of Leven is patron.

Prices of Proviſions, Wages, and Labour, in 1750, and 1790:

	1750.	lb. Dutch.	1790.	lb. Dutch.
Beef	- -	2 d.	- - -	4d.
Mutton	- -	2 d.	- - -	4 d.
Veal	- -	4 d.	- - -	7 d.
Hens	- -	4 d.	- - -	1s. 0d.
New butter	-	4 d.	- - -	8 d.
Salmon	- 1d. & 1½d.		- - -	5d. 6d. &c.
Eggs per dozen	1½d. & 2d.		- -	3d. 4d. 5 d.

And other articles in proportion.

	Per day.		Per day.
Day-labourers -	- 5d.	- -	9d. 10d. 1s.
Maſter wright, or maſon 1s.		- - 1s. 3d.—	1s. 6d.
Maſons, wrights	7d. 8d.	- - -	1s.

	per annum.	per annum.
Farm ſervants L. 2 L. 2: 10:0 and 2 pecks of meal per week		L. 6 L. 7 with meal.

Upper

* The bell is on the eaſt end of the church. It was erected about 40 years ago, when the former one became inſufficient : that bell had been uſed from the days of Robert the Bruce, as appeared by an inſcription on it. The church was new-roofed about 50 years ago.

	1750.			1790.	
Upper family fervants	L. 8 L. 10	-	-	L. 20 L. 25.	
Livery	-	L. 4	-	L. 10 L. 12.	
Maid fervants	L. 1 : 10 L. 2	-	L. 3 L. 3 : 10 L. 4.		

The fuppreffion of vails operated confiderably to increafe the wages of family fervants.——This lift, which applies to Fife in general, is a ftrong argument for the augmentation of minifters ftipends, fchoolmafters, and the falaries of all ftipendaries.

Names of Places.——'The moft, of perhaps all, the old names are Gaelic; *Balintagart*, the prieft's town; *Letham*, the fide of the hill; *Fairnie*, a moift place where alders grow; *Cunoquhie*, head of a corn field, &c. Some are modern. The Bow of Fife is the name of a few houfes on the road to Cupar. Whether this uncommon name is taken from a bending of the road, as fome fuppofe, or, as others, from the meetings of the farmers in old times, to fix the prices of grain, (the bolls being pronounced bows,) cannot be determined. It has been thought, that this fpot is nearly the centre of Fife : this is alfo offered as the reafon of the name.—— Letham is the principal village. On the firft week of June, there is a confiderable fair held at it. Eafter Fairnie is next in fize: Monimail is fmaller. Other clufters of houfes fcarcely deferve the name of villages.

Antiquities.——Near the church, and within Melvill park, there is a fquare tower in pretty good prefervation. Its age is uncertain; but it was repaired by Cardinal Bethune, and was his refidence, 1562. There are feveral diftinct heads of the Cardinal, in his cap, in ftone relievo on the walls. The arms of the family of Bethune are alfo intire. The tower is evidently

evidently part of a large building, the remains of which are very viſible.—The houſe of Fairnie is believed to be one of M'Duff's caſtles. Its walls are uncommonly thick: it is very old, and has been a place of ſtrength.———A ſtrip of land in the farm of Ladifron, belonging to Mr Paterſon of Cunoquhie, is called the temple. There is a tradition, that a prieſt lived here, who had a right to every ſeventh acre of Ladifron, and to the tathing (dung as left on the ground) every ſeventh night.

Tradition ſays, there was a dreadful battle, fought on the N. W. boundary of the pariſh, between the Scots and the Danes. A hillock, called Doulie-cairy Knoll, is ſaid to have received its name from the battle, (*ſorrow and care*).

Longevity.—A woman (Helen Gray) died in this pariſh, in the 105 year of her age. She was born in Tealand, near Dundee. The pariſh regiſter was conſulted, but in vain. The death of Archbiſhop Sharp, ſhe diſtinctly remembered: If ſhe was 3 years old then, ſhe was 105 at her death. She was a little woman, remarkably chearful. Some years before her death, ſhe had a new ſet of teeth. In early life ſhe had been a ſervant in Lord Stormont's family. The ladies of the neighbourhood were much amuſed with her telling them, that Mrs Helen Murray, whom they well knew, as lady directreſs of the Edinburgh aſſemblies, was one of the young bairns ſhe remembered; and that Mr Willie, (Earl Mansfield,) when young, was a very fine laddie—(boy).

Suicide.—There has been but one inſtance of ſuicide for many years. The perſon was old, and in a confuſed, ſtupified ſtate. This event was rendered remarkable by the manner of interment. The body was brought from the houſe, through the window,

window, and buried, under night, at the extremity of the parifh. A proof at once of the force of old fuperftitious cuftoms, and, at the fame time, of the horror fo natural to be felt on fuch an occafion.

Poor.—The funds, for the fupport of the poor, arife from legacies, mort-cloths, marriages, occafional donations, but chiefly from the weekly collections at the church doors. There are 10 or 12 regular monthly penfioners. On emergencies, others are affifted. No begging is allowed. The diftributions, *communibus annis*, are betwixt L. 20 and L. 30 fterling.—In 1782, and 1783, the ordinary funds, with a voluntary and unfolicited donation from the heritors, according to their valued rents, fupplied the great exigencies of the poor, during thefe two unfortunate feafons.

Schools.—The eftablifhed fchool-mafter's falary, and perquifites, as precentor and feffion-clerk, with the fchool-fees, have been reckoned to be worth about L. 14. The number of fcholars varies, according to the abilities and reputation of the teacher; and thofe of the private teachers in the parifh. 30 may be the average. The fees are, Englifh 1s per quarter; writing 2s; arithmetic 2s; book-keeping 10s 6d a courfe; Latin 2s 6d per quarter. It is not doubted but this, and fimilar reports, will evince the neceffity of more encouragement to this ufeful and laborious order of men.

Mifcellaneous Obfervations.——Peats and wood are ufed, but in fmall quantities. Coals chiefly from Balgonie and Balbirnie, in the parifh of Markinck, at 7d per load, of 18 ftone, are the fuel of the parifh. A double cart carries five loads: the carriage cofts nearly the purchafe in money.——Servitudes

tudes are few and dying away. Thoſe that continue, ſuch as aſſiſtance with carriages, &c. during the hay and corn harveſts, are
rather voluntary and diſcretionary than exacted.——The general character of the pariſhioners has always been, that they
are induſtrious, regular, quiet, and reſpectable. There are
mixtures in the pureſt ſocieties, but this character is ſtill merited by the preſent race in Monimail.

PARISH OF MOONZIE.

(County and Synod of Fife——Presbytery of Cupar.)

By the Rev. Mr. Andrew Ireland, *Minister.*

Name and Extent.

THE origin of the name is unknown. It is probably derived from the Gaelic, the language which formerly prevailed all over the peninsula of Fife. There is a parish, with almost the same name (*Monzie*), in the presbytery of Auchterarder, where the names of places are also of Celtic extraction.—Moonzie, in point of extent and population, is perhaps the smallest parochial district in Scotland, and furnishes very slender materials indeed, for statistical observation and inquiry. It is only 1 Scotch mile in length, and about 1½ in breadth. The number of acres is between 1,000 and 1,100.

Surface, Soil, Produce, Cattle, &c.—A great part of the parish is hilly, and the rest is flat and low. The soil is very thin, but fertile. In a wet summer, it produces very good crops, both of corn and grass ; but, in a dry season, all the hilly ground is quite parched. —There are 17 ploughs in the parish. The farmers, now, only put 2 horses to the plough, and 1 man both holds and drives. This is a very great saving. There are about 34 or 36 horses in the parish ; and a very few sheep,

which

which one of the farmers keeps for his own private uſe. There are alſo ſome black cattle bred for ſale.

Farms, Proprietors and Rent.—There are only 4 farms in the pariſh, viz. *Moonzie, Lords-Cairnie, Torr,* and *Colluthie.* The three former belong to the Earl of Crawfurd, and the latter to Mrs. Bell of Hilton. The rent will amount to ſomething more than 1000l. Sterling per annum.

Population.—The population has decreaſed greatly within theſe 40 years, conſidering the number of inhabitants.

The return to Dr. Webſter, in the year 1755, was	249
The number of ſouls at preſent (March 1793), is only	171
Decreaſe,	78

Under 10 years of age,	30	From 50 to 70,	35
From 10 to 20,	32	Annual average of births	3
From 20 to 50,	74	Do. deaths, rather leſs than	3

Church, School and Poor.—The value of the living, including the glebe, is about 90l. Sterling. Lord Crawfurd is patron. The manſe got ſome repairs laſt ſummer, and the kirk and offices will need them ſoon.—The ſchoolmaſter's ſalary is 5l. 10s. per annum. The ſchool dues are very ſmall.—There are only 3 or 4 perſons in the pariſh who get charity; but they do not need much. The fund is very ſmall.

Character, &c.—The people are very decent and regular in their attendance upon divine worſhip. They are alſo very diligent and induſtrious in procuring ſubſiſtence for their families.—This pariſh labours under no particular diſadvantage. It is a great way off from coal; but there is now a fine turnpike road the moſt of the way. It has one great advantage, that it is within 2 ſhort miles of the town Cupar, where the people get a good price for any thing they have to ſell.

PARISH OF NEWBURGH.

(County and Synod of Fife.—Preſbytery of Cupar.)

By the Rev. Mr. Thomas Stuart.

Name, Situation, Extent and Soil.

THE town of Newburgh has evidently given its name to this pariſh ; and the ſignificant term, by which it is denominated, may have been impoſed in reference to ſome more ancient burgh in the neighbourhood. It forms the boundary of the county of Fife, on the N. W.—The extent of the pariſh is inconſiderable, and its figure very irregular, one part of it being detached from the other *. The ſoil on the N. and E. of the town of Newburgh, where the ground is low and flat, conſiſts of rich clay, not inferior in quality to any in the Carſe of Gowrie ; on the weſt of the town, and near to the river, where the ground riſes higher, it is light and gravelliſh ; more ſoutherly, where the ground ſuddenly dips, it tends to moſs ; and ſtill farther ſouth, where the ground again riſes into the Ochil Hills, it becomes, in ſome places, dry and loamy, in others wet and tilly. In the eſtate of Pitcairly, however,

* See Ainſlie's map of the counties of Fife and Kinroſs.

however, owing to the fortunate flopings of the eminences, and the largeness of the interjacent flats, there are many fields well adapted to the purposes of agriculture, which have, accordingly, been brought by the proprietor, into a state of fertility and cultivation.

Climate, Difeafes, &c.—In the hilly parts of the parish, the climate, although cold, is reckoned more healthy, than in the lower grounds, on the bank of the river, where the town of Newburgh stands. *There* the flat is hemmed in on the south, by the Ochil Hills, which obstruct the sun's influence, while it lies open, on the opposite side, to the N. E. winds, that blow up the Frith of Tay with piercing keenness. Notwithstanding this, epidemical distempers are not more frequent, or more fatal in Newburgh, than in other parts of the neighbouring country. Rheumatisms and consumptions may be stated, as the diseases, to which its inhabitants are most liable. The practice of inoculating for the small pox, not having become general, many children are, from time to time, lost by that disease. In the course of spring and summer 1791, no fewer than 56 children died of it, in the town of Newburgh. But it may be expected, that the same distemper will not in future, find so many victims, as the good sense, and well directed affection of parents begin to overturn any prejudices, they might formerly have entertained on that subject, and to engage them in taking that easy step, for saving the lives of their offspring, which experience justifies, and which Providence, from the success attending it, seems to sanction and approve.

Rivers.—No river runs through this parish. The Tay, which washes its northern extremity, more properly forming a boundary to it, than making any part of it. But the
Tay

Tay may find a place in the ſtatiſtical account of any diſtrict, that reaches to its border. This noble river, having received the acceſſion of the water of the Earn, begins at Newburgh, to aſſume the appearance of an arm of the ſea ; and, by the inhabitants of that town and neighbourhood, is denominated the *Broad Water.* When the tide in it, however, has ebbed, it leaves a conſiderable part of its channel dry ; and, collecting itſelf into two currents, paſſes along the oppoſite ſides of its bed, in what are termed the *North* and *South Deeps.* The South Deep, contains by far the greateſt quantity of water, and furniſhes the courſe, which veſſels of burden uſually hold, in paſſing up and down the river. As far up as Newburgh, the Tay admits veſſels of 500 tons burden ; but above the confluence of the Earn, beyond which Perth is ſituated, veſſels of 200 tons burden, when deep laden, proceed with difficulty. Veſſels, however, of about 90 or 100 tons burden, (in which the trade with Perth is uſually carried on,) eaſily make the ſhore of Perth ; and when larger veſſels are employed in that trade, part of their cargoes is diſtributed among lighters, on their arrival at the ſhore of Newburgh.

Salmon Fiſhing.—Beſides being favourable to commerce, the Tay furniſhes great quantities of excellent ſalmon, the fiſhing of which has, eſpecially of late years, become a conſiderable ſource of wealth to all who have property in the river. The proprietor of that part of its channel, on the ſouth ſide, which correſponds to the length of the pariſh of Newburgh, draws about 200 l. Sterling, of yearly rent, for his fiſhings ; and, in ſituations farther up, where the channel is not ſo broad, nor the tide ſo powerful, proprietors receive a much greater rent for a much leſs extent of water. What enables fiſhermen to pay ſuch high rents, is, the great price which falmon bring in the London market. The company at Perth, which rents the bulk of falmon fifhings in the Tay, feldom expofes fifh to fale in Scotland, except at Perth ; but continues to fend them to London through the whole fifhing feafon. When the weather is not uncommonly warm, or the fifh more than ordinarily abundant, they are fent up frefh. For conveying them, the company employs no fewer than 4, and fometimes 5 fmacks, of about 90 tons burden each, which are, in general, navigated by failors belonging to Newburgh. Thefe light, but ftrong built veffels, are kept running at all weathers, with almoft any quantity of fifh ; and, as the voyage, in the fifhing feafon, cannot be long, they generally bring their cargoes to market perfectly found, efpecially fince the practice has prevailed, of packing the falmon in ice.—One fituated on the border of the Tay, is pleafed with obferving this new and gainful trade to the capital; and cannot help admiring the fpirited induftry of that merchant, by whom it was firft rendered confiderable. At the fame time, he may be allowed to exprefs his regret, that any advantages arifing from a monopoly of falmon, fhould prevent the inhabitants of three counties, from fharing in thofe delicacies, which Providence annually fcatters in fuch abundance upon their fhores.

Hills and Woods.—The hills in the parifh of Newburgh, prefent no remarkable appearance. Like the generality of hills, in that extenfive ridge, which runs, with little interruption, from the neighbourhood of Stirling, to the N. E. extremity of Fife, they are broad-topped, green, and in many places, arable.—That abrupt rock near to Newburgh, on the S. E., which excites the furprife, and fometimes awakens the terror of ftrangers, in paffing along the road immediately under it, belongs to the parifh of Abdie. In regard to woods, it does not appear, that there have been any of great extent,

in

in the parish of Newburgh, at least within the period to which
its written records reach ; although it is not improbable, that
the wood mentioned in the history of Sir WILLIAM WAL-
LACE, by the name of *Iron-Side*, may have anciently covered its lower grounds. Above 20 years ago, the proprietor
of Pitcairly, having inclosed the greatest part of his lands, in
that quarter, with ditches and stone fences, run along many
stripes, and intersperfed several considerable clumps of different
kinds of wood, which give a cheering appearance to his estate,
as it unexpectedly opens on the view of the traveller, in croffing a district, otherwife uninclosed, and ill supplied with trees.
Of late years, similar steps have been taken, in the lower
grounds, on the estate of Mugdrum ; and at no great distance
of time, the beauties of that place, naturally delightful, may
be much heightened, by various well difposed, and thriving
plantations.

Antiquities.—At the N. E. extremity of this parish, near
the river Tay, on a gentle rife, in the middle of a rich, and
not unextensive flat of clay lands, appear the ruins of the ancient *Abbey of Lindores.* Concerning the history of this
Abbacy, while it continued under the power of the church, or
after it was erected into a temporal lordship, nothing material
can be difcovered, which has not already been made public.
About the year 1741, the abbey, with a fmall part of the abbey lands, which, till that time, had been retained by the
family of Lindores, paffed into the hands of the fon of a former
minister of Newburgh ; and, by a fubfequent fale, have come
into the poffeffion of the family of Mugdrum. What may
have been the extent of the buildings of the abbey, in former
times, one cannot judge, as part of the grounds, which they
once occupied, is now converted into arable land. Remains
of the church, however, are still extant, which shew, that it

muft

muſt have been a large, if not an elegant building. Parts, alſo, of the garden walls are ſtill ſtanding, which ſuggeſt no mean idea of the wealth of the clergy who inhabited it, and ſtrongly mark the pains they had taken, to ſecure the delicacies and luxuries of the table. Within theſe walls, and for a ſmall ſpace beyond them, on one ſide, the ground continues to be occupied by fruit trees, which, having been long ſince planted, exhibit appearances of decay, that, viewed in conjunction with the mouldering fragments of ſtructures, half covered at top with ivy, and ſurrounded at bottom with thorn and hazel, give an air of melancholy grandeur to the place at large. That dwelling houſe, ſituated in the heart of the ruins, and occupied occaſionally, till of late years, by the proprietors, or their friends, muſt have been repaired from ſome more ancient fabric, or an entire new building of ſtones taken out of the walls of the abbey. If we may credit tradition, it was reared by the firſt Lord Lindores, in the beginning of laſt century, and has received conſiderable additions and improvements ſince that period. Formerly ſtrangers, who viſited the ruins of the abbey, had a ſtone coffin pointed out to them, which was placed within the area of the church, on the north wall, towards the eaſt end, which was ſaid to have contained the remains of an Earl of Douglas; but, in conſequence of depredations lately made upon the walls, it is now covered over with rubbiſh. Whether this coffin did in fact contain the bones of an Earl of Douglas, or of a Duke of Rothſay, or perhaps of ſome dignified eccleſiaſtic belonging to the abbey, no certain information can be procured, as there is not a ſingle inſcription to be found in any part of the church, or of the other buildings, which might lead to the diſcovery of facts of ſuch remote antiquity. Upon the whole, in viewing the abbey of Lindores, nothing is now to be met with, worthy of attaching the curioſity of the viſitor.

tor. If ever it preſented any ſtriking diſplays of the taſte, and magnificence of our forefathers, they have been removed ; and, ſhould the practice of demoliſhing its ruins continue a few years longer, the eye of the moſt prying antiquary, will ſcarcely be able to diſcern the ſituation where it was placed.

Beſides the ruins of the abbey of Lindores, this pariſh contains two croſſes of very ancient erection. One of theſe is placed on a riſing ground, a little weſtward of the town of Newburgh, and within 4 yards of the Tay. The other is ſituated at the diſtance of ſomewhat leſs than a mile to the S. in an opening of the Ochil Hills, on the confines of Strathearn, where the road, formerly leading towards Lindores, ſeparates from that which at preſent leads to Auchtermuchty. The lower croſs, known by the name of the Croſs of Mugdrum, conſiſts of one large ſtone placed upright in another, which has been hollowed for receiving it, and which ſerves to retain it in an erect poſition. Upon the upright ſtone, although mutilated, remains of the figures of horſes may be traced ; but no veſtige of any inſcription appears. The upper croſs, called Croſs M'Duff, conſiſts, at preſent, of one large quadrilateral block of freeſtone, rudely indented in ſeveral places, but is ſaid to have had formerly another ſtone ſtanding upright ; although the ſtone now lying along the the ground, has no appearance of ever having been hollowed, in the manner of that which forms the baſe of the Croſs of Mugdrum. No ſatisfactory account can be given of the various purpoſes, which theſe croſſes were originally meant to ſerve. The tradition, which connects Croſs M'Duff with the juriſdiction of the powerful Thane of Fife, may not be deſtitute of foundation ; but in regard to the Croſs of Mugdrum, even tradition ceaſes to furniſh any information. It were needleſs to quote the lines of jargon, which are ſaid to have

been

been engraved on the Crofs M'Duff. They are to be found in every book, which treats of that ancient monument *.

Town

* Although tradition has retained few particulars, refpecting the hiftory of either of the croffes, it continues to preferve the memory of the fpot, in the lands belonging to the town of Newburgh, on which more than one unfortunate victim fell a facrifice to the fuperftition of former times, intent on punifhing the crime of witchcraft. The humane provifions of the legiflature, joined to the fuperior knowledge, which has, of late years, pervaded all ranks of men in fociety, bid fair to prevent the return of a phrenfy, which actuated our forefathers univerfally, and with fatal violence. But we may well be furprifed, in obferving how near to our own times, it continued to exert its influence over the judgment, not of the common people only, but of thofe too, who, by their education, fhould have been raifed above vulgar prejudices. As late as the year 1653, the records of this parifh, contain articles of an additional charge, brought by the minifter himfelf, againft Katharine Kay, while under procefs of fcandal, before the kirk-feffion, for imprecating curfes upon him, becaufe he had debarred her accefs to the communion, which evidently fhew, that he entertained fufpicions of her being a witch. The articles, or points of accufation, as the records term them, are 5 in number; and as they ferve to exhibit a ftriking picture of fentiments, once prevalent among the people of this country, no apology is requifite for taking the liberty of inferting them.

" Newburgh, September 18th, 1653. The which day, ye minifter gave in, " againft Kathrine Key, feverall poynts yt had come to his hearing, which he " defyred might be put to tryell. 1. That being refufed milk from Chriftian " Orme, or fome other in David Orme's houfe, the kow gave nothing but red " blood; and being fent for, to fie the kow, fhe clapped (ftroked) the kow, and " faid, the kow will be weill, and thereafter the kow becam weill. 2. That " John Philp having ane kow new calved, the faid Kathrine Key, came in and " took forth ane peice fyre, and yrafter the kow becam fo fick, that none expect- " ed fhe fould have lived. And the faid Kathrine being fent for, to fie the kow, " fhe clapped the kow, and faid the kow will be weill enough, and fhe amen- " dit. 3. That the minifter and his wyfe, having ane purpofe to take ane chyld " of theirs from the fd Kathrine, which fhe had in nurfing, the chyld wold fuck " none woman's breaft, being only one quarter old; but being brought again to " the faid Kathrine, prefently fucked her breaft. 4. That thereafter the chyld was " *fpayned* (weaned), fhe came to fie the child, and wold have the bairne (child) " in her arms, and yrafter, the bairne mufned and gratt (weeped fore), in the

" night

Town of Newburgh, its History, &c.—The town of Newburgh arose, in the times of popery; and, at an early period, was erected into a burgh of regality, under the Abbot of Lindores. In the year 1600, James VI. erected the Abbacy of Lindores into a temporal Lordship; and, in the year 1631, his son Charles I. granted a charter to the town of Newburgh, forming the community into a proper royal burgh, with the several immunities and privileges, usually conferred on the royal burghs of this kingdom. At present, Newburgh has no voice in the choice of a representative to parliament; but, in all other respects, it retains the features of a royal burgh. Its revenue, indeed, is very inconsiderable, not exceeding 25 l. Sterling, per annum, out of which the minister receives, yearly, 20 l. Scotch, in payment of stipend. Notwithstanding which, its office bearers make a decent appearance; a court is held in it weekly, with marks of dignity; and it retains a clerk of ability for recording its public proceedings.—One, who has occasion to observe the importance of insuring full respect, to persons cloathed with the office of magistrates, may be allowed to express a wish, that government would devise some method of increasing the revenues of the lesser burghs. A small sum of the public money applied in this way, could not fail of contributing to the preservation of order, in places, which,

owing

" night, and almost the day tyme; also, that nothing could stay her, untill she
" died. Nevertheless, befor her coming to see her, and her embracing of her,
" took as weill wt the spaining, and rested as weill as any bairne could doe.
" 5. That she is of ane evill *brutte* (report) and fame, and so was her mother be-
" fore her." When these points were put to trial by the kirk-session, the evidence of their truth did not, it should seem, come out with such clearness, as to enable the kirk-session to pass sentence against Katherine; and they accordingly referred the matter to the presbytery of Cupar for decision. But in what manner the presbytery of Cupar treated it, no notice is taken in the records of the kirk-session.

owing to the general increase of wealth, and other obvious causes, are in some danger of requiring the authority of an established and respectable magistracy, to preserve them in tranquillity and good order.

The town of Newburgh, consists of one street of considerable length, with small suburbs at each end, and a lane leading towards the shore from its centre. The houses, on each side of the lane, and in the suburbs, have been built within these 30 years. The town itself, does not occupy more ground than it did in the end of last century ; but, in consequence of alterations, that have since been made upon the buildings, it must be capable of containing double the number of inhabitants. Formerly, the generality of houses in Newburgh, were low built, and covered with thatch of straw, or of reeds. Of late years, a better style of architecture has prevailed ; and, at this day, Newburgh has some pretensions to neatness, in the structure of its houses. Sixty years ago, few of its houses concealed their rafters.—At present, scarcely any of them, and none lately erected, present that naked appearance. On the same spot, where 12 years ago a board was placed in the window, to exclude the winter storm, may now be seen, a Venetian blind, attached to the casement, for blunting the rays of the summer sun. Within these 10 years, not fewer than 30 houses have been rebuilt, within the liberties of Newburgh ; some of which might be rented at 12l. and none for less than 5l. per annum. Preparations are also making, for rebuilding two or three more. The street of Newburgh, which has long been paved with stones, having fallen into disrepair, the magistrates and town council, lately, formed the resolution of paving it a new ; and by means of assessments from proprietors within the burgh, together with a small allowance out of the statute labour, leviable upon the inhabitants at large, they have made considerable progress in the execution

ecution of their defign, Some appearances, which would induce one to be of opinion, that coal might be found in the
grounds belonging to the town, having alfo attracted the notice of the magiftrates and town council, they are at prefent
taking the proper fteps, for afcertaining the exiftence of that
ufeful mineral in their territory ; and it is to be prefumed,
that the liberality of the neighbourhood will enable them to
make the moft fatisfactory inveftigation. Various other
meafures have of late been purfued by them, and by individuals in the place, which fhew, that the fpirit of improvement, long dormant, has awoke, and become active in Newburgh, as well as in many other burghs in Scotland.

Manufactures and Commerce.—Till within thefe few years,
a great proportion of the inhabitants of Newburgh, whatever
other trades they might exercife, were a kind of hufbandmen.
But moft of the fmall portions of land, which they formerly
held, and which they generally cultivated with their own
hands, having been purchafed of late by the proprietor of
Mugdrum, and laid out in large parcels, they are now attached more to particular callings. The trade which occupies the greateft number of hands, is that of weaving cloth.
No fewer than 270 of the inhabitants, are at prefent employed in it. The weavers of Newburgh, however, do not yet
abide conftantly by the loom. Accuftomed from their early
years, to handle the oar, as well as the fhuttle, they betake
themfelves, in confiderable numbers, to a fea-faring life, when
the price of thefe kinds of cloth, which they are in the practice of weaving, falls low in the market. While they continue at the loom, they do not, in general, arrange themfelves
under different mafters, who might furnifh them with materials,
and pay them for their work. Some of them do indeed follow
that method ; and work-fhops may be met with, in which
near

near a dozen of looms are employed by one manufacturer.
But the greater part of them weave their own yarn, and
bring their own webs to fale. The webs, which they commonly weave, are of three kinds, termed by the workmen,
Silefias, Ofnaburghs, and Brown Linens. For fuch cloths, there
is, generally, a good, and at prefent, a very great demand in
London and Leeds. The weavers, in Newburgh, however,
have little direct intercourfe with either of thefe places.
They generally difpofe of their webs, at Newburgh, to a few
of their own number, who again difpofe of them at Perth,
Dundee, Cupar, Auchtermuchty, and Glafgow, to perfons
there, who purchafe them, either with their own capital, or
upon commiffion, for the Englifh markets. Not more than
two of them tranfact bufinefs immediately with London. Befides weavers, Newburgh contains its full proportion of fhopkeepers, inn-keepers, fmiths, mafons, carpenters, fhoemakers,
tailors, butchers, bakers, fifhermen, and feamen. Scarcely
any of its inhabitants find themfelves placed beyond the neceffity of employing themfelves in manual labour; although
few or none of them are engaged in manufacturing any materials for exportation, except the linen cloths already mentioned,
and barley into malt. Of the latter, they fend to Edinburgh
market, in the courfe of one feafon, about 1800 bolls. Till
of late years, a great proportion of bread, beer, and butcher's
meat, confumed in Newburgh, was brought from Perth,
Dundee, and the Carfe of Gowrie; but the bakers, brewers,
and butchers, are exerting themfelves in their refpective occupations, and they bid fair for fecuring, in future, the cuftom of the generality of the inhabitants. Formerly, few people reforted from any diftance to Newburgh, for merchant
goods; and the retail trade in it was limited to a few articles,
in the hard-ware and grocery lines, purchafed commonly by
the dealers at Perth, or at Dundee. But within thefe few

years,

years, feveral fhops have been opened, upon a more extenfive fcale ; and there is reafon to believe, that the demands of the town and neighbourhood, will furnifh the keepers of them with employment. Still, however, no trader has as yet appeared in Newburgh, whofe extenfive tranfactions in commerce, would entitle him to the name and character of a merchant ; though perhaps the time is not far diftant, when many will be found here of that refpectable defcription.

Shore.—A few yards northward from the town, and nearly connected with it by buildings, although beyond the limits of its jurifdiction, lies the fhore of Newburgh ; which confifts of three continuous piers, projecting into the fouth deep of the river Tay, with feveral dwelling houfes, ftore-houfes, and other conveniencies for commerce. Thefe piers form very fafe ftations, for the veffels employed in the trade on the river ; and although none of any burden can properly be faid to belong to Newburgh, and but few are freighted to it, except with coals or lime, they are feldom to be feen without fhips, as the generality of veffels, bound for Perth, muft wait at Newburgh the flow of the tide ; and not a few of them, muft unload part of their cargoes there, before they can, even with the tide, proceed farther up the river. Hence arifes a good deal, if not of trade, at leaft of ftir, at the fhore of Newburgh, which proves of advantage to the place at large. The fmacks employed in the falmon trade, alfo, lie to there, at all feafons, and take in all kinds of goods for London market. A trade in wood and iron, is likewife carried on at the fhore, by a dealer, who refides upon the fpot, and who has obtained a pretty extenfive fale. A tannage is likewife forming there, which will revive a trade, that was carried on at Newburgh, in the end of the laft century. Formerly, great quantities of burnt lime-ftone, brought by land carriage, from the inland

parts

parts of Fife, were shipped at the shore of Newburgh, and sold to the farmers in the Carse of Gowrie, for manure. But the lime works erected on the Frith of Forth, and on the English coast, from which the farmers, in the east end of Strathearn, and in the Carse of Gowrie, are more readily and more cheaply supplied, have nearly put an end to that species of traffic. For several years past, great quantities of wheat and barley, purchased from the farmers in the neighbourhood, have been shipped at the shore of Newburgh, chiefly for the Edinburgh and Glasgow markets. This trade seems likely to continue; and while it brings advantage to Newburgh, must operate to the benefit of the country at large. On the north side of Fife, more grain is cultivated, than can be consumed by the inhabitants. Formerly, a market was, with difficulty, found for the surplus; but, by the connexion establishing between Fife and the south country, this difficulty will be removed, and a new spur given to the farther cultivation of a district lately much improved, but capable of being rendered greatly more productive.

Farms.—There are only 4 farms in this parish, the remaining lands, which are not extensive, either continuing in the possession of the proprietors themselves, or being divided into inconsiderable portions among a variety of feuars, tenants, burghal heritors, and other small proprietors. Of these farms, however, it may be with truth, affirmed, that they are at present, in as good a state of cultivation, as any in the neighbourhood. Few farms, in the whole extent of the Ochil Hills, to the westward, have been more judiciously laid out, than two of them, which occupy the estate of Pitcairly; and no farm in the Carse of Gowrie can be kept in higher order, or rendered more productive, than the one which is connected with the Abbey of Lindores. The fourth farm, although

formed

formed but of late, chiefly out of fmall purchafes from the burghal heritors of Newburgh, bears evident marks of improvement.

Rent, Proprietors, &c.—The valued rent of the parifh amounts only to 1958 l. 17 s. 6 d. Scotch. Its real rent may not at prefent be great ; but, on the expiration of fome leafes, it muft rife confiderably, as land, in the lower grounds, on the eaft of Newburgh, lets, at from 2 l. to 3 l. *per* acre ; and, in the higher grounds, at from 10 s. to 2 l. *per* acre. The territory of the parifh is divided among two greater, and about 30 fmaller proprietors, called here, as well as in other parts of the country, *portioners.* The two greater, and moft of the fmaller proprietors, ufually refide in it. Befides the four farmers already mentioned, there are few tenants in the parifh, who do not refide in the town, or at the fhore of Newburgh ; and their number is not great, nor their portions of land extenfive. The four greater farmers pay of rent above 50 l. *per annum* each ; the other tenants pay much below that fum.

Crops.—The principal crops in this parifh are oats, barley, wheat, beans, and a mixture of beans and peafe. Notwithftanding the richnefs of the foil in the lower grounds, it is not long fince wheat made a crop there in rotation. Of late years, wheat has been fown, not only in the lower grounds, but alfo in the hilly parts of the parifh. As turnips are not found a profitable crop in clay lands, they are not cultivated in the lands attached to the Abbey of Lindores. Any trials made to raife them in the higher grounds, have fucceeded. But it is matter of regret, that farmers, in this part of the country, fhew fome backwardnefs, in extending a fpecies of crop, which, when properly conducted, not only meliorates the land, and gives it frefh life and vigour, but alfo furnifhes a delicate and nourifh-

ing

ing food, either for feeding young cattle, and raifing them to a greater fize, or fattening the old, and bringing them to a better market. Clover and rye grafs are generally fown with the barley ; and, after a crop of grafs has been taken for one year, the ground is again broke up for oats. Wheat is fown after fallow or after pulfe, but commonly after fallow. Manure is laid on the fallow, or when the land is undergoing preparation for a peafe crop. When the feafon will admit, beans, or a mixture of beans and peafe, are fown upon the manure, and plowed in. Wheat is not fown fo early as formerly, even upon fallow. Farmers are of opinion, that very early fowing feldom produces the largeft head, or the heavieft grain of wheat. Oats are fown from the beginning of March to the end of April, and the feed, generally made ufe of, is a fpecies of oats termed Grange-bothrey, from a farm of that name, in the county of Angus. Barley is fown in the end of April, and through the whole of May. Moft of the feed employed is a mixture of different kinds, originally imported from England. Though the lands, being under better culture than formerly, yield greater quantities of barley, it is remarked, that its quality feems not to be equal. Whether this be owing to the frequent fowing of wheat, or to the introduction of lime, as a manure, experience has not yet enabled the farmer to determine. The quantity of grain, raifed in this parifh, is by no means equal to the maintenance of its inhabitants ; but the deficiency is abundantly made up by the neighbourhood.

Population, &c.—From the report of one, who, during the indifpofition of the writer, was employed to afcertain the number of the parifhioners, it appears, that the parifh, at large, contains 1664 fouls, of whom 1552 belong to the town, fuburbs, and fhore of Newburgh, and 112 to the country part
of

of the parifh. The inhabitants of the town, fuburbs and fhore, confift of 772 males, and 780 females. Of the inhabitants in the country, 64 are males, and 48 females. The return to Dr. Webfter, in 1755, amounting only to 1347, it is evident, that there has been an increafe, fince that time, of 317 fouls. Owing to the manner, in which the publication of marriage banns is generally regiftered in Scotland, an accurate account of the marriages, that take place in any particular parifh, cannot always be obtained. But the records of this parifh, fupply the following account of births and deaths, for the laft fix years, which there is every reafon to believe, may be depended on.

TABLE of BIRTHS, DEATHS, &c.

Years.	Births.			Deaths.			Ages of perfons who died.										
	Born.	Males.	Females.	Died.	Males.	Females.	Under 2 years.	Between 2 & 5.	Between 5 & 10.	Between 10 & 20.	Between 20 & 30.	Between 30 & 40.	Between 40 & 50.	Between 50 & 60.	Between 60 & 70.	Between 70 & 80.	Between 80 & 90.
1786	46	24	22	32	10	22	2	3	3	4	5	4	1	1	5	3	1
1787	58	34	24	25	13	12	3	2	2	1	3	2	2	3	5	2	0
1788	66	34	32	30	13	17	6	3	3	2	4	1	1	1	7	2	0
1789	61	36	25	27	16	11	5	2	5	5	2	2	2	1	3	0	0
1790	66	35	31	31	18	13	5	2	2	4	3	5	3	2	4	1	0
1791	69	33	36	98	42	56	23	35	13	3	2	4	5	4	5	4	0

Ecclefiaftical State.—There are three clergymen in the parifh of Newburgh ; the minifter of the eftablifhed church, of the Burgher Seceders, and of the Congregational Society, befides feveral others, who, without taking the name of clergymen, teach and exhort, under the denomination of Anabaptifts, and Unitarians. The Congregational Society is fmall. The Burgher Seceders may exceed one third of the whole inhabitants of the parifh. In point of numbers, the Anabaptifts and Unitarians fcarcely deferve the name of focieties. The Unitarians do not exceed four ; and the Anabaptifts are not double that number. The Anabaptifts are connected with a church of the fame defcription, at Dundee. It may be prefumed, that the Unitarians have eftablifhed more diftant connexions. There are alfo, in the parifh, feveral families who belong to the congregation of Antiburgher Seceders at Abernethy. The Antiburgher Seceffion, is of long ftanding in the parifh. But the Burgher Seceffion fprung up in it, on the admiffion of the prefent incumbent, into the Eftablifhed Church. The town of Newburgh, alfo, contains a few Independents, and one or two profeffors of the Epifcopal religion, but no Roman Catholics. Befides thefe various denominations of Chriftians, not a few perfons refide within the bounds of this parifh, who hold communion with no religious fociety, and feldom join in any public acts of religious worfhip. A friend to principles of toleration, and an advocate for liberty of confcience, rejoices in obferving men of different views and opinions, on fubjects of religion, living together in the exercife of mutual charity, and tranfacting peaceably with one another, the bufinefs of civil life.—Thefe are happy times. Even among the common people, perfecution for the fake of confcience begins to be regarded with horror ; and the bigot fhould in vain attempt to inflame them with violence, againft perfons of fentiments, the moft oppofite to thofe which they

have

have embraced. At the ſame time, conviction of the importance of religion, to the preſent comfort, and future happineſs
of mankind, muſt produce the deepeſt regret in the minds of
thoſe, who are called to witneſs liberty of conſcience made a
pretence for neglecting duties; which the beſt, in all ages,
have ever held ſacred.

Lord Viſcount Stormont, and Mr. Hay of Mugdrum, are
vice-patrons of the pariſh. The ſtipend conſiſts of 31 bolls,
2 pecks of oats; 65 bolls 2 firlots of bear; 37 bolls 2 pecks
of meal, (2 bolls 2 pecks of the oats, and the ſame quantity
of the bear being converted to the town, at 20 l. Scotch,) and
22 l. Scotch in money, with a manſe, and a glebe of 4 acres.
The pariſh church is an old Popiſh chapel, ſituated within the
town of Newburgh, which, in conſequence of a late thorough
repair, has been made a very convenient place of worſhip.
The manſe is a new building, erected ſince the admiſſion of
the preſent incumbent, on a moſt delightful ſpot, beyond the
town of Newburgh, to the eaſtward, in full view of the river
Tay, and Carſe of Gowrie.

Schools.—There are two ſchools in the pariſh, and one
teacher in each ſchool. The ſchool, taught by the pariſh
ſchoolmaſter, is attended by 60 ſcholars, of whom 8 are
taught Latin, 22 writing and arithmetic, and 30 Engliſh.
The other ſchool, which is private, and taught by a Seceder, is
attended by 55 ſcholars, of whom 3 are taught Latin, 21
writing and arithmetic, and 31 Engliſh. During the winter
ſeaſon, both ſchools are reſorted to, after the ordinary hours of
labour, by a conſiderable number of grown up perſons, for
the purpoſe of learning Engliſh, writing, arithmetic, book-
keeping, and navigation. Of late years, the advantages of
education, have been fully perceived by parents, and are
eagerly ſought for their children. There is one licenſed
preacher

preacher belonging to the parish, and three young men from the town of Newburgh, have either juft finished, or are at prefent, profecuting the ftudy of phyfic, in the univerfity of Edinburgh.

Poor.—There are no poor on the funds, who refide in the country part of the parish. The number of poor on the parish roll in the town, is confiderable. They are maintained by the intereft of accumulated fums of money, feu-duties of a fuperiority in lands purchafed for their behoof, collections at the church door, and other cafualties. Befides the money given in monthly penfions, confiderable fums are diftributed occafionally, to perfons in ftraitened circumftances, who receive no ftated fupplies ; and the education of about 8 children, is ufually paid for.

Charaɛter and Manners of the People.—In a provincial town, inhabited chiefly by failors and weavers, poffeffed of fmall properties, and nearly on a level with refpeɛt to riches, one does not look for polished manners, and the courtly attentions praɛtifed in great cities. Till of late years, the inhabitants of Newburgh were remarkable for their rufticity, and for the freedom with which they treated their fuperiors. " We will let the beft Lord of the land ken, that when he " fets his foot on Newburgh caufeway, he is Bailie Lyell's " vaffal," was the boaftful language in which they expreffed their emancipation from feudal tyranny, and their enjoyment of political freedom. The prefent inhabitants retain the fenfe of independence, imbibed and cherished by their anceftors ; but having shared in the effeɛts of that civilization, which has recently produced fo great a change on the manners of the nation at large, they are ftudious of difplaying it with moderation and courtefy. They mingle with their neighbours in the

the tranſactions of commercial intercourſe ; and they gradually aſſimilate to the general character of their countrymen.
The bulk of the inhabitants undoubtedly merit the praiſe of
ſobriety and induſtry ; and inſtances of perſons are not wanting, who, by ſignal propriety, in their own deportment, furniſh a daily rebuke to the unprincipled and idle ; and, by ſuperior attention to the education of their children, take the
ſureſt method of producing a thorough reformation on the
manners of the people. No perſon belonging to the pariſh of
Newburgh, has ſuffered the puniſhment of death for any
crime, within the period to which its records extend. In times
of peace, Perth receives its moſt expert ſailors from this diſtrict ; whilſt, in time of war, Newburgh ſupplies the Navy
of Great Britain, with ſteady, well behaved, and gallant
men.

Advantages and Diſadvantages.—The pariſh, and in particular, the town of Newburgh, labours under ſeveral diſadvantages. The country near it, on the ſouth, is hilly, thinly inhabited, and badly provided with roads. Trade being already eſtabliſhed at Perth and at Dundee, militates againſt
its ſpeedy acquiſition of commercial conſequence. The appointment too, of magiſtrates in Newburgh, without a revenue adequate to the ſupport of their authority, may be reckoned unfavourable to it. When perſons in power are dependent,
regulations of police may be formed, but will ſeldom bé executed. In every town, men are to be found of weight ſufficient to thwart thoſe ſchemes of improvement, which muſt
be proſecuted at the perſonal expence of the projectors. But,
notwithſtanding theſe obvious obſtacles, no ſpot on the whole
north ſide of Fife, ſeems better calculated for preparing various kinds of manufacture for ſale, and for ſupplying part
of three counties, with foreign articles of conſumption. It
lies

lies open to the moſt diſtant markets, has convenient ſtations for ſhipping, and admits veſſels of conſiderable burden. The fertile diſtrict of the Carſe of Gowrie, is at no great diſtance, on the north ; and a well cultivated country approaches on the E. and W. There, a malting concern, of great extent, might be eſtabliſhed ; and, in the immediate neighbourhood, might be found no inconvenient ſituation, for any work re-quiring a command of water, while Newburgh might furniſh plenty of hands for carrying on the operations of the manu-facturer ; as there are hundreds in it already trained to the loom, who only want a ſpirited merchant, with an adequate capital, to direct their induſtry into a lucrative channel. The time cannot be far diſtant, when theſe obvious advantages will be ſeized, in an age of ſuch commercial enterpriſe ; and then the town of Newburgh, long poor, though independent, will become diſtinguiſhed for the wealth, the induſtry, and the number of its inhabitants, and better entitled to the atten-tion of the philoſopher and the ſtateſman.

PARISH OF NEWBURN,

(County and Synod of Fife, Presbytery of St Andrew's.

By the Rev. Mr Lawrie, *Minister.*

Extent, Situation, Surface.

THE parish of Newburn, is, on an average, about 3¼ English miles long, and 2 broad, is situated in the Presbytery of St Andrew's, and Synod of Fife, bounded on the E. by Kilconquhar; on the W. by Largo; by part of both these parishes on the N. and on the S. by the sea. The soil in general is very fertile, and produces excellent crops. Almost the whole land in the parish is arable and inclosed. The late Mr Craigie of Lawhill (now Hall-hill) began inclosing, and the farmers seem fully convinced of its advantages. Wheat grew here more than half a century ago; but a far greater quantity is raised now than before. Turnips and potatoes were introduced many years ago likewise; but the former, owing to the

natural

natural fertility of the foil, and the improved ftate of agri-culture, have been cultivated with remarkable fuccefs. The luxuriant turnip-crops in this diftrict in favourable feafons, might arreft the attention of the traveller, who has vifited more fortunate climes.

Population and State of the Poor.—The population in 1755 was 438 fouls. The number of fouls was found by the minifter, in the courfe of his parochial vifitation in April 1794, to amount exactly to 456. From a recent enumeration it appeared, that the inhabitants under 10 years of age were 142. The annual average of births for the laft 10 years appears from the regifter to be 12. The annual average of marriages is 3, and that of deaths 6. Though the climate is favourable to longevity, and epi-demical diftempers feldom prevail, infection is communi-cated when any malignant difeafe does appear, by the common people reforting from all quarters to the apart-ments of the fick, without adopting any means which would tend to prevent its diffufion. Far be it from any Chriftian to difcourage innocent expreffions of friendship to the diftreffed; yet the attendance of many idle vifi-tors on the fick is extremely culpable. They not only hurt *them* in feveral refpects, but alfo endanger their own lives, and thofe of their neighbours. On thefe accounts, the indifcriminate practice of vifiting the fick, whether it pro-ceeds from an impertinent curiofity, or a miftaken principle of benevolence, is often attended with the moft fatal effects. But wherever prejudice or cuftom, in fpite of falutary re-monftrance, leads " every one to do that which is right in " one's own eyes," many of confequence will do wrong.

The number of poor perfons on the parifh-roll is feven, who are fupported by the collections on Sunday, and the

interest

intereft of a confiderable fum of money appropriated to them. The relief granted to each individual varies according to the circumftances of the cafe. Befide their ftated allowance, occafional fupply is given where it is judged neceffary. The poor are maintained in their own houfes ; and, on an average, the annual fum expended for their fupport, may be about L. 13 Sterling. But relief is not confined to thefe penfioners alone. The eftablifhed provifion for the benefit of the indigent, enables the church-feffion to extend their charity, and-receive the applications of families who are reduced to the neceffity of foliciting affiftance, in confequence of accidental misfortunes. Church-feffions are generally allowed to be the moft faithful adminiftrators of the funds for the maintenance of the poor ; and indeed, their judicious arrangements have merited the approbation of the moft enlightened part of the community.

Ecclefiaftical State of the Parifh.—It has been often remarked, that Newburn, for many years paft, has been a nurfery of Seceders ; and remarked with furprife, that a fmall arm of the fea fhould be the boundary between *moderation* and *fanaticifm*. Cameronians, Independents, perfons belonging to the Burgher Congregation, and alfo to what is called the Relief Congregation, are to be found here. The number of Independents is about 20. They are the only fect who have a place of meeting for public worfhip in the parifh. The members of the Relief Congregation are about the fame number ; the Burghers amount to 12 ; and the number of Cameronians is confined to two. It is pleafing, however, to a philofophic and a pious mind to perceive, that the intolerant party-fpirit which has too often characterized fectaries, is far lefs prevalent

valent than in former times. Diverfity of religious fentiments does not prevent focial intercourfe, and mutual good
offices.

In defcribing the general character of the people, it is
but juftice to pronounce them fober, regular, induftrious.
Humanity, too, it muft be mentioned to their honour,
holds a confpicuous place in the catalogue of their virtues.
It is but juftice alfo to add, that of late no addition has
been made to the number of Seceders in this parifh;
on the contrary, one of the elders of the Relief Congregation has returned to the Eftablifhed Church : rational
religion feems to be gaining ground ; and the fmall remainder of enthufiafm will moft probably die with them
who cherifh it.

The patronefs of the parifh is Mrs Halket Craigie of
Hall-hill. There are 7 heritors ; at prefent only 3 of them
refide in the parifh. The benefice here is one of thofe
which greatly requires increafe ; and a procefs of augmentation is about to be commenced. The money-ftipend at
prefent is L. 40 : 11 : 1 Sterling, and the victual-ftipend
confifts only of 7 bolls of wheat, 32 bolls 1 peck of bear,
and 24 bolls, 3 firlots, 3 pecks of oats. The glebe fcarcely
includes 4 acres. The victual ftipend, at an average, is
but L. 40 Sterling *per annum*, as part of the lands which
pay ftipend are of an inferior quality.

School.—The parochial fchool is of confiderable repute.
Several gentlemen's fons refort to it for education, which
they receive on very moderate terms. Englifh is taught
for 1 s. 6 d. ; writing and Englifh for 2 s. ; arithmetic for
2 s. 6 d. ; and Latin for 2 s. 6 d. *per* quarter. The local
fituation is eligible in two refpects : It is favourable both
to their health and their morals. The air is falubrious ;
                                                          and

and the youth are not expoſed to the contagion of thoſe vices which unhappily prevail in large towns.

About the middle of the laſt century, John Wood, Eſq; proprietor of the lands of Orkie, deſtined that property after his death for erecting a free grammar ſchool in the pariſh of Drumelry, *alias* Newburn, and maintaining ſix poor ſcholars thereat. The rent of theſe lands is now about L. 140 Sterling *per annum,* and the parochial ſchoolmaſter educates and maintains the poor ſcholars on Mr Wood's *mortification,* as it is called in Scottiſh law language ; for he officiates in a double capacity, being choſen both by the heritors and the patrons of the mortification already mentioned. By the deed, ' Sir Thomas ' Gourlay of Kincraig,' &c. ' the miniſter of Newburn,' &c. and ' their ſucceſſors whatſomever, are appointed ' lawful, undoubted patrons of the foundation and mor- ' tification in all time coming.' Boys of the firname of *Wood* are always to have a preference.

Price of Labour and Proviſions.—The yearly wages of farm-ſervants is about L. 7 for men, and L. 3 for women, beſide their victuals. The wages of the day-labourer is 1 s.; in time of harveſt they are rather higher ; for mowing hay he gets, *per* day, 1 s. 6 d. The day wages of a maſon is from 1 s. 6 d. to 2 s.; of a tailor 1 s. when he furniſhes proviſions to himſelf ; and when victuals are provided for him, 6 d.

The average price of beef is 3¼ d. *per* lb.; of veal, 3¼ d.; and of mutton the ſame. The price of a hen, at an average, is 1 s.; of a duck, 9 d.; of a pig fit for table, 5 s. Butter is about 8 d. *per* lb. But the price of labour and proviſions, in general, is more than doubled within theſe 30 years.

Improvements

Improvements fuggefted.—Befides putting the roads in better repair, the eftablifhment of a more regular market would alfo be a very confiderable advantage in this part of the country. Another difadvantage, under which not only this, but the adjacent parifhes labour, is the weight of bread being left entirely to the will of the baker. Wherever this is the cafe, the confumer is liable to fuffer lofs; and the very exemption from any regulation on this point is a temptation to injuftice. A remedy certainly exifts fomewhere, and it ought to be fpeedily applied. To remove the local inconvenience complained of, or rather the general evil, might not the bread be occafionally infpected by fome proper perfon appointed for that purpofe by the juftices of the peace? And wherever the weight is found deficient, let the bread be given to the poor. The very idea of being fubject to the jurifdiction of the juftices of peace, or of feeling the confequences of the complaints lodged with them, would operate as a powerful reftraint on men who have it in their power to impofe both on the rich and the poor, it is faid, by charging what they chufe for a loaf, which might be purchafed in other places, where there is a check and controuling power over bakers, for a far more reafonable price. While fome of the people complain of imaginary grievances under the happy conftitution where they live, it is hoped the real one now fpecified will be removed as foon as it is poffible.

Antiquities.—There are veftiges of the eaft part of the church having been a Roman Catholic chapel.

If we may give credit to the records and traditions which have been tranfmitted to us of that early period, the Culdees, who are thought to have been the firft regular clergy in *Scotland,* had a church and refidence in this parifh

fo

ſo early as the time of *Malcolm Canmore.* The earlieſt records which we have of theſe monks mention Hungus the
firſt King of the Piĉts, as their Great Benefaĉtor ; and St
Andrew's, or its neighbourhood, as their chief reſidence.
Brude, the laſt King of the Piĉts, made a donation to them
of the iſle of Lochleven ; Kirkneſs was given to them by
M'Beth, ſon of *Finlay* ; and their Majeſties King *Malcolm*,
and his Queen *St Margaret*. granted to them the village
of *Balchriſtie* *, (or, as it has been interpreted by ſome,
the Town of Chriſtian), in this pariſh. The preſent proprietor of the village (Mr Chriſtie of Balchriſtie) informs
me, that ſome years ago he dug up the foundation-ſtones
of an old edifice near the weſtern wall of his garden, and
in the very place where, according to the beſt accounts,
the church of the Culdees ſtood. Some ſay, this was the
firſt Chriſtian church in Scotland ; and, indeed, the name
of Balchriſtie, as above explained, and the high probability
of the Culdees landing firſt on the adjacent inviting ſhore,
give conſiderable countenance to the tradition.

Additional Obſervations.—This ſituation has been long
admired for variegated ſcenery and an extenſive view.
The ſcene now before me, conſiſting of woods and waters,
and hills and dales, is ſuch as the writer of romance might
have delighted to feign. *Hall-hill* at preſent appears in
ruins ; but a new manſion-houſe, as is believed, will ſoon
add to the beauty of theſe rural wilds. *Hæ latebræ dulces
etiam, ſi credas amænæ.* The gentlemen are elegantly
lodged themſelves ; and their tenants have far better farm-
houſes than in former times. All ranks, indeed, ſeem to
participate

---

* *Vide* Guthrie's Hiſtory of Scotland, and the authorities to which he
refers.

participate more of the comforts and conveniencies of life than their fathers—more than many of themfelves did in the days that are paft. From the communications of the clergy, this feems to be the cafe through all the land, which is one proof, among many others, that might be produced, of the futility and the falfehood of thofe complaints which fome malcontents have been pleafed to advance againft the government of Great Britain. But the period has now fortunately arrived when, in confequence of the vigilance of a vigorous adminiftration, and the good fenfe of an enlightened people, *Britain is faved*, and *Villany*, it is prefumed, will no longer dare to addrefs Ignorance; the period has now fortunately arrived, when the eye of loyalty is gladdened to fee, that they who had flocked to the ftandard of fedition are fcattered: Yes! the aufpicious period has arrived, when the Genius of our favoured ifle, in all her native majefty and magnanimity, can proclaim : " My children abhor the fanguinary fac-" tions of France. They difavow their principles, and de-" teft their practice. Principles fo bafe they leave for mif-" creants to teach, and madmen to believe. The feafon of " delufion is paft, and Britons love their native land. Many " wanderers have returned to the *Houfe of their Fathers*."

PARISH of PITTENWEEM,

(COUNTY OF FIFE.)

By the Rev. Mr JAMES NAIRNE.

Name, Situation, Soil, Air, &c.

THIS parifh is fituated in the prefbytery of St Andrew's, and Synod of Fife. There is no doubt that coal was, in old times, wrought where the town now ftands; and in the town there is a large cove, anciently called a *weem*. The pits produced by the working of the coal, and the ftriking natural objeƈt of the cove or weem, may have given birth to the name of the parifh. Whether Pittenweem originally was a parifh or not, is uncertain. The extent of the parifh is about an Englifh mile and a quarter in length, and about half a mile in breadth. It is bounded by the parifh of Anftruther-Wefter on the E.; by the fame and Carnbee on the N.; and by St Monance on the W.; the frith of Forth bounds it on the S. The grounds in the parifh are flat; the foil is in general black and loamy, and very fertile; the air is dry and healthy; the water remarkably foft, while that of the neighbouring towns is hard and brackifh. The moft prevalent diftemper among

among the inhabitants, is the *phthisis pulmonalis*, or consumption.

Fish, Shipping, &c.—The fish caught here have of late years been in much smaller number than formerly. Quantities are sometimes sent to the Edinburgh market. Within these few months, a plan was formed for catching turbot with nets, and so getting them alive to send up to London ; but the trials have not been as yet very successful. A considerable quantity of lobsters are caught here and in the neighbourhood, and sent to London.—The people here are generally fond of a seafaring life, but few have entered the navy as volunteers. They in general discover an aversion to the army, and I do not think more than 2 or 3 from the parish have inlisted during the last 30 years. At present the number of boats is only 5, and of vessels 4. From a record of the town, it appears that prior to 1639, the shipping here was considerable. From that year to the 1645, the town suffered greatly in that article. It appears from that record, that there belonged at least to the town 13 sail of large vessels ; all of which were either taken by the enemy, wrecked, or sold in consequence of the death of the commanders and mariners at the battle of Kilsyth.

Coal, &c.—The whole surface of the parish is supposed to cover a continued field of coal, which lies in a very extraordinary way, first taking one direction, then a contrary one, with different dipps. The property of it belongs to Sir John Anstruther. When it began to be wrought is uncertain. It is believed to have been wrought by Oliver Cromwell, who took possession of the Earl of Kelly's estate, of which it then formed a part ; and a pit is still to be seen, that goes by the name of Cromwell's pit. In past times, as much coal was taken out as could be procured without

a

a fire engine. After the working had been long difcontinued, Sir John Anftruther, about 20 years ago, erected a
fire engine, and has fince that period put out an immenfe
quantity of coal, and made falt to a large extent. There
are 9 falt-pans. The average expence for the coal and falt
working is about L. 50 weekly. The colliers are all free,
ftand engaged by the year, and are paid in proportion to
the work they refpectively perform. A good and laborious collier will earn about 18 s. a-week.

Population.—According to Dr Webfter, the number was
939. At prefent it is 1157, all refiding in the town, except 4
families. Males, 541; females, 616; that is, nearly 30
females for 27 males. The difproportion between the number of males and females, may be owing to a number of
the young men betaking themfelves to a feafaring life;
and there being no fhipping here, although there is a fea-
port, many of them fix the refidence for their families at
the places from whence they fail, and fo ceafe to appear on
the parifh-roll. Befides, no manufactures being carried on
in this place and neighbourhood, induces another clafs of
young men to repair to thofe towns where manufactures flou-
rifh, and to fettle there. The females are generally ftationary. The average of births is 37, of deaths 25; from
which it appears, that multiplying births by 26, and deaths
by 36, will produce numbers that would fall fhort of the
actual population.

From 1684 to 1690, the average of births is   -   43
From 1699 to 1709,   - - -   33$\frac{1}{2}$
From 1709 to 1719,   - - -   34
From 1719 to 1729,   - - -   38$\frac{1}{2}$
From 1729 to 1739,   - - -   30$\frac{1}{2}$
From 1739 to 1746,   - - -   28
From 1751 to 1761,   - - -   21

From

From 1761 to 1771, the average of births is - 20
From 1771 to 1780, - - . - 30
From 1780 to 1790, - - - 37

From this it appears, that the population at the end of the laſt century was greater than at preſent, and was double what it was at the middle of the current century. The failure of the herring-fiſhing, and of the French and Eaſt Country trade, diminiſhed, and the erection of Sir John Anſtruther's coal and ſalt works has increaſed the population. The average of marriages is 7.

The number of ſouls under 10 years of age, is - 260
From 10 to 20, - - - 200
From 20 to 50, - - - 439
From 50 to 70, - - - 224
From 70 to 90, - - - 34
The number of handicraftſmen, is - - 78
————— Of apprentices, - - 15
————— Of ſeamen, - - 72
————— Of fiſhermen, - - 12
————— Of miners and colliers, - 36
————— Of houſehold ſervants, - - 49
————— Of labouring ſervants, - 18
————— Of perſons born in England, and the
        Britiſh colonies, - - - 10
————— Of perſons born in other pariſhes, about 400
————— Of the Eſtabliſhed Church, - 1024
————— Of Seceders, - - 110
————— Of Epiſcopals, - - - 23

The population has increaſed very conſiderably within theſe 25 years, owing to the colliery and ſalt-works. The proportion between the annual births and whole population, is as 1 to 31; between the annual marriages and whole population, as 1 to 165; between the annual deaths and whole population, as 1 to 46; between bachelors and married
ried

ried men, (meaning by a bachelor, a man at the age of
25, and a houſeholder), as 1 to 18. Marriages, at an a-
verage, produce about 4 children. The number of inhabited houſes is 185, and the average of inhabitants for each
exceeds 6, and does not reach 7.

Agriculture.—Formerly the whole lands in the pariſh
were employed in raiſing corn. Two-thirds of the ground
was ſown with rough bear, and the remaining third with
wheat, oats, peas and beans. Still a larger proportion of
bear and barley is ſown than of any other grain. Of late
years green crops have been introduced. Fields are laid
down with clover and rye-graſs; cabbages and kail are
raiſed in the fields, for winter food. The average rent of
lands may be L. 1, 15 s. an acre. For the beſt, L. 2 : 12 : 6
is paid. The land is generally not incloſed, and the rent
is ſuch, that the proprietors imagine the increaſe would not
be a ſufficient compenſation for the expence of incloſing.

Stipend, Church, Poor, &c.—The value of the living,
including the glebe, and converting the victual at 10 s. the
boll (which is rather a low converſion) is L. 82. The
patron is Sir John Anſtruther. When the church was
built is uncertain. It certainly was not originally intended for a church. Concerning it there are two traditions,
one of which is, that it was ſome of the cloiſters of an
abbey, and the other, that it was the large barn or gra-
nary where the corns of the abbey were depoſited,
which laſt ſeems probable. The manſe was built about
the 1720, and received reparations afterwards. There are
22 proprietors, 7 of theſe are communities, viz. 3 kirk-
ſeſſions, 2 ſea and 2 trade ſocieties; 10 of the heritors reſide in the burgh.—The number of poor in the pariſh is
proportionally great. At the two laſt general diſtribu-
tions,

tions, upwards of 60 received charity. The funds for their ſupport, ariſing from lands and weekly collections, are from L. 50 to L. 60 Sterling yearly. The ſailors have a fund, conſiderably above L. 100 a year, for the ſupport of their own poor. They are able to make a very decent proviſion for the widows, both of ſhipmaſters, and of common mariners. This ſociety obtained about 6 years ago a royal charter. The trades have likewiſe a fund for their poor, which I believe is about L. 20 a-year. There are other two charitable ſocieties, but they are ſtill in infancy, and their annual produce is inconſiderable, but from the nature of them they muſt grow. One of theſe ſocieties is formed by the people connected with the colliery. This ſeems to be a moſt laudable and humane inſtitution, as accidents often happen at collieries, and it were to be wiſhed that it generally obtained at all public works.

Prices and Wages.—The prices of proviſions are nearly doubled within theſe 30 years. Beef, veal, mutton, lamb and pork, are generally ſold at 4 d. the lb.; geeſe, at 2 s. 6 d.; ducks at 8 d.; hens at 11 d.; and rabbits at 3 d.; butter is generally 8 d. the lb.; grain is generally 2 s. the boll below the Mid Lothian fiars. The fuel made uſe of is coal, and the price of 400 weight is 1 s. 3 d. carriage included. The wages of domeſtic female ſervants are generally L. 2, 10 s. a-year.

Miſcellaneous Obſervations.—The people in general are œconomical. Land is often changing proprietors, and the general price is 25 years purchaſe. The people do enjoy the comforts of ſociety, and are contented with their ſituation.—The roads in the pariſh are very indifferent. They

They are kept in repair by the ftatute-labour, which is generally commuted. Laft feffion of Parliament paffed a bill for turnpike roads in Fife, and the great road from E. to W. will pafs along by this town.—Kelp is made here, and the average quantity is 8 tons yearly.—The ifland of Mey, where a light is regularly kept, was a part of the priory, and is in the lordfhip of Pittenweem.—The principal bay neareft this is Largo Bay, and the fafeft harbour is Ely, 2 miles farther up the frith than Pittenweem.—One of the fleet of the Spanifh Armada came to this coaft in great diftrefs, and put in to the harbour of Anftruther Eafter, where the people were hofpitably treated.—In the year 1779, Paul Jones, with his little fquadron, lay for feveral hours off this harbour, about half a mile from the fhore. The pilot and his crew went off, believing they were Britifh fhips, and requefted fome powder, which was given. The crew were permitted immediately to return, but the pilot was detained, treated very uncivilly, and was not fet at liberty, until after the engagement Paul Jones had with our fleet.— There is a limeftone loch to the weftward of the town, which produces a confiderable quantity of lime annually.— The cove or weem within the burgh is fituated half way between the beach and an old abbey. It is large and capacious, confifting of 2 apartments. At the further end of the inner one, there is a well of excellent water. At the junction of the two apartments, there is a ftone-ftair, which carried you up a little way to a fubterraneous paffage, which led to the abbey, where was another ftair, which landed in the great dining hall of the abbey. The two ftairs ftill remain ; but of late years the fubterraneous paffage was deftroyed, by the inpending earth finking, and cutting off the communication. The fubterraneous

paffage,

paſſage, I think, might be about 50 yards in length. —Dr Douglas, the preſent Biſhop of Saliſbury, was born, and received the firſt principles of his education here. His father was in the mercantile line.—Pittenweem was conſtituted a royal burgh, by a charter from King James V. in 1547. In the town's charter-cheſt there are many old writings, which I cannot decipher. The following extraſt from their records I tranſmit:

'*Pittenweem, decimo-quarto Feb.* 1651.

' The bailies and council being convened, and having re-
' ceived information that his Majeſty is to be in progreſs
' with his court along the coaſt to-morrow, and to ſtay at
' Anſtruther houſe that night, have thought it expedient,
' according to their bounden duty, with all reverence and
' due reſpeſt, and with all the ſolemnity they can, to wait
' upon his Majeſty, as he comes through this his Majeſty's
' burgh, and invite his Majeſty to eat and drink as he paſſes;
' and for that effeſt, hath ordained, that the morn after-
' noon, the town's colours be put upon the bertiſene of the
' ſteeple, and that at three o'clock the bells begin to ring,
' and ring on ſtill till his Majeſty comes hither, and paſſes
' to Anſtruther: And ſicklike, that the miniſter be ſpoken
' to, to be with the bailies and council, who are to be in
' their beſt apparel, and with them a guard of twenty-four
' of the ableſt men, with partizans, and other twenty-four
' with muſquets, all in their beſt apparel, William Suther-
' land commanding as captain of the guard; and to wait
' upon his Majeſty, and to receive his Highneſs at the Weſt
' Port, bringing his Majeſty and court through the town,
' until they come to Robert Smith's yeet, where an table
' is to be covered with my Lord's beſt carpet; and that
' George Hetherwick have in readineſs of fine flour, ſome
' great

' great bunns, and other wheat-bread of the beſt order,
' baken with ſugar, cannell and other ſpices fitting; and
' that James Richardſon and Walter Airth have care to
' have ready eight or ten gallons of good ſtrong ale, with
' Canary, ſack, Rheniſh wine, tent, white and claret wines,
' that his Majeſty and his court may eat and drink; and that
' in the mean time, when his Majeſty is preſent, the guard
' do diligently attend about the court, and ſo ſoon as his
' Majeſty is to go away, that a ſign be made to Andrew
' Tod, who is appointed to attend the colours on the ſteeple
' head, to the effect he may give ſign to thoſe who attend
' the cannon of his Majeſty's departure, and then the haill
' thirty-ſix cannons to be all ſhot at once. It is alſo thought
' fitting, that the miniſter, and James Richardſon the oldeſt
' bailie, when his Majeſty comes to the table, ſhew the great
' joy and ſenſe this burgh has of his Majeſty's condeſcend-
' ence to viſit the ſame, with ſome other expreſſions of
' loyalty. All which was acted.'

PARISHES of St ANDREW'S, AND OF St
LEONARD'S

(COUNTY AND SYNOD OF FIFE, PRESBYTERY OF
ST ANDREW'S.)

By the Rev. JOHN ADAMSON, D. D. *firſt Miniſter of
St Andrew's.*

Name, Burgh, Univerſity, &c.

THE pariſh derives its name from the city of St Andrew's, formerly the ſeat of the primate of Scotland,
and alſo of the prior of St Andrew's, whoſe revenue greatly exceeded that of any other churchman in Scotlånd. The
revenue of the archbiſhop in 1651, was money Ster-
ling, L. 242 : 0 : 7$\frac{2}{12}$; wheat, bolls 489 ; bear, bolls 466 ;
and oats, bolls 1072 : and that of the prior in the ſame
year, was, money Sterling, L. 186 : 9 : 10$\frac{4}{12}$; wheat bolls,
bog-bear, bolls 2119 ; oats, bolls 2426 ; meal, bolls 1827 ;
and peaſe, bolls 55. Theſe two benefices were conjoined
in 1635, and the united revenue would now, at a moderate
converſion of the victual, amount to nearly L. 6000 Sterling

ling a-year *. The original name of this city was Mucrofs, *i. e.* " the promontory of boars," from *muc*, fignifying a fow or boar, and *rofs*, a land, promontory, or peninfula. Hence Kinrofs, " head of the peninfula," and Culrofs, back of the fame. But St Regulus, (vulgo St Rule), a monk of Patræ in Achaia, (warned, as is faid by a vifion to fail weftward, and) having landed in this neighbourhood, with fome relics of the Apoftle Andrew, about the year 370; and having been fuccefsful in converting the Piᵿs, Herguftus, the King, changed the name of Mucrofs into that of Kilrymont, *i. e.* Cella regis in monte; or Cella in monte regis; becaufe the king had given to Regulus and his companions a piece of high ground, adjoining to the harbour, on which he alfo erected a chapel and tower in honour of the monk, and bearing his name. The walls of St Rule's chapel, and the fquare tower, ftill remain. The tower is about 108 feet high, without any fpire; the outfide, from top to bottom, is of thin afhler work, the arches of the doors and windows, femicircular. The tower has been, at the expenfe of the Exchequer, within thefe few years repaired, that is, fuch of the afhler ftones as had fallen down, have been replaced, and all the joints filled up with cement; and a turnpike ftair reared within fide, from bottom to top, which is now covered with lead within a parapet of 4 feet. The exemplary virtue of Regulus and his company caufed a great refort of people to his chapel; and the name of the city was foon changed from Kilrymont to Kilrule, (Fanum vel Cella Reguli,) which name is ftill retained among the Scotch Highlanders. The name, Kilrule, continued

---

* A very full account of the archbifhoprick and priory, may be feen in Martin's Reliquiæ Divi Andreæ, M. S. a copy of which is in the Advocates library. Mr Martin of Clermont, the author, was fecretary to 2 fucceffive archbifhops of St Andrew's, and dates his book in 1685.

tinued in ufe till the Picts were extirpated by the Scots, who changed the name into St Andrew's. At this time the Metropolitan church *, which under the Picts had been at Abernethy, was tranflated to St Andrew's ; and the town was new peopled by a colony of Scots, particularly by thofe under the command of Fiffus Duffus, whofe great fervices to King Kennet were rewarded with all the lands lying in that fhire, formerly called Pichtlandia, and which that captain, from his own name, called Fifland. The wall furrounding the priory is pretty entire ; it is filled with baftions, fome round, and fome fquare. Part of the priors and fubpriors houfes yet remain. Adjoining to the priory, are the ruins of the cathedral, which was demolifhed by a mob, inflamed by a fermon of John Knox's. Both towers at the eaft end are ftill ftanding, having lately got a fmall repair. One only of the weftern towers now remains, and a part of the weft end of the outermoft fouth wall. All the arches in the eaftern towers are femicircular; thofe in the weftern tower, and in that part of the fouth wall adjoining to it, are pointed. The pits are very vifible, out of which have been dug the foundations of the 4 great pillars that fupported the cupola, and the foundations of the crofs ailes can be traced. The length of the cathedral from E. to W. as marked by the towers, as nearly as can be meafured, on very rough and unequal ground, is 350 feet ; and the breadth of the crofs ailes from N. to S. 160 feet.

* To the church of St Andrew's was given the Boarchafe; a tract of land fo called, extending from Pitmillie, nearly 5 miles E. from St Andrew's, to the new mill of Dairfie, 6 miles W. from the city, and from 2 to 5 miles in breadth. A confiderable village, and adjacent lands in the E. end of the parifh, have the general name of Boarhills. The arms of the city are a boar leaning on a tree ; likely that this part of the country was infefted with boars.

feet. On the north ſide of the town, a little weſt from the cathedral, on the brink of a perpendicular rock, are the ruins of the caſtle, known by the name of Cardinal Bethune's, be-cauſe therein he reſided, and therein was ſlain, in 1545, by Norman Leſly and his company. From the caſtle, weſtward, there anciently ran a ſtreet, called the Swallow-ſtreet, ſaid to be the reſidence of the merchants. It is now a public walk, between the walls of gardens and fields. The inhabited ſtreets are 3, running nearly from W. to E. but not quite parallel, as they all terminate on the ca-thedral, in the E. end: The South-ſtreet or Shoegate, Market-ſtreet, and North-ſtreet. Theſe ſtreets are inter-ſected at right angles, by narrower ſtreets called wynds. On the ſouth ſide of the South-ſtreet, nearer the weſt end, is a much admired ruin of a chapel, belonging to a convent of Gray friars; the roof is a continuation of the walls formed into a Gothic arch. Within the boundaries of this convent, is the public grammar-ſchool and ſchool-houſe. At the weſt end of the North-ſtreet, was a convent of Black friars, of which nothing now remains but a part of the garden wall. Immediately adjoining to the weſt port of the South-ſtreet, is a ſuburb, called Argyle, Argael, or Northgyle; to which reference is made in ſtating the popula-tion of this pariſh. The reaſon of the name is not known *.

The

* St Andrew's is a royal burgh, and for electing a member of the Bri-tiſh Parliament, is claſſed with Cupar, Perth, Forfar, and Dundee The government of the city is veſted in a provoſt, dean of guild, and 4 bailies, who with the town-treaſurer, are called the office-bearers in the council, and are elected annually at Michaelmas by the whole council. The dean of guild here has the precedence of the bailies, and is preſes of the council in abſence of the provoſt. No one is eligible into the council, who is not a burgeſs and guild brother, aſſeſſed in a portion of the public burdens within the city. The provoſt is the only member of the council who is not obliged to reſide. He has alſo this further privilege, that he

may

The great opulence of this city, in the times of Popery, may be conceived from this single circumstance, that there was an annual fair here, commencing in the beginning of April, which lasted for some weeks; and to which there resorted, from 2 to 3 hundred vessels, from all parts of the then commercial world. After the Reformation, the city gradually fell into

may be re-elected every year as long as he lives, while none of the other office-bearers can continue above 3 years in immediate succession. No councillor, that has at any time enjoyed a higher office, can afterward be elected into a lower. Besides the 7 office-bearers above mentioned, the council consists of 14 brethren of the guild, the convener of the trades for the time being, and the deacons for the time being, of the 7 following crafts, or incorporations, *viz.* smiths, wrights, bakers, tailors, shoemakers, weavers, and fleshers; amounting in all, to 29. The council annually undergoes a partial change, which is made in the following manner; on the Wednesday preceding the Michaelmas election, the subsisting council, of 29, adopt 3 by a majority of suffrages: these new councillors vote with the old council in the subsequent election of office-bearers. The council for the year after said election, must consist of these 3 new members, the new office-bearers, the office-bearers of the former year, the new convener, and 7 deacons of crafts, with such other guild brethren, as the magistrates please to name, for making up the number 29. The magistrates, for time immemorial, have been in use of naming the guild councillors of the former year; excepting 3, who must leave their places to the new members. When any office-bearer dies, his office must continue vacant until the following Michaelmas; but his seat in the council is filled up by another guild brother, at the nomination of the magistrates, who fill up every vacancy in the council occasioned by death; but when a councillor resigns, his successor is elected by the remaining 28. This is the set and established practice of the city. The proper office of the treasurer is that of factor or chamberlain of the town's revenue; and when he is appointed to discharge this office, he has a small salary. But the council, having found much inconveniency in the frequent change of this officer; and having also found, that it was sometimes a very delicate and difficult matter, to call the treasurer to account, when he had a vote in the elections, have of late years established a factor, who is not eligible into the council; and they have left the treasurer merely the name of office, with the political privileges annexed to the name.

into decay, from which it is now emerging, by the ſpirited
exertions of a few individuals. There are as yet no exports from St Andrew's, grain only excepted. But from
this port, chiefly is the eaſtern part of Fife, for 9 or 10
miles, ſupplied with wood and iron, which formerly were
purchaſed at Dundee on the river Tay, or at Ely on the
Forth ; and the ſhore-dues, which 20 years ago did not
produce to the corporation above L. 10 Sterling a-year, are
now let in leaſe for L. 66. Several veſſels, from 40 to 200
tons, have within theſe 2 years been built at this port,
which are employed by the inhabitants in the wood and
coaſting trades. In the ſpring of 1792, Meſſrs Robertſons
of Glaſgow, eſtabliſhed in this city a factory for ſowing and
tambouring muſlin. In a few months, they collected between 3 and 4 ſcore apprentices, girls from 5 to 14 years
of age, who receive weekly from 1 s. 3 d. to 2 s. 6 d.
according to their age and progreſs. The number of apprentices is ſtill increaſing *.

But the chief ſupport of this city is the Univerſity, and
the conflux of ſtrangers, who here find excellent teachers in
all different branches. The Univerſity which is the oldeſt
in Scotland, being founded in 1444 †, formerly conſiſted of
3 colleges, *viz.* St Salvator's, founded by James Kennedy,
Biſhop of St Andrew's, in 1458; St Leonard's college, founded by Prior Hepburn, 1512 ; and St Mary's, founded by
Biſhop John Hamilton, 1552. In each of theſe colleges were
lecturers in theology, as well as in philoſophy, languages, &c.
In the reign of James VI. 1579, under the direction of George
Buchanan, the Univerſity was new modelled ; and St Mary's
college was appropriated to the ſtudy of theology, and is therefore diſtinguiſhed by the name of the Divinity-College, or the

New

---

* Number of apprentices, in May 1793, 110.

† Fordun mentions an univerſity at Andrew's, in 1410.

New College. In 1747, on a petition from the masters of the 2 colleges of St Salvator's, and St Leonard's, the Parliament united these 2 colleges into one society, under the designation of the United College. These colleges are independent of each other in their revenues and discipline. The Senatus Academicus, or University meeting, consists of the principals and professors of both colleges, which have a common interest in the library. The preses of this meeting is the Rector or his depute. The higher academical degrees are granted by the University. The Rector confers the degree of Master of Arts, on the recommendation of the Faculty of Arts in the United College. The Dean and Faculty confer the degree of Bachelor of Arts. The Rector is chosen annually, on the first Monday of March, by the Comitia of the University, consisting of the Rector, Principals and Professors of both colleges, with the students of divinity, of moral and of natural philosophy; all these masters and students are divided, according to the place of their birth, into 4 nations, Fifans, Angusians, Lothians, and Albans, which last class comprehends all who belong to none of the first 3. Each nation chooses an Intrant, and the 4 Intrants name the Rector. If the votes of the Intrants, are equally divided, the last Rector, who is preses of the Comitia, has the casting voice. The only persons eligible into the office of rectorate, are the principals and the professors of divinity, who are designed Viri majoris dignitatis ac nominis, or Viri Rectorales. The Rector immediately after his instalment, (which is performed by his putting on the gown of office *, being a purple robe

with

---

* The principals and professors, in session time, wear black gowns, like those used by the clergy in Scotland The students in the United College wear gowns of red or scarlet freeze, without sleeves. The students of divinity have no distinguishing garb or dress.

with a large hood, the hood and borders of the robe lined with crimson satin; and by receiving the oath *de fideli*,) names deputes, from among the Viri Rectoralis, and affessors from the Senatus Academicus. He is a civil judge in the University, before whom may be brought complaints against masters, students, or supposts of the University. To his court, there lies also an appeal from the judgments of either college, in matters of discipline. In the rectoral court, the affessors have a deliberative voice; but the rector is not bound by their opinion or advice, having the power of decision entirely in his own person. The Court of Session have shown themselves very tender in receiving appeals, or advocations from the Rector, in matters of discipline over the students. The revenue of each of the colleges is partly in tithes, partly in property-lands. The revenue from tithes is always decreasing, by augmentations of stipend, granted by the Commissioners of Teinds, to the parochial ministers. In each college, there are apartments for lodging the students, rent free; there is also a public table for the bursars on the foundation. In the United College, there is a separate table for such students as choose to board themselves, at about L. 10 Sterling for the session, consisting of $6\frac{1}{2}$ months; at each table, one of the masters presides.

St Andrew's has many advantages as a place of study. The University library is well stored with books in all the sciences, to which every student has access, for a small yearly payment. The masters are eminent in their several departments. There are very few avocations to the youth, who are not however restrained from innocent amusements, which are properly regulated by the masters. The person, the character, and actions of every student, are

well

well known by the masters ; so that any tendency to riot
or dissipation is immediately checked ; attention, diligence,
and good behaviour, are observed, encouraged and honour-
ed ; and the public examination of each class, in the Uni-
versity-hall, at the end of the session, excites and maintains
a spirit of application and emulation. The situation of the
place is very healthy ; there are dry walks at all seasons,
the air is pure ; the streets are spacious and open ; and the
water, which in great plenty is brought into the town,
from adjacent springs, by leaden pipes, is excellent. Putrid
or malignant diseases are scarcely ever seen in St Andrew's. Epidemical diseases of any kind are very rare,
and also much milder than in other places of the same size
and population.

Coal is in great abundance within a few miles of the
city ; much also is imported from both sides of the Forth,
chiefly from Dysart, Alloa, and Borrowstounness. The
proper weight of a St Andrew's cart-load, or boll of coals,
is 75 stone, or 1200 pounds. The average price of this
cart-load, including carriage, has hitherto been from the
adjacent mines, 5 s. Dysart, 5 s. 4 d. Alloa, 5 s. 10 d.
Borrowstounness, 6 s. 4 d *. The harbour has of late been
much improved, and the mole extended farther towards
the sea. A spirit of enterprise has arisen among the inhabitants, new houses on an improved plan of size, accommodation, and elegance, are yearly rising, and there is every
reason to believe, that St Andrew's will continue to flourish, and will gradually regain its former lustre.

Extent,

* During the winter 1792-3, St Andrew's suffered under the general
complaint, of scarce and dear coals. The moor coals were raised to 6 s. 6 d.
Dysart and Alloa, to 8 s. 9 d. Borrowstounness as high as 11 s.

Extent, Surface, Soil, Climate, &c.—The parish of St Andrew's forms a parallelogram nearly, the ends of which pointing towards E. by S. and W. by N. broadest at the west end. The length from E. to W. about 10 miles; city of St Andrew's nearly in the middle of the north side; greatest breadth nearly 4 miles. Through the whole length of the parish there is an acclivity from N. to S. forming, with little interruption, one large corn-field, in which are found all the varieties of soil, clay, loam, sand, &c. The sandy soil is chiefly in the neighbourhood of the city, and adjoining to the mouths of Eden and Kenlowie. These sandy fields seem, at some remote period, to have been collected by the small rivers, and, by gradual accumulation, to have diverted or narrowed the course of the waters. All these fields, however, are ploughed, and, by proper attention, produce good crops of corn, excepting a small spot of downs or bents, which is opposed to the sea on the east side of the harbour, and a larger tract of the same running from the N. W. corner of the city, which produces some pasture for sheep, and forms the links, well known to golfers. Along the east side of these links, in a direction nearly S. and N. is a flat firm sandy beach, about $1\frac{1}{2}$ mile long, terminated on the N. by the mouth of Eden. This beach is known by the name of the West Sands, and is almost entirely covered by the sea at spring tides. From the southern extremity of this beach, to the east end of the parish, with the interruption only of the harbour, and another short sandy beach, called the East Sands, running along the first mentioned spot of downs or bents, the shore outward from high water mark is lined with rough and ragged shelving rocks, mostly covered with sea-weed, and the coast inwards is very rocky and bold, the face of it in some places perpendicular rock to the height of 30 or 40 feet, yet the plough comes to the very brink, having a sufficien-

cy

cy of foil. The boundaries of this parish to the W. and S. terminate in moors, covered with short heath and furze. Some parts of these moors have of late been limed and ploughed, and have yielded a few profitable crops of corn. The soil there, however, is in general too cold and wet for retaining clover in winter. The greater part of these moors seem fit only for being planted with wood, and the proprietors are beginning to attend to that useful improvement of waste land. The air, climate, and salubrity of the whole parish is nearly the same with that of the city. In common with all the eastern part of the island, this parish is well acquainted with the cold damp easterly winds, or haars of April and May. These haars seldom fail to affect those who have ever had an ague, though in no part of the world are agues less frequent than here. The air of this corner is, in general, too sharp for phthysical constitutions.

Springs, Rivers, Sea Coast, Fish.—There are several ochre springs on the high grounds in the east end of the parish, some of which have been frequented by scorbutic and scrofulous patients, but few have boasted of benefit from them, more than they would have derived from the moderate exercise of walking a mile or two in the fresh funny mornings of April and May. There are no lakes, canals, or rivers, deserving the name. In Eden and Kenlowie, is a considerable number of trout; in the embouchure of Eden is a flat sandy bay, abounding with large flounders; in this bay, at low water, is gathered a very great quantity of cockles and mussels, both of which are prized as an article of food for the common people, and of delicacy among the better sort. The gatherers, after carrying them two miles, sell them in St Andrew's at 2 d. the measured peck. The mussels are used by the fishermen as bait for haddocks. In the course of Eden, for about a mile from its mouth, salmon

mon are caught, but in no great quantity. The fiſhing, indeed, has not been profecuted with much ſpirit. In the
bay or creek of Eden, the ſea flows ſo high, as to admit
veſſels of 40 or 50 tons, many of which there unload barley for a diſtillery, coals and lime for the neighbouring farmers, who thereby ſave 2 or 3 miles of land-carriage, and
are thus enabled in a few days to convey to their farms as
much of theſe neceſſary articles, as formerly occupied their
ſervants and horſes for the greater part of the ſummer;
which ſeaſon is now ſpent in ploughing and hoeing. In the
eaſt end of the pariſh alſo, are ſome ſmall creeks among the
rocks, where veſſels of inferior ſize deliver lime and coals.
—St Andrew's Bay, until within theſe few years, abounded in haddocks, with which 5 or 6 boats, 4 men in each,
ſupplied St Andrew's, Cupar, and the north ſide of Fife for
10 miles. Theſe haddocks were of a ſmaller ſize than
thoſe in the frith of Forth, but of a better flavour in the o-
pinion of the people of this place ; they formed the chief
article of animal food to the poorer ſort, and were always
ſeen at every table ; but of late this ſpecies of fiſh has almoſt entirely deſerted this bay, as well as many other
parts of the eaſtern coaſt of Scotland ; the cauſe has never
been diſcovered *. Lammas herrings have, in our memory, been caught in immenſe quantities within this bay, on
the coaſt of Kingſbarns pariſh ; but very ſeldom, during
theſe laſt 20 years, has that fiſhing there been worth mentioning. The rocks, from the bottom of the bay to the
eaſtern extremity of the pariſh, abound with limpets and
periwinkles of different kinds ; alſo with lobſters, and
ſome varieties of crabs, of which the partan only is uſed
for food. The ſhallow water, over a ſandy bottom, affords
great

---

* Some old people here ſay, that about the beginning of this century,
the haddocks in like manner deſerted this bay for a year or two.

great plenty of flat fish, such as flounders, soles, skate, halibut, turbot.   Near the rocky shore. many small cod, both red and grey; in deeper water, ling and larger cod.   All these kinds of fish are sold by tale or by hand.   Some of the larger ling, cod, and halibut by weight, from 2 d. to 3 d. the pound.   Since the departure of the haddocks, the fishermen have become poor, and either unable or unwilling to profecute their trade to any extent ; and what adds to their poverty, incapacity, and languor is, that, on many occasions, an unexpected blaft of north-eaft wind, which raifes tremenduous waves in this bay, has torn in pieces all their lines *.

Sea

* The moft memorable cafe of this kind in our days happened on 4th Nov. 1765.   The morning was quiet ; all the boats went to fea, and dropt their lines.   While lying on their oars, about 7 o'clock it began to fcowl in the N. E.; the fifhermen faw reafon to apprehend a ftorm, and immediately began to gather up their fifhing tackle ; but before they could accomplifh this, the gale had increafed fo as to raife immenfe curled and broken waves.   Each boat made for the neareft beach or cove between rocks.   Two of them, very near each other, had got fo clofe to the Eaft Sands, that the people on the beach had begun to wade into the water in order to affift their friends ; when the one boat, raifed on the top of a prodigious wave, was driven right over head of the other.   The uppermoft boat was inftantly either buried in the fand, or carried back by the reflux, fo that no part of it, or of its crew, was ever again feen.   The undermoft boat was drawn afhore by the women, all the people alive. The writer of this has feen and felt the wound made on the head of a boy in the ftern of the undermoft boat, by the keel of the uppermoft.   On this occafion, of 5 boats, 3 were totally loft, and the other two much damaged, and moft of the tackle loft.   Twelve men were loft, of whom one was unmarried, the other eleven left widows and 28 children.   Many of the men who efcaped with life were feverely bruifed.   A fubfcription was immediately fet on foot among individuals and focieties in St Andrew's, which, with donations from other burghs, and from noblemen and gentlemen in different parts of the country, produced L. 317: 7 : 9$\frac{3}{4}$ Sterling. This money the fubfcribers committed to truftees, who, after giving an immediate fupply to the diftreffed families, fettled a half yearly penfion on
the

Sea-weeds.—The fea-rocks in this parifh are covered with the common weed, which ufed formerly to be cut every third year, and burnt for kelp. The demand for this article feems to be diminifhed ; as for feveral years paft, the corporation of St Andrew's have not been able to get their fea-weed let to any undertaker. This weed the farmers never cut for manure ; and the tangle, though its broad leaved tops are feen in great quantities on the furface of the fea, yet is fo fituated at the farther extremity of the rocks, and grows in fo deep water, that they can neither cut nor tear it up. Every gale of wind, however, from any eafterly point, and every violent agitation of the fea, throws upon the beach and into every creek, all the way from the mouth of Eden to the eaft end of the parifh, a great quantity of tangle mixed with many other weeds, which are carefully gathered ; and, according to the feafon of the year, are fpread on the grafs, mixed in dunghills, or tilled down for barley or potatoes. The Corporation of St Andrew's have hitherto permitted the towns people in common to gather, tax free, whatever fea-weed is thrown in between the mouth of Eden and the eaft fands adjoining to the harbour ; the remainder of the fhore is private property of the feveral heritors, according to the extent of their refpective lands.

Land-

the widows and on the children, until they fhould be capable of doing for themfelves. And fo faithfully and prudently has this fund been managed, that though the widows have regularly received fuch a penfion as, with their own labour, has been fufficient for their fupport, though the children have been helped forward in life, though different fums have been applied for repairing the fifhermens loffes at fea, and though the grandchildren of fome of the fufferers have alfo been occafionally relieved, yet there remains of the ftock about L. 60 Sterling, and the number of penfioners is, by death and otherwife, reduced to four.

Land-marks, &c.—On the lands of Brownhills and Kinkell, which form the firſt riſing ground eaſtward from St Andrew's harbour, there are a few inſulated rocks from 20 to 40 feet high, and of nearly equal breadth ; one about half a mile from the harbour, called the Maiden Stone, which ſtands alone ; and about half a mile further, the Rock and Spindle, adjoining to one another. Theſe are cloſe upon the beach, above ordinary high water mark, and are of very little uſe as land-marks, becauſe the cloſely adjacent land is much higher than they. About a mile farther eaſt, among the rocks of Boarhills, near to a creek where ſmall veſſels may enter and unload, is ſuch another inſulated rock, called Buddo, which is generally marked on ſea-charts, becauſe it is better ſeen at ſea, the adjacent land being flat. This rock is perforated by a kind of gateway, 4 or 5 feet wide.

The chief land-marks in this pariſh are the ſteeples of St Andrew's, and a ſmall obeliſk of ſtones, on the higheſt part of the farm of Bahymont, about 2 miles S. E. from the town *.

Minerals, Caves.—Freeſtone is often dug from the ſea rocks ; but in general the texture of it is very open and porous, or it crumbles and diſſolves when expoſed to water or humid air, after the external incruſtation is broken. On Strathkinneſs Moor, about 3 miles from town, and on Nydie Hill, which is a greater elevation of the ſame moor, to the weſtward, are excellent quarries of freeſtone for builders, door-cheeks, windows, ſtairs, and grave-ſtones. Theſe quarries require very little tirring. In ſome places the rock has no covering of earth. Many marks of very old quarries. It is ſuppoſed, that out of ſome of theſe were dug the

ſtones

* There have occaſionally been found on the ſhore ſome petrified ſea-weeds and a few years ago, part of the trunk, at its diviſion into two main branches, of what ſeems to be a petrified tree. It was by the late Honourable Colonel John Nairne, made the door-poſt of a grotto in a garden of this city, now belonging to Mr Erſkine of Cambo.

ſtones wherewith St Regulus's tower is faced all round. On Denhead moor, in the S. W. corner of this pariſh, and on the confines between it and that of Cameron, a coal-mine belonging to Mr Martin of Denbrae, has ſometimes been wrought to a ſmall extent. On the ſame moor, Mr Durham of Largo has a coal. None of theſe are now oc-cupied. Two or three years ago, ſome Engliſhmen, judg-ing from the appearance of the ground, expected to find coal in many different parts of the pariſh, and entered into contract with ſeveral proprietors ; but, after expending a good deal of money in boring, &c. they were diſappointed. In the face of a freeſtone rock, overhanging the ſea-beach between the caſtle and the harbour, there is an excavation ſeemingly artificial; it is nearly round, about 10 feet dia-meter, and the ſame height. On the eaſt ſide of it, the rock is ſhaped into the form of a table or altar, and on the S. W. ſide is an aperture of the ordinary ſize and ſhape of a door, by which you go into a ſmall cloſet, ſuppoſed to have been the cell of a hermit ; the acceſs to it is now ve-ry difficult. In the face of the rock on which the caſtle ſtands, are the remains of ſuch another excavation ; from the eaſt ſide of this, is a perforation through which a man may eaſily creep, into a ſmaller one, which is alſo open to the ſea, over which the rock hangs ; this cave alſo is of very difficult acceſs. About a mile eaſt from the harbour, there is a natural cave of eaſier acceſs, Kinkell cave. The mouth is to the north ; the direction of the cave is ſouth-wards ; the ſhelving of the freeſtone roof makes a croſs ſec-tion of the cave, triangular ; there is a continual dropping from the roof.

Population.—According to Dr Webſter's report, the number of ſouls then was 4590. I have had acceſs to no data, by which the ancient ſtate of the population of this pariſh can be gueſſed at. A proceſs now in dependence before

the

the Court of Seffion, for an alteration and divifion of the
parifh church, has caufed a very minute inquiry into the
prefent population. The numbers reported on oath by the
the tellers, are as follows, *viz.*

Number of fouls in the parifh,
In the town and royalty,	-	2390
In the fuburbs of Argyle,	-	129
In the country,	- -	1431
		3950

Children incapable of going to church,
In St Andrew's,	- -	288
In Argyle,	- -	14
In the country.	- -	202
		504

Suppofed neceffarily detained at home,
In St Andrew's,	- -	189
In Argyle,	- -	16
In the country,	- -	231
		436

Diffenters of all denominations,
In St Andrew's,	- -	91
In Argyle,	- -	5
In the country,	- -	22
		118*

Within

* When the three laft claffes are deduced from the total, there remain
2892, who are or ought to be attending public worfhip in the Eftablifhed
Church, and for that number the purfuing heritors infifted, that there
fhould be accommodation in the parifh-church. The defenders alleged,
that accommodation is needed for no more than 1800, being about two-
thirds of the examinable perfons. The number of parochial communicants at the Lord's Supper, is between 1500 and 1600, and the church, as
now feated, cannot contain above that number The iffue of this procefs
will determine what proportion the Lords of Seffion judge that the fize of
a parifh-church fhould bear to the number of inhabitants. By one interlocutor they have already ordered an architect to vifit this parifh-church,
and report whether he can find accommodation in it for 2500.

Within thefe 12 months, there were alive in the city of St Andrew's, 40 perfons above fourfcore years of age. There is now alive at Boarhills one man aged 96.—By frequent changes of feffion-clerks, and from other circumftances, the parochial records of births, deaths and marriages, are imperfect and defective. There follows an abftract from thefe records at different periods, where any competent number of years could be traced in fucceffion. The marriages are recorded only when the bride was refiding in the parifh, and no regifter of the dead was kept in this parifh, in the beginning of this century.

| Years. | Births. | | | Mar. |
	Males.	Fem.	Total	
1699	45	53	98	26
1700	33	41	74	28
1701	51	57	108	20
1702	60	55	115	23
1703	49	55	104	17
1704	45	53	98	17
1705	52	52	104	24
1706	52	57	109	26
1707	62	48	110	22
1708	57	58	115	28
1709	63	60	123	31
1710	52	48	100	21
1711	54	57	111	39
1712	70	56	126	21
1713	56	49	105	32
1714	70	61	131	34
1715	47	47	94	21
1716	62	58	120	34
1717	69	67	136	34
1718	83	54	137	32
	1132	1086	2218	530

20 years births. Males, 1132. Females, 1086. Total, 2218. Average, 110$\frac{9}{10}$.—Proportion of males to females, as 11 to 10.553.

20 years

20 years marriages, 530.—Average, 26¼.

Average of births, 110.9 × 26 = 2883.4.

Births, greateſt number, *anno* 1718, = 137 × 26 = 3562.

The average of marriages in the above table, differs but little from that in the ſubſequent; but the average of births conſiderably exceeds that of more modern times, and there is no reaſon to believe, that the pariſh was more populous fourſcore years ago than it is now. The reaſon of the difference may perhaps be, that the Seceders negleƈt to have the birth of their children regiſtered in the parochial records:

Yrs.	Births. Males	Fem.	Total.	Deaths. Males	Fem.	Total.	Mar.
1743	56	36	92	24	28	52	27
1744	54	59	113	28	32	60	33
1745	45	41	86	33	39	72	17
1746	52	57	109	45	64	109	27
1747	59	51	110	26	40	66	19
1748	56	54	110	65	62	127	34
1749	57	44	101	50	47	97	38
1750	63	65	128	34	38	72	34
1751	55	52	107	49	44	93	28
1752	51	40	91	55	63	118	24
1753	57	67	124	43	52	95	31
1754	55	54	109	35	52	87	19
1755	58	54	112	38	47	85	22
1756	46	67	113				19
1757	67	47	114				18
1758	38	50	88	57	55	112	
7759	68	52	120	48	29	77	
1760	53	47	100	54	49	103	
	986	937	1923	684	741	1425	390

18 years births. Males, 986. Females, 937. Total, 1923. Average, 106⅝.—Proportion of males to females, as 11 to 10.453.

16 years deaths. Males, 684. Females, 741. Total, 1425. Average, 89 1/16.—Proportion of males to females, as 11 to 11.916.

15 years marriages, 390. Average, 26.

Average

Average of births, $106\frac{5}{8} \times 26 = 2777\frac{2}{7}$. Ditto of deaths, $89\frac{1}{16} \times 36 = 3206\frac{1}{4}$.

Births, greateſt number in 1750,—$128 \times 26 = 3328$.

Deaths, greateſt number in 1748,—$127 \times 36 = 4572$.

Yrs.	Males	Births. Fem.	Total.	Males	Deaths. Fem.	Total.	Mar.
1774	41	34	75	35	46	81	25
1775	50	55	105	41	42	83	24
1776	54	46	100	32	46	78	25
1777	59	53	112	59	61	120	27
1778	55	53	108	24	38	62	22
1779	48	46	94	33	33	66	24
1780	52	48	100	28	48	76	24
1781	47	46	93	37	45	82	27
1782	53	43	96	38	48	86	23
1783	59	44	103	19	27	46	30
1784	72	50	122	52	45	97	26
1785	50	69	119	33	54	87	30
1786	63	51	114	38	38	76	17
1787	68	51	119	41	36	77	12
1788	62	50	112	38	42	80	29
1789	69	63	132	27	35	62	31
1790	51	67	118	41	38	79	26
1791	50	50	100	50	46	96	22
	1003	919	1922	666	768	1434	445

18 years births. Males, 1003. Females, 919. Total, 1922. Average, $106\frac{7}{9}$.—Proportion of males to females, as 11 to 10.078.

18 years deaths. Males, 666. Females, 768. Total, 1434. Average, $79\frac{2}{3}$. Proportion of males to females, as 11 to 12.684.

18 years marriages, 445. Average, $24\frac{13}{18}$.

Average of births, $106\frac{7}{9} \times 26 = 2776\frac{2}{3}$.

Average of deaths, $79\frac{2}{3} \times 36 = 2868$.

N. B. Theſe numbers are far below the actual number of fouls, $= 3950$.

Births, greateſt number in 1789,—$132 \times 26 = 3432$.

Deaths, greateſt number in 1777,—$120 \times 36 = 4320$.

As

As the average of births in thefe two periods is fo equal, the average of marriages fo nearly the fame, and the average of deaths in the latter period is fo much below that of the former, the prefumption is, that the number of inhabitants is increafing. And the reafon why the average of deaths has of late years decreafed, may be, that the common people now ufe more generous food, are better clothed, and more attentive to cleanlinefs in their perfons, their manners, and their dwellings. By the foregoing table it appears, that the modern average of births in this parifh is to the real number of inhabitants as 1 to 37 very nearly; average of marriages as 1 to 160 nearly; average of deaths, as 1 to 49½ nearly.—The number of artificers in the parifh, mafters and freemen, is nearly as follows : Smiths, including 1 watchmaker, 2 tinmen, 2 workers in brafs, and 3 glovers, incorporated with the fmiths, 21; wrights, carpenters, and mafons, 50; bakers, 19; flefhers, 19; tailors, 23; fhoemakers, 34; weavers, 52; faddler, 1.—Befides the profeffor of medicine in the univerfity, there are in St Andrew's other 2 regular phyficians; all the three practife in midwifery and furgery, as occafion offers; one apothecary, who is alfo a practitioner in phyfic. Several fhopkeepers vend a few of the more common medicines, fuch as every neighbour prefcribes to another; 5 writers or attornies; 2 meffengers at arms. The courts of law here are the Bailie court, the Dean of Guild court, Juftice of Peace court, and the commiffary court for the diocefe of St Andrew's, whofe regular place of meeting is the church of St Salvator's College.—There are no known inftances of people dying here for want, nor of murder, nor of fuicide, excepting the cafe of one man who hanged himfelf about fourfcore years ago; his body was diffected, and his fkeleton remains in the univerfity library. No emigrations from this parifh; and though,

though, as in every other town, a few houſes may be occaſionally unoccupied, yet in general there is a demand, and the building of new houſes is found a profitable application of money.—The modern average of ſtudents at the philoſophy college is 100; of ditto at the divinity college is 48. No regular authentic liſt of ſtudents at the philoſophy college has been kept till of late years; but by examining the matriculation book, and allowing that the number of new ſtudents formerly bore the ſame proportion to the total that it now does, it ſhould ſeem that the average of ſtudents at the philoſophy college was, from 1738 to 1747, 56; from 1757 to 1766, 79; and from 1773 to 1782, 88 : Hence it appears, that the reſort of ſtudents to St Andrew's continues to be on the increaſe. The greateſt number in any one year, in recent times, is 137. The number of ſtudents in divinity alſo increaſes, as the average from 1773 to 1782, is only 30. The greateſt number in any one year during that period is 35. Greateſt number ſince that time, 54. The greateſt number of ſtudents at the univerſity in any one year, 179.—Beſides the parochial Eſtabliſhed miniſters, there is in St Andrew's an Epiſcopal clergyman, who has an annual penſion from Queen Anne's bounty, and a miniſter of the Burgher Seceders; there is but one family of Antiburgher Seceders.

Productions.—There are no old' plantations of wood in this pariſh. Several young plantations are going on, particularly in the eaſtern part of the pariſh by Dr John Hill, Profeſſor of Humanity, Edinburgh, on his lands of Kinglaſſie; John Campbell, Eſq; writer to the Signet, on his lands of Smiddygreen; James Anderſon, Eſq; Advocate, on Newbigging; Rev. Dr Duncan, Epiſcopal clergyman in Dundee, on Stonywynd; and Mr Turnbull, jointly with his tenant John Adamſon, on Burnſide fide of Boarhills: In this laft cafe, the moor was under leafe as a part of the farm; the tenant, without any deduction of rent, was at the expenfe of enclofing and planting, and continues to have the burden of defending; at the end of 50 years, the tenant's heirs get half the value of the wood. The ufual varieties of foreft-trees are among thefe plantations; but the Scotch fir is in greateft quantity. All the ufual pot-herbs are in great plenty. Gardening becomes yearly an object of more attention. Every farmer raifes wheat, barley or bear, oats, peafe and beans, turnips, potatoes, clover. The quantity of land fown with wheat increafes every year. Barley is now more cultivated than bear; but perhaps more than either, a mixture of the two, which is called ramble. Rutabaga, or Swedifh turnip, has been tried, but not perfifted in. The drill-hufbandry is followed only with the potatoes and turnip, and a few beans. The parifh, including the city, needs an importation of meal, but it fpares barley.

The number of black cattle in this parifh, as in all the neighbourhood, is yearly diminifhing; as the farmers now do all their work with horfes alone; two of which are yoked in the plough, and guided by the ploughman. Within thefe 30 years, each plough had 2 horfes and 4 oxen, which always needed a goadman. The culture of graffes and of wheat has gradually expelled the fheep from this parifh, all the land that could yield them any tolerable pafture being now fubjected to the plough. There remains not a ftore-flock in the whole parifh. A few are kept on the Links of St Andrew's, chiefly for the fhambles, the prefent tackfman being a butcher. Some of the farmers alfo graze a few for the butchers *.

Stipends,

---

* About the beginning of March, (feldom fooner), the farmers begin to fow oats and beans. The fowing of barley and bear terminates in the end

Stipends, Heritors, School, Poor, &c.—The parifh is a collegiate charge, both minifters officiating in one church, which appears to have been built in the year 1112, in the form of a crofs, the north aile of which was taken down long ago The King is patron of the 1ft charge, to which belongs the parochial ftipend. The magiftrates and town-council, of the 2d charge ; the ftipend of which is paid out of the Town's patrimony. The 1ft minifter's ftipend is wholy victual, confifting of wheat, 14 bolls 2 pecks ; oats, 63 bolls 3 firlots 2 pecks $1\frac{1}{4}$ lippies ; bear, 65 bolls 3 firlots. The 2d minifter's is in money, *viz.* 1300 merks, L. 72 : 4 : $5\frac{4}{11}$ Sterling. The firft minifter has a glebe of 4 acres, now let at L. 2, 10 s. the acre. Nei-ther of the minifters have a manfe; although it ap-pears from the prefbytery-records, that there were man-fes for both 150 years ago. The 2d minifter has alfo the teind of the fifhes brought into the harbour for fale, for which the fifhermen were wont to pay L. 2 Sterling ; of late years they have paid nothing. The church got a con-fiderable repair, with a new roof, in the year 1749. Since that time, fome partial repairs. A procefs, as formerly mentioned, is now in dependence for dividing the area, and enlarging the auditory of the church. The number of he-ritors and portioners in the landward parifh is about 45, of whom 10 are refident The proprietors and portioners of burgh and prior acres cannot eafily be reckoned. Every year makes alterations among them ; and the number is gradually diminifhing, becaufe the acres that fucceffively

come

end of May new ftyle. Wheat feed generally begins about Michaelmas. Wheat harveft for the moft part begins before the end of Auguft ; and barley harveft foon after. Few feafons now permit the fields to be clear-ed before the end of October ; though all the old leafes oblige the tenant; to remove at Michaelmas.

come into market are generally bought up by thofe who
have already fome property in the vicinity.—In the city of
St Andrew's is a grammar-fchool, in the patronage of the
town-council. The rector enjoys, rent free, a houfe, in
which may be, and fometimes have been, accommodated
25 boarders. A garden, fufficiently large for the family,
and a falary of L. 16 : 3 : 4 Sterling, paid out of the funds
of the corporation, out of which alfo are paid all the repairs
of the fchool and fchool-houfe. Mr Mouat, the prefent incumbent, who entered on his office about Candlemas 1791,
has already recommended himfelf fo much to the general
efteem, and to the favour of the patrons, that they have
freely conferred on him an yearly addition of L. 100 Scots,
making his falary L 25 Sterling. The number of his boarders is always increafing. The fchool-fees have not been
raifed for time immemorial; 2 s. 6 d. a-quarter, and a
gratuity at Candlemas, at leaft equal to the quarterly payment. The fcholars, in general, pay at leaft 5 s. a-quarter, and a Candlemas gratuity, according to their rank and
fortune, from 5 s. even as far as 5 guineas, when there is
a keen competition for the Candlemas crown. The king,
i. e. He who pays moft, reigns for 6 weeks, during which
period he is not only intitled to demand an afternoon's play
for the fcholars once a-week, but he has alfo the royal privilege of remitting all punifhments. The number of
fcholars is from 50 to 60. The mafter has no other perquifites but his houfe, garden, falary, and fchool-fees. The
corporation allow him an extra L. 7, in part payment of an
affiftant.

There is alfo in the patronage of the town-council another fchool for Englifh, writing and arithmetic. The prefent fchool was built, chiefly at the expenfe of George
Dempfter, Efq; of Dunichen, late provoft of the city and
member of Parliament for the diftrict. The mafter's falary

is

is 200 merks. *i. e.* L. 11 : 2 : 2$\frac{8}{12}$ Sterling, paid by the Exchequer. This ſalary, however, belongs to him more properly as precentor in the town church, than as ſchoolmaſter. The corporation, out of reſpect to the abilities, aſſiduity, and ſucceſs of Mr Smith, the preſent incumbent, have given him out of their funds an additional L. 5 Sterling a-year. The loweſt fees at this ſchool are 1 s. 6 d. a-quarter, and a gratuity at the new year. Mr Smith has, at extra hours, what is called a private ſchool, or ſecond claſſes, at 2 s. 6 d. the quarter. Number of ſcholars, in the public ſchool, at an average of 7 years, is 120; and in the private ſchool, 55. Mr Smith teaches book-keeping for a guinea. The maſter of this ſchool has no houſe, nor any other perquiſites. Mr Smith indeed is ſeſſion-clerk ; but this office is not neceſſarily connected with the Engliſh ſchool *.

Beſides theſe eſtabliſhed ſchools, there are in St Andrew's three private ſchools, where the children of the poorer ſort are for lower fees taught to read. There are in town, ſchools for needle-work of all kinds, and tambouring ; the miſtreſſes have no ſalary, but depend entirely on their aſſiduity and good behaviour. A muſic-maſter, and dancing maſters, of approved character, during the winter months. There is no eſtabliſhed ſchool for French. Mr Smith, the Engliſh maſter, reads that language at a private

hour

---

* It is worthy of record, that as ſoon as Mr John Halkat, who for many years had, with great honour, held the office of rector in the grammar-ſchools, firſt of Cupar, and latterly of St Andrew's, began to ſhow ſymptoms of decline, his *quondam* pupils, by voluntary ſubſcription, purchaſed for him a very handſome annuity, on which he now lives in St Andrew's with much comfort, and enjoying univerſal reſpect. The corporation of St Andrew's have alſo continued with him half his former ſalary for life.

hour with such as choose to employ him. At Boarhills, in the east end of the parish, and in a centrical spot for the west end of the parish, are schools for English, writing, and arithmetic. The houses have been lately rebuilt or repaired by subscriptions from the neighbouring proprietors and tenants, with a little aid from the kirk-session. The salaries, L. 3 each, are paid chiefly by the session. A patriotic club of farmers, in Boarhills and the neighbourhood, having formed a stock purse, by a small monthly contribution, fines of absentees, &c. purchased an acre of land, a mort-cloth, and a hearse; the profits of these are given for the encouragement of their schoolmaster.

The established roll of those poor, who receive a weekly pension, and are supposed to need that pension during life, is 47. But besides this roll, there are many indigent families, &c. who get occasional supply; and the amount of this supply is in some years not much below that of the weekly pensions. The annual average of the funds under the administration of the session, is, 1. Produce of all donations, mortifications, legacies, &c. vested in one common subject of land, about L. 33. 2. Weekly collections at the church-doors, about L. 76. 3. Rent of seats in the church, marriage-dues, &c. about L. 14. Out of this revenue, amounting to L. 123, besides the supply of the poor, there fall to be paid land-tax, communion-elements, salaries to clerks and village schoolmasters, burials of the poor, repairs of seats, &c. Over and above these funds already mentioned, the late Principal Murison of the New College, who died 30th July 1779, bequeathed L. 100 Sterling to the session as trustees; the interest thereof to be distributed on the 30th July annually to decayed householders *.

Miscellaneous

* Here, as in every other part of the country, the price of provisions has been considerably advanced of late years. Average prices now are,

beef,

Miscellaneous Observations—This parish seems to labour under no particular disadvantages. It enjoys several advantages, some of which will apply to very few other parishes in the kingdom, *viz.* such as are derived from the University. In common with many others, it has all the advantages that result from good schools, for both boys and girls, from a salubrious situation, from a well supplied market, and from the neighbourhood of the sea. Proprietors in this parish have a particular advantage, that they are not burdened with a minister's manse, nor schoolmaster's salary; and hitherto they have been taxed with no more than one third of the expense of the parish-church, the

King,

---

beef, a-pound, 4 d.; in November, 3¼ d.; veal and mutton, from 3¼ d. to 5 d. according to the season; lamb, from 1 s. 6 d. to 5 s. a-quarter; pork, 3 d. and 4 d. the pound; pigs, from 2 s. 6 d. to 5 s.; geese, 3 s. and 3 s. 6 d; ducks, from 6 d. to 1 s.; chickens, 8 d. a-pair; pigeons, 3 d a-pair; rabbits, 6 d. and 7 d. a-pair; butter, from 7 d. to 9 d. a-pound; cheese; 2¼ d. and 3 d. a-pound; eggs, 3 d. and 4 d. a-dozen; hens, 1 s. each; oat-meal, 1 s. a-peck; ploughmen's wages have, within these 30 years, been raised from L. 3 Sterling a-year, to L. 5, L. 6, L. 8, L. 9; common labourers, from 6 d. a-day to 1 s.; masons, from 1 s. a-day, to 1 s. 8 d. 1 s. 10 d. 2 s. according to the demand; others, in proportion. When labourers are sober and frugal, when their wives are industrious and attentive, and the family enjoy a competent measure of health, they seem to live very comfortably upon their earnings. The advance on wages is much greater than that on provisions. When the labourer received 3 s. a-week, and paid for two pecks of meal at 8 d. he had a surplus of 1 s. 8 d. When he now receives 6 s. a-week, and pays 2 s. for his meal, his surplus is 4 s. The fuel used in this parish is coal; the price of which has been formerly stated. There are some mosses in the neighbourhood; and many families lay in a few peats, which are used chiefly for kindling the fires. The cottagers adjoining to the moors use turf for covering or gathering their fires; they likewise cut furze for fuel. The wages of female-servants run generally from L. 2, 10 s. to L. 4. or L. 5 a-year, according to the rank and fortune of their masters; footmen, from L. 10, to L. 15, or L. 20.

King, as fucceeding to the archbifhop, and the corporation
of the city, bearing the other two thirds. This expenfe
of the church, and alfo that of the ftipend, falls light on a
valued rent, which exceeds L. 24,000 Scotch. The difadvantage of the harbour is, that it lies in a rocky fhore, at
the S. W. corner of a deep bay, very much expofed to all
winds from E. and N. The accefs to the port, therefore,
is often very difficult, and the departure precarious.—The
language of this parifh is the common dialect of the Scotch
Lowlands. The Fifans are faid, by ftrangers, to ufe a
drawling pronunciation, but they have very few provincial
words. Very many of the names of places in the parifh,
are evidently modern and vernacular, Denhead, Edenfide,
Northbauk, Bylone, Smiddygreen, Stonywind, Boarhills,
Brownhills, &c. Several places retain the ancient Gaelic
names, Balrymont, Kinglaffie, Kingafk, Kincaple, Strathkinnefs, Balmungo, &c. Kincaple, about 3 miles W. from
St Andrew's, near the road to Dundee, Strathkinnefs a
fhort mile S. from Kincaple, on the old road to Cupar, and
Boarhills, between 3 and 4 miles E. from St Andrew's,
may be reckoned villages: in thefe, befides farmers and
cottagers, you find alehoufes, blackfmiths, wrights, weavers,
tailors, fhoemakers.—On 8th February 1792, in digging a
garden belonging to David Roger, ftaymaker, in the ftreet
leading to Cardinal Bethune's caftle, called the Caftle-wynd,
a fmall pot was turned up, which feemed to be full of earth,
but being immediately dafhed in pieces, there dropped out
8 gold coins, and about 150 filver ones. The gold was
clean, though the colour pale. The filver pieces were covered with thick ruft, and many of them perfectly friable *.

The

---

* One thin gold piece, about the fize of a fixpence, has a lion ram-
pant, or couchant, IACOBVS DEI GRATIA REX SCOTORVM; on
the

The only tumulus recollected in this parish was about 1¼ mile westward from St Andrew's, on the south road to Cupar, called Pitoutie Law. In forming the highway, about 30 years ago, it was thought necessary to remove this tumulus. Nothing was found but stones and earth. —The general size of the people is from 5 feet 8 inches to 5 feet 10 inches. In one family, there are 2 or 3 young men, who measure 6 feet 3 inches; one of them, 6 feet 5 inches. The people of this parish are sober, temperate, and industrious; more addicted to the arts of tranquil life than

---

the reverse, a man in armour on horseback. James I. was crowned 1406. Another, near the size of a half crown, has in the middle, a lion sitting like a cat, with a wide mouth, and stretched out tongue, between two pillars, PHS, (supposed Philippus), DEI GRATIA DVX BVRG : Reverse, a shield, quartered, 1st and 4th. 3 fleurs de lys; 2d and 3d, a lion erect, and a small shield in the middle. SIT NOMEN DOMINI BENEDICTVM AMEN. A third, about the size of a shilling; in the middle, a sun, with 4 flaming crosses, EXVRGAT DEVS ET DISSI-PENT INIMICI EIVS : Reverse, unicorn holding a shield, IACOBVS DEI GRATIA REX. A fourth, a little larger : shield, with 3 fleurs de lys, overtop'd with a crown, CAROLVS DEI GRATIA FRANCO-RVM REX : Reverse, IMPERAT VINCIT REGNAT. The silver pieces are very thin : most of them about the size of a shilling, some of them smaller. On removing the rust, there appears on one side a full face under a crown ; on the reverse, a cross, around which are two circular inscriptions ; outer circle, POSVI DEVM ADIVTOREM MEVM : inner circle, VILLA CALISIE ; crowned head, HENRICVS DEI GRATIA ; or CIVITAS LONDON, HENRICVS, &c.; or, CIVITAS EBORACI, EDVARDVS, &c.; or, VILLA EDINBVRG, IACOBVS, &c. One has the addition of a sceptre to the crown'd head, ROBERTVS DEI GRATIA REX SCOTORVM. Reverse, inner circle, VILLA EDINBVRGH ; outer circle, DNS PTECTOR MS LI-BERATOR MS. (*Dominus protector meus, liberator meus.*) Robert Bruce was crowned 1306. Many of these coins have been sold ; the silver, at 1 s. each, and the gold, at 12 s. and upwards, according to their size.

than to military fervice ; kind and hofpitable to ftrangers ;
benevolent and friendly to one another ; very ready to all
the offices and duties of fociety ; not very forward in making new difcoveries, but willing to improve by the experiments elfewhere made ; peaceable in their demeanour ;
candid and liberal in their judgments ; refpectful to their
fuperiors, without fervility ; compaffionate to the diftreffed,
and charitable to the poor ; contented and thankful in their
fituation ; attached to their religion, without bigotry or enthufiafm ; regular in their attendance on Chriftian inftitu-
tions, and pious without oftentation ; loyal to the King ;
obedient to the laws ; enemies to fedition, faction, or tu-
mult, and deeply fenfible of the bleffings they enjoy as
Britifh fubjects. In no corner of the kingdom, is it more
comfortable to live, as neighbours, magiftrates, or minifters.

The highways through this parifh are fuch only as di-
verge from St Andrew's as a centre, *viz.* to Carrail or Crail
S. E. ; to Anftruther, S. ; to Ely, S. W. ; to Cupar, W. ;
and to Dundee, N. and W. All thefe roads are made and
repaired by the ftatute-labour of the county, which is for
the moft part commuted into money. That to Crail is
always in the beft condition, becaufe it is neareft to good
materials. Acrofs a fmall river or burn, called Kinnefs,
or Netherburn, which runs along the fouth fide of St Andrew's eaftward, are two bridges, of one arch each ; the
one at the eaft end of the town, on the road to Crail and
Anftruther ; the other at the weft end, on the road to Ely.
Acrofs the fmall ftream of Swilian, which runs through
the Golf-links, is another bridge of one arch, on the road
to Dundee. Thefe are the only bridges within the parifh.
In the eaftern extremity of the parifh, on the Crail road,
over Kenlowie, dividing St Andrew's from Kingfbarns, is
a fourth bridge, of two arches ; all thefe are kept in good

repair

repair by the county. In the weſtern part of the pariſh, on the road to Dundee, over Eden, which divides St Andrew's from Leuchars, is a fifth, called Gair, or Guardbridge, built at the private expenſe of a Biſhop Wardlaw (he died in 1444), who eſtabliſhed a family of the name of Wan as hereditary keepers of the bridge, for which they have a perpetual fee of about 10 acres of land adjoining to it. This bridge has ſix arches, is no wider than neceſſary for one carriage, and is covered with cauſeway-ſtones and ſome flags. Acroſs the bridge was wont to be ſtretched an iron chain, which was opened only for chaiſes; carts, &c. were obliged to paſs under the bridge; and as the ſea flows far above this part of Eden, theſe carriages were obliged to wait the reflux of the tide, which cauſed ſo great interruption to the buſineſs of the country, that many years ago the chain was removed. This bridge is maintained by the county. By the recent act the turnpike road from St Andrew's to Cupar, as well as to Dundee, is by this bridge; the bar is on the Leuchars ſide, at the weſt end of the bridge, where theſe two roads ſeparate; there is no bar on this line of road farther eaſt than this bridge.—In the neighbourhood of St Andrew's, land is rented as high as L. 3 the acre, or four bolls of bear, which ſometimes exceeds L. 3. No farms in the country have as yet exceeded L. 2, 10 s. the acre. L. 1, or L. 1, 5 s. may perhaps be the preſent average of farm-land. Rents, however, are advancing very faſt; even to ſix times the ſum at which the lands were let 38 years ago. Among about 60 farms, we have them of all ſizes, from 20 acres to 300. The number of tenants is on the decreaſe; the number of encloſures on the increaſe, though in general the pariſh is uncncloſed.—The people of this pariſh are by no means noted for frequenting taverns or alehouſes: Drunkenneſs is no part of their characteriſtic: The number of drinking clubs decreaſes every

year

year. Number of alehoufes, inns, &c. in the town, 42 ; and in the county, 6 ; which is rather below the average for the laft fix years.—The number of cottages in this parifh has varied very little for thefe many years paft, very few of the farmers choofing to diminifh or to increafe their number; the progrefs of manufactures may, in all likelihood, render cottagers more and more neceffary for fupplying a fufficiency of reapers in harveft, more particularly as at that bufy time the dreffing of their wheat lands occupies many of their ordinary fervants.—1793, May. A failcloth manufacture is now beginning in St Andrew's.

Whatever has been faid above in general, concerning the town and parifh of St Andrew's, muft be confidered alfo as including the parifh of St Leonard's, which is intermixed with the other.

St LEONARD'S PARISH,

By the Rev. Joseph M'Cormick, *D.D. Minifter of St Leonard's, and Principal of the United College.*

THE parifh of St Leonard's confifts of a few diftricts in different quarters of the town and fuburbs of St Andrew's, together with 2 farms in the country, about 3 miles diftant from the town, all originally belonging to the Priory, afterward to the College of St Leonard's, and now to the United College of St Salvator and St Leonard's. It is probable that the erection of the parifh is of the fame date with the foundation of the College whofe name it bears. Although the principal of St Leonard's did not always officiate as minifter of the parifh, and in the inftance of Mr George Buchanan, was not even a clergyman, it is certain, that for fome time before the Revolution, the two offices were held by the fame perfon ; and ever fince that period the principal of the College has been a clergyman and minifter of the parifh.

According

According to my lateſt ſurvey, the number of ſouls in the whole pariſh amounted to 385 ; of theſe, there are in the town, 220; in the ſuburbs called Argyle, 115 ; and in the country, 50. As the inhabitants of the ſeveral diſtricts in the city and ſuburbs, belonging to the pariſh of St Leonard's, are interſperſed with thoſe of the town pariſh, the annual average of births, marriages and deaths in any given period, as alſc the number of males and females who are born and die in that period, muſt be in proportion to the numbers of each pariſh, and need not be repeated.—The number of poor upon the ſeſſion-roll of St Leonard's is from 6 to 9, beſides the occaſional poor ; and the funds for their ſupport are from L. 25 to L. 27 Sterling a-year.— The ſtipend of St Leonard's conſiſts of 5 chalders of victual, one half of which is oats, and about L. 3 Sterling of money, the rent of an acre and an half of land mortified about a century ago to the miniſter of St Leonard's.

PARISH OF St MONANCE,

(COUNTY AND SYNOD OF FIFE, PRESBYTERY OF St ANDREW's.)

By the Rev. Mr ARCHIBALD GILLIES.

Name, Extent, Surface, Soil, &c.

BEFORE the year 1646, the name of the pariſh was *Abercrombie* [*]. With regard to the name St Monance, it has undergone very little variation. In the oldeſt writs

I

---

[*] From which period it has improperly acquired that of St Monance ; the reaſon for which, follows. The lands of Newark (which at preſent give a title to a Lord of that name) were formerly a part of the pariſh of Kilconquhar ; the tithes of which are ſtill paid to the incumbent of that charge. But in the year 1646, when the lands of Newark and Abercrombie belonged to two near relations of the name of Sandilands, the one bearing the title of Lord Abercrombie, now extinct, and the other Sir James Sandilands of Newark ; they, for their conveniency &c. having previouſly agreed with Mr Robert Wilkie, then miniſter of Abercrombie, and a pariſh by itſelf, applied to the preſbytery of St Andrew's to have the lands of Newark disjoined from Kilconquhar, without prejudice to the incumbent, and annexed to Abercrombie : Parties being agreed, the preſbytery

I have feen, being fometimes called St Menin, fometimes St Monan, and in modern times, and at prefent, St Monance. —As to the derivation, amidft the many reports, what to me feems moft probable, is, That it originated from the hermit who ferved at the chapel, and which gave name to the town. And as it became the place of public worfhip for the parifh, and the town the moft populous part of it, through time the parifh came to be called St Monance a-lone. For before the period of annexation, the village of Abercrombie was pretty populous, but fince has very much diminifhed. At prefent, it confifts only of one farm-houfe and offices, the houfes of two other fmall tenants, and a few cottages. The manfe and glebe are ftill in it. The parifh is of fmall extent, and forms nearly a parallelogram, ex-tending from the S. E. where it is wafhed by the frith of Forth, to the N. W. The breadth from W. to E. is about a fhort Englifh mile, and from S. to N. $1\frac{1}{2}$ mile. The land rifes fuddenly from the fea, but of no extraordinary height; after which it is flat, with a very gentle and eafy afcent upwards to Abercrombie, about a mile, and then de-clines in the fame manner towards the N. the furface af-fording a very beautiful appearance. The foil in general is a light loam, and friable, very little clay, all quite free of ftones, and very fertile and manageable. The whole is arable, excepting a trifle in a natural ftate, and which is ca-pable of cultivation, The fea coaft is flat and rocky. The rocks confift of free and lime ftone, and a great quantity of

ironftone

prefbytery granted their requeft *quoad facra.* But whether any applica-tion was afterward made to the Lords of plantation, and the fame con-firmed by them or not. does not appear. After which the name of the parifh in the records of prefbytery, ftood thus : ʻ The parifh of Abercrombie with St Monance.'—At that period, the church (or chapel, as then called) of Abercrombie was fuffered to go into ruin, and an old Gothic chapel at St Monance (of which more afterward) became the place of public wor-fhip.

ironſtone lying ſcattered upon the ſurface. It yields a good
deal of ſea-weed for kelp, which is uſually cut every third
year, and after gales of wind from the N. E. E. and S. E.
a good quantity for manure.

Climate, &c.—The climate is mild and temperate, the
air dry and ſalubrious. But when it blows from the E. and
S. E. it is ſharp and cold, moiſt, and full of ſalt particles.; for the land is much expoſed to the ſea on theſe
quarters, and not covered with trees; which if it were, the
air would not only be more mild, the ſurface greatly beautified, but the ground more early in its productions, which
are much checked in the ſpring by the winds from theſe
points, and which commonly blow for a long time at that
ſeaſon. Yet upon the whole, the inhabitants in general are
very healthy. There have been no inſtances of unuſual
longevity during the incumbency of the preſent miniſter.
But there are many now living of 70, 76, and 80 years, and
ſome died a few years ago, at the age of 90 and 91. The
ſmall-pox uſed to make great ravages among the children,
eſpecially in the town of St Monance. If the contagion
got in during the heat of ſummer, when the air is much
tainted with the refuſe of the fiſhing, it was then peculiarly
fatal, ſweeping off from 20 to 30 children at a time. But
its deſtructive progreſs has for ſeveral years paſt been in ſome
degree mitigated, by that happy invention, inoculation ; and
to which the people in general are now becoming more and
more reconciled.

Rivers.—There are no rivers, but one ſmall brook, which
bounds the pariſh on the W. runs S. interſecting part of the
lands of Newark, and empties itſelf, between the church
and town of St Monance, into the frith of Forth. There
is another in the lands of Abercrombie, which bounds the

pariſh

parish on the eaft fide, runs S. E. between it and the lands
of Balcafkie, and difembogues itfelf between the two An-
ftruthers. Both are in a manner dry one half of the year.
Such is the cafe with all the rivulets in this part of the
county, and which is a great lofs to it, where there are fo
many fea-port towns; there being no river, or running
water of any confequence, eaft fide of the river of Leven.

Mines.—There is abundance of coal in the lands of
Newark, confifting of fplint, cherry, and culm, at prefent
working. It is not level free, but wrought by a fire engine.
Likewife one of the neateft and beft contrived falt-works
upon the coaft, called St Philip's; both are the property of
Sir John Anftruther, Baronet. The coal and falt, befides
what is fold to the country, are exported at Pittenweem.
In the lands of Abercrombie there are feveral feams of
coal, but as yet untouched, and which belong to Sir Robert
Anftruther, Baronet. Coal abounds in this country, both in
the coaft and interior parts, and that neceffary article for
the comfort of life might be obtained at an eafy rate. But
fince of late, coal working has become a trade, by opening
only a few at a time, and thus monopolizing them, the
price is kept up; and there is no other fuel ufed, or to be
had in this place. This winter the inhabitants have been
greatly diftreffed for want of this article, by the difficulty
of obtaining it, and the high price.

Fifhery, &c.—Formerly there was a very plentiful fifhing upon the coaft here, confifting of cod, ling, haddock,
rowan or turbot, fkait, &c. and St Monance ufed to be one
of the principal fifh-towns upon the coaft. But within thefe
4 or 5 years paft, the fifh have in a manner quite deferted
thefe places, (particularly the haddock) and none are now
caught but a few cod, rowan, and fkait. Before, fifh of all

kinds

kinds were in great abundance, and at an easy rate, but now are very scarce, and high priced; not one haddock being taken in a whole year. There has been no sufficient cause as yet assigned for this remarkable change. The shoals of herrings which used with great certainty to frequent the coast, particularly in the autumnal season, and likewise in the spring, are now become very precarious, and of no consequence. This great decrease of the fishing is a vast loss to this part of the country. For as fish was a principal part of the support of the inhabitants, other provisions have greatly advanced in price; and as great quantities of herrings, over and above the home consumpt, were cured and exported, trade has suffered much. Besides, the fishers are threatening an emigration to other places; though as yet only one man and family have left the parish this spring, and gone to the town of Ayr, on the west coast *.

Migratory

* The common market for the fish is Edinburgh. They are bought up by the fishers of Fisherrow, who attend with their boats, purchase at sea, and carry them off. Formerly the practice was, that out of the fleet of boats belonging to the town, two were obliged in their turn to come into the harbour, and offer market for two hours, for the supply of the inhabitants. But that good regulation being now overlooked, the fishers have wholly laid it aside. This has enhanced the price of fish here, that it is but little below the market at Edinburgh, and they are difficult to be obtained. The lobsters are commonly taken in contract from the fishers by a Company, and carried alive in smacks to the London market, and other places in England. The boats used in the fishing consist of a larger and smaller kind; of the former there are about 14, and of the latter about 20. The small are used both in summer and winter, in what they term the white fishing. Each of these require four men for the oars, and one steersman. With them, they fish with great and small line, for cod, rowan, haddock, &c. and with nets for skate. The larger are used only in the herring fishing; and their complements of men are some six, some eight, according to their size, with a steersman. But besides these, there are a number of yawls, with which, through summer, they fish with

the

Migratory Birds, &c.—There are the fwallow and martin, the plover both green and gray, the cuckoo, and but
few woodcock. Through the whole of the year, the fea
gulls, (called by the vulgar fea maws,) frequently come
upon land; but when they do fo, it affuredly prognofticates
high winds, with falls of rain from the E. and S. E. and as
foon as the ftorm abates, they return again to the frith, their
natural element. I faw fome time ago, a golden crefted
wren, and the only one that hath appeared to me in this
country. Its fize was much about that of the common
wren, and nearly the fame in the colour of the body. The
crown of the head was ornamented with a circle of feathers
of a fiery orange, or golden colour, with a beautiful bright
fpot of yellow in the centre. Hares and partridges abound;
a few quails, and fome foxes and rabbits in the light
grounds.

Town of St Monance, &c.—The town is fituated upon a
fpot of a triangular form; one fide of which verges upon,
and is wafhed by the frith of Forth, the other two fides are
covered by the rifing grounds. And as it enjoys a S. and
S. E. expofure, it is defended againft the cold bleak winds,
from the N. E. N. and N. W. Its fituation is thereby
mild and kindly even in winter, when blowing from thefe
points; but quite the reverfe, when the wind blows upon
the fhore. There is a harbour belonging to the town, the
                                                    building

the hand-line for the tanny cod, (or red ware cod, as they call it,) among
the rocks and fea weed. The hands ufed in thefe, are commonly a man
and boy, and fometimes only one man. Of the number of hands ufed in
the fifhing here, only fuch as are advanced in life hold clofe by it. The
young men engage to the fhips employed in the whale fifhing; return
when the herring fifhing comes on in autumn; and, when that is over,
engage themfelves in voyages in private fhips, in different places, during
the winter feafon. By this means St Monance becomes a good nurfery
for fea men.

building of which is of no great conſequence. But what merits obſervation, is the great depth of water. At ſtream tides when full water, it is from 18 to 20 feet deep at the entrance; and in ordinary floods, from 13 to 15, though the building extends but a very ſhort way out to ſea. But though by this depth of water it is capable to admit veſſels of burden, yet none frequent it but in the ſummer ſeaſon; and then but very ſeldom, and when freighted to the place: For the entrance is narrow between two ridges of rocks, the bottom rough, and thereby difficult and dangerous.

Diviſion and Rent of Lands, &c.—The whole of the lands of Newark are incloſed with hedge and ditch, except a ſmall part by ſtone fences. There is no real farmer, who makes farming his ſole buſineſs, but one, and his farm is of no great extent. The remainder is let off in ſmall parcels to the inhabitants of the town. Theſe take it not ſo much for the profit ariſing from farming, as to enable them to keep their horſes, which, by their being employed in driving of coal, fiſh, and otherwiſe, thereby procure their own ſupport, and enable them to pay the rent. Likewiſe, a good number of cows are kept, for the ſale of milk to the other inhabitants. The lands of Newark contain about 266 acres, and they are generally let from L. 2, 2 s. up to L. 3 the acre. The valued rent of this part of the pariſh is L. 1207, 13 s. 4 d. Scots; but the real rent I cannot aſcertain. For, beſides the rent of land, there are the feus in the town, tithes upon the fiſhing, &c. There are already large two thirds of the lands of Abercrombie incloſed, and the people are at preſent engaged in that work, decorating the incloſures with clumps of trees here and there. The whole is done with hedge and ditch, for there is no freeſtone in the grounds, but what lies very deep, The farmers are ſuffi-

ciently

ciently convinced of the advantage of inclofing, which they fhow, by giving higher rents for inclofed than uninclofed grounds. The whole of the lands of Abercrombie are divided into farms, containing from 40 to 60, 80, and 117 acres, and but a trifle in fmall parcels. The rent varies, fome being 15 s. L. 1, L. 1, 10 s. L, 1, 15 s. and fome up to L. 2 the acre. The whole acres are 600, and upwards. The valued rent is L. 1486 Scots, but the real rent I cannot determine. The whole number of acres, therefore, in the parifh is about 866, and the valued rent L. 2693 : 13 : 4 Scots. There is a mill in the lands of Abercrombie, to which all the tenants are thirled, for fuch grains as are mealed for the ufe of their families, and pay multure.

Agriculture, &c.—About 15 years ago, the only plough ufed here was the old Scots plough, of a very heavy and clumfy conftruction. It was drawn fometimes by 2 oxen, and 2 horfes; and fometimes by 4 oxen and 1 horfe. But what is now generally ufed is the fmall Englifh plough with iron mould-board; and the Scots plough, of a fhorter and lighter conftruction than formerly; and a plough, compofed of partly Englifh and partly Scots, having an iron mould-board and head. The Englifh plough makes the neateft work, but does not anfwer in ftony ground; whereas the Scots anfwers all grounds. All thefe ploughs are now commonly drawn by 2 ftrong horfes; except when breaking up ftiff land from grafs that has been down for fome years, then 3 or 4 horfes are ufed. One man both holds the plough, and manages the horfes by a pair of long reins, except when more than 2 horfes are ufed. The roller is frequently ufed here, as the ground is friable, in the fpring upon the wheat crop, to fhut up the furface, and thereby to prevent the fatal effect of the froft at that feafon;

and

and upon the ſowñ barley grounds to preſerve the moiſture from the violent exhalation. All curved and broad ridges are now done away, and the ridges are made ſtraight and narrow ; the ſurface is by far more neatly dreſſed than formerly, and gives pleaſure to the beholder. It is only within theſe few years, that wheat or barley were ſown in the pariſh to any extent ; but now a conſiderable quantity of both. The wheat is generally ſown after potatoes, fallow, and beans or peaſe, and the time of ſowing, from the middle of September even till the end of November ; but the greater portion in October. Beans, peaſe, and oats, from the beginning of March to the middle of April. The greateſt part of the beans are in drills, which are dreſſed with the hand-hoe, and furrowed up with a light plough conſtructed for that purpoſe, with a mould-board on both ſides, in ſummer. There uſed to be a great quantity of flax-feed ſown by the inhabitants, who hired the ground from the tenants. But of late, the price of the ſeed and rent of land have riſen to ſo great a height, that but a ſmall quantity is now ſown in compariſon of what uſed to be, and the return not compenſating their expenſe. The time of ſowing is from the middle of March to the end of April. Potatoes the whole of April ; and bear and barley from the beginning to the end of May, among the latter, graſs-feeds are ſown, and rolled down. Turnips, of which there are now large fields, are ſown from the middle of June to the middle of July. The farmers uſe turnip to fatten cattle with for ſale, and which are bought in ; for having little or no natural paſture, they raiſe few or none. To the ſame purpoſe their crops of hay are applied, and by this means increaſe the fulzie for their grounds. The harveſt generally begins about the laſt week of Auguſt and 1ſt of September, and by the firſt and ſecond week of October the crop is wholly got into the barn-yards. Of wheat,

barley,

barley, bear and sometimes of beans, a greater quantity is raised in this parish than what is necessary for the support of the inhabitants. These are generally sold to the bakers and brewers in the towns upon the coast side, or to persons residing there, who are commissioned by such, in Edinburgh, Leith, and other places, to buy up for them. The fatted cattle are commonly bought by the butchers from Edinburgh, Perth, &c. For Fife of a long time past has been famous for fatted cattle. Since the price of land has increased, the farmers sow little more oats than to serve their own confumpt; it being a low priced grain, and esteemed a scourging crop to the land. The difference between the prices of grain in the market at Edinburgh and this place, being somewhat considerable, together with the ease of water-carriage in transporting it, occasions the demand upon this quarter.

Population.—The return made to Dr Webfter in the 1775 of the population of the parish of St Monance was 780 souls; the number in 1790 turned out to be 832, which is an increase only of 52 since that period. But as there is no evidence in the registers of any particular enumeration being taken of the inhabitants at that time, there is ground to suspect that it has been either superficially taken or exaggerated, for the following reasons: 1st, Because houses in the town of St Monance have of late increased in number above what they then were, and all are possessed. 2d, Since that period, the coal-work has been set a-going, about which several houses have been raised, and the salt-works built, in which are a number of houses for salters, &c. Both of which have brought a number of persons, and their families, into the parish, from other parts of the country. *Lastly,* The inhabitants of Abercrombie, and country parts of the parish, are much the same they were at that period. From all

all which, there is reaſon to ſuſpeẛ that the enumeratiori then made was not juſt ; and that had it been ſo, the in-creaſe now, above what the number then was, muſt havè been much greater. The births, marriages, and deaths, aṡ entered in the pariſh-regiſter for 7 years, are as follow :

Years.	Births.	Marriages.	Burials.
From Oẛ. 2. 1783*			
to do. 1784,	36	7	25
Do. 1784 to do. 1785,	34	12	30
Do. 1785 to do. 1786,	41	3	17
Do. 1786 to do. 1787,	26	6	23
Do. 1787 to do. 1788,	26	7	17
Do. 1788 to do. 1789,	30	11	15
Do. 1789 to do. 1790,	34	6	11
Totals,	227	52	158
Average nearly,	32	7	19

The great increaſe of deaths in 1783, 1784, and 1786, was owing to the ſmall-pox getting into the town of St Monance in the height of ſummer, when the air is tainted by the refuſe of the fiſhing, (as before obſerved,) which, when it happened, never failed to ſweep off a great number of children. It is to be obſerved, that the great exceſs of births beyond the deaths, in the above ſpace of 7 years, is owing to many of the preſent inhabitants continuing ſtill to bury in the pariſhes from whence they came, and the cuſtom of paying the tax upon deaths in the place where the dead are interred. The whole pariſh belongs to two proprietors,

* The reaſon why the calculation begins at the 2d of Oẛober, is, be-.cauſe the tax upon births, &c. did take place then, and the regiſter com-menced.

proprietors, Sir Robert Anftruther, Baronet, proprietor of Abercrombie, and Sir John Anftruther, Baronet, of the lands of Newark ; but none of them, refide in the parifh. In the lands of Abercrombie, all the inhabitants are farmers, and cottagers employed by them ; except in the village of Abercrombie, there are 1 wright, 1 fmith, and 3 weavers.—It was obferved before, that the lands of Newark were let in fmall parcels to perfons who refided in the town of St Monance. Befides thefe, in that place, there are 4 bakers, 3 brewers, 2 fmiths, 4 merchants, 1 wright, and 1 boat-builder ; 2 mafons, 2 fieve-makers, 2 flax-dreffers, 1 fhoemaker, 5 tailors, 6 weavers, and 1 gardener. The reft of the inhabitants are compofed of fifhers and failors, land-labourers and day labourers, and fuch as are employed about the coal and falt works. And it merits obfervation, that there are no lefs than 12 fpirit and ale houfes, the unhappy effects of the keepers of which, by their craft to decoy, are with regret feen upon both the health and morals of the young and inconfiderate.

Church, Stipend, &c.—What is at prefent ufed for the church of the parifh is part of an old convent, on the weft of the town of St Monance ; which is fituated upon a rock, advancing into the frith of Forth. It had been a very ftately and beautiful Gothic pile of hewn ftone, in the form of a crofs, with a fquare fteeple in the centre *. The walls of the fouth and north branches are ftill ftanding, but want

the

* This chapel is recorded to have been a priory of the Black-friars. It was founded by King David II. of Scotland, in the 40th year of his reign, and was ferved by a hermit. By his charter, dated " at Edinbrugh," he grants thereto, the lands of Eafter-birney in Fife, and fome lands in the fheriffdom of Edinburgh. It was given by King James III. to the Black-friars. To it was annexed the convent founded by the Macduffs Earls of Fife, at the foot of the Caftlehill of Cupar of Fife. Afterward,

the roof; of the weſt branch no veſtige remains, and the
eaſt branch, with the ſteeple, ſerves at preſent for the place
of public worſhip. This part of the building has a very
beautiful vaulted roof, with veins jutting out from the ſide-
walls, and meeting in the centre of the roof, where it is
decorated with roſes, and other ornaments. Over the vault,
there is a ſlate roof, to preſerve it from the weather. The
burden of upholding this fabric, was laid by the proprietor
of the lands of Newark upon the feuars of St Monance,
when he let off the ground on which the town-ſtands, having the annexation in view. But the building ſeems to
have been in a manner totally neglected by them. In the
1772, it was in ſuch a ruinous ſtate, that the incumbent
raiſed a proceſs for reparation before the preſbytery, and
obtained a decree for that end againſt the heritors. But
the feuars were reluctant, pretending they were not obliged
to uphold it. This brought on a proceſs between the heritors and them, before the Lords of Seſſion, in which they
were caſt, and found liable to uphold the fabric. During
the proceſs, it received a partial reparation, but nothing e-
qual to what was granted by preſbytery ; and nothing more
has yet been done, either by the heritors, to enforce the
decree of the Lords upon the feuars, or by them, to teſtify
their compliance with it ; and if they continue long ſo to
do, this venerable pile muſt ſink into ruins. What a pity
is it, that ſuch a beautiful monument of antiquity, and
which perhaps has not its fellow in Scotland, ſhould be ſuffered to go to deſolation ! The King is patron of the pariſh.
The manſe was built in the laſt century, has undergone
ſeveral expenſive reparations, but is at preſent in bad con-
dition·

terwards, both were annexed by King James V. to the convent of St An-
drew's, at the weſt port of the ſtreet called the North-gate, founded by
William Wiſhart, biſhop of that city.—Hiſtory of religious Houſes in
Scotland, by a preſbyter under Biſhop Roſs of Edinburgh.

dition. There is no fchool-houfe in the parifh, but the heritors allow the interest of the money appointed by law,
for building a fchool and houfe, to the mafter, to hire one.
The ftipend confifts of 96 bolls, Half bear and half oats,
Linlithgow meafure, L. 11 : 2 : 2$\frac{8}{12}$. in money, and L. 3, 6 s.
8 d. in lieu of vicarage-tithes. But of this laft, the prefent incumbent has never realifed more than L. 2 : 19 : 2$\frac{2}{4}$,
though he has often applied to the heritors concerning it.
The amount of the whole, (taking the victual at the com-
mon converfion,) is L. 64 : 1 : 5$\frac{2}{4}$ Sterling, exclufive of the
glebe, and which, including arable and grafs grounds, and
what the manfe and offices employ, is 8 acres 2 falls.

State of the Poor, &c.—The funds for the poor, are the
weekly collections at the church door. Thefe of late have
greatly diminifhed, owing to the increafe of the different
fects of Seceders in this part of the county, the Relief,
Burghers, and Antiburghers, &c. The teachers and managers of each of which focieties, artfully draw off the ignorant and unwary from the Establifhed Church, by this
means to make up a falary for their teachers ; and pride
themfelves to have it not only equal to, but above that of
the minifters of the church. They give no charity to their
poor ; but the whole of what is collected at the door of their
meeting-houfes, and what arifes from the rent of feats is
applied to this purpofe. When any of their fociety are unfit for labour, by ficknefs or old age, and reduced in circumftances, being unable to pay the heavy affeffments they
lay upon them, and ftanding in need of charity ; finding
they can reap no more pecuniary benefit from them, they
fend them to the church-feffion for relief. Thus their practice has laid the church-feffions under the difagreeable neceffity of acquainting them, that upon their leaving the
church, they will be deprived of the benefit of that fund.
                                                        And

And did they not take this method, the whole would be confumed upon fuch as contribute nothing to it * Befides the above, there are others, fuch as feamen, and of other profeffions, who enter into focieties, and pay into what they call their box, and publicly collect from others, and though they attend the church, give nothing to the poor. Thus the public fund is much injured, and the whole collection which comes from a few perfons, is but fmall ; which, with the rent of four acres of land, and two houfes, cannot be calculated at more than about L. 9 a-year. There are now upon the poors lift three perfons and two orphans. None are allowed to beg publicly. The parifh, however, is much infefted with beggars from towns at a diftance.

* It may be proper to obferve, that the above fectaries are always ready to break the public peace. A flagrant inftance of which they iately gave in this corner. By forming focieties, which confifted, if not wholly, yet moftly of perfons of thefe fects, for circulating feditious pamphlets, and diffeminating difaffection to King, and Government, by thefe meetings, and private converfations.

Mifcellaneous Obfervations.—In the 1782, the harveft was very late, owing to the rains through the fummer, and heavy falls of fnow and intenfe frofts in the end of September, and the whole of October. This did not only greatly injure the crop, but made the harveft uncommonly late in this parifh. And as this weather was fimilar over all Scotland, the country was threatened with a general fcarcity. The meal quickly rofe to 1 s. 3 d. the peck, which rendered it very diftreffing to the poor ; the induftrious labourer and artificer, having a family of children, being above what they could procure by their labour. The feffion, moved with compaffion, and fearing the fatal effects of the fcarcity; came to a refolution to lend their aid for preferving the lives of the inhabitants. For this purpofe, as oats or meal were very difficult to be obtained, they thought it proper to have recourfe to Sir Robert Anftruther, Bart. for his farm-oats to be converted into meal, and to be applied to the fupport of the parifh ; and agreed to give him for every boll of meal the price current, and to give it 3 d. the peck to the inhabitants below the market price. Their requeft he was fo good and humane as to grant. Having thus fecured meal, the feffion, to prevent impofitions, made a furvey of the parifh,

rifh, to find out the moft neceffitous families, without diftinction of fects or parties. They appointed two days in the week for diftribution, Tuefday and Friday ; when each perfon, upon receiving a ticket, and giving the fame to the perfon appointed to diftribute the meal, were to receive the quantity therein fpecified, at 3 d. the peck below the market price. By this means, they not only had it at this eafy rate, but were fure of having it. For, at that time, meal often could not be procured for money. This the feffion continued to do, from the 1ft of February to the end of May 1783, when the fhipping, in the courfe of Providence, arrived more early than ufual from the Baltic, with a fupply for the relief of the country. By this method the feffion became the happy inftruments of fupporting no lefs than 40 families, befides individuals, and preferving the lives of their fellow parifhioners from the general calamity.

PARISH OF SALINE.

(Preſbytery of Dunfermline.—Synod and County of Fife.)

By the Reverend Mr WILLIAM FORFAR.

Extent, Name, &c.

THE pariſh of Saline is 7 miles long from E. to W. and 6 broad at the center from S. to N. becoming gradually narrower towards the extremities. The E. part, and nearly the half, is hilly and marſhy, the W. half very level. The moſt probable account of the origin of the name, according to the opinion of a gentleman converſant in toponomy, is this. Saline is a contraction for *Salvin* or *Salbin*, *bhean or bean*, pronounced *vin* or *bin*, ſignifies in Gaelic a hill or mountain; and it being natural for the Scotch to ſpeak *ore aperto*, *ſel* is eaſily converted into *ſal;* it is alſo habitual for them to ſuppreſs the letter *v*, which may account for the formation of the name Saline as preſently uſed. *Sal* or *ſel* is either Gaelic, ſignifying *great*, or Saxon, ſignifying *great* or *good*. Hence Salin or Salvin will denote a great hill; and as the hill called Saline Hill is of conſiderable height, the pariſh, and the village which lies at the foot of it, may have derived their names from this circumſtance. The perpendicular

height

height of the hill, from the village where it begins to riſe, is more than a quarter of a mile *.

Population.—The number of inhabitants in whole, including the ſectaries, who do not exceed 20 or 30 perſons, is 950, while the return to Dr Webſter in 1755 was 1285. One cauſe of the decreaſe was the removal of a great number of cottars, poſſeſſing ſmall tenements, which obliged them to ſeek refuge in other places. The number of proprietors is 23, including thoſe of the barony of Inzievar, which belongs to this pariſh *quoad civilia*, and to the pariſh of Torryburn *quoad ſacra*, and excluding 10 proprietors who have property in this pariſh *quoad ſacra*, belonging to the pariſhes of Torryburn and Dunfermline *quoad civilia*. Of all theſe, only 10 reſide in the pariſh. There are four freeholds ; Killerny belonging to Major Aytoun ; Nether Kinneddar to Mr Haly ; Hillſide to the Reverend Mr Colvil ; and Inzievar to Mr Ronaldſon.

Soil.—The ſoil is various, in general thin, and of a tilly bottom; ſome parts, however, are remarkably good, of a loamy nature, and eaſily wrought. Wheat, which is now coming more into uſe, has yielded 16 after 1, beans 15, barley 20, though uſually ſeldom more than 8 or 10. There is

an

* The ſame gentleman hazards another conjecture of the origin of the name given to the hill, and conſequently to the pariſh and village. There is an old ruin near the foot of Saline Hill, a little above the village, called Kill-erny. *Kill* and *cell* are known to be ſynonimous terms, to which the name of the founder or ſaint may have been added. Hence Kill-erny literally ſignifies the cell of Erny, and Saline Hill would moſt naturally obtain the name of Cell-vin, or the hill where the cell was. In ſupport of this, the Celtic word for cellar is *ſeileir,* which ſtill ſeems to accord with the preſent orthography of the name Saline.

an inftance of oats yielding upwards of 40 from 1, thinly fown after burnt mofs. Many parts are capable of great improvement, which hitherto have continued almoft in a ftate of nature. There is much need of draining and fummer ploughing. Lime is too little ufed. Even near the village and heart of the parifh, there is much wet and wafte ground, which, though capable of being fertilifed and beautified by fkill and induftry, is likely ftill to excite in the traveller the idea of poverty and indolence. Green crops are but little in ufe. Planting and inclofing have been practifed a little, though they are ftili too much neglected. There are large tracks of mofs, fome of which yield excellent peat for fuel. There are two natural woods; one of which was fold a few years ago for upwards of 500 l. Sterling; befides thefe, there is a good deal of fine old afh, and of young oak, afh, and fir, in a thriving condition.

Minerals.—The parifh abounds with coal in every part; fome of it remarkably good, though little or none is wrought, owing partly to the inactive fpirit of the proprietors, but chiefly to the vicinity of Blairngone, which fupplies all the country round at a low price. There is alfo lime, and a good deal of ironftone; the quality of the latter is remarkably good. Two of the proprietors have given a leafe to the Dovan Company, one at $9\frac{1}{4}$ d. *per* ton, the other at 6 d. the Company working it, and paying damages.

Rent, Manufactures, &c.—The valued rent of the whole parifh is 4078 l. 19 s. 4 d. Scotch. The real rent may be about 2500 l. Sterling. The proprietors affeffed themfelves fome time ago for 48 ploughgates, though the real number may be 20 more. The two horfe plough is now much ufed. Some farms are wholly let for grafs, which, in the hilly parts

of

of the parish, are found to raise much better rents than tillage. There are only 2 farmers who keep sheep. There
are no manufactories. There are 3 wrights, 4 taylors, 3
shoemakers, 3 smiths, 11 weavers, 8 masons, 1 brewer, and
1 maltster. There are three corn-mills, and one fulling-mill.
Wages are much the same as in other places, and have been
on the increase for some time.

Poor, &c.—The number of poor on the roll is 13, regularly supplied by the interest of a fund, amounting to 187 l. 15 s.
6¾ d. Sterling. It was formerly much greater, till more than
100 l. Sterling was lost by a failure. Besides the interest of
the above sum, the collections made on Sabbath, with mort-
cloth money, marriages, &c. may amount to 12 l. Sterling,
annually. There are no travelling poor belonging to this
parish, though there is no want of such from other parishes ;
a practice which ought not to be tolerated in a well regulated state, as it extorts from charitable people, even against
their own judgment, part of what they would otherwise be-
stow with more pleasure and advantage among the residing
poor, whose characters and circumstances are known to them.
Births at an average are about 16 ; deaths 10 or 12. The
climate is healthy. There are no epidemical diseases peculiar
to this parish. There are some instances of longevity, as in
other places. Several have lived above 80 ; some above 90 ;
one or two above 100 years. Within this century, there
have flourished 15 ministers and preachers, 10 surgeons, 12
bred to the law, 6 writers, 6 schoolmasters, who were all
born and received the rudiments of their education in this
parish. For a long period past it has been less prolific of
learned men. At present there are none intended for any of
the learned professions, except one, who has been for some-
time in the line of a writer.

Ecclesiastical

Ecclefiaftical State and School.—The manfe was built about 50 years ago; it is ruinous, and intended to be rebuilt this fummer. The church is alfo in a bad ftate, having got no material repairs for a long period; it will fcarcely admit of repairs now, and probably muft be foon rebuilt. The ftipend, which needs much to be augmented, is only 1000 merks Scotch, including communion element money, which laft is no more than 1 l. 5 s. 9 d. Sterling, a fum four times lefs than the minifter's actual expences on that occafion-: This fmall fum is never paid but when the facrament is adminiftered, even when it is not in the minifter's power to do fo. The whole is paid in money; formerly there was part in victual. There has been no augmentation for 50 years paft. The glebe is fmall but good. There was a confiderable quantity of excellent wood growing on it, planted about 70 years ago, by the Reverend Mr Bryce. Some of the heritors, ignorant of the law and the rights of a clergymen to every thing growing on his glebe, cut it down, and fold it for 30 l. Sterling, immediately after the death of the laft incumbent. The prefbytery, as guardians, interferred; and, by the exertions of fuch of the heritors as had all along difapproved of the unjuftifiable meafure taken by the reft, the matter was at length amicably fettled, and the money, arifing from the fale of the trees, was paid to the prefent incumbent fhortly after his fettlement. There have been only 4 minifters here fince the revolution; Meffrs Wyllie, Plenderleith, Bryce, and Hunter. The laft was fettled in the year 1732, was 60 years minifter in Saline, and died at the age of 95; his wife and children all died long before him. The prefent incumbent was fettled on the 24th of January 1793. The crown is the undoubted patron.

The whole emoluments of the fchoolmafter, including perquifites for marriages, &c. may amount to 20 l. Sterling yearly, a fum by far too little for fo large a parifh, and fo

useful

ufeful an office. School fees 1 s. 6 d. a quarter for reading,
2 s. for writing, 2 s. 6 d. for arithmetic, 3 s. for Latin, which
is feldom taught here *.

Character.—The people, a few excepted, are fober, induftrious, fenfible, difcreet, and peaceable, of as little fuperftition and as much religion as their neighbours. They have
been long diftinguifhed' for their regular and decent attendance on public worfhip, and have not yet forfeited the praife
which

* There are no antiquities in the parifh, unlefs the remains
of two old towers and fome cairns on the tops of hills, may be
reckoned fuch One of the towers called Killerny, part of
which is yet ftanding, feems to have been pretty large. It confifted of two parts, called the N. and S. built at different times.
The date of the S or neweft part, which confifted chiefly of
one large room, all arched and very high, was 1592. That of
the other, which probably was a cell or hermitage, is unknown.
The eftate on which it ftands is faid to have belonged formerly
to one Scot of Balneiry; and fome fabulous ftories are told about
the murder of his lady and child, by the undertaker whom fhe
employed to build the S. part for a fummer-houfe, but did not
pay according to paction. As a punifhment for his crime, he is
faid to have been confined in a part of the tower called the prifon, and fed on his own flefh till he died. Some of the inhabitants have a fong which celebrates thefe fuppofed tragical events,
but its merit is not fuch as to entitle it to a place in the Statiftical Account of Scotland. There is neither record nor oral tradition as to the date or founder of the other tower called the Kirkland tower, part of which ftill remains. It ftands very near the
church, on part of the lands formerly belonging to the bifhop
at Dunkeld, which ftill bear the name of the Kirklands, now belonging to Sir William Erfkine of Torrie. It can hardly be
doubted, were the matter to be inveftigated, but the glebe,
which is faid to be lefs than the law allows, would be entitled
to an addition from thefe lands. The remains of two camps, as
they are called, are ftill to be feen, one on Saline hill, another
on the low grounds; the laft is faid to have been Roman. They
are both of a circular figure, and probably were originally fheep
or cattle folds, built with fome ftrength and art, in times when
rapine and plunder were the means of fubfiftance.

which is due to them on this account. They are averfe to long preachings, long prayers, and long pfalms; their ideas of religion and morality, in general, are tolerably found and rational. Thofe in better circumftances, of whom there is a good number in this parifh, are fociable, polite, and hofpitable.

Mifcellaneous Obfervations.—The village of Saline ftrikes a traveller by its beautiful and rural fituation. It lies in the center of the parifh, in a place which, being moftly furrounded with rifing ground, is fometimes called the Bafon. It confifts, if fmall things may be compared with great, of the old and new town, and contains in all, including the fuburbs, 200 inhabitants. A river, running through the middle, divides the old and new town; which laft has rifen within thefe few years, excels the other, both in the number and neatnefs of its buildings, and is ftill on the increafe; were manufactures introduced, and encouragement given, it might foon become confiderable. The whole village confifts of fmall feus, all belonging to Sir William Erfkine of Torrie, and the ground is ufually let at 2 l. an acre. There are four public houfes, none of which afford proper accommodation either for men or horfes. The chief article which is fold, pernicious frequently both to health and morals, is whifky. It is not long fince an inhabitant of the parifh was killed by it, and was carried from the public houfe to his grave; and foon after, another not more wife, nor warned by his example, had nearly fhared the fame fate. One good public houfe would be better than the whole; and as the great road from Dunfermline to Auchterarder runs through the village, a man of character and fubftance who could afford proper accommodation, might meet with great encouragement. It is the moft central place between the Ferry and Glendovan, for travellers to

halt

halt at ; and if the proprietor were to build ſuch a houſe, and
let it to one who could afford to brew and bake, he would
receive more than common intereſt for his money, would
confer a public benefit on the pariſh and on travellers, beſides increaſing and ornamenting the village, which he has
the pleaſure to ſee in a thriving and promiſing condition *.

* There is a practice here, too common in moſt places, which,
it were much to be wiſhed, was aboliſhed or leſs uſed. When
any one is taken ill, the neighbours think it their duty, or a
piece of civility, immediately to frequent the houſe, and even
crowd the room where the patient lies; which muſt be attended
with very bad effects. Even where the ſmall-pox or fevers are
raging, mothers with their children in their arms attend without ſcruple, a practice rather tempting, than truſting in providence, as it is unneceſſarily expoſing themſelves to danger,
which might be eaſily avoided. On theſe occaſions, they are all
phyſicians; they feel the pulſe, ſhake their heads, and have an
unlucky turn to foreboding the worſt. I have known a man giv-
en up by his neighbours, who, in three or four days after, has
been working in the ſtone quarry ; and ſeveral perſons are ſtill
alive, in very good health at this day, and likely to ſee ſome
carried to their graves, who had long ago pronounced their
doom.
A kin to this is a notion too common, though a miſtaken one,
that the miniſter of the pariſh ſhould almoſt conſtantly attend
the bed-ſide of the ſick. Where perſons are worn down with
age and infirmity, and have been long deprived of public in-
ſtruction, they have a right to ſee their miniſter, to converſe
with him, and receive conſolation, and ſo in other caſes, where
diſtreſs does not wholly unfit for converſation. But what can a
miniſter, if he has not ſome ſkill in phyſic, do or ſay to one in
the rage of a fever? he pretends not to work miracles, the patient means not to make confeſſion, to take the ſacrament, or to
receive extreme unction. When cuſtom is on the ſide of what
is right and profitable, it ought to be preſerved and encouraged;
if otherwiſe, however popular, it ſhould receive no countenance.

PARISH OF SCOONIE.

(COUNTY OF FIFE.)

By the Rev. Mr DAVID SWAN.

Name, Situation, and Extent.

NO fatisfactory account can be given of the origin of the name. In old records, it is written *Skuny*. The old church was fituated upon a fmall eminence, like an artificial mound, ftill employed as a burying ground, with a deep hollow on all fides. Such as are acquainted with the Erfe language may, perhaps, be able to trace fome connection between the name and fituation. Like the names of many other places in this country, it is probably of Celtic origin. The parifh is fituated in the county of Fife, and prefbytery of Kirkcaldy; from which place it is 9 ftatute miles diftant. It is about 5 miles long, from fouth to north; and nearly two miles in breadth. At the N. E. extremity, the three parifhes of Scoonie, Largo, and Ceres, and the three prefbyteries of Kirkcaldy, St Andrew's, and Cupar, meet in one point.

The ground rifes by a gentle flope, all the way from the Forth, nearly to the north end of the parifh; and almoft every part of it commands an extenfive and beautiful view of the Forth, Leith, Edinburgh, and the Lothians, from St Abb's head to the Queensferry: The greateft part of

the

the parifh is inclofed with ditch and hedge: There are no hills, but feveral fwells or rifings of the ground, which, with belts and clumps of planting, afford a finely variegated profpect.

Soil, Climate.—There are not 10 acres of unarable ground in the whole diftrict, but the foil is of different kinds: The fouthern and lower part of the parifh, comprehending about two thirds of it, confifts partly of a dry fharp foil, yielding good crops of all forts of grain, and of excellent quality, except in very dry weather ; and partly of a rich heavy loam, yielding large crops in all feafons. The northern and higher part of the parifh is a moift black foil, of which a large proportion is generally in pafture, for which it is well adapted; and when broke up, after lying 8 or 10 years, yields two or three very heavy crops. The climate in the lower part of the parifh is, in general, very mild and temperate ; but the E. and S. E. winds, blowing from the fea, are, efpecially in the fpring months, extremely fharp and penetrating. In the northern part of the parifh, the climate is more unkindly, and the harveft two or three weeks later, owing to the greater moifture of the foil, and its more elevated fituation. The inhabitants are, in general, healthy, and not fubject to any epidemical difeafe. Inoculation has not yet become fo general as in fome other parts of the country, but the people's prejudices againft it are gradually fubfiding.

Produce, Agriculture.—The crops in the lower part of the parifh are wheat, peafe and beans, barley, oats, potatoes, turnips, cabbage, flax and grafs. Almoft all the ground, defigned for pafture, is fown with artificial grafs. In the higher part of the parifh, the crops are, barley, oats, potatoes, a fmall proportion of peafe, fome turnips and flax.
There

There is ſcarce any flax raiſed, excepting what is for private uſe. The produce of oats, peaſe and potatoes, is wholly conſumed in the pariſh, and a conſiderable quantity of
oat meal is brought from the inland parts of the country.
There is no fixed mode of cultivation. Wheat is ſometimes
ſown after fallow, drilled beans, potatoes, or graſs that has
lain a year or two. Some fields produce wheat and beans
alternately, and generally yield very good crops. Every farmer raiſes a conſiderable quantity of turnips, which are now
employed rather for rearing young beaſts, than in feeding cattle for the market. Since the price of black cattle has been
advanced to ſuch a rate, the farmers have reared a much
larger quantity than formerly. Such as occupy a farm of
200 acres or ſo, raiſe annually 14 or 16 calves, which are
ſold at 2, 3, or 4 years old. Veal is now become a very
rare article in our markets.

Within theſe 20 years, there is a very great alteration in
the mode of plowing. In place of 4 horſes, or 4 and ſometimes 6 oxen, yoked in one plough, the land is now generally plowed with 2 horſes ; one man holding the plough
and managing the horſes.

Rent.—The valued rent of the pariſh is L. 4692, 8 s.
Scotch, and the real rent L. 2000 Sterling. Land lets at from
L. 1, 10 s. to L. 3 Sterling *per* acre. In large farms with
old leaſes, the rent is from 5 s. to 15 s. But as the leaſes ex-
pire, there is always a very conſiderable riſe. Paſture
grounds let at from L. 1, to L. 1, 10 s. *per* acre.

River and Fiſhing.—The river of Leven, which hath its
ſource from the lake of that name, runs along the ſouth
ſide of this pariſh, from weſt to eaſt, and takes a turn to the
ſouth, about a quarter of a mile before it is diſcharged into
the

the fea. It abounds with excellent trout of various kinds;
and at the mouth of the river, there is a falmon fifhing, which
belongs to the eftate of Durie. The greateft part of the
falmon caught here is carried over land to Perth, or Newburgh, where they are fhipped for the London market. On
this river there are from 36 to 40 mills, of different defcrip-
tions, within the fpace of 11 or 12 miles.

Population.—The return to Dr Webfter in 1755, was
1528 fouls. The number of inhabitants in this parifh at
prefent; (*anno* 1791,) is 1675; confequently the increafe
amounts to 147.

Abftraft of marriages and births for the laft 7 years.

Years.	Mar.	Males baptifed.	Fem.	Total baptifed.
1784	16	22	21	43
1785	11	21	20	41
1786	8	26	20	46
1787	18	15	16	31
1788	10	19	13	32
1789	8	24	27	51
1790	14	14	23	37

Of deaths no accurate regifter can be kept, the dead being interred in different burying grounds in the neighbourhood, and no account given of them. It is to be obferved,
that the number of births and marriages has not increafed
in proportion to the increafe of the grofs number; which
muft therefore be afcribed to the great influx of young
people, of late years, employed in the manufaftures. Of the
whole inhabitants, there are not above 150 feparatifts from
the eftablifhed church, of whom nearly the one half are
Burgher Seceders; 35 Antiburghers; 34 of the Relief Society; 2 Independents, and 3 Epifcopalians.

Heritors,

Heritors.—There are ſeven large proprietors in the pariſh, and two ſmall ones : Only two of the greater heritors reſide in it, viz. Mr Chriſtie of Durie, and Mr Tullidelph of Kilmux. The proprietor of Durie poſſeſſes above three fifths of the valued rent of the pariſh. The houſe of Durie is an elegant modern building, ſituated on a riſing ground, about a mile north from the Forth, and commanding a moſt delightful proſpect; with an extenſive policy, laid out in very good taſte. Few places in the country can boaſt of a more eligible ſituation. No eſtate in the pariſh is under entail.

Eminent Men.—Till within theſe few years, the eſtate of Durie had been, for near two centuries, the property of the reſpectable family of Gibſon, ſome of whom were particularly eminent in the law department. One of that family was Lord Regiſter, and another a Lord of Seſſion. Of the latter an anecdote is reported, which ſtrongly marks the barbarity of the times. There being an important cauſe between two noblemen, in dependence before the Court of Seſſion, Lord Durie, while taking an airing on the ſands of Leith, was forcibly carried off by one of them, in order to prevent him from giving his vote at the deciſion of the cauſe, which the party apprehended would be unfavourable to his intereſt.

But of all the eminent men born in this pariſh, none has been more remarkable for genius and learning, than Mr Jerome Stone. His father, (a reputable ſeafaring man,) dying abroad, when Jerome was but three years old, the mother, with her young family, was left in very narrow circumſtances. Jerome, like the reſt of the children, having got the ordinary ſchool education, reading Engliſh, writing and arithmetic, betook himſelf to the buſineſs of a travelling chapman. But the dealing in buckles, garters, and ſuch ſmall articles,

not

not fuiting his fuperior genius, he foon converted his little ftock into books, and, for fome years, went through the country, and attended the fairs as an itinerant bookfeller. There is great reafon to believe, that he engaged in this new fpecies of traffic, more with a view to the improvement of his mind, than for any pecuniary emolument. Formed by nature for literature, he poffeffed a peculiar talent for acquiring languages with amazing facility. By a ftrange predilection, he firft applied to the ftudy of the Hebrew and Greek ; and, by a wonderful effort of genius and application, made himfelf fo far mafter of thefe languages, without any kind of affiftance, as to be able to interpret the Hebrew Bible and Greek Teftament into Englifh *ad aperturam libri*. At this time he did not know one word of Latin. Senfible that he could make no great progrefs in learning, without the knowledge of Latin grammar, he made application to the then parifh fchoolmafter, Mr John Tufcan, (who is ftill alive), for his affiftance. Some time after, by the countenance and patronage of the late Reverend and learned Principal Tullidelph, an heritor of this parifh, he was encouraged to profecute his ftudies at the Univerfity of St Andrew's. An unexampled proficiency in every branch of literature recommended him to the efteem of the Profeffors : and an uncommon fund of wit and pleafantry rendered him, at the fame time, the favourite of all his fellow ftudents, fome of whom fpeak of him to this day, with an enthufiaftic degree of admiration and refpect. About this period, fome very humorous poetical pieces of his compofition were publifhed in the Scots Magazine. Before he had finifhed his third feffion at St Andrew's, on an application to the College, by the Rector of the fchool of Dunkeld, for an affiftant, Mr Stone was recommended as the beft qualified for that office; and about two or three years after, the Rector being removed

moved to Perth, Mr Stone, by the favour of his Grace the Duke of Atholl, who had conceived a high opinion of his abilities, was promoted to the rectorſhip.

When he firſt went to Dunkeld, he entertained but an un-favourable opinion of the Erſe language, which he conſider-ed as a barbarous gibberiſh : But in order to inveſtigate the origin and deſcent of the ancient Scots, he applied to the ſtudy of their primitive language. Having, with his uſual aſſiduity, endeavoured to maſter its grammatical difficulties, he ſet himſelf to diſcover ſomething of its true genius and character. He collected a number of ancient poems, the pro-ductions of Iriſh or Scottiſh bards, which, he ſaid, were da-ring, innocent, paſſionate and bold. Some of theſe poems he tranſlated into Engliſh verſe; which ſeveral perſons now alive have ſeen in manuſcript, before Mr Macpherſon pub-liſhed any of his tranſlations from Oſſian.

He died while he was writing and preparing for the preſs, a Treatiſe, entitled an " Inquiry into the Original of the " Nation and Language of the ancient Scots, with conjectures " about the primitive ſtate of the Celtic and other European " nations ;" an idea which could not have been conceived by an ordinary genius. In this treatiſe, he proves, by the cleareſt reaſoning, that the Scots drew their original, as well as their language, from the ancient Gauls. Had Mr Stone lived to finiſh this work, which diſcovers great ingenuity, immenſe reading, and indefatigable induſtry, it would have thrown much light upon the dark and early periods 'of the Scottiſh hiſtory, as he opens a new and plain path, for leading us through the unexplored labyrinths of antiquity. But a fever put a period to his life, his labours and his uſe-fulneſs, in the year 1757, being then only in the 30th year of his age. He left, in manuſcript, a much eſteemed and

well

well known allegory, entitled " the Immortality of Au-
" thors," which has been publifhed, and often reprinted
fince his death, and will be a lafting monument of a lively
fancy, found judgment, and correct tafte. It was no fmall
ornament of this extraordinary character, that he paid a
pious regard to his aged mother, who furvived him two
years, and received an annual penfion from the Duchefs of
Atholl, as a teftimony of refpect to the memory of her fon.

Village of Leven.—The only village in the parifh is Leven, which belongs to the barony of Durie, and is fituated
upon the eaft bank of the river, where it runs into the fea.
It contains 335 families, and 1165 inhabitants. The rents
of houfes are from 10 s. to L. 8 Sterling. There are 6
trading veffels of from 90 to 140 or 150 tons, belonging to
this port, employed moftly in the Holland and Eaft fea
trade. There is no port on the coaft of Fife better calculated for the timber and iron trade, having eafy accefs, by
roads perfectly level, to a populous adjacent country; and
the head of the river affording a fafe and commodious harbour. The beach is fandy, and the fhore quite flat.

Commerce.—There is a fair in the fpring for lintfeed, and
one every month, from May to October, for white linen.
There are two inns in the town, and fix fmall beer brewers,
befides four or five ale and porter houfes, &c.

Minerals.—There are very extenfive feams of coal in
the eftate of Durie, which have been wrought for upwards
of a century. One feam is of an excellent quality, and ufed to
be exported from Leven to Holland, where it met with a
more ready fale, than moft of the other coals carried from
this

this part of the country. This ſeam, ſo far as it could be drained by the preſent water engine, is now exhauſted. The ſeams now working are of an inferior quality, but an-ſwer for land ſale, and furniſh fuel for two or three ſalt pans, which are very productive. By an additional engine, the proprietor will have the command of a large field of the principal or better ſeam.

Manufactures.—The chief manufacture in the pariſh is that of brown linen, from 8 d. to 10 d. a yard. A conſiderable quantity is whitened, and ſold at from 10 d. to 20 d. and ſome of a finer texture from 2 s. to 4 s. a yard. There are about 140 looms in the pariſh, moſtly employed in that manufac-ture. In the near neighbourhood of Leven, there is an ex-tenſive bleachfield, which may employ about 16 or 18 hands. The buſineſs is yearly increaſing, as the people's prejudices againſt public bleaching are daily wearing off. There is alſo a conſiderable roperie eſtabliſhed at Leven, and a good number of ſhoemakers are conſtantly employed in making ſhoes for public ſale.

Church.—The church, a neat and modern building, with a ſpire, was erected about 16 years ago, in the immediate neighbourhood of Leven, being more convenient for the greater part of the pariſh, than the old ſituation at Scoonie, which is about half a mile diſtant. The Manſe has been in-habited above 15 years, and is ſituated within an hundred yards of the church. The right of patronage, which belonged formerly to the priory of St Andrew's, is veſted in the Crown. The ſtipend conſiſts of 54¼ bolls of bear, 44 bolls meal, 29¼ oats, and 4 bolls wheat, with L. 25 Sterling,

in

in money, and L. 3 : 6 : 8 for communion elements, befides
the manfe and glebe *.

Poor.—There are no begging poor in this parifh. About
15 or 16 families receive from 6 d. to 1 s. of weekly fupplies, according to their refpective circumftances. Three or
four have a fmall monthly allowance, befides occafional charities given to families in diftrefs. The members of the
kirk-feffion are very careful, in guarding, on the one hand,
againft impofitions, and, on the other, that no neceffitous
perfon be neglected. The only funds for the fupport of the
poor, are the weekly collections at the church doors, amounting to about L. 26; the collection at the communion, difpenfed twice a year, L. 11 ; feat rents L. 4, and a trifling
fum arifing from the mort-cloth, amounting all together to
about L. 45 or L. 46 Sterling *per annum.*

General Character.—The people in this parifh are, in general, fober, induftrious, and thriving. If any behave in an
irregular and diforderly manner, they are avoided by their
neighbours, it being reckoned difcreditable to be feen in
their company. They are focial in their tempers, liberal in
their fentiments, refpectful to their fuperiors, and hofpitable
to ftrangers; regular in attending upon the public inftitu-
tions

* As a tribute to the memory of a worthy clergyman, it may be proper to
mention, that Mr Thomas Melvill, the late incumbent, who was fettled in
1718, being, by years and infirmity, laid afide from duty, was obliged to
employ an affiftant; and, underftanding that the admiffion of his affiftant to
be his fucceffor, would be acceptable to the parifh, he, to make way for his
fucceffion, although he had no natural connection with him, readily and generoufly refigned his charge in 1764, ending his days 3 years after, in a ftate
of the moft chearful tranquillity.

tions of religion, and remarkable for external decency in the houſe of God. Few people are more compaſſionate to the indigent, or contribute more liberally to their ſupport, not only by their public collections, but by private donations. Such as ſeparate from the eſtabliſhed church, have little of that reſerve or moroſeneſs, which is the general characteriſtic of ſeparatiſts of almoſt all denominations. There have been, as in all ſocieties, ſome idle worthleſs perſons among them ; but in the memory of man, there has not been one convicted of a capital crime.

Schools.—There is one eſtabliſhed grammar ſchool in the pariſh. The maſter, who is fully qualified for his office, teaches Engliſh, Latin, Greek, writing, arithmetic, book-keeping, the practical parts of mathematics, and navigation. There is a commodious ſchool, and ſchool-houſe furniſhed by the heritors. The ſalary is L. 200 Scotch, and, with the other emoluments, may amount to L. 40 Sterling a year. There are, beſides, two or three ſmall ſchools, in which young children are taught to read Engliſh, at the very eaſy rate of 1 d. *per* week.

Antiquities.—The only antiquities this pariſh can boaſt of, are ſome ſtone coffins, which have been found to the eaſtward of the river, with human bones, ſuppoſed to have been depoſited there in the 9th century, when a battle was fought upon theſe grounds between the Scots and the Danes.

Advantages.—It is no ſmall advantage to this pariſh, particularly to the town of Leven, that they have no connection with corporation or borough politics, which, for the moſt part, are attended with ſuch bad effects upon the induſtry and morals of the people. The manufacturers have the benefit

of

of a ready money market for their cloth, as foon as cut from
the loom, without travelling 100 yards from their own
doors. It is alfo a matter of great conveniency to have a
Poft-office at Leven, with an arrival every day from Edinburgh, Monday excepted, and a departure every day, except Saturday. The turnpike road, from Kirkcaldy to the
eaft coaft of Fife, interfects the parifh in a ftraight line from
weft to eaft, at the diftance of about half a mile from
the town of Leven, and the turnpike road from Kirkcaldy
to Cupar, by Cameron bridge, runs diagonally through the
northern part of the diftrict. In a fhort time, there will be
an excellent road from the fhore of Leven to Cupar, the
county town, which is diftant about 10 ftatute miles. The
principal advantage of the parifh, is, the having abundance
of coal in the near neighbourhood, the ordinary fuel of the
pooreft families. Peats are a fort of rarity, of which fome
families purchafe a fmall quantity yearly, for their conveniency. To all thefe advantages, it may be added, that every perfon in health, may, with moderate induftry, earn a
comfortable livelihood.

Difadvantages.—As Leven is a thoroughfare from the
weft to the eaft coaft of Fife, the inhabitants are much oppreffed with beggars and vagrants. Largely as they contribute to the fupport of the indigent among themfelves, they
complain, that they give three or four times more to ftranger poor. It is an obvious defect in the police of this country, that no effectual method is devifed for reftraining vagrant beggars, who lay the public under fuch heavy contributions. It may, perhaps, be faid, that the people are not
obliged to ferve them : But fuch as are acquainted with the
ftate of the country, know well, that while thefe vagrants are
permitted to go about, the people *muft* give them fomething.

It

It is a conſiderable inconvenience to this pariſh, that there is no bridge upon the Leven, nearer than Cameron, about 2 miles up the river. But there are two good fords in the neighbourhood, always paſſable, except i i h floods, or for an hour or two at high water, during ſpring tides; and near the town, there is alſo a coble or boat for paſſengers. It is likewiſe a very great inconvenie ce, not only to this pariſh, but to travellers in general, that there is no bridge over Scoonie river, upon the great turnpike road to the eaſt coaſt. The water s often regorged with ſuch banks of ice upon each ſide, that there is no paſſage for carriages, but with manifeſt danger. Though in ſummer it is almoſt dry, yet the water ſometimes riſes to ſuch a height, as not to be fordable with ſafety. Some years ago, a farmer and his wife attempting to croſs upon horſeback, were carried a conſiderable way down the ſtream; the woman not leſs than 400 or 500 yards. Had they not been ſeen, and opportunely aſſiſted by the neighbourhood, both of them muſt inevitably have periſhed.

It is to be hoped, for the credit of the gentlemen of the diſtrict, that this inconveniency will ſoon be remedied. The want of good free-ſtone quarries has been a great diſcouragement to building in this pariſh, as ſtones cannot be got, but with much labour and expence. Neverthelefs the greater part of this pariſh have reaſon to acknowledge with gratitude, the goodneſs of a wiſe and gracious Providence, which hath rendered their ſituation, upon the whole, ſo eaſy and comfortable.

PARISH of STRATHMIGLO,

(COUNTY OF FIFE.)

By the Rev. Mr GEORGE LYON.

Name, Situation, Surface, Soil, &c.

STRATHMIGLO is ſo called, as being a ſtrath or valley on both ſides of the water of Miglo, which runs through it from W. to E. and then takes the name of Eden. It is in the preſbytery of Cupar, and Synod of Fife. It is 5½ Engliſh miles long, and 3½ broad, bounded by the Lomond Hill on the S. and on the N. by a branch of the Ochil Hills; and by the pariſhes of Portmoak, Orwell, Arngoſk, Abernethy, Auchtermuchty, Kettle and Falkland. It is partly flat, and partly hilly. The ſoil on the N. ſide of the water is generally moiſt, but tolerably fertile; on the S. ſide dry and ſhallow; but in the eaſtern part of the pariſh, on both ſides of the water, it is deep and fertile. The air, through a great part of the year is rather moiſt, but not unhealthy. The moſt prevalent diſtempers are fevers, attributed to the moiſtneſs; but they are not frequent, and ſeldom mortal. There are no remarkable mountains. The hills are covered

vered with grafs. A bed of freeftone runs along the S.
fide of the water of Miglo for about 3 miles, and is ufed
for building houfes and inclofing ground. There is no
other found, except a white ftone on the N. fide of the
Lomond Hill, which admits of a fine polifh, and is ufed
by the richer fort of people for hearthftones, the corners
of their houfes, and lintels for doors and windows. A
kind of moorftone is fometimes ufed for inclofing ground
with what they call a Galloway dike, or open ftone-fence.

Population.—By Dr Webfter's report, the numbers
were 1695 *. In the year 1754, when I was ordained minifter of the parifh, there were about 1100 perfons in it,
and this year (1790) there are about 980, of whom about
470 are males, and 510 are females. From the 1ft of
October 1783, when the regifter began to be better,
though not exactly kept, to the 1ft of October 1790, the
number of births has been about 225, of burials about
136, and of marriages about 95. There is but one inftance of a very long life well authenticated, that of one
James Beveridge, who lived to 110, and was 7 times married. There are 26 farmers, whofe families may confift
of 182 perfons in all : About 50 manufacturers, 46 handicraftfmen, 24 apprentices, 29 houfehold and 50 labouring
fervants, 4 merchants, and 110 inhabitants in the town of
Strathmiglo. There are about 266 born in other diftricts
or parifhes in Scotland. There are 19 heritors ; 12 of
whom, among which are 2 families of gentry, refide.
There is one writer. About 750 are of the Eftablifhed
Church, about 228 Seceders, and 2 Epifcopalians. The
population of the parifh is materially different from what
it was 25 years ago, and the decreafe is attributed chiefly
to the throwing 2 or 3 fmall farms into one, and the a-
bolifhing of cotteries ; for, though fome of the cottagers
take

---

* Probably a miftake of the pen for 1695.

take houſes in the town of Strathmiglo, others go and reſide in towns, where the encouragement to manufactures
is greater. Each marriage may produce, at an average,
5 children; none have died from want; no murders or
ſuicides have been committed; few have emigrated, and
none have been baniſhed; if any have left the pariſh, it
was not for want of employment. There are about 245
inhabited houſes. At an average, 4 perſons may be to
each inhabited houſe. A few are uninhabited.

Agriculture, &c.—The number of cattle may be about
500, of horſes 190, and of ſheep 300. Within theſe few
years, great improvements have been made in agriculture.
There are about 54 ploughs, all of the common kind;
74 carts, and 2 carriages. The pariſh ſupplies itſelf with
proviſions for common uſe; but at the ſame time, it both
imports and exports.—26 years ago there were only 2
incloſures in the pariſh, and now there are about 63, and
many of them large. Great part of the pariſh is now incloſed. The people generally ſow in April and May, and
reap in Auguſt and September. There is only one wood
about 3 quarters of a Scots mile in circumference: One
piece of marſhy ground, about a quarter of a mile long,
and very narrow: One lake, about a quarter of a mile
in circumference; and no river except Miglo, which is
very ſmall. The pariſh has no peculiar advantages or
diſadvantages that I know; except the advantage of being
in the immediate neighbourhood of hills for the rearing
of ſheep. The land-rent may be about L. 2926 Sterling.
The rent of houſes cannot be exactly aſcertained, as they
are of ſuch different dimenſions; but a houſe of 2 ſtoreys
may rent at L. 3, 4 s. Sterling, and of 1 ſtorey, if of equal
length and breadth, at L. 1, 16 s.

Stipend,

Stipend, Poor, &c.—The living, including the glebe, is, at the ordinary conversion of victual, L. 105, 13 s. Sterling. Lord Stormont is patron. The church was built about 5 years ago, and the manse 2 years sooner.—There are 8 poor families, who receive monthly pensions, .besides some others, who have occasional relief. The ordinary annual amount of the weekly contributions is about L. 8 : 12 : 4 Sterling, and the produce of alms, and other funds destined for that purpose, is about L. 23 : 3 : 4.

Prices, Wages, &c.—Butcher meat 30 years ago was about 2½ d. now 4½ d. ; and so on as to other articles ; a boll of wheat 15 s. now L. 1, 1 s.; of barley 9 s. now 14 s.; and of oats 8 s. now 12 s.—A day's wage for a labourer in husbandry and other work, is generally 1 s. without victuals, and 8 d. with them ; and so on as to other professions.—The fuel commonly made use of is coal. The price on the coal-hill is 7 d. for the load, which is reckoned 16 stone. They are procured from Balgonie, Balbirnie, Lochgellie, and Kettle—I cannot exactly say what the expence of a common labourer, when married, at an average may be ; but if he has 3 or 4 young children, it may be about L. 16, 12 s. ; and if he and his wife are in health and vigour, his wages, with any little shift his wife can make, and it can be-but little while the children are very young, is sufficient to bring up his family. The usual wages of a farmer's principal male servant, are L. 8 Sterling ; of an under male servant, L. 4; of a female servant, L. 2, 5 s.; and of a domestic female servant, L. 2, 10 s.

Miscellaneous Observations.—There are only 2 villages. The people are generally of the middle size. The tallest man I ever heard of, and whom I knew, was about 6 feet 5. They are in general disposed to industry and œconomy.

No

No manufactures are carried on, except by individuals. They are not fond of a seafaring or military life. Property, particularly in land, does not often change. It sells, at an average, at about 26 years purchase. The people are as much disposed to humane and generous actions, as others in their circumstances generally are. On the whole, they enjoy the comforts and advantages of society, and seem contented.—The county roads and bridges are in tolerable good order, and are kept in repair by assessments in money and statute-labour, exacted in kind. There are no turnpikes. The general opinion is, that if the money raised by them is properly applied, it is the only effectual way to make good roads and bridges, and keep them in proper repair.— The farms in general may be at an average of about 150 acres, and the average rent about 10 s. an acre. The number of farms is diminishing rather than increasing.—The manners of the inhabitants are much the same they were 36 years ago, civil and obliging ; but their dress and style of living are very different. At that time, though the rents the farmers paid were very low, they and their families were in general coarsely clad, and lived in a mean style ; but now that the rents are greatly raised, in some places of the parish doubled, and in one farm almost tripled, the farmers are in appearance richer, and their families dress and live much better.

PARISH OF TORRYBURN.

(County and Synod of Fife—Preſbytery of Dumfermline)

By the Rev. Mr. David Balfour.

Erection and Name.

THE pariſh, now known by the name of Torryburn, includes the pariſhes of *Torry* and *Crombie*. When their
union took place, cannot be aſcertained ; but it appears, from
certain papers relating to the ſtipend, that it muſt have been
before the year 1623. The name of the former, *Torry*, ſignifies, in Gaelic, the *King's Height*, and, with the addition of
burn, the Scotch word for a rivulet, is now the general name
of both. This addition ſeems to have been ſuggeſted by a
ſmall ſtream, which runs along the ſouth eaſt part of the principal village in the pariſh, and divides the two baronies of
Torry and Crombie*.

Situation

---

* The names of the places, in the pariſh, are partly Engliſh, and partly Gaelic.
The Engliſh names are expreſſive, either of the local ſituation, or of the name
                                                                        of

Situation and Extent.—It lies on the weſtern extremity of the county of Fife. Its extent is inconſiderable, being only, from E. to W. about 2 miles, the ſame in breadth on the eaſt quarter, and nearly the ſame on the weſt, if the lands, which are in the pariſh only *quoad ſacra*, are included. From N. W. to S. E. it will meaſure between 4 and 5 miles.

Soil and Cultivation.—The ſoil, throughout the pariſh, is naturally good, and in general well cultivated, particularly the lands of Torry, all of which are incloſed, and in the higheſt ſtate of improvement. Theſe lands, when laid down in graſs, make excellent paſturage. The ſucceſſion of crops on the Torry eſtate, (moſt of which is at preſent in the hands of the proprietor), is in general as follows :—turnips, barley, red clover, wheat, beans, oats. The ground is well dunged for the turnips, and well limed for the wheat. This method of cropping, has been found to ſucceed very well. The lands, in general, let from 20s. to 40s. per acre.—The time of ſowing peaſe, beans, and oats, is from the middle of March till the middle of April. Barley is commonly ſown in the month of May,

of the original proprietor. Thus, *Moorſide*, ſituated on the ſide of a moor ; *Grey Crags*, ſituated near a ſtone quarry ; *Milltown Row*, a row of houſes ſituated near where a mill once ſtood ; *Knowhead*, ſituated on the top of a riſing ground ; *Annsfield*, the field of Ann. The Gaelic names, *Torry*, (above mentioned) ; *Inzievar*, a *place ſeen from a diſtance* ; *Drumfin*, or rather *fian*, the ridge of Fingal, and probably *Crombie* and *Pitſoulie*.—There were two perſons belonging to this place, who accompanied Lord Anſon in his voyage round the world, in the years 1741-2-3, and who came to England with him in the year 1744. The proportion of prize-money, which, in the courſe of this expedition, fell to the ſhare of one of theſe men, was pretty conſiderable. Upon his return home, he purchaſed a ſmall piece of ground, and built a houſe upon it, which he called *Tinian*, after the beautiful and fertile iſland of that name in the Pacific Ocean, and to which the crew of the *Centurion*, the Commodore's ſhip, and the only remaining one of the ſquadron, owed their preſervation.

May, turnips in June, and wheat in the months of September and October. In early seasons, the harvest commences about the middle of August; in late ones, about the beginning of September; and the crops are generally got in by the end of October.—In the year 1782, the fields were not entirely clear before the middle of November.

Climate and Diseases.—The situation of Torryburn is healthy and pleasant, and the inhabitants live to a considerable age. There are several persons to be found at present above 80. There are no diseases in the parish which can be called endemial, or peculiar to the people. They are sometimes afflicted with fevers, but these seldom prove mortal.

Coals, &c.—In the lands of Torry, the property of Sir William Erskine, there are many different seams of coal, of various qualities and thickness. Great fields of these coals are still to work, (particularly the main coal of Torry, which is of the best quality), but they are all under level. The lands of Crombie were found to contain 6 seams of coal, of a quality much the same with that of the Newcastle, and, like it, turned out small. The seams above the level are wrought out. Parts of the others still remain, but cannot be wrought but with the assistance of a powerful engine. The following table of the thickness of the various seams of coal, in both estates, was furnished by a gentleman, who was proprietor of the one, and had a lease of the other.

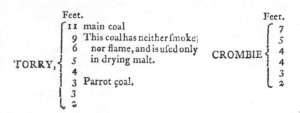

Feet.
TORRY, {
11 main coal
9 This coal has neither smoke,
6 nor flame, and is used only
5 in drying malt.
4
3 Parrot coal.
3
2

Feet.
CROMBIE {
7
5
4
4
3
2

Besides

Befides thefe different feams, there is, on the north parts of Torry, a fine parrot coal, in thicknefs 4 feet, which is very valuable, and is faid to fell in the London market, at a higher price than any other.—There is alfo very good iron ftone in the parifh, fome of which has been wrought.

Population.—This parifh, though inconfiderable in regard to extent, is pretty populous. Upon a furvey of the inhabitants, taken laft year (1791), they amounted to 1,600 fouls. The return to Doctor Webfter in 1755, was 1,635. The following table will fhew the medium of marriages, births, and burials for the laft 20 years.

Years.	Mar.	Births.	Bur.	Years.	Mar.	Births.	Bur.
1772	20	75	34	1782	10	63	44
3	17	67	68	3	6	60	62
4	15	78	30	4	18	66	34
5	15	69	36	5	23	62	56
6	11	63	36	6	16	57	36
7	11	77	62	7	16	66	56
8	15	81	47	8	10	52	22
9	9	70	48	9	12	54	42
1780	11	68	41	1790	17	43	59
1	8	61	34	1	7	57	40
	132	709	436		135	580	451
Ann. Av. nearly	13	70	43	Ann. Av. nearly	13	58	45

From this comparative ftatement, it appears, by the births, that the population of the parifh has been upon the decreafe during the laft 10 years, which is actually the cafe. In the firft period, the coal in the eftate of Crombie was wrought to a pretty confiderable extent; but, when it began to fail, numbers of the workmen went to collieries in the neighbourhood; and at prefent, very few families of them remain in the parifh. With regard to the deaths, (the mediums of which, in both periods, are nearly equal, and which, in the laft, ought

to

to have diminiſhed in proportion), it muſt be obſerved, that
thoſe people who have left the pariſh, ſtill continue to bury
their dead here, whoſe interments, without diſtinction, are in-
ſerted in the regiſter, along with thoſe of actual pariſhioners.
It appears, from the regiſter of the dead, which was begun in
this pariſh in February 1696 *, that in the year 1697, 114
died ; and that of theſe, 76 died in the months of January,
February, March and April. In the year 1699, 81 died ; of
whom 40 in the months of September, October, November
and December. This vaſt mortality is accounted for by a
dearth †, which prevailed, more or leſs, for 7 years in the end
of laſt century ; at which period alſo, great numbers of fiſh
are ſaid to have been thrown in upon the coaſt ; of theſe the
people eat immediately from the want of other food, and thereby became the prey of dyſenteries, and other putrid diſorders.
—The great body of the people is compoſed of day labourers ‡, mechanics, and ſailors.

Proprietors and Rent.—There are 14 heritors in the pariſh,
4 great, and 10 ſmall. The valued rent, as appears from
an extract taken from the ceſs books of the county, amounts
to 5,184l. Scotch. There are ſome lands, in the pariſh only
quoad ſacra, the valued rent of which is 889l. 3s. 4d. Scotch.

Church and Schools.—The value of the living, including a
glebe of two acres and a half, amounts to between 80l. and 90l.
Sterling.

* The medium of deaths might then be about 21.

† The meal is ſaid on that occaſion, to have been ſo high as 2s. per peck.

‡ Day labourers earn, in ſummer, 1s. per day ; and, in winter, 9d. or 10d.
Wrights and maſons, 1s. 6d. ; and the wages of plowmen are from 6l. to 8l.
per annum. The wages of women, are, for turnip weeding, and hay making,
6d.; and ſhearing in harveſt, 7d. and 8d., with their proviſions.

Sterling. The patron is the Rev. Dr. John Erſkine of Carnock, one of the miniſters of Edinburgh.—There is a good
parochial ſchool here for the following branches of education:
Latin, Engliſh, writing, arithmetic, navigation and book-
keeping ; beſides a Sabbath evening ſchool, which is ſupported by ſubſcription, and is at preſent in a flouriſhing condition,
and well attended.

Poor.—The number of perſons at preſent on the poor's
roll amounts to 50 ; 15 of theſe receive each from 3d. to 6d.
per week ; other 15 are allowed 4l. Scotch, to enable them to
defray their houſe rents ; and the remaining 20 are thoſe,
who, though in leſs indigent circumſtances, ſtand in need of
ſome aſſiſtance, and receive from time to time, according as
the funds will allow. The funds, from whence theſe payments
are made, ariſe, chiefly, from the weekly collections at the
church doors, and the profits of the mortcloth, which amount,
in all, to about 30l. Sterling yearly.

Shipping and Trade.—There are 13 veſſels belonging to
this place, viz. 1 ſhip, 3 brigs, and 9 ſloops ; whoſe burdens,
put together, amount to upwards of 1000 tons, and give employment to about 70 ſeamen. The larger veſſels are engaged in foreign trade. The ſloops are coaſters; but ſome of them
occaſionally go up the Baltic for wood and grain. We have
2 paſſage boats, the largeſt of which was built by the merchants of Dunfermline, principally for the purpoſe of tranſporting to Borrowſtownneſs their manufactured diapers, which
are brought here in carts, and carried to London by the Borrowſtownneſs traders, and for bringing over the goods, which
come for them by the ſame conveyance : And the other is
chiefly employed in importing commodities for the conſumption
of the inhabitants. There are no manufactures in the pariſh ;
but

but there is a confiderable quantity of yarn fpun for the manufacturers in Dunfermline, which brings into circulation
here, to the amount of between 400l. and 50cl. Sterling yearly.

Antiquities.—There are no natural curiofities in the parifh,
and its antiquities are but few. In a pretty extenfive plain
field, N. E. of the village of Torryburn, there is a flat ftone,
raifed upon one end, of a fhape nearly oblong, and meafuring,
from the furface to the top, about 8 feet, and about $4\frac{1}{4}$ in
breadth. Round the edge of it there is a deep circle, and on
each of the fides a number of ridges, all of which wear the
appearance of art and antiquity. At about 18 or 20 paces
from this ftone, there is a number of fmaller ones, which,
from their prefent pofition, feem to have formed part of a
circle. This place is thought to have been the fcene of a
battle in fome former period, and thefe ftones to mark the
graves of fome of the chiefs, who had fallen in the engagement. And the fuppofition is rendered highly probable
by the name which it ftill bears, *Tollzies*, which is evidently a corruption of the Scotch word *Tulzie*, which fignifies a
a *fight*.

In the church-yard, there is part of an epitaph, which,
from its fingularity, and at the fame time beautiful fimplicity,
appears well worth prefervation. When the prefent incumbent entered to his benefice, it was entire upon the grave
ftone ; but a gentleman, whofe property the burying ground
now is, perhaps from inattention, caufed part of it to be
erafed, in order to make room for inferting the deaths of
fome of his relations. The following is the epitaph intire, as originally compofed.

E P I-

EPITAPH.

" At *anchor* now, in Death's dark *Road,*
  " Rides honeſt Captain HILL,
" Who ſerv'd his king, and fear'd his God,
  " With upright heart and will.

  " In ſocial life ſincere and juſt,
    " To vice of no kind given;
  " So that his better part, we truſt,
    " Hath made the PORT of HEAVEN."

PARISH OF WEMYSS,

(County and Synod of Fife, Presbytery of Kirkcaldy).

By the Rev. Mr George Gib, *Miniſter.*

Name, Extent, and Surface.

THE name of the pariſh is ſaid to be Gaelic, and ſignifies a *Cave*, in alluſion to the number of natural
caves on ·the ſea-ſhore, near the village of Eaſter Wemyſs.
Hence, too, all that tract of ground between the lower part
of the water of Ore and the ſea, was, in old times, called
Wemyſsſhire. The pariſh is diſtant from the Preſbytery-
ſeat about three miles. Its greateſt length, which is from
S. W. to N. E. will not exceed 6 miles, nor its greateſt
breadth 1¼. It is bounded by the pariſh of Dyſart on the
W.; by Markinch on the N. and E. ; the water of Leven
ſeparates it from a ſmall part of the pariſh of Scoonie on
the N. E. ; and the frith of Forth waſhes it on the S. The
ground, which is in ſome places high along the ſhore, afterwards

terwards riſes gently to the N. The ſhore, from high water mark outward, is lined with rocks, which are not high, being moſtly covered at high water.

Climate and Diſeaſes.—Like all the S. and E. ſhore of Fife, being much expoſed to the E. winds in the ſpring months, it is unfavourable to pulmonic complaints, but in other reſpects, the climate cannot be ſaid to be unhealthy. Some of the fiſhermen are afflicted with calculous concretions : and the reaſon which they generally aſſign for this, is their being ſo much expoſed to cold with wet feet. Many children die of the ſmall-pox in the natural way. In the village of Buckhaven upwards of 30 were lately cut off. It is to be hoped, however, that the prejudice againſt inoculation will not in future be ſo general as it has been. Many perſons live to upwards of 80 ; and within theſe two years, 3 perſons have died above 90.

Villages.—Weſter Wemyſs is a burgh of barony, with 2 bailies, a treaſurer, and council. There are other 3 villages on the coaſt, *viz.* Eaſter Wemyſs, Buckhaven, and Methil. There are 2 villages in the country called E. and W. Coaltowns.

Soil and Agriculture.—The ſoil varies both in the country and on the coaſt. In ſome places it is fine black loam ; in others light and brown, ſometimes approaching to ſand ; and a ſmall part, particularly in the N. W. corner, is cold and wet. It is all arable, and, with a few acres excepted, produces good crops of wheat, bear, beans, peaſe, oats, potatoes, and turnip. The farmers are, in general, active and induſtrious, and attentive to every improvement in agriculture. In farms near the villages, land is let to trades people for planting potatoes, who muſt all afford manure,

hand-

hand-hoe their potatoes, and pay at the rate of L. 3 the acre. By this means the farmer procures a quantity of good manure, has his ground well cleaned, and an excellent crop of wheat or bear the following year. The plough used is Small's, which is drawn by two horfes, and held and managed by one man. There are no fheep, but a few kept by Colonel Wemyfs for family-ufe, and they are of a very fine kind. There are 16 farms, which are rented from L. 25 to upwards of L. 400 a-year.

A confiderable quantity of land near the coaft is rented by land-labourers, who refide in the villages, and though, with many of them, farming is only a fecondary object, yet the land in general is well laboured, and produces good crops. Almoft all fow fome turnip for their cows in winter, and feed their horfes with potatoes, which are generally boiled and mixed up with light corn. The fea-weed, or ware, which is driven in by the fea all along the fhore, makes excellent manure when fpread immediately after it is carried to the land. This land, which is ufually called the Acre-land, lets from L. 1, 10 s. to L. 2, 15 s. the acre.

Plantations. —There is but little old wood, excepting fome at the caftle of Wemyfs. The late proprietor, the Hon. James Wemyfs, Efq; inclofed a great part of the parifh ; fome of it with ftone and lime, and other parts with ditches and hedge, and planted many thoufands of trees; and his fon, the prefent proprietor, is going on with the fame plan. He has inclofed much. and for thefe 6 years paft has planted, of various kinds, upwards of 200,000 trees every year, in different places. All the plantations are in a very thriving way, and in a few years will both warm and greatly beautify the grounds.

Fifhing

Fiſhing and Buckhaven.—From the ſcarcity of haddocks
for ſome years, ſeveral of the fiſhermen have entered into
the navy, or on board merchant-ſhips, and others have become day labourers in country work. Formerly there
were in Eaſter Wemyſs 5 boats, with 5 men each, and
one in Weſter Wemyſs, with 5 men, and now there is only
one boat in Eaſter Wemyſs, and the crew conſiſt of old
men. In Buckhaven, the fiſhing is ſtill continued with
little alteration in the number of fiſhermen; and though
fiſh are much ſcarcer than formerly, yet the fiſhermen are
in ſome meaſure compenſated by the high price, and certain market for thoſe they catch. The fiſh uſually caught
are haddock, cod, turbot, ſkate, whitings, ſoles, flounders,
makarel and herring. A conſiderable quantity of lobſters
and crabs, or partons, (and ſometimes a few cray or craw-
fiſh) are taken, with trap-creels let down into the ſea upon
the rocks near the ſhore. A worthy fiſherman aſſured me,
that he has known, about 40 years ago, 25,000 haddocks
caught by the fiſhermen of Buckhaven in one day, which
were ſold from 6 d. to 10 d. the 100; now more is ſometimes given for a ſingle haddock. At preſent, moſt of the
fiſh caught here are ſent to the Edinburgh market, and the
reſt are ſold in this neighbourhood by women, who carry
them in creels on their backs. When fiſhing was plenty,
few of the fiſh caught in this pariſh were ſent to Edinburgh,
becauſe then the fiſhermen in the Eaſt of Fife carried their
fiſh to that market, and thoſe being taken in deeper water,
and conſequently larger, were always preferred. At that
time moſt of the fiſh caught here were ſold in the neighbouring burghs, or bought up by men who carried them
in creels on horſes to a conſiderable diſtance, where they
found a good market. This laſt gave employment to many
in the pariſh; and a few years ago, ſome of them had got
neat carts fitted up for the purpoſe; but of late, they have

been

been obliged, in a great meafure, to give this up, both from the fcarcity and high price of fifh. Twelve boats, with 6 men in each, ufed in the month of Auguft, to go from this parifh to the herring-fifhing off Dunbar; but the encouragement for fome years paft was fo fmall, that they had entirely abandoned it. There is now, however, a profpect of this fifhing being revived by the appearance of herring in the Bay of Inverkeithing; if there is encouragement, the fifhermen here will not fail to improve it.

The fifhermen in Buckhaven generally marry when young, and all of them marry fifhermens daughters of the fame village. I am particularly indebted to a very ingenious and intelligent General for a letter written by my late amiable and worthy predeceffor, the Rev. Dr Harry Spens *, when minifter of this parifh, (dated Wemyfs, 20th Auguft 1778), from which the following particulars refpecting the original inhabitants of Buckhaven, &c. are tranfcribed:

" As far as I have been able to learn, the original inha-
" bitants of Buckhaven were from the Netherlands about
" the time of Philip II. Their veffel had been ftranded
" on the fhore. They propofed to fettle and remain. The
" family of Wemyfs gave them permiffion. They ac-
" cordingly fettled at Buckhaven. By degrees they ac-
" quired our language and adopted our drefs, and for thefe
" threefcore years paft, they have had the character of a
" fober and fenfible, an induftrious and honeft fet of people.
" The only fingularity in their ancient cuftoms that I re-
" member to have heard of was, that of a richly orna-
" mented girdle or belt, wore by their brides of good con-
" dition and character at their marriage, and then laid afide
" and

---

* He publifhed an Englifh tranflation of Plato, de Repub.

" and given in like manner to the next bride that fhould
" be deemed worthy of fuch an honour. The village con-
" fifts at prefent of about 140 families, 60 of which are
" fifhers, the reft land-labourers, weavers, and other me-
" chanics."

Minerals and Foffils.—There is a great quantity of free-
ftone, but in general of a reddifh colour, open and porous,
and apt to crumble when much expofed to the weather.
There is limeftone, but it is faid not to be of a good quality ; perhaps it would have been more valued had lime been
in lefs abundance in the neighbourhood. Ironftone has
lately begun to be wrought ; but what deferves here particularly to be noticed is the excellent coal with which this
parifh abounds, and which has been wrought for fome centuries. In the weft ground of the parifh, befides what is
called Dyfart coal, (which is 21 feet thick, with 3 feet of
coarfe coal left for a roof) of which a very extenfive field
remains to be wrought in the eftate of Wemyfs, there are
other 10 or 11 workable feams of coal, moft of which have
been wrought above the level of the fea. The principal
feam of the 10 or 11 is now working between 50 or 60
fathoms below the furface. This feam is 10 feet thick,
but 8 feet of it is only wrought, *viz.* 5 feet of very fine
fplint, and 3 feet of free, the other 2 feet being left for a
roof. The water is raifed by a fteam-engine. The coal
is brought to the pit-bottom by horfes under ground, and
then raifed by horfe-gins. Coal for exportation is driven
in large waggons from the pits to the harbour of Wefter
Wemyfs. The other feams in this part of the parifh, which
have been wrought, are all entire below the level of the
fea, excepting one, a fmall part of which was wrought near
the fea, about the year 1656, at which time the water was
drawn off by horfes.

In

In the eaſt ground of the pariſh there are ſeveral work-able ſeams of coal. The Right Hon. David Earl of Wemyſs, (a nobleman of a great and public ſpirit, who kept a particular account of the coal, written with his own hand, mentions ſeven ſeams of coal which he had cut through in making a level mine from the ſea-ſhore, which he drove upwards of 600 fathoms acroſs the metals. In working this level in 1671, he obſerves, " I am ſtill work-" ing that level in ſtone, with two men in it day and night " (except Sundays). I give them 10 s. Scots a-day, their " bearers 4 s. Scots a-day, the windles men get 6 s. Scots " a day or night. I ſharp their picks and furniſh their " candles." The only ſeams that have been wrought in this part of the pariſh for a conſiderable time were, one 8 feet thick, and 20 fathoms from the ſurface, and another much about the ſame thickneſs, and 7 fathoms deeper. The main coal is 12 feet thick, of an excellent quality, and was always preferred at the foreign markets. It was formerly wrought to a conſiderable depth by two engines, at Kirk-land of Methil, which were driven by the water of Leven. To the S. of Kirkland this coal is cut off by a hitch or dike, which throws it down 30 fathoms. This has lately been cut out under the care of a very ingenious and active engineer, and the coal is now working level free. A wag-gon-way of 2 miles from the pits to the harbour of Methil is now completed, and every thing promiſes an extenſive trade ; and indeed, from this ſeam of coal, with others ly-ing contiguous, it would not be at all ſurpriſing to ſee, in a few years, Methil rank among the firſt coal-ports in Scot-land *.

Salt.

* David Earl of Wemyſs, in his remarks on Methil, obſerves, that " the Biſhop of St Andrew's did create it into a free burgh of barony in 1662,

Salt.—There are 9 ſalt-pans at Methil, and 7 at Weſter Wemyſs. Theſe works have been long carried on, and much ſalt is made at them, both for land-ſale and exportation.

Manufactures, Commerce, &c.—Almoſt every ſubſtantial family uſed annually to make a few pieces of good linen, from yarn of their own ſpinning, which was wrought by weavers in the pariſh, and generally bleached by the proprietors themſelves, and then ſold in the public markets held in this and the neighbouring pariſhes for the purpoſe. In this way the weavers had been employed time immemorial till about the year 1750, that ſome in Eaſter Wemyſs began to manufacture linen themſelves, and ever ſince this buſineſs has been extended and improved. The linen now made is generally well known for its quality and fineneſs. Moſt of it is made from Scotch flax, the greateſt part of which is ſpun in the pariſh. It is thought by manufacturers to be ſuperior to any in the country; and in confirmation of this, it may here be obſerved, that the premiums given by the truſtees for linen and ſheeting were adjudged for 5 years ſucceſſively to manufacturers in this pariſh; to one in the years 1785 and 1786, and to another in the 1787, 1788, and 1789. Since the latter period, the number of looms has increaſed, and the manufactory varied; part of the looms being now employed in weaving checks and ticks for manufacturers in this and the neighbouring pariſhes. There are about 120 looms employed.

At

" 1662, called Methil, with a weekly mercate on the Wedneſdays, and
" two public fairs in the year, viz. one on the 22d June, St John's day,
" and 27th December, alſo St John's day in winter, in that year 1662,
" and ſo for ever, holden of him and his ſucceſſors, Biſhops of St An-
" drew's, paying him yearly 20 s. Scots as a feu-duty for ever."

At Kirkland, in the N. E. extremity of the pariſh, on the river Levén, near the ports of Methil and Inverleven, a large ſpinning work has been carried on for ſome time, by ſome gentlemen of London and Dundee, under the firm of Aiſlabie, Nielſon, and Company. They ſpin a conſiderable quantity of cotton and linen yarn, particularly of the latter, which they have begun to manufacture into cloth. Their yarns are approved of, and they are believed to be going on very ſucceſsfully. . The ſituation of this eſtabliſhment is a very advantageous one, and it is capable of great extenſion, as well for bleaching and printing, as for ſpinning the yarns and manufacturing the cloth. The company already employ about 300 people, and the buſineſs ſeems to be increaſing. Previous to the eſtabliſhment of this work, there were at Kirkland only two or three houſes, but now a number of very neat and convenient houſes are built, and in a ſhort time it is probable that it will be a conſiderable village. Kirkland is ſaid to have been the place firſt propoſed by the Carron Company for eſtabliſhing their works.

A little to the weſt of Kirkland is a waulk or fulling-mill, and dye-houſe, where buſineſs has been long carried on, and is conſiderably increaſed of late years. There is only one corn-mill in the pariſh, but there are others equally convenient on Colonel Wemyſs's property, lying in the pariſh of Markinch.

The *maritime commerce* has much increaſed of late. There are 10 ſquare-rigged veſſels and one ſloop belonging to this pariſh, whoſe regiſter meaſure may amount to upwards of 1480 tons. They are moſtly employed in the carrying trade. They are generally loaded with coal outwardly, and bring home wood, iron, flax, &c from the Baltic to the different ports in the frith of Forth. Some of them have been freighted to the Mediterranean, Weſt Indies, and America; and one is at preſent engaged by Government in the tranſport ſervice.

At Weſter Wemyſs *two ſhip-carpenters* began to build ſhips about ſeven years ago. The ſituation is good, and they have found great encouragement. They employ about 18 apprentices, and ſeveral journeymen. Here ſome of the beſt veſſels which have ſailed from the frith of Forth for the Weſt Indies have been built, as well as ſome for the Baltic trade. Other two ſhip-carpenters have juſt begun to build at Methil, a moſt convenient ſituation for the buſineſs, and it is thought that they will meet with equal encouragement with the former.

A gentleman in Eaſter Wemyſs, who carries on a conſiderable brewery, lately began to import wood from the Baltic, which has been of great advantage to the neighbourhood; and from the rapid and extenſive ſale which he has met with, cannot fail to ſecure benefit to himſelf.

There are properly no *merchants* in the pariſh, with the above exception. Some perſons ſell a ſmall quantity of neceſſary articles; but as there are opportunities every day of being provided with theſe at a cheaper rate from Kirkcaldy, they meet with no great encouragement.

The *ſea-weed* on the rocks upon the ſhore is cut every 3 years, and yields about 100 tons of kelp. The time of cutting is in June and July.

There are two good *harbours* in the pariſh. One at Methil, which was built by the Right Hon. David Earl of Wemyſs about the year 1650, ſolely at his own expence. The other is at Weſter Wemyſs, but when built is unknown. It was ſome years ago greatly improved by a baſon for cleaning it.

Exports

Exports and Imports.—Coal and falt are the only exports. The quantity differs according to the demands. At an average there is fhipped at Wefter Wemyfs annually 6000 tons of coal, moftly for Amfterdam, Hamburgh, and Middleburgh, being of a quality particularly fuited for light-houfes. The light on the ifland of May, at the entrance of the frith of Forth, is fupplied from this coal *.

About 40,000 bufhels of falt are annually fhipped from this parifh for the different ports from Dundee to Invernefs.

The imports are moftly oak-timber for fhip-building, Memel and Norway timber, deals, &c. Gottenburgh iron, deals and battons; in all about 10 cargoes in the year.

Bridges and Roads.—There are no bridges in the parifh, but a fmall one over a rivulet that paffes through Eafter Wemyfs, nor is there any need for more. The turnpike-road from Kirkcaldy to Cupar by Kennoway, and to the eaft of Fife, paffes through the north part of the parifh; but from its diftance from the coaft, being near $1\frac{1}{2}$ mile, the greater part of the inhabitants reap little advantage from it.

Inns.—There are properly no inns, but there are a fufficient number of houfes where ale and fpirits are fold.

Price of Provifions and of Labour.—The price of provifions and of labour has confiderably advanced of late years. The price of butcher meat is from 4 d. to $5\frac{1}{4}$ d. a-pound tron, at different feafons of the year; of butter, from $7\frac{1}{2}$ d.

to

* As there is now a pretty certain profpect of the great coal in the eaft part of the parifh being again wrought, it is probable that a much greater quantity of coal will be exported from the port of Methil.

to 10 d. ; of a hen, from 1 s. to 1 s. 4 d. ; of chickens, from 7 d. to 9 d. a pair; of eggs, from 3 d. to 5 d. a dozen.

The wages of men-fervants are from L. 6 to L. 8 a-year; and thofe who have houfes of their own, and maintain themfelves, have 6¼ bolls of meal, with an allowance of milk, and fometimes, in lieu of milk, L. 1, 6 s. Day-labourers have from March to October 1 s. 2 d. a-day, and 1 s. the reft of the year. Mafons 1 s. 8 d. and carpenters or wrights 1 s. 6 d.

Population.—According to the account given to Dr Webfter in 1755, the number of fouls amounted to 3041. The following is a pretty accurate lift taken in the year 1791 :

	Families.	Males.	Females.	Total.
Wefter Wemyfs, -	235	353	416	769
Eafter Wemyfs, -	153	268	289	557
Buckhaven, -	163	277	324	601
Methil, -	81	153	161	314
E. and W. Coaltowns,	93	166	227	393
Country, including Kirkland,	71	191	200	391
	796	1408	1617	3025
Total in 1755,	-	-		3041
Decreafed,	-	-		16

Lift

Liſt of Births and Marriages, taken from the Pariſh Regiſter, for 10 Years *.

	Births.			Marriages.
	Male.	Fem.	Tot.	
1782,	26	32	58	29
1783,	28	36	64	10
1784,	34	20	54	33
1785,	34	43	77	35
1786,	47	60	107	13
1787,	37	35	72	21
1788,	43	53	96	24
1789,	35	39	74	21
1790,	49	55	104	25
1791,	44	33	77	17
Total, -			783 †	228

Population has certainly increaſed in ſome of the villages, particularly in Eaſter Wemyſs and Methil; but it has greatly decreaſed in the country part of the pariſh. In the ſeſſion-records, there is mention of many places, of ſome of which no veſtige can now be traced; and that which remains of others, is only a few aſh-trees, which were uſually planted round their gardens or kail-yards. This decreaſe is owing to the ſame cauſes which have in general operated in other parts of the country, *viz.* the monopolizing

---

* The people in this pariſh are remarkably attentive to regiſter their childrens births; and of the above liſt of marriages, both bridegroom and bride, with a few exceptions, belonged to the pariſh. There being two burying-places beſides the church-yard, and no proper regiſter of deaths kept, the number of burials cannot be aſcertained.

† During the above period there were 8 times twins.

nopolizing of farms, the introduction of two-horſe ploughs,
incloſing, and a greater proportion of land laid out in graſs.

Eccleſiaſtical State, Heritor, &c.—The church is an old
Gothic building in the form of a croſs; there are evident
marks of conſiderable additions to it, but no dates that can
fix its age. It was repaired and much improved in 1792,
and is now a well-lighted, warm, and decent place of worſhip. The church and manſe are in the thriving village of
Eaſter Wemyſs, the moſt centrical part of the pariſh. The
patronage belongs to the Town-council of Edinburgh. It
belonged to the family of Wemyſs till about the 1214,
when Sir John de Wemyſs * gifted it to a religious houſe
at Soltray in Mid-Lothian. The reaſon he aſſigned for this
donation is in theſe words, " pro anima mea, et anima
" Comitis Duncani, et pro animabus patris et matris."

Colonel William Wemyſs of Wemyſs, Eſq; member of
Parliament for the county of Fife, is ſole heritor of the
pariſh, and his family reſides in it at the caſtle of Wemyſs.
The ſtipend, as ſettled by the Court of Seſſion February
1794, is L. 50 of money, 64 bolls of meal, 32 bolls of bear,
and L. 5 : 11 : 1¼ for furniſhing communion-elements.
The manſe was built in 1791, and, to the honour of the heritor, it is one of the beſt in the country. Moſt of the old
offices were removed in the ſame year, and a part of the
old manſe was fitted up to ſupply their place. The ſite
of manſe, garden, and offices includes about an acre of
ground, incloſed with ſtone walls. The glebe contains between

* This Sir John was the firſt who took the ſirname of Wemyſs. Till
about this time ſirnames were not uſed in Scotland. They only added
either their father's name aiter their own, or ſome epithet expreſſive of
ſomething which referred either to body or mind.——BUCHAN, Hiſt. rer.
Scoticar. lib. 7.

twéen 8 and 9 acres, and is all inclofed *. There are fome rocks and fea-weed, which belong to the minifter, and as this property is near the glebe, it is of great advantage for manure. For the kelp from the rocks the prefent incumbent has received about L. 5, 5 s. every three years.

There was once a parfonage and vicarage at Methil, the patronage of which was difponed by Archbifhop Hamilton to Sir John Wemyfs of Wemyfs, who died in 1571 †.

The following Perfons have been Minifters of this Parifh fince the Revolution.

Rev. Mr Archibald Riddell, admitted October 1691, and tranflated to Kirkcaldy June 1697.

Rev. Mr Thomas Black, tranflated from Strathmiglo October 1697, and tranflated to Perth July 1698.

Rev. Mr James Grierfon, ordained September 1698, and tranflated to Edinburgh July 1710.

Rev. Mr John Cleghorn, tranflated from Burntifland February 1711, died at Wemyfs February 1744.

Rev. Mr Harry Spens, ordained November 1744, and tranflated to the Profefforfhip of Divinity in the Univerfity of St Andrew's, October 1780.

Rev.

* A confiderable quantity of flax is raifed in this parifh; and the glebe, from the following remark, will appear to be no unfavourable foil for it. The Rev. Dr Spens fowed one year 9 lippies of lintfeed, which yielded from the mill 18 ftones. In 1787, the prefent incumbent fowed 3 lippies, which he winnowed from his preceding crop, and it yielded from the mill 7½ ftones. The fame year he fowed 2 lippies of foreign feed, which only yielded 2 ftones 10 lb. It may be of fome advantage to obferve, that the lint 1787 was pulled before it was fully ripened, and great care was taken in the watering of it. Much lint is loft from being too long in the water.

† This Sir John Wemyfs, fays Bifhop Leflie, " upon the head of the " Gentlemen of Fife in 1547, gave the Englifh, who landed in the coun- " ty, a confiderable defeat, and killed about 700 of them."

Rev. Mr William Greenfield, ordained September 1781, and tranflated to Edinburgh, November 1784.
The prefent incumbent was ordained March 1785.

Catechift.—The Right Honourable George Earl of Cromartie, in 1705, in teftimony of his great affection and honour to the memory of Margaret, heirefs and Countefs of Wemyfs, and Countefs of Cromartie, his deceafed Lady, mortified a fmall fum of money for founding a ftipend or falary to a catechift, for catechifing and inftructing the coaliers and falters, and others in the parifh of Wemyfs, to be paid yearly to the kirk-feffion of Wemyfs, under the care and direction of the family of Wemyfs, and minifter of the parifh, for faid ufe, and the payment to be made on the firft day of January Old Style, being the birth-day of that illuftrious Countefs. The gift of prefentation is in the family of Wemyfs, and the prefentee to be tried and admitted by the minifter and kirk-feffion. The prefent catechift is the firft on the eftablifhment; he was admitted in 1749; his falary is L. 250 : 3 : 4 Scotch money, and the intereft of L. 50 Sterling.

School.—The fchool-houfe was built in 1694. The fchoolmafter's falary is L. 6 : 13 : 4. He has a houfe and garden. The number of fcholars in winter is about 60, and in fummer 40. The fees *per* quarter are, for Englifh, 1 s. 2 d.; Englifh and writing, 1 s. 6 d.; arithmetic, 2 s. Latin, 2 s. 6 d.; book-keeping and navigation, a guinea for each. As precentor and feffion-clerk, he has yearly L. 2, 10 s. and 12 s. 6 d. every time that the Lord's Supper is difpenfed; for each marriage 2 s. 3 d. and each baptifm 10 d.; for parochial certificates about a guinea a-year. There are feveral private fchools.

Poor.

Poor.—The number of poor who receive regular fupply from the kirk-feffion on an average is 39, each of whom receive from 1 s. to 2 s. 6 d. the month. There are others, not upon the roll, who receive annually 5 s. fometimes more, to enable them to pay their houfe-rent ; and feveral others receive occafional fupply, as circumftances require ; the annual amount of all which is from L. 50 to L. 60, raifed by the weekly collections at church, the dues of pall or mortcloth, and the intereft of L. 300.

Diffenters.—There are but few Diffenters in the parifh. There is a Burgher meeting-houfe at Buckhaven, but has no minifter. Thofe of the Antiburgher perfuafion have places of worfhip in the parifhes of Dyfart and Markinch. There are about 24 who join the Prefbytery of Relief, and 6 of the Epifcopal perfuafion.

Antiquities, Caftle of Wemyfs, &c.—Under this article may be ranked the ruins of the caftle of Eafter Wemyfs, ufually called Macduff's Caftle, and faid to have been built by Macduff, who was created Earl of Fife about the 1057, and on whom King Malcolm Canmore conferred many very uncommon privileges. Two fquare towers, and a confiderable part of a wall that has furrounded the caftle, ftill remain. It is fituated on a delightful eminence, about 100 yards from the fhore.

In the 1290, on the death of King Alexander III. the Eftates of the kingdom fent Sir Michael Wemyfs of Wemyfs, and Sir Michael Scot of Balweary, in the parifh of Abbotfhall, as ambaffadors to Norway, to bring home Princefs Margaret, grand-daughter to the late king, and undoubted heirefs of the Crown of Scotland. Fordun, in his hiftory, fays, " Nobiles Scotiæ duos milites, fcientia et mo-" ribus præclaros Michaelem Wemyfs et Michaelem Scot " ad Regem Norvegiæ, folemniter direxerunt." Buchanan

nan ſtyles them, " Equites Fifani illuſtres." They went to Norway; but unhappily for them and their country, the Princeſs died at Orkney on her paſſage to Scotland. As a monument of this honourable embaſſy there is ſtill preſerved in the caſtle of Wemyſs a large ſilver baſon, of an antique figure, which was given by the King of Norway to Sir Michael Wemyſs.

Perhaps, under this article ſhould alſo be mentioned a ſtone, on the turnpike-road, about one-third of a mile after entering the pariſh from the eaſt ; it has ſtood time immemorial ; is 4 feet in height above ground, and 3 feet diameter, by ſome called the Standing Stone, by others the Half-way Stone between Kirkcaldy and Kennoway. For what reaſon it was placed there, the writer could never learn any thing ſatisfactory.

The caſtle of Wemyſs, ſituated a little to the eaſt of the burgh of Weſter Wemyſs, and cloſe by the ſhore, on a cliff between 30 and 40 feet above the level of the ſea, is a large and magnificent building. When it was built is uncertain, but part of the eaſt wing is ſaid to be near, if not as old as the caſtle of Eaſter Wemyſs. It received conſiderable additions about the beginning of the 17th century, from the Right Honourable David Earl of Wemyſs, and his grandſon, being Lord High Admiral of Scotland, raiſed a good wall, in the form of a fort, upon a beautiful bowling-green; and placed a few cannon to anſwer ſalutes from ſhips as they paſſed. The preſent proprietor laid out a piece of ground, ſome years ago, in a garden, with high walls, an elegant green-houſe, hot-houſes, &c.; and it is ſaid that there are few, if any gardens in Scotland, where there is ſo much forcing as in this. It was in the caſtle of Wemyſs that Lord Darnly had his firſt interview with Queen Mary, 13th February 1565. The Queen was at this time on a tour of viſits in Fife, which, ſays the famous John Knox,

cauſed

caufed wild fowl to be fo dear, that partridges were fold at a crown a-piece.

Perhaps in few parifhes has land been longer in the pof-feffion of one family than in this. Hugo, or Eugenius, fecond fon of Gillimacheal, 4th Earl of Fife, and grandfon of Macduff, the firft Earl, got from his father the lands of Wemyſsſhire, &c. &c. and his defcendent is prefent pro-prietor of them. Gillimacheal was witnefs to the founda-tion-charter of the Abbey of Holyroodhoufe in the 1128. The lands of Wefter Wemyſs have been uninterruptedly poffeffed by the noble family of Wemyſs fince the above period. The lands of Eafter Wemyſs went off from the family, and were poffeffed by a family of the name of Li-vingſton, and then by the Colvills of Ochiltree ; but after 200 years feparation, they were again added to the eftate of Wemyſs, by the Right Honourable John Earl of Wemyſs, who was High Commiffioner to the General Affembly of the Church of Scotland in the year 1641.

Caves.—It was obferved, that the parifh derives its name from the number of natural caves in it. There are feven a little to the eaft of Eafter Wemyſs, and all but one about 100 yards from high-water mark. Four of them were long ago fitted up for, and ftill are pigeon-houfes. There are two at the bottom of the cliff, and immediately under the ruins of the caftle of Eafter Wemyſs ; one of them is called Jonathan's Cave, from a man who, with his family, refided fome time in it ; the entrance to the other is very narrow, but after having got through it, you find yourfelf in a very fpacious place, in which is a well of excellent water ; it is annually vifited by the young people of Eafter Wemyſs, with lights, upon the firft Monday of January Old Style, but from what this cuftom took its rife the writer could never learn. The feventh (the neareft to the
　　　　　　　　　　　　　　　　　　　　　　　　fhore)

ſhore) is called the Court Cave, and two reaſons are aſſigned for the name; one is, that when the lands of Eaſter
Wemyſs were the property of the Colvills, they here held
their baron-court; another, that King James IV. in a fro-
lick once joined a company of gypſies, who were here
making merry, and when the liquor began to operate, the
gypſies, as uſual with people of their character, began to
quarrel among themſelves; upon this his Majeſty attempted
to mediate between the parties, but they, ignorant of the
rank of their new aſſociate, were about to handle him
pretty roughly for his goodneſs, which obliged the King to
diſcover himſelf; in alluſion to this affair, the cave was
afterwards ironically called the Court Cave. There is another cave a little to the eaſt of the caſtle of Wemyſs, and
much about the ſame diſtance from the ſhore as the former. This cave, which is about 200 feet in length, 100
in breadth, and 30 in height, was fitted up about 60 years
ago by a tackſman for a glaſs-work; but ſoon after the work
commenced, the man became bankrupt, and the buildings
were allowed to go to ruins.

Advantages and Diſadvantages.—The pariſh derives
great advantage from the abundance of coal; and when
fiſhing was plenty, living was much cheaper here than in
moſt places. One diſadvantage which the commercial part
labour under, is the want of a poſt-office. Though Dyſart,
which is the neareſt poſt-town, is not at a great diſtance,
yet as letters cannot be anſwered the ſame day on which
they are received, without ſending them by expreſs to the
office, much inconvenience is thereby occaſioned, which
could be eaſily remedied at a very ſmall expence, as the
poſt-boy paſſes through Eaſter Wemyſs on his way to
Leven.

Character.

Charaſter.—The people in general are ſober and induſtrious, regular in their attendance upon public worſhip, and apparently contented with their ſituations *.

---

* At a period when the abolition of the ſlave-trade has become the ſubjeſt of Parliamentary conſideration, the following anecdote may not be diſagreeable, as being perhaps the firſt proceſs of the kind that came before the Court of Seſſion :—A gentleman from the Weſt Indies, reſiding ſome time at Methil, a negro ſervant, whom he had brought with him, embraced at that time the Chriſtian religion, and was baptized in the church of Wemyſs, September 10. 1769, by the name of David Spens. Soon after this his maſter reſolved to ſend him back to, and ſell him as a ſlave in the Weſt Indies ; but Spens getting information of it, immediately left his maſter, and went to the houſe of a farmer in the pariſh. The maſter then raiſed a proceſs before the Court of Seſſion againſt Spens to return to his ſlavery, and againſt the farmer for adviſing him to deſert, and alſo for protecting him. To defend Spens from the oppreſſion of his maſter, and to aſſiſt him in aſſerting, what they conceived, his juſt rights and privileges as a Britiſh ſubjeſt, the inhabitants of the pariſh readily eſpouſed his cauſe, and raiſed a conſiderable ſum of money. The cauſe was enrolled January 1770. Four lawyers were engaged ; and on the 2d February, the cauſe was ably pled on both ſides. Memorials were appointed to be given in for both parties ; but ſoon after this the maſter died, and the cauſe was dropt. To the honour of the lawyers engaged, for the defendant, viz. Meſſrs Croſbie, Al. Ferguſon, Hay and Belſches, Advocates, and Mr Walter Ferguſon, writer, agent, none of them would accept of a fee.

TRIAL of WILLIAM COKE and ALISON DICK for
Witchcraft.—Extracted from the Minutes of
the Kirk-Seſſion of Kirkaldy, A. D. 1636.

Omitted in the Account of Kirkaldy,

September 17*th*, 1633.

T HE which day, compeared Aliſon Dick, challenged upón
ſome ſpeeches uttered by her againſt William Coke, tending
to Witchcraft ; denied the ſamyne.

1. Compeared Alexander Savage, Andrew Nicol, and George
Tillie, who being admitted and ſworn, deponed as follows :
The ſaid Alexander Savage, that he heard the ſaid Aliſon
Dick ſay to her huſband William Coke, " Thou has put
" down many ſhips ; it had been gude for the people of
" Kirkaldie,

" Kirkaldie, that they had knit a ftone about thy neck and
" drowned thee."

2. Andrew Nicol deponed, that he heard the faid Alifon fay
to him, " Thou has gotten the woman's fong laid, as
" thou promifed; thou art over long living : it had been
" gude for the women of Kirkaldy, that thou had been
" dead long fince. I fhall caufe all the world wonder
" upon thee."

3. George Tillie deponed, that he heard her fay to him,
" It had been gude for the women of Kirkaldy, to put
" him to death; and that he had died 7 years fince."

Also compeared Jean Adamfon, Kathrine Spens, Marion
Meafon, Ifobel Murifon, Alifon Kelloch, who being admitted and fworn, deponed as follows :

4. Jean Adamfon deponed, that fhe heard Alifon Dick fay to
her hufband William Coke, " Thief! Thief! what is this
" that I have been doing? keeping thee thretty years
" from meikle evil doing. Many pretty men has thou
" putten down both in fhips and boats; thou has gotten
" the woman's fong laid now. Let honeft men puddle
" and work as they like, if they pleafe not thee well,
" they fhall not have meikle to the fore when they die.

5. Kathrine Spens deponed, that fhe heard her fay to him,
" Common thief, I have hindered thee from many ill turns
" doing both to fhips and boats."

6. Marion Meafon deponed, that fhe heard her fay, " Common
" thief, mony ill turn have I hindered thee from doing thir
" thretty years; mony fhips and boats has thou put down :
" and when I would have halden the ftring to have faved
" one man, thou wald not."

7. Ifobel

7. Ifobel Murifon deponed, that fhe heard her fay to him,
" Thief, thief, I have keeped thee from doing many ill
" turnes. Thou has now laid the woman's fong."

September 24*th*, 1633.

8. Compeared Janet Allan, relict of umquhile John Duncan
fifher ; deponed, that Alifon Dick came in upon a certain
time to her houfe, when fhe was lying in of a bairn, and
craved fome four bakes ; and fhe denying to give her any,
the faid Alifon faid, Your bairns fhall beg yet, (as they do).
And her hufband being angry at her, reproved her ; and
fhe abufed him in language ; and when he ftrak her, fhe
faid that fhe fhould caufe him rue it ; and fhe hoped to fee
the powarts bigg in his hair ; and within half a-year, he
was caften away, and his boat, and perifhed.

9. Janet Sauders, daughter-in-law to the faid William Coke,
and Alifon Dick deponed, that William Coke came in to
her ; and fhe being weeping, he demanded the caufe of it,
fhe anfwered it was for her hufband. The faid William
faid, What ails thee ? Thou wilt get thy gudman again ;
but ye will get him both naked and bare : and whereas
there was no word of him for a long time before, he came
home within two days thereafter, naked and bare as he
faid ; the fhip wherein he was being caften away.

4, 10. Jean Adamfon deponed, that when her gudman failed
with David Robertfon, the faid David having fent him
home with a fhip to come for Scotland, there was a long
time that there was no word of that fhip ; fo that David
Robertfon coming home, and the other fhip not come,
nor no word from her, he faid he would never fee her.
The faid Alifon Dick came in to her, (fhe with her bairns
being weeping,) and faid, What ails ye Jean to weep ?
She anfwered, We have all good caufe to weep for my
hufband,

hufband, whom we will never fee more. The faid Alifon faid, hold your tongue, your gudman and all the company are well enough; they are in Norway loading their fhip with timber to come home; they will be here fhortly: and fo it fell out in every point as fhe faid.

5, 11. Kathrine Spens deponed, that William Coke came in to her, after that his wife had fpoken fo much evil to him, and faid, Kathrine, my wife has fpoken meikle ill of me this day, but I faid nothing to her again. If I had fpoken two words to her the laft time fhe was in the fteeple, fhe would never have gotten out of it.

Minutes of 24th September, Ordains Mr James Miller to ride to Prefton, for the man that tries the witches. The expence to be paid by the Town and Seffion.

October 8th.

12. Compeared Ifobel Hay, fpoufe to Alexander Law, againft Alifon Dick, who being fworn, deponed, that fhe having come in to her houfe, her hufband being newly failed, fhe craved fome money of her, which fhe refufed, and boafted her. The faid Alifon faid, It fhall gang wair geats; and that fame voyage, her hufband had great lofs. And thereafter, the faid Alifon came in to her houfe, fhe being furth, and took her fifter by the hand, and fince that time, the maiden had never been in her right wits.

13. William Bervie declaired, that Robert Whyt having once ftricken William Coke, Alifon Dick his wife, came to the faid Robert, and faid, Wherefore have ye ftricken my hufband? I fhall caufe you rue it. The faid Robert replying, What fayeft thou? I fhall give you as much—you witch. She anfwered, " Witches take the wit and the
                                            " grace

" grace from you : and that fame night, he was bereft of
" his wits."

14. Janet Whyt, daughter to the faid Robert, compearing,
affirmed the faid dittay to be true upon her oath. And
added, that fhe went to the faid Alifon, and reproved her,
laying the wyt of her father's ficknefs upon her. Let him
pay me then, and he will be better ; but if he pay me not,
he will be worfe. For there is none that does me wrong,
but I go to my god and complains upon them ; and within 24 hours, I will get a mends of them. The faid Janet
Whyt declared, that Alifon Dick faid to her fervant, Agnes Fairlie, I have gotten a grip of your gudwife's thigh ;
I fhall get a grip of her leg next ; the faid Janet having
burnt her thigh before with lint : and thereafter fhe has
taken fuch a pain in her leg, that fhe can get no remedy
15. for it. Whilk the faid Agnes Fairlie deponed, upon her
great oath to be true.

Alifon Dick herfelf declared, that David Paterfon, fkipper,
having ftruck William Coke her hufband, and drawn him
by the feet, and compelled him to bear his gear aboard,
the faid William curfed the faid David, and that voyage
he was taken by the Dunkirkers. Alfo, at another time
thereafter, he compelled him to bear his gear aboard,
and a captain's who was with him : and when the captain
would have paid him, the faid David would not fuffer
him ; but he himfelf gave him what he liked. The faid
William curfed the faid David very vehemently : and at
that time he himfelf perifhed, his fhip, and all his company, except two or three. Alfo fhe declared, that when
his own fon failed in David Whyt's fhip, and gave not his
father his bonnallie, the faid William faid, What ? Is he
failed and given me nothing ? The devil be with him :—
if ever he come home again, he fhall come home naked

and

and bare: and fo it fell out. For John Whyt, who had that fhip freighted to Norway, and another wherein him-felf was, declared, that they had very foul weather; and the fhip wherein the faid young William Coke was perifh-ed; and he faved all the men in the fhip, wherein he was himfelf. And albiet the ftorm increafed two days before the perifhing of the faid fhip, and fix days after; yet, the two hours fpace in the which they were faving the men, it was fo calm in that part of the fea, that they rowed from one fhip to the other, with two oars; and the fea was all troublefome about them. And the faid William Coke the younger, was the firft man that came a fhip-board.

Paction.—The fame day, Alifon Dick being demanded by Mr James Simfon Minifter, when, and how fhe fell in covenant with the devil; fhe anfwered, her hufband mony times urged her, and fhe yielded only two or three years fince. The manner was thus: he gave her, foul and body, quick and quidder full to the devil, and bade her do fo. But fhe in her heart faid, God guide me. And then fhe faid to him, I fhall do any thing that ye bid me: and fo fhe gave herfelf to the devil in the forefaid words.—This fhe confeffed about four hours at even, freely without compulfion, before Mr James Simfon, minifter, William Tennent, baillie, Robert French, town clerk, Mr John Malcolme, fchoolmafter, William Craig, and me the faid Mr James Miller, writer hereof.

October 15*th.*

16. The which day, compeared Chriftian Ronaldfon, againft Alifon Dick, who, in her prefence being fworn, deponed, that fhe having fet ane houfe to the faid Alifon, and when

the

the gudman came home he was angry, and said, he would not have the devil to dwell above him in the close; and he went and ftruck up the door, and put forth the chimney that fhe put in it. And thereafter, Alifon came to the faid Chriftian, and chopped upon her fhoulder, and faid to her, Chriftie, your gudman is going to fail, and he has ane ftock among his hands; but ere long, his ftock fhall be as fhort as mine. And fo it fell out; for he was caften away in David Whyt's fhip, and faved nothing.

October 22.

17. Compeared Merjory Marfhall againft Alifon Dick, who being fworn, deponed, that Alifon having brought her gudman's cloaths once from the Caftle-haven, fhe offered her 12d for her labour, who would not have it; and fhe faid to her, Alifon, there is not many of them. She anfwered, they fhall be fewer the next time: and the next voyage, he was caft away in David Whyt's fhip.

18. Compeared alfo Kathrine Wilfon, who being fworn, deponed, that fhe and Janet Whyt being fliding together, Alifon Dick came to them, and afked filver from Janet Whyt, who would give her none, but fled her company into the faid Kathrine's houfe, and fhe followed, and fhe gave her a piece bread, and Janet Whyt bade her give her a plack alfo, and fhe fhould pay her again. And when fhe got it, fhe faid, is this all that fhe gives me? If fhe had given me a groat, it would have vantaged her a thoufand punds. This is your doing, evil tidings come upon you. And fhe went down the clofs, and piffed at their meal-cellar door; and after that, they had never meal in that cellar, (they being meal-makers). And thereafter they bought a horfe at 40 lib.; and the horfe never carried

ried a load to them but two, but died in the *butts, louping to death,* so that every body said that he was witched.

October 29th.

19. Euphen Bofwell being sworn, deponed, that her gudman being to sail to the East country, loaden with salt, the said Alison Dick having born some of the salt aboard, she came to her and craved money from her, who gave her meat; but would give her no money, saying to her, Alison, my gudman has paid you himself, and therefore, I will give you nothing. She replied, Will ye give me nothing? I hope in God, it will be better sharp (cheaper) sold nor it was bought: and so it fell out; for the ship sailed upon the morn; and the day after that, she sank, salt and all, except the men, who were saved by another ship that was near by them.

20. Thomas Muftard being sworn, deponed, that James Wilson going once to sail, Alison Dick came to him, and desyred silver from him, he would give her none; she abused him with language, and he struck her; she said to him, that that hand should do him little good that voyage: and within two days after, his hand swelled as great as a pint-stoup, so that he could get little or nothing done with it. The next time also when he was to sail, the said Alison went betwixt him and the boat; and he said, Yon same witch thief is going betwixt me and the boat; I must have blood of her: and he went and struck her, and bled her, and she cursed him and banned him; and that same voyage, he being in Caithness, standing upon the shore, cleithing a tow, and a boy with him, the sea came and took him away, and he died; and the boy was well enough.

Desires

Defires Mr Robert Douglas to go to the Archbifhop with this procefs, to get his approbation thereto, who takes upon him to do the fame.

Minute of November 19th.—5s given for a load of coals to Alifon Dick; 14s. for her entertainment this week bygone, being this day, with her hufband William Coke, burnt for witchcraft.

————

In the Minute of 17th December, there is a particular Account of the Town and Seffion's extraordinary Deburfements for WILLIAM COKE and ALISON DICK, Witches.

In primis.—To Mr James Miller, when he went to
   Preftowne for a man to try them, 47s. L. 2 7
 Item.—To the man of Culrofs, (the execu-
   tioner,) when he went away the
   firft time, 12s. - - 0 12
 Item.—For coals for the witches, 24s. - 1 4
 Item.—In purchafing the commiffion, - 9 3
 Item.—For one to go to Finmouth for the
   laird to fit upon their affife as judge, 0 6
 Item.—For harden to be jumps to them, - 3 10
 Item.—For making of them, - - 0 8

   Summa for the Kirk's part L. 17 10 Scots.

The

The Town's part of Expences Deburfed extraordinarily upon
WILLIAM COKE and ALISON DICK.

In primis.—For ten loads of coals to burn them,

5 merks, - - L. 3	6	8

Item.—For a tar barrel, 14s. - - 0 14 0

Item.—For towes, - - - 0 6 0

Item.—To him that brought the executioner, 2 18 0

Item.—To the executioner for his pains, 8 14 0

Item.—For his expences here, - 0 16 4

Item.—For one to go to Finmouth for the

laird, - - - 0 6 0

Summa Town part, L. 17 1 Scots.

Both, L. 34 11

Or L. 2 17 7 ſter.

INDEX

Index

Charitable societies, 28, 170, 282–284, 341, 487, 556, 613, 614, 698

Cloth manufacture, 5, 21, 124, 322, 332, 333, 388, 500, 532, 674

Coal industry, 2, 19, 35, 51, 52, 62, 73, 87, 99, 110, 115, 120, 129, 138, 142, 149, 155, 160, 239, 246, 261, 263, 276–277, 309, 310–319, 325–326, 328, 337, 339, 342, 348–349, 376, 394, 396, 398, 399, 424, 432, 442, 455–457, 468, 485, 496, 517–518, 569, 624, 629, 633–644, 693, 694–695, 710, 717, 738, 745, 754, 767–768, 780–781, 781, 791–792, 805

Communications: roads, bridges, 6, 16, 19, 44, 63, 73, 93, 114, 123, 130–131, 150, 155, 174, 181, 192, 199, 200, 211, 219, 228, 235, 248, 275, 303, 320, 322, 331, 342, 385, 404, 424, 425, 428, 439–440, 457, 469, 518–519, 598, 622–623, 647, 683, 690, 698–699, 730, 731, 732–733, 758, 771, 772, 777, 796, 803

Costs—food, 4–5, 33, 40, 46, 47, 62, 82, 136, 229, 237–238, 258, 319, 337, 389, 426, 433, 469, 477, 492, 497–498, 557–559, 580, 619, 631–632, 656, 689, 690, 698, 728–729, 750, 776, 796–797
—fuel, 5, 19, 47, 62, 73, 92, 102, 129, 130, 192, 235, 261, 276, 277, 319, 320, 349, 375–376, 386, 398, 432, 455, 456, 468, 490, 496, 518, 614, 619, 659, 662, 698, 699, 729, 776

Cotton manufacture, 5, 61, 92, 489, 539–540, 581, 707

Crop rotations, 18, 31, 42, 43, 75, 79–80, 118–119, 225–226, 256, 359, 412, 445, 465, 490, 497, 513, 516, 595, 655, 677, 744

Common land, 520, 546

Courts of law, 722

Dairying, 18, 43–44, 83, 580

Dearth, famine, 40, 189, 210, 426–427, 442, 750–751, 782

Depopulation, 12, 66, 75, 88, 103, 110, 252, 470, 483, 491, 662, 798–799

Diet, 25, 32, 47, 55, 87, 136, 150, 229, 388, 470, 498, 574, 722

Dress, 150, 173, 235, 321, 344, 442, 560, 592, 574, 722, 777

Dry docks, 94

Elections, 205–206, 273

Emigration, migration, 185, 186, 722, 740, 775

Eminent persons, 133–134, 148–149, 175, 299–302, 401–402, 561–565, 575–577, 700, 755, 764–767

Enclosures, 3, 14, 18, 43, 88, 102, 107, 119, 128, 133, 139, 155, 191, 227, 228, 237, 250, 255, 264, 329, 330, 331, 348, 359, 395, 425, 438, 447, 453, 481, 491, 497, 498, 508, 590, 600, 601, 602, 646, 667, 685, 697, 724, 733, 742, 754, 761, 774, 775, 779, 788

Index

Index

References to Plants.

p. 19 - Furze (Aberdour)

p. 54 - "Heath" (A/muchty).

p. 65 - "Heath" } (A'tuol)
        whin

p. 85 - - Trees (Balmerino)

p. 101 - "Heath" (Cameron)

115 - Trees (Carnbee)

117/8 - Trees & "Heath" (Carnock)

157 -   "   (Ceail)

188 - 'Heath' & bent-grass (Cults)

190 -   "   & whins   "

220 - Ash (Cupar)

237 - Furze & heath (Dalgety)

249/25?-Moor (Dunnind). (ass Lens)

262 - The King's Muir (")

303 - Moor & morenss (D'luie).

304 - Trees   "

331 - Weeds (Dysart)

352/3/4 - Heath, Furze, moss (Falkland).

367 - whins (Ferryport)

387 -   "   (Forgan)

419 - Furze, broom & trees (Dunn Der -Kenback)

463-4/5- Trees = Casts of (Kilmany)

482 - Furze (Kinghorn)

497 -   "   (Kinglassie)

567 - "Usalon marsh & deceitful bog" (Largo)

568 - "Thorns, briars & furze"   "

600 - Grass, heath & furze (Leuchars)

602-6 – Tent moss or Shengly-dykes

712 – Heath + Furze (St Andrews)

715 – Seaweed (")

723/4 – Woods + Scotch fir (")

754 – Trees + moss (Salvie)

788 – Trees (Wemyss)

p. 31 - Birds (Anstruther W.)
55 - " (D'mochty).
111 - " (Carnbee)
121 - " (Carnock)
151 - " (Ceres)
153 - " (Collessie)
189 - Fish (Cults)
368 - Rabbit (Ferryport)
370 - Birds (")
431 - Fish (Kettle)
453 - Birds (K'bar)
458 - Fish (")
497 - " (Kinglassie)
591 - " (Leslie)
605 - Rabbit (Leuchars).
622 - Fish (Markinch)
712 - Trout (St. A.)
741 - Birds & Mammals (St Monans)
763 - Fish (Saline)